Reggie

Reggie

The Life of Reginald Maudling

LEWIS BASTON

SUTTON PUBLISHING

First published in the United Kingdom in 2004 by
Sutton Publishing Limited · Phoenix Mill
Thrupp · Stroud · Gloucestershire · GL5 2BU

British Library Cataloguing in Publication Data
A catalogue record for this book is available from the British Library.

ISBN 0-7509-2924-3

Typeset in 10.5/13pt Photina MT.
Typesetting and origination by
Sutton Publishing Limited.
Printed and bound in England by
J.H. Haynes & Co. Ltd, Sparkford.

CONTENTS

List of Illustrations

PREFACE

I first became interested in Reginald Maudling in early 1999, when I was asked to write a book to accompany a Channel 4 television series called *Sleaze*. It was a commission with a rapid turnaround (although for various reasons the book itself did not appear for nearly a year), and in researching it I read a lot of biographies of postwar politicians who had fallen from grace in one way or another. I was puzzled that nobody had written a life of Maudling, who after all was the most senior British politician to be felled by scandal in the twentieth century. Although overshadowed in most perceptions of Maudling, I also discovered that he was the first minister to admit that Britain's future role was as a top second-division nation; the Tory Chancellor whose budget was popular with the trade unions; the Home Secretary on whose watch the Northern Ireland Troubles got out of control; the Tory who pondered the massive extension of state control of the economy and the permissive society in the 1970s. Everyone who knew him said what good company he was, what a nice man: an intelligent, decent, gentle character who believed in consensus. There was also a darker view of Maudling. The journalists covering the Poulson affair found him a devious adversary and believed that behind his bonhomie lay, to put it bluntly, a greedy criminal.

When I became serious about this project I contacted Caroline Maudling, Reggie's daughter, and I also sent her an early version of a proposal for the book. It was a distressing business for her, particularly at a time when she was dealing with the tragic death of her brother William. Caroline Maudling does not believe that it is her place to give or withhold 'official' status, but she has helped considerably and given me access to other family members and personal friends. I am most grateful to her. I also respect and admire her. She has inherited her father's charm, wit and generosity of spirit. She will not like everything in this book, but I hope that she and others will accept that I have always tried to be fair to him and to write a rounded, balanced account.

My relationship with the Maudling family was the least of my problems. It seemed obvious to me that he was an interesting subject, but this appeared to be a minority opinion. My literary agent, Simon Trewin (successively of Sheil, Land and Peters, Fraser and Dunlop), believed in it even when I had become a bit dispirited, and eventually came to agreement in 2002 with Sutton, who have displayed faith and a certain amount of bravery in publishing the book. I owe Simon (ably assisted by Claire Scott) and Christopher Feeney of Sutton many thanks. At the other end of this long road, my thanks to Hilary Walford for shepherding *Reggie* through the production process, and Mary Worthington for her skilful copy-editing. Niri Shan and Nicky Goodey of Taylor Wessing had the no doubt intriguing task of offering their legal advice.

While conducting my research I have found out why such an apparently promising subject has not had a biography, while other more obscure politicians of the same era have been written up. It helps a lot if one's subject has a collection of papers, catalogued and archived by a professional archivist, available for consultation. Some politicians kept everything, neatly filed, and as a result have disproportionate influence on the historical record. Reggie Maudling's papers are held at Churchill College, Cambridge, and are still closed even with an authorisation letter from the family. The archivist assured me that these were solely constituency casework from Barnet, not general political papers, and thus of limited interest even if I could gain access to them before the year 2079. If they are indeed constituency correspondence from the 1970s, they should be renamed the Arthur Fawcett–Viv Walker papers, as Reggie was not the most diligent of constituency MPs during the period. There are lots of boxes of papers there, frustratingly locked up. There are apparently no other sets of Maudling papers, although I was told a most intriguing tale at one point about a mechanical digger and a hole in the ground somewhere in Hertfordshire.

To add to the problem of no accessible papers, Reggie was not much of a letter-writer or diarist. His stationery was an unusual, small size that deliberately encouraged brevity of expression. There are only a couple of ministerial appointments diaries. He was rather disorganised in his approach to filing, and he lived in and for the moment. There is remarkably little that gives much of an insight into Maudling's personality in the archives. His contemporaries when they came to write their memoirs rather shied away from grappling with the real, problematic Reggie and either ignored him or told well-polished stories. For such a large, heavy man, he walked lightly through the historical record.

I am not a Conservative, which in writing a life of Maudling I tend to regard as being a positive attribute. Some very good political biographies have been written by biographers who support different parties from their subject – I think here of Anthony Howard's *R.A. Butler*, or Michael McManus's *Jo Grimond*. The late, great Lord Jenkins wrote a workmanlike *Attlee* and splendid books on Gladstone, Asquith and Churchill, but then his wide experience of politics gave him a special authority in writing across party lines. The contemporary Conservative Party has, with one or two exceptions such as – greatly to his credit – Kenneth Clarke, given up honouring Reggie Maudling. My attempt to claim Maudling as a distant ancestor of New Labour will probably please nobody. I hope it is taken as a

serious comment; Hegelians like Maudling and the advocates of the Third
Way adopt, chameleon-like, the colours of their surroundings. Maudling
may be to the left of Blair, but this is more a function of the political
climates in which they operated rather than revealing any deep ideological
distinction between them.

I have to say a few words about the attitude of the Conservative Party. The
Conservative Party nationally has taken pains to make their records accessible
to contemporary historians through the Conservative Party Archive at the
Bodleian Library in Oxford, and for this anyone writing recent political
history should be grateful. I appreciate the help of their archivists and
officials. I would also like to thank members of the Feltham and Heston
Conservative Association for their efforts, largely fruitless but still appreciated,
at tracing Reggie's first election campaign in 1945. Individual members of
the Chipping Barnet Conservative Association have been a great help. Some
Conservative associations have been very unhelpful. Perhaps they feel justified
in their paranoia on seeing what I have written, but all they did was to
deprive me of a few witnesses and papers that would have probably put
Reggie in a positive light. I am glad that the national party, and many senior
figures, took a different attitude. They probably also have enough perspective
to realise that, although there is much they will not like, the book is
balanced, even sympathetic.

Thank you to all the librarians and archivists who helped with the book by
doing their professional jobs, particularly those at the British Library, the LSE
Library (BLPES), Kingston University Library, the Library of Congress and the
public libraries of the City of London, the boroughs of Barnet, Bromley,
Camden, Hackney, Hounslow, Kensington & Chelsea, Southwark and
Westminster, and the counties of Carmarthenshire, East Sussex and
Hertfordshire. The internet-based services of LEXIS-NEXIS, J-STOR and the
Google search engine are indispensable research tools, so thank you to their
authors wherever they may be.

The specialist and private collections consulted include those at Merchant
Taylors' School (Geoffrey Brown), OMT Society (Jeremy Birch), Merton College
Oxford (Michael Stansfield), Oxford Union Society, Middle Temple Library
(Lesley Whitelaw), Royal Academy of Dance (Eleanor Jack), Churchill College
Cambridge (Allen Packwood and Andrew Riley in particular), the Bodleian
Library (Jill Spelman), British Newspaper Library, National Museum of Labour
History (Stephen Byrd), Linen Hall Library (Yvonne Murphy), University of
Kent at Canterbury (Sue Crabtree), Birmingham University Library (Chris
Penney), University of Leeds Library, Hull University Library, London
Metropolitan Archive, Family History Centre, Barnet Museum, University of
Tulsa Library (Gina Minks), Cheddi Jagan Research Centre, Georgetown
(Dudley Kissoore), University College London Archives section, Glasgow
University Archives Service, Trinity College Cambridge and the West
Yorkshire Archives Service at Wakefield. The assistance of Andrew Brown

and his colleagues at the Metropolitan Police Records Management Department in the closing stages is greatly appreciated.

Particular thanks to the National Archives (formerly Public Record Office) of the United Kingdom, among whose professional and unfailingly helpful staff I have spent much time, and their equivalents at the National Archives of Ireland in Dublin, the Public Record Office of Northern Ireland (PRONI) in Belfast and the National Archives and Records Administration (NARA) of the United States. Stephen Twigge and Mark Jarvis were particularly helpful in the later stages of the book.

Some individuals have helped by granting me access to various documents, including photographs: Sir Clive Bossom, David Butler, Trudi Fawcett Kotrosa, Murray Martin, Caroline Maudling, Michael Melville, Michael Rice and Richard Stott in particular. Thank you to Denys Blakeway and Leonie Jameson for access to transcripts of interviews for the television programme *Sleaze*, which they made in 1999 and for which I published a companion book.

For permission to reproduce copyright material I am grateful to the above-named persons and institutions. Some extra specific acknowledgement is due to the policy of the Controller of The Stationery Office (TSO) in relation to papers held in the National Archives and the West Yorkshire Archives Service, and to the copyright department of Pan Macmillan regarding the rights to Reginald Maudling's *Memoirs* published by Sidgwick & Jackson in 1978. I gladly acknowledge the help of Frances Cairncross, who gave her permission to quote from the unpublished diaries of her father Sir Alec Cairncross. The Macmillan Trustees gave permission for several quotations from Harold Macmillan's diaries, and Sheridan Westlake of Conservative Central Office cleared the quotations from the Party's papers. Lord Weatherill kindly gave his permission to quote from Whips' Office papers. For photographs, I would like to thank Trudi Fawcett Kotrosa, the Press Association, Associated Press and Hulton Getty. If I have inadvertently failed to trace or credit any copyright holders for material going beyond the 'fair dealing' rule, I can only offer sincere apologies and promise to make amends in any future edition of this book.

Many people have given interviews, of varying length from a short phone call to several hours of intense conversation. Thanks above all to Caroline Maudling, Edward Maudling and Melissa Maudling for their help. I am grateful to everyone who helped with their reminiscences of Reginald Maudling, including Leo Abse, Lord Allen of Abbeydale, Lord Baker of Dorking, Ann Brum, David Butler, Sir Peter Carey, Lord Carlisle of Bucklow, Lord Carr of Hadley, Lord Carrington, Tom Caulcott, Sir Sydney Chapman, Sir Robin Chichester-Clark, Peter Duplock, Raymond Fitzwalter, the late Sir Sandy Glen, Sir Philip Goodhart, David Graham, Joe Haines, James Haw, Maurice Hayes, Anthony Howard, Jack Howard-Drake, Sir Tim Kitson, Trudi Fawcett Kotrosa, Charles Longbottom, John Marshall, Murray Martin,

Michael McManus, Stratton Mills, Sir Derek Mitchell, Dennis Nicholson, Lord Parkinson, Tony Poulter (and the officers of Alpha Delta Plus who produce their website), Michael Rice, Andrew Roth, Alex Saville, Daphne Seillier, Robert Shepherd, Corinne Souza, Mr Stone, Richard Stott, Viv Walker and Ken Williams. Several others have helped on condition of anonymity, and I am equally grateful to them – particularly those with whom I came into contact late in the process. If there is anyone I have neglected to thank for their help, please forgive this accidental discourtesy. I would have liked to do more interviews, and there are a few cases in which either it did not prove possible to arrange a meeting for whatever reason, or when pressure of time has meant that I did not talk to people who had expressed their willingness to do so. My apologies to these people as well.

A few have refused. I had a peremptory, but not wholly uninteresting, letter from Sir Edward Heath, and a charming letter from Lord Callaghan of Cardiff, each of whom answered some questions I had put. It is an elder statesman's prerogative to respond to requests as he wishes. I also had an exchange of correspondence with the late Sir Frederic Bennett, in which he advised me to wait until the publication of his memoirs, and it is to my great regret that I did not have the opportunity to explore his point of view. George Wilson, who was John Poulson's administrator in 1968–70 and returned to the civil service in 1970, also refused. Muir Hunter, QC, understandably, was not willing to talk about the Poulson affair, although at long last some of the results of his enquiries can see the light. My descriptions of his thinking are inferred from the transcripts of the bankruptcy hearings rather than any interview with him.

Very late on in this project, in July 2003, the Lord Chancellor's Department released forty-two case files from the Poulson prosecutions at Leeds Crown Court in 1973–4. These files contained an astonishing mass of detail, including many Poulson papers seized during the bankruptcy and several private examinations in bankruptcy which cast new light on the entire affair. There may be more to come in the future. One Poulson case file (J291/102) has been closed for 100 years, and a file referred to during the bankruptcy hearings in 1972 entitled 'Correspondence mainly between debtor and the Right Honourable Reginald Maudling between 1st December 1966, to 2 July 1970' has not surfaced. Reading the files that have been released, and some papers in the West Yorkshire archives in Wakefield, has cast a new and very harsh light on Reginald Maudling's behaviour. When I saw the case files in September 2003 I was forced to reassess some of the judgements I had made about Maudling's conduct and character, although I have still tried hard to understand rather than merely condemn. But to read a letter Maudling sent while Home Secretary to a company director, saying that '£3,000 will meet all my cash requirements for the foreseeable future' was still a shock to the system.

For most of the period I have been writing *Reggie*, I have been on the staff of Kingston University. My colleagues Ilaria Favretto and Brian Brivati were particularly helpful, as was Kingston's Vice-Chancellor Peter Scott. Thank you also to Sue Simms and her colleagues for their efficiency. Long-term research is becoming increasingly difficult to organise in British higher education. What research does go on is to the credit of grant-giving foundations, including the Nuffield Foundation. I received a grant of a little under £5,000 in 2002, for which I would like to express thanks. It helped with research costs, including many visits to archives, including those in Washington, DC, the discovery of the Arthur Fawcett diary in Baltimore on the same trip, and with the employment of Alice Ceresole as my researcher for a few months in 2003. I would also like to thank Ken Ritchie and colleagues at the Electoral Reform Society for their patience concerning my outside interests. I would also like to express my gratitude and respect for David Butler and Anthony Seldon, who have taught me so much about politics and historical writing.

I am grateful to several individuals for answers to particular questions, advice on earlier drafts and various suggestions about writing the book: my agent Simon Trewin and editor Christopher Feeney. Vic Baston, Jill Baston (who took a particular interest in Beryl Laverick's acting career), Hannah Nicholson, Ros Baston, Donna Sharpe, the late Sir Alexander Glen, Karen Baston, Thomas Gijswijt, Alice Ceresole, Peter Neumann, Brian Brivati, Sir Peter Carey and John Marshall read bits and commented on them. Thanks also to Karen for the bibliography. Michael Crick, an avowed 'early life' enthusiast in his own work, inspired me to take Reggie's early career seriously, I think with good results. Michael Rice, Andrew Roth and Leo Abse all helped with psychological insights. Robert Shepherd, biographer of the other two musketeers of the Conservative Parliamentary Secretariat, Macleod and Powell, decided that he would not write a life of Maudling – but talked to me about him several times. He has written Reggie's new *Dictionary of National Biography* entry, to replace Edward Boyle's rather over-indulgent 1981 effort.

Writing *Reggie* has imposed great demands. He was a man of many parts, a quick intellect who grasped an astonishing array of arcane and detailed subjects as his life went on. I have scrambled in his wake, probably in many cases less sure-footedly. As well as the obvious intellectual and financial demands, it has been occasionally quite draining emotionally. I have spent countless hours agonising over what I should say about him, what is fair, what is supported by the evidence. I have generally opted for candour. When something is undeniable, but unpleasantly true, I have written it. When the evidence points towards a conclusion, without quite getting there, I hope I have indicated where it stops. There is more 'perhaps' in this book than in many such books; Reggie was that sort of man, and I am that sort of writer. I can't elevate speculation into fact, or reconstruct dialogue wholesale, but then I can't just abandon the trail either. I trust the readers are capable of making their own judgements about things. I thought hard, and I hope fairly.

I never met Reggie Maudling, and I have harsh things to say about certain aspects of his behaviour, but I am confident that I would have liked him. One of the best moments, although itself tinged with sadness, I have had in the writing of the book was when I showed Sir Sandy Glen, a friend of Reggie's for whom I have enormous admiration, a draft version of what has become Chapters 2 and 3. I was honoured that he recognised his old friend in what I had written. Likewise, Ken Williams – one of life's truly original characters Reggie and I have both got drunk and talked about big ideas with – felt that Reggie was in a funny way fortunate to have me on the case, as I had understood something about him. Reggie himself, in the final page of the epilogue of his memoirs, comments 'Tout expliquer, c'est tout détruire'. I prefer Madame de Staël's original version of 'Tout expliquer, c'est tout pardonner'. While I am sure there is still much that one does not know, and cannot know, to understand Maudling is I hope to forgive more than to destroy.

Finally, some deeper debts. My girlfriend (May 2001), fiancée (October 2002) and wife (August 2003), Hannah Nicholson, has been a (sometimes brisk) voice of common sense, a support and a distraction. A writer needs these. Reggie and Beryl were married, devotedly, for nearly forty years, and I hope that in this they can be an example. Reggie's parents are less inspiring. I am grateful that my mother has so little in common with Elsie Maudling, and that my father's own fine qualities include some he shares with R.G. – compassion, calmness, integrity and optimism. I dedicate this book to Vic and Jill Baston.

Lewis Baston
January 2004

ABBREVIATIONS

APG	active, permanent and guaranteed (Northern Ireland)
BCCI	Bank of Credit and Commerce International
BLPES	British Library of Political and Economic Science
CIA	Central Intelligence Agency
CP	Construction Promotion (Poulson)
CPA	Conservative Party Archives
CPRS	Central Policy Review Staff
CPS	Conservative Parliamentary Secretariat
CRD	Conservative Research Department
DTI	Department of Trade and Industry
ECGD	Export Credit Guarantee Department
ECSC	European Coal and Steel Community
EEC	European Economic Community
EFTA	European Free Trade Association
EPU	European Payments Union
ERM	Exchange Rate Mechanism
ESRC	Economic and Social Research Council
FCO	Foreign and Commonwealth Office
FTA	Free Trade Area
GLC	Greater London Council
GATT	General Agreement on Tariffs and Trade
HCSC	House of Commons Select Committee
IBA	Independent Broadcasting Authority
IMF	International Monetary Fund
IOS	Investors Overseas Services
IPD	Inter Planning and Design (Poulson successor)
IRA	Irish Republican Army
ITCS	International Technical and Constructional Services (Poulson)
JCR	Junior Common Room
KADU	Kenyan African Democratic Union
KANU	Kenya African National Union
Memoirs	Reginald Maudling, *Memoirs* (London: Sidgwick & Jackson, 1978)
NARA	National Archives and Records Administration (USA)
NATO	North Atlantic Treaty Organisation

NEDC   National Economic Development Committee (Neddy)
NIC   National Incomes Commission (Nicky)
NICRA   Northern Ireland Civil Rights Association
NUM   National Union of Mineworkers
OECD   Organisation for Economic Cooperation and Development
OEEC   Organisation for European Economic Cooperation
OPS   Obscene Publications Squad
OSB   Open System Building company (Poulson)
PESC   Public Expenditure Survey Committee
PPS   Parliamentary Private Secretary
QPM   *Questions of Procedure for Ministers*
REFA   Real Estate Fund of America
RIBA   Royal Institute of British Architects
RPM   Resale Price Maintenance
RUC   Royal Ulster Constabulary
SDLP   Social Democratic and Labour Party (Northern Ireland)
SDR   Special Drawing Right
SIH   Shipping Industrial Holdings
UAE   United Arab Emirates
UDA   Ulster Defence Association
UDI   Unilateral Declaration of Independence (Rhodesia)
UVF   Ulster Volunteer Force

THE MAUDLINGS AND THE PEARSONS

Reginald George Maudling was an unusual character in his chosen profession. He had a puckish sense of humour, a social conscience and a restless interest in new things, be it modern architecture or novel entrepreneurial ways of doing business. He had a talent for explaining complicated subjects in terms that people could easily understand, but he quickly became bored by formality and routine. His career was briefly disrupted by involvement in a firm with a prestigious board of directors, which was not all that it seemed. He married a woman who was acutely ambitious and in constant need of money. And he had a son, who shared more than just his name, who nearly became Prime Minister.

Despite being so much his father's son, Reggie Maudling had remarkably little to say about his family in later life. Sir Sandy Glen, who became close to him in the mid-1950s, does not remember him ever talking about his parents beyond mentioning the bare fact that his father was an actuary and had a firm of his own.[1] The Maudling family itself lacks much of an oral tradition, and the current generation do not know much about their family history.[2] Reggie gave little away in his *Memoirs*. There was nothing personal in his description of his origins, which reads more like a sociological analysis of the mores of the upper middle class: 'narrow, closed, and class-conscious in both directions, up and down. But it had high standards of integrity, and a deep belief in patriotism, in honest hard work, and in the virtues of saving. No doubt it was in many ways intolerant, and could be described as complacent.'[3]

This dispassionate, generalised version of his childhood failed to reveal what Reggie inherited from his family background. Thanks to R.G.'s[4] hard work, he and his family had a good standard of living. Reggie's earliest memories were of a large house with a tennis court and a full-time maid, but not of love. His mother was cold; his father was distant despite his good humour. Reggie's outward personality was very similar to that of his jovial father, a legacy he embraced, but his mother's snobbery and intolerance inflicted deeper wounds. The Maudlings may have been complacently well off, but his mother Elsie was anxiously aware of her side of the family's far from grand provincial origins, and the failure of her father's dreams of big business success.

Reggie Maudling was a fourth-generation Londoner and a third-generation City professional on his father's side. The Maudlings were middle-class dwellers in the big city, lacking in traditions of blue blood and manual labour, who felt their identity was English without prefix or suffix denoting class or region. Their jobs – in the law, the City and politics – were all London occupations. Reggie's branch of the family is a story of north London and the City of London for the most part; there is another branch of the family in County Durham but the two are not closely connected. There are two main theories about the distant origins of the surname. One is that it is a derivation of 'Maud' originating in Central Europe ('-ling' is a German diminutive form), and that, way back, the Maudlings might have been Jewish. The other is that it comes from 'Magdalen', meaning 'woman from Magdala', suggesting that, way back, the Maudlings might have been Palestinians (or possibly come from a 'Magdalen' home for fallen women).[5] Reggie himself showed little sign of knowing or caring; he was more concerned about where he was going than whence he came.

Reggie's grandfather was George Terry Maudling, who was born in Woolwich in November 1855. George moved north of the river, working as a solicitor's clerk in the City and marrying Ellenor Price in 1881. George gradually worked his way up from his position as clerk, taking his law examinations in 1898 and becoming a partner in the City firm of Morley, Shireff & Co., based at Old Broad Street, in 1919. George's parents were William Maudling, a Woolwich iron founder, and his wife Elizabeth who lived to the age of 87. In the family's history Reggie was from the third comfortable generation; George Terry carried them from the working to upper middle class and after him the Maudlings belonged to the respectable middle class of City professional services which had grown up to service the capital city of the Empire. George's son, Reginald George, was born on 20 September 1882, and went to Merchant Taylors' School in the City from 1894 to 1900, where he was noted as a cricketer.[6] After he left school he worked as a clerk for the London & Lancashire insurance company; one of the attractions of this work was apparently that he expected to be able to get off easily to play games.[7] R.G. was bright and ambitious, and studied for qualifications of his own while at the firm, becoming a Fellow of the Institute of Actuaries in 1909.

The role of an actuary is essentially to advise insurers about the statistical complexities of risk that underlie insurance, and to forecast financial returns. A good actuary has to be a good mathematician with a strong grasp of statistics, while also having a sense of the way in which real life disrupts the orderly world of risk tables. Despite their other similarities, R.G., the professionally cautious calculator of risks, had a different nature from his son, whose career was destroyed by careless risk-taking.

The actuarial profession has long been the butt of jokes along the lines that it is for people who can't stand the excitement of accountancy, but R.G. Maudling, at least, had an interesting career. Not long after he left London & Lancashire, he was appointed head of the Life Department at a newly formed insurance company called Omnium, which, as its name suggests, intended to deal in all forms of insurance business. It was launched with something of a splash in October 1909 with an illustrious board of directors including the Earl of Chichester and Prince Francis of Teck.[8]

Omnium soon ran into difficulties. It was one of the biggest cases in a spate of insurance company failures in the early 1910s that provided the backdrop for Forster's *Howard's End*. General insurance was a crowded market and a contemporary analysis thought that for success 'a modest beginning, great patience in the early years, and a low ratio of expenses are absolutely necessary'.[9] Omnium had none of these features, displaying grand ambitions and big spending, with well over £10,000 on 'initial expenses' and over £1,000 in each category of 'general expenses' and 'office furniture and fittings' out of its initial capital of £100,000.[10]

Omnium closed down in April 1912 and R.G. had the distinction of being the only head of a life insurance business never to have paid out on a claim. Most of the business was sold on to the United London & Scottish group, which in turn went bust a couple of months later. In 1913 Conservative MP John Norton Griffiths asked a question in the Commons about the Omnium affair, alleging that 'severe losses have been incurred by tradesmen, working men, and other policy holders, who are unable to obtain payment of losses insured against or return of premiums paid'. The government replied that because Omnium had been put into voluntary liquidation the Board of Trade had no jurisdiction to launch an inquiry.[11] There was a distinct whiff of malpractice about Omnium, but at that time there was little that could be done.

Maudling's own part in the collapse seems innocent. The life business was disposed of separately from the rest of the company; it was transferred to the London & Lancashire, his former employers and a more substantial company than United London & Scottish. Maudling's Omnium venture came to nothing, but he escaped with his reputation intact, or even enhanced because of his insistence that the life business was put on a secure footing. He was soon back in business thanks to the intervention of Sir Alfred Watson, the doyen of the actuarial profession. Watson was the senior partner in the oldest – and for a long time the only – firm of consulting actuaries, R. Watson & Co., who were free to take on business independently rather than working in-house for an insurance firm. Watson recalled that Maudling was the only candidate who had answered correctly a question he had composed in an exam paper, and was impressed by his conduct in the Omnium affair. He made R.G. a junior partner, and then quickly left the firm on his appointment as the first ever Government Actuary, a post created because of the Liberal government's National Insurance Act passed in 1911. In 1912, at the age of 30, R.G. Maudling had one of the highest positions in his profession.

R.G. shared with his son Reggie many of his more endearing and impressive qualities. He lacked pomposity: 'he had an amusing dislike for formal conferences and when they became unduly irritating to him he would keep up a running fire of funny asides.'[12] A reputation as a wit may be more easily acquired among actuaries than other professions, but he was certainly one of its freer spirits.[13] He also had a gift for turning the dry technicalities of his work into plain language and working well with clients. The Watson firm grew steadily during Maudling's control and further partners were taken on. R.G. also contributed to the work of the Institute of Actuaries as a senior Fellow, serving on the executive and writing an important article in its journal about sickness compensation in the mining industry in 1929.[14] His wider interests were apparent in his election as a member of the Royal Economic Society in 1923[15] and the Royal Statistical Society in 1928.[16]

In the early 1920s R.G. established an entrepreneurial offshoot, Commercial Calculating Ltd, which worked from the same offices in the Temple. Commercial Calculating offered the statistical and mathematical expertise to do bulk and specialist number-crunching, outside actuarial work as such, to firms who would pay for it. The ventures prospered and in 1927 the firms moved into a prestigious headquarters at Empire House, a newly built office block in St Martin-le-Grand on the western edge of the City of London, opposite the imposing Telephone Exchange. Empire House was not one of the best examples of a 1920s office block, with a clumsily designed interior, but it is still imbued with the flavour of its times.[17] R.G. Maudling was a devotee of modern architecture, as demonstrated by his move into Empire House and his choice in the late 1930s to buy two newly built flats in modernist blocks at Mandeville Court in West Hampstead and the Art Deco Hastings Court development in Worthing.

Though prosperous, R.G. Maudling was a generous man. Reggie had a scholarship at Merchant Taylors' but his father still paid school fees, which went instead to a 'Maudling fund' to support boys whose fathers had died or run into financial trouble. In the financial arrangements in his 1940 will, R.G. insisted that any funds of his not be invested in the mining industry. When he died in 1953, early in retirement like many driven, hard-working men, he left nearly £71,000 in his will; he would count as a millionaire if his legacy were denominated in the currency of the early 2000s rather than the 1950s.

Reggie Maudling's mother, Elizabeth Emilie (usually known as Elsie), was born in Crouch Hill, Hornsey in north London, on 15 March 1885, the daughter of Charles Pearson and his wife Annie (née Cooper). Charles Pearson was in the printing trade, an upwardly mobile man originally from Derby who described himself as a 'stationer' when he married in 1884 and a 'managing director of a printing company' in 1910. Annie was from Huddersfield, the daughter of James Cooper, who was alternatively 'gentleman' and 'general waste dealer' depending on which official document one consults. The Pearsons were managers and businessmen, rather than professionals, and of perhaps noticeable provincial origins and accents in turn of the century London.

Charles Pearson owned a printing works on Mansell Street in Aldgate, where the City of London ran up against the East End; he would claim that it was in the City while it was actually a few yards inside the borough of Stepney. Wherever it was, it was an impressive building which signalled to all who saw it that 'Chas. Pearson & Son Printer and Manufacturing Stationer' had arrived. After the war, in 1921, the Pearson firm had two branch offices in the City proper and described its work as 'wholesale, export, manufacturing and retail stationers, commercial and art printers, die sinkers and engravers and sample bag manufacturers'.[18]

The Pearsons lived in Stoke Newington, the other side of Finsbury Park from Crouch Hill. The small borough consisted of solidly middle-class, even a little snobbish and exclusive, areas of north London, but even so it was not Millionaire's Row. Charles Pearson did not manage the next step up and make the big time as a captain of industry. Pearson's business boasted an imposing façade but it somehow failed to generate much in the way of profit for its founder. It did not grow much more after the early 1920s and from the 1930s onwards it declined. Pearson himself retired in poor health and lived in modest suburban comfort in the same North Finchley as his daughter at the time Reggie was born. He died of lung cancer in December 1928 and left a relatively meagre £7,982 in his will. His widow Annie had enough to live reasonably well, but she did not leave much either when she died in March 1941 in a coal gas poisoning accident.

R.G. Maudling was a suitable husband for the Pearsons' daughter, a respectable young professional with prospects and a pleasing nature. He lived literally around the corner from them in Queen Elizabeth's Walk, his parents' house in Stoke Newington, and the Maudlings were established members of local society – the sort of people who were invited to civic and mayoral banquets. R.G. and Elsie were married on 5 October 1910 at the imposing parish church of Stoke Newington, an occasion recorded in the local newspaper as one of the district's 'interesting weddings . . . The couple were married very quietly. The presents were very numerous and several were of quite a costly nature.'[19] Quiet weddings became something of a family tradition; compared to Reggie's own nuptials, his parents' marriage was positively showy. The best man was the groom's brother Leonard Hugh Maudling.

Elsie's character is more elusive at this distance than her husband's. She was ferociously status-conscious and seems to have been as harsh and cold as her husband was jolly, but we only have Reggie's – indirect – word for her authoritarian, smothering attitude to him as a child.[20] Like R.G., Elsie Maudling had unusual preferences in wills, but in contrast to his ethical issues with mining she used wills to make personal points. She intervened in her mother's arrangements, and at Elsie's 'express request' her benefit from Annie's will was restricted to £1,000. What Elsie may have meant by this is open to interpretation. It is possible that she wanted to help her brother keep the business going, and knew that she and R.G. were comfortably off; also possible that it was a gesture of contempt as much as generosity. When she died, she surprisingly left no will. It is impossible to believe that someone in her position, the wife of a City professional who had drawn up a complicated will, would have been accidentally intestate. At some time between his death in 1953 and hers in 1957 she almost certainly destroyed her will, in order to avoid expressing anything that might be taken as love for her only son.

Elsie's warped feelings towards Reggie were no doubt intensified by his status as her only child, repository of all her hopes and ambitions. Theories about birth order effects tend to be rather speculative psychology, and attempts to link birth order with future leadership or political views have amounted to rather little of substance. However, Reggie was something of a stereotypical only child – sociable but with an elusive, self-contained quality, and rather indulged and indulgent. He clearly found the experience of being an only child stifling and reacted against it in his own family:

> Only children get many advantages which parents cannot provide for a large family, but they are constantly in danger of being spoiled and attracting too much attention to themselves, and taking too much for granted. This is fine while it lasts, but when you grow older and move out into the world, it sometimes calls for rather painful adjustment.[21]

A 1970 study of the family background of past Prime Ministers suggested that ambition for high office was related to the deprivation of love in childhood through the death of a parent.[22] For Maudling, political ambition burned with a flickering, rather than constant, flame; his loss was of a different nature. He was also more intelligent and self-aware – for good or ill, acknowledging Freud as one of the great intellects of his age – than most men in politics. He did not seek a simulacrum of love in the adoration of a crowd. He sought it instead in his own family, and his friends. Reggie chose as his motto for life some lines of Hilaire Belloc:

> From quiet homes and first beginning,
>   Out to the undiscovered ends,
> There's nothing worth the wear of winning,
>   But laughter and the love of friends.

Unusually for a man of his generation Reggie Maudling did talk openly of 'love'. For him, it was something to be striven for, something that he needed effort to achieve – not something unconditional. His search for love was part of what made him such a kind, charming man, such a healer rather than a warrior in politics. But it also led him 'out to the undiscovered ends' – to disgrace and an early grave.

Chapter 1

'FROM QUIET HOMES AND FIRST BEGINNING', 1917–1937

Reginald Maudling – he had no middle name[1] – was born on 7 March 1917. His parents Elsie and R.G. were then living in Finchley in the north London suburbs, at 53 Westbury Road, a quiet street of Edwardian family houses near Woodside Park station. However, only a few weeks after Reggie was born they moved out of London, frightened by German air raids, to the sleepy town of Bexhill on the Sussex coast. They remained for a few years after the end of the war and Reggie briefly attended the Harewood infants' school in Bexhill. Reggie's earliest memories are of a feeling for the sea, an appreciation of the waves rolling onto the beach and an awareness of comfort and security on water and land.[2]

In the mid-1920s the Maudling family moved back to the London area. They settled in Southborough Road, a prosperous avenue of early twentieth-century villas near to Bickley station in the Kentish suburbs of London of the sort where City professionals frequently chose to live. Reggie was enrolled at a local preparatory school, Bickley Hall, which occupied a Georgian building in nearly 30 acres of its own parkland just up the road from his parents' house.

Bickley Hall was a traditionalist, muscular Christian school, founded in the Victorian era as Sidcup Hall College, but which moved to the Bickley Hall buildings in 1918.[3] It was a family-run school. The Farnfields were eight brothers, all of whom became teachers and clergymen and six of whom won sporting Blues at Cambridge. Bernard 'Bunny' Farnfield was an international amateur footballer before the First World War, and also gifted at cricket, tennis and hockey. Undaunted by a severe heart attack in his final term at Cambridge, he remained a keen sportsman all his life and when he became joint Headmaster of Bickley Hall he did his best to instil an obsession with sport in his charges.[4] His brother, Archie Farnfield, was the other joint Headmaster and a man of firm religious views. 'Mr Archie' and 'Mr Bunny', as they insisted the boys call them, were in charge during Reggie's period at the school.

In the 1920s, Bickley Hall was a pretentious establishment. At 40 guineas a term, plus extras, it was expensive.[5] Boys were required to wear Eton suits on Sundays, dark tweed in winter and grey flannel in summer. Its promotional material was, with false modesty, written by a supposedly independent observer rather than being an honest puff from its Headmasters.[6] The ethos of the school, reflecting the interests of its Headmasters, revolved around Christianity and team sports. From this angle, Reggie Maudling was a total failure for the school in that he took next to no interest in either of its founding principles.

There were two religious services a day, conducted by the school chaplain, who was, according to the PR brochure from the 1920s, 'particularly selected for his understanding of boys'.[7] The school's grounds contained a swimming pool, tennis courts, pitches for football and cricket and a miniature golf course. Whatever its faults, Bickley Hall was at least well equipped; it also had an oak-panelled reading room, a fine flock-wallpapered dining hall and civilised showers and changing rooms. It had a reasonably high-quality teaching staff and was described by government inspectors in 1933 as being 'a normal Preparatory School of a good type, in which boys are brought to a standard at which they pass comfortably on to Public Schools and a creditable proportion of them to Scholarship standard. They are particularly well catered for in the matter of games, and have every appearance of being healthy and happy.'[8]

Manly competition was another virtue the school intended to instil. The school described its purpose in terms that were supposed to have died in the trenches: 'Every boy is made to feel that when he does go on to a Public School, 'Varsity, and finally into Professional, Business or Public Life, he must not "let down" his old school, but must always "play the game" and do his best.' The school brochure promised that the Headmasters ensured that 'a particularly watchful eye is kept on a boy's conduct and habits' and that 'the Dormitories are personally supervised by the Headmasters, and the Dormitory discipline is very strict'. Reggie's own memories of the place were not fond, and he refused to lift a finger when he was petitioned to save it from closure in the early 1960s.[9] But he was well able to keep up with his studies: 'I found the scholarship relatively easy, because I had a quick mind and an ability to absorb facts, and that was what was then meant by scholarship.'[10] But he disliked the sport, especially compulsory rugby, and the discipline at the school scared him into conformity. The school sent weekly reports to all parents and enlisted their support for its discipline.

Reggie was at Bickley Hall because of the social aspirations of his parents, but perhaps because he was not there for long he was not scarred by it. It seems likely that he was a day boy and therefore spared the worst of what was predominantly a boarding school.[11] He did learn, even if by rote, the basics of classics, maths, French and history. He also absorbed one of the better lessons the place offered: 'At Bickley Hall they are taught how to lose as well as how to win. They accept defeat with the same spirit as they rejoice in their victories. If the words "bad luck" are heard in their conversation, it is only used in speaking of their opponents.' Reggie was always able to shrug

his shoulders and move on from his defeats without lapsing – until the very
end – into self-pity. The adult Maudling behaved graciously to those he had
beaten, or lost to, in competition, such as electoral opponents and rival
ministers during government disputes.

Reggie escaped at the age of 11. He took an examination for school
entrance and performed spectacularly well – he was elected to an entrance
scholarship in December 1928 and started at Merchant Taylors' in January
1929 in the Upper Fourth form. He was a year and a quarter younger than
his nearest rival. The school separated out pupils into broad streams,
concentrating on different aspects of the syllabus, and Maudling was in the
classical division. The choice of Merchant Taylors' was a matter of
Maudling's father following a family tradition – he and his brother had both
gone there – but it also placed Maudling socially. When Maudling started, the
school was based at Charterhouse Square in the City of London, but in May
1933 it moved to purpose-built buildings amid acres of playing fields at
Sandy Lodge in Northwood, north-west of London on the Metropolitan Line
of the Underground. It was mainly a day school, and Maudling commuted
back and forward to the City each day from Bickley. When the school moved
it became practically impossible to commute, as he would have spent at least
four hours each day in transit. His parents moved out of Bickley, and for a
few years after 1933 they lived somewhat temporarily in places such as the
Moor Park Club and the Bushey Hall hotel quite close to the school,
suggesting an unusually close relationship with their son.[12]

The school was founded in 1561 by the City of London's Merchant Taylors'
livery company and it retained strong links with the City. Its ethos was, for a
public school of the time, quite academic and its products tended to be solid,
upper-middle-class City professionals – the senior Maudling was far from the
only actuary to have had a Merchant Taylors' education. The school was
respectable rather than fashionable, not a training ground for social and
political ascendancy but a serious-minded establishment that was particularly
geared towards educating pupils in the classics. The young Maudling's
academic success in such a school is therefore a sign of his high intellectual
ability, not a reflection on the dullness of his contemporaries. Almost
effortlessly, Maudling rose towards the top of his form (second out of twenty-
eight, with a special commendation, in his first term). His form teacher in
Midsummer Term 1929, Rex Cherrett, recalled him as 'A mere twelve year
old, dark, solid, self-possessed but the owner of a very cheerful smile, clearly
very able but not making himself unpopular by being too eager to prove it,
slightly inky in appearance and a little untidy in his handwriting'.[13]

In those days bright boys were accelerated through the school and within
his first year Maudling had risen to the Classical Fifth, the most senior form
outside the Sixth. In the Easter Term of 1930, at the age of only 12, he was
second from top in a form of twenty-three which contained boys up to the
age of 17. His academic triumphs continued with his gaining his School

Certificate at the age of 13 in summer 1930; when the school returned from vacation in the autumn he was in the Lower Sixth, still only at the age of 13. It was then that he encountered the teacher who gave him his strongest memories of the school, Billy Lumb. Maudling remembered Lumb's ferocious anti-Catholic opinions, but also his love for the classics and his ability to inspire the boys in his class to share the enthusiasm, and his opinion that 'the purpose of an education is to learn how to learn'.[14]

In 1932, at the age of 15, Maudling passed his Higher Certificate exams. Even at a time when schools were more flexible, this was an extraordinarily rapid progress – he was an exceptional young man in something of a hurry. His Headmaster, Spencer Leeson, recognised the risks of such heady early success, telling him after he had done well in some exams, 'Maudling, you suffer from two dangers, vanity and selfishness, beware of them both.' Maudling wrote that he had never had better advice from anyone.[15] Perhaps in later life he avoided these undesirable traits too diligently, not noticing that he had acquired other, maybe more serious, faults.

Maudling was not often in trouble with the authorities at Merchant Taylors'; there were no instances of him being reported in the surviving caning books from the period. The school was nowhere near as harsh as Bickley Hall and for the most part boys were treated reasonably, but there were occasional acts of unfairness. Anthony Greenwood, then an older pupil but a Labour minister in the 1960s, once arbitrarily gave Maudling fifty lines. Greenwood had been told off by the Headmaster for not using enough punishment to maintain his authority and angrily dished out the punishment to the first three small boys he saw: 'they were not behaving unduly boisterously and looked hurt and surprised when I descended on them . . . It was the only time I ever administered punishment, and I had forgotten about it until Reggie Maudling turned up in the House and reminded me.'[16] A small act of injustice of a peculiar sort – was Maudling more the victim of the system of discipline imposed by the school authorities, or of Greenwood's idealistic protest?

More usually Maudling's engaging personality saw him through any trouble. According to a contemporary in 1929–32, Andrew Powles, 'he was generous with his talents, always willing to explain some problem with homework'.[17] Even when he was clearly misbehaving, people found it difficult to be hostile to Reggie. In a revealing story Donald Sherriff, another boy who went up to school on the same train and later became a vicar, remembered Reggie as a prankster:

We sometimes travelled together, and on one occasion I got into his compartment at Bromley South, and he kindly offered me a chocolate. I took one with silver paper, threw the paper out of the window and took a bite. It was then that I discovered that it was not cream inside but soap . . . I spat it out, but I still foamed at the mouth. There was no water to rinse my mouth, and I re-spat, and spat again, but by Penge East the compartment was packed. He was sitting opposite me, and really enjoying the situation. For the next twenty minutes I sat speechless, but still foaming. It was only when we reached Holborn that I was able to wash my mouth out. But there was something about him that made it impossible to be cross over the situation – and I quite often used it as an illustration of things not being quite what they seem . . .[18]

Behind the glittering academic achievement and the occasional practical joke, it is possible to discern a complicated, solitary boy who left little impression on most of his contemporaries. While not unpopular, Maudling was out of the mainstream because of his youth and his lack of interest in group activities of any sort. Dennis Nicholson, who was a few years younger than Maudling, remembered that 'he seemed to spend most of his time trying to get out of doing things'.[19] Reggie recalled when Chancellor that 'I'm afraid I wasn't good at corporate activities outside the scholastic. My outside interests were very undignified and few in number.' The mind boggles as to what he might have meant. He emphasised his feelings about organised games: 'My attitude to games? I was lazy. I was very fat and a very bad player of games, and my eyesight is rather short, so I didn't find rugger or cricket very agreeable. I preferred golf, where the ball is stationary and easier to see, and easier to hit.'[20] Golf also suited a measured, solitary temperament. It avoided direct physical confrontation, the need for coordination between players in the team and demanded less continuous attention. Maudling as a golfer could talk and make jokes with opponents, while enjoying a leisurely walk. The clever schoolboy, with the connivance of most teachers who take no pleasure in inflicting team games on the unwilling and incompetent, can often choose congenial games options. By the end of his time at Merchant Taylors', Maudling was quite an accomplished golfer, with a low handicap, and was the captain of the school team in a match against the masters. He also, strangely given his bulk and apparent lack of physical grace and coordination, excelled at ice skating. He once appeared in an ice pageant of some sort before the Prince of Wales, a tale he was fond of telling his friends over a drink and revelling in the incongruity.[21] To the end of his life, he kept hold of a bronze national medal for figure skating.

While he did not like team games, he positively loathed the Officer Training Corps (OTC), the quasi-compulsory military training for public schoolboys. He told the school newsletter: 'I was the worst of the lot. Most unco-operative, I'm afraid, and very incompetent. My puttees never stayed up. I was generally thoroughly bad, I'm sad to say.'[22]

His amateur interviewer noted that, 'behind the cigar smoke, he looks unrepentant'. Maudling's OTC career produced several characteristic anecdotes – he didn't see the point of getting rained on at the parade ground, so he took an umbrella with him when it looked wet. In his *Memoirs* he recalls having fainted on a parade because he had over-indulged in the tuck shop at lunchtime, although one of his contemporaries remembered that 'he used to go on field days with a couple of bottles of beer secreted about his person and that this rather slowed down his movements in attack', which could provide an alternative explanation for his sudden unconsciousness.[23] Reggie could have been the model for the 'fat owl' Billy Bunter, with his schoolboy enthusiasms, rotundity and – perhaps – his lifelong fixation about an imminent postal order bringing him comfort, fame and fortune. Young Reggie even appeared in the costume of a brown owl at a Hallowe'en ice skating ball.[24]

It is intriguing to note that the mentality of the mid-century Conservative Party was perhaps more influenced by the spirit of rugger and the OTC than any political philosophy. In his political life Reggie would be among people who would have despised boys like him, and who respected institutions and symbols that the young Maudling in turn had rejected. It is speculative but it is certainly imaginable that exposure to a less congenial public school – more snobbery, more rugger – might have tipped Maudling's individualism into a hatred of the system. But the young Reggie had already learned how to make peace with the system and work his way around the unpleasant aspects of it.

Maudling spent four years in the Lower and Upper Sixth Forms. Very belatedly, the delay probably because of his youth, he became a 'Prompter' (junior prefect) in Christmas Term 1934. During his long Sixth Form, he matured and developed a certain amount of confidence. He became more willing to express his opinions, speaking for the Conservatives in the school's mock election in October 1931 when the schoolboys mirrored the national result – a Tory landslide.[25] Others recall him 'always talking about politics', and having an ambition to be 'a Cabinet Minister, and I intend to be Prime Minister'.[26] Leeson fostered wider interests among the Sixth Form by chairing the debating society, and encouraging students and guest speakers to give lectures. The pages of the school magazine, *Taylorian*, at the time are full of accounts of these events. Each summer several students had travelled abroad and returned to school with social and political portraits of where they had been, including several from Germany in the early stages of the Nazi regime.

Maudling's first recorded contribution to the debating society came in October 1933 in a debate on the proposition 'That this House has no confidence in the League of Nations'. The minutes recall that when the debate was open to the floor of the House 'Mr Maudling, in a burst of withering sarcasm, made it quite clear that his faith in the League had gone'. At the time, the League had been discredited by its failure to do anything about the Japanese attack on Manchuria, although particularly on the left in Britain illusions persisted about its effectiveness. Maudling then bobbed up in two successive debates to defend capitalism against a rhetorical assault from several left-wing Taylorians: 'It was idle talk to say that capitalism had failed.

It had been misused. Such events as the Great War had dislocated the system. Communism was no more likely to succeed than capitalism. Communism simply meant the mass production of everything.'[27] Having distanced himself from communism, the young Maudling also felt an early distaste for fascism. He was a member of the dissenting minority (37–17) who opposed the motion that 'This House has more sympathy with the German point of view than the French'. The general pro-German feeling in Britain in the early 1930s, of which the trend of the schoolboys' debate was but a tiny part, was more about the harsh treatment Germany had received in the Versailles Treaty in 1919 than support for Hitler's regime. Maudling returned to criticise Nazi Germany in two further debates, saying that 'State control generally does not benefit an art, quoting as an example the present position of the Berlin State Opera' (which was being forced to conform to Nazi racial and cultural ideology) and deploring Jew-baiting in Germany.[28]

Maudling's opinions at this stage of his life could cause him no embarrassment whatsoever. They are in line with the humane, liberal-conservative approach to politics that remained with him throughout his life. His last two appearances at the Sixth Form debating society were flourishes in which he expressed rather less orthodox ideas. He spoke against blood sports, in a memorable performance:

> When the debate was thrown open to the House, the floodgates of sarcasm were raised, and torrents of rhetoric poured forth. Mr Maudling, coming into action like a machine gun, fired at such a rate that most of us heard nothing more than a low rumble, punctuated now and then, like the cracking of individual bullets, with 'the German sport of Jew-baiting', 'hunting the Capitalist in Russia' 'the OTC' 'that immortal trio, huntin', shootin' and fishin'' 'disguised as an apple tree' 'the *Bystander, Sketch* and *Sphere*' 'Society photographs' 'large mass of bleeding birds' 'charging off on a motor bicycle' 'why not use armoured cars?' 'Lucretius and the Classical Side' and 'Gad, sir! Lord Beaverbrook was right!' Eventually Mr Maudling, who is not water-cooled and cannot fire for ever, dismantled his 'cannons overcharged with double cracks' and subsided.[29]

Maudling's tendency to incoherence and gabbling in his school debates was mentioned several times in *Taylorian* debate reports, including – engagingly – one signed off as 'R.M.'. He always spoke rapidly in debate even as a more practised performer in the House of Commons, where the writers in the Gallery reckoned he spoke at 200–250 words per minute, compared to the average MP's 120–140.[30] He was more languid and conversational on television, but when animated his words sometimes spilled out in chaotic fashion.

His swansong at the school debating society was as seconder of the motion 'in the opinion of this House the literature, art and music of the present days will be condemned by posterity'. Perhaps his desire to be a scheduled speaker led him to argue a case he did not believe with much conviction, but the adult Maudling would not have agreed that jazz was a 'cacophony', nor that 'Turner was the first impressionist and his ideas were followed, until to-day we have meaningless designs. The artist tries to express his personality, but personality cannot be communicated, therefore modern art cannot last.' A true son of R.G. Maudling, though, Reggie did hail 'the beauty of modern architecture'.[31]

In spring 1935 he left school a term early, to the fury of the school authorities. He felt it was hardly worth his while staying on, as he had already finished his exams and in February 1935 it was confirmed that he had been awarded a scholarship to Merton College, Oxford to start that autumn. He took the chance to go on a trip to the USA and Canada, visiting friends he had made through golfing and through his father's neighbours and business contacts. He spent much of it in Hamilton, Ontario, socialising and playing golf with the Dalley family, who were prominent in local business. He returned via a couple of days in New York, commenting forty years later that he 'learnt how lonely you can be in a big city when you are young and mystified'.[32] Maudling came back from this trip telling tales of the wonders of the New World: Steven Watson, a friend from school who also went on to Oxford, recalled that 'he held us enraptured with his description of American and Canadian girls'.[33] From Maudling's own rather elliptical account in his memoirs, it sounds as if he made more progress on this front in Canada than he did in the United States.

Maudling went up to Merton College, Oxford, in autumn 1935 to read classics. Merton scholarships are called 'Postmasterships' and at that time entitled the holder to £100 a year (equivalent in 2003: about £4,000). Merton, like Merchant Taylors', valued academic achievement in the 1930s and the tutors were trying to build up what might now be called a 'centre of excellence' in classical studies. Its social composition was changing a little as well, with the major public schools being less dominant than in previous years.[34] Another feature of Merton was its insularity as far as Oxford student life was concerned, which in the late 1930s seemed to be dominated by Balliol. Arguably the oldest collegiate institution in Oxford, its pleasing gardens and quads screened from Merton Street by forbidding walls, Merton was and is traditional but rather quirky.

The classics degree at Oxford is called Literae Humaniores, usually known as Greats. Unlike most degree courses, it lasts four years and has two sets of examinations, Honour Moderations in the middle of the second year and Finals after four – hence the ability of those taking it to claim a 'Double First' if they do well in both. The first few terms are largely concerned with classical literature, but the content after that broadens out into philosophy and ancient history. Maudling started out studying Greats, but swiftly became bored with classical literature – perhaps understandably given the length of time he had spent academically treading water in the classical Sixth Form at school. Maudling persuaded his tutors to allow him to proceed directly to the second part of Greats and ended up doing a three-year classics degree, something which is not really supposed to happen in Oxford.

Maudling's switch of degree had several consequences. He could never claim the somewhat meaningless academic distinction of a Double First, although later in life people would sometimes assume he had one, but this was a minor loss. The academic pressure was off in his first year and a half and he had more time to develop other interests. He was exposed earlier to philosophy, which made a deep impression on him. But Maudling had also found a way of beating the system. The Postmastership he had been awarded was on the assumption that he would be reading the full four-year Greats (although technically it was for two years and renewable for another two) but he would only actually study in Merton for three years. He walked off at the end of his studies in summer 1938 with a year's extra money and the blessing of his tutors.

A clue to Reggie's distinctiveness as a politician comes with an examination of what he did in the political ferment of Oxford in the 1930s. The notorious 1933 'King and Country' vote at the Oxford Union debating society was followed by several years of passionate, serious politics. There was some youthful communism and a growing consciousness of the menace of fascism, particularly after the start of the Spanish Civil War in 1936. Two by-elections, for Oxford University in 1937 and the City seat in 1938, rallied progressive students of all parties and were a training ground for distinguished, powerful future leaders like Denis Healey and Edward Heath.

All of this passed Maudling by. Merton was certainly a college where one could close the doors on the outside world, but it was also the young Maudling's choice not to get involved. According to a contemporary, he then found student politics a bore and adult politics somewhat repulsive.[35] He joined the Oxford Union debating society but surprisingly, given his enthusiasm for the Merchant Taylors' debating society, he hardly participated. He recalled that 'I made only one speech in a Union debate – it was very, very bad'.[36] The rather full records of debates in the *Isis* student newspaper, perhaps out of kindness, do not record any contribution. Maudling's erratic machine-gun style delivery, while passable at a school society, would have floundered at the Union amid the poised, fluent – if facile – oratory of the elegant products of the major public schools. Edward Heath, starting from a lower social position and without Maudling's easy charm, managed to impose himself on the Union through force of will; but Maudling could not be bothered with the disagreeable business of fighting his way through and decided to relax and enjoy life. It is not hard to see a parallel with what happened when they confronted each other for the Conservative leadership in 1965.

Maudling's principal university activity was golf. He would often get up at eleven in the morning, walk across the quad to his bath and then get his clubs and disappear for a leisurely round of golf, leaving his friends baffled as to when he got his work done;[37] his ability to succeed without apparent effort was established early. His prowess at Merchant Taylors' made him one of Oxford's best golfers and he frequently appeared for the university team. He made a splash early on, as *Isis* reported in November 1935: 'we congratulate R. Maudling on his golfing success at Southfields last week where, playing from a handicap of 3, he tied for the St. Andrew's Vase with a net score of 70.'[38] Further successes were reported in autumn 1936, but his team showings became sporadic. Maudling could easily have had a golf Blue (a mark of sporting distinction regarded with absurd levels of respect later in life) but could not be bothered to turn out for the team on quite enough occasions to manage it – he was also less than diligent at attending practice sessions.[39] It may sound a truism, but Maudling was not particularly good at things that were difficult for him. Some people are, and have the perseverance to practise and become good at them in the end, but Maudling found that a lot of life came easily to him. He could not be bothered with the 'inconvenience' of practice for golf, or much else.[40]

Maudling was not one of the big men in college. He had lost the clear academic superiority he enjoyed at school – his contemporary Alan Meredith was regarded as the intellectual of his year, and another Mertonian of the time Richard Cobb went on to become an eminent historian. Socially, the debonair Etonian Airey Neave dominated Merton. The minute books of Merton's societies of the time are a record of Neave's relentless tendency to join something and then take it over. The Myrmidons were an elitist dining society of the sort which the well bred of Oxford have often established in order to behave badly. The Sir Richard Steele Society, re-established in 1935, was a small group which met occasionally for heavy drinking under the transparent cover of being a debating society. Despite its congruence with Maudling's interests, he never seems to have become a member of this group. He did, though, take some interest in the Merton Floats dramatic society (inevitably run by Airey Neave).[41] If anyone had said then that a Merton man would one day become effectively Deputy Prime Minister, there would have been surprise that Airey wouldn't make it to the top job. In March 1937 *Isis* reported satirically that Neave had already turned down a position in the Cabinet; in the same piece Maudling was merely teased for an unsuccessful attempt to grow a moustache.[42] After heroic service in the war Neave had an oddly insignificant ministerial career, his public offices peaking at Under-Secretary for Air in 1959, although it was cut short when he was assassinated in March 1979. From the perspective of Merton life their political careers were a vivid example of the race between the tortoise and the hare.[43]

It is hardly a criticism of Maudling to note that he did not go in for the dreary and self-aggrandising business of undergraduate politicking, or of 'hacking' college or university societies. His interests were more normal, human ones – making friends, having a pleasant time involving mild bad behaviour, and thinking about ideas in a beautiful and rather carefree place. This, after all, is what the majority of people did and do while at Oxford. Maudling's social character, of a gregarious loner – someone with 'no enemies, but really no close intimate friends'[44] – was already established. While he had a lot of chums, he did not forge any intense, lifelong bonds of friendship with his Oxford contemporaries.

Maudling and his friends casually disregarded the ridiculous prohibition in the university regulations from going to pubs and would enjoy driving out to village pubs, singing and drinking vast quantities of beer. Maudling fondly recalled the poetical line 'meum est propositum in taberna mori' as something of a motto of the period.[45] 'I propose to end my days in a tavern' seemed a lot less funny and charming as he lay dying from alcohol-related disease in February 1979 than it did on those carefree 1930s summer evenings.[46]

Maudling also enjoyed a jolly and boisterous social life in Merton, occasionally sitting up in the common room or private rooms drinking and arguing with friends. He often went to parties and his birthday celebrations were quite excessive occasions involving much drinking, high spirits and falling over.[47] There were also parties at the end of terms, which sometimes degenerated into drunken rowdiness. In March 1936 at the end of his second term in college Maudling was reprimanded and fined twice in short succession for participating in such revels, first for throwing bottles from his windows into the quad and then for noise at a lunch party. The fines amounted to £2 and £1 (sizeable sums, considering that £1 in 1936 money is nearly £40 in current terms). Maudling's misdemeanours were overshadowed by those of Airey Neave and chums, who drunkenly climbed the Chapel Tower and threw bottles from that considerable height into the quad.[48]

A revealing documentary record of the escapades and preoccupations of Reggie and his contemporaries survives in the form of the Merton College JCR suggestions book. This rested on a table in the junior common room, and although its ostensible purpose was to allow students to make comments about college facilities, it served as a general noticeboard for juvenilia, showing off and drunken abuse. The JCR steward would reply in the spirit of the original comment. From May 1936 until the end of his time in Oxford Maudling was a regular contributor, his neat, narrow writing and the wayward dotted 'i' and crossed 't' of his script[49] easily recognisable even when he had not signed himself as 'RM'.

Maudling started with relatively serious suggestions, to become more facetious as he went on. A revealing early comment was: 'Sir, Would it not be possible for either the Stores or the Buttery to stock Schweppes Tonic Water, it being now necessary for those who do not like Lime Juice to drink their gin neat?' Reggie would have been well aware that it is never a necessity as such to drink neat gin, and was gently sending himself up, but there was a point to the enquiry as well as demonstrating that he was already quite keen on spirits. Later interventions also showed concern with the availability of beer, wine, port and sherry, although in later life sherry was one of the few drinks he professed to dislike, perhaps for the usual reason people find themselves unable to stand a drink they rather liked at university. Another of Maudling's causes was the provision of indoor pub games at college, a campaign which proved successful and of – perhaps dubious – benefit to Merton students to this day.[50]

Maudling would also use the suggestions book to engage in occasional satirical sallies poking fun at political posturing such as Neville Chamberlain's national keep fit campaign, the excesses of pomp and ceremony of the 1937 Coronation and – most daring of all – the sanctimonious attitudes on display during the 1936 abdication crisis. The Archbishop of Canterbury was the external Visitor of Merton College and Maudling suggested that his 1937 formal visit be marked by 'Presentation by such betrothed members of the College . . . of gold mug embossed FIDES MARITORUM ET FORNICATIONIS DEFENSOR in commemoration of his noble fight for morality v the American widow.' While hardly radical – and allowing for the fact that there are few less obtrusive or effective forms of protest than writing smart alec comments in a student suggestions book – Maudling's contributions prove that he did not take the government, Church or monarchy too seriously. His conservatism was never about slavish respect for traditions or institutions.

The greatest influence Maudling took away from Oxford was academic, which is a rarer phenomenon than generally imagined. Reggie wore his intellectualism lightly at Merton and most contemporaries had no idea that he took philosophy and classics so much to heart. His philosophy tutor at Merton was Geoffrey Mure, who was something of a living legend, even then, as the last surviving Hegelian. It was said in the 1930s that some questions on the philosophy finals exam papers were specially tailored for the unusual perspective of Merton men. Maudling became a disciple of Mure's distinctive philosophical school. He admired Mure and gave him credit as the man who had done most to shape his attitude to life.

Mure for his part respected Reggie's intelligence and interest in philosophy ('a fresh and interesting mind', he wrote in 1937) and was also obviously charmed by his personality. In support of Maudling's scholarship applications he referred to his 'pleasant personality and good manners' and regarded Reggie as 'a very likeable pupil'.[51] Geoffrey Mure became a lifelong friend and had the sad duty of writing his pupil's obituary for the College magazine.

Mure's teaching methods would not receive the approval of the agencies that now monitor every aspect of higher education:

When it came to setting essays Mure simply announced a subject, with very little or even no reading. As for the tutorials themselves, they might start on Socratic lines but rapidly developed into an unrehearsed meditation, a monologue with pregnant and alarming pauses, carried on by the tutor himself. Not surprisingly, the less gifted pupils were very soon lost, and even the more able found it hard to follow what was going on.[52]

Maudling had no difficulty in coping; he was bright and also motivated by a deep interest in the ideas with which he was dealing. He paid close attention to tutorials, and was even known to interrupt Mure to point out inconsistencies with what the tutor had been saying in previous weeks. His essays were 'economical, brief but usually to the point'.[53]

Mure was unusual in clinging to a system of philosophical idealism while those around him in Oxford inclined to empiricism or even narrower linguistic concepts of philosophy. His tutorials were a tour around the greatest texts of Western philosophy, with particular emphasis on the foundations laid by Aristotle and Plato, progressing quickly to a detailed examination of Hegel's thought.[54] Under the influence of Mure, and Mure's particular perspective on Hegel, Maudling became a Hegelian. 'As a young philosophy student I was immensely interested in and attracted by Hegel's work. A dangerous guide you might think as the ills of Fascism and Communism have both, at various times, been construed as derivations from his philosophy. But those were monstrous distortions of his dialectical concept.'[55]

Hegel's writings are frequently difficult and obscure, and their metaphysical discourse admits many interpretations. Briefly, his view of history is as an evolution through stages of political development (each in turn reflecting a stage of mental and philosophical development) with 'the progress of the consciousness of freedom' as the ultimate meaning of history. The culminating stage of this progress, of which the Enlightenment and the rationalism of the French Revolution were the latest stages, was the complete freedom of the individual within an 'organic community'. But the Hegelian concept of freedom was different from the absence of restraint, or the ability to follow individual desires. Hegel thought that individual desires of this sort were not an expression of true freedom, but themselves were the product of the immediate circumstances of the time. In *Philosophy of Right*, Hegel commented:

What the English call 'comfort' is something inexhaustible and illimitable. Others can reveal to you that what you take to be comfort at any stage is discomfort, and these discoveries never come to an end. Hence the need for greater comfort does not exactly arise within you directly; it is suggested to you by those who hope to make a profit from its creation.[56]

Maudling proudly confesses in his memoirs to having thrown his copy of
Adam Smith out of a porthole on an ocean-going ship during his student
years,[57] and it is clear that classical economics went out of the window pretty
early in his life.

According to Hegel, true preferences are those which accord with
rationality and can be expressed as being in line with a universal idea.
Freedom and duty would coincide exactly in a situation where a rationally
ordered state and a society of free, self-actualising individuals meet in the
form of an 'organic community'. Here, with Hegel's concept of the state as an
instrument of divine will, lies the risk of totalitarianism within his philosophy.
Communism saw itself as the highest stage of human development and felt
itself entitled to override the preferences of individuals to serve the greater
good; the Nazi state claimed to be the representative of a German racial
organic community.

However, it is easier to join Maudling in seeing Hegelian origins in welfare
state democracy and One Nation Conservatism. An 'organic community'
nurses its members who fall upon misfortune back to health. In repeated
references in his speeches and articles to concepts like the need for the
voluntary acceptance of standards, or 'the self-discipline of a responsible
society' – the willingness to accept coordination for a greater good[58] –
Maudling shows his Hegelian colours. However, the Hegelian concept that
most intrigued Maudling was the dialectic. This posited that the essential
dynamic of intellectual enquiry, and of history, is a threefold process of thesis,
antithesis and synthesis. A 'thesis', a state of affairs, a customary way of
thinking, exists but eventually shows itself to be incomplete or not internally
consistent. This gives rise to an 'antithesis', which challenges and contradicts
it, but is itself not sufficient as an organising principle. The collision of the
two produces a 'synthesis', which transcends the differences between them
and moves things forward.

Reggie's Hegelianism had several consequences for his politics. Broadly, he
believed in progress and had a faith in the future and human nature that is
lacking in traditional conservative philosophers. He thought, admittedly to no
startling conclusions, about what society would be like, and politics would be
for, once the problems of scarcity had been solved through technology and
organisation, the next stage of the march of history. He expounded a
Hegelian version of British political history and analysis of current
developments in his first public political statement in 1943, which is explored
further in another chapter.

Hegel's ideas resonated with Reggie at an emotional level as well as with
his intellect. The idea that out of conflict could, or even must, come
agreement was congenial to him, and he was bewildered by, and retreated
from, conflicts that seemed to lead nowhere – such as the one he encountered
in Northern Ireland. Hegelianism, in Reggie's version at least, is a rather
passive doctrine, not a call to arms of any sort but a rational structure of

thought that justified moderation and consensus while recognising that the challenge of the extremes could have its place in bringing about progress. Rather than supporting totalitarianism, to Maudling Hegel offered a reason for calmness, almost Zen passivity, about political conflict, and an accepting attitude to political opponents. It becomes hard to draw boundaries when all is recognised as being part of a dialectical process out of which comes progress. Maudling himself believed that Hegel was central to his thought, and indeed he was, but Hegel provided an intellectual framework for Reggie's inner nature that was there before he ever met Geoffrey Mure or opened *Lectures on the Philosophy of History*.

Chapter 2

BETROTHAL AND THE BAR, 1935–1940

A turning point in Reggie Maudling's life came in his first college vacation. Some time during the 1935 Christmas holidays he went to a supper party in London and met a 16-year-old dancer-turned-actress called Beryl Laverick, who was currently appearing at the Lyric Theatre, Hammersmith, in a children's play called *The Magic Marble*.[1] She was playing the lost little sister of a fairy queen, imprisoned by a friendly ogre called the Woblin until she was rescued by Sir Galahad.[2] The position of romantic lead in her real life was unoccupied, and Reggie stepped quickly into the role. For him, it was love at first sight. He was quietly determined that she would be his girlfriend. Although she initially found him a little pompous, she did not resist for long; the first present he gave her, quirkily and obviously endearingly, was a porcelain armadillo they named Ernest.[3] Reggie's college friend Steven Watson noted that Reggie seemed to have captured Beryl's fancy almost immediately.[4]

There were some similarities between the pair, some coincidental and some significant. Both were only children. Neither had a middle name. Both had jolly, amiable fathers and cold, snobbish, ambitious mothers. But while Reggie was a Londoner through and through, Beryl was of Geordie origins. Her father, Eli Laverick, was born in Newcastle in 1889, the son of a foreman in the Tyneside shipyards who was also called Eli. Further back, the family's origins are rather mysterious. James Haw, Beryl's cousin, believes that Eli senior was a Jewish refugee from Russian pogroms who ended up disembarking from the ship at Cobh (then called Queenstown) in Ireland, and the family certainly has a tradition of closeness and sympathy with Jews. Eli senior, like many Jewish refugees, was a reformer if not a radical, who campaigned for women's suffrage and Irish Home Rule and had a fierce faith in education. His daughter Margaret, Beryl's aunt, was an early feminist pioneer, who served on local public boards and was the first woman to be made head of a mixed grammar school.[5]

The junior Eli (often called Billy) Laverick worked on the white-collar side of shipbuilding, becoming a draughtsman and a naval architect. During the First World War he moved between military ports as his talents were called upon by the war effort, spending some time in Portsmouth and marrying Florence Ridge, the daughter of a railwayman, in distant Barrow-in-Furness in 1917. The couple moved again and ended up in New Malden, in the Surrey suburbs of London, where Beryl was born on 12 June 1919.

Beryl Laverick was a pretty little girl with a round face and an appealing smile. She was poised and outgoing and her mother drove her from a very early age to become a ballet dancer. This was not as common then as it is now, for ballet was in its infancy in Britain in the 1920s, the first foundation of a professional ballet establishment in Britain being Marie Rambert's Ballet Club of 1920.[6] There had been a few schools before the war, but in 1920 the Association of Operatic Dancing (later to become the Royal Academy of Dance) was founded to regulate and improve ballet schools and promote the art form. In Blackheath, a pleasant part of south-east London not far from the Woolwich dockyard, where the Lavericks lived for nearly all their married life, there was a school run by Mrs Freda Grant, who specialised in teaching very young children how to dance. Beryl joined the Grant ballet school at the age of 3 or 4, and was quickly successful, being awarded a *Dancing Times* medal as the winner of the 'Special Baby Class' in national competition in April 1924 when she was only 4 years old.[7]

Beryl won medals in most of her years in ballet school, with the exception only of 1927 when, as she self-deprecatingly remembered in an interview, she appeared as a grasshopper: 'it was a bit of a disaster. I lost my bulrush.'[8] In the late 1920s she was awarded a scholarship by the Association of Operatic Dancing. The scholarship meant, as well as her lessons with Mrs Grant, two extra dance lessons each week, and one whole week each year, spent at the Association's headquarters at Holland Park Avenue in west London.[9] Her scholarship moved her into the elite of British ballet. Her coach for the special lessons was Noreen Bush, a young dancer and teacher, but the most senior ballerinas in Britain, such as Ninette de Valois and Adeline Genée, would often sit in on the scholars' lessons. Genée tried to come to all of them and get to know the students, and regarded Beryl as something of a favourite. Genée left a strong impression on little Beryl Laverick, who admired, even hero-worshipped, her.

Adeline Genée had a theatrical, operatic manner, 'as regal in private as on the stage'.[10] The Association's office manager, Kathleen Gordon, recalled their first meeting, observing her 'incredibly immaculate appearance which always distinguished her. She extended a hand gloved in snowy whiteness, into which I placed my grubby paw, and in her deep and husky voice (so unlike a dancer's) said, "That curtain is damnable! Get rid of it!"'[11] Her haughty manner was redeemed by impish humour and her generosity with her efforts towards colleagues and, particularly, her young students. Adeline Genée was of Danish origin, born Anina Jensen and adopted at an early age by an uncle and aunt, who were noted dancers, and who had themselves taken on the surname Genée as a tribute to a composer, Richard Genée.[12] Genée's affectations and tenuous relationship with the reality of her own origins were not all that unusual for a grand performer of the times, but she was a particularly seductive role model for Beryl, a little girl already inclined to fantasy and make-believe.

As a dancer, Beryl Laverick specialised in 'demi-caractère' work, which involved dressing up in costume and performing ballet versions of folk dances. Her party piece, which she developed in the late 1920s, was called 'See Me Dance the Polka' and was by all accounts a winsome and delightful performance from 'a very clever little character dancer'.[13] She spent her childhood learning how to please and impress adults through her dancing – even the title of her act was about drawing attention to herself.

Beryl's *annus mirabilis* as a dancer was 1932. She won the *Dancing Times* competition and achieved the highest ballet qualification in Britain, the Solo Seal, in the spring. In the summer she became the second ever winner of the Adeline Genée Gold Medal, an award which is not given every year and is the world's most prestigious ballet medal. Beryl danced several times at showcase ballet events, including on two occasions before King George V and Queen Mary, who was a patron of the ballet. In February 1933, at Adeline Genée's last public dance season at the London Coliseum, Beryl had a prominent role in *The Debutante*, playing Lutine, 'a favourite pupil'.[14]

While it appeared that Beryl could look forward to great success in British ballet, her dancing career seems to have ended not long after Genée's own last dance. Her reasons can be guessed at. As an adolescent, Beryl had curves and rather stocky legs, more like a chorus girl than the sylph-like ideal represented by the ballet. At 13, she had already spent nearly ten years in the ballet and perhaps she was bored. Perhaps all those years of training had inflicted some damage on her body – later on, she did seem wistful about having to leave the dance. Other opportunities were opening for her at the time.

At Christmas 1932 Beryl played the title role in *Alice in Wonderland* produced by Nancy Price at the Little Theatre in the West End. Her dancing ability was one factor in her choice, against stiff competition, but so too was her physical appearance – a small girl with long hair and a passing resemblance to Tenniel's famous engravings of Alice. *The Stage* review commented that 'A very charming, fresh, natural and sweetly unsophisticated embodiment of Alice was given by Miss Beryl Laverick, who went on from success to success'.[15] She appeared in other West End productions,[16] including two reprises of her role as Alice. The rather slighting 'sweetly unsophisticated' was replaced by outright admiration in some other reviews; a year later she delivered 'a wholly delightful impersonation of Alice, and one could hardly imagine anyone with a more complete appreciation of the part'.[17] During 1933 and 1934 she also played small parts in a couple of films, travelling to Austria with her mother to appear in *The Constant Nymph* and as Mary Esterhazy in *Unfinished Symphony*, a biopic about Schubert made by Willi Forst and Anthony 'Puffin' Asquith in Vienna in 1933/4.

Beryl was never a particularly famous or prominent actress, and her film career never really took off. But for all that, she was successful on the stage, appearing regularly in various productions and attracting favourable notices. In the late 1930s she worked quite often as a radio actress and announcer, and appeared on several occasions on *Children's Hour* and even featured in 1938 on a cigarette card in the Churchman *In Town Tonight* series.[18]

As well as being a micro-celebrity, Beryl was physically very attractive and a lively, outgoing young woman. Reggie could hardly believe his luck. His physical self-image was always rather negative and self-deprecating; to himself, he was always the fattest boy in the school, an inky character with undignified and unimpressive interests. In reality, the young Maudling was an impressive, even handsome man. He was tall and broad-shouldered, with a large frame that could bear a certain amount of filling out. He had intelligent, gentle eyes and an infectious smile. But to him, Beryl seemed a dream come true – a girl from out of his league who had somehow ended up with him. All his life, he was devoted to her, and even oblivious to other women who found him attractive. His devotion came with a certain edge of insecurity that prevented him from ever standing up to Beryl or denying her what she wanted. Reggie's love for his wife, itself an admirable and touching quality, became part of his tragedy. His friend Sir Sandy Glen said that Reggie had never had an affair, and that perhaps he should have done.[19] What Glen meant is that it could have cured Reggie of the illusion that he was unattractive and that Beryl's love for him was some sort of freak occurrence, and helped him put this aspect of life into perspective.

However, in his late teens and early twenties Reggie's relationship with Beryl gave him inner confidence and distinguished him from most male Oxford students, who found the large ratio of men to women daunting. Reggie wrote in 1937 that Merton should introduce divans to the common room: 'think how useful they might be at Commem [Ball] time. At any rate I should be – which is the most important consideration to my mind. RM'. Another student added, 'What, useful at Commem time?' to which Reggie replied 'Yes, without doubt RM.' He contributed again on behalf of the 'betrothed' members of College. Reggie was comparatively free of sexual hang-ups and would make mild allusions to sex that stuffier politicians of his age would have avoided. For instance, when he was called 'the great unmade bed' by Ian Paisley and others for his rumpled appearance, he said that he quite enjoyed it as an unmade bed was a sign of recent happy times.

Reggie was enjoying life in the late 1930s. During his summer vacations he would go on long adventurous voyages as a passenger on cargo ships, for six weeks in the Mediterranean in July and August 1937 and then for a similar period in South America in summer 1938. He would spend the long sca crossings reading improving books – it was a good way for him to work his way through his student reading list with few distractions. When he hit a port it was a different matter; he joined the ship's crew drinking and gambling in nightclubs and casinos. In Santos, Brazil, he woke up on the wrong ship and had to rush back by train to where he was supposed to be and catch up with his ship. Later on that trip, he says in a particularly teasing and mischievous passage of his memoirs, 'the other valuable experience I had was being arrested in Buenos Aires by a local customs officer'. When he was searched at the dockside, the officer found two semi-precious stones he had bought and was taking home for Beryl, and Reggie's companion, a German student, made matters worse by insisting that they were diamonds. The fuss was smoothed over, Reggie signed a statement in Spanish and ICI's man in Buenos Aires[20] recovered the stones. Reggie tells us: 'When in trouble with the police, particularly in a foreign country, patience, amiability and an infinite desire to please are the essential ingredients of escape.'[21] Given Reggie's own later brush with the law, and even the astonishing coincidence that in 1974 a policeman was trying to investigate him for alleged diamond smuggling, this tale has the ring of an elaborate joke, told at whose expense one can never quite be sure. On the summer voyages in general, suffice it to say that they were broadening, eye-opening episodes of his life, part of the process of growing up and spreading his wings.

When he came back from holiday in October 1937 for his final year Maudling started to pull ahead academically. Until then Mure 'had regarded him as the safest of seconds', but now he realised that Maudling was a certain first. When he took Finals in summer 1938 Maudling achieved one of the top firsts in his year. He was runner-up for the John Locke prize in mental philosophy, so could with justice claim to have been the second-best philosopher of the class of 1938.[22] Reggie toyed with the idea of becoming an Oxford don, a lifestyle which could have been very suitable for his personality and talents. In 1938 he took the examination to enter All Souls College, Oxford's most elite institution. The College takes no students and its Fellows engage in research and teaching in conditions of modest luxury. Fellowships are for seven years and give the Fellows considerable freedom and economic independence. The examination is not only a major academic challenge but also involves joining the Fellows for a formal dinner to see how the candidate's face fits. For whatever reason – and no papers survive – Reggie did not enter All Souls.[23] However, academia was not his main interest at the time, as he aspired to become a barrister.

Maudling's brief legal career began when he was accepted to join the Middle Temple in October 1936, at the beginning of his second year of studies at Merton. In those days it was quite common to take academic and legal studies concurrently, and it was particularly convenient in allowing the student to eat the requisite number of dinners in Hall to qualify for the Bar. Reggie started dining with some enthusiasm, clocking up his termly requirement of three dinners in the first term and maintaining a steady rate of progress for the next few years. Quite apart from satisfying the requirements of the Bar, the dinners were congenial occasions in which the meals were washed down with wine and brandy and topped off with a fine cigar. It was no hardship for Maudling to attend every few weeks and exchange banter with his randomly selected colleagues in his 'mess' table of four.

As with his application to All Souls, Maudling was confident enough to aspire to the best institution of its kind in Britain. He applied for the prestigious Harmsworth Scholarship in 1937. The scholarship had been established by the newspaper baron in the 1920s and at that time awards were restricted to men from Oxford and Cambridge Colleges who were members of the Middle Temple. The conditions of an award stipulated that 'In selecting the candidates for nomination the Vice Chancellors shall take into consideration their studious habits, their disposition to follow loyally the traditions of the English Bar, and the necessity or probable necessity for financial assistance to enable them to become practising Barristers.'[24] Reggie had a supportive but not hyperbolic reference from the Oxford authorities, and several personal testimonials including one from his father's actuarial colleague Victor Burrows, who was 'greatly impressed both as regards his ability and character'. Competition for the scholarship was stiff and Reggie was turned down after an interview in October 1937.

Undaunted, he applied again in June 1938 and received a more fulsome tribute in his reference from the Vice-Chancellor:

> Mr Maudling is a Classical Scholar of Merton College. He took Pass Moderations because he is only able to stay at Oxford for three years. He is taking the Final School of Literae Humaniores this Term, and his Tutor, Mr G.R.G. Mure, tells me that a First Class is not an impossibility for him. Mr Mure says that he has very considerable ability and vigour of mind, and some natural aptitude for philosophy, with a pleasant personality and good manners; and is likely to make a really good barrister and to uphold the best traditions of the Bar in character, brains and social aptitude.

Maudling was one of Oxford's favoured candidates this time. In October 1938 the Harmsworth board confirmed that he had been fortunate, and he started legal studies in earnest with the aid of a £200 (present value around £8,000) annual scholarship grant and the prestige that came of being, once again, one of the elite even within a traditional and highly respected institution. Satisfyingly, Maudling had triumphed over Airey Neave, who also applied but had an unenthusiastic reference because his tutors had to explain away his poor examination performance. Knox Cunningham, another future Conservative MP, also failed.

Maudling moved back with his parents when he returned from Oxford to London. They had moved again in 1936 to a newly built block of flats called Mandeville Court, on Finchley Road. West Hampstead at that time was an intriguing area. Refugees from Nazi Germany – and from 1938 Austria as well – had established an intellectual, Jewish ambience to the area which was sometimes referred to as Finchleystrasse. The artist Oskar Kokoschka was one of the Maudlings' neighbours for a while in Mandeville Court. It was an enjoyable area for R.G. Maudling, a devoted modernist, to live in, and it was central enough to be very convenient for Reggie to pursue his legal studies. He became something of a library regular, to the extent of spending most of his Saturdays there in the first half of 1939, and large parts of July and August too, studying law books.[25] As in his previous educational institutions, he was clearly capable of bursts of considerable energy and application when it mattered. He made rapid progress with his courses and by summer 1939 he had completed the bulk of what was required. He was well advanced with dinners as well, so a future as a barrister seemed assured.

At this time Maudling also started to think again about politics. The revival of his sixth-form interest after his non-political college days has no obvious explanation, and was certainly not rooted in any passionate partisan views. On 19 July 1939 he went to see Harold Nicolson, the independent-minded (not to say dilettante) MP for Leicester West, who recorded him as: 'A young man from Merton who has got a first and wants to know what political party he should join. I say that he had better wait. Every party today is crushed by its own old men; out of all this there may emerge a party which young men can join with fervour.'[26] Maudling's own comment on being shown the extract before publication in 1965 was that 'As I recall it, my concern was not quite so vague as the note suggests. I had never contemplated joining the Socialists, but although by temperament Conservative, I was interested in the National Labour concept. In fact, I was thinking of the parties of the centre, or right of centre, and asking advice on this.'[27]

There is no reason to disbelieve Maudling's gloss. It seems unlikely that he was ever interested in joining Labour, which was then completely culturally alien to him. He had no emotional connection to the worlds of nonconformity, trade unionism or left-wing intellectuals that made up the party, and was clear in his own mind that he believed in a reformed capitalist system. Labour, ostensibly, stood for Socialism, which was incompatible with capitalism.

The parties of the right and centre comprised the independent Liberals and the supporters of the so-called National Government, whose name suggested a broad coalition although it was in fact dominated by Conservatives. There were a few supposed independents and two smaller parties also under the National label – the Liberal Nationals and National Labour. Maudling's interest in National Labour deserves some exploration. The party was the small fragment of the Labour Party that had followed Ramsay MacDonald into coalition with the Tories and Liberals after the collapse of the Labour government in 1931. A 'National Labour' party fought the elections of 1931 and 1935 in an electoral pact with the Conservatives but despite attempts to establish a party organisation it remained a top-heavy band of ex-Labour notables. After MacDonald ceased to be Prime Minister in 1935, and even more after his death in 1937, the purpose of his National Labour vehicle was in serious doubt. The party was also a flag of convenience for Harold Nicolson, who had sought election for three other parties in the four years before his election in 1935; Maudling could not have been surprised by the dispassionate but indecisive advice he received from such a man.

National Labour's propaganda stressed cooperation in industry and the party aspired to be a synthesis of political approaches. It would, for instance, accept the traditional Conservative policy of tariffs while also creating publicly owned corporations like the London Passenger Transport Board.[28] The attraction of such an approach to Maudling's Hegelian cast of mind and lack of reverence for traditions is obvious. There were also cross-cutting political divisions in the late 1930s which fragmented the National bloc, such as the abdication crisis in 1936 and the opposition to the government's policy of appeasing the dictators. Nicolson was one of a relatively small band of anti-appeasers on the National benches.[29]

Maudling seems not to have been inspired to sign up to National Labour, or any other political party, by his conversation with Nicolson, although there is no practical way of proving this negative. He was not in any hurry to make a political decision, because his personal and professional lives were on the point of great change and occupying a lot of his energy. He spent most of that summer closeted in the library of the Middle Temple studying for his final Bar examinations. His deepening commitment to Beryl had led them at some point to declare their engagement, to the fury of his mother. But the first change came from a less expected direction. The headlines of the newspapers Reggie, and everyone else, were reading that summer were full of Hitler's threats against another neighbour, Poland, and the nervous determination of the British government that this time they would put up more of a struggle. On 1 September German tanks crossed into Poland and, when they failed to withdraw by 3 September, Britain declared war on Nazi Germany.

Reggie Maudling, like most men of his generation, volunteered for the armed services in September 1939, but was turned down because of his poor eyesight. He returned to his legal studies amid the gloom and fear of blacked-out London during the 'Phoney War' while the government came to a decision about what it could do with Maudling's services.

The war was not the only shadow over the wedding of Reginald Maudling and Beryl Laverick. They married on 9 September 1939 but despite their mutual devotion the wedding was a strange occasion. Reggie's own lack of religious belief – and unwillingness to feign it for the purposes of obtaining a church wedding – meant a register office ceremony. Civil weddings were relatively uncommon in 1939. Even more unusually, the Maudlings arranged to tie the knot in a town they hardly knew. Reggie's father had allowed them to live in his new flat in Hastings Court in Worthing for a few days and on their wedding certificate both Reggie and Beryl claimed to be resident there (itself a slightly scandalous arrangement for 1939).

However, the strangest aspect of the wedding was the absence of the groom's mother. Elsie's opposition to the relationship remained completely implacable. The reason for her hatred of Beryl was essentially snobbery,[30] though a certain element of anti-Semitism cannot be ruled out. The provincial background, evoking her own not too distant origins, cannot have helped, but the worst thing was that Beryl was earning her living on the stage. Acting was not considered respectable and one can easily imagine comments, made with a curled lip, about a 'little dancer' or worse. It was hardly a dynastic, social climbing 'good' marriage; perhaps Elsie believed that Beryl was a pretty, flighty girl who had used her wiles to ensnare her inexperienced son. But probably no girl would have been good enough for Elsie's boy.

Elsie tried as far as she could not to recognise the marriage and refused to come to the ceremony; there is a blank space on the register entry alongside the signatures of Beryl's parents and Reggie's father. She had threatened never to speak again to Reggie if he married Beryl and had the perverse, masochistic determination to carry out the threat for the rest of her life. She never spoke again to her only son, despite his achievements that would have made any normal mother extremely proud, and she never saw her grandchildren.[31] When she died, in a Worthing nursing home on 7 September 1956, without a will,[32] Reggie, her only son, inherited the money anyway, and he delivered a final snub, an act of symbolic revenge, by refusing to attend her funeral and going on holiday instead.[33]

Elsie's hatred had not dissuaded Reggie from marrying Beryl, but instead had driven them even closer together. Reggie was deeply hurt by his mother's rejection but he had made his choice and kept to it. His happy relationship with Beryl came at a shocking emotional price for him and the effects of the trauma lingered, subtly, for the rest of his life. In his memoirs, affectionately dedicated to Beryl, he does not mention their wedding, one of the proudest moments of his life. While his childhood was comfortable and stable, he learned as a young man that, for him, there was no such thing as unconditional love and that even a mother's love can sour into cruelty.

Elsie damaged her own marriage in her campaign against Beryl. The inner workings of a mid-century middle-class marriage are impenetrable. The contrast between Reggie's father's support and his mother's hostility is as sharp as it could be. Suggestively, around 1939 and 1940 the confusing pattern of R.G. and Elsie's residences is at its most tangled. From Mandeville Court, they acquired the Hastings Court flat in Worthing and in 1940 R.G. Maudling is also found registered at a house in Reigate in Surrey and in the plush filing-cabinet apartments of Cranmer Court in Chelsea. It looks likely that there was some sort of quiet separation between the two of them at this time, and that the marriage endured out of inertia and the need to keep up a respectable appearance. Later, they do seem to have lived together genuinely in Worthing, so perhaps the differences were patched up. Interestingly, Reggie's first substantial speech in the House of Commons that did not concern constituency or economic issues was a compelling argument for the liberalisation of the law on divorce, which at the time required proof of adultery and often involved the parties to the case in sordid, sometimes literal, public washing of dirty linen.

It is not clear where Reggie and Beryl Maudling lived when they returned to London and he finished off his legal studies waiting for the call-up. They lived in several different flats during wartime, although for some purposes, such as his calling to the Bar, Reggie regarded his official residence as being with his father in Reigate.[34] They told their children about small flats and a tyrannical landlady, and a place shared with another couple, during the war. The Maudlings started married life with very little money, particularly during Reggie's last few months as a law student. There was the occasional subvention from the Harmsworth fund, the odd dribble from his father's businesses or Beryl's radio acting, but not much to live on. When they did get hold of some money they would tend to spend it right away by buying a bottle of champagne and drinking it together.[35]

It is a poignant image. Reggie and Beryl, man and wife both barely in their twenties, sitting in a cramped and dingy blacked-out flat somewhere in London, drinking champagne they couldn't afford, perhaps listening on the gramophone to some of the romantic songs that were so popular at the time; a little island of warmth and love amid the spreading darkness. He and Beryl would transport themselves into a private little world where there were no money worries and they could live in style. In this charming, romantic way an element of wish-fulfilment and *folie à deux* first appeared in their relationship.

Reggie took his Final Bar examinations at the end of 1939 and his not unexpected pass was announced in January 1940. Having also eaten sufficient Middle Temple dinners to be allowed to qualify, he was called to the Bar on 26 January 1940 at the precociously early age of 22. He intended to specialise in international law, becoming a member of the Grotius Society, which was a forum for intellectual discussions on the subject.[36]

Through his diligence at his studies, Maudling had managed to play the scholarship system to advantage again, after his extra year's money from Merton College in 1938–9. The Harmsworth scholarships were tenable for three years, and Maudling finished his studies less than halfway through the period. This was quick, but not completely abnormal. The scholarship period had been set long so that scholars were not faced with a cash crisis between qualifying as pupil barristers and gaining enough of a reputation to be given sufficient briefs to make ends meet. Maudling, however, walked off with £300 while drawing a civil service salary.

Maudling, though a qualified barrister, did not actually practise. The fact that he had qualified, even though he had never darkened a court door, protected him in the early 1950s when the Harmsworth scholarship committee had something of a purge on people who had taken the scholarship but failed to become barristers.[37] He was not even present at his own calling in 1940 because a suitable national service post had come up in RAF intelligence. He gave his occupation as 'barrister-at-law' on an official document in 1944 and remained on the Law List until 1963, but never seriously contemplated resuming his legal career after the war. His circumstances were rather different then, having a small child as well as a dependent wife, and it would have been difficult to sustain a family on the uncertain earnings of a junior barrister with five years' interruption to his career. 'I hoped to be a barrister, but the war put paid to that,' he recalled in a 1976 interview.[38]

Chapter 3

'CONSERVATIVES AND CONTROL', 1940–1945

The total mobilisation of Britain for the Second World War changed every life it touched. The generation of Oxbridge graduates who went down in the late 1930s (or up in the mid-1940s) had a unique insight into life. Some, like Denis Healey, Edward Heath and Tony Crosland, saw war at its most elemental – kill or be killed in hellish environments on the front line in Europe. Maudling's Merton colleague Airey Neave escaped from Colditz, and his postwar best friend Sandy Glen was dropped behind enemy lines in Yugoslavia with instructions to close the Danube, blow up the Romanian oil wells and stir up a revolution while he was at it.[1] The psephologist David Butler, a callow youth in 1945, found himself in charge of a tank group of grizzled veterans who had fought across the Western Desert and were now smashing their way through Holland (VE Day was celebrated with the liberation of a Dutch gin factory). These men had seen the skull beneath the skin of civilisation; they were at once egalitarian, consensus-minded and tough to the point of brutality when fundamental values were involved.

The experience of those who stayed behind and served in other capacities gave them a different perspective. The British government managed to use extraordinarily diverse talents. Crossword experts and theoretical mathematicians, most notably Alan Turing, did their best in Bletchley Park and other establishments, and their applied intelligence was an immense service to the war efforts. Sefton Delmer and Richard Crossman cooked up ingenious and occasionally obscene propaganda to demoralise the enemy; scientists, economists, such as Harold Wilson and Hugh Gaitskell, and engineers had free rein to think up ideas to serve their country. The period 1940–5 was an explosion of state-sponsored creativity and ingenuity that has few parallels.

Maudling's physical shortcomings had ruled him out of active combat in September 1939, but in January 1940 he was called up to one of the intellectually interesting but rather peculiar departments that flourished during the war. He joined Fighter Command as a member of its Operational Research department, based at Northwood, not far from Merchant Taylors' new buildings. Operational Research was essentially the use of mathematical and statistical techniques in conducting military operations. The OR section had been instrumental in the invention of radar, and its leader, Harold Larnder, played an unsung role in the Battle of Britain. By drawing up graphs of aircraft production and combat losses, Larnder helped Field Marshal Hugh Dowding to persuade Winston Churchill not to throw more British planes into the doomed defence of France in May 1940, with the result that they were available to defend Britain that summer and autumn. The OR section seemed an obvious marriage with Maudling's analytical, undogmatic intelligence, but Maudling did not last long. His arrival was something of a surprise to the group and Harold Larnder recalled him as having been a 'misfit' in the section with considerable ability but no aptitude for operational research: 'After only a few weeks, in which his main assignment was to visit searchlight sites in the south east of England to investigate reports that they had seen mysterious zeppelin-shaped objects in their searchlight beams, Maudling moved on elsewhere.'[2]

After his short spell in Operational Research Maudling was transferred to RAF intelligence in spring 1940. Air intelligence was a rapidly growing part of the RAF; there were forty officers at the start of the war and over 700 at its end. It was composed almost entirely of outsiders brought in on war service. Maudling was set to work in Deputy Directorate 4, which focused on the Mediterranean war and later became exclusively concerned with signals intelligence.[3] The main focus of his work was on decrypted Italian Air Force signals, probably more on analysis of the results than on the actual code-breaking. Maudling said that during this time 'I learned a great deal about the methods of Intelligence',[4] but the details of what exactly he did during this eighteen months are not clear. He was promoted at some stage from pilot officer to flight lieutenant. While it is likely that he did all his work in and around London, his children remember seeing some furry RAF flying boots among his limited memorabilia[5] and it is possible that he went on the occasional intelligence mission to RAF stations elsewhere in Britain.

When the opportunity arose for a transfer into Whitehall in 1941, Maudling took it eagerly. There was a vacancy for an assistant Private Secretary in the office of the Secretary of State for Air, the Liberal Party leader Sir Archibald Sinclair, and Maudling was seconded out of the RAF and into the civil service to fill it. To gain this posting he needed to have given a good account of himself as intelligent, discreet and hard-working, and he continued to show these qualities in the Air Ministry. A junior officer who worked with him then had a strong impression of him, enough to talk about him frequently to her fiancé, Derek Mitchell (who himself later served as Reggie's private secretary). Reggie's image at the Air Ministry would have been no surprise to anyone who had encountered him at work elsewhere:

When he worked there he gave a great impression of being laid-back and idle. But he could switch on and concentrate and work at a tremendous pace. After he was done he would wander off again and once more seem idle. People who knew him and worked with him knew there was a lot more to him than met the eye from his laid-back manner.[6]

Much of Maudling's work in the ministry's headquarters in King Charles Street was routine. He would deal with constituency cases forwarded by MPs (including Winston Churchill) and other personal cases thrown up by wartime service in the air force.[7] He saw at close hand the development of the relationship between business and government. After a shaky start in 1940–1, when the disruptive presence of Lord Beaverbrook at the Ministry of Aircraft Production had caused problems for Sinclair and the Air Ministry, the air campaign was an example of the effective use of private industry subject to government control and direction. Having seen Whitehall at work, Maudling was confirmed in his dim view of the prospects for direct state control of industry. What he believed in was control and coordination of the economy by the state – not ownership – and conversely that government should be open and accessible to business expertise, and to some extent should organise itself to accommodate the interests of business.

He was also given security clearance to see Cabinet papers. Reggie on occasion took responsibility for extremely sensitive communication within the government about wartime strategy. There was one such occasion in August 1942, when one of Churchill's constituents wrote to Number 10 with the suggestion that electricity power stations would be a suitable target for bombing raids. The letter was treated seriously in Number 10, as the author was the Chief Electricity Inspector of the Electricity Commission, and passed to the Air Ministry for comment. Reggie Maudling wrote back in 'Secret' terms to Downing Street about the bombing strategy, noting that the Air Staff were aware of the importance of such targets but they were difficult to hit, being small and often well defended. 'Moreover, we have been compelled recently to divert a large proportion of our effort to objectives more directly related to the U-boat offensive, and in particular, our daylight operations, in which alone we can expect to obtain a really high degree of accuracy against precise targets, have been mainly against U-boat building yards and Diesel engine works.'[8]

Maudling's relationship with Sinclair was proper and professional, but not warm.[9] The Secretary of State was a dignified, rather aloof Scottish baronet and Maudling found his way of doing business not congenial. Sinclair was a night owl, doing much of his most important business between 10p.m. and 2a.m., and Maudling at that time would rather have worked early in the mornings to leave the evenings free to be with Beryl. More seriously, Sinclair was not decisive enough for Maudling's liking, tending in a rather Liberal way to see both sides whenever a choice of action was put before him. He was also a bad delegator, allowing minor matters to pile up on his desk for decisions. By the end of the war, Sinclair was exhausted by his punishing and unproductive routine.[10] Many of the effective decisions ended up being made by Sir Charles Portal, Chief of Air Staff. What Maudling did admire about Sinclair was his sense of principle and integrity; 'he convinced me that politics was a profession that could be pursued with honour'.[11]

Soon after his arrival at the Air Ministry Maudling's vague and inconsistent interest in politics became a serious ambition. His own comment is true as far as it goes, in that his experiences with Sinclair did show him that there was a positive side to politics; that it was not the boring and 'repulsive' business he and many others had believed in the 1930s. But his admiration for some of Sinclair's qualities is of the sort that grows over time and it cannot explain his new, more determined, sense of political ambition. Put bluntly, he felt he could do the job better himself. Here he was, an exceptionally intelligent young man of 24, not without traces of vanity and arrogance, among the leaders of British political life, bearing witness to their indecision and inefficiency as well as their integrity. Maudling saw, early on in the Air Ministry, that even the leaders of Britain's heroic struggle in the 1940s were not superhuman and that he could walk confidently even in such company. Sinclair's Principal Private Secretary, Ronald Melville, became a friend as well as a colleague to Reggie during their work together, and encouraged him to follow his political ambitions.[12]

Before going into politics Reggie had to make a final decision about which party he wanted to join. Maudling's political views were not far from Archibald Sinclair's own. In March 1941 Sinclair told a Liberal audience:

After the last war everybody wanted to get back to 1914. Nobody now wants to go back to 1939. That is a great difference – people are looking forward – they are *looking our way* – they are looking forward to a world structure founded on the rule of law and buttressed by force as the servant not of selfish imperialism but of international justice . . . So at home – war, that most sweeping of revolutionaries, is breaking up the old order and we shall have to construct a new world in which we must see to it that we realise our ambitions for social justice and equality of opportunity, and make life fuller and happier and richer than it has been for the masses of our fellow countrymen.[13]

Some of Reggie's own political ideas followed the Liberal creed of Sinclair; the last part quoted here about social justice and 'fuller and happier and richer' life is particularly reminiscent of Maudling's utterances as Chancellor in the early 1960s. Maudling evidently gave some thought to why he did not join Sinclair's Liberals, for he gave a long and reasoned reply to a letter from a Liberal in his prospective constituency a few years later:

During the war I saw quite a lot of the Liberal Party. For some three years I was one of Sinclair's Private Secretaries at the Air Ministry and I had, therefore, a very good opportunity of learning about his political outlook.

At the same time in contact with many other Liberals like Wilfred Roberts, Geoffrey Mander, Hugh Seeley, all of whom explained to me their views of the virtues of the Liberal Party and the defects of the Conservatives. Quite frankly, *I was never able to discover any great matter of principle on which my own views differed greatly from those of my Liberal friends.*[14]

Maudling's objection was not so much to liberalism, or even organised Liberalism, but to the Liberal Party. He saw the present Conservative Party as a synthesis of the forces of Conservatism and Liberalism which had been in competition during the nineteenth century; a party that respected tradition and freedom, providing for democracy and the rule of law with a 'One Nation' view of society. The differences between the two had become obsolete and were insignificant in comparison with the new threat to 'our major social institutions' from socialism. 'I believe in present circumstances the type of society, which to my judgement both of us want to see developing in this country, can best be developed and the things that we cherish in common can best be defended by the Conservative Party.' Maudling also knew the Liberals well enough to realise that they were a chronically divided party. Even when it was a contender for national power the Liberal Party was frequently split, and the internal problems had not been resolved by the party's steep decline since 1916. These splits were replayed on Lilliputian scale throughout the 1940s. Were they an anti-Socialist party, upholding the traditional Liberal values of free trade? Or were they the creators of the British welfare state and the repository of progressive ideas? Maudling told his Liberal questioner in 1946 that 'There is an extraordinary diversity of opinion between the traditional liberalism still strong within the ranks of your party, and the views, for example, of Wilfred Roberts and T.L. Horabin. Quite frankly, I find it extraordinarily difficult to distinguish between the views of Horabin and of the Socialist Party. Yet only recently he was your Chief Whip.'

Horabin, the Liberal MP for North Cornwall, came to the same conclusion in 1947 and joined the Labour Party, to be followed by fellow senior Liberals Edgar Granville, Geoffrey Mander and Megan Lloyd George. Others drifted into alliance with the Conservatives – Churchill, himself a former Liberal, spoke for Violet Bonham Carter in 1951 and invited Liberal leader Clement Davies to join his Cabinet. Maudling's Liberal correspondent, Mr Booth, wrote in a second letter that 'I think that if you younger and modern-minded Conservatives could show that you were in the ascendancy in your Party, then the outlook would be different'. Reggie cultivated Mr Booth and won his personal support in the 1950 and 1951 elections; Booth joined the Conservatives in 1952 once he was sure that the moderates were in charge.[15]

The Liberals, therefore, were not capable of making a united and effective contribution to British politics at the time, and it is hard to fault Maudling's logic in deciding not to fly under their colours for pragmatic, political reasons. There was also an important personal reason – Maudling's ambition. Having decided that he was interested in a political career, it would have been quixotic to join a party with such poor electoral prospects if his views would fit somewhere else. Liberal MPs were a scattered band, drawn from the Celtic fringe and a few other outposts held by sheer force of personality. Reggie Maudling, a middle-class Londoner, could not expect to be selected for a far-flung Celtic rural seat, and would have found the practical difficulties of representing such an area a great obstacle. He did not have the love of, and aptitude for, electioneering that enabled Jeremy Thorpe – an ambitious man who did join the Liberals – to gain a personal victory in his chosen constituency. The Liberal Party could do little for Maudling, and Maudling could not offer them what they needed at the time.

Maudling did not trifle with the Liberal Nationals, who occasionally pondered merger with the proper Liberals but were becoming indistinguishable from Tories. He joined the Conservative Party, which after all was the party supported by the vast bulk of the upper middle classes of southern England, a category to which Reggie and his parents belonged. It is not possible to give an exact date for when Reggie decided which of the parties of the 'centre and right of centre' was for him, but it is likely to have been between July 1939 and December 1941.[16] However, constituency party organisation was in abeyance during the war and even in normal circumstances it has been known for candidates to be adopted despite not being members – Colonel Michael Mates, for one, promised his Petersfield selection committee in 1974 that if selected he would join the Tory party.

Certainly by December 1941 Reggie was taking active steps to get into Parliament. He was fortunate in having a useful connection to Conservative Central Office through Sir Patrick Gower, whose son was at Oxford with Reggie. Gower had served as a Private Secretary in the Treasury and Number 10 until 1929 when he joined Central Office as Director of Publicity. Gower was also Chairman of Charles Higham, one of the leading pre-war advertising agencies in Britain. Although he left Central Office in 1939, Gower was still an influential figure with the party.[17] The opening provided by Gower got Maudling an interview on 17 December 1941 at Conservative Central Office with Thomas Dugdale, MP, at the time the Conservative official in charge of the candidates' list. Dugdale was impressed by Maudling and noted that 'His ambition is one day to enter Parliament and make it his career. He possesses a good personality, is obviously very intelligent and I think he will one day make a good Member.'[18] One can detect a hint that Dugdale thought Reggie was not quite ready for the responsibility, but further references the Tories took out left them in no doubt that Maudling was suitable. Gower in particular put in a strongly worded endorsement of Maudling's qualities. Conservative Central Office also asked for references about Beryl, in that old-fashioned Tory way, to see if she would be a suitable adornment. John Miles, the Warden of Merton College, told them that, although he did not know Beryl, Reggie 'is a man of first rate ability, very industrious and would get up with accuracy a most complicated subject. He is a strong young man and a very fine golfer. He is not shy, but is not pushing. He has good manners and address and was a popular member of the College.' Miles was sufficiently impressed by Maudling that he added in his own hand 'I think he should be an excellent candidate' to the typed letter. Louis Greig, the swashbuckling former sportsman, royal equerry and exotic fellow bird of passage in the Air Ministry, added his own endorsement: 'I am quite confident that he should make a good Member. He is very intelligent, hard working and well informed. I have not had the pleasure of meeting his wife, but I have learnt from a good friend of his and mine that she is all that could be desired.'[19]

At no stage in the process did Reggie's political views seem to count for much; his ability as a golfer and the attractiveness of his wife were more important. Reggie had made it onto the candidates' list, although he did not turn immediately to seeking a seat because few, other than Tory seats falling vacant in by-elections, were selecting in 1942. Another reason was that he was under civil service rules, which precluded seeking election, although he assured Dugdale that if he were selected he could arrange to transfer back to the service side of the RAF. This, however, would have meant leaving his interesting posting in Whitehall, and he was reluctant to do so. Having secured this rung on the ladder, Reggie carried on working in the Private Office, where attention was focusing on the great bombing onslaughts against Nazi Germany, and also thinking through his ideas about domestic politics to which he remained constant throughout his life.

Unusually for a civil servant – but there were many unusual civil servants during the war – Maudling wrote an article about political philosophy for the *Spectator*. It was published in November 1943 under the title 'Conservatives and Control'. The essay is a recognisable product of a Hegelian with an Oxford philosophy education. Maudling's starting point was the transformation of party politics since 1900:

> In the last century it was the parties of the Left that unfurled the banner of individual liberty in their assault on the stronghold of privilege manfully defended by the Right. Now it is the party of the Right, still on the defensive, that is fighting the cause of individual liberty against the threatening collectivism of the Left.

The eclipse of the Liberal Party, after it had achieved its goal of gaining political freedom and equality, demonstrated to Maudling that 'the social need which the party had expressed had been satisfied'. To Maudling:

> The 'century of the common man' has seen the emergence of two political facts: the first, that political and economic liberty are interdependent, so that the achievement of the one is valueless without the other; the second, that whereas in the political sphere liberty and equality are

complementary, in the economic sphere they seem to be ultimately irreconcilable.

Socialism, for Maudling, meant making the choice for equality over freedom in economics, and if this means that political liberty has to be sacrificed with economic liberty, so be it. The authoritarianism of socialism meant that it was opposed to both liberal and conservative ideas; however, it took over as the progressive force in British politics because the Liberals were incapable of meeting the legitimate demand for a struggle against economic privilege, which Maudling was sure would be the motive force of politics in the rest of the twentieth century. This is a tendentious account of the politics of the Labour Party in Britain, which risks restating more subtly Churchill's notorious 1945 broadcast about the need for a Gestapo 'no doubt humanely administered in the first instance' to implement a socialist programme. The young Maudling sometimes wrote, as many Tories did at the time, as though the advent of Attlee, Morrison and Bevin was an awful threat to freedom and British institutions. This shows a lack of knowledge of, and sensitivity to, the British Labour movement and its traditions – in free trade unionism and in the 'New Liberal' intellectual movement in the early twentieth century, which started to produce the welfare state, as well as socialism. A reading of Evan Durbin's 1940 tract, *The Politics of Democratic Socialism*, would have set him right about the fact that Labour intellectual discussions took the great questions of economic, social and political liberty exceptionally seriously, but this enlightenment had to wait until long evenings in the 1950s and 1960s spent talking to Roy Jenkins and Tony Crosland in the bars of the House of Commons. It was just a different intellectual culture.

Maudling believed that the Conservative Party had already declared in favour of individual liberty, but could see two ways in which it might develop the position. One route would be an emotional appeal to impatience with regulations and controls imposed during the war ('Do you want your entire existence, private as well as public, from the cradle to the grave ordered and controlled by the hordes of State bumbledom?'). In 1943 Maudling asked of this line of argument: 'can anyone of intellectual integrity maintain that it represents a serious contribution to political thought?' Despite this, in 1945–51 and even later, there was all too much of this kind of talk from the Conservatives, particularly from Churchill and Charles Hill. The second possibility, the one that the Conservatives ended up doing rather than saying, was to reject indiscriminate opposition to controls and attempt to compromise and draw spheres of influence in a consensual way between the claims of freedom and control. But Maudling felt that this was a mere compromise, which, while it had its place in practical politics, was not suitable for questions of principle.

Maudling thought he had a third way. Every philosopher is taught the distinction between negative freedom (freedom *from*, aka liberty) and positive freedom (freedom *to*). The negative idea of freedom was an undesirable legacy from Liberalism. Maudling had a radical rather than liberal approach to society:

> For all too many of our people freedom from control has meant nothing more than freedom to be poor, to be workless, to live in discomfort, insecurity, squalor. They have been free to vote, free to a remarkable degree from the interference of the State in their lives: yet their lives have been circumscribed and dictated from the moment of birth by economic necessity, and they have been condemned to a perpetual struggle against poverty and the threat of unemployment. The truth is that to speak of freedom in such circumstances is a travesty. Freedom for civilized man is not a mere negative, not just freedom *from*; it is freedom *to* live as a member of an organized society, freedom to think, speak, work and worship and to develop his individual personality in conditions that befit the dignity and greatness of the human race.[20]

To Maudling, 'control is part of the machinery of freedom and in the freedom of civilized man control is absorbed and transcended . . . [the Conservatives should argue that] the purpose of State control and the guiding principle of its application is the achievement of true freedom'. To more doctrinaire modern ideologues, this statement cannot be considered compatible with the Tory faith. Even at the time, Hayek's 1944 free market tract *The Road to Serfdom* was dedicated 'to the socialists of all parties' and he would certainly have included Maudling among that number. From a different starting point, Maudling had ended up at much the same place philosophically as Labour's social democrats. His politics recognised as appropriate the demand for economic equality and accepted the validity of the most usual left-wing critique of negative freedom. He accepted that the state has a major role in remedying social injustice. Where he parted company with 1940s social democrats was in his dislike of direct state control of economic enterprises; he felt that his experiences in Whitehall taught him that 'State enterprise is not a good thing for the economy as a whole'.[21] Another distinction was his emphasis on individuals, as opposed to thinking about people in groups, as the left tended to do at the time. These differences became more blurred over the years. New Labour would certainly have reservations about Maudling's faith that the route to freedom could be via controls and state intervention.

It is a fine distinction between transcending a thesis and antithesis to produce a synthesis, and the elevation of compromise into a principle, and Maudling was to return to the question in future discussions, such as his attempt to define the 'extreme centre' in 1970.[22] To what extent he, and others, managed to do more than produce a lowest-common-denominator consensus in practice is a question that underlies his entire career. He always felt that he did find something better than splitting the difference. While some

Conservatives felt that their post-1945 outlook was a necessary accommodation to political circumstances, Maudling positively believed in the welfare state and social equality. Although he belonged to a party of the right, and rose nearly to the top of it, he was never really a man of the right. Such Tories existed then, back when the party was a national institution.

However, Reggie may have been a bit too non-partisan and consensus-minded to appeal to Conservative audiences. The *Spectator* piece earned a blast from the high Tory Earl of Mansfield, who wrote: 'Mr Maudling does not give any real guidance to the Conservative Party, nor is there any indication that he is qualified to do so, as no tinge of Conservative spirit appears in the article.'[23] His lack of 'Conservative spirit' may have damaged his attempts to find a constituency. In July 1944 he was keen to apply to his home constituency of Greenwich, which had not yet selected a Tory candidate. Greenwich was then a marginal seat, held by the Conservatives in 1935 but which had gone Labour in 1923 and 1929 (and never went Conservative again after Labour gained it in 1945). Reggie told Central Office that if he were to be unsuccessful in Greenwich he would be quite prepared to fight a 'difficult' seat for the experience.[24] He was indeed turned down at Greenwich, despite his charm, local connections and very presentable family, which now boasted an infant addition. Reggie's first son was born in March 1944 and christened, like his father and grandfather, Reginald; he could have, if he had wished, called himself 'Reginald Maudling III' but he used his middle name and was generally known as Martin Maudling. A number of unsuccessful attempts to get selected followed, and Reggie's offer to fight a safe Labour seat looked in danger of being taken up as victory, and a general election, came closer into view.

Reggie Maudling's tour of duty in the Private Office came to an end as 1944 turned into 1945, and he moved to a section of the RAF called S6, which provided the secretariat for the Air Staff. By then the Allies had established air superiority over Germany and ground forces were on the borders of the German Reich itself. The end was near but the air offensive continued, most controversially in the firebombing of Dresden in February 1945. Maudling did not talk much about the bombing later on, or mention it in his memoirs, but he was close to the centre of RAF strategy in the Private Office and S6 as it evolved from 1942 to 1945 and grew steadily more brutal. Sinclair had reconciled himself to inflicting massive civilian casualties, comparing himself privately in May 1942 to Cromwell who would 'slay in the name of the Lord' by bringing the horror of war back home to the cities of Germany. He was less frankly bloodthirsty than Sir Arthur Harris, and in public pronouncements would attempt to portray the offensive in terms of the destruction of the Nazi war machine rather than as killing civilians. Sir Ronald Melville told Sinclair's biographer, Gerard De Groot, that while telling the truth to Parliament is easy, telling the right lie well and sticking to it is much more difficult. De Groot wrote that 'in defending air policy, Sinclair's perception of his duty to his country overrode his duty to the truth and for that matter to liberal values'.[25] Maudling saw nothing in this that was inconsistent with his view of Sinclair as a man of principle and integrity. Maudling learned early on in political life that the ends could justify the means, if necessity and a higher moral purpose demanded it; as Home Secretary in charge of Northern Ireland he felt that one should not be too squeamish when waging war.

As the war in Europe drew to an end, attention in Britain started to drift to the resumption of normal political activity. Germany surrendered on 7 May, and the coalition government arrangements clearly had to be renewed on some basis or brought to an end. Churchill offered the Liberal and Labour leaders the opportunity to continue the coalition until the end of the war with Japan (at that stage seemingly a distant prospect); Sinclair was willing to accept but Attlee followed strong Labour feeling that continued coalition was undesirable and pulled out. The coalition ended on 23 May. Churchill, a veteran coalitionist, regretted this, as did many moderate Conservatives such as Maudling, who had admired the spirit of progress and consensus that the wartime government had created.

The end of the coalition precipitated a general election, the first for nearly ten years. The electoral map had last been redrawn in 1918 and by 1945 it was severely out of date. The coalition government had acted to remedy the worst anomalies by splitting some of the most oversized seats and creating new ones. The changes resulted in twenty-five last-minute selections in the weeks leading up to the election, many of them in suburban areas around London. One such was Heston and Isleworth, hewn mostly from the Tory redoubt of Twickenham. The constituency seemed a promising prospect for the Conservatives when its borders were drawn out on the political map. It consisted of suburbs that had sprung up between the wars either side of the Great West Road stretching west across Middlesex from London towards Slough and Reading. The constituency was a mix of residential areas and modern industries, an area of growth and low unemployment that had prospered throughout the 'depressed' 1930s. The main local landmark was Heston aerodrome, where Neville Chamberlain had waved his famous piece of paper on his return from Munich in 1938. The Tories would have been well ahead in the seat in 1935, and given that the Tories were expected by most observers to win the election on Churchill's coat tails, it was one of the best seats on offer at the time.

The newly formed Heston and Isleworth Conservative Association had, nearly as its first item of business, to select its candidate. Two local men applied for the Conservative nomination, among them a young RAF airman, Flight Officer John Day, who seemed the early front-runner.[26] Central Office sent the selection committee eleven names from their list. The selection committee narrowed it down to four candidates: Day and another local, George Willment, and two from the Central Office list including Maudling. On the evening of 9 May the four spoke at a meeting of the selection committee and Maudling was a runaway winner, with an overall majority on the first ballot. While Day and Willment rallied round and supported Maudling, there was some carping in the local press about his lack of local credentials.[27]

The main contest in Heston and Isleworth was between Maudling and the Labour candidate, W.R. Williams, the assistant secretary of the Union of Post Office Workers who, like Maudling, was not a local candidate. No Liberal came forward to fight the seat, but a local retired army major, Wallace Drake-Brockman, stood as an 'Independent National' candidate on a platform concentrating on the grievances of ex-servicemen.

The Conservative organisation in Heston was rather a scratch affair. The chairman and agent, Bob Salisbury, was according to Reggie 'a cheerful extrovert . . . who gave me an early warning that I should disregard anything he said after nine o'clock at night. We got on very well.'[28] The poor state of national Conservative organisation in 1945 gave candidates an unusual degree of freedom to mount their own electoral appeal. As Maudling had predicted, there was a lot of simplistic sloganising about freedom, but some of the emerging young moderate Tories took the opportunity to emphasise that things could not go back to 1939 and that there had to be more state provision of social services and more intervention in the economy. Maudling's speeches during the campaign were unashamedly from the progressive wing of the Conservative Party. He was in favour of the Beveridge Report and a government commitment to maintain full employment.

Maudling's economic philosophy in 1945 was a decidedly left-wing and progressive version of Toryism, along the lines he had sketched out in his *Spectator* article. In the short term he believed in an economy with extensive government controls over industry to oversee the transition to an affluent peacetime order, and also in the desirability of the government intervening to secure social objectives:

During the period of scarcity the Government would have to retain a lot of control over the economic life of the nation. One of the reasons why economic controls had functioned very well in war time was that British industry, built up by private enterprise, was easily adaptable. Such controls were not needed for a period of abundance.

Maudling believed in a mixed economy, with ownership primarily in private hands but a role for the government in directing its progress:

A blind belief in nationalisation that rejected all the merits of private enterprise was foolish; a blind belief in private enterprise that saw no good at all in government was equally foolish. The truth of the matter was that in the years to come we would need all that was best in state action and of individual enterprise. There was no need for a clash between Government organisation and individual initiative: they should be complementary.

We could go forward only by harnessing all the driving force of private enterprise and all the organising power that a modern State could wield.

Although fighting under Conservative colours, Maudling had imbibed some of the radical spirit of 1945, commenting that 'We had regained our faith in our country – a faith that seemed to be flickering in the dismal years between the two German wars'. Maudling believed that Britain should contribute forces to a new international police force, 'strong in the defence of justice' and that 'the friendship should become closer' with the Soviet Union.[29] In all his speeches he stressed the Coalition programmes of national insurance, child welfare and family allowances. Although opponents recognised his sincerity, he was vulnerable to the charge that the Conservatives would revert to pre-war type should they win.

The most exciting moment in the Heston campaign was on the Monday evening before polling when Winston Churchill passed through as part of a campaigning swing around marginals in the London area. A vast crowd, running into thousands, assembled at Busch Corner in Isleworth, while Reggie and family, plus election agent Robert Salisbury, waited on the roof of a surface air-raid shelter at this unglamorous road junction. Despite Churchill being nearly an hour late he had a tumultuous reception; the police line broke and cheering crowds surrounded his car. Reggie and his party struggled through to meet the Prime Minister. Churchill greeted Maudling 'very warmly' – although not personally close at this stage, Churchill was aware of Maudling because of his wartime work at the Air Ministry. Ever the politician, Churchill gave fifteen-month-old Martin 'an affectionate pat on the cheek'. Reggie joined Churchill for a short drive on what seemed a triumphal progress through the suburbs.[30]

Although the exhilaration of that day provided a boost for the Tories of Heston and Isleworth, there were worrying signs on election day. Labour's local activists were youthful and energetic, and were well supplied with cars to help voters to the polls. Reggie and Beryl committed a polling day faux pas by starting to drive around the constituency in a loudspeaker van at 6a.m., offering early morning greetings and perhaps counter-productive encouragement to voters to get to the polling stations. In future general elections in Barnet, a bit scarred by his experiences in west London, Reggie completely foreswore the use of loudspeaker vans.[31] Whether roused by the Maudlings or not, voters were keen and queues had formed outside polling stations before they opened. When the polls closed Maudling seemed less confident of victory than Williams, but they both had a long wait to see who had won.[32]

There was a three-week delay before the votes were counted while ballots were returned from British armed forces scattered around the world. This was a time of anxious speculation, although it was generally reckoned that Churchill's popularity had brought the Conservatives victory. When the ballot boxes were opened on 26 July, the votes told a different story. Labour were not only winning traditional strongholds and target seats but scoring unexpected gains in previously safe Conservative areas. Heston and Isleworth was swept away in this tide. Reggie Maudling had unexpectedly lost his first election by a considerable margin and Williams became the constituency's first MP. In his victory speech Williams congratulated his opponents for having 'played a good straight game and put up a clean fight' and expressed pride in the high level of debate and discussion that had characterised the local contest. Maudling made a gracious speech of concession, wishing Williams well, and commented that although it was his own first election it would not be the last, by a long way – he promised that he would be back after his defeat.[33] Maudling, however, did not return to Heston. Williams was unseated in 1950 by a new Conservative candidate, Richard Reader Harris, who had campaigned with considerable energy for four years.

W.R. Williams	Labour	29,192	54.3
Reginald Maudling	Conservative	22,623	42.1
W. Drake-Brockman	National	1,919	3.6
Labour majority		6,569	12.2
Electorate		72,219	
Turnout			74.4

The election result left Maudling in a difficult position. He had resigned his civil service position and was unsure about what to do next. Reggie and Beryl, with Martin, were living in a rented flat in New Court, in the Middle Temple where he had read for the Bar, and the idea of starting legal practice was still theoretically open. However, there was no shortage of more qualified barristers returning after the war; it was a particularly troublesome moment to try to enter the profession. Beryl was helping make ends meet by doing a little acting; despite what she said later she had not entirely given up her career on getting married. She had a couple of minor film appearances during 1944 (*English Without Tears*, and uncredited in *Fanny by Gaslight*) and fairly frequent *Children's Hour* radio broadcasts. At the time of the 1945 election she had appeared as Princess Elizabeth in a *Children's Hour* series *The Little Stuarts*.[34] It was not enough to live on. During summer 1945, the demobilised Reggie Maudling appears to have done some work for his father's firms, R. Watson and Commercial Calculating, presumably giving legal advice and perhaps commenting on political matters relating to the Labour government's proposed changes to the national insurance system. However, Reggie's ambitions were focused on politics – winning an election and developing his high-level contacts. Reggie remained in contact with Tory politics as the party picked itself up, talking to people at Central Office, undertaking speaking engagements, being generally helpful, biding his time until the Tories realised how useful he could be to them. It did not take long.

Chapter 4

CHURCHILL'S PINK PANSY:[1]
CONSERVATIVE RESEARCH,
1945–1949

Although Maudling was naturally disappointed at losing the 1945 election, on further reflection he could see the positive side of the result, nationally and personally. 'It may well be that the strange political instinct of the British people proved right again on that occasion.'[2] Although he still sometimes spoke and wrote as if Labour were a threat to British liberty and democracy in the 1940s, these were reflexes rather than a considered position. Maudling recognised, as the less subtle partisan does not, that there is intrinsic value in alternation between government parties, no matter how painful or undesirable it may seem at any particular juncture. His Hegelian passivity in the face of great historical changes gave him a broad perspective on the rise of socialism in Britain.

Maudling also felt, again on reflection, that the Conservatives had not deserved to win in 1945. They had traded too heavily on Churchill's prestige as war leader and 'had not much to offer at that time to those who wished to see change'.[3] Reggie's apprehension in 'Conservatives and Control' that the Tories would try to campaign on rhetoric without offering anything of substance had proved correct. He was on record as having mocked this approach in his 1943 article and could not be dismissed as merely wise after the event; the 1945 election result seemed to have proved his point. After 1945, Maudling had a more receptive audience for what he had to say, and he was in a position to make sure that he could be heard. He had impressed J.P.L. Thomas, the Conservative Party's vice-chairman in charge of candidates, and Thomas tried to recruit him to help organise the 'Junior Movement', which eventually became the Young Conservatives. Maudling extricated himself from this commitment, with some good grace, when a job with a new and more interesting organisation called the Conservative Parliamentary Secretariat came up.

The CPS was a response to the desperate problem the Tories faced in adjusting to opposition after having spent only three of the last thirty years out of power. Many of them had no idea of how to operate without an army of civil servants backing them up. They were demoralised by defeat and the confident swagger of the Labour majority in Parliament and the sense, which carried on for most of 1945 and 1946, that the socialist tide was still running strongly. The Research Department, established by Joseph Ball in 1929, had been run down before and during the war. Under Neville Chamberlain it had become an adjunct of Number 10, and it was not active from 1940 until shortly before the 1945 election, when the Conservative policy machine amounted to David Clarke, Henry Brooke and two secretaries.[4]

The party's priority in 1945 was to get back on its feet and act like an effective opposition; the longer-term thinking that was associated with the work of the Research Department could wait for another day, when money was less tight. The idea of having some research support for the Shadow Cabinet originated with Winston Churchill, who proposed establishing a small research staff and rooms available for himself and ex-ministers; a kind of Shadow Cabinet office. David Clarke noted in 1951 that 'This plan was so unpopular both among Mr Churchill's colleagues and among backbenchers, who felt they were being left out, that it was dropped'.[5] It would indeed have been a centralising move, but a large part of the problem was that Churchill proposed that Duncan Sandys, his son-in-law and former MP for Norwood, should head the new body. This gave the original secretariat plan the air of setting up a personal staff, and Sandys was not universally popular. The Sandys plan having been killed at the Shadow Cabinet meeting of 30 October, the party chairman, Ralph Assheton, was left to make the arrangements.

The resulting organisation, the Conservative Parliamentary Secretariat, was actually quite similar to Churchill's original idea, but Sandys did not feature and its research assistance was available to the party's backbench policy committees and occasionally MPs as well as to the Shadow Cabinet. Accommodation was found at 24 Wilton Street in Belgravia, a brisk 15-minute walk from the Houses of Parliament; a room was kept for the use of ex-ministers, but it was hardly ever used and the Secretariat staff annexed the room almost unnoticed as their numbers grew.

Recruiting staff for the Secretariat was a haphazard process. Assheton told David Clarke to go and find people, but he found it surprisingly difficult. Reggie Maudling, who was hanging around Conservative politics wanting to find something to do, was an obvious choice given his Whitehall experience. He became the first member of the Secretariat in November 1945, temporarily under David Clarke. Maudling was joined early in 1946 by a more senior if less effective figure, Henry Hopkinson, who volunteered to leave the diplomatic service and join the party staff: 'Eden's nominee' sniffed Rab Butler in his memoirs.[6] Other members were recruited as and when they turned up – Enoch Powell started in March 1946 with Iain Macleod joining in April. There were other, less famous and high-powered, members of the Secretariat like Philip Bremridge, Mr Stebbings and Brigadier Blunt, but in Maudling, Macleod and Powell the office had a nucleus of intellectual and political strength – and ambition. The Secretariat opened a new career route in British politics. Before 1945 the parties employed few professional researchers, and those that did exist seemed not to aspire to front-line political careers themselves. Maudling and his colleagues were the first backroom boys to make the leap, and they have been emulated by generations since. There had been people born into politics, like generations of Churchills, and people who had always had political ambitions but first did other jobs, like F.E. Smith, but the professional politician was born on the day in November 1945 when Reggie Maudling sauntered into the Wilton Street office and put his feet up on the desk.

A professional politician needs a seat, and Maudling, Macleod, Powell and Hopkinson were all selected for promising parliamentary candidatures during the 1945 parliament. Reggie, again, was slightly in the lead and was one of the very first new candidates to be adopted, in February 1946. He was not keen to return to Heston and Isleworth, with its memories of defeat and its rather large Labour majority, despite his bravado at the count. The constituencies which wanted to select candidates as soon as possible were generally much better prospects, seats which were surprise Labour gains in 1945 where the Tories would be back even if there was hardly any change in public opinion. Central Office graded such constituencies 'Marginal +',[7] and this sort of seat in the London suburbs was the dream of many ambitious young Tories, including Reggie Maudling.

Maudling had an interest in two such constituencies. He had spoken at a Conservative meeting in Uxbridge, north-west of London, in autumn 1945 and attracted the support of some local Tories, one of whom wrote to him inviting him to enter the selection. Labour had won the seat by only 1,084 votes in 1945. It was even more attractive than it seemed because it was oversized and would surely be divided in the review of parliamentary boundaries that the Labour government was conducting. The northern part of it consisted of some extremely safe Conservative territory at Ruislip and Northwood, including the hinterland of Merchant Taylors' and Fighter Command, which after 1950 became an utterly reliable Tory stronghold. By getting the Uxbridge selection, Maudling would have been able to have first refusal on the new Ruislip Northwood constituency. His Secretariat colleague Iain Macleod pulled off a similar trick in Enfield, whose division in the 1948 review created a safe Tory seat out of what looked to the uninitiated like a Labour-inclined marginal in 1945.

The other option was Barnet. Jim Thomas had passed Reggie's name to the Barnet selection committee and Reggie was unsure about whether it was done to put his name in for Uxbridge as well, asking Thomas, 'Is this against the rules? Uxbridge is not so good a bet as Barnet, but it's a seat that should be won back, and I imagine that I shall be facing very high-class competition at Barnet.'[8] Barnet was an exceptionally attractive constituency from Maudling's point of view. It was technically a county constituency of Hertfordshire but in fact most of the population lived in outer London suburbs at the far end of the Underground's Northern Line. It consisted of Barnet itself, a pleasant suburban town on a hill, some elite areas like Hadley and Totteridge and some less select areas of Victorian and inter-war housing at East Barnet and New Barnet. It extended a little out into the countryside at Elstree and Borehamwood. Reggie himself had been born just outside the boundaries of the constituency, and his background gave him an affinity with the sort of people who lived in the area – prosperous middle-class professionals and commuters. It also meant that he could live in the constituency while travelling to Westminster, which saved a lot of expense and effort when he had a young family. There was little agriculture or manufacturing in Barnet, although there were some modern industries in the area, such as the film studios at Elstree.

Labour had won the newly created Barnet seat in their 1945 landslide by only 682 votes. The Labour MP, Stephen Taylor (later Lord Taylor of Harlow), was a doctor who became one of the most impressive of the unlikely winners of 1945, and it had been suggested that he might move to a more reliable constituency because of the probability of the seat going to the Tories at the first opportunity. Taylor decided to defend the seat and face the probability of defeat with dignity, for he had already decided that he did not love parliamentary life.[9] The redistribution of seats in 1948 made Barnet even better for the Conservatives, because the area around Hatfield, including the wealthy villages of Brookmans Park and Cuffley, came into the constituency. Hatfield in those days was a rather Tory village, based around the seat of the Marquesses of Salisbury; the Labour government's New Town was still mostly on the drawing board. On the new boundaries it is doubtful whether Labour could have won Barnet even in 1945. If Reggie won the Tory selection he would be securing a strong base for a parliamentary career.

The final stages of the Conservative selection took place in February 1946.[10] Maudling travelled up to Barnet on the evening of St Valentine's Day, Thursday 14 February, to address the constituency executive and answer questions alongside four other candidates, whittled down from twenty-one applicants. It was an unusually thorough and formal selection procedure, painstakingly fair although of course each of the prospective candidates engaged in a bit of socialising and lobbying. It was an open seat because the previous candidate, a rather stuffy barrister who had been a surprise winner at the previous selection, had put on a poor showing during the 1945 campaign and the local Conservatives were anxious to go for a completely different type to demonstrate that the Tories were changing. According to Robert Carr (now Lord Carr of Hadley), who chaired the Barnet Young Conservatives and reached the final round of the selection:

They wanted a progressive, modern party – they were 'One Nation' before the phrase was coined. They also wanted to do the selection by a proper structure of internal democracy rather than just by a clique. We all wanted to increase party membership and build up an organisation, which had run down during the war. Barnet dropped the practice of asking candidates for financial contributions to the Association and election expenses, which was banned by the party only in 1948. They wanted a young, moderate, progressive figure as their candidate.[11]

Reggie and two others were chosen to go forward to the final stage, a special general meeting of the entire Conservative association the next day where they would again speak and answer questions. The three finalists were very much in the youthful, moderate mould – Reggie Maudling, Robert Carr and Ian Orr-Ewing. As Maudling had anticipated, the quality of the competition was high but in the event he was the leading candidate because of his experience in contesting the 1945 election and his work for the Secretariat. On the night of the selection meeting the three drew lots and Reggie went first. Robert Carr remembers that Maudling 'was the best performer on the day, but people were favourably inclined to him. The officers were pretty determined to see him selected, and it was clear that they were voting for him. He was introduced very favourably . . . His standing was high and that's why he won.'

It was a very gentlemanly contest and the three Barnet finalists became close friends. Robert Carr was surprised a couple of weeks later when the Conservatives of Mitcham wrote inviting him to contest the selection, and even more surprised when he was selected there despite telling the committee that he would not give the association money or move to the constituency. Maudling, on the other hand, had accepted the request of the Barnet Tories that he find somewhere to live locally. Robert Carr lived in a modest house in Totteridge Green, one of the most attractive and expensive parts of Barnet, and when he saw that another house in the small development was for sale he told Maudling. The Carrs and Maudlings became near neighbours, and the Orr-Ewings lived not far away.[12]

Reggie was a keen and energetic candidate once he was adopted, plunging straight into a run of speaking engagements across the constituency and corresponding frequently with the *Barnet Press* to get himself known. On 25 February he spoke at his first public meeting, at St Mark's Hall in New Barnet, on the subject of foreign policy. He observed that an atomic war would bring all plans of social improvement to nothing, and that 'For that reason foreign affairs were not a matter of contention between the main political parties. Mr Bevin commanded the confidence of all save possibly the lunatic fringe of Communists.'[13] The young Conservative aspirant praised Labour's Foreign Secretary as a man whose policy was frankness rather than appeasement. It was an unusual note to strike for his first speech as the local Tory candidate. He did offer a little criticism of the Labour government, calling nationalisation a simple solution to a complex problem and saying that government should work on the 'solution of practical problems of work,

food and homes, rather than misdirecting its energies to widespread schemes
of industrial reorganisation'. Maudling expounded his faith in state
organisation for the Tories of Barnet:

> The future would undoubtedly see a great extension of state activity, and
> that could bring much benefit to individual citizens, but in a completely
> socialist state personal liberty would be at a discount. The greatest problem
> facing the country was how to exploit the benefits of modern government,
> while avoiding the loss of individual initiative and liberty. The Conservative
> Party believed that a solution avoiding both extremes could be found, a
> policy which would be in harmony with our long and great political
> traditions.

It was a speech along these lines that drew a comment from a Labour-
supporting heckler at a meeting in Barnet: that it was the most socialistic
thing he had ever heard. Reggie quipped back that at least he could be sure of
the man's vote at the next election.[14] Maudling believed in keeping his
language moderate, which was fairly unusual at the time when allegations of
'Gestapo' and 'lower than vermin' were traded back and forward. The
chairman of Potters Bar Conservatives, just across the border in Iain
Macleod's Enfield, talked of 'this Nazi, fascist, totalitarian government we
have at Westminster'[15] and many Conservatives were driven to irrational fury
merely by the presence of Labour in power.

Reggie's first speech in Barnet demonstrated his general approach to
politics in the 1940s, and his work at the Parliamentary Secretariat showed
the same qualities of restrained language, a preoccupation with balance and
moderation and a distrust of simple solutions to complex problems. Maudling
saw his role at the Secretariat as being to provide intelligent arguments to his
party – to some extent rationalising the party's prejudices in a more
convincing way than in the past, to some extent educating the party out of
those prejudices and making it fit once more for power. He had a chance to
nudge the Tories towards the third way he had advocated in his 1943
Spectator piece – away from windy rhetoric about freedom but without falling
into simple me-too politics.

For all his moderation, he was a loyal servant of his party, aware of and to
some extent sharing the sensibilities of the traditional Conservative. In 1946
he wrote at length to Eden to oppose the current proposal to change the
name of the party to give a more modern image and to facilitate the
absorption of what remained of the Liberal Party. Reggie argued that people
'are looking to us for leadership. They will not be pleased with a trick of
salesmanship. They are looking to us for an idea, for a faith. They will not be
happy with a mere change of colour.' After only about five years in the party,
and all his hesitations in 1939–41, Reggie had already put down strong Tory
roots and condemned the prospective 'spectacle of the Conservative Party

apparently running away from its own name and, by implication, from its own past'.[16] Reggie was an instinctive loyalist, and in this he was perhaps at his most deeply Tory.

Although the Conservative research work was important and productive, it was also – not to be underestimated – great fun. Maudling loved his time in Conservative research. It was a jolly, optimistic period in his life, rather like Oxford except he was now doing some teaching, and his students included Winston Churchill and Anthony Eden. In the mid-1970s, when his career was on the slide, he would pop into his old office when passing, standing amid the old furniture and heavy black Bakelite telephones that still furnished the place.[17] He relaxed, lost in pleasant memories of happy days and bright-eyed enthusiasm that had long since faded.

Maudling found the work extremely interesting. He started off well in the winter of 1945/6, even though the Conservative Party was at a low ebb in electoral appeal and self-confidence. The Labour government's National Insurance Bill was newly published and Reggie was able to bring in his father's actuarial expertise to the technical aspects of the legislation and to making connections between the Conservatives and the private pension funds industry.[18] He then became the officer in charge of everything relating to economics, including trade and industry questions and the Conservative response to the Labour government's nationalisation programme. He also had some responsibilities for the civil service and industrial relations. The Secretariat and the Research Department were regarded as a sort of shadow civil service, and they aped the civil service tradition of the 'able generalist'. They were not appointed as experts. Maudling had studied classics and philosophy rather than economics, although his war work had involved coordination with industry. Brigadier Powell would have been a natural choice for defence (and, had it not been for his eccentric views on the Empire, for foreign policy too) – so he covered a ragbag of domestic issues including town and country planning. The main task of the researchers was to provide briefing papers on issues as and when they came up in Parliament, which required a quick survey of existing literature, a little original thought and the ability to synthesise the information into a written essay with evidence. It was one of the few jobs for which an Oxford arts education can be considered vocational training.

In covering economics and industry Reggie had the most pressurised job. Many Conservative MPs had no clue about modern economics and needed careful nursing through debates. The Labour government was implementing its programme of nationalisation of industries such as coal, gas, electricity, transport and eventually iron and steel, each of which required a complicated, detailed piece of legislation. The Conservative leadership set the overall policy, usually of half-hearted opposition to the principle and more spirited attempts to amend the detail. Coming up with possibilities for opposition amendments was part of Maudling's job. As well as briefings on specific issues as they came up, he would provide surveys of the economic scene to inform the front bench for budget and economic policy debates. Maudling's briefing papers are for the most part detailed and serious assessments of some quite difficult issues such as the proper role of parliamentary accountability in nationalised industries:

> With few exceptions these Acts give Ministers general powers of direction, unlimited powers of demanding information and certain specific powers of direction. They can be questioned on the use, misuse or failure to use any of these powers. Beyond this, however, they have no responsibility, and, therefore Questions cannot be in order . . . if industries are to be nationalised, the new set up should be as practical as possible and should be as closely as possible in line with a commercial undertaking . . . To press now for extended Ministerial powers of detailed direction (and unless Ministers' powers be extended, Parliamentary control during Question time cannot be) would be completely to reverse the policy that we have consistently followed in the matter of nationalised industries.[19]

Their tone tended to be academic, or civil service, with the thinnest veneer of partisan comment; if anything his papers were rather too detailed and dispassionate for many of their consumers' needs. Some ran to thirty densely typed pages. Maudling's output was astonishing. In 1947 there were 64 briefings on fuel and power, and in 1948 there were 48 about the gas industry. The research staff produced 319 briefings in 1947, 248 in 1948 and 243 in 1949.[20] Most of these, and many of the longest, were in Reggie's fields.

Reggie never gave the impression that he was working hard at the Secretariat. As at Oxford, he was able to get the job done in bursts of concentrated mental activity. An hour of him working at full speed was worth several hours of most people's time. He had a habit of returning from lunch in mid-afternoon, wreathed in cigar smoke and brandy fumes, putting his feet up on the desk and reeling off a word-perfect memo for the party leader in 20 minutes. He also studied rather furtively, reading at evenings and weekends, and put in more hours than he was willing to admit. He certainly did not impress his colleagues as a slave to duty while he was working for the party. Despite the pressure, he was the calm centre of the volatile team at the Secretariat. Enoch Powell, with whom he shared an office, found Maudling 'an admirable colleague at work: easy-going outwardly and unruffled, always with time to listen to other people's problems, and genuinely kind in matters personal'.[21] Powell was not an easy man to get on with, and in many ways was temperamentally Maudling's opposite – driven, fanatically hard-working, and logical to a fault. Maudling once tried to convince Powell that he was being 'too logical', but Powell refused to recognise that this concept made any sense.[22] Powell lacked Maudling's inbuilt ideological stabilisers and, as

Macleod commented, pursued his trains of thought until they went crashing into the buffers at the end of the line. Powell was also highly strung and, in the 1940s, was in emotional turmoil about his relationships with women; that he still thought of Reggie as a kind confidant when he wrote his appreciation in 1979 says something about Maudling's calmness and maturity as he turned 30 in 1947.

Although Maudling liked Powell, with a kind of bemused affection for his eccentricities, he was closer to his fellow researcher Iain Macleod, with whom he would frequently disappear for long, bibulous lunches, sometimes at Macleod's club, Crockford's. Reggie remembered that 'we talked, and argued, and thought, and discussed about politics day after day, but we were never, I believe, solemn, because we realised that you do not have to be solemn in order to be serious'.[23]

Maudling thought of Macleod as a 'strange, lovable and complicated character',[24] words that suit their author as well as their subject. Macleod was the big brother Reggie never had – a little older and certainly in the 1940s more worldly wise than him: a professional gambler, a ladies' man, a wartime soldier who nearly shot a friend dead in a fit of drunken rage.[25] There was an aura of danger and romance about Macleod that Reggie simply did not have; Macleod's speeches crackled with passion, scorn and bitter partisan emotion, while Reggie's tended to be blandly agreeable. Macleod inspired young Conservatives in the 1960s, such as John Major, who wore out the grooves of a gramophone record of Macleod's speeches through excessive listening. Maudling was much less of a leadership icon and role model even before his political career started to fade in 1965.

Maudling and Macleod, despite these personal differences, shared a lot, including a rather feckless love of the good life – meaning large quantities of excellent food and drink – regardless of whether they could actually afford it. Their political views were very similar, although Macleod expressed his faith more aggressively. Maudling regarded Macleod as 'substantially to the right' on economics (which indicates that Reggie viewed anything much further to the right, such as the economics of Powell and Joseph, as not being legitimate). On some social matters, such as hanging, it was Macleod who was the more 'left-wing'.[26] These were differences of emphasis rather than profound principle.[27] Rab Butler thought more highly of Macleod ('the most ambitious and maybe the cleverest of the three') than Maudling, 'more dilettantish, he would take lunch from 12 to 3',[28] even though Macleod was frequently Reggie's partner in crime at lunchtime. Perhaps Butler saw in Maudling too much of a reflection of himself, his easygoing vices as well as his virtues, and in Macleod a harder-edged, improved version. Maudling was often thought of later as a Butler man, like Macleod and Powell, but his allegiance was always more complicated than that. In 1954, when the image of Maudling as a Rab sidekick had already caught on, he surprised Treasury official Robert Hall by telling him that he hardly knew Butler personally.[29]

Reggie did not depend on Butler as a patron; he had already, by the time Butler absorbed the Secretariat into the Research Department in 1948, forged links with the leader of the party, Winston Churchill, and the man who was effectively the deputy leader, Anthony Eden.

Reggie's ability and his amiable personality meant that his activities quickly went beyond the formal grind of writing briefing papers. In 1945–6 he helped Anthony Eden with speech-writing on domestic subjects. Eden had long experience in foreign affairs, but as the de facto deputy leader to Churchill, who was spending a lot of time abroad and was, to put it mildly, disengaged from politics, Eden ended up having to cover some domestic territory as well. Eden's first major postwar speech on Conservative philosophy, at his constituency association in summer 1946, contained passages that read like pure Maudling:

> As this twentieth century develops it becomes ever more apparent that the problem of the relation of the individual to the state is the most urgent and vexatious problem of politics. It is not a problem to which one can give a single answer. It is as foolish to say that the state should have no authority over individual lives as it is to say that the individual has no right to freedom from the state.[30]

Maudling gave strong support to Eden's emerging line of thought about a new big idea for the Conservatives, to enable them to put up a positive alternative to socialism that would have electoral appeal, intellectual solidity and its roots in Tory tradition. He urged Eden to give the Conservatives a strong lead at the 1946 conference: 'I think there is no doubt that people expect a statement of the first importance on our domestic policy to be made at Blackpool, and there is widespread hope that this statement will contain some broad but definite general principle on which Conservatives throughout the country can work in explaining what our policy is.' Maudling and Eden talked frequently about domestic policy and Maudling picked out something Eden had said as being a particularly important point that could form the basis for a new Tory appeal: 'If I may say so, I think that such a principle is contained in your expression "a nation wide property owning democracy". In the principle of the diffusion of ownership rather than its concentration we have something wholly opposed to Socialist principles which we can develop and which can be made fully understandable to the average elector.'[31]

Eden's concept of the diffusion of ownership was not just related to housing, but it reflected his great interest in 'co-partnership' in industry. Eden returned again and again to his desire to break down the barriers between managers and managed in industry and found Maudling highly receptive to his thinking. Reggie helped Eden work up 'nation wide property owning democracy' into an important passage for his conference speech, which was much noted after the 1946 conference and has become a central point of reference for Conservative philosophy ever since. Eden had a habit, which Maudling seemed to pick up, of omitting or mangling the best sound bites from his speeches, but this time he delivered it as intended.[32] His speech-writer on domestic policy deserves a considerable share of the credit.[33]

Despite Reggie's role in Eden's domestic speeches, and Oliver Stanley's joke that being around the Conservative research establishment was 'like being educated at Eden (Eton) and Maudling (Magdalen)', Reggie was not a particular protégé of Eden. Robert Carr, who knew both well, thought that: 'There was not a particularly close relationship between them; at the Research Department he worked primarily for Winston rather than Anthony. But it was clear that Eden respected him and regarded him as a top calibre person, he always spoke well of him. And there was never any awkwardness or tension, unlike with Enoch.'[34]

Winston Churchill tended, as admiring assistants to President Roosevelt observed during the war, to 'roll his own' as far as speeches were concerned. Certainly, no speech-writer can take much credit for Churchill's most celebrated flourishes of oratory, but even for him a 40-minute speech needed legato passages between the swelling crescendos. He would pace up and down his study at his Kent home, Chartwell, dictating passages to his assistants, and for factual content on domestic policy needed considerable research support. This is where Maudling came in.

Reggie's first speech-writing task for Churchill was in 1946, when he was summoned to Chartwell. Churchill, clad in his off-duty garb of a boiler suit, greeted him, '"Ah, Maudling, I see you have arrived, come and have a whisky and soda. Of course," he said, after a moment's reflection, "there is tea if you would prefer it."' Reggie did not prefer it, and got off to a good start with Churchill.[35] Churchill liked strong drink, and strong drinkers, and Reggie quickly found a place in his affections. Churchill had an avuncular relationship with Maudling and enjoyed his company. Alone amongst the Conservative research staff Maudling received a copy of his book *The Gathering Storm* in November 1948. Churchill personally added his name to a draft list of 'personal friends' to send to the publisher.[36] He gave Maudling his hospitality on several occasions, and it bothered Reggie that there seemed little he could offer in return until he hit upon an appropriate solution.[37] Each year from 1947 until the early 1950s, Reggie sent Churchill a present of cognac – which varied from the good to the excellent – purchased during his annual September holiday in south-west France, which Churchill showed every sign of appreciating. In 1949 Reggie sent some speech ideas along with the bottle, and received a reply thanking him warmly for his 'notes and draught'.[38]

As well as liking Maudling personally, and relying on his help with speeches, Churchill sought out his advice on economics, and praised Maudling's gift of making economics comprehensible to him. Tory MP and *Express* journalist Beverley Baxter could say in 1949 that Maudling 'is a real power behind the party scenes. In fact, he is one of only three people to whom Mr Winston Churchill ever listens.'[39] When Churchill received memorandums on economics, or even on general political strategy, he would often pass them to Maudling, asking the younger man what he thought of their ideas.

It would be too much to call Maudling Churchill's Peter Mandelson, but he did undertake the occasional image-making task. J. Arthur Rank suggested to Churchill that television cameras could be used to film and transmit his 1947 conference speech to an overflow audience – the conference hall was not big enough to accommodate all those present – at a nearby theatre. Churchill was worried about the heat from the lights and sent Maudling to find out for him 'if the things are as beastly as they sound'. Maudling made enquiries and came back satisfied that the lights would not bother Churchill, although it might be a wise precaution to type his speech notes on matt paper to avoid glare. The experiment went ahead; it was the first time television had been used in politics for this purpose.[40]

Maudling was also involved in Westminster social life, meeting journalists and planting the occasional story. A particular contact at this stage was Hugh Massingham of the *Observer* (and *Tribune*).[41] Most of his spinning was on behalf of the party, but he gained a little publicity for himself on this occasion with the appearance of a *Sunday Pictorial* article with the slightly provocative headline 'Speech by Churchill: Facts by Maudling'. Churchill's Manchester speech 'like most of his major public speeches in this country, was studded with facts and figures about our economic situation. Who provides him with this material? The answer is: Reginald Maudling, thirty-year-old prospective Tory candidate for Barnet.' Maudling was quoted as assuring the journalist that the generally accepted idea that he also wrote Anthony Eden's weekend speeches was not true; a somewhat artless denial, revealing that Reggie had inspired the piece and causing some amusement in Central Office.[42]

Maudling's main function as economic adviser was to enable Churchill to perform more effectively in big domestic policy debates in the Commons and big set-piece speeches through statistical briefings, checking references and verifying facts. Churchill came to rely heavily on Maudling for support and advice on domestic policy. He bombarded Reggie with comments and enquiries before his keynote speech to a major Conservative rally in Manchester on Saturday 6 December 1947, and kept him at his side on the morning of the speech and for dinner on the train on the way back from Manchester to London.[43] Maudling accompanied Churchill to many of his major domestic speeches.

Maudling's proudest speech-writing achievement for Churchill was over the most notable piece of Tory ideological renewal in the 1940s – the Industrial Charter of 1947. Industrial policy was obviously an area requiring a new Conservative policy, given the nationalisation policy of the Labour government. Butler set up a study group of MPs in 1946 and arranged for it to be given secretarial and research support by David Clarke and Reggie Maudling. The group held meetings with business leaders in various industrial areas, including Birmingham in December 1946 where Maudling took the note of the meeting. He noted that the business leaders believed in works committees, but not workers' control as such, were concerned about the practical aspects of profit sharing and, surprisingly to Maudling, willing to consider profit limitation running alongside a wages policy.[44] Maudling, as one of the researchers-cum-secretaries, was not a particularly influential voice in the writing of the Charter. That was primarily the work of much more senior figures – Butler, Harold Macmillan (whom Butler credited with providing the intellectual background), David Maxwell-Fyfe and Derick Heathcoat-Amory in particular. They knew what they wanted to say, but in Maudling they had a committed assistant and no doubt something of a calming influence on what could have been a difficult committee, but actually turned out to be very comradely. Its right-wing members, Sir Peter Bennett and James Hutchison, contributed to its work and helped persuade their wing of the party that it was acceptable.[45]

The document was published in May 1947, written in rather flat prose (Maudling had warned a Barnet audience to expect something that appeared to be dull, but honest).[46] It aimed to bury the charge that the Conservatives wanted to go back to the miserable inter-war economic conditions or that they stood for a devil-take-the-hindmost individualism. The Industrial Charter endorsed the maintenance of full employment, the government's responsibility for economic management, and the principles of the welfare state. While doing so, it also struck some traditional Tory notes in favour of an orderly end to rationing and controls, restoration of the market system in areas such as food and commodities, and reducing taxation to improve incentives. The most controversial part of it, at least within the Tory party, was the 'Workers' Charter' which, while stopping well short of promising legislation, at least endorsed the principles that Eden and Maudling had been talking about when they mentioned cooperation in industry.

The Charter was generally well received when it was launched, but its authors were concerned as to how it would fare among Conservative activists at the 1947 party conference in Brighton. Maudling's main contribution to the Charter was not so much in his research and drafting before it was published, but through a classic piece of stage management to get it accepted at Brighton. Reggie's first approach was to write and pass round model resolutions backing the Charter to his friends so that they could get them submitted through their local associations. This was not as successful as he had hoped. The eventual wording that went to the conference, and was published in the agenda, had been submitted by his friend Ian Orr-Ewing but somewhere along the line it had been altered to make it a bland resolution on the Charter, 'welcoming it as a basis for discussion'. Reggie was puzzled, telling Butler that 'I know it was not in the original resolution Orr-Ewing submitted because his was one of the ten or twelve that I helped to instigate'.

The feebleness of the resolution was embarrassing to the Tories, who were now exposed to criticism from Labour and the press that the Charter may have been full of good intentions but did not represent the true face of Toryism. As Reggie wrote, 'it seems to me that nothing could be worse than to have this resolution put to the vote at Brighton. Either way the Charter would be killed; openly if the resolution is defeated; quietly laid to sleep if the resolution is passed.' Reggie blamed the old right, represented by Sir Herbert Williams and Sir Waldron Smithers, who hated Butler and his new policies. Maudling moved quickly and submitted an amendment of his own which endorsed the Charter more explicitly 'as a clear restatement of the general principles of Conservative economic policy, [and] recommends that the Committee which prepared it should be kept in being in order to revise it in detail in the light of the discussions at this conference and thereafter to keep it fully up to date'.[47]

Reggie's political cunning, which he had in abundance as a young man, had been brought to bear on the conference stitch-up. It looked like an innocuous procedural motion – the moderate right could persuade themselves that the prospect of further amendment meant that the Charter was not officially part of Tory policy. But the motion had been cleared with Butler and was acceptable to him. When the conference came round Reggie popped up as a delegate from Barnet and spoke in favour of his amendment. He had already fixed things with Orr-Ewing: 'My intention will be to move it in a conciliatory manner as being mainly a drafting amendment designed to make quite clear what the conference is deciding. Orr-Ewing will accept the amendment, although I shall arrange for his acceptance to be disclosed only as the seconder of the amendment finishes speaking.'[48] Maudling moved the amendment, saying that it would make it clear that the Charter was Conservative policy and would be the basis of the policy for the next election.[49] It was one of Maudling's best conference performances. Mark Chapman-Walker, a Conservative official observing the mood of the conference, reported that it was 'a vigorous speech, enthusiastically acclaimed'.[50] It won a favourable notice for its 'gusto' in the Daily Mail.[51] The stage management worked perfectly – the right didn't know what hit them. There were only three dissenting votes and Waldron Smithers was left spluttering impotently in the wilderness, sending long eccentric letters to Butler and Eden about the hijacking of the Conservative Party from its true path.

The crowning moment for Maudling that year at Brighton was a little way into Winston Churchill's speech on Saturday 4 October: 'In our Industrial Charter, which is the official policy of the party, we have shown quite plainly the broad democratic view we take of current affairs and the many forms of social activity which we espouse and encourage in our free, tolerant, and progressive association.'[52] Churchill's words had been scripted by none other than Reginald Maudling, wearing his hat as adviser to the party leader. Maudling told a rather polished version of the story in his *Memoirs*:

> I was working for Winston on his concluding speech to the Conference and we came to the topic of the Industrial Charter. 'Give me five lines, Maudling,' he said, 'explaining what the Industrial Charter says.' This I did. He read it with care, and then said, 'But I do not agree with a word of this.' 'Well, sir,' I said, 'this is what the Conference has adopted.' 'Oh well,' he said, 'leave it in,' and he duly read it out in the course of his speech.[53]

In actual fact, there was little in the Charter that Churchill would have had trouble swallowing. It was more that, through wounded pride and a hardening of the ideological arteries, Churchill was not convinced that the Tories needed much new policy at all, and tended to think that all the Tories needed to do was to sit back and wait for the swing of the pendulum; so much the better if they could return to power with a minimum of specific commitments and a 'doctor's mandate'. If he really was reluctant, Churchill was a good sport about being bounced – he invited Butler to his room for copious champagne on the evening the Charter was adopted,[54] and his fondness for young Maudling if anything increased during 1948 and 1949.

After the conference, Reggie spent a little more time developing his knowledge of industrial questions. He volunteered to conduct a Central Office speaking tour around Lancashire in October while he gained some first-hand experience of the county's industries and familiarised himself with a part of the country he did not know well. Maudling's Lancashire trip was a great success. A Conservative regional official reported back to Central Office that Reggie

> addressed a number of meetings and I have had most appreciative reports from Chairmen and members of the audiences he addressed. Lancashire audiences can be very critical, especially of strangers, but Mr Maudling handled them admirably. Several people have remarked to me that he has the great gift of considerable knowledge and the ability of putting it over to his audience in terms which they can understand and appreciate. We will welcome a return visit at any time.[55]

Maudling could look back on 1947 with considerable satisfaction, personally and politically. He and Beryl had a new baby daughter Caroline, a reasonably high standard of living that allowed a holiday in France in September, and they were settling comfortably into Barnet. Reggie had scored several successes such as the Industrial Charter and the Lancashire speeches, and was pleased to have established the good terms with Winston Churchill that were so clear at the time of the Manchester speech.

The political climate had also changed during the year. In 1946 Tories had to take comfort where they could find it – Reggie himself in a letter to *The Times* in December had resorted to hailing 'the very significant vote at the Scottish Universities' in an obscure by-election.[56] In 1947 there was a lot more to go on. Labour government had suffered through an unusually harsh winter and coal shortages which coincided with the nationalisation of the industry. The coal crisis at least made voters more willing to listen to what the Conservatives had to say about industry and nationalisation, even if they did not agree entirely with the jibe that it took a rare genius to organise simultaneous fuel and fish shortages in a country that was built on coal and surrounded by sea. Labour had hardly recovered from the coal crisis when a premature move to full convertibility of the pound at the rate of £1 to US$4.03 in July led to a massive outflow of foreign exchange, followed by the suspension of convertibility and a series of painfully restrictive economic measures. Among these measures was the introduction of rationing on items which had been freely available even at the lowest point of the war; by December 1947 nearly all foodstuffs were rationed and petrol almost unavailable. Some of the self-confidence and belief of the Labour government had gone and the Conservatives were now taken seriously as an alternative government not just by themselves but by the electorate.

Maudling's work at the Secretariat turned increasingly towards general economic analysis during 1948, although he was of course still working on industrial matters such as gas and electricity in response to government bills. Much of this work is ephemeral and reveals little about its author, but there is the occasional illuminating passage. A long memorandum on the state of play in January 1948, written primarily for Churchill, is the most revealing.[57] In it, Maudling warned the Tories, some of whom had been anticipating another financial crisis and the imminent collapse of the Labour government, that Labour Chancellor Stafford Cripps had the short-term situation sufficiently under control to see Britain safely through to the arrival of Marshall Aid from the United States later on in the year. 'Any political tactics based on the assumption of a financial crash are liable to fail.'[58]

Maudling warned against adopting a gloom-and-doom style of opposition:

Let us not be trapped into carping criticism. The one thing Morrison would like us to do is to get up all the time and say: 'Oh, things are not really doing as well as all that, you know.' What we should say is that things are going better in this country, not because of the Government but despite the Government. It is the magnificent efforts of management and workpeople that are increasing production in this country. What right have the Socialist Government to claim credit for the achievements of private enterprise industries . . .?[59]

Maudling put it more simply to a public meeting: 'You can survive with the Socialists, but with the Conservatives you can survive and prosper.'[60] This was good politics, an elegant escape from one of the most alluring traps of all-out opposition, all the better for being an easily grasped argument with a considerable degree of truth on its side. The Conservatives had been given an open goal in 1947 and they could not rely on this in future. Maudling had been thinking to the next set of problems, and finding solutions.

Another line of attack, which Maudling referred to but did not develop at great length, was on the prevailing ethics of the Labour government. Chancellor Dalton, who had resigned because of a minor indiscretion – an inconsequential premature disclosure of some of his November 1947 Budget – was restored to office in May 1948. In his notes for Churchill's Luton Hoo speech in June 1948 Maudling reminded the leader that 'The Dalton episode is fresh in the public mind and has, I believe, caused deep resentment in the country, particularly among the middle classes. They feel that it is discreditable for a Prime Minister to restore to office at a munificent salary a man who has so discredited himself into a position of trust.'[61] Maudling made another comment in January 1949, that standards of conduct in public life had become 'rather lost and tarnished in Britain'; Conservatives had to carry part of the burden of 'restoring respect for the law and respect for the efficiency and common honesty of public life in the country'.[62] This was a response to the Tribunal of Inquiry into alleged corruption at the Board of Trade, which found no pattern of corruption but did find that a junior minister, John Belcher, had unwisely accepted gifts from shady businessmen. Churchill took rather the opposite view, namely that the Tribunal had found that standards in British government were higher than anyone had expected. Like many young political researchers, Maudling could be bumptious and arrogant, and he must have cringed if he was ever reminded of some of these comments, but in general he kept to economic policy and broad ideas; other than with Dalton he seems to have avoided making personal attacks in private or in public.

Lord Woolton, the Chairman of the Conservative Party since 1946, was an industrialist who became famous as Minister of Food during the war, a difficult and potentially unpopular position with the great responsibility of enforcing rationing and economy in the nation's eating habits. A 'meat pie with no meat in it' became known as a Woolton pie in his honour. His efforts for the Conservative Party were in quite a different direction, as funds started pouring in from companies, rich individuals and a growing army of party members to fund the party's operations. At the October 1947 party conference he challenged the party membership to raise £1 million (a massive project in postwar Britain; the sum's modern value would be approaching £20 million) – and succeeded well within a year. In 1948 the party set up a complex network of front companies to store and channel the money, so great was the inflow of cash.

All this meant that the financial constraints that were so pressing in late 1945 had largely been lifted by the late 1940s. The Research Department resumed activity in summer 1946 and it, the Secretariat and the departments grouped at Central Office all took on staff; in 1950 the Conservative research establishment amounted to fifty people, including twenty-four research officers. By summer 1948 it had become apparent that there was some duplication of functions between different bits of the party's research and information operation, which became increasingly important now that a manifesto had to be written. All the most dynamic members of the Secretariat having been selected as parliamentary candidates, the organisation would not be able to function as it stood during the next general election.[63]

The obvious solution was to merge the departments into a single Conservative Research Department, and this step was proposed in June 1948 and taken in October. Rab Butler, who had previously been involved with Conservative studies on postwar policy, took overall charge. While the new body was called the CRD, the section heads who ran its policy and propaganda functions were drawn largely from the Secretariat, including Maudling, who headed the Economic Section. In retrospect Maudling, Macleod and Powell were sometimes referred to as 'Butler's backroom boys' but in fact most of their time as Conservative researchers had not been spent working directly for Rab. Maudling was the least committed to Butler of the three officers because of his prior links with Churchill and Eden.

The amalgamation meant a significant pay rise for him, because the pay arrangements at the Secretariat had been rather unsettled. The rule had been established in March 1946 that the 'customary maximum for junior staff is £700. But salaries above £800 are personal to the individual.'[64] There had been some feeling among the staff there that they were underpaid, so Reggie was at one stage deputed by Powell and Macleod to argue for a rise with the management. Powell told him that he mustn't sell the two of them out if he was offered a deal that was advantageous to himself; Reggie, looking slightly shocked, said that of course he wouldn't. Powell thought that, even then, he had seen something soft and greedy in Reggie's character.[65] As it happened, the three got their pay rise, although with individual bargaining it was hard to know if it was the same pay rise for all three.

Maudling's salary at the Research Department was not bad – £1,250 (2003 value: around £24,000). This was supposed to include £100 for local travel and entertaining two or fewer people at a time, but longer journeys and larger parties could be claimed for in addition to the salary. David Clarke, who signed off the expenses, wrote that he interpreted the arrangements for travel expenses 'very liberally'.[66] Even leaving aside the ability to claim expenses, Reggie was actually getting more than backbench MPs were paid – their salary had increased after the 1945 election from £600 to £1,000. He was also receiving a £2,000 per year allowance from his father, who had agreed to help Reggie make ends meet in the early years of his political career.[67] He also maintained directorships in the family firms, although he might not have received any money for these in excess of his allowance. Reggie's annual income while at the CRD was certainly comfortable, if not outright affluent. He cultivated the impression of high living and expensive tastes; he had already developed a taste for fine cigars, good brandy and expensive restaurants, and annual foreign holidays in the late 1940s were a luxury few could afford. Life for Reggie was pleasant; he felt he was doing well by doing good.

As head of the Economic Section Maudling acted as a guardian of the Conservatives' commitment expressed in the 1944 White Paper to the 'maintenance of a high and stable level of employment'. He was aligned with Butler and Clarke on this and favoured making the commitment to avoid mass unemployment as explicit as possible on the grounds that they were already committed to it and that 'if mass unemployment returns to this country, the government in power at the time will become so unpopular that the fact that undertakings have previously been given on the subject will be of no significance whatever'.[68] Maudling's argument about the 1944 full employment guarantee was tailored to appeal to Tories hungry for a return to power; its realism hastened its acceptance by reluctant elements within the party. Like Machiavelli, Reggie smuggled wisdom and moderation under a cloak of cynicism.

While many Conservatives did accept the welfare state and a large government role in the economy as a necessary but not desirable aspect of the way things were – like bad weather – and a minority raged against it, Reggie was different. As a Hegelian of his particular stripe, he believed in consensus per se, as a method of transcending the current set of arguments and therefore the engine of historical progress. In the context of the 1940s, he saw the welfare state as the next stage in the grand narrative of history, a synthesis between the thesis of liberty and the antithesis of equality. His approach to political questions derived from his belief in the dialectic: 'In politics it may be called the Middle Way, Butskellism or Consensus. By any name it makes sense to me.'[69] A more explicit commitment to consensus by a senior politician cannot be imagined. Unlike other politicians who held moderate positions, like Macleod and Gaitskell, Maudling did not feel obliged, either from tribal emotion or political calculation, to conceal his moderation when he spoke. Maudling's career is evidence that, at the highest levels, there were Conservatives who did believe, consciously, in consensus politics.

The question as to whether a political 'consensus' existed or not by the end of the 1940s – or indeed at any other time – is a matter that has itself not resulted in a consensus among historians.[70] Did 'Mr Butskell' – the *Economist*'s fusion of Labour Chancellor Hugh Gaitskell (1950–1) and Conservative Chancellor R.A. Butler (1951–5) – really exist? Sceptics about consensus point to the sharp Conservative emphasis in the 1950s on

economic freedom, as against Labour's belief in planning, and controversial
episodes like the early denationalisations under the Churchill government and
the Rent Act of 1957 as indicating that free market Toryism was not in
abeyance in the postwar period. What continuity there was in policy was
more to do with the recognition of the electoral, economic and international
constraints working on British politicians than a voluntarily accepted set of
ideas in common between Labour and Conservative elites. After all, it was
Butler who described politics as 'The Art of the Possible'.

In the 1940s, albeit in a relatively junior role to Butler, Macmillan and
Eden, Maudling steered the party in the direction of accepting much of the
Attlee government's legacy and set the course for the next twenty to thirty
years. The Conservatives were at a historical juncture when they needed the
skills and the consensual views of someone like Maudling in order to adapt to
new circumstances. His career over the next quarter-century is an indication
that consensus politics in economic, colonial, social and, particularly, foreign
policy, did exist to a significant degree; and his political demise in the 1970s
was a signal that the consensus era was coming to an end.

Maudling's first constituency speech made plain his high opinion of Bevin's
foreign policy, and behind the scenes he also rather admired Chancellor
Stafford Cripps, who in 1948 and 1949 was presiding over an austerity policy
intended to rectify Britain's external balance of payments. Maudling
expressed a confidence in Cripps that he lacked in Dalton. In January 1948
he wrote that among the Labour ministers, 'Stafford Cripps, the best of them,
may well think well and accurately, but he cannot think on the grand scale'.
The contrast there was with Churchill, rather than a self-aggrandising claim
for his own superior powers.[71]

Maudling believed, like other Conservatives, in the price mechanism. Food
subsidies were a point of ideological confrontation – to the Tories they were
an undesirable interference in the market which had outlived their rationale,
but the problem was that their abolition would make the poorest worse off
without any means of compensating them, given that working-class people
were below the income tax threshold anyway and paid little purchase tax. It
was a thorny problem – they basically wanted to cut or preferably abolish this
expensive programme, but feared that it would instantly revive their heartless
image from the 1930s. Cripps cut food subsidies in his 1949 Budget, a move
that Maudling welcomed for economic and political reasons. As with Harold
Wilson's 'bonfire of controls', the Labour government was moving away from
central direction and towards some use of the price mechanism – it was not
only the Conservatives who were giving ideological ground. Maudling made a
characteristically ironic observation on the food subsidy cuts, which were
accompanied by a reduction of alcohol duties: 'I must say I never believed
that any politician could increase the price of food in order to decrease the
price of booze and now a teetotal Chancellor has actually done it – and what
a lot of trouble he is getting into as a result.'[72]

To Maudling at the time, the 1949 Cripps Budget, by drawing the limits of taxation and regulation, was 'a turning point in the political history of this country',[73] – perhaps, in retrospect, the birth of consensus. Maudling always rather liked Labour Chancellors, like Cripps, Jenkins and later Healey, who put the brakes on, but his own Chancellorship in the early 1960s was far from austere. The Chancellor who alongside Mr Butskell might have been dubbed Mr Crippling never even had Butskell's virtual existence. Maudling's admiration for Cripps was partly his ability to tell his party hard truths, but partly also an acknowledgement that his puritanical example was not something Reggie himself could emulate. However, Maudling also had a subconscious partisan attitude towards prosperity and austerity. The Conservatives, being the natural party of government, were responsible and capable of controlled economic expansion; under Labour similar policies looked like socialist profligacy. Maudling was not alone in this perspective, then or later. There was also something deep within Reggie's psychology, about his attitudes towards austerity and self-restraint against instant gratification, but these are reflections best left to a later chapter.

The parliamentary year in 1948–9 was dominated by the Labour government's Iron and Steel Bill, which unlike the other nationalisations aroused sustained Conservative opposition both to principle and detail. During the last few months of 1948 Reggie worked prodigiously on briefing papers to analyse the government's bill, and its arguments, and develop counter-arguments for the Conservative front bench. His principal briefing on steel is an impressive accomplishment; a logical exposition which marshals economic statistics, quotations from Hansard and the history of the industry into a well-organised whole.[74] It was all a bit much for Churchill's House of Commons speech – he used little of it – but it did provide the framework of the Conservative case against iron and steel nationalisation. Maudling did not advocate the unrestricted free market, but instead favoured a continuation of government supervision and price control over a privately owned industry. His general attitude was that questions of nationalisation and private enterprise should be dealt with pragmatically, and that there should be no 'tit for tat'.[75] A more elaborated version of his attitude to state industry came in a note to Churchill during the 1950 general election:

We will not de-nationalise for the sake of de-nationalising. Our concern in every case will be the public interest – in other words, the greatest possible efficiency and the best conditions for those employed in the industry. As a general rule, we believe this can best be ensured through enlightened private management, working through a competitive system, but clearly it will not be possible in every case to return to private ownership. Where this can be done, it will be done.

Maudling's agenda for privatisation stopped at road transport and cancelling the nationalisation of iron and steel. For the remaining state industries, interestingly, he insisted that they be reformed to give greater consumer protection and parliamentary accountability, and that 'every nationalised industry will observe the worker's Charter'.[76] Maudling had some common ground with those who criticised the Morrisonian nationalised industries from the left.

Churchill's thoughts in opposition turned more to grand international themes than the details of domestic policy. In his 1947 conference speech and other utterances he proclaimed himself an 'earnest advocate of a United Europe'.[77] Maudling's first known thoughts on the Europe question showed signs of intoxication with Churchill's vision. He wrote in January 1948 of a vision of the future in which the United States and Britain together were leading 'a close and living harmony between a united Empire and a united Europe'. Maudling noted that 'the possibilities of international co-operation in economic matters have hardly yet been realised', and also that 'Britain must take the initiative in these matters and press on all the time with all possible strength. For it is only by this close political and economic harmony of the whole non-Communist world that the fabric of our society and our economy are going to be held together in the years to come.'[78] Maudling seemed a potential recruit for the Euro-federalist wing of the Conservatives, but away from the Churchillian influence Reggie's thinking evolved in its own unique direction. He was always firm in his support for international economic cooperation and trade, but only at the end of his life did he seem interested once again in the European ideal.

The other great issue of postwar politics, the Cold War, was, however, emerging clearly by 1948. Maudling had no doubt that Churchill had been accurate in describing the 'iron curtain' in 1946 and in the late 1940s Maudling was at his most hawkish on Cold War issues. The seemingly limitless threat of Soviet expansion, apparent in industrial disturbances in France and Italy in 1947–8, the Berlin blockade, and the takeover of power in a succession of Eastern and Central European countries caused fear even in Britain. Maudling's own Hegelian attitude had some of the same teleological certainties as the communists. To him, the pattern of communist takeovers – the bullying and absorption of social democratic parties into 'unity' organisations – showed that the future would lie in a great clarification of politics between communist and anti-communist, and social democracy would therefore be torn in two along this fault-line. He wrote scornfully to Churchill in January 1948 that 'Socialism differs from Communism only in degree and technique. Experience all over Europe has shown how Socialist Parties disappear or crumble in the face of the growth of Communism. There is no reason to suppose that Attlee and his party can succeed where all other Mensheviks have failed.'[79] Reggie made overheated speeches along similar lines several times in Barnet in 1948 and 1949,[80] but it was a line that he abandoned when it was falsified by the course of history. It was a rare excursion into this sort of strident partisanship. On foreign policy at least, the young Maudling did not yet know quite what he thought and was rather buffeted by Churchill's enthusiasms.

Maudling was, even in the late 1940s, well connected in the City – partly through his family connections, and partly because he was a useful man to know given his party responsibilities for economic policy and industry. Reggie was involved in organising an informal dining circle through which leading industrialists and City people could meet senior Conservatives; as he put it to Churchill in May 1949, 'one of the main purposes of these meetings is to strengthen the existing contacts between the City of London and the Conservative Party'. Eden and Woolton were among the guests, but Churchill declined rather formally when he was asked.[81] Maudling's contacts, and his knowledge of international economics, proved useful in September 1949. Cripps had gone to the IMF discussions in Washington and, given the continued strain on gold and dollar reserves, Maudling was surprised that the talks were reportedly so cordial and Cripps was so optimistic at their conclusion; he could not see how this could be justified and signalled to Churchill that something strange was going on.[82] A few days later the government announced that the pound would be devalued from $4.03 to $2.80. Fixed exchange rates, as a civil servant observed after 'Black Wednesday' in 1992, make liars or fools out of politicians. They need to deny any intention to devalue until after it happens, because the markets would collapse at any sign of weakness; they are obliged, like Catholic priests when a doctrinal statement is issued, to move directly from one state of certainty to another. Even someone of the integrity of Stafford Cripps saw his reputation unravel as his statements to the House of Commons denying any intention to devalue, even as late as July 1949, became indefensible. Churchill, when Cripps advised him privately, congratulated him but in his Commons speech attacked him for lying to the public.[83] At the time, Maudling thought devaluation would not do much good, and was surprised that Cripps had gone for it. Maudling, although a 'soft money' man, never thought much of devaluation as such as a policy option. Immediately after the crisis, Maudling felt that it was so disastrous that the Tories should promise, and the country would be ready for, a more radical programme of cuts in health and social services and harder work all round for no extra reward.[84] Maudling was caught between two competing instincts of the progressive Tory of the times – the desire to find something, anything, to do that would stop Britain running into perpetual economic crises on the model of 1947 or 1949, and the desire also to maintain a decent welfare state. In the backwash of devaluation, the first instinct took over; as time went on, he softened his hawkish attitude and even by the end of October 1949 he was talking more in terms of a rationalisation of housing subsidies than a radical series of cuts.[85] As Chancellor, Maudling faced many of the same problems as those which had vexed Cripps; but Maudling thought he had found a synthesis of economic progress and social compassion that would enable him to escape.

When Parliament broke up for the Christmas recess in 1949, there was no expectation that it would resume before a general election. Both parties were in good fighting spirit and looked forward to the campaign. Attlee saw no reason to delay because the government had completed its legislative programme and he was advised that Labour would win whenever the election came.[86] Labour's support was solid among working-class voters, who were proud of the government's achievements and who had benefited from its social policies and full employment. The Tories were also confident of victory. They knew that Labour had a problem with middle-class voters, who were chafing under the pressure of austerity and rationing to which, as 1950 began, there seemed no end in sight. Reggie had presciently observed this trend as early as December 1946 from a study of by-elections and local elections. He wrote then that 'in the traditional Socialist strongholds, such as Rotherhithe and Aberdare, the Government's position is as strong as ever. In the residential and middle class areas, which formerly would have been expected to vote Conservative and whose capture by the Socialists in 1945 came as a surprise even to them, the Conservative position has greatly improved and the Government has lost a great deal of ground.'[87]

On 10 January 1950 Attlee announced that the election would take place on 23 February. The Conservative Research Department team of Hopkinson, Powell, Macleod and Maudling dispersed to Taunton, Wolverhampton, Enfield and Barnet. The calling of the election marked an end to Reggie's idyllic Research Department years and his duties at the feet of Winston Churchill, but he left confident of winning Barnet and of even better times to come.

Chapter 5

A BRIEF STAY ON THE BACKBENCHES, 1950–1952

Reginald Maudling, having done his bit for the renewal of the Conservative Party at headquarters, now found a powerful Conservative machine at his disposal in Barnet. The Conservative campaign in the suburbs in 1950 probably marked an all-time peak of mass political organisation in Britain, with literally thousands of Tory activists turning out to give support to their candidates. Even in this context the Barnet Conservatives were conspicuously well organised. Arthur Fawcett, an experienced and highly professional agent who had previously worked with Churchill in Epping, arrived in the constituency at the beginning of 1949. The Barnet Conservative organisation built up to a formidable level during the late 1940s. To take a small example, the Well House ward was organised as a branch from November 1948, with eighty members; within a little over two months membership had risen to 147. The territory was so good that Maudling and other members would canvass door-to-door asking people to join the party.[1] In the constituency as a whole membership stood at around 12,000 by 1950. Across the country the Tories were attracting floods of new members, but Barnet's achievement was exceptional and its membership figures were among the highest in the country. Something like one elector in five in Barnet was a Conservative Party member.

Reggie played his part in the Conservative revival in Barnet. He was a particularly dedicated, diligent candidate. Hardly a week went by without one or more speaking engagements and the pages of the *Barnet Press* in 1946–50 are testament to Reggie's hyperactive attention to the constituency. As well as formal speeches and ward dinners, he would work his way slowly through the constituency, street by street, knocking on doors and talking to residents.[2] Another striking feature of Maudling's long campaign in Barnet was the frequency of top-name visitors who could be persuaded by the eager young researcher to travel out to the suburbs or stop off on a Friday evening on the way north. Harold Macmillan, Henry Willink, Peter Thorneycroft and Beverley Baxter all came and spoke, and in June 1948 Reggie, via the good offices of Clementine Churchill, prevailed upon Winston to stop for tea and a photo-opportunity at the Maudlings'

Totteridge home.[3] Beryl loved playing hostess to the Churchills; she beamed as the great man appeared on their suburban doorstep. It was quite a coup, and encouraged the Barnet Tories in their view that their candidate was someone who was going to the very top.[4]

Beryl was taking a close interest in politics in the late 1940s. She was adopted as the Conservative candidate for the East Barnet ward of Hertfordshire county council, which had returned a substantial Labour majority in the previous elections in 1946. The Conservatives did well in the spring 1949 local elections, aided by Cripps's harsh Budget, and recorded their best ever results in several wards for the Hertfordshire county council and the smaller local authorities. One particular high point was Beryl's gain in East Barnet, on a high swing, with a record majority of over 1,000.

As the first elected Maudling, Beryl helped the Conservative cause in East Barnet in particular. She was assigned to two county council committees, the Care of Children committee and the Welfare committee, both of them regarded as suitable for women – indeed, in 1951 the Children committee had a female majority of eleven to five which was extraordinary for the time. Beryl was happy enough with the traditional female role in this as in other aspects of her life. The most prominent stand she took was in December 1949 over the provision of play centres. These were a wartime service to help working women with childcare, and Hertfordshire county council now proposed to scrap them with only a month's notice. Beryl spoke up strongly against the plan, pointing out that the play centres were helping Britain's effort to increase industrial production and that they were a valuable social service for working parents. She warned her colleagues: 'If we close these centres some mothers will give up their jobs rather than risk their children's health and safety, and those mothers who simply cannot afford to cease work will be forced to let them roam the streets with a consequent increase in accidents, illness and juvenile delinquency.'[5] Her objections were voted down, with one male councillor saying dismissively that 'these married ladies' place is in the home and not in the factory'. Three letters from women in support of Beryl were published in the next week's *Barnet Press*. Although Beryl's own home life was very conventional, to speak out in 1949 in favour of childcare provision for working women put her considerably ahead of her time.

In general, Beryl was not one of the most active councillors, attending about half her assigned meetings. She was less inclined to go to Welfare, which dealt with old people's homes and housing for evicted families, than Children which dealt with increasing provision of children's homes and some difficult individual cases of whether to take children into care.[6] When she did attend she spoke up in county council debates about several issues and was praised by the local paper as showing 'considerable knowledge and balanced judgement'. When the next elections came round in spring 1952, she gave up her seat, commenting that 'I feel – much as I would like to carry on – that it is increasingly difficult to give the time I think should be devoted to the important duties of a county councillor. The work is important and I should hate to feel I was neglecting it.'[7] Her decision spared her an electoral defeat, for Labour did well in the 1952 elections and Ron Ledger (later elected MP for Romford) regained East Barnet for the party.

The county council elections were a prelude to the main event – the general election of February 1950. Elections were fought differently then, with less of a central strategic plan of campaign. The main party speakers would tour the country, making speeches on the issues as they saw them, Attlee famously driven in erratic fashion from place to place by his wife Vi. The evening speeches, as reported on the radio and the next day's press, were the focal point of the campaign. There was little central strategy, and little sense of the ebb and flow of a campaign, in contrast to the elections dominated by the mass media since 1959 and even more since 1974. Constituency campaigning was different as well. Candidates spoke to their electorates at public meetings, sometimes at several in the same evening, and people actually came. The local paper, in Barnet at any rate where the *Barnet Press* was a substantial and politically neutral read, would give detailed coverage of the points made by each speaker. Party activists would canvass from door to door. Barnet in 1950 was a textbook example of a well-run traditional election campaign.

Reggie spoke at a succession of public meetings, often with the assistance of a leading Barnet Young Conservative, a fluent and engaging young man called Michael Rice, whose path would keep crossing Reggie's in future years. Those, including Rice, who were present in 1950, recall a tremendous feeling of enthusiasm and hard work about the Tory effort.[8] A local newspaper noted one of the surprises of the campaign in Hertfordshire and north Middlesex as being 'the rapid growth in support for Barnet Conservative Mr Reginald Maudling. He expected much – but not an Army.'[9]

The Barnet campaign was hard fought but took place in a positive atmosphere and without rancour. Maudling, Taylor and the Liberal candidate, W.H. Jones, all got on well personally, and the campaign started warmly with a joint meeting on 30 January at which Maudling and Jones congratulated Taylor on the birth of his third child, Reggie joking that 'a man who has a family of three should spend as much time as possible at home'.[10]

The slogan Reggie adopted for the campaign, which he used in speeches and as the main point of his election address, was 'It's the future that matters'. While utterly banal on one level, it did signify Maudling's determination not to get bogged down in arguments about the past. The future Maudling offered was based on the agenda set by his favourite Labour politician, Stafford Cripps, whom he quoted in his election address: 'unless we can all quickly produce more and get our costs down, we shall suffer a tragic fall in our standard of living, accompanied by all the demoralising insecurity of widespread unemployment.' Maudling's thinking in 1949–51 was based around this overwhelming need to increase production, and the solutions he offered were mostly orthodox Conservative ones: lower taxation, an end to the wage and profits freeze to give incentives ('This is the only really effective way of encouraging output and efficiency'), more competition and a halt to nationalisation. The address was short on specifics, although it did have a consistent attitude of favouring a regulated market system (in housing and industry, for instance) rather than direct controls or a free-for-all. He disclaimed any intention of slashing the social services, although there was an obvious problem in reconciling this with the desire to cut spending and taxes; as always when people argue along these lines, vague 'efficiency' savings were called into aid.[11] Reggie spent a lot of the campaign defending the Conservatives against allegations that they would create mass unemployment and abolish food subsidies.

Reggie worked extremely hard during the campaign, as he had for four years. He also made the maximum donation allowed under the party rules, namely £85 in cash and £15 in kind through the services of his secretary.[12] He was helped by Beryl, who was constantly at his side. She drove herself so hard that she had some sort of breakdown when it was all over, and on medical advice had to take two months away from any official or social duties. In future she decided not to take such a public part in campaigning, although she contributed a slightly embarrassing but, in those days, expected 'Message from Mrs Maudling' with family photo on the election address, aimed at the women of Barnet.[13]

As a crucial marginal, Barnet received visits from two leading figures. Anthony Eden came by to give Reggie support, adding a splash of aristocratic glamour to a Tory committee room full of envelopes and cardboard boxes as he passed through. Late in the campaign, possibly at a rare nervous moment, Reggie attempted to persuade Churchill to visit Barnet but the leader did not oblige.[14] Stephen Taylor was Herbert Morrison's Parliamentary Private Secretary and he had more luck in persuading his boss to come and help. Morrison spoke at an election meeting on 20 February, at which he tried to appeal to the middle-class vote and stressed the tax-cutting of the Labour government in reducing the standard rate in 1945, and increasing allowances since so that 3 million people were taken out of tax.[15] Yet it was to no avail. Maudling's campaign fell on fertile ground in the villages and suburbs of Barnet and on polling day floods of Conservative voters poured into the polling stations. It was clear by the evening that there had been an exceptionally heavy poll, in Barnet and nationwide.

While most constituencies now declare overnight, in 1950 most counting took place during the day on Friday. The overnight results suggested that Labour had won comfortably, but they were misleading because most of those constituencies were urban, and as declarations streamed out from lunchtime onwards it was clear that the Conservatives were doing a lot better in rural and suburban areas. People followed the 'battle of the gap' on the radio as the

Labour lead slipped throughout the day.[16] The result in Barnet came in the early afternoon and contributed to the sense of Tory momentum. The Conservative gain in Barnet came as no surprise, although Maudling's majority of 10,534 was much larger than expected. Maudling spoke briefly and conventionally after the result, thanking the returning officer and his opponents for the clean nature of the contest. Taylor and Jones also paid tribute to the good nature of the election and wished Maudling well. Taylor commented admiringly that in Barnet 'The Conservative Party has done an amazing organising job in the last four years', and added that, although he was sorry that the voters' decision had gone the way it did,

I am glad that my Conservative opponent should have been Mr. Reginald Maudling. My only criticism of him is that he is not a Socialist. I am sure that as Member of Parliament he will serve you faithfully and well without regard for party opinions. Take your problems and difficulties to him; I know he will do all he can to help.[17]

Electorate		70,687	
Turnout			87.4
Reginald Maudling	Conservative	32,953	53.3
Stephen Taylor	Labour	22,419	36.3
W.H. Jones	Liberal	6,441	10.4
Conservative majority		10,534	17.0

Shortly before his thirty-third birthday, Reggie could at last add 'MP' to his name. He had won an overwhelming victory against a strong candidate, by methods that did him credit. He had personally taken trouble to talk to, and just as important to listen to, as many electors as possible, although he was duly modest about it, telling a branch meeting 'I do not think the candidate makes much difference. He can make a mess of it if he tries really hard, but the result is determined by the party's work in the years before the campaign.'[18] He was a respected young figure in the Conservative ranks, and had the Tories done as well nationally as he had in Barnet he might well have been appointed immediately to a junior ministerial office.[19] However, nationally Labour had won a second term with a precarious majority of six. Maudling's victory came alongside his Parliamentary Secretariat colleagues Iain Macleod in neighbouring Enfield West and Enoch Powell at Wolverhampton South West. The other two Barnet finalists from February 1946 had also been elected: Ian Orr-Ewing became a constituency neighbour by winning Hendon North and Robert Carr won Mitcham. Reggie took his oath on 2 March, between two adventurous MPs – Tory soldier and explorer Fitzroy Maclean, and Labour journalist Phillips Price.

Reggie, although he was familiar enough with Westminster, was a little overawed by joining the House of Commons as a member. Conscious of his junior status, he went into the Smoking Room, the bastion of old-fashioned Conservatism, and found it full of senior MPs taking coffee. 'I was so impressed that I hid behind the *Daily Mail* until somebody ordered a drink,' he told a Barnet meeting. Maudling's anxiety about fitting in socially at the top tables of Conservatism never quite disappeared. The 1950 election was a moment of transition for the Conservatives, sociologically as well as politically, as the first clutch of professional politicians entered the House but still found it operating according to the complacent assumptions of school tie and old money. Although Reggie was distinctly upper middle class, well-off, and went to a good school, he was still not quite top drawer as far as the Tories were concerned. Maudling's very intelligence and professionalism were reasons for him to be below the salt; 'how awfully *clever* of you' is, in an aristocratic drawl, an insult rather than a compliment. Maudling was a player rather than a gentleman.

Despite his sociable, easygoing exterior, Reggie had a serious view about why he was in politics. He had many of the qualities of a natural mandarin: intelligence, adaptability, calmness, and the ability to master a subject quickly from a cold start. What made him a politician was the desire to steer the ship, to make the choices rather than advise or second-guess them from the sidelines. The slight whiff of contempt that went with the old school's regard for Maudling was reciprocated. He liked clubs and clubmen, and enjoyed that aspect of the Commons, but he did not fall abjectly into regarding that as the most important thing in political life. 'He tended to find his colleagues in the House really rather trivial – although he was never discourteous to them, he never felt he had much in common with them either.'[20] He wanted to achieve things, not sit around scoring debating points and drinking in the Commons bars, and it broke his heart when he was reduced to doing just that.

Reggie decided to get his maiden speech over quickly, rushing to speak on 10 March in the debate on the Labour government's 1950 King's Speech. This was only the fifth speaking day of the new Parliament. While a scintillating maiden speech can make a reputation, as it did most famously for F.E. Smith, and a disastrous one carried off with defiance can be burnished into a fine anecdote as Disraeli did of his, a moderately good maiden speech brings with it no particular benefits. Reggie neglected to deliver the usual pro forma tributes to his predecessor and the natural and social wonders of his constituency, although that was less of a fixed tradition then than it is now. Neither was his maiden completely uncontroversial, although it was hardly partisan or provocative. Reggie simply started as he meant to go on. It was a calm speech expressing his point of view and offering a couple of suggestions which he hoped could win acceptance on either side of the House.

Maudling's principal subject was inflation, which the Labour government had been suppressing by wage and price controls and in Keynesian fashion by running a budget surplus to take demand out of the economy. His main argument was that 'a Budget surplus is not necessarily the best way, in every case, to counter the danger of inflation'. He was not challenging the emerging acceptance of Keynesian ideas, but was against the 'one club golfer' view of economic policy, whether it be exclusive reliance on fiscal policy in 1950 or the fashion for monetarism in the late 1970s. The maiden speech suggested a couple of alternatives to a budget surplus to damp down inflation. One was improving the interest rates payable on National Savings, to encourage people to save rather than spend, and the other was to reduce the burden of taxation on people on moderate incomes, so that they would have incentives to increase production. He picked up on this latter point when he had the power to do so as Chancellor; he was consistent in believing that direct taxation on middle-income households was a disincentive to enterprise and production. He concluded the speech:

> The main point I wish to make is that a Budget surplus is, in many cases, a good way of tackling the problem of inflation, but not always, and not irrespective of the means by which it is achieved. The method of applying leeches, when first used by the medical profession was a great advance, but it became customary to apply leeches whatever the patient or the complaint. I think there is some analogy here. If financial leeches, if I may use such an expression to describe tax gatherers, are applied they may be very useful indeed with a patient suffering from galloping inflation, but if applied too long and too assiduously the effect may not be to increase production or reduce inflationary pressure, but to drain strength from the patient and make ultimate recovery more painful and more prolonged. We cannot, in this country, tax ourselves into prosperity.[21]

Reggie said that he found making the speech 'easy'. He conquered his nerves during the speech by adopting the mannerism of taking off his spectacles, a technique he used frequently, particularly at events he disliked, such as party conferences. He found that if he could see clearly, he would tend to establish eye contact with a member of the audience and address the speech to that person; for his maiden speech he was thankful that he could not see Sir Hartley Shawcross, the imposing Labour Attorney General who was winding up the debate, across the floor of the House.[22]

Reggie quickly became a good performer in the House. The Commons chamber is a surprisingly small room, very different in atmosphere from a public meeting, and his agreeable, calm and authoritative manner stood him in good stead in a place that was 'chaps talking to other chaps'.[23] It was another institution with its own rules and codes, rather like an oversized Oxford college, and Reggie felt at home there without becoming an abject slave to its traditions. He talked rapidly but clearly, with an agreeable manner. His voice then was rather clipped, almost BBC English, but it mellowed over time under the influence of whisky and cigars and developed a deep, languid, almost sensual quality that promised friendliness, warmth and good humour.

Reggie was also quick-witted enough throughout his time in Parliament not to rely on notes, and so short-sighted that he had a strong incentive to develop the ability to think on his feet. Maudling could often give a perfectly formed, witty, reasonable speech, accurate in detail, with only a few words scribbled on the back of an envelope.

During the 1950 Parliament the frustrated Conservatives used rough parliamentary tactics which they called 'harrying', with the aim of making life impossible for the government. Divisions would be called at short notice, and ambushes sprung by Tory MPs who had pretended to go home but in fact gathered in the Westminster house of a colleague. The Tory whips would even take advantage when ministers were out of the country on national business, forcing them either to return home or concede the vote. Maudling, and another new boy of 1950, Robert Carr, disliked these tactics enough to complain to the Chief Whip, Patrick Buchan-Hepburn, that they were not prepared to exploit such absences but were given a telling-off by Buchan-Hepburn and 'given fairly clearly to understand that ours was not to reason why'.[24] Given that one whip was the infamous Sir Walter Bromley-Davenport, a former army boxing champion who was known to use his pugilistic skills while enforcing party discipline, this took some courage on Maudling and Carr's part.[25]

Maudling's bipartisan and gentlemanly attitude to the absence of Labour ministers abroad in 1950–1 was of a piece with his later career. Even in 1976, shortly before his sacking by Margaret Thatcher as Shadow Foreign Secretary, he was roused to incandescent rage when she summoned him back from what he thought were promising talks about Rhodesia to take part in a futile vote of censure. Maudling always believed that foreign policy was not a suitable subject for party combat, and when travelling abroad as a shadow spokesman was scrupulous about reporting useful information back to the Foreign Office and not undermining the government.

Maudling's expertise in economics was acknowledged by his being given a prominent role in the Conservative parliamentary response to the 1950 Budget; he spoke repeatedly in the Finance Bill debates that followed from May to July, on many issues of detail such as taxation of commercial vehicles and transfers under the European Payments Union. One of the issues of debate during the Finance Bill arose from a tax avoidance scheme that had come to light at the very end of 1949 involving Messrs Lord and Black, directors of the Austin Motor Company. They had received payments that purported to be covenanted capital transfers but were actually disguised income, and the government proposed retrospective legislation to make the payments taxable. In January 1950 Reggie had written to Eden that 'these payments are difficult to defend in any circumstances and at the present time quite outrageous. I have made fairly widespread enquiries in the City and in industry and I have encountered unanimous condemnation, at any rate of the timing of these payments.' Reggie warned Eden that the Tories needed to dissociate themselves from this sort of behaviour,[26] but in the debates some Tories defended Lord and Black. Reggie was not among them, but he made an interesting point that while he would support retrospective legislation to recover the lost tax, he did not feel it was right to exact an additional penalty. He illustrated his point with a rather personal parallel:

> Suppose someone was trying to pass a bottle of brandy through the Customs when on the way back from a holiday, and he was detected by an officer. The person carrying the brandy might be compelled to pay the full rate of duty. That is not a penalty, but if subsequently he is fined for bringing in the brandy, then he has been punished for what he has done.[27]

Given Reggie did in fact bring brandy back from France every year, this was an intriguing comment to make. In Maudling's thoughts on the Austin Motors case, political expediency, principle, rule-bending and honesty, all seem to be apparent.

On arrival in Parliament Maudling made a useful ally, a man of well-documented and grotesque faults[28] but sentimentally loyal to Reggie in good times and bad: John Junor. In 1950 Junor was writing the Cross-bencher column in the *Sunday Express*, which was then a dominant mass-market newspaper, and Cross-bencher carried considerable weight in Conservative circles. One of the first columns to be obviously inspired by Reggie was on 13 August 1950, in which is described an 'Eden Orchestra' of four MPs, including Maudling, promoting Eden's claims. The column notes that the five MPs closely associated with Rab Butler and the Charters 'Do not root for "Rab". They warm to his policies but not to his personality. For Mr Butler, with his timid smile, is an aloof man who does not easily inspire friendship or loyalty.'[29] This was true for Reggie, but not for an incandescent Iain Macleod who telephoned Butler with news of Reggie's apostasy and later wrote angrily that 'I'm sure in any case I needn't bother to tell you that my loyalties are not so volatile'. Butler was a bit calmer, advising Macleod not to take precipitate action but warning him that 'there are always jackals in politics as there are in the jungle'.[30] Reggie had the advantage over Macleod and Powell of the Eden and Churchill cards up his sleeve, but in inspiring the Junor pieces he had played them much too crudely. Perhaps Macleod gave Reggie a tongue-lashing – an impassioned, abusive Macleod was a formidable spectacle – but this incident was soon smoothed over and seems to have done no permanent damage to Reggie's career. He remained on close terms with Junor and frequently gave him stories, but he managed in future not to leave his fingerprints quite so obviously on them, particularly if they reflected at all on rivalries within the Tory leadership. One of the election analyst David Butler's early memories of Westminster life was seeing Maudling talking to the *Observer*'s Hugh Massingham in the early 1950s, and then next Sunday reading a piece that, while perfectly loyal to the government, subtly promoted

Reggie. It was an education in how things were done.[31] Reggie also managed to mend relations quickly with Macleod (their friendship continued to be close in the 1950s and Macleod was godfather to Reggie's son Edward who was born in 1954) and Butler. It was difficult to stay angry with Reggie for very long.

In his first few years as MP for Barnet Reggie Maudling was an adequate, or even pretty good, constituency member. During 1950 he attended as many constituency events as the whips would allow, and set aside every other Friday evening to meet constituents and sort out their grievances.[32] Soon after he was elected he started holding surgeries on this basis, on a rotation system in the four local government areas within the seat – Barnet, East Barnet, Borehamwood and Hatfield.[33] Constituency service on this scale would now be regarded as a little lackadaisical, but it made Maudling more energetic than average for 1950. Iain Macleod, for instance, never bothered with surgeries.[34] The Tories and the people of Barnet seemed appreciative. A May 1951 Central Office routine report found that, 'Mr Maudling has improved his position very considerably in this Constituency. Is generally very popular and attentive to Constituency matters.'[35]

Maudling involved himself in local issues such as traffic on the Barnet bypass, the problems faced by local doctors and – jointly with Iain Macleod – lobbied the Transport ministry about the inadequacies of suburban train services to New Barnet and Potters Bar. In May 1951 he asked the minister if he was aware of the problem of sheep worrying in Hertfordshire, to which the answer, politely given, was not really. Reggie quickly developed an interest in the British film industry because the largest concentration of studios and production facilities in the country was at Elstree and Borehamwood in the constituency, and in 1950 the industry was at a low ebb, with most of the studio space there vacant and many skilled workers without employment. His second Commons speech was in a debate on quotas for British films, which had been a vexed issue for Harold Wilson at the Board of Trade since 1948;[36] and he also welcomed the support that the new National Film Finance Corporation was giving to the industry.

Reggie's only speech in his first term as an MP that did not concern either economics or the film industry was on 9 March 1951, on the subject of divorce.[37] The law as it stood was extremely restrictive and required long terms of separation and proof of fault, and in 1951 Labour MP Eirene White sponsored a Bill to effect a mild liberalisation of divorce. It would mean that one party to the marriage could obtain a divorce, unilaterally, after seven years' separation with no prospect of reconciliation. On private members' bills like this, particularly when a divisive 'moral' issue is involved, there is a free vote and a premium on gaining cross-party support. Reggie was White's principal Tory supporter – indeed, he wound up the debate for the reformers. By the time Maudling spoke, the government had already conceded that they would set up a Royal Commission on marriage and divorce, and the White Bill was shelved – but he still delivered a brilliant exposition of a secular, liberal argument that was a brave statement for a Tory MP to make in the early 1950s: 'It is not divorce that is the tragedy, but broken homes. It is the rupture of this union between man and wife and not the legal position which creates the tragedy in this country. Every broken marriage is tragic, because either a great happiness has been destroyed or it has never been created.' Maudling even said that it was not necessarily a bad thing that there should be more divorces. He made a forthright statement of the role he saw for the Church: 'surely it is for the Church to maintain among the members of the Church her own view on the sanctity of marriage and not to try to impose it on other members of the community.' He also expressed a humane attitude to the complexities of life, in contrast to the moral certainties of the traditionalists: 'It is unwise in these circumstances in discussing these matters to think in terms of innocence and guilt in every instance. Broadly speaking, we are dealing not with the misdeeds of men and women but their follies and misfortunes, which are much harder to deal with.'

He also expressed the view that the House should always recognise the rights of the individual in discussing these matters. The March 1951 speech was an early and unusually public expression of Maudling's social liberalism. A year later he was in government and no longer able to range freely across whatever policy issue took his interest, but his libertarian instincts foreshadowed his response to the reforming legislation of the 1960s and his own term as Home Secretary. The early public role Maudling took on divorce may have owed something to his parents' circumstances, but it was a fair reflection of his approach to the range of moral and personal issues. However, the debate did not lead to divorce reform. The 1951 Royal Commission was a classic of its 'takes minutes, wastes years' kind – it reported in December 1955 to no effect, after the brief glimmer of liberal reform had been submerged by a tide of New Elizabethan traditionalism. By then, there had been two elections and politics was very different.

Speculation about an election had ebbed and flowed during 1950 and 1951 with the fortunes of the government and the parliamentary position. The government's victories in the votes on the 1950 King's Speech reduced the probability of another immediate election; after the result it had been widely believed that it would be impossible to run a government with such a small majority, but the Labour whips were able to manage. After the economic troubles that followed the outbreak of the Korean War in June 1950, and the political turbulence accompanying the resignation of Nye Bevan, John Freeman and Harold Wilson in April 1951, an election seemed more distant than ever. In summer 1951 the betting was still on there not being an election until 1952 or 1953. In the middle of September, *The Times* reported that 'there is a growing feeling that the odds are lengthening against an election this year'.[38] Behind the scenes, however, Attlee had already decided that he would dissolve Parliament, largely as a courtesy to the King who was due to go on a long tour of the Commonwealth in early 1952 and feared being recalled in the event of a government collapse.[39] Attlee's timing had once again been unlucky. Within weeks the King's illness had led to the cancellation of the tour, and the King died in February 1952. Labour would have done much better to hang on through the economic storms of 1951 and have an election in calmer, prosperous times.

The election was a surprise to Maudling, who never had much of a knack for prediction of this sort. He had confidently and repeatedly stated that there would be a second election in 1950, and then said that there would be no election in 1951. In September 1951 he went on his now traditional two-week holiday in France and Spain, clocking up, he reckoned, 2,800 miles. He wrote to Churchill:

I heard the news of the Election in Cognac, in the office of Jacques Delamain, the doyen of the brandy trade. He gave me this bottle of his 1906 and I said I would convey it to you in the hope that it may help to sustain you during the campaign. Although it is a Petite Champagne it is, I think, quite exceptional and equal to any of the Grandes which I sampled in Delamain's cellars.[40]

Relaxed and refreshed, Maudling returned to Barnet for his first fight as an incumbent, only to find that burglars had struck at the family house and stolen clothes, linen and the contents of the children's money boxes.[41] For the Maudlings, this literally added insult to injury, as summer 1951 had started badly when Beryl broke her shoulder blade in an accident on the Barnet bypass in May.[42] Once they had cleared up after the burglary, Reggie's general election campaign went smoothly.

The 1951 election in Barnet was, as in 1950, a matter for the three main parties only. Maudling and the Liberal W.H. Jones had fought the seat before but there was a change in Labour candidate. Stephen Taylor had not been particularly enthralled by the House of Commons and decided not to attempt to regain his seat from Maudling. Cyril Fenton, who had fought Banbury in 1950, carried the Labour banner in Barnet in 1951. While Taylor was an orthodox supporter of the government, Fenton was a pacifist who promised to resign his seat rather than ever vote for war.

For Reggie it was another hectic campaign, with twenty-seven meetings in Barnet and three engagements in other constituencies. The 1951 election was to some extent a continuation of the 1950 campaign, with the same arguments about the record of the Labour government, the state of the economy, the social services and nationalisation. However, there was an unusual focus on foreign affairs in 1951. Bevin had resigned because of ill health and his successor Herbert Morrison was not performing well in the Foreign Office; there was also a succession of crises – the nationalisation of the Abadan refinery in Iran and a developing argument with Egypt over the status of the Sudan. Conservative criticism over foreign policy was answered with a sharp Labour counter-attack, alleging that Tory belligerence could lead to war. Although the 'warmonger' charge was not made as such by the party leadership, it became an increasingly prominent election argument, culminating in the *Daily Mirror* headline 'Whose Finger on the Trigger?' Fenton, in Barnet, had raised the question of where we would be if Churchill had been Prime Minister during these crises.[43] Reggie called the warmonger allegation 'a pretty dirty business', arguing that the best way to prevent war was to be strong and deter aggressors. That said, Reggie – like many Tories – tried to have it both ways by denouncing Labour's 'bungling' of Abadan: 'It is difficult to speak of what has been going on in Persia without feeling very angry. Seldom has this country been so humiliated.'[44] It was feelings such as these, in the breast even of so calm a Tory as Maudling, which led within five years to the even greater humiliation of Suez.

Reggie had changed his tune a little on unemployment. In 1949 and 1950 he had not been entirely convinced that full employment was here to stay, but in 1951 he expressed complete confidence that advancing economic knowledge meant that unemployment caused by deficient demand was a thing of the past. 'I do not think we shall have any serious argument with our opponents over the question of employment. The difficulty today is not to find jobs for people, but people for jobs.'[45] These remarks show that Reggie was now a card-carrying Keynesian who believed in consensus on how to steer the economy; it is a more orthodox statement of Keynesian ideas than appears in his Research Department output.

The 1951 election campaign was a strange one. Attlee had called it despite Labour being twelve points behind in the polls, but Labour gained steadily as it went on; the core Labour vote rallied round and by the end it was becoming a second extremely close election. Even so, Maudling's hold on Barnet never looked in the slightest danger. Polling day in Barnet was warm and sunny and people poured out to the polls in droves. When the overnight seats were declared, in many places both the Labour and Conservative numbers were even higher than they had been in 1950, and while the Tories were gaining it was not clear until quite late that they – or indeed anyone – would be able to form a majority government. As in 1950, the Barnet result came in the early afternoon on Friday. It was no surprise that Maudling had held the seat, on another extremely high turnout.

Electorate		72,408		
Turnout			86.1	
Reginald Maudling	Conservative	35,327	57.0	+3.7
Cyril Fenton	Labour	22,375	35.9	−0.4
W.H. Jones	Liberal	4,463	7.2	−3.2
Conservative majority		13,152	21.2	+4.2

The Labour vote had been surprisingly resilient and the Conservatives had gained a bit from the slippage of the Liberal vote. This was pretty symptomatic of the national picture – a very similar result to 1950 but this time with the Conservatives making just enough headway for a thin overall majority of seventeen seats despite Labour actually having polled more votes. Maudling had done substantially better than the national average, with a swing of 2.1 per cent compared to only 0.9 per cent nationally, a reward for his work as a new MP and the strength of the Barnet Conservative organisation.

Contrary to some expectations, Maudling was not given a place in the Churchill government when it was formed, but he was obviously not destined to stay on the backbenches for very long, and his ambitions had outgrown Barnet. Even as early as 1951, his devotion to constituency matters was waning. Maudling did have a tendency to work hard and make his mark at something, but then slacken off once it had become a bore. Reggie and Beryl bridled at being expected to do the rounds of Tory cheese and wine parties and dinners, their duty to trot around like show ponies, giving their attention in equal measure to the interesting and the dull. In December 1951 Arthur Fawcett had to warn Reggie, contrary to the impression given by the report to Central Office, of 'restiveness in the division about his failure to attend social functions. He loathes them, but he will do himself no good if he does not start attending them more frequently.'[46] At the end of November 1951 the Maudling family moved out of Totteridge.[47] The area's appeal had waned, as indicated by some sarcastic references in a New Year speech, and living in the heartland of the Barnet Conservative organisation and constantly on call was proving wearing.[48] The constituency activists were quite right to worry that Maudling's victory in the 1951 election and his house move signalled a reduction in his commitment to local affairs.

The house the Maudlings bought was in rural Essendon in the far north of the constituency not far from Hatfield House. It was a rambling seven-bedroom house called Bedwell Lodge. They managed to secure it and move in within weeks after the election. Reggie modestly described it as an 'overgrown cottage', but it was rather more than that. The core of it was a sixteenth-century Jacobean brick house with a fine carved oak staircase, but it had been much added to over the centuries and was a *mélange* of styles and ages – an English Heritage officer told its next occupants that the house had been 'messed about with too much' to be a really historic building. It did, however, have a literary history that was unknown to the Maudlings. In 1891 the family of Beatrix Potter had rented Bedwell Lodge and sketches of it and the area inspired Potter's famous illustrations for her children's books. Peter Rabbit's potting shed was apparently based on the outbuildings at Bedwell Lodge.[49] The garden extended over two acres. It was a rural retreat, a house with a sense of warmth and cosiness that appealed to Reggie and Beryl when they were looking for a place to bring up their children. It also had rather more grandeur than the little suburban house at Totteridge. It was on a scale that could serve as a base for weekend socialising with business and political friends from outside Barnet.

Having been denied ministerial office, Reggie increased his other activities, to the point that a newspaper would comment on his 'budding career in the City'.[50] He was a director of Land Improvement, Planet Assurance and the shipbuilding firm of J. Samuel White on the Isle of Wight, which was run by a Laverick relative in the family line of business. Although he had been fortunate in timing his purchase of Bedwell Lodge – the property market was at a low ebb and it is estimated that it cost something like £9,000 – he would still have trouble affording it on the salary of an MP.

Maudling did not neglect political activities, confident that he would get a ministerial job within a reshuffle or two. He became vice-chairman (under Ralph Assheton) of the backbench Conservative finance, trade and industry committee and also raised his public profile. He had done a little radio broadcasting before the election. His first appearance in January 1951 had not gone over very well; he seemed diffident and ill at ease,[51] but it was a skill he knew he had to master and, with the advantage of being married to an actress, he did. By the 1951 election he was regarded as one of the best Tory broadcast speakers and put the party's case in a 15-minute address on Canadian radio.[52] His first television appearance came after the election, in the *World Survey* programme on 19 November, when he was commenting on economic matters. He said that he did not blame anyone in particular for the current economic situation, which drew the understandable retort that this was not the impression that he or the Conservative Party had given in the recent general election campaign.[53] Reggie was on the television again for the *In The News* programme in January 1952, and the same month he and Iain Macleod went on a short speaking tour of the Midlands.[54] He got involved in some backbench politicking, joining a lobby favouring the introduction of commercial television to compete with the BBC.

Maudling is sometimes assumed to have been, with Macleod, Powell and Cuthbert Alport, one of the founding members of the One Nation Group in the early months of the 1950 Parliament. Perhaps he should have been, but he was not. He was a member of the purely social 1950 Dining Club of new MPs, and this was sometimes confused with One Nation; even Reggie got this wrong in his memoirs. The aims of the group concerned providing a more professional approach to opposition (which Maudling had long urged as a member of the party staff) and a more considered view of social issues. The founding paper, *One Nation*, was subtitled 'A Tory Approach to Social Problems' and did not have chapters on industry or the economy, Maudling's specialist areas. After publishing their paper the authors decided to continue as a dining group and in April 1951 started to consider whether they should produce a wider 'socio-economic Tory theory'.[55] Reggie had strong 'One Nation' views in this area, and this was indeed one of his principal objections to the Labour Party. He always saw socialism as divisive, as stressing conflict between labour and capital rather than their common interests.

Maudling did eventually join the One Nation Group, but not until after the 1951 election, when he and John Vaughan-Morgan were added to its membership following Edward Heath's appointment to the Whips' Office. A rule had been created that frontbenchers were ineligible for active membership. During his short membership of the group Reggie was a regular attender, chairing it twice, including the occasion in February 1952 when Chancellor Rab Butler was the guest of honour. On 7 April 1952, when Reggie next chaired the dinner, Enoch Powell's terse minutes record:

At 9.45pm: A waiter entered and whispered to Mr Maudling, followed by a Whips' messenger who announced 'He wants to see you sharpish.' The Chairman went.[56]

Chapter 6

'THE FIRST DIMPLED CHILD OF BUTSKELLISM', 1952–1955

When Maudling heard what the Chief Whip had to offer him that evening in April 1952 he wondered whether it was worth giving up a dinner for, let alone all the other inconvenience it could cause. Buchan-Hepburn told him that he would be appointed to the Ministry of Transport and Civil Aviation as Parliamentary Secretary. It was hardly a meteoric promotion, but on the other hand it was a government job at last. Reggie was reluctant to accept the position and asked the whips for some time to think it over. His main interest was in economic policy and he feared that his career would be shunted into the unproductive siding of transport policy and never get out onto the main line again. Chancellor Rab Butler advised Maudling to accept it as a first step towards a Treasury post,[1] dangling the prospect of a fairly quick move in front of him and assuaging some of his career worries. Another consideration was money. Maudling had to consider whether it was worthwhile giving up his earning prospects in the City for such a job. He told fellow Tory MP William Teeling a little later that he had decided to accept and that he would be unable to come with him in future to lobby the Foreign Office. 'I'm rather pleased but my bank manager isn't, as I was just beginning to make some money.'[2] Maudling's appointment was announced on 18 April, over a week after the initial offer.

Maudling's first ministerial boss was Jack Maclay, a kindly, moderate Scot who was nominally a National Liberal rather than a Tory, but Maudling had only been in the ministry a few weeks before Maclay resigned. Maclay was a casualty of the misbegotten governmental reorganisation that Churchill introduced in 1951 grouping responsibilities into areas covered by 'Overlords' as well as departmental ministers. This scheme was intended to streamline government but in fact did the opposite, creating an extra tier of interference and causing confusion in developing and implementing policy. Maclay was surprised in 1951 to be given responsibility for both Transport and Civil Aviation while the two remained separate ministries and was severely overworked as a result. He was constantly subject to the interference of Ted

Leathers, 'Secretary of State for the Co-ordination of Transport, Fuel and Power', and Churchill himself who tended to support Leathers against him and pressed for faster progress on the denationalisation of road transport (a particular pet cause of the Prime Minister). With exquisite moderation Maclay wrote to historian Anthony Seldon in 1980 that 'While there is no denying that Winston's methods did make life difficult I do not want to get things out of proportion. He could be very endearing as well as, at times, the opposite! I should have handled the situation differently.'[3]

Maclay's sense that he was not master in his own house must have been heightened when Reggie showed up and introduced himself as the new Parliamentary Secretary. Not only had Maclay not been consulted, but Number 10 also did not even bother to inform him that Maudling had been appointed. Maclay did his best to welcome Reggie to the department, but he was not enjoying the job and his health had started to suffer from stress and overwork. Later in April he had a nervous breakdown and became unable to conduct ministerial business.[4] Churchill accepted his resignation on 5 May, appointed Alan Lennox-Boyd in his place and gave Maclay the curious consolation prize of an appointment to the Privy Council on the occasion of his leaving ministerial office. At the same reshuffle, Iain Macleod vaulted ahead of Maudling and the rest of the class of 1950 by being promoted from the backbenches to Minister of Health.

As dull junior posts went, Transport and Civil Administration was one of the better ones. Maudling was able to keep out of the Churchill–Leathers–Maclay fiasco and as his responsibilities covered aviation he could also stay relatively clear of the complex and controversial transport White Paper. He could not keep completely out of it, and in December 1952 ended up defending the measure in its committee stage even after he had left the ministry.[5] While allowing private road haulage might sound a simple concept, it actually meant tampering with the entire complicated structure of transport finance and cross-subsidy created by the coalition and Labour governments. Even those who welcomed denationalisation were often angry at a special haulage levy that was imposed to keep funds flowing to the railways, and the issue meandered on well into 1953.[6]

Maudling, however, concentrated on the aviation side of this logical but cumbersome double ministry. Aviation fitted in well with his constituency interests because some of the most advanced civil aviation research in the country took place at Hatfield. He could please the local press, and electors in one of the weaker parts of the seat for the Tories, by praising the aviation industry, and had a good start by seeing one of Hatfield's projects come to fruition. He welcomed the start of the first jet airline service in the world, the BOAC De Havilland Comet between Britain and South Africa in May 1952. Reggie compared the new age of British aviation to the beginnings of England as a great maritime power, which was an appropriate New Elizabethan note for the time and reflected high hopes that were, however, quickly disappointed.

The main issue in civil aviation policy in 1952, as it has been ever since and probably evermore shall be, was the provision of airports around London. The problem was that traffic was increasing at a rapid rate and capacity on the ground was going to be cut because Northolt airfield would revert to the RAF by 1956. The principal idea was to designate Gatwick in Sussex as London's second airport, and a public inquiry into the scheme followed. It reported long after Maudling had left the ministry. Lennox-Boyd was interested in opening up opportunities for private airlines, but resisted some pressure to denationalise the state carriers.[7] Reggie was more involved in this aspect of business, winding up debates on the subject in July and October, but he was in the ministry too briefly and at too low a level to have much influence.

Reggie was in high spirits in May 1952, which in an age with more watchful media might have got him into trouble. At a question and answer session for teachers in Barnet, he was told by a swimming teacher that 50 per cent of people couldn't swim and quipped back, 'Well, 80 per cent of them can't think, either.'[8] This could easily have been blown up into a splendid gaffe, but Reggie got off lightly and only faced public criticism from W.H. Jones, the leading Liberal in Barnet, who commented that 'it is shocking that a young man of 36 should say a thing like that. Mr Maudling should be taught to think again himself.'[9] Reggie learned to control his tendency to make casual remarks like this in public and, certainly until he was Home Secretary, was regarded as a safe pair of hands. He meant no harm by his remark, which was received in the spirit it was intended by the teachers in the audience, but it did display traces of bumptiousness and intellectual arrogance that came ill from a plump young Tory minister.

Maudling's self-satisfaction in May 1952 had more to do with his anticipation of future progress than his day job at Civil Aviation. He was confident of his own talents and thought that, in the natural way of things, they would be recognised and now that he was in government he would progress upwards quickly.[10] Trains, planes and automobiles were all very well, but Reggie still had his eyes on a position in the Treasury. Despite his disappointment in April 1952, Maudling was reassured that he was in favour with Butler by Butler's decision to involve him in the parliamentary work that followed the 1952 Budget. He had already spoken as a backbencher in the 1952 Finance Bill debate, and given his interest in economics he was drafted in to handle the committee stages of the Finance Bill. Starting in mid-May, he spoke on behalf of the government on a series of detailed amendments proposed by government departments or MPs, and acquitted himself 'with distinction', according to The Times.[11] Despite not having ministerial responsibility for what he was discussing, Maudling frequently would promise to study suggestions by MPs or look again at the Treasury's proposals. It was an unusual arrangement, in fact the first time that a non-Treasury minister had taken this role; Labour MP Tony Crosland commented acidly: 'we are glad to see that the hon. Member for Barnet has so little to do with civil aviation that he has time to come to speak on matters of finance in which we know he is interested'.[12]

Maudling's appearance in May as a virtual Treasury minister had much to do with another of the blunders Churchill had made in forming his government. Conscious that Butler had little experience in economics, Churchill told him that 'I am going to appoint the best economist since Jesus Christ to help you'. When Butler asked who this might be, Churchill told him: 'Sir Arthur Salter'.[13] Salter became 'Minister of State for Economic Affairs', and nominal second in command at the Treasury. In practice, though, he was irrelevant. Although he had been a distinguished public servant as early as the First World War, at the Treasury Salter was over 70, out of touch with contemporary economics, lacking in energy and a 'difficult, crabby old man' according to his civil servants.[14] Butler thought little of the long memorandums, written in green ink, he received from Salter, and in the House of Commons Salter was little short of disastrous. There was no question of Butler, or the whips, allowing him to take the committee stage of the 1952 Finance Bill. The other Treasury minister, Financial Secretary John Boyd-Carpenter, had his hands full with the public spending negotiations and the civil service, and in any case was at that stage no expert on economics and taxation.[15] Maudling was exactly what the Treasury needed.

Reggie's competent handling of the Finance Bill led him, and others, to wonder why the position should not be made permanent. No doubt stimulated by Reggie himself, reports appeared in the press during May that he was being groomed for Salter's job of Minister of State for Economic Affairs.[16] Maudling's allies in the One Nation Group, who had become increasingly ready to express views about the merits and demerits of ministers and governmental organisation, resolved in July that the Overlord system should be scrapped and that Salter should be replaced by Maudling.[17] Salter was in the way of Maudling's ambitions, but not for long. Butler delivered on his intimation of a rapid move before 1952 was out: on 25 November Salter moved on to another insubstantial post as 'Minister of Materials', his job title disappeared and the office of Economic Secretary, vacant since the election, was restored for Maudling. Reggie's promotion was welcomed in a *Times* leader, which opined that 'Mr Maudling is well qualified for his new post and may be expected to serve the Chancellor well. All in all, the Government appear to have been strengthened by the changes.'[18]

The Treasury ministerial team was a lot smaller in 1952 than it is now. The Chancellor was the only minister in Cabinet (there are now two) and there were two deputies, the Economic Secretary and the Financial Secretary. The Financial Secretaryship was something of a drudge. It involved responsibility for administration, the tax system and also the parliamentary management of a large part of Treasury business. Reggie's job as Economic Secretary covered:

1. Overseas financial questions, including exchange control administration
2. The work of the Overseas Co-ordination Section
3. Questions arising in certain Supply Divisions which involve consideration of external finance, e.g. imports etc.
4. Particular questions dealt with by the Economic Planning Staff as the Chancellor of the Exchequer may from time to time direct
5. Currency and banking policy.[19]

It was thus essentially the international side of the Treasury. In 1958 – when Reggie had temporarily taken over the duties of Economic Secretary once again – a secret official review of the distribution of work within the Treasury described the situation as follows:

At present the Financial Secretary is so over-burdened with routine administration that he has quite inadequate time to devote to thought on administrative improvements, much less to wider aspects of policy. On the other hand, the Economic Secretary, dedicated mainly to City dinners and high thinking, has often had insufficient to occupy his full time; work on his side has already lessened and is likely to decrease more as we move to a still freer economy.[20]

Reggie's style of working was very relaxed. A journalist commented that he would 'slump into his chair at the Treasury and put his feet up on the desk with [a] rag-doll like capacity to relax'.[21] Stafford Cripps had frequently summoned officials for meetings at 8.30 in the morning, and to the relief of Reggie's staff it rapidly became clear that he was not of the same mind. Unless there were early afternoon meetings in the diary, Maudling would usually wander over from the Treasury to the House of Commons for a two-hour lunch break, and work could not compete with the rival attractions of family and social life in the evenings. He would always tend to say yes if he was invited to cocktail parties, both because he enjoyed them and to get the opportunity to do a little social climbing – he was particularly pleased to get an invitation for a party where Prince Philip was going to be in attendance.

The leisurely schedule and the socialising did not interfere with his ministerial duties. According to his then Private Secretary John Marshall: 'The job was not a strain for him. He was never rushing, never running, and he was fully on top of the job. Some ministers always seem stressed and in thrall to the red boxes but he did not.'[22] Although Economic Secretary was hardly the most stressful job in government, it did have its tedious and pressurised aspects, and Reggie's ability to deal with its demands so calmly was more to do with his intelligence and sense of perspective than the inherent easiness of the job. Maudling's duties involved dealing with foreign economic relations, the balance of payments and sterling convertibility, which were highly important, possibly disastrous if mishandled, and involved a command of detail and the ability to get on with people. Maudling was a highly talented occupant of the post, backed up by Marshall, an experienced civil service Private Secretary who had served in the Chancellor's Office under Gaitskell and Butler since 1950. While a good Private Office can prop up an idle or stupid minister, there was never any question of this with Maudling, who was clever and easily able to master complicated briefs. With him, it was more of a problem to stop his mind from wandering off on intellectual tangents when he was posed with a complex issue.

The volume of paperwork and the level of detail that came to the Economic Secretary could be deadening. Things that were not complicated, while still being time-consuming, tended to bore Reggie, and making him focus was a bit of a battle for Marshall:

In the Economic Secretary job all the overseas and balance of payments stuff came to him, and if – as they could be – they were dreary Reggie would tend to put things aside for tomorrow. If they were dreary and important he needed pushing to get him to pay attention. He would say 'let's not do the dull bits, they'll wait.' But sometimes they didn't.[23]

Maudling was never the most disciplined minister in government. From the beginning to the end of his career, he was always inclined to avoid the boring and routine aspects of government work if he could. It was the price to be paid for his balanced, human attitude to politics and administration, part of his very normality. It put him at a disadvantage in the promotion stakes during the 1950s when compared to more diligent, if duller, rivals, but strangely he served a great deal of time in rather technical posts during the decade where his abilities were given less opportunity to shine.

Being a junior minister in a large department can be a thankless job, because there is little that one can do to affect policy as opposed to administer, and defend in the House, policies that have already been decided upon. Much depends on the personality of the minister in charge, and in Butler the Treasury had an enigmatic captain who tended to take the most important decisions himself rather than delegate responsibility. Maudling was frustrated when budget time came around and he found himself 'out of the loop' and hardly aware of what was going on; having been involved from outside the Treasury in 1952 he expected some input once he was officially in the Treasury. In a restive mood, he enquired what was going on and received the dustiest of fob-offs from the Chancellor's Private Office.[24]

International finance in the early 1950s was a different world from the contemporary environment, in which most European countries share a single currency, there is no difficulty in trading any currency from the industrialised West with any other, and most international flows of money are to do with short-term capital investment rather than trade. In 1952 the European economies were in the process of picking themselves up from the destruction of war, arrangements for accepting each other's currencies were tentative and physical trade in goods could be handicapped by the availability or otherwise of the appropriate currencies. Everyone in international economics was worried about repeating the mistakes of the 1930s, when international trade was hobbled by tariff barriers and exchange problems. After the war the problem of how to increase trade (and hence prosperity and peaceful links between countries) while maintaining social stability consumed the attention of economists and finance ministers, but few others – despite its importance it could be a dry, technical subject. Maudling could see both sides of the partially convertible coin: the monetary technicalities and the underlying purpose of preserving a benevolent postwar order.

The environment in which Maudling was operating had been established early on in 1952 by two sets of decisions, one of which was not proceeded with, the other being the budget Maudling had piloted through its committee stages. The one that never saw the light of day was the infamous 'Robot' plan. This was essentially to make sterling (or at least overseas holdings of sterling) convertible into dollars at a floating rate, and – in order to stop the reserves draining off in days as happened when it was convertible in 1947 – raising interest rates, cutting public spending and blocking the 'sterling balances' held by Commonwealth countries in London. What was essentially a simple idea was, of necessity, hedged around with complications, and it would have been horrendously unpopular at home and abroad. Even its advocates talked of its necessity rather than its desirability, and when Butler took it to Cabinet he was defeated by determined opposition, notably from Churchill's close ally Lord Cherwell.[25]

The eventual, non-Robotic 1952 Budget was moderately harsh, and certainly gave a more abrasive impression of Tory priorities than the subsequent record of the government bore out. Food subsidies were cut dramatically, to the embarrassment of Tory chairman, Lord Woolton, who had said during the campaign that no such thing would happen, the temporary import controls that had been introduced in November were tightened even further and interest rates were raised to 4 per cent. It led to a spike of unpopularity for the government ('Not only have we hid our light under a bushel, but we have scratched all over the place to find a bushel under which to hide it', joked Reggie in May 1952),[26] but this proved of short duration. The budget measures had, by happy chance, hit upon the solution to the 1951–2 crisis; it may not have been as permanent a solution as the advocates of Robot believed their plan to be, but the crisis was over none the less. Capital flows were a lot more easily influenced by interest rates and irrational sentiment than anyone had realised at the time, and the outflow stopped and then reversed shortly after the budget. As well as the budget, Britain also benefited in 1952–3 from a sharp change in the terms of trade; commodity prices fell back and the inflationary pressure generated by the Korean War and rearmament dissipated. The sense of crisis and urgency that had pervaded Tory thinking, Maudling's in particular since the 1949 devaluation, dissipated as well. The end of the sterling crisis of 1951–2 without the need for the rigours of Robot was a crucial moment. Since 1949 Reggie had spoken and written about economic affairs in alarmed tones, in terms of the need for radical action to fix Britain's long-term problems. He had, from the sidelines, contributed to the mood that led Butler to endorse the Robot plan. As a backbencher in March 1952 (after the first defeat of Robot in secret Cabinet meetings at the end of February) he had urged the government to

> Move in the direction of the floating value of the pound on the Canadian level, because I do not believe that there will ever be the full confidence there should be in the pound sterling, nor shall we be able to check speculation, and particularly one-way option speculation, until we have the floating rate of the pound instead of moving, as it does at the moment, in a series of hiccoughs from one rate to another.[27]

Although Maudling remained throughout his life an advocate of floating rates, it now became a desirable policy rather than a burning necessity. He never regarded any future economic crisis with the seriousness he had regarded the 1949 devaluation and the 1951–2 drain on the reserves. His 1952–5 Treasury years were spent in calmer conditions than he envisaged, where his tendency to pragmatism could have full rein. Reggie himself described the main lessons of his period as Economic Secretary as confirming his ideas 'That money should be the servant of human beings and not their master, that economics is about people, not ideas, and for that reason there are really no economic problems, only political ones'.[28]

After the demise of 'Robot' an alternative, more gradual international financial policy was developed that became known as the 'collective approach to convertibility'. It was an even more complicated undertaking, launched at the Commonwealth conference of November 1952 shortly before Reggie arrived at the Treasury, which would progressively make Commonwealth and other 'sterling area' holdings of the pound convertible into US dollars, underpinned by a US loan. The incoming Eisenhower Republican administration in Washington was not keen on the plan, and Western European governments were flatly opposed, and the 'collective approach' unravelled; as one Treasury wag put it at the time 'it was getting less collective every day'.[29] Reggie devoted considerable effort to this unproductive venture, which stood very little chance of success. The collective approach withered away during 1953 but according to Maudling the idea of some sort of Commonwealth sterling zone floating with respect to the rest of the world did not die until Butler was 'knocked off it by the hard money men in 1955'.[30]

From the start part of the problem of the collective approach was its half-acknowledgement that Britain was in a supplicant position, and had to look to the United States or to the IMF (International Monetary Fund) for loans to support any of its monetary schemes; however, this was coupled with a sense of entitlement that no longer carried much weight. Financially, Britain was no longer in the top flight, and as Maudling made his way around the world he was repeatedly reminded of this disillusioning fact. He also was given intimations of the changing balance of economic power during his travels, being told repeatedly in Scandinavia during a 1954 visit that while potential customers had no complaints about the quality of British exports, 'the universal complaint was that our salesmanship is nothing like as aggressive as the Germans'.[31] Earlier than most, Maudling was forced to adjust to Britain's reduced power in the world, and started to think about how exports and industry could be assisted by government action.

Maudling went to Washington in summer 1953 to attend the meetings of the World Bank and the IMF. Butler's decision to send him aroused the jealousy of Sir Arthur Salter and Butler had to reassure the older man and explain his reasons – first among them that Maudling was a Treasury minister and that there had already been too many cases of ministers deputising for other ministers in recent weeks. Butler also saw Maudling's foreign role explicitly as career development:

I am very anxious that Maudling should get as much experience as he can in the international field and should become known to our opposite numbers both in the Commonwealth and foreign countries. I think it is only in this way that he can get the experience and standing which will enable him to give me the day-to-day help that I must have.[32]

Reggie followed the IMF trip with a long visit to Asia, calling at Baghdad, Karachi, Colombo, Bombay and New Delhi, that led the *Economist* to remark that he was 'beginning to rank for the title of Britain's peripatetic financial envoy'.[33] The basic point of the trip was the meeting of the Colombo Plan, a Commonwealth international development body, but he stopped off in the other places for meetings and to view other development projects. He was impressed by India's democratic chaos, and admired much of the British political legacy, including its disciplined army; it was one of the first occasions when Reggie had thought much about the Empire. He particularly enjoyed his visit to Bombay, where the state government had clamped down on the sale of alcohol; the Private Office had arranged for him to obtain a permit, which, he recalled in 1978:

I still cherish, authorizing me, as a foreigner, to acquire, transport and consume one pint of foreign liquor. There were a number of conditions on the standard form, one of which, in my case, had been struck out.

Curiosity aroused I managed to decipher what had been excluded; it was the condition that 'the holder shall not get drunk in a public place.' I wonder how many other people can claim to have received an exclusive licence to get drunk in public in Bombay in the 1950s.[34]

Just in case, he did also carry a bottle of whisky in his official briefcase, which, with the help of diplomatic status, he took through in addition to his allowance. It was rather discourteous of him to his hosts, who had made considerable allowances for him, but he got away with it. Reggie also enjoyed the picaresque delights of nightlife in royal Baghdad, including a live sex show performed by two ducks that had waddled onto the stage.[35] He did also get some work done during this trip, as Treasury briefs of stupefying dullness survive at the Public Record Office to testify.[36]

Maudling's job also involved him in Europe to a greater extent than most others in the British government. While Britain did not join the European Coal and Steel Community (ECSC) in 1950, the European Payments Union (EPU) seemed a technical enough institution not to threaten national sovereignty and Britain became a member. EPU members agreed to accept the currency of any other member in payment for exports, which cut through the need for a web of bilateral agreements. The EPU acted as a clearing-house, giving credits to countries in overall deficit within the system (which, increasingly, meant Britain). It was supported by the USA, who tolerated a little discrimination against their own exports in order to promote trade and growth in Europe.[37] It was a successful transitional system, but its continued existence was a matter of tortuous negotiations most years and there were significant strains within it on trade liberalisation and progress to convertibility. Reggie's experience with EPU gave him as much experience as any minister in government in multilateral European negotiation, which was put to use a few years later in an attempt to construct an agreement on European free trade.

Reggie spent much of his last year and a half as Economic Secretary out of the country, on the treadmill of ministerial foreign travel. Butler's project of developing Maudling's career was continuing, but the Chancellor was himself under strain and depressed by his wife's failing health and could not spend long away from her out of the country. It was no hardship for Reggie to deputise at international conferences as he enjoyed foreign travel immensely. Reggie was very English, with that middle-class form of xenophobia that regarded foreign ways of doing things as quirky and amusing rather than threatening, but he liked new places and new experiences. Some of Maudling's travels were a heady opportunity to sit at the top table with the leading figures of world finance and get to know officials and ministers more informally. Reggie went down well wherever he went.[38] He was often better briefed on the detail than most of his seniors, and had the happy ability to correct people when they were wrong without causing offence or showing off.

Maudling bore no relation to the caricature of the stiff, formal, emotionally repressed Englishman abroad, and to meet him in person – expansive, informal, happy and friendly – was an unexpected pleasure for his counterparts. His reputation spread quickly, and in June 1954 he was the subject of an admiring profile captioned 'A Man to Watch' in the US news magazine *Fortune*.[39]

Reggie's performances in the House of Commons were another reason for favourable comment on his prospects. From the very beginning of his ministerial career in 1952, he frequently wound up parliamentary debates, a sign that his ministerial bosses and the whips regarded him as a reliable performer who could be trusted to think on his feet and respond appropriately to the tone of the debate. He often appeared in budget debates and Finance Bill committees in this capacity. Reggie tended to wind up in as non-confrontational a way as possible. *Hansard* on Maudling's principal debates in the early 1950s is studded with pleasant remarks traded across the floor; Reggie always took care to make obliging comments about the previous ministers in his departments when he could. George Lindgren, the Labour MP for Wellingborough who had served in the Civil Aviation ministry, lived not far from Reggie and was an occasional opponent for a round of snooker in local pubs as well as good-natured parliamentary argument. Reggie formed a parliamentary 'pair' with Douglas Jay, a fellow financial expert and intellectual. Pairing meant that the two could be absent by arrangement for non-essential votes, cancelling each other out. Given Reggie's frequent absences abroad and his social calendar, it was a good deal from Jay's point of view. Reggie was generally popular on the Labour benches, with several MPs, including Gaitskell, paying tribute to his reasonableness and charm. A notable tribute came in April 1953 from Jim Callaghan – with whose career Maudling's was intertwined – who commented: 'The Economic Secretary is so amiable that it is difficult to be rough with him. His acute mind, which we have so often admired, must have caused him to realise that he is in difficulty in trying to refute our Amendment.'[40] Reggie's bipartisanship did not go unnoticed. Henry Fairlie observed in the *Spectator* that Maudling was: 'less the protégé of Mr. Butler (though he is certainly that) than the first dimpled child of Butskellism. Mr Maudling is able, and one could forecast a promising future for him if it were not for the fact that he has never yet said anything which could not equally well have been said by Mr Gaitskell.'[41]

Like the construct of Mr Butskell, this was not entirely fair, but there was indeed little in any of Reggie's contributions that had much of an ideological edge. After the course correction of 1952, the 1953 Budget was designed to stimulate the economy through tax cuts, and it worked sufficiently well for 1954 to be as near a standstill budget as could be imagined.[42] There were some steps towards a more free market economy, such as the final removal of rationing in 1954, but for the most part these were changes that a Labour

Chancellor could have endorsed. The post-Robot (or, rather, non-Robot) Treasury was a fine school of consensus politics for Reggie. Some of Reggie's own approach as Chancellor is prefigured by the Butler of 1953–5, who said in 1954 that 'The truth is that we must not be frightened at a little more ease and happiness, or feel that what is pleasant must necessarily be evil'.[43]

Maudling's public profile increased in 1954. He was chosen as the front man for an experimental form of party political broadcast at the start of July. Viewers were invited to call the party's switchboard with questions about any subject, and Maudling would provide the answers. In the history of party broadcasts open-ended questions to a single politician has been a little used format because of the risks of gaffes or inability to answer. As far as one can tell, the questions were genuine and Maudling had not been apprised of them before going on air, and he carried it off with considerable skill. The response was so overwhelming that the Central Office switchboard was overloaded, but the Tories arranged for individual responses to over 600 questions that were not answered on air to be sent, signed by Reggie. The broadcast itself introduced Reggie to a wider audience, who saw him dealing confidently with a range of questions, from purchase tax on bicycles to pig meat subsidies. A couple of the answers revealed a bit more than ephemeral political points. Reggie gave a ringing defence of commercial television, one of his pet causes, and a pragmatic argument for the relaxation of rent control: 'We have been building a lot of new houses in this country in the last year, but it isn't awfully sensible to build a lot of new houses and at the same time to let a lot of old houses fall into disuse and disrepair because the rents are not high enough to enable the owners to keep them in proper repair.'

Another issue of the moment was parliamentary pay and expenses. A Select Committee had recently recommended an increase because the pressure on MPs with no other resources was becoming untenable; about £750 of the £1,000 they were paid went straight out in expenses, leaving some MPs and their dependants virtually on the breadline. Reggie tried to put a reasonable construction on the government's failure to act on its recommendations:

Q: Do you consider that the Conservative Party in the House of Commons has shown class prejudice in refusing the MPs' pay rise?

RM: No, no. Most certainly we haven't. I'm very glad you asked that question Mr Rymers because I'd like to get this as clear as we can. I think there's no doubt that the case for more remuneration in one form or another for Members of Parliament is a strong one. . . . But we felt – the Government felt – that an increase of salary of five hundred pounds at the present moment really could not be justified. Mr Churchill – I beg his pardon Sir Winston Churchill – announced that in the House of Commons and said that we'd be very glad to enter into discussions with the Opposition about alternative methods of meeting the genuine cases of hardship that no doubt exist at the present moment. That's the Government's point of view, and I think it is a fair point of view, and no question of – what do you call it – class prejudice – no question of class prejudice comes into it at all – I really can assure you of that.

This was not the whole truth by any means. The Select Committee was overruled because of party political feeling among Tory backbenchers. The Chief Whip reported:

I am sure that our Party in the House, with the exception of about 40 Members who probably need it badly, will not be willing to agree to any direct increase in salary as suggested by the Select Committee . . . However, this does not end the matter from a Parliamentary point of view. There are cases of hardship on our side, but on the Socialist side hardship is widespread. The 'crunch' of the matter is that many Socialist members, and some of ours, cannot afford, with only their Parliamentary salaries, to live in London during the Session and also to keep up a home and family somewhere else.[44]

A few days later, the Chief Whip was even blunter when reporting a 1922 Committee meeting: 'There was a majority in favour of action on expenses. There was a strong majority in favour of postponing any action till after an Election. There was virtual unanimity on the need to ensure that the Socialists should be forced to initiate any action.'[45]

For the moment, Reggie was adequately provided for, with a £2,000 ministerial salary plus a legacy and trust fund from his father, who had died in April 1953, and the expectation of the balance of his father's considerable money on the death of his mother. However, he was on the edge of a category that Buchan-Hepburn warned was 'a new and valuable type of Member in our own Party whose circumstances do not greatly differ from those on the Socialist side of the House'. The Tories' decision on parliamentary pay *did* have an element of class, and political, prejudice about it. The feeling of the old-style Tories that Parliament was essentially a voluntary activity rather than a career or profession prevented something sensible being done about the question in 1954. The poor pay and crushing expenses, coupled with the lack of pension, severance pay, predictable earning scales and all the other requisites of civilised employment, amounted to a serious problem dealt with in a trivial way. For all the appreciation of Maudling and those like him who had entered in 1950 and 1951, there was very little thought about how to make life easier. Although he was complacent about it in 1954, it was not long before Reggie experienced the rough end of the system.

The pace of ministerial meetings and travel picked up again in autumn 1954. In September he sailed across in the *Queen Mary* with most of the British Treasury delegation to the IMF meeting and was the senior minister on the ship, as Butler took a plane. The government's Economic Adviser, Robert Hall, recalled in his diary that 'We did very little work there: I saw quite a lot of Maudling who is a pleasant man but rather self-indulgent. He is a reasonably good economist and has some political sense but I doubt if he will reach the top of the Ministerial ladder.'[46]

More meetings followed. In December 1954 Maudling attended a NATO meeting in Paris, and returned there in January 1955 with Butler to the OEEC meeting. In March he was in Geneva. Reggie was now a familiar figure on the circuit and it was hardly surprising that he started to attract even more attention as a coming man in international politics. In early 1955 Reggie joined another international group, this time a private one. He became a member of the Bilderberg Group, a sign that he was taken increasingly seriously by influential political leaders in Europe and the United States as well as in Britain. This group has latterly been infamous because it serves as a focus for theories about a secretive elite who supposedly control world events. While it is difficult to take the idea of a world conspiracy run by Reggie Maudling terribly seriously, his Bilderberg involvement deserves some exploration and was a significant advance for his career.

The group was founded in 1952 by Dr Joseph Retinger, a Polish exile living in London, and drew together in the first instance pro-American political figures from Europe such as Prince Bernhard of the Netherlands, Guy Mollet and Antoine Pinay of France and Hugh Gaitskell and Lord Portal from Britain, plus some business involvement and financial backing from Paul Rykens, Chairman of Unilever. The first meeting in 1952 was something of an experiment and the May 1954 meeting at the Bilderberg Hotel in Oosterbeek near Arnhem in the Netherlands is often thought of as being the founding conference of the organisation. Maudling was not present at this conference, but attended the March 1955 meeting at Barbizon, near Fontainebleau in France, and a further meeting in September 1955 at Garmisch-Partenkirchen in Germany. As well as attending the meetings, he also, with Denis Healey, joined the inner 'Steering Committee', which discussed matters in a smaller group and decided whom to invite and what to discuss at the main meetings.[47]

Maudling described the group's purpose in a letter to Anthony Eden in April 1956 as 'working to strengthen relations between Western Europe and the United States',[48] and this was the main focus of its discussions in the mid-1950s. It was one of a number of initiatives in the postwar decade intended to bind the Western alliance together. Its agenda on domestic policy, in so far as it had one, was mildly progressive; its members recognised that social injustice was wrong in itself and likely to provide fertile soil for communism. While its members shared a commitment to the Atlantic alliance, expressions of opinion within the group were heterodox enough to allow the Italian ambassador to France, Piero Quaroni, to make a plea for what would now be called an ethical foreign policy[49] and Denis Healey to argue that NATO should pull out of West Germany on condition that the USSR withdraw from its European satellite states.[50] Its European founders were generally keen on European political and economic union, although this was not a party line by any means – Maudling certainly did not share this view. Retinger inspired the European Movement and the idea of a European single currency was discussed at the Buxton meeting in September 1958 to which – hardly a sign of a secret right-wing gathering – Nye Bevan had been invited.

In February 1956 the British members, including Maudling, persuaded the Foreign Secretary, Selwyn Lloyd, to give his official blessing to the group, which inspired British firms (and the Corporation of Lloyd's) to contribute money to its running costs.[51] Maudling was most heavily involved in the group in the late 1950s, frequently attending steering committee meetings, which took place every few months, usually at Claridge's, one of his favourite London haunts, or in Paris, which he enjoyed visiting. Maudling dropped out of the inner circle in 1959 as he rose higher in government and the Bilderberg organisation grew in complexity. By then, over 300 people had attended one meeting or another and the steering group had become too large, so that a yet smaller 'Advisory Committee' was set up with Denis Healey rather than Maudling taking the British place. Reggie continued to attend Bilderberg meetings when he could, through at least to the early 1970s.

Reggie, anxious for promotion, kept closely in touch with domestic political gossip as well as moving in international circles, which for most of the Parliament had consisted largely of speculation about when Churchill was finally going to resign. The Prime Minister had given countless indications of retirement in 1953 and 1954, but each time decided that he could not step down just yet, to the ever-increasing frustration and fury of his designated successor, the Foreign Secretary, Anthony Eden. It was a tragic situation, as after 1953 neither man was really fit for office, Churchill because of his declining powers following a severe stroke, and Eden because of his increasingly neurotic personality that close observers felt was unlikely to stand up under pressure. At long last, in March 1955, the deal was done; it would have been ludicrous to go through another election under Churchill. Reggie's election agent recorded in his diary on 11 March that 'Reggie Maudling has warned me to be ready for a General Election on 26 May. (Winston was going to go.) There is considerable pressure being brought to bear for a May election.'[52] Reggie's information was good.[53] Churchill stepped down and Eden became Prime Minister on 6 April. The succession was a muted affair, mainly because the national press had been shut down by a strike. When the papers resumed publication, they printed catch-up editions to cover the main stories during the blackout and the end of Churchill's ministerial career after nearly fifty years was marked appropriately. Eden had also, as Reggie predicted, called an election for 26 May, so the details of his initial reshuffle were a lower priority to the press. But most coverage found space to note that Harold Macmillan stepped up to the Foreign Office, Selwyn Lloyd went to Defence and Lord Home to the Commonwealth Relations Office. Butler stayed at the Treasury – with ill consequences for his reputation – but his Economic Secretary was now to be Edward Boyle. Reggie Maudling's apprenticeship was over; he had a department of his own at his command and he became the Right Honourable Reginald Maudling, Her Majesty's Minister for Supply.

Chapter 7

MINISTER OF SUPPLY, 1955–1957

Supply was a disappointing reward for Maudling's Treasury service, given his prior relationship with Eden and the support of Butler. He had told Arthur Fawcett that he 'had hoped for a seat in the Cabinet. I think this is bound to come to him, probably at the next reshuffle . . .'[1] on the pattern of his brief stay at Civil Aviation in 1952. While musing over the composition of his government, Eden had actually considered a steep promotion for Maudling to the Board of Trade,[2] but there were too many other pieces of the jigsaw to be fitted in and at Supply he remained just outside the Cabinet.

The Ministry of Supply was in Reggie's own words in 1978 'a strange Department, and the target of a good deal of criticism, much of it justified'.[3] Even at the time, he said in the Commons that 'I do not mind very much if someone shoots my horse from under me'.[4] Maudling left advice, not heeded, that the ministry be abolished on his departure. It had been established in July 1939 as part of the Chamberlain government's belated rearmament effort and the bulk of its routine work was concerned with what is now known as 'defence procurement' – the supply of materials to the army, navy and air force. Reggie could find himself from one moment to the next talking about compressors on experimental missiles, supplying tanks to Germany and expediting sales of weapons to Iraq, at that time a British ally. He had to offer apologies to the Foreign Office over one occasion when arms were sent to Iraq under unsuitable cover:

> The incident of the three-ply wood made in Israel and bearing markings of the Star of David is, I am afraid, one of those things which no amount of organisation is likely to foresee. I think it is really asking too much of the people who make up packing cases in our establishments to expect them to maintain a political awareness of this kind, but I am sorry it should have happened and we will do our best to make sure it doesn't happen again.[5]

However, most of the top-level political effort in the ministry went on aircraft. It had acquired, on the dismantling of the Ministry of Aircraft Production in October 1945, some responsibilities for civil aircraft production and aviation research, which produced most of the political problems of the department.

The boundaries between this role and Nigel Birch's Ministry of Air were far from clear, and the ministry sat uncomfortably with other ministries with responsibility for research and development (R&D) in non-aviation matters. Reggie hoped not to be there very long, and did not bother to disguise the feeling from his civil servants who regarded him as a bird of passage, hoping to move on to something better.[6] Reggie would certainly have been surprised if he had been told that he would last there as long as Anthony Eden served at Number 10.

Maudling's investiture as a Privy Councillor at Windsor Castle was the first occasion at which his casual fashion sense drew public comment. Charles Hill, also being sworn in, recalled that Maudling caused some raised eyebrows by turning up to the ceremony wearing 'some ancient brown shoes. We had been advised to wear "country clothes" and no doubt he thought brown shoes would supply the authentic rural touch.'[7] Reggie was never much of a countryman. If anything his shoe faux pas showed that he was trying too hard, as he was very conscious that the Privy Council was a great honour at the age of only 38. Reggie's promotion was well received by his colleagues and the weekly press. The *Economist* thought him and Selwyn Lloyd 'almost automatic choices for advancement'.[8] The US news magazine *Time* wrote of 'bouncy young Reginald Maudling, 38, BA Oxford, the bespectacled financial wizard who was one of Chancellor Rab Butler's policy-framing backroom boys'.[9] He was the subject of admiring profiles in several weeklies. *Time and Tide* commented that 'Mr Reginald Maudling . . . is high on the list of future Chancellors of the Exchequer – a man with a present and a future'.[10]

A burst of favourable publicity was an excellent way for Maudling to start the election campaign. This 1955 campaign was probably the sleepiest of any in Britain since 1900. It was widely regarded as a foregone conclusion, with the Conservatives strongly tipped to increase their slender majority to more comfortable levels. Labour did not present an impressive challenge, with Attlee a respected but now elderly figure who had led the party for twenty years, and bitter divisions unconvincingly papered over. The attempted expulsion of Bevan weeks before the election was not a good start. The Tories, on the other hand, were in good heart, pleased that Labour's prophecies of war and unemployment in 1951 had been disproved and proud of their new leader, Anthony Eden.

The 1955 election was the last in Britain that was primarily conducted through speeches and public meetings; television election coverage was confined to the parties' own party election broadcasts. ITV was not yet transmitting, and the BBC laboured under absurd self-censorship.[11] Reggie Maudling, as one of the most prominent young Conservative ministers, played a larger role in the national campaign than in previous elections. He certainly kicked off the campaign during the remaining Commons debates on Butler's tax-cutting Budget. On 21 April after a gentle introduction – he joked that he did not want to seem 'the bad penny that keeps turning up in our financial debates' – he laid into Shadow Chancellor Hugh Gaitskell's speech: 'I observed in a weekly paper recently that I was criticised for never saying anything which the right hon. Gentleman could not equally say. I hope this afternoon to dispose of that particular criticism.' It was one of Reggie's parliamentary high points, a display of aggression mixed with good humour. He accused Gaitskell of inconsistency in claiming that the budget was to buy votes but also did not help many people; that it would be naive political tactics to target a vote-winning budget on the City of London. He challenged the opposition to vote against the tax cuts if they disapproved of them and accused Labour of offering, with or without intending to from the outset, the alternative policy of 'a return to controls, rationing and higher taxation'.[12] His speech was compared in a Tory weekly to another famous political confrontation that made a ministerial career:

> Mr Iain Macleod's clash with Mr Bevan is still remembered after three years and another noteworthy battle took place last week when Mr Reginald Maudling smote Mr Gaitskell hip and thigh during the Budget debate. A stocky, dark man with a pleasant smile, Mr Maudling has been described as 'a charming man who is also something of a political genius.'[13]

Maudling took the lead for the Tories in accusing Labour of either planning for, or having policies that would inevitably lead to, rationing. Some Tories went so far as to print up mock ration books for campaign purposes. The allegation that Labour would reintroduce food rationing through choice or necessity was angrily denied by the opposition. The claim was denounced in the Labour manifesto as 'a deliberate lie'. It was electoral sharp practice, but not a completely outrageous smear; a lower-key version of the 'warmonger' charge Labour supporters had levelled at the Tories in 1951. The 1955 election was unusual in Maudling's career because of his relatively fierce partisan tone; he had realised that if the image of being the 'first dimpled child of Butskellism' took hold it would do his career no good.

When the campaign moved out into the country, Reggie, now developing as an effective platform speaker, accepted as many speaking invitations as he could and spent eight days of the campaign in other constituencies. When Reggie spoke in marginal Wycombe, he attracted further international attention in *Time*, which quoted him as summing up the elections as 'Either go with us – less controls, more freedom, less taxes – or with Labour – more nationalisation, rationing, more controls'.[14]

Maudling's campaign in Barnet was a more highly charged affair than his genteel contest with Stephen Taylor in 1950. The boundaries had changed yet again, to the disadvantage of the local Conservatives. Most of the new territory around Hatfield and Cuffley gained in 1950 was lost again to the Hertford constituency and with it went some of the areas with the highest

Conservative vote and membership. The constituency now consisted of Barnet, East Barnet and the Elstree district. Elstree was increasingly dominated by Borehamwood, effectively a small and rather working-class New Town composed of estates built from 1949 onwards under the auspices of the London County Council. The growth of Borehamwood had provided Maudling with the bulk of his constituency casework in the previous Parliament, particularly housing cases, and an increasingly disadvantageous social composition of the constituency. The Tories were well aware of the problem but could not think of how to counter the threat. A meeting of MPs affected by New Town building came to no better outcome, according to a wry aside from Maudling, than 'we seemed to reach the startling conclusion that socialists in the New Towns were a bad thing'.[15] The boundary changes knocked about 6,000 off Maudling's majority according to local observers,[16] making it theoretically vulnerable if Labour were going to do well.

Maudling was also a much slacker constituency MP than he had been when he first arrived. Attendance at his surgeries had started to tail off: 'in the end I had just this one chap who came every week to tell me about his operation. So I shut the surgery – and nobody seems to mind. As I say, they know where to find me.'[17] Some constituency duties fell by default to Arthur Fawcett, who started writing letters to ministers on individual cases in 1953 and noted that in October 1954 Maudling 'is particularly unpopular now as he is not spending enough time in the constituency'.[18] The constituency's annual reports recorded plaintive cries from the local Tories that 'the only regret your Council has is that the Constituency sees so little of him', although they did recognise the problems that overseas travel, ministerial duties and a small parliamentary majority posed.[19] In November 1953 criticism that Maudling had seen very little of Barnet since the election was reported to Central Office, but this was investigated in the most cursory fashion. 'I would have thought that these allegations were utterly unfounded, but I would be grateful if you will make very tactful enquiries,' was the brief to the Tory official looking into Barnet, and he did little more than consult the 1952 annual report.[20]

The Barnet Conservative party was still exceptionally strong and well organised, despite Reggie's neglect and several minor local splits and scandals, and the more general problem that television was creating for membership organisations. As early as January 1953 Fawcett had noticed that long-term trends were undermining local activism:

The advent of television is already having an effect on attendance at meetings and social functions. I think it will revolutionise our [concept] of social life. Already the public houses are feeling the pinch, theatres and cinemas will probably do likewise, it is now nearly impossible to canvass when any big programme is on, and as I say meetings and socials begin to suffer.[21]

It was as much as anyone could do to hold back the ebb tide. Maudling was fortunate with his agent and his constituency party, and also that in the new age of television politics he could benefit from a good public image and be heard by thousands more Barnet voters than he could in years of knocking on doors.

The local campaign was lively, in contrast to the somnolent national contest. Maudling's Labour opponent was a journalist, Sydney Hyam. Like Cyril Fenton in 1951, Hyam was a left-wing candidate who had particularly strong opinions about foreign affairs. Hyam was completely opposed to German rearmament, favoured a neutral and demilitarised Germany and wanted a complete ban on all testing and research for the hydrogen bomb, which put him to the left of Nye Bevan. Hyam's emphasis on the bomb put him alongside Richard Acland, who had resigned from the Labour Party to fight Gravesend on the issue, but Hyam remained within the party and received a supportive visit from Bevan. Hyam seemed 'short, dark and dogmatic' to the local reporter; 'an idealistic individualist' and potential thorn in the side of the Labour whips.[22]

Maudling stuck to the main lines of the campaign and refused to engage Hyam on his own territory of nuclear weapons: 'I do not intend to waste the time of the meeting by answering the rather hysterical outbursts of my Labour opponent.' He even said that there was little conflict between the parties on foreign affairs. As in his Wycombe speech, the thrust was about Conservative freedom against Labour controls and the differences between the parties as alternative governments. He also repeatedly looked back on the Conservative record of 1951–5 and the contrast with Labour's dire warnings from the 1951 campaign:

We have done the things we have said we would do. The wars and troubles abroad have been settled. At home, taxes have been cut, controls lifted and more houses than ever built. The charge of being warmongers was made against the Tories, but we have ended the wars we inherited. It was said that there would be a million unemployed under a Conservative administration. In fact, employment is at a record level. We have spent more money on education than the Labour Party ever did, and we are providing school places at the cost of providing three under Labour. Far from cutting the social services, we have improved them.[23]

The Conservative future Maudling promised was of freedom and incentives, accompanied by expansion in all the social services 'on progressive lines'. Maudling's message, including the scare about Labour rationing, was attractive to middle-class voters. There was no Liberal candidate in Barnet in 1955, which helped the Conservatives. Given the national trend, the Barnet Conservatives felt confident enough not to spend up to the limit of allowed election expenses, and their confidence was rewarded on election day, 26 May.

Labour turnout in Borehamwood fell well below expectations while in Barnet and East Barnet the Conservative organisation did well at getting supporters to the polls. This time, Barnet's count took place the same night and the result was declared rather early, at shortly before 12.30a.m. Reggie turned up to the count, resplendent in evening dress after an election-night dinner out, and gave a short conventional speech of thanks.[24] He had exceeded the national swing yet again and made even the new version of Barnet a safe Conservative seat – the majority was several thousand more than he had expected.[25] When the national vote was counted, Eden's Tories had won a majority of fifty-eight and polled 49.7 per cent of the vote – as near as any party has come to having the support of half the voters in any election since 1935. The party had won on a progressive manifesto very much in tune with Maudling's views. In some academic analysis of party manifestos the Tories in 1955, uniquely, produced a programme that was to the left of the ideological spectrum. Even some Labour figures, such as Richard Crossman, would admit in private that 'from the country's point of view this was palpably the right result'.[26] Never has a government won re-election so placidly, with such a consensus, and then wrecked it so completely through incompetence and malice.

Electorate		61,255	
Turnout			81.4
Reginald Maudling	Conservative	30,299	60.8
Sydney Hyam	Labour	19,570	39.2
Conservative majority		10,729	21.5

After the excitements of the election campaign, Maudling settled back to ministerial work in his imposing office at Shell-Mex House, on a curve of the Thames with views over Westminster and the City. Despite the peculiarities of Supply, the ministry did do things that could have been interesting, given Maudling's general beliefs about the relationship between government and private industry. For the few years after the end of the war, the boundaries between government, state-owned corporation and private enterprise were thoroughly scrambled in the aviation industry. While the aircraft manufacturers were in private hands, the ministry provided a large quantity (£210.5 million in 1954/5) of public finance for R&D and the production of prototypes. If the design proved commercially successful, the money would be recouped through a levy on sales. If it did not, the government and the firm swallowed their respective losses, as they repeatedly had to in the early 1950s – twelve projects were cancelled in 1952–5.[27] The ministry's decisions about what research to fund were important to the entire industry. The government's involvement did not stop there. Supply was a buying agency for equipment used in aircraft production, which it then supplied to the firms as 'embodiment loan'. It also acted as a buying agency for purchases made by the state-owned airlines.[28] Since a review of policy in 1948, and particularly the return of the Conservatives to power in 1951, the ministry had backed away from such direct involvement in the industry: the production companies were encouraged to conduct R&D using their own private resources and some of the central purchasing functions were lost. It remained, however, a key ministry for an important sector of British industry.

In the early postwar years the future of British aircraft construction looked bright. While the Americans had a better-developed industry, British designs were attractive and the development of the Comet, which Reggie had seen launched into commercial service in his brief passage at the Ministry of Transport and Civil Aviation in 1952, was highly promising. Orders started to come in from across the world, even including the US airline Pan-Am, and Lord Swinton could declare to the House of Lords in July 1952 that 'we may have collared the market for a generation'.[29]

By the time Maudling came to Supply the picture was very different. Comets had been involved in a worrying number of crashes since the launch and in January 1954 they were temporarily withdrawn from service after a Comet fell into the Mediterranean near Elba; within weeks of resumption of service in March 1954 another Comet failed over the Mediterranean. A radical redesign was obviously necessary, and the British aircraft industry never really recovered from the blow.

BOAC, the principal British carrier, responded to the failure of the Comets by announcing that it would now be primarily interested in turbo-prop planes, which, as it turned out, was a technology much less capable of progress than the jets the Americans were still working on.[30] The airline's decision meant that, unless it could be cajoled into changing its mind, the British aircraft manufacturers had lost a large part of their market for their planned new designs of jet plane. Another problem arose when the Treasury started looking around for cuts in summer 1955. The warm fiscal climate with which the Tories had won the election turned colder once the votes were counted, and defence was far from immune. Aircraft under development were frequently designed in both civil and military forms, to economise on the enormous development costs and build in a very understanding, high-volume client from the start; this had been the case with the Vickers jet aircraft project known alternatively as the V1000 or the VC7.

This all started to be Reggie's problem when the Royal Air Force announced that they were no longer interested in the Vickers V1000 transport aircraft. The RAF had been signalling for several months before Reggie arrived at Supply that they were dissatisfied with progress on the plane and felt that it was no longer fulfilling the specification – Reggie's old RAF department, S6, were particularly vocal against the military version. After the death of the military version the question remained as to what to do with the proposed civilian plane.

The V1000 was Maudling's first major executive decision in government. It was a difficult one to make, but by autumn 1955 he had decided that the whole project would have to be axed. The clinching argument for him was that, given BOAC's strong prejudice in favour of turbo-props and its lack of interest in a new jet aircraft, there was no market for the V1000. Reggie also accepted the Treasury and air force criticisms of the cost and timing overruns on the project, although he realised that it was a decision he would need to have ratified at Cabinet level because it was so controversial. On 14 October he wrote to Butler that 'I do not feel, therefore, that I should go ahead and cancel the further development of this aircraft which is my present intention unless I have the agreement of my colleagues who are affected'.[31] The colleagues, Butler included, agreed and Reggie announced the cancellation of the V1000 in November. Maudling briefed the specialist aviation correspondents and expressed his 'great regret at the demise of the V1000, but explained that with the Treasury wielding the economy axe and both potential customers unwilling to order, he had no alternative'.[32] Reggie's tears for the V1000 were, to some extent, crocodile tears, but he was utterly convinced that there was nothing he could do about the situation, that he could not drum up customers out of nowhere.

The decision was controversial and much criticised, both at the time and with hindsight. Vickers were understandably furious, with managing director George Edwards calling it 'a decision we shall regret for many years'. This could be discounted as commercial disappointment, but more worrying was an outspoken attack from Tory MP for Sunderland South, Paul Williams, in an adjournment debate on 8 December, when he called cancellation 'one of the most disgraceful, disheartening and most unfortunate decisions that has been taken in relation to the British aircraft industry in recent years'.[33] Very soon after the destruction of the V1000 production line, jets suddenly came back into fashion with the British airlines, but there were no British models approaching suitability for the fast, high-volume North Atlantic routes. By February 1956 Miles Thomas of BOAC was approaching Maudling, asking if the airline could use Boeing airframes fitted with British-made Rolls-Royce Conway engines. Maudling's initial response was dismissive,[34] but in the end this was the solution adopted and announced by the Minister of Transport and Civil Aviation, Harold Watkinson, in October 1956.

Hindsight has tended to favour the critics of the decision. 'Looking back on it,' Maudling wrote in a particularly vague passage of his memoirs, 'I suppose one could argue that they may have been right, but who can say?'[35] It was less than a ringing defence of his action, but he did have the defence of necessity. There was little that he could do, given the fragmentation of responsibility for the various decisions between the manufacturers, the airlines, Supply, Transport and Civil Aviation, Air, the air force, the Treasury . . . It was a decision taken by default rather than any malice or incompetence on Maudling's part. That said, the arguments he used in the House do seem astonishingly short-sighted and complacent: 'We can offer a greater variety of civil aircraft than they can. The only aircraft that we cannot offer in the early sixties is one that can do flights both ways across the Atlantic non-stop.' One might naively think that such an ability would be useful, and form the basis for a large-scale aviation industry – but Reggie brushed the concern aside by saying that in winter conditions it was all very well to cross the Atlantic in one go, 'but landing when one gets there is another matter. Anyone who thinks there can be guaranteed regular operations across the Atlantic is rather optimistic.'[36] It was all a long way from Reggie's confident talk in 1952 about a new era comparable to England's maritime age; on reflection he concluded that it was the United States, with its wealth, military-industrial complex and large internal distances, that was in a position to lead the aviation age.[37]

Reggie's relations with the ministers in adjacent departments, Watkinson in Transport and Nigel Birch at Air, were not particularly warm. 'I had from time to time considerable battles with Nigel Birch,' he wrote in his *Memoirs*.[38] In February 1956 Harold Watkinson wrote to him criticising him for talking to Miles Thomas of BOAC without reference to him, and a wry note on a briefing paper in August 1956 commented that Reggie 'might conceivably, for once in a way, get the support of the Secretary of State for Air'.[39] The problem was not so much with Reggie's conduct, as with the unworkable complications of the division between the three ministries. Reggie told Watkinson in February that 'I am at present engaged in trying to clear my mind about the future of civil aircraft production in this country, with a view to putting up a paper to the EPC or the Cabinet',[40] but there is no record of such a paper in the Cabinet minutes for the time.

Watkinson, at any rate, was unsatisfied with the outcome of Maudling's thoughts and became increasingly worried about the aviation industry. The V1000 affair had been a turning point, after which the British aviation industry was not a serious competitor to the big US firms. The Boeing and Lockheed designs became the standard models while the airline industry took off. Watkinson wrote to Maudling in June 1956 that: 'I think that we must at least envisage the situation where the big American jet is so well established in world airline operation that it will be almost impossible to supplant it unless the British aircraft industry can come forward with some phenomenal development which puts it four or five years ahead.'[41] Ironically, the search for a 'phenomenal development', something that would leapfrog over the American models, led directly to Concorde – a project that might have been better cancelled. In October 1956 the decision was taken that Britain could not compete in the subsonic aircraft market and that 'we had to go above the speed of sound, or leave it'. The attitude of the aircraft manufacturers, after the V1000 experience, was 'It's a bright idea as long as the government pays for it'.[42] The public spending costs of finishing the V1000 were as nothing compared to the development costs of Concorde.

After the V1000 affair Maudling was an unobtrusive departmental minister, with his public profile lower if anything than it had been in the later stages as Economic Secretary. 'He did not enjoy this time. It was a bit dull,' was the firm impression he gave to his friend Sandy Glen.[43] He was easily distracted and feeling a bit underemployed, and for the first time in his life there were signs that lassitude and self-indulgence were starting to affect his public image. In March 1956, after a long and agreeable dinner and wine tasting, Reggie had to go back to the House of Commons for an evening debate. It was not the most inspiring debate and Reggie quickly fell asleep and started snoring; at 11p.m. Labour MP Fred Willey, who was speaking, said, 'I think it is probably kinder to allow the Minister of Supply to slumber,' but other Labour MPs shouted 'Wake up' at him, and he stirred himself to go through the government lobby when the vote was taken.[44]

It was at this point in his career that Reggie formed a relationship that was to expose him to the temptations of easy money and financial chicanery. As a departmental minister Reggie now had the opportunity to appoint a Parliamentary Private Secretary (PPS) from the Conservative backbenches. The relationship between minister and PPS varies with each partnership, but the basic idea is to give the minister an MP as an adviser and conduit of information from the parliamentary party. Maudling's choice in 1956 was a controversial character, Frederic – usually known as Freddie – Bennett, the MP for Torquay since a by-election at the end of 1955, although he was first elected for Reading North in 1951. Freddie Bennett was a crusty cold-war right-winger, with a whole hive of bees in his bonnet from the Channel Tunnel (for) to Gibraltar (for), Kenyan federalism (for) and 'subversion' (against). In later years he mellowed and drifted to the left, endorsing proportional representation in 1987 and New Labour in 1997.

Maudling's relationship with Bennett baffled many of Reggie's friends and admirers, few of whom have anything positive to say about the man. Bennett was also generally regarded as being unscrupulous with his financial affairs. 'As shady a character as I ever came across,' thought Tom Caulcott, one of Maudling's Treasury civil servants in the early 1960s, and it was a verdict shared by many Conservative MPs.[45] In 1981 a *Sunday Express* poll which identified him as the most unpopular Tory MP found him 'universally and deservedly disliked'. Bennett sued.[46] He was truculent, fussy and difficult to get on with,[47] qualities that made him an unlikely ambassador for someone as emollient as Maudling to employ as his House of Commons eyes and ears. Sir Frederic Bennett died in 2002, and chose not to say anything about Maudling to the author except to note that he was a friend 'Who I readily admit I knew extremely well in his good times and bad. I believe that British Politics and the British Nation itself lost a great deal when he disappeared from the scene.'[48]

Bennett was working on memoirs at the time of his death, which when they appear should present his side of the story. Bennett's father had married into money, in the shape of the Kleinwort banking family, and Freddie was one of the richer, and certainly among the flashiest, Conservative MPs in Parliament, with four houses and a private island in the Bahamas. It was, admittedly, a small and rather insalubrious outcrop called Rat Island, which had a persistent problem with a creeping green algae patch, but even so it was Bennett's personal island in the sun. Reggie's first dealings with Bennett, in 1954, should not have given a positive impression. Bennett was petitioning the Treasury to give special dispensation to allow him and Kleinwort to conduct a share swap in Canada, and was extremely persistent in pressing his case with Reggie and with Treasury civil servants. Officials eventually decided that having delayed a decision for too long it would be unfair to turn him down.[49]

Much as Reggie disliked being taken out of the mainstream of economic policy during the Eden government, it was not a bad time to be away from the Treasury. Butler took back most of his tax concessions in his 'pots and pans' special Budget in October 1955, a humiliating retreat from his ill-advised confidence of the spring. Butler's reputation as Chancellor never recovered from this and the brutal parliamentary beating he took from Hugh Gaitskell in the budget debate. Reggie, who had supported Butler to the maximum earlier in the year, could only offer support from the sidelines. He wrote his old boss a little note during the debate: 'Magnificently spoken and – with respect – just right. Your best ever.' It was a considerate gesture at a difficult time, and Butler showed every sign of appreciating Maudling's support.[50] The Budget was followed by a slide in the fortunes of the government and by January 1956 there was a chorus of press complaint about its lack of direction and a bizarre statement from Downing Street denying rumours that the Prime Minister was about to resign. The year 1956 was shaping up to be rather bleak, even before the Egyptian government announced on 26 July that the Suez Canal, which ran through its territory but was owned by an Anglo-French firm, would be nationalised.[51]

In the early stages of the crisis, there was consensus in Britain that Egypt (rapidly personalised into 'Nasser') had acted wrongly, and that something should be done by the international community. The principal step in this direction was taken in August, with an international conference in London at which Egypt was not represented. The outcome was the Dulles Plan, which proposed internationalising the canal and running it by a board associated with the United Nations, but Egypt did not accept the Plan and in September Britain and France referred the Suez issue to the UN Security Council. Part of their resolution was vetoed by the USSR, and in October Britain joined secret discussions between France and Israel about taking military action against Egypt. The deal was sealed at Sèvres, near Paris, on 22 October and on 29 October Israeli forces crossed into the Sinai peninsula heading towards the canal. Next day, Britain and France sent a hypocritical ultimatum to Israel and Egypt demanding withdrawal from the area around the canal and when Egypt refused bombing commenced.

At this point what was left of the domestic consensus in Britain collapsed. The debate in the House of Commons on 1 November, suspended amid uproar, was one of the most bitter and vicious in history – Reggie's memoirs claim that steam issued from Denis Healey's ears, he was so angry.[52] At the United Nations the Americans distanced themselves from the Anglo-French actions. On Sunday 4 November the *Observer* wrote that 'We had not realised that our government was capable of such folly and such crookedness'. The next day British and French paratroops landed at Port Said. Even within the government, there was a groundswell of disgust from some of the more liberal Tories, such as Anthony Nutting and Edward Boyle, and Eden's Press Secretary, William Clark, resigned, in what to date is the only resignation from the Downing Street staff on a point of principle. Then, on 6 November Harold Macmillan, who had previously been confident and bellicose, announced to colleagues that the Bank of England's sterling reserves were draining away at an alarming rate (Macmillan's figures actually overstated the crisis). No support could be expected from the Americans. While the military operation was technically going well, the cost of continuing could have been the collapse of the pound. The invasion was halted.

Maudling's own part in the Suez debacle was minor, but he was privy to more of it as Minister of Supply than he would have been as a domestic minister. Supply had to ensure that the invasion forces had enough equipment to do their job, and was therefore part of the planning of the operation. There is no evidence that Maudling was aware at the time of the dirtiest aspect of Suez – the secret collusion with Israel in the form of the Sèvres agreement. Eden 'played his cards pretty close to his chest', he recalled in his memoirs. But Maudling's recollection is interesting in that he thought his greatest difficulty was 'to persuade the military that the politicians really meant business. The job of my Department was to ensure that they would have the necessary munitions to carry out their task, but when we approached them to ask if they had all they needed, their reaction was always calm to the point of scepticism.'[53] It was probably because they had more sense. Not for the first or last time, the senior military were more sensitive to political reality than the politicians; the same was true in 1971 when Maudling was more directly involved in the great blunder of internment in Northern Ireland.

Maudling was unapologetic about Suez, even in his 1978 *Memoirs*, despite his general sympathy for the Arab cause. He was making, obscurely, a point about his political integrity, that he would put British interests first in his ideas about foreign policy. He was still manfully defending the action, and the Prime Minister, even in January 1957 when Eden's time was obviously running out. His constituency speeches argued that the government had realised the costs of Suez, but had also measured the costs of doing nothing. 'There was an urgent job to be done and the Government were aware that no one else was willing or capable of doing it. That was the real underlying reason for events in the Middle East.'[54] 'In intervening in the Middle East, we were doing for the rest of the world what the United Nations really should have done.'[55]

This defence of Suez has some uncanny contemporary echoes, given that the invasion of Iraq in 2003 was justified in terms of doing the UN's job for it; the Anglo-French-Israeli invasion was a kind of coalition of the willing when it came to tackling Egypt. The difference is that the USA were leading in 2003 but pulled the plug in 1956, and that Nasser, although autocratic, was no bloodthirsty dictator. Maudling's defence of Suez in the *Memoirs* concludes: 'I certainly believe it was a morally correct action. It was intended to protect Western interests in a way that was perfectly justifiable.'[56] For Maudling to talk about morals in connection with Suez is peculiar. He was always more comfortable in foreign affairs when talking of interests rather than principles, a common feature of members of the foreign policy establishment. There is a case to be made in terms of Western interests. It is much harder to see a moral case for the bombing and invasion of a foreign country for commercial and strategic reasons, still less to make a secret agreement with a third country to start a war and give us an opportunity to strike a hypocritical pose as peacemakers. Suez was one of those incidents, rare in Reggie's life but revealing of a strand in his character, where he displayed a capacity for brutality at a distance; saturation bombing in 1942–5, and incidents in Northern Ireland in 1970–2 have the same quality. His conscience was simply not particularly troubled by such things.

Maudling's one regret about Suez was that it took too long for the forces to arrive: 'if we could have acted more quickly and decisively, it probably would have been all right.' In other words, if the colluding parties had managed to present the world with a fait accompli they might have got away with it. This seems a wrong, as well as repellently cynical, judgement. An earlier invasion, which had managed to get further into Egypt and 'secure' the canal, even if militarily successful, would surely have encountered some guerrilla opposition and led to rising casualties. It could have been the start of Britain's Algeria or Vietnam. Even as it was, the Suez crisis was the start of a more aggressive strand of Arab nationalism and as Anthony Nutting wrote, 'By making Nasser a martyr and a hero, we had raised him to a pinnacle of power and prestige unknown in the Arab world since the beginning of the eighteenth century.'[57] Opposition within Britain would have been just as strong if the invasion had taken place in mid-October, and the French foreign minister, Pineau, listed the division of British public opinion as first among the factors that led to the operation being aborted.[58] Perhaps, as Reggie wrote, the Americans might not have put such pressure on the British and French had the invasion come earlier and not in the closing stages of a presidential election, but there would still have been ill consequences for Britain's financial and moral standing, Middle East politics and Eastern Europe – Soviet tanks rolled into Budapest under cover of the Suez operation. At least the lesson was over quickly, and the price was paid more in pride than blood.

The Eden government had two more months of existence after the Suez ceasefire. Like the proverbial headless chicken, it had sustained a fatal injury but staggered around in aimless motion for a short time afterwards. Another question over Maudling's attitude to Suez is his continued evident admiration for Eden throughout it all. Maudling seems to have been one of very few people who were determined to keep Eden. Most other observers recognised that Eden had developed an irrational fixation with Nasser early in the crisis and as events wore on his mental and physical health deteriorated alarmingly. His doctors advised him to take a complete rest and he flew to Ian Fleming's retreat at Goldeneye in Jamaica on 23 November. Meanwhile in Britain the economic situation continued to deteriorate; petrol rationing was introduced and on 3 December the Foreign Secretary, Selwyn Lloyd, announced the withdrawal of forces from Port Said and the arrival of a UN force to monitor the canal. If Eden insisted on staying on it was doubtful whether the government could survive. Reggie's agent, Arthur Fawcett, felt that further association with the humiliated government would serve no purpose:

> Personally I would like him to resign his ministerial office so that he is available in a few years' time to come in again as one of the party's leaders. However, he thinks we will be able to pull through without wrecking the party as it is . . . He agreed that the whole operation had been a failure but he thinks the UN can be trusted to deal with Nasser and establish an acceptable form of international control.[59]

Resignation would only have made sense for Maudling if it were part of the more general collapse of the government, given that he agreed with the policy and had been implicated in its execution. Reggie decided, as was his usual tendency, to hang on, but when Eden returned his health collapsed again and he could not continue long in office. His final breakdown came on 8 January 1957. Reggie attended the first Cabinet meeting of the day, at which the Prime Minister burst into tears. Reggie told a friend that it was like the Farewell Symphony – one by one the ministers quietly slipped away. Reggie as a junior was conscious of his rank and remained until he was one of the last to go. As he left he looked back, and Eden was there sobbing, with Harold Macmillan holding his hand.[60] Eden announced his resignation the next afternoon. Reggie, more than most people, was deeply saddened by Eden's departure.[61]

Reggie was not so sentimentally loyal to Eden as to fail to secure his position under the likely successors. Reggie's ambition at this stage was to be President of the Board of Trade, and he took both of the potential candidates to lunch in December 1956. He told the story to Michael Rice years later:

> He found it difficult to interrupt the flow when Rab was talking but he did manage to make his request. Rab carried on regardless and took no notice of what Reggie had said. A week later, Reggie took Harold Macmillan to lunch in the same place. Macmillan was very courteous and it did not take

too long to get to the point of putting in his bid for the Board of Trade in the event that Macmillan became Prime Minister. Macmillan said 'But of course, dear boy! The job's made for you, etc etc – but it won't happen. Rab will become Prime Minister; I am too old and frail . . .'[62]

Maudling might have seemed a natural Butler supporter because of his Treasury experience. He owed Butler a lot for having fostered his international financial career, and believed him to be the man to steer the party in the right direction, but was wary of him despite their intellectual agreement and mutual respect. He also knew that Butler was not popular among the Tory grass roots because of his image as being on the left. Reggie also felt that Rab 'gave the impression that he was lifting his skirt to avoid the dirt', and failing to take responsibility for Suez.[63] Maudling could also find positive things to say about Harold Macmillan, leaving aside the prospect of getting the job he really wanted. He said of Macmillan at the time that 'throughout his life he has been a very progressive minded person indeed'.[64] Maudling's insight into Macmillan's political views was more accurate than the conventional wisdom of the time, which was that Butler was the candidate of the left while Macmillan stood to the right. Reggie's own views were in harmony with the Macmillan of *The Middle Way*, his 1938 tract advocating economic intervention and the welfare state. Both men were instinctively in favour of an expansionist economic policy and domestic consensus. It seemed that Reggie leaned a little towards Macmillan in 1957, although this was far from certain, and he could retain a certain amount of ambivalence as Lord Salisbury's peremptory 'Wab or Hawold?' consultation extended only to the Cabinet. Maudling's election agent Arthur Fawcett recorded Reggie's initial feelings:

Whilst we were at the Barnet civic dinner this evening, news that Anthony Eden had resigned. Reggie Maudling came after Cabinet, he looked very tired. I had a brief word with him after dinner. To my surprise he referred to the remark I made to him at the Borehamwood dinner that I did not trust Butler in the present situation one inch. He thought that Macmillan would probably be sent for.[65]

Reggie had jumped the right way. While much of the press predicted that Butler would become Prime Minister, the choice was for Macmillan and the new Prime Minister took office on 10 January. Reggie welcomed the new regime, but when he went to see Macmillan he had a shock in store. Reggie capped the story of his lunch with Macmillan before he won the leadership by explaining, 'I got Paymaster General and I've never trusted him since!' With exquisite irony, Rab Butler's private notes suggest that he had intended to give Reggie the Board of Trade.[66]

Chapter 8

MINI-MINISTER OF
EVERYTHING, 1957–1959

Maudling's disappointment in January 1957, his first serious political setback, was of considerable importance to his life and career, and requires some examination. He had convinced himself that he would, at the very least, join the Cabinet and hopefully thought that Macmillan would deliver on his promise to make him President of the Board of Trade. Other observers wondered whether he might not leap straight into the Cabinet as Chancellor of the Exchequer. Reggie had been longing, with little subtlety, for a Cabinet post for several years.[1] All this made what Macmillan had to say a degrading shock, much as Reggie tried to make light of it. Macmillan's first thought was to leave him at Supply, as he was something of a spare piece in the initial reshuffle. Maudling had by now come to the conclusion that Supply was a foolish ministry that should be abolished, and he had no wish to continue in office there. Macmillan, on the other hand, had an almost mystical belief in its significance after his own experience in a junior role in the ministry in 1940–2.[2] After Maudling rejected Supply, he turned down Minister of Health: 'it was a field in which I had no experience and, quite frankly, no interest.'[3] It was also rather below his dignity, as Macleod had been appointed to that post in 1952 and to accept it would suggest that he was five years behind his rival's career. Maudling eventually ended up with the sinecure job of Paymaster-General. At least at Supply, he had his own department to command. Now this was taken away from him.

Reggie's own little attempt at manoeuvring himself into office had been outclassed by a master of the art. He should have known that Macmillan was a devious operator, and seen through his doddering old man routine, but Macmillan, having seemed to be one of the most bellicose ministers on Suez, turned tail shortly after the actual fighting started when the reserves drained out of the Bank of England. He scared the Cabinet with inaccurate figures and threatened to resign unless the action was stopped. 'First in, first out' commented Harold Wilson. Then, when Eden had retreated abroad and Butler was picking up the pieces as acting Prime Minister in London, Macmillan concentrated on rallying shaky Tory morale, particularly at an infamous 1922 Committee meeting.[4] 'The sheer devilry of it verged on the disgusting,' to the fastidious Enoch Powell,[5] but Reggie had not seemed all that bothered. Now he realised that he had been conned.

Reggie was cross enough to consider resigning but Macmillan appealed successfully to his loyalty and ambition. When Maudling agreed to take the post, Macmillan thanked him fulsomely and trailed the possibility that, as in 1952, he might take a seemingly undesirable job but parlay it to his advantage before the year was out. The full context for Macmillan's view of Maudling as clever, lazy and vain is in his diary entry for 3 February 1957 on that first reshuffle: 'He "goes down" nominally in the hierarchy. But he really is in the interesting part of the game. I hope he will do well. He is very clever; a little lazy; and a trifle vain. But I believe that if he buckles to he *will* do very well.'[6] Maudling and Macmillan were always polite to each other, with the less pleasant aspects of their relationship seeping out mostly in private comments. He later commented to Sandy Glen, without fully explaining what he meant, that Macmillan had 'sold his soul to the devil'. He felt in retrospect that the Tory party was not as safe in his hands as it would have been under Butler.[7] Macmillan, for his part, affected lofty disdain for Maudling's middle-class origins ('no background', he would sniff), despite his own dubious aristocratic credentials. Maudling – bouncy, rather too obviously happily married to someone who loved him – was also something of an affront to a Prime Minister inclined to depression with a dynastic marriage to an unfaithful alcoholic. Macmillan was also a 'good war' snob, and Maudling's Whitehall service was not quite the ticket. His respect for Maudling's cleverness was tinged with disdain.

Paymaster-General is one of several ministerial posts with few specific functions, in this case, not much beyond providing a specimen signature to appear on government payment orders. 'I don't pay anyone and I'm not master of anything,' Reggie grumbled in May.[8] Posts like this are used to get the occupants of non-ministerial positions like party chairman into the Cabinet, and to allow people to take responsibility for specific projects not directly related to a single government department. Rather unusually, Maudling's role as Paymaster-General was to deputise and speak in the House of Commons for a minister based in the House of Lords who had taken overall responsibility for fuel and power.

Sir Percy Mills was an early experiment in bringing business experience into government. He was a Macmillan crony who had worked with him at the Ministry of Housing to deliver his pledge of building 300,000 new houses a year in the early 1950s. Macmillan decided to bring him into the Cabinet in charge of the splendidly Orwellian Ministry of Power, and promptly gave him a peerage. Few of these experiments have proved entirely successful. Business leaders are unused to the constant questioning and challenging that goes with political power, and tend to lack the articulacy and street wisdom of the professional politician. So it was with Mills. 'Percy Mills certainly needed propping up,' according to an experienced civil servant. He was not entirely respected by his colleagues either. Quintin Hailsham wickedly observed that Mills was more suitable to open a debate than to wind up, as 'Percy's a muzzle loader' – you could cram the information into him and fire it off, but not expect him to do anything more complicated than that.[9]

Dealing with energy was hardly ever a good thing for a minister's career at the time; only Gaitskell had emerged in recent years with his reputation much enhanced. Speaking on the coal industry in the House of Commons was particularly risky, because Maudling faced a solid crew of Labour backbenchers from mining seats. Although the mining MPs were rarely great orators, and not renowned as intellectuals, there were many men among them who could speak with real experience and authority about the coal industry and who could easily trip up an arrogant Tory minister from the suburbs. Reggie's introduction to the mining side of his job came in a technical debate on the Coal Mining (Subsidence) Bill on 31 January 1957. Labour MP Harold Neal, Dennis Skinner's predecessor in the Derbyshire coalfield seat of Bolsover, gave Reggie a warm welcome:

> I am in some doubt as to whether courtesy requires me to congratulate the Paymaster General upon his entry to the field of Power or to commiserate with him on his demotion . . . We on this side have always had a profound respect for the right honourable Gentleman's superlative courtesy and his excellent ability in discussing affairs relating to economic and financial matters. Today, he has entered a new field of controversy and has successfully walked the tightrope between technicality and practical experience, so successfully indeed that he might almost have been mistaken for an authority on mining subsidence.[10]

Another mining Labour MP Maudling encountered in the coal debates of 1957–9 was the representative of the Normanton constituency in Yorkshire, Albert Roberts. As with many of them, Reggie remained on friendly terms for years afterwards, although his acquaintanceship with Roberts was more important than most in his own career.

Reggie acquired a deputising role over another part of the energy sector in March 1957, namely the civil nuclear power programme. Lord Salisbury, as part of his miscellany of responsibilities as Lord President of the Council, had been the ministerial overseer of the Atomic Energy Authority (AEA) since its creation in 1954. After his resignation Macmillan assumed Prime Ministerial control over nuclear power, but announced that Maudling would be assisting him.[11] The government had decided in 1955 to build nuclear power stations, fearing that the coal industry would not be able to accommodate anticipated rising demand for electricity and that oil-fired power stations could only be a short-term measure.[12] The vulnerability of oil supplies revealed by the Suez crisis added impetus to the drive for nuclear power, and the programme announced by Maudling in March 1957 was at the upper end of the menu of options given to the government by the Central Electricity Authority (CEA). It effectively trebled the 1955 programme.

Maudling himself bears only limited responsibility for the decision, which was the result of a review that began in October 1956, and for which he was understudy to Macmillan and Mills rather than a prime mover. Macmillan and Mills were both men who were attracted to big gestures and big projects, such as the housing programme, and nuclear power had a modern, futuristic feel to it. Independence from the goodwill of the National Union of Mineworkers and Arab oil producers was no doubt an added attraction. There was a clear sense of political will about nuclear power in the post-Suez period, exemplified by a speech made by Mills's predecessor, Aubrey Jones, in December 1956: 'the Government are anxious to move as far and as fast as we practically can in this matter. The whole national situation absolutely demands it.'[13] Maudling himself told a television interviewer in January 1957 that there should be an all-out drive to build power-generating resources through nuclear power.[14] It is, however, disingenuous for Maudling to claim as he did in his *Memoirs* that all the politicians did was essentially to ratify a technical decision.[15] This was true in so far as he did not feel able to intervene à la carte in the detail of the programme, but to decide between set menus is still a decision and Maudling was involved in it to some extent.

The early 1957 decision to build up nuclear power soon ran into problems. One was the Windscale accident in October 1957, in which a fierce fire consumed one of the generating piles and released a cloud of radioactive material over a large swathe of northern England and Ireland. Gallons of milk had to be poured down drains. It was the first ever major reactor accident, and although it was a military reactor producing plutonium it was still bad for business. It could have been worse. Macmillan, Lord Mills and, one must presume, Maudling as well decided that the report of the inquiry into the accident was better left unpublished.[16] Another problem was financial. Maudling himself conceded in the House, in his statement announcing the programme, that calculations on the costs of generating electricity using nuclear power were liable to 'a considerable margin of error in either direction'.[17] The error involved was, not surprisingly for a technologically intriguing project with political will behind it, in the optimistic direction. By 1959 it was clear that far from being roughly comparable with the cost of burning coal to generate electricity, it was significantly more expensive and the programme slowed down. As Reggie said of his time at the Ministry of Supply, the evil that men do lives after them, and even more than with Supply the consequences of Maudling's announcement in March 1957 are still with us in the form of colossal decommissioning costs, which nobody seems to have thought or cared much about in 1957.

There was injury to add to insult, in the form of a hefty pay cut. Reggie's ministerial salary fell by £2,000 (current value: nearly £29,000) to £3,000, plus a partial parliamentary salary. Maudling's financial embarrassment in January 1957 gave him a harsh education in the instability of the personal finances of the politician, who at the whim of the Prime Minister could suffer large pay cuts overnight with no measures to cushion the loss, even without being sacked. Losing a place in government, or seeing one's party lose office, would be even worse and the blow of a constituency defeat would be harshest of all. His downward move was an unpleasant bump in the road for his own family; he was always determined to provide the best he could for his wife and children and saw this duty to a large extent in financial terms. Demotion struck at the heart of Reggie's self-confidence and even his purpose in life.

An *Evening Standard* diary item based on an interview with Beryl commented that 'no economies in the Maudling household are envisaged as yet; for the Maudlings have some private means'.[18] The Maudlings were more capable of withstanding the financial blow at this time than earlier, as his mother had died in September 1956 and her estate was worth over £11,400 (2003 equivalent: over £165,000), which came to Reggie in December.[19] With her death, a cord that had been a restraint on Reggie's behaviour was snapped. His decision to go on holiday rather than attend her funeral was a final rejection of Elsie's puritanical harshness, and an embrace of Beryl, leisure and pleasure.

The Maudling household was rather grander in early 1957 than it had been a year previously. When Selwyn Lloyd, Reggie's predecessor at Supply, had become Foreign Secretary in December 1955 he acquired an official residence at Carlton Gardens, into which he moved in February 1956. The Lloyds left their imposing rented flat in Chester Street, Belgravia, and the Maudlings moved in. Chester Street was very close to Wilton Street, where Reggie had first worked at the Parliamentary Secretariat, and it was an area that Reggie and Beryl liked and regarded as prestigious. Lloyd's biographer signals Lloyd's arrival in Chester Street with the comment that it was the start of his 'grand' years,[20] and the same could be said for Reggie. Chester Street was large enough and close enough to Westminster to throw receptions and large dinner parties, and was a considerable step up. The Maudlings now had an impressive place in town as well as a rambling country house, and a more lasting solution to financial problems than consuming the capital from his legacy had to be found.

Fortunately for Maudling, the pay cut was temporary. In July 1957 Chancellor Peter Thorneycroft announced increases in pay for junior ministers of £750 for Ministers of State and £1,000 for lesser ministers. The move was welcomed from across the floor by Harold Wilson: 'What is being done for junior Ministers generally is something which has long been conceded as necessary and I am sure that none of us wants to see an able Member, in any party, feeling that he has to turn down junior ministerial office on grounds which we have reason to think have been all too familiar in the past.'[21] Although the January pay cut did not drive Maudling from public office it did leave him determined that he and his family should not again suffer from the vagaries of political life. As well as uncertain earnings, Reggie suffered from taxation complications during 1957, which transparently inspired a long article in *Truth* magazine in November, anticipating Reggie as a great tax-reforming Chancellor.[22]

At the end of July, Macmillan decided that the government needed a minister who could devote nearly all his energies to the complex problems of Britain's relationship with the emerging European Economic Community (EEC). In early August it was announced that this would be Reginald Maudling, given that the energy policy reviews were essentially over. The invitation came as a surprise to Reggie, although he accepted it with alacrity. He altered his travel plans for September to get on with the job and have meetings in The Hague and Paris.[23] The new role would be, at least officially, a coordinating one, representing the Prime Minister and the departmental ministers concerned. The announcement drew positive press coverage in Britain and mainland Europe, which pleased both Maudling and Macmillan.[24] In a small government reorganisation in September 1957 Macmillan decided that, given his European job, Maudling should now, at long last, enter Cabinet, which was good not only for Maudling's status (the *Daily Telegraph* hailed his 'restless energy and drive',[25] possibly for the last time) but also for his bank balance: now he was on a full Cabinet salary of £5,000 a year.

The situation Maudling faced in September 1957 resulted from earlier British miscalculations about what was happening in Europe. In 1951 the European Coal and Steel Community, a supranational agency, came into existence without British participation. The Foreign Office had expected little to emerge from the 1955 Messina conference, but the outcome was an agreement in principle between six states (France, West Germany, Italy and the Benelux countries) to have a common market in all products. Discussions moved quickly, and the scope of agreement widened to cover agriculture, transport and other heads of policy; again, British diplomats stood aloof from the discussions and were surprised by the outcome. In March 1957 the Six signed the Treaty of Rome creating the EEC with effect from January 1958.

Having stayed out of the creation of the EEC, the British nevertheless had to take an interest in this new entity. British trade policy had generally been focused on world organisations such as GATT, but as a condition of Marshall Aid in the late 1940s the Americans obliged Britain to join the Organisation for European Economic Co-Operation (OEEC), which in turn came to administer the Payments Union, and also had a general mission of promoting trade, reducing tariffs and looking into the possibility of creating a customs union or free trade area.[26] The Six creators of the EEC were also among the Seventeen members of the OEEC, and the issue of trade relations between the Six and the others needed to be addressed. The particular British problem was the existing network of trade agreements with the Commonwealth, which would have to be torn up if Britain joined a system with a common external tariff, but which Britain was reluctant to abandon for reasons of cheap food as well as sentiment. Britain wanted the best of both worlds – free trade in industrial goods with Europe, plus retaining Commonwealth preference on food and raw materials. It was not surprising that others were disinclined to concede this.

The initial British response to the Treaty of Rome, proposing vague parliamentary links to NATO, was widely seen as an attempt to torpedo the emergent EEC of Six and caused great suspicion of Britain. A more serious prospect was the revival of what had in 1956 been dubbed 'Plan G' – free trade in industrial goods within the Seventeen, but agriculture to remain separate. The idea now was that the Free Trade Area (FTA) would come into existence parallel to the creation of the EEC and contain all the OEEC countries. It was this enterprise Maudling was instructed to handle in August 1957, with as much media management as possible 'to build up Mr Maudling as the embodiment of a positive and forthcoming British policy towards Europe'.[27] At an OEEC ministerial meeting in October 1957 Maudling was given an international as well as British negotiating commission. The organisation, which contained ministers from the Six, expressed itself in favour of a trade agreement covering the seventeen countries and the 'Maudling committee' was formed to reach agreement.[28]

The essential problem with the Maudling mission was the mismatch between the scale of the issues and the means that were chosen to deal with them. Maudling's approach was essentially technical, as it had been perforce when he was dealing with the European Payments Union three years previously. The theory was that this was a trade agreement, and with enough goodwill, negotiation over points of detail, and concessions on either side, something acceptable if perhaps unduly complicated could be cobbled together. The reality was that the relationship between Britain and Europe needed to be sorted out on a grand level of principle, and all the talks about the appropriate tariff level for British goods manufactured using Australian materials and exported to Belgium could not resolve the issue.

Maudling cannot be entirely blamed for the failure to understand the nature of the European problem – the Treasury and Foreign Office were not greatly interested in the issue. As a junior member of Cabinet he was not empowered to take decisions of the scale that was necessary. Reggie had been instructed to build a bridge but he was only equipped with a bucket and spade to do it. With the best will in the world, it was not possible; and Britain had already exhausted large amounts of the available goodwill by dithering and attempting to dilute or sabotage the emerging European union.

The central issues of the FTA negotiations were disagreements between Britain and France. For Britain it was Commonwealth preference, particularly over food and raw materials, and political sovereignty. For France, the EEC project as it had developed since Messina was splendidly suited to their needs. A solid European trading bloc behind a high external tariff suited them very well, as did free trade in agricultural produce within the bloc. The Six were essentially under French political leadership; Chancellor Adenauer of West Germany was a Christian Democrat Rhinelander who saw a strong axis between Bonn and Paris as being essential to European peace and progress. Any deviation from existing plans centred on the Treaty of Rome was by the end of 1957 going to be a very difficult sell in Paris, especially if it involved any kind of special terms for Britain. Maudling had an almost impossible job, as he realised from the outset; he wrote to Eden's former Press Secretary, William Clark, that 'it certainly is going to be an interesting job that I have taken on and, at the worst, it will be an exciting death'.[29] If he failed, he would be tarred with that failure and lose his image as a 'success man'; if he succeeded, it would be at the cost of offending traditional Conservative feelings about kith and kin in the Commonwealth.

While he was preparing for his European mission, Maudling was also giving some thought to his personal finances after the year's fluctuations in his income and the legacy from his mother. His decisions at this time ran up against the boundaries of acceptable conduct for ministers. Acting on advice from Freddie Bennett, who remained his PPS and made the introductions and recommendations, he became an underwriting, non-working 'Name' at Lloyd's.[30] Membership in those years was very restricted; it rose gradually in the two decades after 1945 from under 2,500 Names to 6,500 and still had something of the quality of a social register. The ability to subscribe sufficient capital to join kept membership exclusive, and even with Essendon, the legacy and family shareholdings Maudling must have been a marginal case when he joined. In return for a nominal investment, Lloyd's on average produced a healthy return, and any loss-making years could be set against the highest rate of tax, so it was a very attractive investment for Maudling.[31]

There had been several previous cases of MPs and peers who were already Lloyd's members taking office, such as Lord Leathers in 1941, and in general it was tolerated as not being sufficiently specific an outside interest to worry about, as long as their involvement was kept passive. There were several more cases when the Conservatives returned to power in 1951 and the whole subject was reviewed. The government decided in 1952 that inactive membership was permitted for all ministers except the Chancellor of the Exchequer, the President of the Board of Trade and the Minister of Transport, because their ministerial responsibilities were close enough to be regarded as being a more direct conflict of interest. Maudling was in line with the letter of these rules by becoming a Name in December 1957 as Paymaster-General, but there were three ways in which his action was open to criticism.

The first problem was simply that when the rules had been drawn up nobody had imagined that a serving minister would conceive of joining Lloyd's. Once again, Maudling had spotted a loophole in the regulations and exploited it, as he had with his scholarships to College and the Middle Temple. More seriously, Maudling had breached the rules that applied in 1957 in the way that he did it. He did not bother to tell Macmillan, Number 10 or the Cabinet Office and the civil servants who monitored these things only found out when it was noted in *The Times*.[32] The government had decided this issue in 1955 when a minister, Harmar Nicholls, was in the process of joining Lloyd's when he was appointed. Nicholls was allowed to join because of the circumstances, but it was ruled that:

> While we find it hard to explain just why, we feel that there is something rather inappropriate in the idea of a Minister becoming a 'name' at Lloyd's for the first time during his period of office . . . we do not think that there is any Ministerial authority for the doctrine that there is no objection to a Minister becoming a 'name' for the first time during his period of office. Similar cases in future should not be approved without further consideration by Ministers.[33]

It was agreed that any future cases should be referred to the Prime Minister for adjudication, with some presumption that a 'more restrictive practice' would follow. Number 10 were concerned that it was not only an outside interest but there was also the possibility that ministers might use their positions to gain favourable treatment from syndicates.[34] Maudling did not. The precedent of the Nicholls case, and the rules established then, were rather conveniently forgotten when Maudling's case came up in 1957 and he was only given an informal reprimand from Macmillan.

The third problem was noted at the time by the Cabinet Secretary, Norman Brook, but escaped general attention. Maudling's European responsibilities arguably put him in a different category with a more direct conflict of interest arising from Lloyd's membership: 'It is perhaps an additional complication that British insurance companies stand to benefit from the Free Trade Area negotiations.'[35] There is no evidence that Maudling acted in any way to further his financial interests during the European negotiation, and Lloyd's was probably the last thing on his mind as he shuttled around Europe in 1957 and 1958. This noted, Freddie Bennett rather irregularly accompanied him on several visits in connection with the European negotiations at official expense in late 1957.[36] The 1957 Lloyd's affair was hardly being seen to be pure, and in a more restrictive climate, such as that operating forty years later, Maudling's actions could have got him and the government into serious trouble. But in 1957 Maudling had shown that he could ignore a ministerial guideline and get away with it. There were not even any Parliamentary Questions.

While the European negotiations were under way, a political crisis in Britain gave Maudling even more work to do in January 1958. Chancellor Peter Thorneycroft and his two junior ministers, Nigel Birch and Enoch Powell, resigned in protest against rising public expenditure in what Macmillan famously called a 'little local difficulty'. Thorneycroft had been insisting on cuts in welfare in particular, and proposed abolishing family allowances for second children and raising prescription charges. Macmillan had no intention of allowing him to do this, and the Treasury position attracted little support in Cabinet, only Reggie speaking in favour of doing away with the family allowance.[37] It was a smaller-scale Tory version of the 1951 crisis in which Bevan had resigned over similar issues, except this time the resigning ministers were in favour of the cuts and the rest of the government opposed them. Unlike the Bevan crisis, it did not lead to a lasting split in the party. The proto-monetarist economic ideas of the Thorneycroft Treasury remained a minority heresy, stamped on by official pronouncements such as the Radcliffe Report, for another fifteen years. Maudling's uncharacteristically hard line on spending during the 'little local difficulty' may have been influenced by his hopes of promotion in the event of the Chancellor resigning; he would be in a better position if he came with a reputation for toughness and loyalty to the previous incumbent. But Reggie was passed over and the mild, unambitious Derick Heathcoat-Amory became Chancellor.

However, Reggie was not unaffected by the 'little local difficulty'. Strangely, no Economic Secretary was appointed to replace Nigel Birch, and Reggie, already notionally a Treasury minister as Paymaster-General, was asked to take over most of the position's responsibilities for an interim period. A Treasury note at the time detailed that Heathcoat-Amory had talked and:

2. it was agreed that Mr Maudling would take the parliamentary work, including the Parliamentary Questions, which would normally fall within the Economic Secretary's sphere.
3. Mr Maudling will take the papers which normally went to the last Economic Secretary for an experimental period, but with some relaxation as far as Capital Issues Committee papers are concerned.
4. Mr Maudling will receive copies of submissions to the Chancellor on major questions.
5. Mr Maudling will be kept informed of the Chancellor's engagements and of any meetings in which he might be interested.
6. The office of the Economic Secretary will be kept open and manned in the Treasury.
7. The Financial Secretary has agreed to take all deputations from trades unions and organisations in connection with the 1958 Budget.
8. These arrangements are provisional and are subject to review in a few weeks' time.[38]

The provisional arrangements in fact remained in place until late October 1958, when Freddie Erroll was appointed to fill the Economic Secretary vacancy. With Europe as well, Reggie was riding three horses at once. Two Labour MPs expressed concern in March 1958 about his workload,[39] but

Reggie found it all well within his capabilities; he never lost the taste for trying to do several things at the same time. Reggie was, for most of 1958, in the unusual position of being a power behind the throne at two completely different departments, Power and the Treasury, each under a chief with a reputation for being pleasant and methodical but short on inspiration and perhaps also on brain power. Heathcoat-Amory frequently consulted Maudling about policy. Government Economic Adviser Robert Hall noted in his diary in March 1958:

> The Chancellor has a habit of collecting people, quite often [Roger] Makins, me and Maudling, quite late in the day and sitting on indefinitely, long after others want to get back to their work or go to dinner. He seems to be quite unaware of any engagements others may have though he is the soul of politeness when his attention is called to it.[40]

Although this could have been infuriating for Reggie, with a young family (Edward was born in October 1954 and William in March 1957) and a social life, it was impossible to take against Heathcoat-Amory and Reggie regarded him affectionately. After the rigours of Thorneycroft, government economic policy moved more towards expansion, with the cautious 1958 Budget setting the scene for a more generous effort in 1959. This was in line with Reggie's instincts, but he was not one of the most insistent voices for expansion – Macmillan was strongly of that opinion for electoral and other reasons, and he was urged on by Lord Mills, who – erroneously – feared a slump, and Roy Harrod, both of whom had Macmillan's ear. Maudling was there to give Heathcoat-Amory general advice and explain technicalities, and also handle the sort of parliamentary business for which the unassuming Chancellor was ill-equipped.

One such incident came among Maudling's first parliamentary appearances for the Treasury. In February 1958 the Commons debated the report of the Tribunal of Inquiry into the 'Bank Rate' affair. This had started in September 1957, when Thorneycroft had raised interest rates by 2 per cent (to 7 per cent) in a deliberately dramatic move to damp down a sterling crisis. When interest rates rise, the price of government fixed-interest gilts falls and just before the September 1957 increase there had been some fishy ('inspired' noted the press at the time) trades in which gilts had been offloaded. Rumours were rife that the decision had been leaked, and the finger was pointed at a political source for the leak; Lord Poole, the party's deputy chairman, was suspected. Harold Wilson as Shadow Chancellor made the most of the affair, and as a result an official tribunal was appointed, chaired by Lord Parker, but when it reported it dismissed the alleged political connection and cleared Poole.

When the Parker Report came to the Commons to be debated, Conservative MPs were in angry mood and Macmillan had given instructions that Labour and Wilson should suffer 'the maximum political punishment' for what in truth had been unsupportable innuendo against Poole.[41] It was a rowdy and bitter debate; Wilson came out battling and turned a potential disaster into a rallying attack on the way business was done in the City. Maudling wound up for the government, facing determined heckling and repeated points of order, defending the honour of the City and accusing Wilson of 'performing a Socialist ritual of a very atavistic kind' in attacking business. Reggie indignantly denounced Wilson for failing to apologise to Poole and called his conduct 'deplorable'.[42]

Bank Rate did Maudling nothing but good – he was himself indignant about the allegations against Poole and took the opportunity to show some fighting spirit to Tory MPs. His stout defence of the City did not go unnoticed either; Wilson's hostility had made him a marked man as far as many bankers were concerned,[43] and conversely Maudling had reaffirmed his credentials as a man of the City. It was itself a less than perfect example of avoiding apparent conflicts of interest, given Reggie's recent recruitment to Lloyd's. In the light of later knowledge about the extent of insider dealing and the propensity of official reports to whitewash uncomfortable matters, the Bank Rate case does not seem as open-and-shut an acquittal as it did in 1958. Maudling refused to state in his speech whether any of the firms with advisory members on the Bank of England's Court had sold gilts at the relevant time. Wilson, in extricating himself from trouble, pointed to the evidence in the Parker Report that showed that there was an uncomfortably small and incestuous network, consolidated through grouse shoots and the old school tie, that ran the City. There were so many points at which leaks could take place that it was nearly impossible to imagine that it had not happened from time to time. Paul Ferris, writing a few years later about the City, pointed out that even in the Parker Report the possibility of 'individual cases in which dealings were prompted by the improper use or disclosure of confidential information' was not ruled out.[44]

Meanwhile, Maudling was involved in his complicated attempt to come to a European free trade agreement. Maudling's negotiations reflected, and in all fairness tended to confirm, his initial feelings. According to his friend Sandy Glen, himself an experienced businessman: 'His attitudes to other Europeans were rather traditional English prejudices – that the Norwegians, Swedes and Danes were all right and pretty much like us, that Germans should be approached with caution but the French were both clever and nasty.'[45] Reggie liked the Scandinavian ministers, some of whom he had met in his 1954 visit, and enjoyed long, happy dinners with them. His principal diplomatic service adviser on European negotiations, John Coulson, was also a man with an affinity for Scandinavia in general and Sweden in particular. Reggie also warmed to the Austrian Chancellor, Julius Raab. An appealing passage in his *Memoirs* records a brief, successful chat in Vienna, which ended with Raab asking him, 'Mr Maudling, do you like sausages and beer?' The answer, of course, was 'Yes', and Reggie joined Raab for a reception for a visiting oompah band from the Chancellor's constituency.[46]

Reggie also found considerable although ineffective support for some of his ideas at a lower level among the rest of the Six. He got on well with the Dutch, and although German Chancellor Adenauer was tightly bound into the alliance with France, his Economics Minister, Ludwig Erhard, was more of a free trader. Maudling always suspected that Erhard would have liked to reach agreement on a large FTA in Europe. Some Germans were also sympathetic to arguments about the undesirability of dividing Western Europe economically and politically. Guido Carli, the Italian representative on the Maudling committee, was particularly helpful in March 1958. The 'Carli plan' proposed to retain internal tariffs on goods sourced from outside with preferential agreements with one country, and in principle seemed a promising way to square the circle, but after exhaustive investigation it proved complicated and probably impossible to administer.

While Maudling did find chinks in the armour of the Six, it was unrealistic to hope that he, or indeed any British effort, could detach the other five from France and his efforts to do so only led to resentment.[47] For them, it was an unacceptable political risk to abandon the solid prospect of the EEC as it stood to erect a contrived structure on the urgings of the British – whose attention was still basically elsewhere, in the Commonwealth or the relationship with the USA. There was no alternative, if the FTA project was to go ahead, to doing a deal with the EEC through the French.

In contrast to his warm feelings about Erhard and Carli, Maudling did not take to Walter Hallstein, the first President of the European Commission, whom he found cold and formal; Hallstein once pompously rebuked Reggie for referring to him as 'Doctor' rather than 'Professor'.[48] Maudling felt with some justice that French tactics were all about throwing up obstacles, and that, as Sellar and Yeatman said of the Irish Question, they would secretly change the Question every time he was getting warm. Having persuaded the British government, in response to a French negotiating point, to relax its insistence on unanimity in the new institution, he came back to find that France was now adamant on just that point. Reggie found his equanimity under severe strain at moments like that. He was unable to make any headway on the French insistence that agriculture should come under the free trade agreement, and unable to offer an acceptable formula that would allow an agriculture deal.[49]

Prospects for an agreement had been dim before May 1958, but they became nearly invisible at that point. No negotiations took place between March and late July as a result of the political crisis in France. The previous French government had been committed to the Treaty of Rome and uncooperative with projects that seemed to threaten it, but the new regime of Charles De Gaulle was more nationalist and protectionist, as well as more decisive. The Maudling committee trundled on, producing detailed studies about the impact of external tariffs and agriculture,[50] and the EEC still as a body endorsed a general trade agreement in a position paper known as the Ockrent Report published in October. Maudling gave more and more ground, offering to go along with the French idea of sector-by-sector agreements that would have produced a system of baroque complexity.[51] However, alternatives clearly had to be considered; in any case, there was now little prospect of any sort of agreement before the EEC tariff arrangements started in January 1959. Maudling spoke in October at Baden-Baden and stated that in the absence of agreement Britain would have to take some sort of unspecified defensive action in 1959. In November 1958 he revealed some of his personal feelings about the negotiations that, contrary to his expectation in September 1957, had proved to be a boring, lingering death rather than an exciting one: 'these negotiations have dragged on a weary, disappointing and almost unconscionable time.'[52]

They did not do so for much longer. The project of an overall European free trade agreement embracing the Six and the outer countries finally crashed two days after Maudling's comments in the House. On 13 November Jacques Soustelle, De Gaulle's Minister of Information, announced that it would not be possible to form a free trade area without a common external tariff and economic and social harmonisation. Two days later at an OEEC meeting David Eccles kicked over the traces with a bad-tempered attack on the French foreign minister.[53] The Maudling committee's activities were suspended and it never met again. At first, Reggie tried to deny that this was the end, and in December he and Erhard met in London to try to revive the FTA process. But in February 1959 Maudling and Hallstein read the official last rites.

Opinions about Reggie's culpability for the collapse varied at the time. An American diplomat reporting in November 1958 found Louis Joxe of France claiming that 'the basic reason for the current impasse was the rigidity and negotiating inadequacies of Mr Maulding, the British Postmaster-General [sic]', Ernst van der Beugel, from the foreign office of the Netherlands, thought that Reggie 'had exhibited a very high degree of patience and skill during the past 18 months of frustrating negotiations with the French'.[54] Maudling can be criticised for failing to do enough to reassure the Six that Britain had moved away from its dog-in-the-manger attitude to European unity that was so apparent in 1955–7, and for sticking too rigidly to his brief during his initial discussions in autumn 1957, for a lack of subtlety in working on fault-lines within the Six and for giving the impression that the EEC Commission and Hallstein were not important.[55] But even if he had played all his cards to maximum effect, it is doubtful whether he could have brought off an agreement.

The failure of the FTA project had lessons for the future of the debate about Britain and Europe. It was an attempt to build in, right from the start, a two-speed Europe, which involved a programme of economic and political union for the core countries and a looser form of economic association for the outer countries. From the perspective of the Six, it is easy to see that it had little to offer. Why should trading concessions be given away to the outer countries without the economic and social safeguards that had been elaborately agreed within the Six? While a system along Carli lines could, albeit with difficulty, cover the manufacturing process from start to finish, how could it deal with the less tangible inputs in the form of cheap food or indeed social factors? What is 'free trade' and what amounts to a level playing field? The EEC in 1959 argued, and even such a non-federal organisation as EFTA found it to be true, that a Free Trade institution sets up its own momentum that leads to the acceptance of common practices in matters such as product standards, external tariffs, labour law, regional adjustment funds, and central executive and judicial authorities.[56] There was no need for, and in fact no long-term way of sustaining, anything between an integrated common market on a regional level and a world system of free trade that would in effect be dominated by the United States. It was an uncharacteristic error of Reggie to forget that the economic is at root political.

If, somehow – by a show of goodwill and humility that was beyond any British politician at the time – Maudling and Macmillan had managed to agree a European Free Trade Area of the Seventeen before De Gaulle came to power, perhaps European issues might have remained at a technical level and not led to the kind of divisions that wracked Labour in the 1970s and the Tories in the 1990s. It was the last chance before Europe became a big issue; that if there had been a middle ground between 'in' and 'out' the issue would have bored all but the most dedicated enthusiasts in a morass of detail about certificates of origin and regional aid, rather than polarising the debate. Perhaps if the FTA had been allowed to develop for a while back then, fewer in Britain would now be inclined to imagine that it was an uncomplicated business that offered the best of both worlds. But the core issue would still have to be faced at some point, and there was no way of doing it entirely painlessly. The Maudling committee was an attempt to please everyone in Britain, and its failure should have been sufficient demonstration that this could not be done in the real world where the EEC was already in existence.

The government published an account of the negotiations and its aspirations for further progress on free trade in White Papers in January 1959.[57] The detail of the Maudling committee negotiations had been confidential while they had been going on, and Reggie had been criticised in the House for giving so little away about them, but there was an opportunity for a debate in February 1959 to discuss the issues. Reggie, most unusually, both opened and wound up the debate, as David Eccles, the President of the Board of Trade, was too ill to wind up as intended. Reggie's speech was notable for its rather Euro-sceptical tone, and Douglas Jay, a redoubtable Labour anti-European, said later that the Maudling speech alerted him to 'the full economic dangers' of EEC membership.[58] Maudling spelt out the problems of the negotiations, principally the complex arrangements necessary if a free trade area was to exist without a common external tariff. The idea of joining the EEC was put to him, and he objected on several grounds: Britain's trading policy would be determined by majority voting in Europe, which accounted for well under a quarter of Britain's trade; that Commonwealth free entry would be a casualty of the common external tariff; and that the consequences would be unacceptable for farmers and involve intervention in industrial relations questions that in Britain were left to employers and unions. There was also the political dimension:

> The whole idea of the Six, the Coal and Steel Community and Euratom is a movement towards political integration. That is a fine aspiration, but we must recognise that for us to sign the Treaty of Rome would be to accept as the ultimate goal, political federation in Europe, including ourselves. That, as I have said, does not seem to me to be a proposition which, at the moment, commands majority support in the country.[59]

It was a practical though unimaginative speech, which tried to claim – as politicians tended to at the time – that there was no contradiction between the Commonwealth and 'Europe'. Maudling, however, stressed the economic objections over the political ones; at another point in his speech he praised the effort to 'increase, sustain and strengthen European sentiment in British public opinion. I believe that to be a good thing, but it is still a delicate plant.'[60] What his remarks about federation suggest is that if public opinion did come round to share that goal, then it might at some point be acceptable to sign up for it, but that the government should not make such a commitment in advance of public opinion. But, in the circumstances of the time, the Commonwealth and economic arguments were crucial for Maudling. Since his brief intoxication with Churchill's vague vision of a United Europe in the late 1940s, Maudling had lost the ability to feel idealistic about international affairs, and could not understand the almost magical hopes vested in the EEC.[61] He was also, privately, heartily sick of the process of negotiating with Hallstein and the French and wanted nothing more to do with it. Edward Boyle and William Barnes, Reggie's Private Secretary at his next job, both recalled Maudling's 'passionate hatred of the EEC',[62] which suggests the emotional rather than material root of his Euro-scepticism and the possibility that in different circumstances the objection might not apply.

With the collapse of the negotiations in Paris in November 1958, Reggie had sought solace in a characteristic fashion. He repaired to a Paris restaurant with three Scandinavian trade ministers for lunch, at which the idea of going it alone and setting up a free trade area among the outer countries was raised.[63] There were no immediate results, although confidential talks at civil service level began and it was announced in March 1959 that the proposal was under discussion. The formation of what became the European Free Trade Association (EFTA) followed rapidly during 1959.

The Seven met at Saltsjobaden in Sweden in June 1959 and the negotiations
were quickly concluded, although the signing of a Treaty did not take place
until after the October 1959 general election in Britain.

In March 1957 Reggie told Arthur Fawcett that he had little hope of the
Conservatives winning the next election[64] and even Macmillan was not sure
he would have more than a few weeks in power. These initial fears were not
realised, but the Tories had a wretched time for much of 1957 and 1958.
After the Suez fiasco came public divisions in the party, with the resignations
of Lord Salisbury in 1957 and the Treasury ministers in 1958, and an
unpleasant spell in the economic doldrums that made Macmillan's boast that
'most of our people have never had it so good' seem somewhat hollow. The
idea of the Tories winning the next election on prosperity seemed fanciful for
much of the 1955–9 Parliament, but in autumn 1958 things started to turn
around and the 1959 Budget was something of a give-away. Reggie wound
up the budget debate on 8 April, commending the proposals as 'a very
powerful stimulus indeed to the economy'.[65] He also commended the spread
of consumer goods, like televisions, that was so changing everyday life in the
late 1950s. Labour sometimes gave the impression in this period of
disapproving of consumer spending and improving living standards, while the
Conservatives could address these aspirations. Gradually the party-political
tables were turned and it came as no great surprise when Harold Macmillan
called an election for October 1959 with considerable grounds for optimism
about the result.

Maudling's national role had increased again with his Cabinet status, and
he spent an even greater proportion of the campaign out of Barnet than he
did in 1955. The European issue was not a matter of much partisan opinion,
and Reggie said little about it, although Freddie Bennett lashed the Liberal MP
for Torrington, Mark Bonham Carter, in one speech, for supporting British
entry.[66] However, as an economic minister Reggie played a part in the central
debate of the election campaign, the ability of Gaitskell's Labour Party to pay
for its promises. How could the improvements in public services and social
security be paid for, other than through tax increases? Gaitskell disclaimed
any intention to raise taxes, and talked instead about a crackdown on
expenses fiddles and tax dodges. Maudling spoke to the effect that tax fiddles
were not confined to business fat cats: 'How much casual decorating work, for
example, is done at the week-ends and paid for in cash that never reaches the
ears of the Inland Revenue? Will Mr. Gaitskell set his blood-hounds after all
these people too?' The *Daily Sketch*, a shameless Tory propaganda rag,
followed this up with a scare story about 'Odd Job Gestapo if Labour Wins'.[67]
While more traditional Tories such as Derick Heathcoat-Amory claimed
complacently that British taxpayers were the most honest in the world, Reggie
responded with a more realistic but somewhat grubby appeal to the public to
identify with tax evaders. But the central Labour promise was to raise growth,
so that revenue would flow in without tax rates rising, but this was widely

disbelieved as being essentially something for nothing. However, Maudling himself managed to spend more than Gaitskell had promised without raising taxes, and within three years was talking about planning as a mechanism to achieve a higher rate of growth.

Unlike the national contest, the Barnet campaign was a quiet business. It was a straight fight again between Reggie and Labour. Labour started off badly when their prospective candidate, Cyril Bibby, had to give up because he was offered a job in Hull, although his replacement, Roy Prideaux, was equal to the occasion and put Labour's case well at public meetings.[68] Compared to 1951 and 1955 there was a lack of needle in the Barnet contest, although the higher national temperature brought out more Conservative workers. Reggie had to write over a thousand letters of thanks after the election, compared to around eight hundred in 1955, but as ever his greatest debt was to Arthur Fawcett, whose overwork had contributed to a heart attack earlier in the year. As Maudling rose up the ministerial ladder and grew more bored with constituency routine, Fawcett increasingly took over constituency work and Reggie felt a pang of guilt about how he had let the burden pile up on his willing agent.[69] During the 1955–9 Parliament Reggie suffered more serious criticism than before about his failure to show due respect to his constituency activists, particularly his tendency to appear as briefly as possible at local party functions.[70]

Electorate		64,739		
Turnout			81.7	
Reginald Maudling	Conservative	33,136	62.7	+1.9
Roy Prideaux	Labour	19,737	37.3	−1.9
Conservative majority		13,399	25.3	+3.8

Despite the small local groundswell of grumbles, and the exciting national campaign, the outcome of the election nationally and in Barnet was an unexpectedly emphatic Conservative victory. Maudling had, for the third election in a row, beaten the national trend with a swing of 1.9 per cent compared to 1.1 per cent nationally. His increased majority was particularly noteworthy as Borehamwood had provided the bulk of the 3,500 extra electors since 1955 and these were expected to be mainly Labour supporters. The 1959 election confirmed Barnet as a safe Tory seat, which despite the addition of the working-class estates of Borehamwood, had swung to the Tories by double the national average over the years since 1945. Party organisation across the country had declined over the past ten years, but Barnet's Tories remained a formidable campaigning machine.[71]

Nationally, the Conservative majority was hoisted to 100. To the victors went the spoils. In the post-election reshuffle Reggie Maudling at last became President of the Board of Trade.

Chapter 9

TRADING UP, 1959–1961

Maudling finally got his due for his work in the European negotiations when he was promoted to President of the Board of Trade. It was, after his 1955–7 spell in what he and many others believed was a joke ministry and his 1957–9 period as jack-of-all-trades, a serious departmental job at last. It was one of the largest ministries in government, with wide responsibilities over industrial regulation, foreign trade, a certain amount of regional policy and competition policy. It was not the Treasury, which was Reggie's real ambition at this time, but it gave him an opportunity to involve himself in economic policy and understudy for the role of Chancellor of the Exchequer. Reggie's overriding mission in 1959–61 was to promote exports, as he announced in the Queen's Speech debate in October 1959: 'I am sure that the expansion of export trade is the first objective of an economics Minister.'[1]

Maudling's Minister of State was Freddy Erroll, the genial Tory MP for Altrincham who had been his Parliamentary Secretary at the Ministry of Supply until November 1956. Maudling and Erroll quickly became good friends; Erroll was a kindred spirit socially who enjoyed holidays in the sun, eating, drinking and half-heartedly working off the effects in a game of tennis. Maudling joked that they were the heaviest ministerial team in government, weighing in at 35 stone between them and when they played tennis together in Cadogan Gardens 'the earth shook as we trundled from side to side, and small children and animals using the garden were known to take fright and flee'.[2] They also saw eye to eye politically. Erroll was if anything even keener on promoting exports than Maudling, and wrote the slogan 'Exporting is Fun!' into the press release of one of Macmillan's speeches in 1960, although the Prime Minister baulked at actually uttering the sound bite.[3]

Reggie was always able and willing to delegate his work to junior ministers and only step in when they ran into trouble. Erroll was a godsend. As well as being agreeable he could cope with detail. At the Board of Trade he gave Erroll a free hand over the complex trade treaty with Japan that was under negotiation; Erroll's role in the treaty was recognised when he was allowed, against protocol, to be one of the signatories in November 1962.[4] However, despite Erroll's abilities as a junior minister he was not really cut out for higher office and was over-promoted when he became President of the Board of Trade in October 1961 after Maudling moved on. His time in charge was a trough in the reputation and effectiveness of the ministry between two strong ministers, Maudling (1959–61) and Heath (1963–4). Erroll's over-promotion was largely through Reggie's own machinations. Reggie lost no opportunity to press Erroll's case with Macmillan, no doubt with sincere regard for his friend in mind, but also to prevent any competitors, such as Macleod or Heath, from gaining experience of economic policy and emerging as rivals for the position of Chancellor.[5]

Macmillan, unlike Maudling, did not have much faith in EFTA and the attempt to construct something from the ruins of the FTA talks. He looked for an alternative, and considered some fairly wild ideas. In October 1959 just after the election he sent a minute to Maudling: 'What do you think of GATT? I know the Americans always cheat where their interests are concerned. Some people feel that on the whole we do better without all the various GATT agreements. Do you share this view?'[6] The General Agreement on Tariffs and Trade (GATT) was the cornerstone of the postwar world trading system, and a safeguard against the competitive tariff barriers that had damaged trade in the inter-war period. A British repudiation of GATT would have been an unbelievably radical step, particularly if undertaken in an anti-American frame of mind without any specific alternative in view. Maudling stamped on the suggestion, starting with an echo of Butler's famous remark about Eden:

> The GATT is the best set of international trading rules that we have, and we should be unwise to get rid of it until we can see something better to put in its place. By and large we need the things we import more, or more urgently, than our customers need the things we export. We must have food and raw materials day in and day out. They can postpone the purchase of bicycles, motor cars, textiles or sewing machines. So I deduce that any contraction of international trade does us more damage than it does to other countries. Our aim must be the expansion of international trade and this implies the removal of barriers to that trade.

Reggie warned that such a move would alienate not only the Americans but the Commonwealth, and that while the Americans did cheat a bit, countries did not like to break the rules too blatantly. Macmillan may only have been playing devil's advocate, but he found Maudling's minute on GATT so convincing that he wanted to circulate it as a Cabinet paper straight away until Maudling persuaded him not to.[7] It was a sign that Macmillan had come to respect and rely upon Maudling's judgement, but the European issue still divided them.

There was a provisional air to the European trade arrangements that had been set up in 1959. Reggie took responsibility for Europe with him when he moved from Paymaster-General to Board of Trade. He moved a few weeks before the signature of the European Free Trade Association (EFTA) convention in Stockholm in November 1959. Seven countries (Britain, Sweden, Norway, Denmark, Austria, Switzerland and Portugal) signed, and with the Six EEC countries Europe was now, as headline writers loved to say, at Sixes and Sevens. The concluding negotiations on EFTA were rapid because EFTA was able to draw heavily on the work of the Maudling committee on creating a Free Trade Area covering all the OEEC countries. The EFTA of the Seven remained a small, British-dominated trading entity separate from the EEC until an overall free trade agreement between the two blocs was made in July 1972. By then, of course, Britain had decided on full membership of the EEC.[8] EFTA did some good for Britain, being the one identifiable area in which Britain's share of the market rose between 1959 and 1965, with the EFTA markets being significant for British manufacturing and chemicals, and it did no harm despite the fears at the time of the Stockholm treaty and the 1960 rebuff that it would create a rigid division into two trading blocs.[9]

EFTA was an acknowledged second-best to a trade agreement encompassing all of Western Europe. Maudling's rationale for it, expressed in the House of Commons and to Douglas Dillon of the US State Department in December 1959, was that it stopped further fragmentation and would provide a better platform for trade negotiations with the Six than could be arranged by each member country acting separately. But this proved a vain hope. In May 1960 the Seven, under the guidance of Maudling who had not given up on the idea of a wider free trade pact, approached the Six with the offer of negotiations on a trade agreement. Within a month, the EEC rebuffed the offer and stated plainly that there was no future in the OEEC as an economic area. The EEC, particularly France whose European negotiator Robert Marjolin had resigned as Secretary-General of the organisation to pursue the Messina project, believed the organisation had outlived its usefulness. In 1961 it transmogrified into the Organisation for Economic Cooperation and Development (OECD), taking in non-European members and becoming a vehicle for general cooperation and research.

Maudling's hostility to the EEC was at its most determined in 1959–60, particularly in the Commons debate on the EFTA treaty in December 1959. He referred to the EFTA Treaty as a second-best outcome, and when a Liberal MP asked whether joining the EEC would be the best or the worst, he replied 'The best answer I can give to the hon. Gentleman is that it would be the third-best. At the moment I am concerned only with the second-best.'[10] This offhand comment was most revealing of Maudling's attitude at the time to Europe. In his prepared speech he said that 'we have responsibilities going far beyond the confines of Western Europe alone', and implicitly criticised the EEC as favouring the interests of rich countries over poor: 'Could it make sense, in world terms, to begin putting duties on raw materials, in particular, putting duties on raw materials coming from the so-called underdeveloped countries? I can think of no more retrograde step, economically or politically.'[11] The last sentence is sometimes quoted against Maudling. While he did have a sentimental attachment to the Commonwealth as a geopolitical and economic institution and an inflated view of Britain's place in the world, like many politicians of his time, this comment was not a mere reflex. He was genuinely and increasingly concerned at this time about world poverty, and was actually talking about the effect of depriving poor countries of markets for their products. It was a real drawback to the idea of Europe as a protectionist bloc, which was recognised and addressed by the expanded EC in 1975 with the Lomé convention.

However reasonable a case Maudling made, it did not reflect the emerging realities. The idea that the Commonwealth would remain as it was for ever – with Britain importing raw materials and exporting manufactured goods and services – could not be sustained. The other states, particularly newly independent former colonies, were intending to develop their own industries. Of more immediate concern was the attitude of the United States. The Americans had always been willing to tolerate a measure of discrimination against their own products, in the greater interest of promoting peace and growth in Europe. This was why they had fostered the European Payments Union and OEEC, given more than they received from GATT and also looked with favour on the EEC. But from Washington the Maudling dream of an FTA without much political superstructure spanning Europe and roping in the Commonwealth looked like a design to cut them out. Dillon told Maudling in December 1959 that the Americans would not be willing to support it, in a conversation that chilled Maudling.[12] In March 1960 Maudling angrily told the Chancellor that Dillon was 'working against us' by encouraging the Six to accelerate their plans to reduce tariffs with respect to one another, which would create further disadvantage for British exporters to the EEC.[13] Macmillan unsuccessfully appealed to De Gaulle to halt the move. American policy seemed to be in favour of building up the Six, and encouraging Britain to join the Community.

After the complications and rebuffs of 1957–9, EEC entry also started to attract influential support in Whitehall and the press, and Macmillan started to look with more and more favour on the idea and see it as a solution to Britain's political isolation and a spur to economic growth. In a July 1960 Cabinet meeting, after the failure of the proposal for association between EEC and EFTA, the majority in Cabinet were still opposed, with Maudling arguing against an application on political grounds – that it would be 'disastrous' for several reasons, including likely opposition from the French.[14] Perhaps he personally feared having to return to the negotiating tables where he had wasted so much energy since August 1957. Maudling had little to offer at this time by way of creative thinking on Europe or trade. He had confessed to a journalist in February that 'he had nothing new to suggest' and was utterly disheartened by French negativity.[15] He had not even written the paper that was put before the Cabinet; extremely unusually it was credited entirely to an official committee under Maudling's Permanent Secretary, Frank Lee. As former diplomat Roy Denman put it, 'It must be the only occasion in British history when a memorandum by an official was largely responsible for a momentous change in British foreign policy.'[16] In the parliamentary debate that followed, Maudling was still holding out hopes for some sort of association, perhaps the Six deciding to join EFTA as a collective unit, and claimed that 'No one is advocating joining the Common Market as it is'.[17]

Maudling's comment reflected an over-optimistic hope that the 'third-best' plan had been seen off in the Cabinet debate. But the idea of full UK entry had now become thinkable, and Macmillan made an important choice a couple of weeks after the discussion. Maudling having outlived his usefulness, a new Europe minister had to be appointed. Macmillan considered Maudling's sidekick at Trade, Freddy Erroll, for the job.[18] Erroll would probably have continued Maudling's scepticism about the project and his attitude of regarding it as a detailed trade negotiation. Instead, he transferred responsibility for EFTA and the next phase of European policy from Maudling to Edward Heath, who was an utterly convinced supporter of British participation in European unity.[19] Heath was freer and more able than Maudling to pursue the political dimensions of the project. Exploratory negotiations began at the invitation of Adenauer in August 1960. Maudling consistently argued against making an application, both on its merits as he saw them and on the practical point that despite some positive signs from De Gaulle France would ultimately use her veto, but Maudling was in a minority when the time for decision came in July 1961.

The formation of the EEC without Britain, and the failure of the wider FTA negotiations, created a problem for British exporters. The progressive dismantling of tariffs on trading goods between members of the Six was giving members a widening competitive advantage over outside countries attempting to export goods into the Six. In the long term, this would harm the economy, but it also posed a short-term problem in that Britain's weak export performance was undermining the balance of payments. When the British economy expanded it sucked in imports at a faster rate than it could generate export trade, leading to a deficit and therefore putting pressure on sterling. Action taken to reduce import demand or induce capital flows dampened down economic growth, particularly as world trade rules developed and direct quota control of imports became less respectable. This British 'stop-go' cycle was wearily familiar by 1961. More exports would help stabilise the pound, allow a more expansionary domestic policy and enable Britain to import more for the purposes of investment or consumption. A dramatic rise in exports would free Britain from many constraints on economic expansion. Maudling saw the Board of Trade's mission during his time predominantly in terms of promoting exports, but locked out of the EEC (partly his own fault) he only had secondary tools at his disposal, namely EFTA, supply side policy, intervention and exhortation.

To deal with the supply side, Maudling's preoccupation with exports led to some rather free market attitudes towards industry, in the hope that freer competition would make British industry more competitive in international markets. He came to the conclusion that the system of Resale Price Maintenance (RPM), a system by which producers could specify the prices charged in shops for their goods, should be scrapped in the interests of free competition, efficiency and lower prices. The Board of Trade's departmental ethos was always rather economic-liberal, and they put up a closely argued paper for abolition to Maudling when he took office. Maudling said he agreed with it entirely but stood no chance of getting it through Cabinet.[20] Maudling made sure that the Treasury knew about his views; in January 1960 the Government Economic Adviser, Robert Hall, noted that 'Maudling favoured the abolition of Resale Price Maintenance and wished he could do something about it'.[21]

The problem with moving on RPM in 1960 was opposition from Reggie's old boss Percy Mills, who carried weight with Macmillan, and Lord Hailsham, who was an important voice in Cabinet. The policy was controversial in Cabinet because of its presumed bad effects on small shopkeepers and thence on natural Conservative supporters. Reggie was unwilling to go into battle against the odds on something that might make him unpopular. He also undertook a review of monopolies regulation, with a view to encouraging more competition, but this proceeded in a most leisurely fashion and had produced no results by the time he left the Board of Trade. The whole area of competitiveness and pricing had to be revisited later with the establishment of a Cabinet subcommittee to look into it in May 1963.

Maudling's tentative free market instincts were also apparent in his attitudes to the unions. The Board of Trade had been his first prolonged encounter with the trade union movement and it could not escape Reggie's attention that there were problems in working practices and labour relations that were impeding the ability of British industry to compete internationally. Unusually in his career he favoured taking a hard line with strikes, including a railway strike in February 1960 that he wanted to resist, but Butler and Heath favoured settling on generous terms. In June 1961 he told Macmillan that while industry had been under the scrutiny of the Restrictive Practices Court since 1956 there had been complaints that 'nothing comparable has been done about the restrictive practices of labour. For my part I share this point of view . . . I believe myself that the time is rapidly approaching when we should take some important new initiative in the matter.'[22]

Maudling and Macmillan were musing about the possibility of dramatising the amount of action that had taken place against the restrictive practices of business as a means of preparing the way for a wider freeing up of the economy. There was a certain amount of alarm within his ministry at the prospect of a confrontation with the unions. Maudling's civil servants warned that although the Restrictive Practices Court had made an encouraging start, there were still plenty of restrictive practices left, either unofficially or in areas not covered by the 1956 law, and that the unions' case was different, as the supply of labour at an agreed price was the basis of collective industrial bargaining.[23]

Maudling certainly had no wish to tear up the system of industrial relations from the roots. Despite his belief that the unions were a monopoly supplier of labour, he knew that they were a social as well as an economic institution. A few years before, asked about communism in the trade unions, he replied:

> I'm not sure it's a question for a politician to answer. I think it's a question for the trade unions themselves to answer. I think it would be a very bad thing indeed if Governments started trying to interfere in our Trade Union Movement in this country, which after all is one of the real fundamental bases of our democracy in this country.[24]

Even though the Conservative government at the time he spoke (1954) was almost obsessively obliging to the unions, Reggie's answer went well beyond formal pleasantry. He basically thought of the labour movement as part of British heritage and society, a social institution not to be trifled with, for what seemed sound Conservative philosophical reasons. Maudling's tentative June 1961 flicker of interest in trade union reform did not last long. Within a month the general economic climate had deteriorated to such an extent that Chancellor Selwyn Lloyd introduced a restrictive mini-budget and a 'pay pause' on 25 July 1961. There was no appetite within the government for antagonising organised labour any more than that. Maudling's own relations with the trade unions became much warmer when he returned to economic policy in 1962. He had the same aims in mind, of increasing productivity at the 'micro' level through getting rid of restrictive practices and improving the 'macro' climate of policy by making Britain less inflation-prone, but he chose different methods from those hinted at in his 1961 memorandum.

While the free market side of Reggie's political ideas had more exposure in 1959–61 than in other ministries, he was still a convinced interventionist and his main legislative achievement in the post, the Local Employment Act 1960, served to increase the state's powers over the location of industry. Maudling's attitude to industrial development showed his essential optimism and belief in the positive power of the state, and his view of economics as subordinate to political and social matters. Introducing the Local Employment Bill he said:

> In these matters we cannot be guided only by pure economic doctrine. That is why we have this legislation. Although, no doubt, to the economist a house is only a house, we know that a house is more than a house – it is a home. A town is more than a collection of houses – it is a collection of homes, a community. Social capital and human capital are not adaptable

and changeable to the extent and at the pace which economists might sometimes assume.[25]

Maudling's purposes were interventionist, but the Bill itself was not particularly dramatic. Its main significance was as an indication that the Conservative government had started to change course. The coalition government had passed a Distribution of Industry Act in 1945, and the Labour government in 1945–51 had actively embraced a regional policy that was intended to direct industrial development towards areas suffering, or at risk from, high unemployment. When the Conservatives returned to power in 1951 this policy withered away and was even put into reverse with the development of the New Towns around London. There seemed little cause for concern during the 1950s, and those concerns that arose among Board of Trade officials were ignored because all seemed well and previous Trade ministers such as Peter Thorneycroft had ideological aversions to intervention.[26] However, in 1959 the decline of coal, cotton, shipbuilding and heavy engineering was causing problems for vulnerable areas like western Scotland, the north-east and parts of Lancashire.[27]

Even on existing legislation the government already had powers to offer investment incentives and even direct provision. In October 1960 Maudling announced more 'advance factories' – government-built factories in favoured areas in advance of demand to fill them. These had taken place on a small scale since February 1959 but the programme was greatly expanded by Maudling. A number of large-scale industrial enterprises were directed towards development areas at the behest of Maudling or Macmillan, although it was Macmillan's 'judgement of Solomon' that instead of one huge new steel plant, capacity should be divided between Llanwern in south Wales and Ravenscraig in Scotland. This decision, according to the history of the industry, involved more public money than had been spent on regional policy in total during the entire 1950s.[28]

Maudling's personal involvement was greater in the case of the car industry. Motor production was expanding at the time and he decided that new plants would be located in depressed areas, particularly around Liverpool where the local economic climate was colder than the general prosperous atmosphere. Reggie told colleagues that although it meant higher costs it was justified in terms of 'social policy'.[29] He confidently hoped that 'the car companies taking their new factories to Merseyside would probably have cured Merseyside's unemployment completely'[30] He did not insist that the car manufacturers built more factories – this was left to market forces and he was personally sceptical about whether such a massive expansion of car production capacity in Britain was justified. Maudling's role came in telling them in which areas they would be permitted to build the new factories. He also expanded the government's use of Industrial Development Certificates to prevent development in areas with full employment already.

Maudling's complacency about Merseyside was symptomatic of the flaws in the government's regional policy at the time. While the Conservatives were willing, as they had not been for most of the 1950s, to throw public money at the problem, they now had an unrealistically short-term view of the issue. Maudling's Local Employment Act 1960 focused assistance on those relatively small areas with unemployment over 4.5 per cent.[31] His thoughts on Halewood indicate the prevailing view that the small pools of high unemployment that existed in 1960 could be mopped up by deploying the odd factory here and there. There was no sense of the problems of particular regions reliant on declining industries, which without a more radical overhaul of infrastructure and economy would continue to generate areas of high unemployment faster than large employers could be cajoled into moving in. Economic historian Peter Scott called regional policy at this time 'the worst of both worlds' – neither the flexibility of the market nor the coordination of a proper regional policy. In the north-east, a charismatic Labour politician called T. Dan Smith had started to argue for a more comprehensive approach. In 1962 the Conservative government decided there was something in it, and Lord Hailsham was put in charge of strategy for the north-east.

Maudling's complacency about the effectiveness of pinprick regional policy interventions in general, and the future of Merseyside in particular, was proved incorrect. The docks were in terminal trouble and their decline dragged the local economy down. Halewood did provide an anchor of sorts for employment – the consequences of its closure or non-existence in the early 1980s would have been terrifying. But this was at the cost of giving the Ford motor company the ability to demand even further government support to keep it open. It also created a factory whose public image for militancy and low productivity frightened other employers away from Liverpool. Reggie Maudling is the unacknowledged godfather of Halewood, Linwood and those other centres of 1970s industrial unrest.

Maudling's time at the Board of Trade has elements of free market and interventionist policy, which indicates that he did not see its role primarily in ideological terms. His overriding priority was to increase British exports, and if this end was served by a particular policy, it was appropriate. Thus, Maudling found himself arguing in the same period, summer 1960, that the government should consider setting up a state-owned lending organisation to provide funds for exporters, and also that the Inland Revenue should go easier on expenses deductions for foreign business travel. It was a 'what matters is what works' approach that had definite merits, but there is always the risk that lack of ideological prejudice can shade into lack of principle, as it did when Maudling himself was a businessman involved in export promotion.

Somewhere between intervention and exhortation was talking to industry and setting up tripartite institutions to try to reach agreement on measures to increase exports. In its consensus format and its reliance on personal relationships, it was a characteristic Maudling method. Within the Department of Trade, he set up an Export Promotion Group, and he also reached outside for advice. There had been a Dollar Export Council since 1948, when obtaining dollars was a fundamental object of Britain's international economic relations. During the late 1950s attention turned to trying to get a share in the rapidly expanding West European market. Maudling established the European Export Council, with representation from industry and the trade unions, in 1960. He put his friend Sandy Glen, who was involved in the shipping and travel industries, onto the new body:

> It was his choice of people and it built his friendships in industry. He showed a lack of pretension and pomposity that was attractive in a minister. Reggie played a part in getting the City, business and the trade unions (represented by Harry Douglass). He was enthusiastic and the members of it worked, unpaid, with a great sense of purpose. That stemmed from Reggie . . . It was government intervention that worked, it was pragmatic, suited to him and he did it <u>exceptionally</u> well. He felt Whitehall didn't know Birmingham or Glasgow and the fault ran both ways. It was not a corporate structure, just a way that doors could be opened. Reggie's door was unusually widely open to everyone, regardless of politics, or whether someone was small or big in industry. He was a very welcoming minister.[32]

This welcoming attitude had its risks. Particularly with the export promotion groups, Maudling could be naively trusting because he felt that everyone was on the same side and as interested as he was in the cause of exports. Fortunately for him, this tended to be the case. But in a situation where he was involved in distributing investment incentives and financial support for industry, it could have generated questions – Maudling stepped up subsidies for shipbuilding, an industry with which Beryl had family connections, and Sandy Glen was much involved, but there is no evidence that he did so for any reasons other than his perception of the good of the economy.

There was a troubling overlap between Maudling's social life and his business links as President of the Board of Trade. His favourite businessmen were those he got on well with socially, like Sandy Glen, and their relationships could take on layers of complexity – from official dealings in the Export Council, other official business affecting the firms, private social encounters and the ever-present potential of Maudling's later employment should he lose office. Maudling thought he knew what he was doing, but he was placing a lot of faith in his own integrity and that of his business contacts. Not all were as upright as Sandy Glen. Maudling's civil servants, as Edward Boyle put it in 1981 when researching Maudling's old *Dictionary of National Biography* entry, 'were worried even as early as the late 1950s about his failure to distinguish between the industrial <u>monde</u> and the <u>demi-</u>

monde'.[33] Stripping away the undue delicacy, what the officials at the Board of Trade, from Permanent Secretary Frank Lee downward, were worried about was Reggie's tendency to accept hospitality from all manner of business interests, and the difficulty they had in persuading Maudling to comply with the rules on receiving gifts while on overseas trips. A certain amount of mixing with industrialists is normal, and indeed desirable from a trade minister, but they felt that Maudling was sailing dangerously close to the wind. Too much eating and drinking at the expense of others could create, or more likely appear to create, obligations and the possibility that favours would be repaid later. Rather arrogantly, Maudling assumed that his own certainty that he could distinguish between public and private interests, and act in his ministerial capacity only in the public interest, was sufficient safeguard.[34]

Maudling's own financial arrangements as President verged on the improper. He had got away with becoming a Lloyd's Name in 1957 while a minister, but on appointment to the Board of Trade in October 1959 his position according to the government's guidelines since 1952 was unambiguous. Trade involved direct ministerial responsibility for the insurance market and it was clear that even an inactive membership was not permitted. Maudling dragged his feet about divesting himself of this interest, and when Peter Carey arrived in his Private Office in 1960 he found that it was still a live issue and Maudling had to be told firmly that being a Name was not acceptable.[35] Reggie made a face and grumbled that it was depriving him of a substantial source of income. The issue seems not to have been resolved.[36]

Maudling never really got the point of not just being pure, but being seen to be pure, although it was clearly stated in the rules of ministerial conduct at the time because of the contemporaneous case of Ernest Marples.[37] The conflict of interest between his family building firm Marples Ridgeway and his road construction projects as Minister of Transport raised eyebrows. Marples was an out-and-out rogue in his sexual and financial affairs, but on this occasion he resolved the problem by removing himself from any verifiable involvement with the firm. The basic rule from the secret Questions of Procedure for Ministers was read into the record in the House of Commons in January 1960:

1. It is a principle of public life that Ministers must so order their affairs that no conflict arises, or appears to arise, between their private interests and public duties.[38]

Maudling was in a shaky enough position himself, but, to use Boyle's genteel term, the industrial *demi-monde* had an ambassador at court at the Board of Trade in the form of Freddie Bennett, still serving as Maudling's PPS. In 1960 he was trying to persuade the Board of Trade to change its mind and allow a property company to use the word 'British' in its title; the Public Record Office documents on this 'President's Case' seem to have vanished.[39] Board of Trade civil servants thought of Bennett as an 'unfortunate influence', who, while a sociable sidekick for Reggie, failed to check Maudling's own tendency to indiscipline. Maudling needed little encouragement to attend lunches in the City, but Bennett made sure that he got as much as possible, particularly courtesy of Kleinwort Benson where he was introduced to a large number of City people and industrial clients of the merchant bank.[40]

Maudling's political as well as departmental work sometimes brought him into doubtful company. As did other Cabinet ministers, Maudling spent many evenings, particularly on Fridays and weekends, speaking at party engagements. In November 1960 he was guest of honour at the National Liberal Forum at Caxton Hall in Westminster. The National Liberals had become even less distinguishable from Conservatives during the years since Maudling considered joining them in 1939 and were rather to the right of Maudling in their adherence to old-fashioned free market economics. They also tended to be pro-European and wanted to hear what he had to say about the subject. It was only when Maudling was introduced to the meeting by a senior Yorkshire National Liberal, a balding businessman who bore a strong physical resemblance to the Russian leader, Nikita Krushchev, that he discovered he had to tear up his notes for his usual speech on trade and exports and talk on Europe instead. He charmed the meeting without giving anything away, another example of his ability to think on his feet. After the meeting the Yorkshireman, whose name was John Poulson, took Reggie and Beryl to dinner with several of the National Liberals at his favourite London base, the Dorchester Hotel. 'They were excellent company, and obviously enjoyed themselves,' Poulson recalled in unhappier times, 'though he probably remembered little of the evening the next morning.'[41] Maudling did indeed forget he had met Poulson, but probably not because he drank too much; at that stage in his life he had an enormous capacity to absorb alcohol without ill effects. It seemed an inconsequential and commonplace political engagement, but when he later came to curse the day he met John Poulson, 15 November 1960 was the moment.[42]

Some more Maudling characteristics were apparent in his approach to exhorting British industry to make more of its opportunities. As President of the Board of Trade he was an inveterate attendee at trade fairs, expos and openings, from British Fashion Week to the Earls Court Motor Show to cutting the ribbon on the hideous Carlton Tower Hotel in Knightsbridge. He would take his speech about exports and productivity to wherever he could, including innumerable Chambers of Commerce and industry association dinners. Ministers, principally Maudling, made over eighty speeches in Britain between July 1960 and the end of 1961 wholly or partially concerned with export promotion.[43] Sandy Glen commented that 'There were indeed a lot of trade fairs and visits. He went down well, no pomposity, rather American in that way.'[44] Maudling did not need much persuasion to go on foreign trips in pursuit of export markets. It was an agreeable way of spending time, particularly if Beryl came along too, and he believed that the visits improved trade relations and therefore accomplished something for the British economy and world trade. The trip which involved most preparation, and that he most enjoyed, was to the Soviet Union in May 1961. In his memoirs he devoted nearly half his description of his Board of Trade time to recollections of this enjoyable event.

The British Chambers of Commerce – led by Sir James Hutchison who had served on the Industrial Charter committee – and the Board of Trade had made painstaking preparations for the first British Trade Fair in Moscow. The Eastern Bloc was a largely untapped market for British exporters and the centralised economy of the Soviet Union meant that there were potentially enormous deals if agreement could be reached with Russian industry, and it was both the largest trade fair in Russia and the largest UK overseas trade fair to that date. It was an impressive occasion and Reggie spoke well at its opening, hitting all the right notes about the quality of British goods and the potential of trade to promote friendship and understanding between the USSR and Britain.[45] A surprising bonus was the presence of the Soviet leader, Nikita Krushchev, who had kept the British guessing about whether he was coming because he had neither accepted nor declined the invitation. Reggie and his civil servants realised that it was all going well when they noticed twenty-odd empty seats on the podium at the opening and sure enough a fleet of Russian limousines swept in containing Krushchev and several other senior ministers.[46] In the course of showing Krushchev around, Reggie traded good-humoured banter, a lot of it about football, with the earthy Soviet leader, who asked him if the tight-fitting Gossard corsets exhibited were a new British weapon to terrorise Russian women.[47] It was an agreeable, successful occasion for Reggie.

After opening the British trade fair, Reggie and Beryl had a long tour of Moscow and the western USSR. Beryl rather enjoyed the palaces and museums, but Reggie wandered around like a laid-back tourist – he took a polite interest in culture but did not take it very seriously. He and Beryl left Moscow in the company of Nikolai Patolichev, the Minister for Foreign Trade, travelling down to the Black Sea and then back up to Leningrad before returning home. In Dnepopatrovsk Patolichev announced that now they were out of Moscow the serious drinking could begin, and showed Reggie into a formal dining room for a feast of caviar, sturgeon and various Soviet delicacies, with six glasses lined up at every place setting. Reggie's Private Secretary, Peter Carey, who accompanied him throughout the trip, remembered a long and punishing round of vodka drinking and endless toasts that certainly tested his and Patolichev's livers. Reggie, on the other hand, said he was disappointed when it was over: 'Oh no, I was just getting started.' Reggie felt a bit rougher the next morning, and asked for a breakfast of dry toast, but perhaps through a linguistic glitch or a desire to restore

Russian honour, when he came down it was set up exactly as it was the night before, with another round of toasts to be drunk in vodka. Reggie stayed for a few, but then the British delegation really had to get going to the next stop on their tour.[48]

Beryl also enjoyed her Soviet trip, and returned there a few years later with Caroline. Mrs Maudling was rather a hit with the Russians, who liked her stylish dress sense and her charm. One particularly rapturous reception was in the republic of Georgia, where the mayor of Tbilisi presented Reggie with a large drinking horn full of Georgian brandy and he downed it in one. Beryl received a smaller one, empty, and in her reply to the toast commented that she was disappointed to find that there was not more equality in the Soviet Union; it was filled up and she too polished it off in one, to great laughter and applause.

The Maudlings naturally appreciated a culture in which heavy social drinking plays such an important part, and he responded to the sociability and black humour that are also Russian characteristics. He found communist earnestness amusing, asking a guide at a 'peace' exhibition featuring pictures of anti-nuclear demonstrations in London, New York and other Western capitals where the picture of peace protests in Moscow could be found.[49] He approached communism without much by way of ideological preconceptions, and believed in the positive potential of East–West trade. He was pleased with his Russian expedition and when he returned he, together with his son Edward, officially opened a pioneering Russian shop in London. His efforts did help to expand East–West trade over the next few years, although from a low base.

Maudling's last official visit as President of the Board of Trade was to Canada and the USA in September 1961. Beryl did not come on this rather routine trip, which involved a speech and a dinner at the conference of the Institute of Chartered Accountants of Canada – 'rather heavy handed', as a bored Peter Carey summed up this event.[50] When Reggie arrived in Washington for a series of meetings with Kennedy administration figures he found a telegram waiting for him, with the ambassador under instructions to decode it personally. It was a message from the Prime Minister. Macmillan had artfully waited until Reggie was out of the country to tell him something he knew he would not like. The message told Reggie that Macmillan was making some changes in the government, and he wanted to put Maudling in the Colonial Office. He said he felt that it would be helpful for Reggie to develop his career by gaining some foreign experience. If Maudling accepted, he need only telegram back 'Yes'. Although he was not supposed to tell anyone, Reggie did consult Beryl before he rather reluctantly accepted a job which took him away from his main interest of economic policy.[51] He admitted later that he had no previous interest in colonial questions.[52] It was not what he wanted, but he could take some comfort from Macmillan's intimation that he was being groomed for a position at the very top.

Although it had brought him closer to where he really wanted to be, Maudling's career marked time at the Board of Trade. He enjoyed less personal publicity than he did during his European mission in 1957–8 and, while it was an important ministry, he seemed a little distant from the main currents of politics. He was not seriously considered for the Treasury when Heathcoat-Amory resigned in 1960; compared to his position in 1958 his chances for advancement seemed to have slipped back.[53] He did not have a particularly good reputation in Whitehall as a manager of a large department, however jolly it was to be in his Private Office:

> He didn't care for the management side of running the Department. He left it largely to Frank Lee and Richard Powell, he had no taste for the organisation of a department, he did what was necessary but that was it . . . He was quite genial, but he didn't appeal so much to the lower ranks. He declined to attend the Board of Trade Christmas party, saying that he 'didn't like mixing with the lower orders.' He was half joking. But the attitude did not go down well. He was liked by officials who saw his genial side. The juniors thought him arrogant.[54]

Where Maudling did well as a departmental minister was in winning battles in Cabinet, and presiding over a smoothly running team of ministers and senior officials at the core of the department, but he did not leave much of a mark on policy or the ministry he commanded for nearly two years. He had ideas, like RPM abolition, further anti-monopoly legislation or trade union reform, but he lost interest on encountering the first obstacle. Despite his exhortations, the export performance of British industry was not noticeably improved and struggled to cope with the boom he unleashed two years later as Chancellor. Although he was a strong minister, his successor was not and until Edward Heath arrived the ministry lacked dynamism.

Although on first inspection Maudling's two years at the Board of Trade are one of the least dramatic periods of his life, they are extremely revealing of Maudling's virtues and his developing flaws. He was working well in Cabinet, he was thinking deeply about national problems such as poor export performance and structuring all his policies with that aim in mind, and he had no political enemies. But in his attitude to Lloyd's, in his ready acceptance of hospitality and his eagerness for overseas jaunts, there are traces of the arrogance and greed that proved fatal to his political career. There was also, particularly after July 1960, an intimation of his uncertain commitment to political life, an incipient despair about his prospects, that makes his relationship with business all the more suspect thanks to his anticipated future career. Even in 1955, a fellow MP Robert Cary wrote that 'Reggie just held the scales even between the boardroom and the Treasury. He was convincing because he would be happy in either.'[55] The scales seemed to be tipping in 1960–1 towards the boardroom. It was at about this time that

Cecil King offered him the chairmanship of Reed International 'but after long hesitation he turned the offer down . . . [Cecil King thought] he used this offer to get a promise of the Exchequer from Macmillan'.[56] A news magazine commented a little later that 'having missed the Treasury when Lord Amory and then Selwyn Lloyd were selected, he probably abandoned private hope that the third time would prove lucky. Indeed, there was an impression at Westminster that, having reached his ceiling, he would in due course depart from politics and accept a top chair in business.'[57] Reggie had not given up on politics, and he still dearly wanted to be Chancellor, but he was looking over his shoulder at the alternatives.

Chapter 10

THE MAUDLING CEMENT MIXER,[1] 1961–1962

The Colonial Office was one of the hottest jobs in British politics in October 1961 and Maudling's appointment was a sign that Macmillan, reluctantly, had come to think highly of his ability. The Conservative government had only recently implemented a radical change of colonial policy. Before 1959, the Tories envisaged another ten or twenty years of colonial rule in Africa and had worked out ingenious but unworkable interim constitutions and federal structures in the West Indies and Central Africa. Maudling's old colleague Iain Macleod was appointed in October 1959 with the mission to accelerate progress towards independence, and in February 1960 Macmillan proclaimed the African 'wind of change' to the South African parliament. Independence came rapidly in Nigeria, Sierra Leone, Cyprus and Tanganyika (although taking the Bill and implementing it through Parliament fell to Reggie), and was well on the way in most of the rest of the British Empire in Africa and elsewhere.

By October 1961 the Tory right were in increasingly open opposition to Macleod. The right-wing Conservative MP for Haltemprice, Patrick Wall, wrote to Roy Welensky, the Prime Minister of the Central African Federation, that Macleod's position 'was rapidly becoming untenable'. The brutal relish with which Macleod was pursuing his policies, and telling uncomfortable truths, was dividing the party at a time when the government's domestic position had started to deteriorate. Reggie Maudling was a felicitous choice for the position of Colonial Secretary. Macleod argued strongly with Macmillan that Maudling would be the best replacement. In his justly celebrated valedictory speech on colonial affairs to the October 1961 Conservative Party conference, in which he declared 'I believe quite simply in the brotherhood of man', Macleod expressed his:

Great delight that my successor in this office is to be my friend and colleague for so many years, Reggie Maudling. If I leave him many problems – and I do, even as you will see in Tristan da Cunha – I leave him also in utter confidence a most inspiring trust, because I think that the development of British colonial policy over the years and the development of the British Colonial Territories are among the noblest things in our history.[2]

The right also welcomed the announcement. Patrick Wall wrote to Roy Welensky, the white Prime Minister of the Central African Federation:

> To let you know how delighted I am at the appointment of Reggie Maudling as Colonial Secretary. He is a man of integrity, has a first class brain, is willing to listen and will, I think, do an excellent job . . . I believe that although the new appointment will not herald a change in general direction of British Colonial policy it will certainly mean a modification of the ruthless pro-African Nationalist line which has been pursued recently.[3]

Wall's opinions were influential, and the Federal government refrained from mounting personal attacks on Maudling as it had done against Macleod.[4] Welensky's relations with Macleod were poisonous, but with Maudling there was a trace of friendship despite his verdict that Reggie was 'amiable, completely ignorant about Africa, not aggressively opinionated, but certainly neither strong enough nor independent enough to make any stand against the wishes of the majority of his senior colleagues'.[5]

Freddie Bennett had been a strong ally of Welensky, and the African settlers in Rhodesia and Kenya, and the traditionalist right took some heart that he would still have influence over Maudling, although Bennett himself was obliged to step down as PPS because it would have inhibited the expression of his strong views about the colonies. He was replaced by Francis Pym. When Maudling entered the Colonial Office, he said with apparent benevolent scepticism to his colleagues and officials, 'I suppose I'm looking at a lot of people who believe in the "brotherhood of man".'[6] The description certainly fitted his two junior ministers, Hugh Fraser and Lord Perth, but Reggie was enjoying a little joke, for he too was a firm believer in the brotherhood of man, although he would never have chosen to phrase it in such a way. He uttered the considerably less ringing phrase 'homo sum humane nihil a me alienum puto – I am a man and I count nothing human indifferent to me' in his first Commons speech.[7] Reggie lacked racial prejudice, and was able to found easy, unforced relationships of friendship and respect with African leaders such as Kenyatta, Kaunda and Nyerere. Maudling knew that it was impossible to make everyone happy in colonial policy, and quickly committed himself to continuing Macleod's policy, which, as Maudling said firmly in his first Commons statement on Africa, was established government policy rather than a personal flight of fancy.[8] Maudling looked at the circumstances he found, and sometimes judged that things needed to go even faster than Macleod had envisaged. Macmillan noted in his diary in February 1962 that Maudling was 'plus noir que les nègres, more difficult and intransigent than his predecessor'.[9]

Maudling's job at the Colonial Office was made more complicated by the existence of a separate Commonwealth Office under Duncan Sandys. The division of responsibilities between the two ministries was complicated, particularly in Central Africa with the overlapping existence of the Central African Federation and the separate entities of Northern and Southern Rhodesia and Nyasaland. Macmillan was bombarded with advice that the division of Colonial and Commonwealth was untenable, from within the ministries, and from the Cabinet Secretary, Norman Brook, who told Rab Butler that 'the present system imposed an unwarranted strain on Cabinet government itself. He felt also that the Prime Minister could not go on with the effort and anxiety involved.'[10] When Maudling moved onwards in July 1962, the leadership of the two departments was combined under Sandys. At the Colonial Office Maudling was well served by two principled, liberal ministers, Hugh Fraser and Lord Perth, who shared the burden of the enormous mass of details that needed to be determined in divesting Britain of its colonies.

Although Reggie had got used to frequent overseas travel in his past couple of ministerial jobs, and the Board of Trade was a major post, the Colonial Office was a new departure for him. He sat at the top of an elaborate, though admittedly crumbling, pyramid of power and protocol. The Colonial Office ran territories scattered across the world, and as well as geographical variety it also covered the full range of domestic policies – health, education, transport, community relations, constitutional development, law . . . Colonial Office civil servants could end up with as wide an experience of government as anyone in Whitehall. The Cabinet post covered a lot of ground and as a result Maudling had three Private Secretaries. Reggie did not, however, have to adjust his style of working very much. Shortly after he arrived he had to speak in the House on a Bill he inherited, and as one of his Private Secretaries, Jack Howard-Drake, recalled:

> I fetched the briefs for him, a big bundle. He did not use them in the debate but made some notes on a small, scrappy piece of paper. He made a good speech. I came to him as well with the red boxes, and he said, 'What are these?' He insisted that he did all his work in the office and did not take it home, but it was impossible and it couldn't stick. He was relaxed. He was on top of the work without too much effort, but his reputation for idleness was unfair.[11]

One of the lighter moments of Reggie's term of office came when he received a letter from the author Ian Fleming, asking if the crew making the forthcoming James Bond film *Dr No* could shoot some scenes in Government House in Jamaica. Reggie wrote back to tell Fleming that as the Governor was portrayed as a fool and his secretary as a spy, the Colonial Office could not give permission.[12] Despite this, Reggie counted himself a friend of Ian

Fleming and an unqualified admirer of his work; while he had little time to read for pleasure as a minister he always enjoyed reading Fleming and Simenon: 'I'm a great fan of James Bond. I've often thought he'd be an asset to the Government. Even the Cabinet.'[13] This idle statement was quite revealing about Maudling. The Bond of the books was a different creature from the dashing, open-minded, rather caring figure portrayed by Timothy Dalton and Pierce Brosnan, and the tone of the books lacked the whimsy and self-parody that quickly crept into the films. Fleming's Bond was callous, even sadistic, in his spying escapades, with morality sacrificed to patriotism and expediency; with women he was ruthlessly exploitative in his behaviour while occasionally professing sentimentality.[14] Bond was a brutal character who wanted to believe he had a soft centre; Maudling was a soft man who had, when it came to it during the war, Suez and the Irish Troubles, reserves of callous expediency.

However, what really appealed to Maudling about Bond was his unrestrained enjoyment of luxury and pleasure. Puritans of left and right considered Bond a decadent, amoral influence; to Paul Johnson (probably in both modes) the books were 'a systematic onslaught on everything decent and sensible in modern life'.[15] Bond's consumption was always conspicuous, always the 'best', his on- and off-duty world one of smoking jackets, yachts and the nervous hush of the casino. Maudling himself loved this world; by the early 1960s Nice and Monte Carlo had replaced pottering around south-west France in a car as his preferred type of holiday. Quirkily, when Reggie moved into dubious international business in the late 1960s, he also acquired, in best Ernst Stavro Blofeld style, a fluffy white cat. Like Reggie, although he was a cosmopolitan, Bond was also essentially English (despite his and Fleming's Scottish roots), the fantasy of what David Cannadine calls a 'Tory imagination'; he had a basket of prejudices about foreigners, some of them pernicious and some of them not, and a sense that the natural, settled order of things was the comfortable rule of a Tory establishment. Bond's world was one that Maudling recognised and enjoyed; he was distinct from most of the left (with the notable exception of Hugh Gaitskell, for his own personal reasons), and the old-fashioned right, in doing so. But then again, perhaps Reggie just liked escapist spy novels.

There was more for Reggie to deal with in the Caribbean than location requests for a James Bond film. Macleod had hoped to do a package deal on independence for the Caribbean islands as a Federation of the West Indies, but this came undone in September 1961 shortly before Maudling took over. The electorate of Jamaica, the largest element of the Federation, voted 54–46 in a referendum to secede from the Federation and the government of Trinidad also decided not to participate. The larger territories were unwilling to federate with the smaller and poorer islands, fearing that they would be a drain on resources and that they would have too strong a voice in a federal arrangement. However, without Jamaica and Trinidad the federation concept collapsed and a change of mind was forced upon the British that perhaps each island could after all become an independent micro-state. For the larger islands, Macleod told the Cabinet in September that there was no alternative to acceding to any requests for independence and that Britain should offer to sponsor their membership of the Commonwealth.

Maudling's role with Jamaica and Trinidad was to take over Macleod's policy and smooth the way to independence on good terms with both islands. In January 1962 Reggie travelled to the West Indies 'to break up the Federation and say that was the end, and to see what best could be salvaged from the wreck'. It was a pleasant, sunny if hectic trip in January 1962. Reggie flew into Port-of-Spain, the capital of Trinidad, on 13 January to be greeted by an enthusiastic calypso choir. They had composed a special Reginald Maudling calypso in his honour. The last three verses of the song went:

> A Big Reception for him by all is in store
> Something he will never forget we are sure
> We are indebted to him for his expressions of sympathy
> To the flood victims in the Diego Martin vicinity.
>
> We in Trinidad & Tobago got Britain's consent
> To reach the stage of full internal Government
> So we have no cause for alarm or to make a row
> As Independence is on our door steps now.
>
> From the depths of our hearts we are honest and true
> In this hymn of welcome we dedicate to you
> And sincerely trust wherever you may roam
> That Providence may safely take you and charming wife back home.[16]

Reggie stayed with Lord Hailes, the Governor of the Federation, who, as Patrick Buchan-Hepburn, had been Reggie's austere Chief Whip in the early 1950s. There were dinner parties and receptions nearly every evening during the two-week tour, and a round of meetings with the premiers of the various islands, including the leaders of tiny Montserrat, and colonial officials. Reggie did not think much of the 'Little Eight' leaders: 'they were always having rows, those chaps'[17] and had to dismiss Eric Gairy of Grenada for financial corruption. The man had embezzled some funds and bought a piano with the proceeds, and burst into tears when Reggie told him he had to resign.[18]

Beryl joined Reggie in the islands for most of the time, making the best of an appealing winter break. One night Reggie and Beryl felt unable to cope with another night of official hospitality, and to the consternation of the Governor and the civil servants they disappeared off to a dubious local nightclub. When they came back they reported to Jack Howard-Drake, who was travelling with them, that they hadn't been very impressed by the stripper.[19]

Reggie's talks with most of the political class of the remainder of the Federation confirmed his view that the Federation was a dead duck, and it was duly wound up in May 1962. The islands would thereafter progress at their own speeds towards independence. Barbados gained it in 1966; most of the others followed over time, although Montserrat was still a British dependent territory in 2003. In 1968 Reggie conceded that the outcome was far from ideal: 'I think when you get a man who calls himself Premier of a country with 10,000 people in it, it does become a little unusual.'[20] However, nowhere did it prove a disaster.

Maudling's return to Britain on Saturday 27 January did not mark an end to his Caribbean preoccupations, for it was only a few days until the Jamaican independence conference opened at Lancaster House in London on 1 February. Jamaica was Maudling's first time presiding at an independence conference and it was a fairly gentle introduction to the experience. Two main political parties, the Jamaica Labour Party under Alexander Bustamante and the People's National Party under Prime Minister Norman Manley, were well established and there was a 'Westminster'-style democracy, although disagreements between the parties were occasionally very heated. The Jamaican parties had reached substantial agreement between themselves on a draft constitution before they turned up to Lancaster House. Maudling got on particularly well with Bustamante, a cheerful pragmatic politician with more than a touch of Irish machine politics about him. It was only just over a week before the independence deal was finalised and celebrated with a joyful photo-opportunity of Reggie, junior minister Hugh Fraser, Manley and Bustamante engaging in a four-way handshake outside Lancaster House. Jamaica became independent on 6 August 1962.

Trinidad (with Tobago), the other large splinter from the Federation, was more troublesome. Prime Minister Eric Williams was distrusted as a potential dictator by political opponents, particularly those drawn from the white and Asian minorities. The result of the 1961 election was disputed, with the opposition alleging that it had been rigged and demanding new elections before any independence conference. Some among the Indian minority were demanding parity of representation and public employment with the Afro-Caribbean majority. Attempts to agree a draft constitution within Trinidad fell through, and the arguments continued in London when the independence conference met at Marlborough House on 28 May 1962 under Maudling's chairmanship. Maudling sat back and bided his time, giving little away and uttering the occasional reassuring platitude about the need for national unity, tactics he also used successfully in the even more difficult Kenya conference. The bickering, disputatious Trinidad conference dragged on, and when Reggie called a halt for a tea break one day to avert an imminent collapse it seemed that things were going nowhere. Reggie was as astonished as everyone else when Williams and opposition leader, Rudranath Capildeo, returned from a private session over tea with a fully worked out compromise solution. Island politics being the intimate business it is, the two men ('equal in both academic brilliance and arrogance' according to Trinidadian observer J. O'Neill-Lewis) knew each other well from when Williams was Capildeo's college tutor. It was one of those cases when the best solution really was to lock the two opposing leaders in a room and only let them out when they had agreed. The opposition gave up on several demands and let the 1961 elections stand, and allowed Williams to claim for public consumption that he had made no concessions, while Williams gave way on an independent judiciary and an entrenched Bill of Rights.[21] Maudling delightedly wrapped up the conference that day and Trinidad & Tobago moved quickly to independence.

Maudling's work in clearing up after the implosion of the Federation, and implementing a transition to independent democracy in the Caribbean ex-British colonies, was a success story. However, the other British colony in the area – a Caribbean nation physically located on the South American mainland – was not. This was not because of any reluctance on the part of Maudling, nor other members of the government, to see it take the normal path to independence, still less a desire to cling on to its resources – the sparsely populated colony was a chronic loss-making enterprise. The reasons why the colonial status of British Guiana (Guyana) survived Maudling's term of office and only ended in 1966 have more to do with American than British politics.

British Guiana was a more complicated business than most of the other western hemisphere colonies. Part of the reason was the ethnic division in the country between people of African and Indian origin, but this was a familiar issue to the Colonial Office from their experiences in other territories; the difference in British Guiana was that it was caught up in superpower politics to a greater extent than the other colonies. In the early 1960s a major complicating factor in British Guiana was the involvement of the United States. The 1959 revolution in Cuba that overthrew the American-backed Batista dictatorship installed Fidel Castro and, after initial uncertainty, a pro-Soviet regime. The Americans resented the financial losses from the Cuban revolution and feared that the island would become a communist bridgehead in the western hemisphere, exporting revolution and posing a direct geopolitical threat to the USA. American thinking about Cuba carried over into its attitudes on British Guiana. Those who had trusted Castro's initial noises about a democratic regime felt betrayed, right-wingers wanted to stamp on any other manifestations of socialism in the western hemisphere, and the Caribbean and Latin American department of the Central Intelligence Agency (CIA), a particularly buccaneering, not to say amoral, branch of the agency, wanted to redeem its failure in Cuba.

The dominant force in the politics of British Guiana at the time was Cheddi Jagan, the leader of the People's Progressive Party. Jagan was well to the left of other nationalist leaders in the Caribbean, and had a history of poor relations with London since local autonomy was suspended in 1953 after his first election victory. In August 1961, shortly before Maudling arrived at the Colonial Office, Jagan's party won another election victory and with the timetable in place for independence in 1963 it seemed highly likely that Jagan would be Prime Minister of independent Guyana before long.

British Guiana was an expensive place to run. It was estimated in 1962 that without a price-fixing Commonwealth agreement on sugar, the colony's principal export, 'most of its economy would probably collapse within two years' and that it was dependent on British government loans and grants of £3–4 million a year.[22] As an independent country, it would clearly need aid from somewhere, and given its position there was some eagerness in Britain to see the United States assume the primary burden. The alternative, it was feared, was that Jagan would seek support from communist Cuba and the Soviet Union; Jagan himself was ambivalent and perhaps not fussy about where he could find support; Maudling accurately summed him up as a 'naïve London School of Economics Marxist filled with charm, personal honesty and juvenile nationalism'.[23]

In October 1961 Jagan visited the USA, and was promised American aid for British Guiana, in line with an agreement between the USA and Britain in September.[24] The Americans, as Maudling's junior minister Hugh Fraser put it, then reneged on their pledges to help; Congressional opponents of foreign aid in general were complaining about any assistance to a leader whom some in Washington regarded as a communist, a position that could have been calculated to drive Jagan into seeking support from someone else who could deliver on their promises. Divisions opened up in the Kennedy administration between elements who wanted a productive relationship with Jagan and an independent Guyana, and those who favoured his overthrow and were willing to see independence delayed. John Kennedy himself, according to Fraser, who spent a sweaty two hours in the presidential hot tub talking about British Guiana in March, did not seem much bothered, but the State Department and Bobby Kennedy were more concerned and there were some strong feelings in the CIA and in Congress.[25]

In December 1961 Jagan visited Maudling in London to discuss progress towards independence, and Maudling – against some reservations from Cabinet colleagues and the Governor of British Guiana – agreed that an independence conference should take place in May 1962, which was three months earlier than in the timetable laid down by a constitutional conference in 1960, with a view to full independence by the end of 1962.[26] Jagan stressed at the time that he was 'keenly aware of the benefits that have flowed to this country from the association with Great Britain and of the further benefits which will accrue to us in the future if circumstances allow us to fulfil our desire to remain within the British Commonwealth of Nations'.[27] Maudling's new timetable was soon destroyed. Even though

Maudling had consulted the Americans and they seemed to agree, the Foreign Secretary, Lord Home, received an outrageous letter in February 1962 from Dean Rusk, the US Secretary of State, in which he told the British that 'I have reached the conclusion that it is not possible for us to put up with an independent British Guiana under Jagan . . . new elections should now be scheduled and I hope that we can agree that Jagan should not accede to power again'.[28] This was too cynical even for Macmillan to stomach, and the 14th Earl was a better democrat than to accept this contempt for the electoral process. He also issued a prescient warning that it was doubtful that any alternative regime 'will be more stable and more mature'.[29] Maudling emphasised these points, about democracy and the undesirability of alternative local leaders, to Presidential Special Assistant Arthur Schlesinger when he visited in March, but added flippantly that 'if you Americans care about British Guiana so much, why don't you take it over? Nothing would please us more.'[30]

Crude American pressure on London failed, but when riots and strikes erupted in Georgetown, the capital of the colony, in February, they poisoned the political atmosphere, preventing a consensus from being constructed on the constitution. The British sent troops to help the colony's government quell the disturbances, but the commission of inquiry into the events was not due to finish until July. The disturbances were prompted by a tax-raising budget, and in the background there were American private and trade union interests which had clearly decided that Jagan should be destabilised; whether or not there was covert official support from parts of the State Department or the CIA at this stage is still not clear. High-level discussions within the Kennedy administration had not reached a clear conclusion on whether to try to work with Jagan or overthrow him, although in March Schlesinger reported that 'both State and CIA are under the impression that a firm decision has been taken to get rid of the Jagan government'.[31] The British were suspicious that the CIA had been involved; Hugh Fraser asked CIA director John McCone, and Maudling told Schlesinger that although he did not believe it himself 'responsible people' were accusing the CIA.[32] Both enquiries received assurances that the agency had not intervened.

Maudling was still keen to see progress towards independence, and offered Jagan constitutional and economic advisers from Britain to assist on the drafting of an independence constitution at the start of May.[33] Independence was envisaged at the latest in mid-1963. Maudling's line on rapid independence for British Guiana caused irritation at Number 10; Macmillan's Foreign Affairs Private Secretary noted in May 1962:

The Colonial Office still treat the place as if it were in Africa or Asia whereas it is in the US backyard and politically very important to the Administration with the mid-term elections coming in the autumn. It is perhaps worth bearing in mind that the President now seems willing to help to get a reasonable Congo solution in a situation which is politically difficult for us and we ought to try to help him in return. But I am not hopeful of finding a better solution – unless the US would pay us to stay in Guiana![34]

Macmillan himself was cynical about American motives: 'they are probably moved by internal political consideration as much as by genuine fear of Communism. It is surely to our interests to be as co-operative and forthcoming as we can. In the future the Americans will have to carry the burden of British Guiana and so it is only fair that they should have a share in shaping its future.'[35] The anger at heavy-handed American intervention in February had dissipated, and the British essentially decided that Georgetown wasn't worth a mass, let alone a rift in that fabled special relationship; the place was essentially sacrificed to please Washington.

The US State Department pressurised the British not to agree to independence without another election that would supersede Jagan's victory in August 1961, and following the February 1962 disturbances the British accepted this.[36] There were two tracks to this policy – one was direct interference, although the problem was that 'it is unproven that CIA knows how to manipulate an election in British Guiana without a backfire'.[37] The other, which had some support from Hugh Fraser in the Colonial Office, was that it would be invidious to grant power in such a divided society to Jagan and his party on 42 per cent of the vote,[38] which had given it a parliamentary majority under the first-past-the-post system. The solution was Proportional Representation (PR) – that the two opposition parties, one predominantly Afro-Caribbean under Forbes Burnham and one European under Peter D'Aguiar, could form a coalition government. Fraser saw clearly that the demographic trends would soon produce a considerable Indian majority and therefore, given the racial dimension of politics in British Guiana, a majority for Jagan, and that there was ultimately no other way round but to persuade Jagan to keep out of the communist camp.[39]

Maudling left the Colonial Office still hoping for a rapid transition to independence, whether under Jagan or a short-lived Burnham coalition, but it was not to be. While there had been no official CIA involvement in the February disturbances, in July 1962 Dean Rusk advocated letting the agency loose, and at the June 1963 Birch Grove meeting Macmillan acceded to Kennedy's determination not to see British Guiana independent under Jagan. The Americans got what they wanted in 1964, when new elections under PR produced a government led by Burnham and independence was granted in 1966. Having evicted Jagan, they stopped caring about Guyana and allowed Burnham, ironically, to make a sharp turn to the left and start nationalising as many industries as he could. The Burnham government became steadily more corrupt and oppressive but it was allowed to do what it liked as long as it posed no threat to American geopolitical interests. Burnham died in 1985 and Jagan returned to power in 1992; nearly forty years after his first election victory, Jagan was at last able to govern his country without interference and did so in an impeccably democratic fashion. Maudling had been right about Jagan – who was indeed basically a Caribbean Bevanite – when others had been disastrously wrong. Guyana paid a heavy price to save the anti-communist face of the Kennedy administration and give the CIA something to do after the Bay of Pigs fiasco. The British, often criticised in retrospect for giving independence too quickly to their colonies, actually failed in Guyana by not acting quickly enough to hand over power – or, rather, handing power to Washington, DC, rather than Georgetown. It was one of the less noble episodes in the history of decolonisation, but Maudling at least can bear little of the blame, having done what he could to settle the Guiana question in the normal fashion.

Guyana was not the only place to pose intractable political difficulties. Maudling also found Zanzibar utterly frustrating[40] and Malta little better. The Mediterranean island was an unusual British colony, in that in 1956 it had been seriously proposed from the Maltese side that it be absorbed into the UK; it was also economically dependent on British naval shipyards, which were themselves a vexed issue between the government and the Bailey firm that managed them. Politics in Malta was bitterly disputed between the National Party and the Malta Labour Party, with issues to do with the role of the Catholic Church and the status of the British royal family proving divisive. The constitution had been suspended since 1959. Maudling did not enjoy his first encounter with Maltese politics:

> I think on Malta I wasn't very well advised – one doesn't want to blame one's civil servants obviously, one shouldn't take unwise advice, I think in my negotiations with Borg Olivier I was probably too tough on detail, too pernickety on details. And the Maltese themselves tend to be a little critical sometimes and I think if I had been sensible I would have agreed a little earlier on a number of things. They were all bedevilled by this blasted Bailey Docks business, which had an awful enquiry about that and it wasn't really very pleasant.[41]

Maudling found Maltese politicians an awkward, difficult lot. Nothing much was achieved on Malta during Maudling's time, although his successor Duncan Sandys oversaw its move to independence in 1964 cushioned by promises of extensive British aid. Maudling's next venture in Malta, in 1966–8, was in an entirely different capacity.

The West Indies and these other scraps of territory were relatively minor concerns beside the big issue of the future of the African colonies. There were particularly knotty problems in two areas: Kenya and the Central African Federation, which comprised Northern Rhodesia (now Zambia), Southern Rhodesia (now Zimbabwe) and Nyasaland (now Malawi).

The Federation was a cock-eyed creation of the Conservative government in 1953. It added a layer of complication to colonial matters in the area, and caused great administrative confusion because the Colonial Office had responsibility for Nyasaland and Northern Rhodesia but not Southern Rhodesia, which had been granted a significant degree of autonomy in 1923, nor the Federation as such. The Federal government was a white minority regime, although it lacked many of the pernicious features that had developed in South Africa or indeed in the domestic policy of the Southern Rhodesian government. It also had a powerful advocate in its Prime Minister, Roy Welensky, who had influential friends on the Tory backbenches and a strong line in threatening bluster which masked his political intelligence. Welensky tried, and sometimes succeeded, in playing the Commonwealth Relations Office, under the more right-wing Duncan Sandys, off against the Colonial Office under Macleod and Maudling.[42]

However, the Federation was a hopeless anachronism, given the rise in African nationalism. Nyasaland, with a negligible white population, not much by way of natural resources and a united and effective African nationalist movement under Hastings Banda that formed an autonomous majority rule government in 1961, sat particularly uncomfortably. British use of force in the colony in the 1959 'emergency' was denounced by an official report for turning it into a police state. There was little reason to cling onto it, and every sign that the cost would be high. Had it not been for the Federation, Nyasaland's independence could have been sorted out in 1960 or 1961 in not much more than five minutes. Even Welensky was ambivalent about hanging on to the place. When Maudling met him for the first time, at the start of November 1961, Reggie noted wryly that 'he spent much time emphasising to me what a liability Nyasaland is (though he didn't seem to want to get rid of the liability)'.[43]

Northern Rhodesia was more complicated. Welensky himself had lived for most of his life in the colony, working as a railwayman and getting involved in local politics. The country was sparsely populated and potentially extremely rich, with large copper and other mineral deposits; exploitation of its wealth was one of the attractions of membership to the other members of the Federation. But it also had an overwhelming black majority, and an African nationalist movement ably led by Kenneth Kaunda was becoming impatient with the lack of movement towards majority rule, let alone full independence. Both Kaunda and Welensky had been talking in alarming terms about the possibility of violence in Northern Rhodesia. Reggie thought that Northern Rhodesia had been 'a pretty muddled situation' when he took office; there had been serious disturbances and the relationship with the Federation was complex. 'What I did try and do, having gone out there and talked to all the people concerned, [was] to try and start logically from the beginning again to assess what the problem was and produce a solution tailored to meet it, rather than trying to produce a solution related to one or other of the previous proposals.'[44] Maudling felt free to discard the government's White Paper published as recently as June 1961 because of the threat of force from Welensky that had surrounded it.[45] Welensky saw Maudling in London at the start of November, and impressed him as being reasonable and capable of compromising over Northern Rhodesia. Maudling wrote a handwritten afterthought to a note to Macmillan on the meeting with Welensky that 'I think we should be <u>firm</u> now with him about N. Rhodesia'.[46] Maudling's firmness was only stiffened by a visit a month later, when he was greeted by a large crowd of demonstrators at Lusaka airport, who expressed their disapproval of Maudling by, he recalled, pushing 'before them into our gaze the oldest and ugliest woman of their tribe, totally naked'.[47] For some reason, Northern Rhodesia got to Maudling, and he became unusually passionate about the place.

Maudling decided quickly that the normal glide path towards independence should apply in Northern Rhodesia – elections for a majority-rule autonomous government being the first step. He was 'immensely impressed' on meeting Kaunda, and had faith in his intelligence and commitment to multiracial politics.[48] A government elected by a black majority in Northern Rhodesia altered the basis of the whole Federation, which would then comprise two African nationalist governments and the minority regime in Southern Rhodesia – an even more obvious absurdity than it had been before. This was strongly opposed by Welensky and his backbench allies, and aroused the displeasure of Duncan Sandys at the Commonwealth Relations Office. Reggie ran into what Rab Butler called 'doubts and perplexities' about Central Africa in early 1962;[49] in January and February he threatened resignation on more than one occasion, telling Macmillan that nothing short of a rapid move to majority rule in Northern Rhodesia was good enough. Maudling became inflexible even about the details of the electoral system to be used. He recruited his predecessor to endorse his new policy, although even Macleod thought Maudling's insistence was 'extreme'.[50] Maudling became quite heated about the issue, Macmillan's press secretary Harold Evans noting that he came back from the West Indies in a good mood but within a few days 'had become very angry again'.[51] Maudling won through, and in February 1962 he announced in the House of Commons that Northern Rhodesia would have a majority-rule constitution.

In March 1962 Macmillan finally decided that the division of responsibilities for Central Africa between Colonial and Commonwealth Relations offices was unsustainable and appointed Rab Butler as head of a Central African Office which took functions from both ministries. The problems on the ground, and the strains that had shaken Whitehall, had become too great. In October 1962 Butler reported that the alternatives available were either the secession of Northern Rhodesia and Nyasaland from the Federation, or a dismal cycle of unrest and suppression. Nyasaland left in December 1962 and became independent in 1964 as Malawi. At the end of

1963 the Federation was formally dissolved, and Zambia claimed its independence in 1964. The residual problem was that while it was unacceptable to grant independence to the white regime in Southern Rhodesia, the British government had no effective means of forcing it to reform. The Rhodesian conundrum continued as an issue in British politics for the rest of Maudling's life.

The parallel of the French experience in Algeria was an awful one for the British government in dealing with the colonies that had a significant settler presence. It certainly weighed heavily on Reggie, whom Patrick Wall found in January 1962 brooding about possible parallels between Algeria and the Central African Federation.[52] The French failure to introduce legitimate constitutional structures in Algeria after 1945 had led to the initiative passing to the radical *FLN* (National Liberation Front) movement and the start of civil war in 1954. Torture, used by the French army to suppress the Algerian uprising, brought shame on France, and the radicalisation of the army had destabilised French politics. By 1961 the Algerian situation was polarised between the implacable, brutal *FLN* and the nihilist terrorism of the settlers' *OAS* (Secret Army Organisation). Ultimately, in February 1962, De Gaulle was obliged to cut the cord and concede Algeria to the *FLN*. The settlers were given the choice of 'the suitcase or the coffin' and repatriated to France without compensation for their property. The harkis, Algerians who had fought for the French, were abandoned to a worse fate.[53] The lesson for the British was to establish constitutional structures that could be transformed into an independent, majority-rule government relatively quickly, and to negotiate as soon as they could with the hardest-line people they could find who were open to reason. The alternative was to attempt to hold on to the colonies by force, which, while technically possible, was not worth the cost in money, blood and international odium. There could be no guarantees to the settlers enforceable after independence – for the point of independence was that Britain no longer had control. It was better to abandon the settlers while some goodwill existed, and create an atmosphere in which the majority rulers would not want to get rid of them or expropriate them.

Molly Ryan, a Kenyan white, remembered attending a dinner with Maudling during his visit to Kenya in November 1961, and attacking him for his attitude to colonial issues: 'You know, Mr Maudling, one can only believe that you in England think of us as wooden pieces on a chessboard, without soul or feeling, to be moved backwards and forwards at the whim and will of our English masters in London.' Maudling shot back: 'And what else, indeed, are you Mrs Ryan! If we didn't think of you in this way, and if we thought of you in flesh and blood, we would never be able to carry out the work that we have set ourselves in England to do!'[54] Mrs Ryan had a rare glimpse of the cynical, even brutal side of Maudling, that would not let sentimentality get in the way of necessity. Just like Macleod, Maudling would do what had to be done.

Kenya was, after Rhodesia, the most intractable case in Africa. It was demographically complicated, with several tribes among the African population, the largest being the Kikuyu, plus a significant Asian population and 30,000 white settlers including farmers as well as administrators. Violent conflict had broken out in 1952 with the 'Mau Mau' revolt, a campaign of nationalist terrorism against the white settlers and their interests. It was bloodily suppressed by a British military campaign in the mid-1950s, and British administrators tried to remove some of the sources of discontent by political and agricultural reforms. The constitutional changes were working towards a 'multiracial' system in which there would not be a universal franchise or majority rule, but an intricate balance between whites, Asians, the Kikuyu and the minority African tribes. But in January 1960 the principle of eventual majority rule was conceded and in 1961 an autonomous Kenyan government took office, based around a coalition between the multiracial New Kenya Group, led mainly by liberal whites, and the much larger Kenyan African Democratic Union (KADU) party whose principal support came from the smaller black tribes.

In August 1961 Iain Macleod had arranged for the release of the imprisoned nationalist leader, Jomo Kenyatta, who had been locked up under suspicion of being the intellectual inspiration of the Mau Mau movement. The decision was bitterly opposed by Kenyan whites and took intricate negotiations with the Governor, Patrick Renison, to accomplish, and was denounced by many Conservatives. In October 1961 Kenyatta assumed leadership of the more radical, Kikuyu-based Kenya African National Union (KANU) party. In a Cabinet meeting in November 1961 Maudling ran into heavy opposition for his intention to allow Kenyatta to participate in parliament; one of his colleagues said that Kenyatta was 'an evil man who must be held responsible for the brutalities of the Mau Mau movement'.[55]

Maudling met Kenyatta later in November, which aroused some discontent among people who objected to friendly gestures towards a man so recently demonised as violent and bloodthirsty. Reggie tried to avoid being photographed in scenes that suggested that he and Kenyatta were getting on well, 'Not because I had any particular objection but simply because it would have made my task as Colonial Secretary more difficult if I had done so'.[56] Reggie was not initially particularly impressed, but found himself revising his opinion upwards every time he met Kenyatta. Reggie faced political facts, telling the Cabinet in November 1961 that 'Kenyatta will become Prime Minister whether we like it or not'.[57] A deal with Kenyatta was essential, and it needed to be done relatively quickly. Kenya's economy was going downhill rapidly in the winter of 1961/2,[58] and the fear was in the background that Russian or Chinese communist influence would gain the ascendancy within the Kenyan independence movement if things were left to slide.

The Lancaster House conference on Kenya was the most complicated independence conference Maudling dealt with. It opened on 14 February

1962. It was in fact the second such Kenya conference, a previous meeting having been convened by Macleod in 1960. The 1960 conference had established a complicated electoral system of fancy franchises, but while doing so it had conceded the principle of African majority rule in Kenya and prepared the way for independence. The 1962 conference was about providing a constitution that would take Kenya through independence.[59]

The basic points at issue at the Kenya conference were less to do with relations between black, Asian and white than with the nature of the central government of Kenya. The main nationalist movement, KANU, proposed a strong central government with majority party rule and a unicameral legislature, hedged around with a Bill of Rights to preserve individual and civil rights. Reggie envisaged that KANU was popular enough to control the central government however it was organised. However, KANU's support was strongest among the majority Kikuyu tribe, and the minority tribes of Kenya – including whites and Asians – feared that a strong central government would become an instrument of Kikuyu domination. As Maudling put it: 'The whole battle in Kenya all the time was that people used to run round in groups holding up great banners saying "Regionalism for ever" – you know, misspelt and upside down – regionalism simply meant "Don't let the Kikuyu run our village for us".'[60] To Maudling, it was all an illustration of a general Hegelian principle:

> Federation is a reaction really to thesis and antithesis. You have that thesis of independent feeling, suspicion of one's neighbours, coupled with the antithesis of the unviability of small units, and the only reaction to give you the synthesis of the two is to try and get the small units into a large organisation which can live internationally but given enough autonomy to live in their own communities. It is a natural reaction.[61]

The KADU party, based around minority tribes – Kalenjin, Maasai, the coastal tribes and Somalis – made 'democratic regionalism' the centre of its constitutional framework; there would be six regional authorities with legislative powers, and a second chamber in the national parliament in which all regions would be equally represented. The liberal whites under Michael Blundell broadly supported the KADU decentralised structure. However, KADU's proposed guarantees of individual rights were weaker than KANU's, leading opponents to point out that local authorities might be just as capable of arbitrary tyranny as central government.[62]

When they turned up at Lancaster House, the KANU and KADU positions seemed miles apart, and it looked as if general agreement might not be possible. Maudling felt the situation required a deliberate show of being unruffled. He conducted the Kenya conference in a calm fashion, without much of the psychodrama that often goes with important conferences. He did not like working through the night, or making other people work through the night: 'No, I don't like that sort of style. We did sit up quite late at the Kenya conference once or twice, but on the whole people found that intelligence doesn't increase as the evening wears on.'[63] Neither did he get involved much in minute details; on one occasion when he received a full briefing from all the senior figures involved he concluded that the only progress it had achieved was that 'I'm now confused at a much higher level'.[64] Nor was Maudling constantly engaged in talking to people behind the scenes in an effort to broker an agreement – his approach was that if you are doing this all the time it gets discounted, while the occasional, exceptional 'dinner with a couple of chaps' can have a greater effect.[65] Maudling's talent for masterly inactivity had met the moment.

The conference dragged on for weeks of seemingly unproductive discussions, reaching sixteen plenary sessions by mid-March, during which Reggie aimed to give as many groups as possible the impression that he agreed with them, including the Tory right, represented by Freddie Bennett and Patrick Wall, who supported KADU regionalism.[66] Reggie listened intently to advice that was offered him – Philip Goodhart, a Tory MP who knew Kenya well, came to him with serious worries about the existing plan, particularly concerning landownership, and found Maudling very receptive.[67]

But in fact, through their meandering discussions the two principal parties were getting closer to a basis for agreement. The possibility of a synthesis between their ideas was there from the beginning. KADU had come with a statement of principles, while KANU had made a fairly detailed sketch of a draft constitution. Maudling came to the conclusion that, nice people as KADU were, they simply did not have the political intelligence of their KANU counterparts.[68] Maudling and his officials anticipated that the likely outcome was an adaptation of the KANU draft to reflect some of the principles that were important to KADU, and chose their moment to produce their own draft that each party could claim as a victory for their principal ideas. KANU legal adviser, F.R.S. de Souza, thought the Maudling constitution 'as near perfect as could be obtained under the circumstances' and had a vivid memory of his advocacy in a conversation with Reggie about the merits of a second chamber to the legislature: 'You know, Fitz, a second chamber is required not only as a brake on inexperienced exuberance but also to kick upstairs a veteran politician whose contribution had now diminished through age or drink, but whom the community wished to honour and provide status.'[69] Maudling did not get this suggestion past the Kenyan politicians, and the regional element of the 1962 constitution was pretty much dead on arrival. It became less and less important as the constitution was revised in 1963 and after independence. KANU's concessions were fairly meaningless as Kenyatta told his colleagues that they could be reversed after independence. The regions had been obliged to adhere to central rules in the first place, and they lacked fiscal autonomy. The uneven economic development within Kenya created vast differences in the potential of each region – as KANU delegate Tom

Mboya commented, the region's reserved revenue from fuel tax was not much use if the principal mode of transport in the region was by camel.[70] Maudling was a little surprised that his 'odd' constitution, probably the most complicated left by a departing British administration, lasted for such a short time, but not too disappointed. He reconciled himself to it with the apparently cynical claim: 'The whole object of the Constitution was not to have a Constitution, but to have agreement. Which I think was worked out. Worked out very well.'[71]

The lasting legacy of the Kenya conference was indeed the agreement that was evolved there, not so much on constitutional details but on a common understanding. Politicians who had made demagogic, even bloodthirsty, speeches against each other realised that they had a lot in common, and the minorities realised that the fear of Kikuyu domination was overstated. Kenyatta, in particular, emerged as a figure of high standing even among whites, who had feared him as a 'leader unto darkness and death' only a couple of years before. KANU and KADU formed a coalition central government in Kenya in June 1962, and in July as one of his very last acts as Colonial Secretary Maudling visited to see how it was working in practice, and was pleased to see that teamwork and 'thinking nationally' were developing quickly among Kenyan politicians. He also announced that the land settlement scheme would be tripled, with 15 per cent of the former 'White Highlands' being bought out in the interests of landless African farmers with fair compensation to the white farmers.[72] He was praised by a local newspaper as 'The Maudling Cement Mixer' for his constructive work on building up for independence.

Cooperation at central level in Kenya was institutionalised under independence. The KADU party itself dissolved rapidly in 1963–4, finally winding itself up and merging into KANU in November 1964. KANU radicals in turn split away and formed their own party a little later. The Lancaster House conference succeeded in forming a consensus and preventing the breakdown of Kenya on tribal lines. While Kenya's history even under Kenyatta was not perfect – the arbitrary powers of the central government increased, to be an outspoken dissident was to risk one's life, and the government squandered the talents of its Asian population by a hasty 'Africanisation' policy – it remained relatively stable, peaceful and prosperous. It was only after 1978, under Kenyatta's successor Daniel arap Moi (once of KADU) that Kenya became corrupt and oppressive, and even after decades of Moi's rule the solution to the problem came through a democratic election rather than violence. Constitutionalism, if not the 1962 constitution itself, was and is a strong force in Kenyan politics. Maudling was cited with great respect for his contribution in 1962, when Kenya conducted its constitutional review in 2001.

Maudling always felt proud of what he had helped accomplish in Kenya. He had a principled, determined objective and he pursued it with all his considerable abilities. He was intellectually flexible and willing to listen to reasoned arguments from wherever they came, and in the conference he used his charm and ability to think quickly to advantage. He had a clear view of the important points that needed resolution. Looking back on his political career in 1976, when asked what made him most proud, he chose the independence of Kenya.[73]

In contrast, Kenya's neighbour Uganda offered little to be proud of, although the arrangements for its independence slid past almost unnoticed compared to Kenya. There were few whites in Uganda, and while the internal politics of Kenya was a complicated, multifaceted matter, Uganda seemed a relatively simple business of balancing the claims to separate authority of the traditional kingdom of Buganda with the formation of a Ugandan government. In recent years the British had tried to undermine the kingdom and promote an all-Ugandan consciousness, but this was reversed in the rapid transition to independence. Under Macleod there had been elections and a commission of inquiry into the constitution, which in June 1961 recommended federal status for Buganda and gave the traditional aristocrats control over its parliamentary representation. 'Oh, I don't know, one always has Committee Reports – what the hell!' was Reggie's rather negligent comment in 1968 about the Uganda inquiry.[74] Macleod had set a timetable for independence by October 1962, and assured Maudling that Uganda was all wrapped up. A government under Milton Obote was formed in May 1962, a ramshackle alliance between the Buganda hierarchy and a party representing the scattered tribes in the rest of Uganda. In June 1962 Maudling presided over another constitutional convention, which conceded federal status to other smaller kingdoms. The Ugandan constitution was a dog's dinner, but it sufficed to put a government in place that could accept independence in October 1962, the date specified in the timetable set down in September 1961.[75] It is hard to escape the conclusion that the British simply wanted rid of Uganda, quickly, and that as long as there was a reasonably acceptable set of people to shake hands with when the flag was hauled down, that was good enough. But there was no essential agreement in Uganda on constitutional matters, the one party that had support across the country had been robbed of its victory in elections in March 1961, and the constitutionalist tradition was extremely weak; autocracy, and racism against Asians, were already apparent in Buganda in 1960. Within fifteen years Uganda had completely collapsed under the insane regime of Idi Amin. There was little that Maudling could have done to avert disaster; the course had been set before he took office, and if he had wanted to renegotiate the constitution it would have meant delaying independence, which was briefly considered in April 1962 but was unacceptable not so much in Uganda – where there was little nationalist pressure and some concerns among local leaders about the haste of the pullout[76] – as at the United Nations.

Sometimes, in retrospect, and with the Ugandan case in mind, it seems that the rush to independence was too rapid. Britain bailed out before the rule of law, constitutions, democracy and neutral administration were established, and many newly independent states fell quickly under autocratic, charismatic leadership, and misguided economic policies, even if nowhere else degenerated to the same extent as Uganda. But the logic expressed forcefully by Macleod, and in softer tones by Maudling, is still compelling. What was the alternative? The suppression of revolt in Kenya was costly enough, but the awful comparison in Maudling's mind was the doomed French resistance to Algerian independence. To cling on, to spit in the wind of change, was inconceivable. Maudling was the ideal man to come to terms with necessity, and do it with dignity. The settlements with which he was most involved, the West Indies and Kenya, are among those that have been most successful. In Kenya the success was all the more notable because of the fears, shared by Macmillan, that the country would collapse into violence and poverty. Maudling's jovial personality, and his ability to take people as they came, served Britain and several former colonies well.

Maudling never gave the impression of being gripped by colonial affairs; even his Private Secretary, Jack Howard-Drake, felt uncertain about whether Reggie ever really wanted to be there, or whether he was much interested in what he was doing. 'Macleod was an innovator, Maudling was implementing a policy.'[77] But once Macleod had made the historic shift, Maudling was ideal as a consolidating minister who would continue the policy while smoothing ruffled feathers among those who had been alienated by the change of direction.

Maudling calmed down the internal conflict within the Conservative Party. The Tory traditionalists knew full well that Maudling and Macleod had been playing a classic good cop/bad cop routine, but they could not hold it against Maudling. He treated them with courtesy and respect and was always willing to listen, while Macleod had seemed to enjoy the fight. The old right were, for the most part, Maudling supporters when he ran for the leadership in 1965 and some of them even favoured his cause in 1963. There was something reassuring about the way Maudling could advocate what had a few years earlier seemed wild radical ideas and make them seem thoroughly moderate and reasonable. This talent was first brought to bear on colonial affairs, but Maudling also played the great conciliator in persuading the Tories to accept a large measure of intervention and planning in the economy, and the permissive society. After his short, eventful term at the Colonial Office, imperialism was dead as a force in British politics.

Chapter 11

'STOP DAWDLING, MAUDLING!': CHANCELLOR OF THE EXCHEQUER, 1962–1963

W hile Maudling had been pondering the minutiae of federalism in Africa, the government's domestic political position had been deteriorating. There were signs of mortality as early as summer 1961 with the unpopular 'pay pause', and the Conservatives no longer enjoyed the easy dominance of the eighteen months after October 1959. The government continued to accumulate discontents, as the economy was stalled and impatience grew with Britain's apparent state of general stagnation. In March 1962 slow political decline became crisis for the Tories with the Liberal by-election victory in the previously safe Conservative seat of Orpington. The Conservative candidate, Peter Goldman, a bright Research Department staff member trying to follow in Reggie's footsteps to a safe seat in the London suburbs, was trounced.

During the last forty years, governments, the press and voters have become accustomed to dramatic reversals of fortune at by-elections, but in 1962 the transformation of a Conservative majority of 14,760 into a Liberal margin of 7,855 was a complete shock to the system. As Maudling himself put it, 'the ice broke under our feet and all could see for the first time how thin it had become'.[1] Nobody really knew what to make of it at the time. Given that the 1959 election had seemed such a demonstration that long-term social change determines electoral behaviour, people looked for a social factor that would explain Orpington and other lesser by-election shocks, and explain why 'Orpington Man' was up in arms. Different people found it, implausibly in the right-wing colonel angered by the government's 'betrayal' of the African whites, and more sensibly in the home-owning, modestly affluent lower middle class, who had accumulated grievances such as Schedule A taxation on housing, commuter railway fares and the like, and who believed that Tory Britain was in danger of obsolescence in the newly inaugurated 'space age'.[2]

In May 1962 the local elections demonstrated Liberal strength once again, particularly in middle-class suburbs reminiscent of Orpington. Barnet was socially not too dissimilar from Orpington, as an outer London mixture of established suburbs, commuter areas and new housing. In Finchley, bordering on Barnet, the Liberals swept the board and new MP Margaret Thatcher was one of the most vulnerable-looking targets for the resurgent party. However, the Liberal tide only lapped around Barnet, with the Liberals taking a lead in the combined Chipping Barnet and East Barnet area. According to the careful calculations of Arthur Fawcett, the Tories would still be somewhat ahead in the constituency as a whole in a general election, and Reggie could hold it by something like 3,500.[3] It was still worrying and close enough to home for Reggie to take a particular interest in the causes and contours of the Liberal revival.

Reggie was also chafing under the constraints of the Colonial Office. He was becoming a bit bored and his attention was wandering back, as it always did, to the central questions of economic policy and social organisation. Politics after Orpington presented Reggie, like many Tories, with the threat of electoral defeat, but for him in particular it was an opportunity. He was perhaps the leading Tory with the closest affinity for 'Orpington Man', in his modernity and materialism. If he could re-engage with domestic politics, he would be in a strong position to present himself as the answer to the problems that faced the government. Reggie developed his thoughts in several speeches in May 1962 in which he reflected on Britain having become steadily more prosperous but also the seeming lack of purpose and the 'general feeling, somehow, that we are not giving the dynamic leadership to the country that people wish to have at the moment'.[4]

Reggie followed his speeches with an open letter to the electors of Barnet, an old-fashioned device that he felt was a more considered way of ventilating his thoughts on important issues than he could manage in any speech. It also had the advantage that attention would not be distracted from the content by any deficiencies in delivery. Friendly newspapers, like the *Daily Mail* in 1962 and *The Times* frequently thereafter when he wrote these letters, respectfully reprinted their contents. In the 1962 letter, Reggie stressed the gravity of 'a period of sudden and rare political turmoil':

I am convinced that there is one fundamental reason which underlies all the individual complaints and grievances that are the substance of by-election controversies. It is this. We are seeing the close of one political era and the opening of another. The problems and the needs of our country will be very different in the 1960s from the 1950s: they call for a new outlook and new policies.[5]

Reggie saw the way out of the turmoil of 1962 very much along the same lines as he had seen the Tory position in 1943; he was trying again to convert the Tory party to his way of thinking. To anyone who had read his 1943 *Spectator* piece, the thrust of his 1962 letter cannot have come as much of a surprise; it was the party that had to do the rethinking rather than him.

He returned to his familiar philosophical territory of the difference between negative and positive liberty, and the Hegelian concept of self-discipline providing a balance between order and freedom. He also made, in updated language, his case for controls and coordination in the economy:

> Freedom without order is meaningless in the economic field as it is in the political. No one save an anarchist believes that the right to individual liberty includes the right to destroy society. Nor does it include the right to undermine the economy. When old disciplines go new ones must be found unless freedom is to destroy its own purpose . . . It is the responsibility of Government in the 1960s to drive this fact home by constant explanation of the rights and the duties of the free individual in the free economy and by determined action if powerful groups or organisations attempt to override them. To do this may be inconsistent with classical laissez-faire Liberal doctrine. But it is essential for true freedom and a sound economy in the 1960s.

Maudling stated the purpose that he believed should be the organising principle, the dynamic project to which society's resources should be devoted: 'This must be the sense of purpose for an affluent society. To clear up the remaining areas of poverty and squalor in our own society, to take a lead in the long process of freeing the impoverished majority of mankind from the material shackles that stand in the way of decent human existence.'[6]

It was a well-calculated time for Reggie to publish a political testament. Macmillan had for some time been losing confidence in his Chancellor, Selwyn Lloyd. The Cabinet had overruled the Chancellor on the 1962 Budget, an extremely unusual occurrence, and the Prime Minister started to resent what he saw as the slow progress of the Treasury on incomes policy. As more bad by-elections followed Orpington, including a humiliating slump at depressed West Lothian in mid-June, and the economy continued to stagnate, Macmillan started to brood about the position, and came to the conclusion that something drastic had to be done to encourage the economy to perform and to produce a more dynamic image for the government. Maudling was one minister – with a track record in economic affairs – who was talking a new language and whose recent disquisitions had been treated with respect, and he was no longer being as obstreperous as he had been over Northern Rhodesia in February. Macmillan had essentially decided in early July that he would replace Lloyd with Maudling very soon, and also clear out some of the Cabinet dead wood such as Lords Kilmuir and Mills, Harold Watkinson and one or two others later in the summer. The plans, though, were blown by the indiscretion of Rab Butler, which led to a story in the *Daily Mail* on 12 July about a reconstruction of the government that would soon take place.[7] That evening, Selwyn Lloyd was called to Number 10 to receive the bad news, but he talked to friends and the story spread, alongside the realisation that the

Conservatives had suffered a collapse from a close second to a poor third in a by-election in Leicester North East. In a piece of panicky butchery on Friday 13 July, Macmillan disposed of a further six Cabinet ministers, some with negligent brutality – when he heard that the former Lord Chancellor Kilmuir was dismissed with less notice than he would give a cook, he commented, 'Ah, but a good cook is so hard to find . . .'.

For all its ugliness the July 1962 reshuffle did at least produce quite a good government that was a significant tilt to the left from its predecessor. 'The liberal wing of the Conservative Party is now unmistakeably in the ascendant, both in the Cabinet and outside it, with no more than the minimum of reassurance handed out to the more cautious and traditionally conservative,' commented the *Spectator*.[8] Edward Boyle was a strong, committed liberal at the Education department; Keith Joseph an expansionist minister at Housing and Local Government. It was also a strong government; it had a higher than usual proportion of ministers who were relatively young, intelligent and knew what they were doing in their own department. Paradoxically, although the dismissal of Lloyd was widely regretted, the appointment of Maudling as Chancellor was perhaps the most popular aspect of the reshuffle. He received some of the best publicity of his life. The American Embassy noted that 'Maudling, his reputation as a negotiator slightly tarnished when he tangled with the Europeans on trade matters, is resourceful, energetic and honorable. He is of open nature, and dealings with him by our Treasury people should be both intimate and pleasant.'[9] Maudling's political career was back on track, after some speculation during the previous couple of years that his days as the coming man were over. As a news magazine, the *Statist* commented: 'Until recently he has been inclined to feel that time and opportunity had passed him by.'[10] Now it had come, out of the blue, to Reggie's surprise and delight, and he had the job he had always wanted.

The summer of 1962, and the two years after it, was the happiest time of Reggie Maudling's life. It was a joyful, optimistic period for the Maudling family. Beryl confided to a Tory meeting in a branch of the Barnet constituency party that the 'happy chaos' of family life kept them sane when affairs of state were most pressing.[11] For Caroline he had been a benevolent but distant father when she was smaller:

He did not spend much time with us. He viewed that world rather as the domain of women; they handled home and family while men dealt with work and politics. I was usually away at boarding school except during the parliamentary recess. He didn't talk to us about elections, politics and so on; it would not have occurred to him that we might be interested.[12]

As with his political life, Reggie was trying harder and getting it more right than he had before, or would do afterwards. Reggie and Beryl were both softening their approach to parenting and there was an uncomplicated joy about Reggie's relationship with the younger boys in the early 1960s. He would drive them to school most mornings, keeping step with the rhythm of normal family life among the electorate. For William's seventh birthday in 1964 (which coincided with Reggie's own forty-seventh) there was a cake made in the shape of a castle, 'Fort William' with seven candles from its towers and turrets. William gave his father some walnut whip cakes, Reggie complaining to a newspaper, 'There are hardly any left. All the family have been eating them.'[13] William wanted to follow his father's footsteps into Parliament, while Edward had ambitions to be a fireman. Martin, now 19, was less sure about what he wanted: 'I don't really know what I'll end up doing but I don't have any political ambitions at present.'[14]

Beryl's life was bound up with Reggie's to an unusual degree for a political wife. She would often accompany him on overseas visits, and was usually present at his side at cocktail parties and receptions. She was widely regarded as being sociable, charming, attractive and good company if a bit flighty. Beryl was very much a part of Reggie's family and social life, although she was not interested in politics and not really capable of offering much by way of advice or comfort to him as a politician. She was not as strong-willed and intelligent as, for instance, Eve Macleod or Rab Butler's formidable second wife, Mollie, both wise counsellors and stabilising influences on their political husbands. Although he was always in Beryl's company, Reggie had to bear a lot of the burdens of his life alone.

However, Reggie was besotted with Beryl, on a deep romantic and sexual level that nothing seemed able to disturb, and he was oblivious to other expressions of interest from women. 'If I had married that man, he would have been Prime Minister,' sighed Christobel Berry, who had married into the *Telegraph* dynasty, to a friend.[15] Some other admirers without a direct interest in the matter thought that Reggie would have been better off getting a divorce and marrying someone more supportive and suitable,[16] but there is no sign that the idea ever took the first step in crossing his mind. He devoted his energies to making Beryl happy, which was becoming a progressively more difficult job as she became used to grand living and being the centre of attention at receptions. Beryl became very high maintenance, with a round of hair stylists, manicurists, massages and suchlike, and also demanding that her expensive tastes in fashion, furnishing and antiques were satisfied. Reggie hated displeasing her or denying her anything.

Now that the older children were practically grown up, and the two younger boys were at school, Beryl had considerably more free time and energy to do what she thought she should as a leading society lady. She could be pushy in good causes, such as the Westminster Hospital, and was an effective organiser and fund-raiser. She also gave of her time and could be extremely sympathetic in her charity work, with a mixture of warm-heartedness and affection that recalled her childhood role model, Adeline Genée. Beryl tried to develop herself as a patron of the arts, particularly ballet; she did not forget her extraordinary career as a child dancer. She was still in touch with ballet teachers and dancers, such as Noreen Bush, who now ran a ballet school on the outskirts of East Grinstead in Sussex, and there would be the occasional theatrical reception where they met. At one, in 1962, Beryl learned that the Bush–Davies school were building a small studio theatre and needed a bit more money. By Beryl's account, 'I made a little speech about forming the trust to build a theatre on a piece of land in Sussex, and the whole thing started from there.' Beryl and her ballet friends and some local figures in Sussex formed a charitable trust. Beryl threw herself, almost obsessively, into raising money:

By having fetes and jumble sales. We arranged Dior dress shows, people gave lunch parties, one with Irene Worth. We held whist drives, wine and cheese parties. And, of course, I wrote an enormous number of letters. Not circulars. That would not do at all. Personal letters. Then I had Reggie to advise me. He told me whom to approach. He was a great help and also wrote to people.[17]

There was a champagne reception at Number 11 in 1963. As the fund-raising progressed, the scale of the theatre project spiralled even more rapidly, until the little stage for the Bush–Davies girls had become a 330-seat ballet theatre with a large, specially designed stage. There was never a chance, even with Beryl's intense fund-raising, of the finances adding up for what had become the Adeline Genée Theatre. It started off as a way of occupying Beryl's time, but by 1964 it had become a burden; things had gone too far to pull out without great embarrassment, but to see it through became a greater and greater stretch, as the dream grew in scale and as the costs inevitably overran. The theatre (and the underlying purpose of the theatre, which was to make Beryl happy) was, a few years later, to lead Reggie into disaster, but for now it seemed an expression of the fact that Reggie and Beryl had finally arrived in society.

The Maudlings were blessed by having good friends as well as a warm family. Only a few friends were political, including particularly Ian and Joanie Orr-Ewing, the Macleods, the Errolls and the Carrs, plus Freddie Bennett. Some Chester Street neighbours, Stephen and Mrs King-Lewis, also became close. Reggie also remained on close terms with his college tutor, Geoffrey Mure, and fellow student and now businessman Michael Clapham. Beryl had friends from the worlds of dancing and the theatre. The Maudlings also picked up friends among people they met, including Sandy Glen. Glen was in the shipping and travel business, but before going into business had been an explorer and a war hero; he and Reggie met at a dinner in the early 1950s and hit it off almost immediately. Sandy Glen was left with a tangible sense of the warmth and happiness of the Maudling family life in the late 1950s and early 1960s:

Every New Year we would come to 'first foot' them with their black poodles. It was a simple, enormously happy, good atmosphere, the children bustling around, always bare footed. There was a great sense of normality and goodness about the scene. There was a lot that was wonderful in Reggie's family life early on, tremendous happiness. Their marriage was based on great love. It seemed like the Garden of Eden before the serpent appeared.[18]

As Chancellor, Reggie had a reputation for being, as well as a family man, a bit on the louche side, although in a rather harmless and appealing way. He would venture the occasional sartorial experiment, including on one memorable occasion a bright yellow dinner jacket that appalled his friends. Another experiment was a velvet, midnight-blue dinner suit that he wore to a meeting at Number 10: 'Ah, Reggie,' Macmillan greeted him, 'off to the 100 Club again?' 'Plays the drums, y'know,' the Prime Minister muttered to his neighbours at the Cabinet table. Reggie was, quietly, rather hurt at the time, but enjoyed telling the anecdote. Reggie was no stranger to the late-night, smoky bonhomie of London's jazz clubs, which were growing in popularity in the early 1960s. He enjoyed eating, drinking, puffing at fat cigars and occasionally dancing the night away, and saw no reason why high office should make him solemn. When in Paris on Board of Trade business, officials put a night at the opera in his programme but he told them that he would much prefer to go to the Crazy Horse, a famous upmarket cabaret and strip club. The Crazy Horse story practically became part of his official biographical summary at the time.[19] It was quite a good metaphor for his rather sensuous liking for mild decadence and spectacle; for a lack of prudery or sexual inhibition combined with devoted fidelity to Beryl, who accompanied him on some of his expeditions to strip clubs. It also signified his refusal to feign an interest in high culture; while most ministers would probably have gladly exchanged an opera trip for the chance to watch chorus girls clad only in large feathers, few were willing to admit to it as publicly.

Maudling would admit to being mildly philistine. His non-political pursuits did not compare with the 'hinterland' of widely advertised cultural knowledge of someone like Denis Healey or Roy Jenkins. His hinterland was lightly cultivated. High culture requires a certain amount of investment of time and intellectual energy that Maudling could have afforded had he been so inclined. Reggie refused to make the effort. However, there is no rule that says that members of the political elite have to have refined tastes that differ from those of the mass of the electorate. His tastes were defiantly 1960s middlebrow: he liked jazz, James Bond and Kingsley Amis. To relax, there were also the detective novels of Georges Simenon and the *Eagle* comic, supposedly for boys but enjoyed by Reggie – particularly the strips featuring the Mekon.[20] He liked watching westerns on the television, and other favourites were *Doctor Who* and *Tom and Jerry*.[21] Reggie said in 1973 that

'I watch TV mostly at weekends and find it compelling. I keep thinking there must be something else I ought to be doing but find it very difficult to switch off. My favourite programmes are pretty low-brow but then I look upon TV as a medium for entertainment not education.'[22] This was one of the strands running through his career – in the 1950s one of his pet causes as a backbencher had been commercial television.

Reggie's holidays had become, by the early 1960s, what a profile called 'the expensively simple kind' – villas, yachts, nightclubs in the more exclusive resorts of the Mediterranean, often courtesy of rich friends such as the Yugoslav shipping owner Vane Ivanovic in Majorca, or Neville and Christobel Berry in the south of France. He was seen 'dancing barefoot on the Riviera', an appealing image of a relaxed, uninhibited man enjoying life.[23] Maudling was aware that too obvious a taste for luxury might not be an entirely good thing and while private indulgence was one thing, coming across in public as a plutocrat was another. Peregrine Worsthorne recalled a dinner at the particularly image-conscious moment of the 1963 party conference in Blackpool when Reggie 'Had just lit up a fat cigar when a television crew started filming our table. To my disgust, instead of boldly continuing to puff away, he furtively hid this symbol of affluence under the table.'[24] Reggie also sometimes risked not appearing affluent and suave enough. Even though his holidays were increasingly spent amid luxury, he still wore notably tatty swimming trunks, and he did not greatly care about the impression he gave with his work clothes. He admitted that he got more crumpled as the day went on, and that his policy with suits was to 'wait until my present suit is getting a bit too shabby and then I buy another one'.[25] His taste in cars was similarly understated. He and Beryl would cram themselves into a Triumph Herald, which, given his bulk, took a certain degree of effort and looked mildly ridiculous. Perhaps in reaction, Martin became a devotee of fast cars and, for a time, a most unsuccessful racing driver.

Not all Reggie's pleasures were of the senses. He was intellectually curious, perhaps particularly in the changing world of the early 1960s, reading a lot of politics, economics and philosophy – although very little highbrow literature. He would often just sit and think about things, weaving connections between ideas, creating new ways of looking at what he had read about and pondering what were the central questions. Sometimes, even when apparently switched off and not thinking about anything, he would suddenly grab a scrap of paper and write down a thought that had occurred to him. He could listen to a discussion, apparently not contributing much but contributing a brilliant summing up of the most important points that left little more to be said. His reputation for laziness was spreading in the early 1960s, but at that stage it was largely undeserved. Ministerial office was well within his mental capabilities and he saw no reason to put on a show of effort when something came easily to him. His Treasury Private Secretary, Tom Caulcott, remembered Maudling as efficient rather than lazy: 'What he was not was lazy as a minister. He was faster than any other minister I knew, and it wasn't because he didn't really do the work. He did it, and got through the papers extremely fast. He could run rings around most other people intellectually.'[26] When there was an issue with which he was wrestling, he was perfectly capable of putting in the hours. His children recall occasions when he was shut away in the study, working on his papers early in the morning or on a weekend afternoon. He probably hid how much he worked from his colleagues, something that ultimately did him little good. An August 1962 interviewer found him relaxed and confident behind the Chancellor's desk in the Treasury 'looking like a benign, oversized furry cat, too well fed to pounce'. In the same interview, asked whether he was ambitious, he said 'Perhaps I am, but not in any out of the ordinary way. I don't think you have to be ruthlessly ambitious to get to the top in politics. Do you?'[27]

Maudling's career up to this point illustrated that ability, a pleasant temperament and 'ordinary' ambition could get one a long way. Maudling seemed, more than anyone else in politics, to be lacking in anger. Although it was part of the reason for his broad (but perhaps shallow) popularity, this disappointed some political allies, such as Charles Hill who wrote in 1964 that 'I am sorry I have never seen him angry, for his equanimity suggests to some that he lacks fire in his belly leading them to wonder whether the stuff of leadership is in him'.[28] Reggie himself said that 'any man who cannot feel anger can never achieve anything in this world. On the other hand it's one thing to feel it, and another to show it. It's often better to feel it and conceal it, rather than to show it.'[29] Maudling's undercurrent of anger was only rarely glimpsed, and it was possible to know him quite well without seeing him as anything other than pleasant, good-humoured and obliging, but the suppressed anger of the nice man can be a very dangerous force. Reggie, at least overtly, reacted to most things, even those that many others would consider tiresome, absurd or wrong, with a kind of amused tolerance about the varieties and follies of human existence. His broad shoulders were often shrugged. He did not resent defeats or brood, choosing instead to move on to the next matter. Reggie did not think of political life as a battle, or of himself as a fighter.

Most politicians, even as a piece of glib retrospection, can claim to have been brought into the profession by anger at some act of injustice or oppression. But Maudling's motivation was always obscure. His Private Secretary, Derek Mitchell, accompanying him to a formal speech, remembers adjourning afterwards for a drink in his hotel room. Reggie turned on the television and *Come Dancing* was on; the Chancellor watched with a rapt expression on his face and said, over his whisky, 'Derek, this is what Conservatism is all about!' Mitchell was never quite sure what he meant.[30] What Maudling might have meant was, to borrow John Prescott's phrase, 'traditional values in a modern setting': the preservation of an English, cosy and reassuring way of life while adapting to a time when everything was changing fast. Maudling was not ideologically driven – although he had a profound sense that the Conservative Party should be at the centre of public life as the natural party of government, but also that it should govern from somewhere on the centre-left. Reggie would never have put it this way himself, and would have resisted any attempt to describe what he was in politics to achieve. Politics was management, steering the ship, seeking consensus, adapting to new circumstances, and he knew himself well enough to know that he was good at it.

The Treasury had been revolutionised since Reggie's last substantial involvement as acting Economic Secretary in 1958. Tom Caulcott, who had been on a scholarship to the USA in 1960–1, recalled:

> The change had come over economic policy in 1960/61 . . . When I came back things had changed. There was more interest in government intervention in the economy; in the 1950s the Conservatives had reacted against the detailed Labour controls in 1945–51 and talked more about encouraging enterprise, but in 1961 attention turned back to broad planning and intervention. There was a lot more discussion about managing the economy, a sea change in attitudes had taken place in the official attitude and the line in policy papers.[31]

Selwyn Lloyd, a quiet, conservative minister who appeared to lack political and intellectual confidence, was an unlikely person to preside over such a radical change in the framework of policy. Even so, he was a considerable innovator. In July 1961 the Plowden Committee examining the treatment of public spending reported, and recommended a longer-term planning system. Even before the final Plowden report was published Lloyd had already started work on a five-year plan for public spending, and the Tory government had set a course for substantial increases over the medium term. In 1961 it was already clear that a choice had been made between any possibility of significant tax cuts in the 1960s and the expansion of the social services – the Tories chose to expand the social services.[32]

As well as the public spending regime, Lloyd – Prime Minister Macmillan always in the background – changed other aspects of economic management. In 1961 the Chancellor took powers to use the 'regulator' – the ability to vary indirect tax rates between budgets, and proposed the establishment of a National Economic Development Committee (NEDC, aka Neddy), which brought together government, management and unions. Its first meeting was in March 1962. The next month, the Budget set out a growth target of 4 per cent (Lloyd had argued that it might as well be 5 per cent, but was persuaded that this was completely unrealistic) and announced the government's conversion to some form of planning. In February the government had announced a formal pay policy, with the publication of a 'guiding light' to indicate the future overall path of earnings. Running an incomes policy was a volte-face not only for the Tories but for the Treasury – in mid-1962 the

Chief Economic Adviser, Alec Cairncross, reflected on the 'excessive zeal for a policy they formerly would have none of'.[33] Alongside Neddy there was Nicky – NIC, the National Incomes Commission, which Macmillan had taken the lead in preparing for but whose public announcement fell to Reggie as Chancellor. The purpose of the NIC was to police the incomes policy by assessing the validity of pay claims that exceeded the guiding light, but it never operated at full strength because it was boycotted by the trade unions and only heard four cases before Labour abolished it. But economic policy was a very different environment from the 'set the people free' of Conservative politics in 1951.

There are parallels with the state of affairs in Maudling's previous job at the Colonial Office. There had been, over the last couple of years, a revolution in policy which had abandoned previously totemic items of the Tory faith – the Empire, and now even the pretence of removing government controls from the economy. However, while the imperial changes had aroused considerable heat within the party, the shift in economic thinking had been less openly contentious. Still, it was once again Reggie's task to take over after the revolution, reconcile everyone to the new way of doing things, and pursue the new direction even further. It was a task he relished.

Maudling's regime behind the solid walls of the Treasury was calm and benign. He had good relations with his junior colleagues, John Boyd-Carpenter, Edward du Cann and Anthony Barber, all of whom became supporters. He was happy to delegate and take them into his confidence, in contrast to his own experience under Butler in 1952–5. Maudling was popular with his Private Office and a refreshing contrast to Selwyn Lloyd, who had a reputation for being neurotic and *de haut en bas* with his civil servants. Reggie was much warmer and more democratic in manner and shared light-hearted banter with the Private Office. Tom Caulcott, a Private Secretary to both men – and then ('Oh, you poor bugger!' as Reggie told him on the day of the changeover), to George Brown at the Department of Economic Affairs in 1964–5 – recalled that:

> He was a great guy to work for. He was totally unflappable. He never lost his temper. Selwyn Lloyd was petulant, always complaining, and then there was the nightmare of George Brown and his explosions. Reggie was so calm. It was a straightforward couple of years' work. Crises happened and things would go wrong, things that would have been huge nightmares with Selwyn Lloyd or George Brown, but they went calmly with Reggie. He would just do what was necessary without fuss.[34]

Caulcott, who served throughout Reggie's Chancellorship, recalled two pieces of modernisation that followed Reggie's arrival: he allowed them to acquire the Treasury's first photocopier – in 1962 – although he was more interested in another machine he installed in the Private Office. Reggie found that there was no fridge to go with the drinks cabinet, so he instructed Caulcott and the Principal Private Secretary, Derek Mitchell, to see to it that they acquired one, preferably one which didn't make a lot of noise. Whatever else Reggie achieved at the Treasury, at least from then on the gin was cold and there were ice cubes when the Chancellor was entertaining.

The Private Secretaries also enjoyed trips out of town with Reggie, even to the dull civic events that frequently fell to the Chancellor, because somehow or other they would end up having a good time. Another rule was devised within the Private Office stating that a Private Secretary should accompany the Chancellor to cocktail parties, not because they feared any gaffes but because it was such fun.[35] Reggie introduced the civil servants to one of his principles of social life:

> Always accept any invitation to free alcoholic drinks, even if you don't think you can go. You never know, it might turn out that you could make it that evening after all because other plans change. And even if you don't turn up to a party people often think that you did anyway, and it makes sure you stay on their invitation list.

Reggie, although he liked a good party as much as ever, exercised some caution and discipline in his financial and personal affairs, which had been seriously slipping during his time as Paymaster-General and at the Board of Trade in 1957–61. The Chancellorship was largely free of the feeling that Reggie was sailing close to the wind that had developed in his previous jobs. His Private Secretary, Tom Caulcott, recalled a circumspect Maudling, rather more so than he had been at the Board of Trade:

> He always had an eye for money but he was perfectly proper at every stage as Chancellor. There was only one incident, which was around the time of the purchase tax reduction on cars. He wanted to get a car for his son Martin, and he called up Harrison who was chairman of whatever BMC/ Leyland was called then and said he couldn't afford a new one, were there any ex-demonstration models available for sale? Harrison said that, 'We'd do anything for you, sir.' After this conversation Reggie got a bit worried and asked me and Derek Mitchell whether it would be all right. We told him that he'd better make sure he paid for it. He did, but he did get a nearly new MG for a good price. It was the only incident I remember about him sailing at all close to the wind.[36]

Being distanced from Freddie Bennett – his PPSs in 1961–4 were very respectable, Francis Pym and David Gibson-Watt – was part of the reason, but it is more than this. Maudling was taking his responsibilities seriously. He was at last in a position to do what he wanted to in politics and it was the time he was most interested in politics and policy. Reggie's full-hearted commitment to political life in 1962–4 was a high point of his life, the ambivalence about whether he belonged there or in business temporarily dispelled. He had his hands on the levers of economic power and could put his ideas about growth, modernisation and liberalising society into practice.

Maudling's approach to the Treasury was casually commanding, even arrogant. He enjoyed taking decisions and wielding power and had no problem with overruling the permanent Treasury and Bank of England establishment. When asked why he disagreed with official advice he replied that that was the reason one had ministers. Alec Cairncross, the Chief Economic Adviser, found Maudling a contrast to Selwyn Lloyd, who was more amenable to general discussions on the state of the economy. In January 1963 he noted:

> The Chancellor keeps his own counsel. I've seen very little of him except over the electric power settlement but there is undoubtedly some coolness between him and the Department. They don't like his preference for gimmicks, for putting his own individual mark on things. But he has also been fairly free in rejecting advice (e.g. on social service benefits) or in indicating distrust (e.g. over the amount of slack in the building industry).[37]

The most senior Treasury officials, such as the successive Permanent Secretaries Frank Lee (who left, as he had planned, after only a few weeks of Maudling but could have stayed longer), and his replacement William Armstrong, found Maudling a puzzling man to deal with. Although he often talked about productivity and efficiency he took very little interest in the detail of these subjects. He was bored by such details and had endured two years of this sort of thing at the Board of Trade and took the view that he was there as Chancellor to have a broad view, to see the wood rather than the trees. Financial commentator Samuel Brittan once said to William Armstrong that one needed to stick pins into Maudling to get him to respond. 'Very long pins', said Armstrong.[38] A caption to a photograph of Maudling playing croquet in the magazine Time and Tide, 'Mr Maudling: A Powerful Stimulant Required', was referring to economic policy but must have amused the mandarins greatly.[39]

The lack of enthusiasm for Maudling at the Treasury was as nothing compared to what the Bank of England made of him. The Governor, appointed in 1961, was Lord Cromer (Rowley Baring), one of the most controversial Governors in recent history. Cromer saw himself as a practical, common-sense banker but was actually a deeply ideological advocate of free markets, particularly capital markets, and the fixed exchange rate system. His advice to Maudling, including a March 1963 letter expressing concern about the growth in public spending, was repeatedly ignored, and Cromer resorted to trying to see Macmillan behind Maudling's back.[40]

According to Maudling's successor, Jim Callaghan, Reggie 'did not get on with Cromer, nor Cromer with him. Maudling felt the City had too strong a grip on British industry.'[41] Maudling detested the conservatism of the Bank of England and the old City banks as institutions: 'too much marble and monopoly', he sniffed.[42] He had little personal regard for Cromer. Cromer in turn had feelings bordering on loathing for Maudling, whom he thought 'was one of the worst Chancellors I met. Not completely the worst . . . He was very idle, very opinionated and very conceited. It was he that created the crisis that Wilson inherited really and Wilson knew it.'[43] Tom Caulcott, who observed the dysfunctional relationship between the two, felt it was simply down to Cromer's resentment of Maudling's all too evident intellectual superiority.[44]

Maudling's tasks as Chancellor were clear. The *Economist* wrote after his appointment that the three priorities were to build stronger defences for incomes policy against wage claims and cost-driven inflation, to increase international liquidity and to reflate the domestic economy.[45] Few disagreed. Macmillan had made it clear that he was expecting Maudling to be a more active and forward-looking Chancellor than Selwyn Lloyd, whose relationship with the Prime Minister had collapsed, thanks in part to his dour, depressing attitude. By 'forward-looking', Macmillan meant that he expected Maudling to come up with ideas and make the running in questions like incomes policy, but more than this to implement an expansion programme to reduce unemployment. However, in summer 1962 Macmillan's pressure was comparatively light. Alec Cairncross recorded at the end of August that in his opinion and that of Tim Bligh, Macmillan's Private Secretary:

> the PM having appointed RM was content to let him get on with the job and had no great interest in how he did it (except that he was worried about unemployment) over the next couple of months because he had the Conference in September with Commonwealth Ministers and then the Party Conference to prepare for.[46]

Maudling also knew that he had to establish credibility with the financial markets. The opinion of Tory MP Nigel Birch ('For the second time the Prime Minister has got rid of a Chancellor of the Exchequer who tried to get expenditure under control. Once is more than enough') had influential support and to be identified early on as an unthinking inflationist would have done Maudling considerable damage. There were a substantial number of Conservative MPs, not all of them by any means from the unreconstructed right, who felt that Selwyn Lloyd had been cruelly used for taking a responsible attitude to the national finances. Maudling intended all along to be a bold, risk-taking Chancellor, but there were some dues to be paid first. Maudling's first moves were cautious, and his first Commons speech notably complacent.[47] Lloyd had contemplated a reduction in Bank Rate to take effect in August, but over the summer and early autumn Maudling twice refused to take this step. At his first meeting with business leaders in the National Production Advisory Council just after he took office, he said that 'business was living from hand to mouth, suffering from a complete lack of confidence in the future' and needed stimulus.[48] He also rebuffed the advice of Alec Cairncross to take some immediate action to expand the economy, and decided to bide his time by 'reviewing the situation, consulting officials and industrialists, and considering possible lines of action'.[49] They all told him the same thing.

Maudling returned early in his Chancellorship to the question of international monetary liquidity, a subject which had exercised him considerably during his stint as Economic Secretary in the early 1950s. The problem was essentially in funding expanding world trade. The system established after the war had gold plus two international reserve currencies, the dollar and sterling, which required Britain and the USA to run up external debts to keep the international payments system functioning. As world trade grew, the total level of overseas indebtedness needed also rose, to an extent that worried Maudling as exposing the British economy to risks. The answer, it seemed to Maudling, was to transfer the burden to a kind of international reserve currency, administered by the IMF. It made no sense to him that real prosperity, in terms of international trade and UK economic stability, could be put at risk because of utterly technical factors. While there was no immediate shortage of liquidity, he believed that something had to be done if world trade were to continue to expand.

The 'Maudling Plan' was developed with great speed within the Treasury over the summer of 1962 – as late as the end of July, the prospect of going to the IMF meeting in Washington in September 1962 with a plan was regarded as highly uncertain. Reggie was advised against being too specific in a speech on 26 July, but decided to signal his intention 'to take the initiative in discussing with representatives of the other main countries involved what positive measures we can take in this field'.[50] Maudling was determined to be seen to take a bold initiative in Washington, which would be a first step towards a long-term solution to the liquidity problem, backed up, as he was anxious to stress, by a thorough analysis of the issues. He intended to establish himself early on not only as a British political figure but also as a serious authority in international finance.

Maudling's plan faced misgivings, rather than outright hostility, from other countries. The Americans were anxious not to see the role of the dollar diminished. Maudling's emphasis on the IMF was controversial in Europe, where the IMF was perceived as being an Anglo-American institution which served the geopolitical interests of its dominant powers. This resentment caused the 1961 IMF meeting in Vienna to be an 'almost humiliating' occasion because of European suspicions about the borrowing scheme and Britain's own bid to borrow $1.5 billion from the fund, at the time the largest drawing of IMF resources in the organisation's history. Strong official advice to Maudling before the speech urged that it should not be portrayed in any way as a response to any short-term issues, but a longer-term arrangement, and Reggie was obliged to tone down his draft of the speech that dismissed the threat of world inflation and expressed more concern about world deflation caused by a lack of liquidity. Maudling was anxious to move quickly to alter the international financial system to facilitate expansion, but his officials were aware that this would worsen the risk of the speech being badly received by the Americans and Europeans.[51]

Maudling's speech to the IMF on 19 September outlining what became known as the Maudling Plan was received politely at the conference, with some admiration for 'the extremely skilful deployment of a view which was known in advance to be unpopular to most of the leading personalities here', the Americans calling it a 'constructive suggestion' but pointing out some pitfalls. The German delegate pointedly referred to a 'tendency to look to institutional panaceas to remedy defects in the international monetary system. The real need was for sound policies in member countries.' Other commentators concluded that it offered more to potential creditors to the system, and, as the *Guardian* commented, 'it can and will be construed primarily as a device for easing Britain's path'. Most of the press back home gave it a cautious welcome.[52]

Historian and former Labour Treasury minister Edmund Dell has criticised it as being a plea by Britain to the rest of the world to allow it to run an inflationary domestic policy in conditions of greater safety.[53] Perhaps, but it was not inconsistent with the desire of Maudling (and Callaghan) to escape from a constraint which had aggravated the stop-go cycle. Some of the most successful high-growth economies of Europe, such as France and increasingly Italy, had been run on an 'inflationary' basis. It was not a mere expansionary flight of fancy by Maudling; Sir Frank Lee, not an admirer of Reggie, thought at the time that a new international reserve asset was needed and that the Maudling outline was 'a soundly conceived and sensible scheme which we could well support without misgivings'.[54]

The Maudling Plan was not adopted by acclamation in Washington, but that was never its intention − it was a draft, outline proposal to meet a need that the British Treasury and others had identified. It was the start of a long process that was taken up by Callaghan and others after Maudling had gone, and eventually saw daylight, duly modified and evolved (the French Ministry of Finance produced a revised international system in 1964), as the Special Drawing Right (SDR) of the IMF. Maudling hailed the SDR agreement in 1967 as the culmination of the process he had started in 1962.[55] While the SDR never quite achieved the prominence that its early advocates had hoped, and the structural problem of the US deficit, aggravated by the Vietnam war, destabilised the international financial system in the late 1960s, it was still a useful contribution. Maudling was entitled to take some credit for the achievement.

Back at home, the economic situation had continued to get worse after Maudling's arrival at the Treasury, as Britain's latest 'stop' phase of the cycle ran into a period when the world economy was on the edge of recession. Output was stagnant or falling, industrial investment was falling rapidly and unemployment was rising in the second half of 1962. Unemployment had risen over the politically sensitive level of 500,000 and was particularly concentrated in depressed areas such as the north-east of England and the west of Scotland, where heavy industry was suffering from falling orders. A dismal air of pessimism had gathered by October, which posed the risk of becoming a more general crisis of confidence in economic prospects. Commentators had started to make comparisons with the 1930s, when the same industries and regions had been crippled by the economic slump.[56] The calls for action to head off this threat grew louder as the autumn wore on, the *Daily Mail* urging 'Stop dawdling, Maudling!' This slogan was first used by car workers at a protest in January 1961,[57] but it now entered popular currency.

Maudling's speech to the Conservative Party conference did nothing to restore confidence; it was another dull, passionless conference speech that troubled his admirers. In more junior ministerial office, his inability to turn in a good performance or even to pretend to like the Conservative Party conference had not been a serious problem, but, as one of the most senior ministers in government, it was now becoming an embarrassment. His lack of respect for the Tory conference was obvious in 1962. An American diplomat at the conference recorded that it was an 'ineffective, inert performance in replying to the debate on economic policy, withdrawing nothing concerning past government policy and disclosing nothing new about future changes in what appeared to be an ill-prepared and discursive speech'. 'The greatest disappointment of the conference was Maudling. Since he had been so widely touted as bringing brilliance, energy and youth into the Treasury, his failure to produce any evidence of change came as a particular disappointment. Although undoubtedly inhibited by the need to wait for the recommendations of NEDDY and NICKY it seems surprising that he had not been able to pull a single rabbit out of his hat.'[58]

Reggie was pilloried a little later in the BBC's *That Was the Week that Was*, which mocked him for leaving a meeting with some unemployed people with the quip, 'Well, I've got work to do if you haven't'.[59] The dawdling, however, was coming to an end. If he had wished to, Maudling could have tried to convince the conference that the economy had turned the corner. Within the Treasury the advice in favour of a touch on the accelerator had grown more insistent over the summer, and the first tentative action came at the very end of September when a quantity of 'special deposits' were returned to the clearing banks. These special deposits had been called for as a way of restricting bank lending, and their return allowed the banks to lend against these reserves and thereby encourage private sector spending. On 2 October in his formal Mansion House speech in the City, Reggie announced that the public sector would be called upon to assist in reflating the economy. A kick-start programme of investment had been drawn up, with £15 million of spending in what was left of financial year 1962/3, a significant £40 million boost in 1963/4 which tailed off to another £15 million in 1964/5. The forecast growth in public spending generally was adjusted upwards and there was no significant effort at imposing any cost cutting on the 1963/4 spending estimates.[60]

The October loosening was only a prelude to the main event, a set of measures announced in November 1962 that amounted to a mini-budget. The two most important changes Maudling announced in November were intended to stimulate areas of the economy in which surplus capacity was most apparent. The motor industry Maudling had done so much to expand while at the Board of Trade was helped by a cut in the purchase tax on cars from 45 per cent to 25 per cent. This tax had wavered back and forward around 50 per cent in recent years, and Maudling's move brought it back in line with most other goods. Car registrations leapt by nearly a third between summer 1962 and autumn 1963,[61] and, with the motorways that Maudling's public investment boom paid for, a radical step had been taken towards what Thatcher called 'the great car economy'.

The other major change was on investment allowances. Capital investment by British industry had slumped following the 1961 measures and Maudling stepped in with what amounted to £50 million of investment tax cuts in a full year. Investment in development areas, and capital spending on scientific research, were particularly generously treated, with firms now able to write investment off fully within the first year of it taking place; some of these changes were introduced by the unusual procedure of announcing that they would be in the 1963 Finance Bill but retrospectively applied back to November 1962.[62] The net effect of the October and November measures was the equivalent of injecting £200 million into the economy, and as the Economist said, it could at the time plausibly be called 'the third largest sudden injection of tax reliefs in British fiscal history' after the budgets of 1945 and 1959: a 'Not so Little Budget' indeed.[63]

Maudling's November package was widely welcomed, the stock market notching up gains and Nicholas Davenport writing in the Spectator that 'Mr Maudling has instituted a new regime at the Treasury. He has abandoned the stupid stop-go monetary policies; he is working on more rational lines.'[64] The mini-budget was a classic piece of Keynesian fine tuning. The dangers of recession were fought with a calibrated piece of fiscal demand management aimed particularly at the sectors and regions that had been suffering most severely. However, they were arguably over-fine in their focus; a more general economic stimulus might have done more to restore general confidence, and by leaving it to November Maudling had allowed things to drift and a pessimistic mood to become established.[65]

The November measures were followed by further expansionary measures in the next couple of months. In December Maudling allowed local authorities in the north of England to spend money over the winter on public works to counter the threat of unemployment, and cut purchase tax to 25 per cent on radio and television sets. In January 1963 a considerably above-inflation uprating of state pensions and benefits was announced, and Maudling even attempted to devise a way of paying the increases early for maximum reflationary effect, although this did not prove practical.[66] This was a marked increase in public spending, and the combined effect of the measures since November, and the government's adoption of the 4 per cent growth target, meant that over the winter of 1962–3 projected future spending was pointing upwards at a much sharper angle than it had in July 1962.

An opportunity for a much more radical break with past policy was offered by the French veto, on 14 January 1963, of British entry into the EEC, on which Macmillan and his European negotiator, Edward Heath, had pinned many hopes. As an experienced European negotiator Maudling had a good idea of what was coming. In November 1962 he had observed privately that 'the French didn't want us in. They'd been trying hard to push us into a position where we would have to refuse.'[67] He was not particularly distressed by this prospect. He had come round to the view that there was a strong economic case for joining but disliked the political baggage that went with it, saying that 'he wasn't ready for federation' and feared Labour scoring points about whether the Treaty of Rome really did imply a federal commitment. Gaitskell, after all, had made a notably popular speech at the Labour conference in October, which opposed EEC entry on the grounds that it would end 'a thousand years of history'.

The EEC decision was a *terminus' ad quem*, after which new options would have to be considered one way or the other. Maudling called the 'Non' 'a great disappointment, but not a disaster'.[68] Publicly, he accentuated the positive, talking of working with the Americans to reduce tariffs all round, and with the Commonwealth and EFTA countries, and saying that Britain did not need an external pressure of this kind in order to modernise.[69] Privately, Maudling thought it was a good opportunity to float the pound. Within the Treasury there was advice from Alec Cairncross, supported by Maurice Allen of the Bank of England, to the effect that if British entry to the EEC was rejected they should go over to a floating rate,[70] and some inconclusive contingency planning had already taken place in January 1963. In early February Cairncross put his thoughts down on a 'Top Secret' note on devaluation and floating. Under the Conservatives, he wrote, 'We have never explicitly ruled out devaluation as an act of policy; but the circumstances would obviously have to be very special before we thought such an act appropriate and justifiable.' The collapse of the EEC negotiations seemed a reasonable pretext for a sterling float. The position was complicated by sterling's role as a reserve currency, but Cairncross felt that there was a case for a 'downward float' – in effect, a market-driven devaluation – of approximately 10 per cent.[71] In February 1963 Maudling told Macmillan, in a Top Secret discussion on economic policy, that he 'had asked the Treasury to consider other measures on the balance of payments side, including straight devaluation, a floating rate, multiple rates and an import surcharge'.[72]

Somehow by 1963 floating the pound had become a vaguely left-wing position, rather than being associated with the right as it had been in the early 1950s. Maudling was now keen on the idea because it would remove a constraint to the policy of headlong economic expansion that he was intending to implement. Out of office in 1968, he stated his point of view more plainly than he ever could as Chancellor:

> In the first place it seems illogical that exchange rates should remain fixed because there is no logical reason why the economies of the various countries should advance at precisely the same pace or that they should be equally successful in maintaining their internal purchasing power. In the second place I believe a floating rate can give more room for manoeuvre to a Government in dealing with balance of payments problems.[73]

Macmillan, on balance, opposed the idea of a float in the circumstances of 1963 'since people might think it a gimmick and might take on a mood of indiscipline at the loss of moral pressure implicit in a fixed rate of exchange'. Maudling also had reservations, as it would be very difficult for him to defend to his international colleagues and could mean that IMF drawing rights would be withdrawn, but he did conduct a serious examination of the pros and cons of floating as a means of responding to the EEC snub and unleashing domestic expansion. Instead of a float in 1963, Macmillan and Maudling decided to do all they could to strengthen British reserves so that they could be confident that an expansionist policy would be allowed enough time and international confidence to succeed.

The decision not to go ahead with the float had a significant unanticipated consequence. Westminster journalist Andrew Roth had got hold of the story that Maudling and Macmillan were planning to float the pound but heard at a late stage, just before his deadline on 8 March, that it had been cancelled. This left his newsletter *Westminster Confidential* with a gap to fill at a few hours' notice and instead of the pound Roth chose to lead with the rumours that had been circulating for a month about a link between a good-time girl, a Russian military attaché and the Secretary for War, John Profumo.[74] The Profumo story circulated at a higher velocity at Westminster, and finally broke open on the night of 21 March when three Labour MPs mentioned allegations in the Commons chamber. The next day, under pressure, Profumo made his fateful statement that there had been no 'impropriety' in his relationship with the girl involved, Christine Keeler. The Profumo story then seemed to go away; but Profumo's denial was untrue and enough people knew or guessed to make the situation untenable. In the meantime, political attention turned to Maudling's first Budget on 3 April.

Maudling's two budgets have gone down in popular history as examples of irresponsible pre-election excess. In neither case is this fair. The economic signals before the 1963 Budget were extremely confusing. Maudling's Chief Economic Adviser, Alec Cairncross, was in gloomy mood about the prospects for the UK and world economies in January. While unemployment had not risen in the previous month it was not clear that the rising trend of the previous year had come to an end, and production had, according to the latest information, fallen although nobody was sure whether this was down to the exceptionally bad weather that had struck Britain over the winter of 1962–3. On the other hand, consumption seemed to be starting to recover, with retail sales rising and car registrations also up in response to the November measures.[75] Popular perceptions of the economy were still that it was, in the words of an ITN commentary on 30 March, 'in a depressed state' and 'a dangerous state of stagnation'.[76] This perception was shared in Number 10, where Harold Macmillan was always worried about unemployment, particularly in the region of his pre-war constituency of Stockton. 'The economy is not really moving forward yet at all,' Macmillan wrote to the Treasury on 6 March.[77]

Official advice was strongly for generosity in the 1963 Budget. Lord Cromer was arguing that 'the need for a Budget to stimulate the level of the activity of the economy is abundantly clear at home and abroad', and added that £200–300 million of concessions would be appropriate.[78] The Treasury's budget committee recommended £250 million or thereabouts. Advice from political colleagues tended to be more generous; in February Macmillan urged Maudling to consider 'the big stuff – the national plan, the new approach, the expand or die' and to give away £400 million, as the National Institute for Economic and Social Research also suggested.[79] In March the Prime Minister was still urging Maudling to give more away in the budget; Macmillan 'wondered whether in view of the recent production figures it might not be right to go for a more extensive range of tax concessions. The Chancellor of the Exchequer thought this would be unwise and said that the important factor here was the underlying trend and not the month-to-month figures.'[80] Maudling was resisting pressure to do more rather than insisting on expansion at all costs. He stuck closely to the official guiding lights, and the concessions he settled on in his budget were worth £269 million.

Before the budget speech Maudling caused apoplexy among Treasury civil servants by suggesting that he could make some of it up as he went along. He had once confessed the ambition to be the first Chancellor in history to make a budget speech without notes.[81] Budget speeches are 'magnificent official works of art', every word weighed and considered by civil servants and the package designed to be released stage by stage through a well-oiled routine.

Mitchell and Caulcott persuaded him that this was one speech he simply could not do off the back of an envelope.[82] During the speech, Maudling spoiled the fun of journalists who enjoyed commenting on what the Chancellor was drinking during the budget speech by not disclosing the contents of his glass. Selwyn Lloyd had owned up to whisky, and Derick Heathcoat-Amory drank a sweet concoction of rum, milk and honey.[83] But Reggie did not keep them waiting for the big news – while most budget speeches run through a review of the last economic year and announce minor changes first, Reggie chose to hit his audience with the main tax changes first. While it lacked suspense, it was one of his more effective public speeches.

Among the tax changes Maudling announced was the timetable for the abolition of 'Schedule A' taxation on owner-occupied property, the principle of which the Cabinet had wrung from Selwyn Lloyd in 1962. It gained Reggie some more popularity among the middle classes and the Conservative Party. Abolition of Schedule A was not accompanied by any move on the tax relief on mortgage interest payments, which lasted until the 1990s. The 1963 Budget was a further encouragement, if one was needed, for a rush into mortgaged home ownership and left the fiscal treatment of housing unbalanced. Maudling, despite his intentions in 1957 after his own fluctuating income had caused problems and his thankless task of fielding Gerald Nabarro's tedious but justified parliamentary questions about the anomalies of Purchase Tax,[84] was not much of a tax-reforming Chancellor. He was sceptical of the view, soon to be institutionalised by the Institute for Fiscal Studies, that taxes should be relatively simple and should not be used as indirect levers of social policy. In November 1962 he told the *Guardian*'s Francis Boyd, who offered jokingly to build him up as the greatest Chancellor since Gladstone if he simplified taxation, that 'one couldn't be both fair and simple. The complexities had to be introduced to allow for fair cases.' Reggie believed that nothing much could be done about simpler taxation,[85] or rather that he could not do much without compromising on fairness.

Perhaps the most controversial aspect of the Budget within the Cabinet and among economic experts was the way in which Maudling chose to distribute the tax cuts. There had been endless arguments within the Treasury about how it should be done, with Maudling calling for an exhaustive range of briefing papers from the Inland Revenue to illustrate the different options and how they might be implemented. The basic choice was between a cut in the standard rate of income tax, probably by 6*d* although there were some in the press and the Conservative Party arguing for a dramatic reduction of 9*d*, and an increase in the tax-free personal allowance. The arguments for the former were that it would grab headlines and was easier to explain to people, and that it would increase incentives to work. The arguments for the latter were that it would help the poorest in society most, and probably have a larger stimulating effect on the economy because more of it would be spent immediately. Chief Secretary to the Treasury, John Boyd-Carpenter, and Lord Cromer from the Bank of England, argued for a standard-rate cut. Cromer phrased his plea in very strong terms: 'I am gravely concerned that concentration on Income Tax Allowances will stimulate home demand without contributing in any way either to competitiveness in prices or producing any effect on business that will be constructive in increasing our overseas earnings. I venture to suggest that such a measure may indeed sow the seeds of the next structural exchange crisis and will be so interpreted abroad.'[86] Maudling in the end decided that he would go for the increase in the allowance and not the standard rate cut.

In the pre-budget Cabinet several ministers made last-ditch arguments that it would be better to make a cut in the standard rate rather than increase allowances, but of course by that stage there was nothing that could be done. Maudling was a stronger minister than Selwyn Lloyd, who had been humiliated by late alterations to his 1962 package. Maudling's tax cut was the most egalitarian available. It made a big difference to those on low incomes just above the tax threshold, while not giving much to higher earners. A total of 3,750,000 wage earners were taken out of income tax altogether. It was less showy but more effective at stimulating demand than a standard rate cut. 'As it happened, it lacked political effects. Maudling was insistent that it wasn't about making a political gesture, it was about spreading wealth,' according to Tom Caulcott.[87]

Maudling had a choice, and chose a redistributive tax cut[88] when there were strong arguments being made for making a less egalitarian choice. His choice very clearly reflected his values. He resisted parading his social conscience around in speeches but it is impossible to understand why he pressed so strongly for raising allowances without accepting that he had a strong sense of fairness and equality. He accepted to a large extent the right-wing argument that high marginal tax rates are a disincentive to work. He commented in 1967 that 'it would only cost £4 million for the Chancellor of the Exchequer to say "No one in this country to pay more than 70 per cent of his income in taxation." It brings us in line with every other country in the Western world. This is not an economic matter, it is a political matter.'[89] Perhaps he felt more strongly about high marginal rates in 1967, but in 1963/4 he neglected to do anything about the matter. Neither did Maudling do anything significant to satisfy the view expressed in the City, and endorsed by Cromer, that something should be done about the short-term gains tax introduced by Lloyd, Maudling dismissing the argument with the comment: 'There is a certain amount of grumbling on the Stock Exchange, for which I feel very little sympathy.'[90]

Maudling was without the unpleasant hypocrisy of proposing tax cuts to encourage the rich to work while favouring punitive measures to make the poor work. He opposed the 'trickle-down' theory. To Maudling, 'incentives operate all the way down'.[91] He did not believe in the incentive argument strongly enough to expend any effort after his cuts in autumn 1962 and spring 1963 in going any further with tax cuts.

The other 1963 Budget measures included 'free depreciation' – i.e. a generous tax write-off on investment – in the development areas, a continuation of the Macmillan government's progressively more generous approach to regional aid. He also gave special dispensation to shipping and shipbuilding, an industry whose appeal to Reggie's sentiment was made easier by Beryl's family connections, but in retrospect it was not a particularly good decision.[92] There were several minor tax cuts and changes scattered around the Budget, which some Treasury civil servants sourly regarded as gimmicks. One of the smaller ones which Reggie took pride in and which had a long-lasting effect on British life was the lifting of the requirement for people brewing beer in small quantities to obtain an expensive excise certificate. The entire home-brewing hobby owes its existence to Reggie Maudling.[93]

'Expansion without inflation' was Maudling's overall headline for the Budget, but at the time the Budget was seen as a rather cautious package. 'Half Speed Ahead' commented the Economist,[94] and Labour's economic thinkers such as Roy Jenkins and Anthony Crosland criticised it for being insufficiently expansionary.[95]

The Budget, as a whole, was intended to fit into the government's strategic framework for the economy. Macmillan had suggested to Maudling that they should produce a 'national plan' for economic growth. While Maudling stopped short of talking in such terms, he was effectively doing something not dissimilar. The first NEDC report of 6 February 1963, endorsed by the government, had approved the objective of 4 per cent growth in the economy, and by boosting demand the Budget was attempting to reach this target. There was a problem in the detail, namely that the target covered 1961–6, and thanks to disappointing performance in 1961–2 there was some catching up to do which meant a growth rate for a time of 5 per cent. After the Budget, Maudling made a number of optimistic pronouncements about the economy, some of which advisers feared were premature or excessive. In terms of the short-term progress of recovery from the low point of the winter of 1962–3, Maudling was generally right, but the larger problem was that everyone was now committed to the 4 per cent growth target, and to carry any credibility the government itself had to behave as if it was going to happen.

There was another piece of the strategy, which never quite fell into place. A Number 10 note on a meeting between Macmillan and Maudling at the end of November 1962 recorded that:

The vital need for an incomes policy was apparent throughout the [Neddy] report. He [Maudling] was not without hope that it might be possible in the course of next year to reach some kind of agreement with the trades unions on an incomes policy though he could not foresee what kind of terms they might want and whether they would be at all acceptable to the Government.[96]

Part of the reason for the distribution of the tax cuts had been that it would be most likely to appeal to the trade unions, and indeed the TUC's Economic Committee gave an unusually warm reception, amounting practically to an endorsement, to a Conservative budget. But the welcome fell short of actually getting involved in the workings of the incomes policy or issuing any signals supporting a period of restraint in wage negotiations. The new, higher, guiding light in the Budget of 3.5 per cent was nearly as widely ignored as its predecessor, and discussions trailed on into the summer to try to achieve a measure of consensus around an incomes policy.

What Maudling and Macmillan were left with was a policy of expansion, without the protection of an incomes policy – although hopes were still being held out – and without the flexibility that floating the pound would have offered. The hope, after summer 1963, had to be that a virtuous circle of expansion, expectations and investment would be firmly established by the time the balance of payments constraint became too pressing.

Maudling's expansive personality and forthright attitude to increasing prosperity set the mood for expansion, in contrast to the outlook of his sombre predecessor Selwyn Lloyd and indeed the three Conservative Chancellors between Butler and Lloyd. His public profile enabled him, as Cairncross admiringly noted, to 'convince everyone that he was an expansionist while at the same time pursuing a policy that was markedly more cautious than the one Mr. Lloyd would almost certainly have accepted'. Maudling's profile as a risk-taking expansionist served him and the government well at the time, but left him exposed if things were to go wrong. Reggie, of all people, was not someone who cut a plausible figure as an advocate of belt-tightening, and his later actions to rein in expansion passed almost unnoticed and unappreciated.

Maudling's confidence communicated itself to commentators, the public and the financial markets. Alec Cairncross told Per Jacobsson of the IMF that 'the Chancellor had a great advantage over his predecessors that he was able to impress public opinion as knowing what he was about. He commanded the respect of the Press.' The Budget did Reggie's public reputation considerable good, with Gallup polls finding that 59 per cent of the electorate thought the Budget was fair and that Maudling was doing a good job; only 24 per cent did not think it fair, and only 19 per cent thought Reggie was not doing a good job. After the Budget Maudling was far and away the most popular Conservative in the country, with 33 per cent liking him most compared to 25 per cent for Macmillan, 23 per cent for Butler and 13 per cent for Hailsham.[98] The complaint, voiced before that Budget in the *Sunday Express*,[99] that Maudling was 'almost unknown to the public' was silenced.

In June, the Profumo affair returned to haunt the government. John Profumo's resignation on 4 June, confessing that he had indeed had an affair with Christine Keeler, was followed by an orgy of rumour and recrimination. The government even ended up involved in the scandalous divorce case of the Duchess of Argyll. Some of the evidence in the case consisted of explicit photographs of the Duchess engaged, as the more discreet tabloids sometimes say, 'in a sex act' with a man whose head was not in the picture; that of the Duchess, by the nature of the occasion, was. Rumours were rife about who the 'headless man' was (oddly, the identity of the photographer has never been much of a subject of discussion) and the name of Duncan Sandys came up frequently. Although he was not the 'headless man', his prolific sexual life had probably involved an earlier encounter with the Duchess, and the delicate Education Secretary, Edward Boyle, wrote to a friend in this context, commenting on 'the utter brutishness, moral philistinism and virtual nihilism of a number of wealthy people where sex and life generally are concerned'.[100]

In the bizarre circumstances of the time, the case seemed a threat to the government and Sandys came close to resigning. Reggie was less bothered than Boyle about the sex life of Duncan Sandys and was 'terribly amused' by the whole business. He was, in a slightly schoolboyish way, intrigued by what his colleagues had been getting up to. After one Cabinet meeting at Admiralty House Reggie, in a state of some astonishment, summoned Derek Mitchell to meet him there. 'My God, we've had an extraordinary meeting. The whole agenda was swept aside and we spent the time talking about the Duchess of Argyll!' The photographs were spread on the Cabinet table and passed around and people were terrified. 'Poor Duncan Sandys was in tears, and said it wasn't him but it could have been.'[101] The government felt compelled to appoint Lord Denning to conduct an official inquiry into Profumo and the other rumours and the inquiry team set up in the rooms at the back of the Treasury building, a suite of offices often used for governmental odds and ends. Reggie was curious about 'those girls' – Christine Keeler and Mandy Rice-Davies – and had his Private Office set up an early warning network so that he could take a look at them on the way in to see Denning. The alert came and Reggie ran down the corridor ('as fast as I've ever seen him move' according to Tom Caulcott) but he was too late.[102]

Maudling could forgive but not very easily understand the trouble that Profumo and Sandys had got themselves into through their strong sexual drives. 'What does the bloody man think he's doing?' he would ask his civil servants when some new revelation or rumour reached his ears. Reggie was besotted with Beryl and felt no need to look elsewhere, and seemed oblivious to any expressions of interest from other women. Reggie's drives ran in different directions – for comfort, for money – and he was as powerless in the face of these temptations as Profumo had been when he first met Keeler.

As Macmillan's grasp on power weakened there was a surge in support for Maudling to take over as Prime Minister. As Chancellor he was associated with one of the few areas in which the government could claim much success – the economy was responding to his expansionary measures in the Budget and the November package, and unemployment was falling fast. June 1963, ironically, saw a record fall (73,000) in the jobless total, taking it below the 500,000 mark. Reggie's public image also seemed to be the answer to the problems that the Profumo affair caused the Conservative government. He was certainly no prude, as his well-publicised liking for the Crazy Horse saloon indicated, and he had a relaxed and jokey attitude towards sex. For all this, he was also happily married and devoted to his wife and children. He was a modern man and could never seem as out of touch as Macmillan and the old establishment. Although he enjoyed shooting weekends in the country as much as any of them, he did not have a tweedy, grouse moor image. Reggie's aspirations and lifestyle were recognisable as normal and human to the bulk of Tory voters and the electorate at large. Harold Wilson was seriously worried about the threat from Maudling, telling his ally Richard Crossman: 'Well, you know what our directive is – to keep Macmillan as our most valuable asset.' He added, 'The one thing I am really frightened of is Maudling.'[103]

The tide was running very strongly for Maudling in June and July. Reggie was only a point behind Butler as the public favourite for the succession, if Macmillan were to resign, with 23 per cent naming him as their choice in July.[104] But Reggie's public standing was as nothing compared to his domination of the Conservative parliamentary party. On 20 June the *Daily Telegraph* reported its polling of Tory MPs as indicating that Maudling was streets ahead of any rivals for the succession, and the 1922 Committee's own soundings showed similar results.[105] On 11 July Andrew Roth's well-informed private newsletter *Westminster Confidential* reported that he enjoyed the support of 'at least two thirds of the Conservative MPs' and probably more.[106] On 12 July the *Daily Telegraph* survey put his support at 70 per cent, with more than half of the MPs who had not supported Maudling in June switching their support towards him in July.[107] The *Telegraph* surveys, interestingly, allowed MPs to be conventionally loyal and back the incumbent, Macmillan; very few did so. There was considerable feeling in July that Macmillan should go, and the argument was made that he should do it now and allow Maudling to take over without a struggle, so that the new leader could be ratified at conference in October. One MP, writing anonymously, commented that 'already we are talking at Westminster as if Mr Maudling is about to move into Number 10 Downing Street'.[108] How could things possibly go wrong from here?

Chapter 12

BLACKPOOL OUT OF SEASON, 1963

R eggie Maudling had an endearing and infuriating personality trait, which determined that when he did something out of character he did it in an artless, ham-handed fashion that defeated the apparent purpose. In July 1963 Freddie Bennett was urging him to capitalise on his strong position and establish himself as heir apparent. According to Reggie's Private Secretary, Tom Caulcott: 'Reggie, Beryl, Freddie Bennett and I ended up at Chester Street. Bennett was saying that Reggie had to make a push, that this was our chance, and he said he would manage the campaign.'[1] His appeal to youth, they decided, given the criticism of Macmillan for being old-fashioned and out of touch, was the key theme. A Saturday speech on 6 July at Sawston, in the Cambridgeshire constituency of his former PPS Francis Pym, would be the moment when Maudling burst onto the stage as the voice of youth. The speech was built up as a major event. According to Maudling at Sawston, the Profumo affair was of minor importance in explaining the current problems of the Conservative Party – he felt that people did not blame the government as a whole for one man's misdeeds or accept that there was general corruption. The Conservatives had been falling behind because of the desire for change and also because 'We have not been successful in obtaining the allegiance of the younger generation of voters, because we have not yet found a way of talking to them in language they understand, or in terms of the ideals they cherish.'[2] 'It is all too easy to get a distorted picture of the generation now growing up. Behind the vulgarities and the sensationalism,' said Reggie, 'there is developing a new seriousness and sense of purpose.' Maudling was always conscious of Harold Wilson's gift for political presentation, and had realised that there was a risk that Labour were transforming their image away from being tired and backward-looking and towards youth, meritocracy and a scientific approach. Maudling felt that there was no reason why the younger generation of Conservatives, such as himself and Macleod, could not appeal to the idealism he was talking about, to which Kennedy had spoken in the United States.

Many Maudling supporters approved of the speech. According to the *Sunday Times* a week later: 'Mr Maudling's courage in speaking in strong leadership terms, and in aligning himself so decisively with the younger generation, is welcomed by his supporters at Westminster. They are convinced that the time has come for him to declare himself willing to take over the leadership, in response to the party's call.'[3] However, others were not impressed. The *Daily Telegraph* commented on the rather woolly and platitudinous nature of Maudling's actual suggestions of what to do: 'Fair enough, but what form is this offensive to take? At times it is difficult not to feel that the constant call for new action has become a substitute for the action itself.'[4] Maudling's spin of the speech as being an appeal to youth exposed him to ridicule. Lord Poole, a chieftain of Central Office, made fun of middle-aged people 'prancing about' pretending to be young and saying that 'the best way to spoil the picnic is for Dad to go along'.[5] But these were strange times, and even Rab Butler felt obliged to claim that he was 'with it'. On 10 July an Illingworth cartoon for the *Daily Mail* depicted Reggie as Elvis on stage playing to an audience of three unimpressed stereotypical Tories; 'Rab and his Bongo Boys' wait in the wings while 'Closing' is written across a poster for 'Mac and his Happy Wanderers'. The months leading up to the Conservative leadership contest of 1963 did have something of the air of a talent show, in which successive hopefuls perform on stage, whipping up strong but transient enthusiasm. Reggie's position was never so strong again as it was in the first two weeks of July 1963.

Maudling's overwhelming lead was the product of a very particular conjunction of circumstances in the first half of 1963. Conservative MPs were not thinking particularly clearly at the time. The fear and panic of the Profumo affair caused sudden swings of emotion and the rush for Maudling was one of them, albeit one of the more rational responses to the situation. The strong feeling that it was time to switch to the next generation, which was nearly universal in June 1963, did not last. A curious possibility opened up with Royal Assent on 16 July to Tony Benn's Bill that allowed hereditary peers to disclaim their titles. Now Conservatives could think about some new options, including the conference darling, Lord Hailsham, and the experienced, understated Foreign Secretary, Lord Home. Maudling was flavour of the month in July, but the problem with being flavour of the month is that it can only be a transient honour, and in the Tory leadership stakes all depended on being the favourite when the incumbent finally departed.

The sharp decline in Maudling's standing over the summer of 1963 has puzzled even such seasoned commentators on leadership elections as Alan Watkins.[6] It certainly baffled Reggie, who found that his colleagues were, though still cordial, a lot less so after the recess than before it.[7] They no longer saw him as being the man who would shortly have their ministerial future in his hands. The Maudling movement suffered a complete loss of momentum during July and August, and by the time political life was resuming in September Reggie was back to being among the second rank of potential leadership candidates.

Once the political temperature had cooled some more, critical attention was brought to bear on Maudling's suitability as party leader and Prime Minister. Butler supporter Sir Ted Leather had said even in July that much as he liked him, Maudling 'is not ready for it. I'm no old fogey, I'm two years younger than Reggie, but I think we're in danger of letting the glamour of President Kennedy's youth go to our heads.'[8] Leather's view gained increasing support over the summer, and somehow by the time the political season started again in September the conventional wisdom had swung round to the feeling that Maudling was rather short of experience. There was a steady movement back to Butler among people who had briefly rallied round Maudling in June and July but who were fundamentally admirers of Rab, such as Enoch Powell.[9] Support reverted to the more established options as it became clear that the Profumo affair was not necessarily the end of life as the Tory party knew it. The boom in support for Maudling also lacked the backing, essential in the Conservative Party of the time, of a significant element of the party establishment – if Maudling had taken over in July 1963 it would have had some of the elements of the Peasants' Revolt that installed Thatcher in 1975, a defeat for the conventional Tory way of doing things rather than a new face fronting the operation. While this seemed possible, even desirable, to many MPs in June and July, it looked much less so the further one moved on from the Profumo debate.

Over the summer recess, questions were raised about what Maudling's vision of where the Tories and the country should be going really amounted to, and about whether he was competent to lead. Hubert Ashton, MP, wrote to Butler in September that 'some quite sensible people feel that he might prove disastrous'.[10] Henry Brooke doubted whether Maudling had what it took to bear the strain of such high office.[11] Some MPs, like Enoch Powell's PPS, Martin Maddan, were concerned that the lack of support for Maudling at Cabinet level was an indication that Maudling might be a flawed candidate, and reconsidered their support. Maddan, unusually, chose Heath.[12] Frank Lee, who had briefly overlapped with Reggie as Treasury Permanent Secretary, had strong doubts of a sort that were shared in political circles. According to Alec Cairncross, 'F.G. Lee on Sunday [13 October 1963] said he thought Maudling had no principle in him and when I said he might be the sort of man to put in the ring against Harold Wilson he said that was the trouble – he was "too like him – a kind of rich man's Harold Wilson".'[13]

A closer look at Maudling had also proved off-putting to some potential supporters on the reforming Bow Group wing of the party, who tended to agree with him about most matters of importance but were not so keen on his laid-back manner and apparent complacency about the state of Britain. According to William Rees-Mogg, a perceptive writer about internal Tory party politics at the time, most progressive Tories 'would regard his leadership with benevolent depression and some with benevolent despair. They like him as a man, and like his intelligence, but differ from him altogether on the range and urgency of reform.'[14]

Maudling's support, although strong among MPs, was less solid among the constituency activists, who thought of Maudling as rather an unknown quantity.[15] Reggie had been less than diligent about making himself known on the circuit of constituency dinners; it was hard enough work to persuade him to attend Barnet events, let alone sacrifice a Friday or Saturday night to the proverbial rubber chicken somewhere unglamorous. Tory activists liked what they saw, but did not feel they had the measure of the man. They preferred the passion of Lord Hailsham, or Iain Macleod. Reggie's support also became thinner if one looked higher than the level of the backbench MP. Richard Crossman divined from across the floor that even at its peak, although the majority of backbenchers were in favour of Maudling, the 'officer class behind the revolt' were not as keen.[16] In the Cabinet, Maudling's position was even worse. Rees-Mogg wrote about the slippage of Maudling's support in favour of Butler at the end of July: 'In a straight election in the Cabinet Mr Butler would have at least a two to one majority. Indeed I have heard of no member of the Cabinet who is more than a tepid supporter of Mr Maudling's claims.'[17]

After the slightly embarrassing Sawston offensive, Maudling reverted to public diffidence, although he was trying in his own rather obscure way to shore up his position among the party grandees. He did little to entrench the loyalty of those who had rallied to his support in the spring, although he did start to expend some more attention on securing his position. There were risks in his sudden status as the favourite for the succession, principally in the fact that the incumbent showed no sign of wanting to depart. Macmillan played a rather cruel game of building up and knocking down potential successors, and Maudling had good reason to fear that the Prime Minister, with a well-placed bitchy comment here and there, could undermine him severely. Maudling assured Macmillan that while he did want to succeed him as Prime Minister he would not play any part in intriguing to displace him.[18]

Another important visit before Westminster shut down for the summer was to Rab Butler, at the very end of July. According to Butler:

> I had a strange visit from Reggie Maudling himself about which I have not spoken to anybody in which he started by saying that if I got the job could he continue at the Treasury and then went on in a very friendly atmosphere to say that if it went the other way he could imagine no one he would wish to have by him more than me. He referred to our happy working together at the Treasury and hoped that he could produce as good results there. As might be expected the interview did not get very far. I said that I had been at the top of affairs and acting head of the Government long enough not to have gained a certain calm of mind but I did not think we could carry the matter any further at present. I said that as between us there was no personal issue this was very fortunate.[19]

However, after these tentative meetings, Reggie entirely characteristically decamped with the family to the south of France, where he was staying with rich friends, the Berrys, and abandoned politicking for some uncomplicated leisure. Meanwhile, passions had subsided and when the Denning Report into Profumo and other rumours was published it acted as an effective bromide to that summer of sexual scandal. The Labour lead in the polls deflated to normal proportions and Maudling – and others – assumed it was back to politics as usual. In late September he travelled to Washington, DC, to attend the annual IMF and World Bank conferences, dispensing reassurance about the British economy and circulating in his usual friendly fashion around the social circuit.

However, the leadership question had not been resolved. Macmillan dithered about whether he could carry on and lead the party into the next election. In early September he felt he no longer had the strength, and started casting around for a non-Butler, non-Maudling option: 'It needs a man with vision and moral strength – Hailsham, not Maudling. Yet the "back benches" (poor fools) do not seem to have any idea, except "a young man". Admirable as Maudling is, I doubt if he could revive our fortunes as well as Hailsham.'[20] During September he seemed to change his mind, and want to carry on after all; but on 7 October the Prime Minister started to feel unwell, and unable to urinate. During the Cabinet meeting on 8 October he was in obvious pain, as both Maudling and Heath noticed. His usual doctor being absent, he had sought advice from Stephen King-Lewis, who was a friend and neighbour of Reggie Maudling, who treated the immediate problem and called in a specialist. The advice was that he had a tumour of some kind in his prostate. Macmillan took alarm at this, and became despondent about the possibility of carrying on. The Conservative conference began in Blackpool knowing that Macmillan was ill, but not how serious the condition was, nor whether he intended to resign – which was only officially confirmed in a statement read from the platform by Lord Home, the Foreign Secretary, on 10 October. The conference was a circus without a ringmaster.

Maudling passed through the Treasury on the way up to the Conservative Party conference. He told William Armstrong that 'the rat race was on' and that his chances were about fifty-fifty, and then caught the train north from London on 9 October in the company of several other ministers.[21] Reggie arrived in Blackpool and went to the Imperial Hotel. David Gibson-Watt was waiting there for him at the door and bounded up to greet him. He had arranged television interviews and meetings for the rest of the evening to promote Reggie's leadership chances but Reggie was tired and wanted to relax. 'There's a really good fish bar up the coast and I really have to visit.' He was suitably grateful to Gibson-Watt for his efforts, but they were going to eat fish and chips rather than do the rounds of the conference television broadcasts.[22]

Reggie scorned the Conservative Party conference and quickly became disgusted with the feeding frenzy that had broken out that year in Blackpool.[23] He did not think much of conference as a social occasion and he disliked the excesses of political enthusiasm it involved in a normal year, let alone torrid, conspiratorial 1963. Reggie dabbled in plotting; he was often to be seen, puffing cigars and drinking champagne with journalists, friends and assorted Barnet and other Tories in the Imperial Bar, vaguely dispensing the wisdom that it was time for the Conservatives to find a young, progressive leader.[24] The situation at Blackpool was shaping up as a confrontation between Hailsham supporters, whose man was more inspiring to the Conservative Party workers in the constituencies, and Butler supporters who believed he would be more likely to appeal to moderate voters in the next election. But each man aroused strong opposition as well as support, with Hailsham's judgement and Butler's firmness both being open to question. Butler was particularly unpopular among Conservative activists.[25] In other deadlocked situations a compromise candidate – Bonar Law in 1911, John Major in 1990 – has managed to come through the middle. Maudling was not a bad choice as compromise candidate, although he shared rather too many of Butler's virtues and vices. If he could remind the audience why he had been so popular only a few months earlier, if he could manage to fill the hall with enthusiasm for his speech on Friday, he would have won half the battle.

Reggie was not unaware that the 1963 conference was turning into a beauty pageant in which people's chances of becoming Prime Minister were affected by the quality of their speeches and the excitement they generated among the 'representatives' in the Winter Gardens. Too much excitement was almost as bad as too little, as Hailsham found out when colleagues including Maudling reacted with disgust and comparisons to Hitler's Nuremberg rallies to an over-the-top burst of rabble-rousing in Blackpool. But there was little danger of Reggie whipping up a hysterical mob. He took greater than usual care over preparing his speech, and he had been deluged with advice about it. Arthur Fawcett, his faithful Barnet agent, wrote to Reggie on 21 September, before the overt leadership crisis resumed:

Whatever may be the circumstances in which the Conference is held I do hope that you, yourself, will spare no pains to make the speech of a lifetime. Whatever may be the situation in Parliament, in the constituencies the issue of the succession to the leadership is still wide open – and this because all too little is known of the personalities concerned. I think that Hailsham is certain to get an ovation as soon as he appears on the platform; but I think, on the whole, that the Conference will be watching points, and that the impression made by individuals is going to play a large part in determining the succession, particularly if the issue is delayed until after the election.[26]

Edward Du Cann, his Economic Secretary who had a better sense for what Conservatives wanted, and the journalist Patrick Sergeant presented him with a speech draft as a gift on the way back from New York after a few days there following the IMF conference. According to Du Cann, 'he was a little embarrassed but seemed nonetheless pleased. He promised to read it with care, but he never promised to deliver it. In the event he used not one word of it.' Reggie later said to Du Cann that his speech had suffered from too much preparation[27] – it was certainly not one of the occasions on which he worked from the back of an envelope.

The speech was not in fact a bad one. Wilfrid Sendall, one of Reggie's friends in journalism, read it and thought it was a 'cracker'.[28] But it was milder than the usual conference fare. Its content can be faulted for being too reasonable. Maudling failed to exult in Britain's economic performance over the previous year, and merely commented that he hoped he had obeyed the instruction given last year to 'stop dawdling' before reeling off some facts and figures to prove it.[29] He dwelt rather more on some Treasury issues such as the problems he saw impeding growth – the measures he had taken to increase resources to sustain sterling as a reserve currency and the need for an agreed incomes policy, and even issued a warning to the Tories that they should not expect much by way of tax cuts in the next few years because of social expenditure: 'Our plans for education, housing and overseas aid will lay a heavy burden on the Exchequer and, of course, they must reduce the scope for tax reductions.' This was a very responsible line to take in the circumstances. Reggie seemed to imagine that the Conservative Party conference could be used as a forum for a bit of political education. Another part of his speech should have been able to excite them a bit more. Maudling provided a strong riposte to Harold Wilson's invocation of the white heat of the technological revolution at the recent Labour conference in Scarborough. 'The rapidly changing world of modern science and technology is the last place for socialism' because the flexibility of response to new ideas could only be provided by private enterprise. Imposing nationalisation and government controls could only retard technological progress. True to form, Maudling refused to bring out the worst in his audience, and criticised Labour's policies as misguided rather than motivated by wickedness.

As in his much-admired 1962 letter to his constituents, he mused on the future of society in the technological age and the 'human purpose' behind economic expansion. Sometimes these thoughts veered into vague generalities and platitudes, but he closed with a fine, progressive statement of intent:

> There are great things to be done; meeting the passion for education, clearing up the pools of squalor that still disfigure some parts of our national life, bringing light and air and beauty to our cities, bringing aid and succour to the people of Asia and Africa who live at the edge of subsistence. These are the purposes which we disguise under the name of economic policy. They are noble purposes.[30]

What was really wrong with Maudling's speech was its delivery. It was said of Michael Heseltine that he could always find the clitoris of the Conservative Party conference. Reggie Maudling could barely manage to undo its bra-strap. His deficiencies as a conference orator were, for once, in the peculiar circumstances of Blackpool in 1963, of crucial importance. Reggie ran through his speech flatly, not allowing the audience much chance to applaud or draw breath, not bothering with much by way of rhetorical devices, and failing to adjust the microphones so that his speech – coming from higher because he was taller than most of his colleagues – could be heard clearly. The Tories in 1963 wanted to forget about the horrible year of scandal and disastrous opinion polls they had endured, and be sent out from Blackpool full of optimism and fighting spirit. Neither the content nor the delivery matched the demands of the occasion. There was dutiful applause for the Chancellor when he drew to an end. Maudling supporters in the hall leapt to their feet, hoping to inspire a standing ovation for their man, but nobody joined them and one by one they sat down, rather embarrassed.

The instant judgement at Blackpool was that Maudling had muffed his chances of becoming leader. Potential supporters such as Powell and Macleod concluded that Reggie had 'lost too much ground to be recovered' and lined up behind Rab Butler.[31] Arthur Fawcett's daughter Trudi, a Young Conservative delegate at Blackpool, remembered 'even I as a young girl – and I really wanted him to be Prime Minister – could tell it was a lousy speech and that it wouldn't help'.[32] The press and other commentators agreed. 'Mr Maudling had left the mute stuck in his trumpet,' said *The Times*.[33] 'If not the dullest speech in history, it would do until the dullest was made,' quipped Bernard Levin on *That Was the Week that Was*. Maudling's failure was made all the more conspicuous by comparison with Lord Home, who had stormed the platform earlier that day. Home's speech was no less platitudinous than Maudling's, although he mixed in rather more red meat for the right wing, and he delivered it competently. The prospects of Home becoming leader had not been taken seriously before Blackpool, but he was increasingly in play after his conference success and Macmillan was using the apparatus under his control to influence matters in Home's favour. Butler, having persuaded his colleagues to let him do the closing speech on Saturday, followed Maudling in disappointing his supporters. A meeting of the 1922 executive towards the end of the conference found that Maudling's support was running at only two, as against two for Hailsham and ten who had decided to support Lord Home. There were apparently none for Butler.[34]

Still, all was not lost for Maudling. He had not emerged as the favourite, but he was not completely out of the game either. On Monday, Tuesday and Wednesday of the week after Blackpool (14–16 October) the contest was still on and the candidates continued to promote their claims. At Ladbroke's the odds on Lord Hailsham had lengthened after the conference fiasco, while there was backing flowing in for Lord Home. Maudling was still a long shot, but there was heavy betting on him at 16–1 and by the Tuesday afternoon his odds had shortened to 8–1.[35]

However, Cabinet met on the morning of Tuesday 15 October, and Butler read out a note from Macmillan about the process to be used for the selection of a new leader; Butler and the rest of the Cabinet agreed that what were called 'the customary processes of consultation' would be the right way to proceed.[36] The problem was that nobody had a very clear idea about what the process should be, other than that a senior figure with no direct personal interest in the result should be commissioned to canvass opinion. The results, except for who would become leader, would be confidential. This sort of politics was, even before the leadership crisis, widely regarded as out of date. A Conservative MP, Humphrey Berkeley, had suggested in early 1963 that the party should conduct proper elections, and in July even the establishment *Times* mocked 'the picture of a small closed world, plutocratic as well as political, where power is valued and exploited. The outside public do not enter there; they are to be excluded from knowledge of the private mystery.' Next day the paper reported, 'Conservative doubts on way of selecting leader'.[37] In 1963 the customary process was broadened out somewhat from the small sampling that Lord Salisbury had conducted in 1957 but remained in essence unchanged. The person entrusted with the task was the Lord Chancellor, Lord Dilhorne, who until a couple of years earlier had served in the Commons as Sir Reginald Manningham-Buller, often known by the spoonerism 'Bullying-Manner' and not such a respected figure as 'Bobbety' Salisbury. By their general agreement to the 'customary processes', though, the Cabinet were complicit in the fiasco that several of them later disowned. It was a missed trick for Maudling, whose chances were best if the decision could somehow be thrown to Conservative MPs.

After the Cabinet meeting, Macmillan saw a few of the potential leadership candidates. Whatever he said to Home and Hailsham, he did not – contrary to press reports – discuss the leadership with Maudling. Nor did he discuss Maudling's claims in his own contemplative essay on the succession he wrote that day.[38] Dilhorne was conducting more systematic interviews with individual Cabinet ministers. Dilhorne's gathering of opinions from the Cabinet on 15 October has become notorious for its incompetence or dishonesty. Dilhorne had already expressed his view to Macmillan that in the event of the Prime Minister resigning 'our only hope is Quintin',[39] but after the collapse of the Hailsham campaign switched his allegiance in accordance with his master's wishes, towards Home. He recorded ten Cabinet members supporting Home, four for Maudling (Reggie himself, John Boyd-Carpenter, Freddy Erroll and Keith Joseph), three for Butler (Rab, Henry Brooke and Enoch Powell) and two for Hailsham. Dilhorne ran various permutations of second preferences, none of which showed Maudling scoring at all well. When Dilhorne asked Maudling whom he would prefer if Reggie himself were eliminated from contention, Reggie replied 'Butler', but added almost as an afterthought that he would be entirely prepared to serve 'under Alec'.[40]

The oddest aspect of the Dilhorne Cabinet survey was that Iain Macleod was counted as a Home supporter. This was extremely hard to reconcile with Macleod's behaviour over the succeeding days and months. Apologists for the way in which the succession was organised have suggested, correctly, that Macleod could be devious and mercurial, and speculated that he might have changed his mind or indulged in some singularly inept tactical voting for some mysterious purpose. More convincing is the account of Macleod's biographer Robert Shepherd, who argues that for whatever reason Dilhorne got it wrong.[41] Shepherd also points to the fact that Edward Boyle – a much more straightforward character than Macleod, whose private papers abound with evidence that he favoured Butler – was also listed as being for Home.[42] John Hare, also listed by Dilhorne as a Home supporter on the first count, was almost certainly not either – he telephoned Maudling on the Friday morning, 'greatly disturbed by the way in which the Prime Minister was handling the situation' and telling Reggie that at least ten of the Cabinet were solid for Butler.[43] Switching these three votes to where they belong produces Home seven, Butler five, Maudling four, Hailsham three.[44]

The Chief Whip Martin Redmayne's canvass of MPs had asked not only for definite but also for second and third votes in the event of the chosen candidate being unavailable, and for 'definite aversions' – people who would have difficulty stomaching particular candidates. The first report via Dilhorne did not give concrete figures, but on 18 October, after a request from Macmillan, they were reported to Number 10 as in the table.

Candidate	First choice	Second or third choice	Definite aversions
Home	87	89	30
Butler	86	69	48
Hailsham	65	39	78
Maudling	48	66	6
Macleod	12	18	1
Heath	10	17	1

Three candidates were considered eliminated – Heath and Macleod for low levels of support and then Hailsham, presumably because his 'definite aversions' were so numerous that his appointment would have alienated a fifth of the parliamentary party. When first preferences for these candidates were reallocated, Home's narrow lead survived with 113 votes to 104 for Butler and 66 for Maudling. There was no way in which Redmayne's advice to Macmillan, that 'the position of second man varies between Maudling and Butler according to how the figures are read', can have been true, without even more extreme distortions of the will of Conservative MPs.[45] The figures are dubious in themselves, as a one-vote lead for Home was convenient for the party establishment, and the expression of second preferences on such a scale for Home is an indication of the 'guided democracy' that the whips' consultation exercise involved. Backbench MPs recalled being prompted, and being suspicious that mild expressions of liking for Home ended up being noted down as second preferences even if they were strong supporters of another candidate.

While Maudling attracted hardly any strong opposition, neither did he have a sufficient level of solid, positive support. Redmayne also reported to Macmillan that when he examined where support for each candidate came from, 'Maudling's is almost exclusively from the younger and more junior element'. The more 'mature' chaps favoured Home or Butler.[46] Maudling also had very little support among Conservatives in the House of Lords, where a parallel survey found only two supporters, to 14 for Hailsham, 15 for Butler and 31 for Home. Percy Mills, his old boss at the Ministry of Power, could not abide the thought of Maudling as Prime Minister at any price.[47]

On the Wednesday, political affairs were still turbulent and, except to those privy to the thinking of Harold Macmillan, little seemed to have been decided. For Reggie it was a lull during the crisis, as he had a long-standing official engagement at the annual Mansion House dinner for the Lord Mayor of the City of London, at which Chancellors normally give a speech. Reggie's Mansion House speech was better received than his recent effort at the party conference; there were a number of technical changes to local authority loans to announce, but some items of more general interest such as an optimistic progress report about the economy since the Budget, and a look forward to the next problem of avoiding a repetition of the 'stop-go' cycle in 1964/5. Reggie noted that 'the tide is on the turn' for private sector investment, but seemed less concerned than Lord Cromer, the Governor of the Bank of England, about the continuing high levels of public sector investment.[48] Preparing for and delivering the Mansion House speech proved a healthy distraction from the leadership crisis for Reggie.

On the morning of Thursday 17 October the situation still seemed unclear. Hailsham was out of the running, Maudling was still in the picture and seemed to be recovering some of the damage from his conference showing, and the balance between Butler and Home was debatable. During the day things would be resolved in a way that came as a surprise and a shock to Maudling and his allies. Maudling tried to concentrate on his Treasury work but at noon Iain Macleod turned up in a state of high anxiety having learned from a source in Buckingham Palace that it was looking as if Lord Home would soon be asked to form a government. The Lord Chancellor, Dilhorne, was going to present the results of his consultation, and those that had been carried out among MPs and peers, to Macmillan that afternoon. Freddy Erroll came over as well and there was a small conclave – one of many to take place in the week after Blackpool – to discuss what should be done.

Just before 1p.m. Maudling asked his Private Secretary to get hold of Dilhorne on the phone. He did, and Maudling told Dilhorne that he and some colleagues were concerned about the way Macmillan was going about advising the Queen about the succession. He wanted a Cabinet meeting chaired by the Lord Chancellor to discuss the succession in an open, collegial manner but Dilhorne 'disliked the idea intensely' and resisted, saying that he had been going about gathering opinions and that the open expression of views within the Cabinet would be 'divisive' and was opposed by other colleagues.[49] Dilhorne had good reason to oppose Maudling's suggestion of an open discussion of the Cabinet's preferences.

Maudling and Macleod were near to open revolt at this point. They retreated to the Mirabelle restaurant to meet Beryl and chew over the situation. Meanwhile, Derek Mitchell met Philip de Zulueta, the Number 10 Private Secretary who dealt with foreign affairs, for a lunch of their own and was told *sotto voce* that the odds were shortening on the 14th Earl. Mitchell found this difficult to believe and expressed some of Maudling's worries about the possibility of bias in the process to Tim Bligh. Bligh confirmed that Macmillan had come to a decision – although he professed to be unsure as to what choice he had made – and that it was too late for 'anything short of open revolution in the Conservative Party' to change the Prime Minister's mind. Mitchell hurried to the Mirabelle, where both ministers still remained at around a quarter to three, and imparted this knowledge to Reggie and Macleod, who were both 'astonished' and 'depressed'; Macleod said that if it was true the Conservatives would be exposed to 'derision'.[50] About half an hour after Reggie had returned to the Treasury, Macleod telephoned with the news that he had spoken to William Rees-Mogg, who had got wind of what was going on, and that Rees-Mogg reckoned that it would be a disaster if Home was selected.

At 4.15p.m., Maudling heard from Dilhorne that he had prepared a document for Macmillan in connection with the succession. This document summed up Dilhorne's own soundings, the whips' canvass of the MPs, and opinion in the House of Lords. Maudling was curious not only about the contents of the document, but its status. He and the other dissenting ministers wanted to know whether it would be presented to the Queen or whether it would just be propped up on the sheets of the Prime Minister's sickbed and used as an aide-memoire. Maudling tried to get an answer from Number 10, but it took a couple of hours to do so. He met Bligh face to face in the early evening to ask about the process, and was told that the document would 'point unmistakably in the direction of Lord Home' and that the Prime Minister endorsed its contents. The upshot was that it was likely to result in Lord Home being summoned to the Palace.[51]

By this point Reggie realised that he would not emerge from the 1963 crisis as Prime Minister, and that even if Home was somehow blocked, Butler would have to be the beneficiary – Maudling did not have enough support. An angry Freddy Erroll complained that it was appalling, and that 'it was disgraceful that the leadership of the Party should be determined by an old man lying on his sickbed', but Reggie seemed calm. He walked down the main steps of the Treasury, Derek Mitchell at his side. He was 'obviously sad, but with every sign of being resigned to losing out this time'. His mind turned immediately to seeing the bright side of what had happened, commenting that it was 'something of a relief not to have to take on the responsibility' and that he could continue to enjoy life; something that the pressures of Number 10 would have made more difficult.[52] Reggie rationalised his disappointment in a very balanced, calm way. As was his wont, he shrugged his shoulders and moved on to what life next had to offer.

Reggie may have considered himself personally out of the running, but he still had strong views about the future of his party. He now enlisted in Rab Butler's army for the final struggle. After a dinner with Lord Cobbold, the former Governor of the Bank of England, Beryl and Lady Cobbold, he returned home to Chester Street but was summoned at midnight to a famous meeting at Enoch Powell's house, a short walk away in South Eaton Place. The press, camped outside while the meeting took place, had discovered the fact that the meeting was on when journalist Henry Fairlie called Chester Street to try to speak to Reggie. Caroline gave Fairlie the number Reggie had left her, and Fairlie recognised it as being Powell's. Reggie told the others at the meeting – Macleod, Erroll, Powell and Lord Aldington from Central Office – that he was out of the running and that Butler was the only acceptable successor.[53] At 1a.m. those present, plus Hailsham by telephone, told Redmayne that they all reaffirmed their support for Butler.

If Thursday had been confusing, complete chaos reigned on Friday 18 October. Almost as soon as he returned to the Treasury in the morning Maudling started to field telephone calls from other Cabinet ministers who favoured Butler. There was a confused discussion at one point, when Macleod had two telephones and was talking to Maudling with one receiver and Powell with the other. A small black box came in to the Treasury with the notice of the government's resignation in it. 'The Chancellor glanced quickly at the letter and then threw it back at me without comment,' recalled Derek Mitchell.

Maudling had by now counted himself out of the race, and his decision had got through to other Conservative MPs. John Hall, a potential supporter, called the Treasury and asked whether it was true that Maudling had pulled out and was throwing his weight behind Butler. Maudling, overcome by fatalism, decided it was not worth saying anything about this 'or any other' rumour, as it was all too late.[54] Given that Maudling had by now withdrawn from the contest as far as he could, in any sensible electoral system his supporters' preferences as between Butler and Home should have been taken into account. They would have been, in all probability, heavily in Butler's favour, but time was running out.

Maudling then left to go to the Overseas and Defence Committee, at which he had been led to believe Butler was presiding, but found that Butler had passed the chairmanship to Home. Macleod went round to the Treasury clamouring for Maudling to be pulled out of the meeting; Butler also called, and at lunchtime a Treasury 'council of war' was convened between Maudling, Butler, Macleod and Hailsham; Macleod suggested Downing Street but Reggie offered the Treasury as a less public and provocative venue, and came along with Erroll and Boyd-Carpenter in tow. During the meeting, news came through that Home had been called to the Palace to be given the commission of trying to form a government – not at this stage an actual appointment as Prime Minister. To become Prime Minister, Home needed to secure the consent and participation of most of the Butlerites. This, for a while, was far from certain. The meeting continued over Treasury pork pies and sandwiches, Macleod desperately trying to work out how to stop Home.

Butler and Maudling were the key men for Douglas-Home to convince to sign up for office in a new government. At 2.45p.m. Butler saw Home and reserved his position rather than refusing outright. Maudling was next in, at 3.15p.m., for what turned out to be an alarming interview with Alec Douglas-Home. When Maudling refused to commit himself about whether to serve, Home said that if he was holding out in the hope of Rab becoming Prime Minister he was mistaken. If a Home government could not be formed, the job of making the next attempt would fall to Reggie himself.[55] It was a dizzying moment, but Maudling quickly calculated that under these circumstances the commission to form a government was not worth much. To wreck Home's attempt for what would look like personal ambition would not be a good start for Maudling's own government. He would have had difficulty in persuading several of his Cabinet colleagues to join. His support was stronger on the backbenches and among junior ministers than in the Cabinet, and a Maudling government formed in bitterness would have lacked several important figures, probably the admittedly disposable Dilhorne, Redmayne and Brooke among them. If he failed to put together a government, his career was over. If he managed, he could see that it would have split the party and probably lost an election within a year. More than any of this, Reggie would have known what it was to be hated. The rationale for sending for Maudling, rather than Butler, if Home failed is far from clear, as Maudling was clearly third in the consultations and Butler second, even taking them at face value.

During the afternoon there was a steady flow of ministers through the doors of Number 10, where Home was seeing the Cabinet one by one to see if they would serve. At six o'clock a slightly menacing call came through to the Treasury from Number 10. Tim Bligh said that the bandwagon was rolling well. Constituency feedback and the meetings with ministers had gone well so far, and a Douglas-Home government could be formed. 'It would be unfortunate if anybody delayed jumping on the bandwagon so late that bad blood was created.'[56] It was a well-placed thrust at Reggie's weakest point. He was comfortable and happy where he was, and the insinuation that he could be evicted from the Treasury to somewhere less appealing was worrying. Butler and Maudling were both summoned for further meetings at Number 10 in the early evening, in conditions of considerable confusion.

After yet another hectic day Reggie adjourned to the home comforts of Chester Street, but he did not manage to have a peaceful evening in. After dinner the tortuous discussions, on the one hand to form a Douglas-Home government and on the other to prevent it, went on. There was such heavy traffic through the doors of Number 10 that officials lost track, and a certain amount of telephoning and plotting among the Butlerites. This culminated in yet another meeting at 9.45p.m., this one of a different character from Tuesday's midnight meeting. Reggie, who was not generally a diary keeper or note taker, did write an account of this meeting but, he claimed preposterously in his memoirs, it was in pencil and had faded hopelessly a couple of years later.[57] Douglas-Home met the other leadership contenders, Butler, Maudling and Hailsham, for a 'quadripartite' meeting at Downing Street, in which Hailsham agreed to serve but Maudling and Butler reserved their positions. Maudling remarked to Butler after the meeting that 'things were closing in'.[58]

Having slept on it, Maudling continued to delay making a definite statement on Saturday morning. His comment to Dilhorne on Tuesday, that he would be happy to serve under Alec, weighed on him and he was reluctant to go back on his word despite the strong feelings of his friends that the process had been a fraud. He stalled a bit more, but after Butler himself had accepted office Maudling saw no reason to stay out. Macleod and Powell disagreed, disgusted with what had happened, and refused. In a way, Maudling was the truer Butlerite than his two more zealous fellow disciples from the Research Department years. Butler did after all recognise the result of the manoeuvres, by accepting office, and his instinct was always to go along. Butler, like Maudling, found his ambition sometimes overpowered by ambivalence and fastidiousness during the 1963 crisis.

Maudling's failure to rise to the occasion at the party conference was not because he did not care about making a good speech, or fail to realise the importance of the occasion. He knew all this very well himself, and was repeatedly told it by his friends. On some level the realisation that it was so important seems to have frightened him into over-preparation and bad delivery. After Blackpool, he was utterly calm, with only the occasional half-amused exclamation such as 'What a muddle!' or 'What extraordinary confusion!'[59] He was impassive, unexcited by the political whirlwind, a calm influence at a time when his colleagues Macleod and Powell became extremely heated, just as he could be when they were all Conservative researchers together. Reggie could have been a role model for the qualities extolled in Rudyard Kipling's *If.* He even managed to do some Treasury work that dramatic week.

Whatever caused the failure of the Blackpool speech, it was not laziness or a lack of conscious ambition to succeed. If one is to look within Reggie's character for an explanation, there was a strand of self-sabotage in his nature that manifested itself at the crucial moments when he had an opportunity that needed taking, a fear of too much, too conspicuous, success. However, Reggie was an intelligent, highly ambitious politician, who dearly wanted to be Prime Minister. Despite Reggie's protestations to the contrary Beryl, whose feelings were always of deep importance to him, would have loved to be the hostess of Number 10. But Reggie was not blinded by his ambition. He had not lowered himself by scattering promises of preferment to others. Nor had he pretended to be other than he was during the leadership contest, which was a deeply significant matter for him. His sense of the integrity of his personality meant that he wanted the Conservative Party to come to him, conscious of what it was doing and not because he had manipulated the outcome. 'To thine own self be true' was an important motto for Reggie. In a way, if Reggie had made an abnormally rabble-rousing speech, taken Blackpool by storm and won the leadership, the Conservative Party would not have taken the real Reggie to its heart. Once the fuss was over he felt reassured that he had not sold his soul in pursuit of power.

After he had decided to stay and serve in the Douglas-Home government, Maudling felt some pangs of doubt as to whether he had acted correctly. Enoch Powell noted that on Saturday, 'Mr Maudling shortly afterwards telephoned me and submitted his whole course of action for the last 48 hours. I assured him that he had not acted inconsistently with anything which he had professed.'[60] Nor had he. He had given no undertakings to fight in the last ditch for Butler and had pressed the Butler case strongly. If Butler had refused to serve, Maudling would have been placed in a real dilemma – between his comment to Dilhorne that he would serve under Alec, and his loyalty to Butler. But Rab absolved him of this problem by agreeing to serve. There was only one way, once the focus had shifted from Blackpool back to Westminster, that Maudling could have stopped Home, and that was by disclaiming his own ambitions and throwing all his weight behind Butler – *before* Thursday. But the results of the consultations were not known, and given Maudling's pre-recess landslide advantage among MPs, there was every reason to stay in until the game was definitively up for his own prospects.

The result of the leadership contest was actually the best outcome, short of victory, from Maudling's point of view. Reggie's return to the Treasury, his favourite job in government, had not been a foregone conclusion, because an unpleasant surprise would have awaited him had Butler made it to Number 10. The July meeting with Butler had not, on Butler's understanding, produced a deal. Rab intended to appoint Iain Macleod, whom he had always admired more, as Chancellor of the Exchequer. Butler thought that 'Maudling was too slack, with his cigars and burgundy'.[61] Where Maudling would have ended up in a Butler government is unclear. He would have been a most unsuitable party chairman because this job requires at least the ability to simulate strong partisan feelings. The other option fitting his status might have been Home Secretary, where Henry Brooke was a much-criticised incumbent, or possibly as a Deputy Prime Minister to succeed Butler, with an accumulation of grandiose titles to soothe his pride. In the circumstances Maudling might have chosen to resign from office and leap into making money at that stage rather than doing so after October 1964.

There was another layer to the silver lining for Reggie. Sir Alec Douglas-Home was likely to be a short-term leader, because he seemed likely to lose the election or step down in a few years even if he won. Maudling was assured another bite at the cherry some time in the 1960s and was now the leading prospective candidate from the left of the party. Reggie had been toying all through the last week of the crisis with the idea of taking Beryl to the pictures, to see the latest James Bond film, *From Russia with Love*. This proved impossible as chaos descended on Thursday night, and the movie trip had to wait for a calmer evening. From the point of view of Reggie's leadership ambitions, it was more a case of *You Only Live Twice*. He could get on with his life and try again another day.

Chapter 13

'SORRY, OLD COCK': THE MAUDLING BOOM, 1963–1964

By a peculiar coincidence, the Saturday morning in October 1963 on which the Douglas-Home government was formed was the very day the rebuilding of Number 11 Downing Street was finally completed. It had been fixed months in advance, on the assumption that it would be a quiet weekend between the party conference and the start of parliamentary business.[1] Reggie moved into Number 11 in the morning and at eleven o'clock Derek Mitchell came in to see him, finding him 'in an armchair in the morning room, surrounded by dust sheets and with the last hammerings of the Ministry of Works' contractors in the background as they finished putting up curtains'. Reggie bustled around his new house, exploding – for the first time during the leadership crisis – at the unduly complex newly installed telephone arrangements in Number 11 'which were clearly going to call for a training course for the Maudling family and were likely forever to be beyond the comprehension of the new Portuguese cook'.[2]

The Maudlings quickly came to love Number 11. Reggie had tried to convince himself that Beryl would not have enjoyed the burden of being hostess of Number 10, but she would surely have relished every minute. She certainly rejoiced in her role as hostess of 11 Downing Street, and was proud to have had such a large say in the decoration of such an important house. She loved holding receptions, particularly for artistic and theatrical people, and became more and more involved in raising money for the charitable causes she supported, such as Westminster Hospital and the Adeline Genée Theatre. Her mother, Florence, basked in the reflected glory, and came round more frequently than ever. Beryl's cousin James Haw remembers one occasion very clearly:

Aunt Florence was a social climber (and a good one too – her daughter had married well). The culmination of her feelings of success I thought I saw when I visited Beryl at Number 11 in 1963. There was a room with two windows separated by a chimney that looked out over St James's Park and Horseguards' and she sat there on a wide sofa looking out. It was as if she said to me out loud, 'look, I made it.' The satisfaction oozed from her.[3]

Reggie and Beryl's older children were growing up in autumn 1963 when the family moved into Number 11. Martin was admitted to Merton College, his father's Oxford college, and went up just before the leadership crisis broke. Martin's academic record at Harrow was too mediocre to merit his admission to Oxford, but at that time ability was not the only consideration. Martin was accepted at the insistence of the Warden, Reggie's old tutor Geoffrey Mure, because he was the son of a noted old member and would be part of a 'rounded' college. This string-pulling indulgence did Martin, in the long run, no favours. There was something strangely unformed about Martin's character. He lived in his father's shadow, and followed in his footsteps, although he did not have his father's intellect. 'He seemed a nice bloke but he seemed also to have no personality – there was a blank there,' was a not atypical verdict on Martin at the time. He could not manage Reggie's understated success at college and spent most of the time idling with friends, acting and developing an interest in racing cars. He went down in 1966 without a degree, whereupon he became a serious headache for his father.

Caroline turned 16 in 1963 and 'came out' at a debutantes' ball. She was a beautiful and charming young woman who was extremely popular in politics and society. She enjoyed the opportunities that came her way, including some journalistic work as the *Daily Mail*'s 'travelling teenager' in 1964 and an appearance alongside John Lennon on *Juke Box Jury* in June 1963. Lennon was in a negative mood and the only one of the records to be voted 'Hit' was Elvis Presley's 'Devil in Disguise'. Caroline studied acting in Bristol. Like her mother, Caroline had a brief cinematic career, adding some glamour to *It's All over Town*, a 'light-hearted pop-music vehicle'[4] released in 1964, also featuring Willie Rushton of *Private Eye*, Acker Bilk and Frankie Vaughan.

For the two younger boys, family life in Downing Street was no end of fun. They were fascinated by the armed police guards who stood outside the door. William inadvertently got one officer, Tony Poulter, into some trouble when he told Beryl about witnessing Poulter trying to shoot a pigeon that had emptied the contents of its stomach over his uniform. News got back to the Inspector and Poulter was carpeted, although Reggie himself had nothing but sympathy for his actions.[5] Edward managed to persuade another officer to lend him his whistle and promptly ignored the condition of the loan that he shouldn't blow it – policemen came running from all over Downing Street. The children had the run of the Downing Street garden, often cheering up the Prime Minister as he looked out from the Cabinet room, and a balcony overlooking the street from which they would sometimes give impromptu press conferences.[6]

The Maudlings' relaxed approach to parenting had been an issue when the arrangements were being drawn up for access to the new Number 11 building. Reggie and Beryl wanted to allow Martin and Caroline free access to and from the building at all hours of day and night, to give them some privacy if they came back drunk or with company. The Maudlings requested a system by which there could be a buzzer on the lock, but this was vetoed on security grounds. They grudgingly accepted a compromise whereby the door would be staffed until 9p.m. and after that access would be via Number 10.[7] One evening Martin and some friends rolled back at 4a.m. from a fancy dress party in ancient Roman costume – 'all back to mine' is particularly appealing if 'mine' is 11 Downing Street – to the consternation of the security authorities.[8]

The Maudling family added some much missed glamour and laughter to Downing Street that had not brightened up the centre of British government since the Asquith children. It was a pleasant year in the family's life. The press were still sufficiently kind and discreet for the children to make their mistakes and grow up reasonably privately. Edward and Caroline still have fond memories of their father's time at Number 11.

After the excitement of the leadership contest Maudling returned to his office at the Treasury. Douglas-Home also, notoriously, had little interest in or knowledge of economics and gave Maudling free rein at the Treasury. In a 1962 interview Douglas-Home had admitted that 'When I have to read economic documents I have to have a box of matches and start moving them into position to simplify and illustrate the points to myself'.[9] Most Prime Ministers chose to chair the Economic Policy committee of the Cabinet but under Alec Douglas-Home this was left to the Chancellor.[10]

The only inhibiting factor in Reggie's dominance of economic policy was the new role that had been given to Edward Heath at the Board of Trade. Heath took over responsibilities for regional development and industrial policy as well, to become the Secretary of State for Industry, Trade and Regional Development.[11] There were briefings to the press at the time stating that Heath had a wide, general brief to oversee modernisation and a kind of overlord role on economic policy. Maudling took this invasion of his territory badly and asserted at the end of October that he retained 'overall responsibility for economic policy' regardless of what might be said about Ted Heath's new job. There was an incipient power struggle between the two economic ministers, with Maudling's adviser Alec Cairncross unimpressed by his attitude: 'Fact is he wasn't consulted by PM about Heath's title (or presumably functions) and Heath suggested it himself. Can't see that this kind of squabbling will put him in a stronger position to contest PM'ship when it comes up again in 5/10 years' time. Just pique.'[12]

The rise of Heath had a significant effect on Reggie's chances of winning the leadership. Once Heath was in the running, Maudling had lost some of his political advantage from being young. Heath was only a year older, and also had most of the qualities the Tories were associating with youth – vigour, determination – in greater measure than Reggie. Everyone knew that Heath believed in Europe and modernisation, but when it came to what Reggie's big ideas were, there was less certainty. From being the candidate of youth,

Reggie was subtly transformed over the next two years into being the quiet life, steady as she goes candidate. Where Reggie still scored in 1963–5 was for normality. The very qualities that were attractive about Heath as a leader also set him apart from the electorate; a bachelor, a music buff, a driven man compared to Reggie, who obviously loved leisure and family and was rather proud of not having much interest in high culture. The contrast between the two affected their personal relationship. 'On the surface they seemed to be like-minded colleagues, but there was always an edge when Ted Heath came into the Chancellor's office for a meeting, as he often did, and the temperature dropped,' recalls Tom Caulcott.[13] They had astonishingly little in common. Maudling admired Heath's qualities and recognised their place in politics, but he did not seek out opportunities to see Heath socially. Maudling's outgoing, matey personal style, and his confidence about physicality, grated with Heath's chilliness and reserve, and theirs was never a close friendship. Heath, according to someone with whom he discussed the matter, 'never rated Maudling much, in any capacity' but still had a great appreciation for Maudling's loyalty and sense of honour.[14]

Heath was a much more stubborn politician than Maudling, and lacked his ability to shrug his shoulders and move on. This quality was ultimately an element in Heath's downfall, but the positive side of Heath's stubbornness was a certain quality of political courage that Reggie lacked. The most controversial of Heath's modernising proposals was the long-delayed abolition of Resale Price Maintenance, announced in January 1964. The Labour government had proposed abolition in 1951 but the plan had not gone far by the time the Tories returned to power and it was then dropped. Maudling had ineffectively proposed abolition in 1960 but given up on the idea. In summer 1962 it was still being inconclusively kicked around the Cabinet, the economic case for it being balanced by a political case against it because it was opposed by most small traders, who were influential in Conservative constituency associations.[15] The Treasury and the Board of Trade, even under the gentle regime of Freddy Erroll, continually argued in favour of making RPM illegal and ending the problem in the interests of competition and consumer choice, but in January 1963 after a conversation with Reggie, Erroll was persuaded that nothing could be done for the time being. '*Requiescat in* temporary *pace*' was Reggie's comment to Derek Mitchell.[16] It was not one of Maudling's better moments – his desire for a quiet life triumphed over a measure that he knew was a good idea; he was right but irresolute.

The political changes of 1963 ended the logjam on RPM, and finally Heath was able to get the measure – a short and simple Bill – onto the legislative agenda. Douglas-Home asked Maudling's advice before proceeding. Maudling replied that the economic arguments were decisive and it would not necessarily be bad for the small shopkeeper, and that the political arguments were changing because Wilson might take up the issue as part of his modernisation campaign.[17] Maudling's advice was still hedged around with qualifications and caveats, but Douglas-Home allowed Heath to go full steam ahead. It was a brave move for a Conservative government so close to an election. At a meeting of the backbench 1922 Committee in January 1964 Rab Butler's PPS, Paul Channon, reported that 'There was almost unanimous criticism of the government's proposals on the ground of timing. Members appeared almost equally divided on their merits.'[18] But it was an intelligent calculation that there were many times more consumers than small traders in the electorate, and that a modernising image was of itself worth more than pandering to the traditional heartland. It did not spell the end of the High Street as we know it, and despite the apocalyptic predictions it cannot have cost any Tory seats in 1964.

Now that Heath had pushed the issue, Maudling offered the support he had withheld from Erroll a year earlier. As a department, the Treasury were almost as strongly in favour as the Board of Trade, and Reggie was perfectly happy to see the market free up, however uneasy he had been about being seen as the origin of the move. The Treasury line was to stiffen the resistance of the Board of Trade to any watering down of the policy for political reasons,[19] and Maudling stood solidly but not particularly energetically behind Heath in the interdepartmental and political battles that followed before the measure was passed into law in July 1964. Reggie wound up the Second Reading debate on 10 March, commending it for its effects on the consumer, but while Reggie had avoided the initial blame for being associated with a controversial measure, he also forfeited to Heath the credit for bravery and modernity in the longer term. 'Mr Heath's victory' said the *Economist*.[20]

Maudling was even less inclined to do much about two other reforms that were being considered in late 1963 – he came out 'strongly . . . but half in jest', according to Cairncross, against decimalising the currency and building a Channel Tunnel.[21] His objections to decimal currency at the time were primarily concerned with the public spending implications – he feared that given the high projected levels of spending anyway, the additional sums involved in a changeover in the mid-1960s would lead to higher taxes. But he realised that it had to be done at some stage.[22] Similarly with the Tunnel, Maudling took a basically positive paper to Cabinet in January 1964 despite his own instincts. It is admirable for a politician to transcend his prejudices, but when he did so Reggie somehow did not carry a great deal of conviction, and neither decimalisation nor the Channel Tunnel got much further under the Douglas-Home government.

Although he was constrained on some of the ancillary economic issues, Maudling was firmly in control of the central issues of economic policy – the government's own fiscal position and the decisions on whether to restrain or encourage demand in the economy as a whole. He had won international sympathy for the strategy of aiming for high growth during his September 1963 visit to the IMF and World Bank meetings, again in Washington, DC.

Maudling went around dispensing cheerful reassurance to the Americans and anyone else who was interested that the British economy was doing well and was on its way to escaping the 'stop-go' constraint. He managed to convince the American Treasury, who had been sceptical about his international financial ideas a year earlier, that his domestic policy was on course and not in danger of overheating.[23]

However, over the summer of 1963 Reggie had concluded, despite urgings for more expansion from the TUC and some commentators, that the economy was already responding well to the reflationary measures he had taken since November 1962. Maudling now started playing the role of the strict Chancellor in the new government, giving a public warning on 26 October about inflationary trends in prices and incomes. On the same day, the Prime Minister – in a by-election speech in Kinross and West Perthshire, where he was the candidate – talked in terms of Britain 'right in the van of modern progress' and that his policy was neither right nor left but 'straight ahead, fast'.[24] Maudling and his Treasury advisers were concerned about these mixed messages.

Reggie hoped that there might at last be a general agreement on incomes policy, so that inflation might be capped while growth in the real economy took hold. The tide was flowing more strongly in favour of incomes policy, with the TUC (ambiguously) and Labour during the conference season endorsing the principle of planning incomes and ensuring that wages growth did not exceed output growth. The TUC General Secretary George Woodcock himself believed in a voluntary incomes policy, so long as there was a wider system of agreement encompassing prices, profits and rents and it was not just focused, as the NIC had been, on wages. During Woodcock's time, the TUC never repudiated the principle of voluntary incomes policy.[25] But there was a strong tradition within the trade unions of free collective bargaining, and the TUC's authority over member unions was very limited. The Conservatives also would have trouble with extending government intervention over as wide a range of economic issues as the TUC wanted. If it had been left to Woodcock and Maudling personally to sort matters out, it could probably have been done within weeks, but Woodcock in particular was operating under severe constraints. Frank Cousins, the leader of the Transport and General Workers, the largest union at the time, bluntly told the TUC in September 1963 that 'We will not have wage restraint, whoever brings it and wraps it up for us'. Cousins was aiming at Maudling, whose efforts to reach agreement through the NEDC he believed were a snare that might endanger Labour's electoral prospects, but the warning note for a future Labour government was unmistakable.[26]

Maudling seems not to have been entirely clear about what would be regarded as acceptable reasons for a particular settlement deviating from the overall policy. While he approved of the principle, he gave the impression of being cynically relaxed about granting exceptions. His Economic Adviser, Alec

Cairncross, noted: 'what I think important is that the Chancellor should not in his public speeches give approval to the efforts of workers to cash in on an improvement in productivity to which they have in no real sense contributed'.[27] On 11 December 1963 Alec Cairncross noted:

> Chancellor yesterday said incomes policy had to be simple enough for Harry D. [Douglass] to understand. We needed a non-aggression pact for the next year with Trade Unions agreeing not to raise wages beyond a certain proportion and employers not to put up prices both with exceptions that could be justified. Agreed that might be few cases in private sector for next six months and this means that railways not setting the fashion but coming at tail end! I think that he deceives himself here and that 6% railways settlement is more serious than he imagines. At Thursday's Cabinet (so T.B. says) he was alone in defending a 6% settlement – the others were quite prepared to sack Beeching. He thinks of productivity and profitability to justify what he regards as realism.[28]

Reggie tried to persuade the union leaders he encountered through the NEDC that, even if they could not sign up formally to an incomes policy, they should exercise restraint and not start a cycle of competitive pay claims by trumpeting each good deal. He told Douglas-Home in December 1963 that 'He would try to draw out Bill Carron on the wages front and would try to get him to say that the engineering settlement was really 3.9% since it covered a period of 16 months and it was the employers who had for their own purposes presented it as 5% rather than 3.9%.'[29] Maudling started the process of micro-managing not only wage settlements in both public and private sectors, but also the presentation of those settlements, which would be part of the economic policy environment until the early 1980s. He also took the initiative of giving the *Sunday Times*'s William Rees-Mogg a long, detailed briefing about the aims of the government's incomes policy, which resulted in a considered piece 'Real Wages – or Dummy Money'.[30] The aim was to establish a broader consensus that incomes policy was a good idea, but his efforts were overshadowed by the first strong attack from a senior Tory on his economic policy.

In January 1964 Enoch Powell spoke at the National Liberal Forum, John Poulson's political discussion group, and boldly denounced prices and incomes policy as 'hocus pocus', declaring that short of going to a communist system these matters would be determined by the market mechanism.[31] Reggie was understandably cross at this fundamental attack by someone so recently a minister:

> My dear Enoch
> Many thanks for sending me a copy of your full text. I'm sure your intention, as you say, was helpful: unfortunately our friends in the press have not taken it so! But that is not unusual. Reggy.[32]

Although the tone of Maudling's note to Powell was friendly, it conceded little and the National Liberal Forum speech was a parting of the ways between the two old friends, who had been fighting on the same side so recently during the leadership crisis. While not bitter – he seldom was – Reggie did have something of a talent for genial contempt, and occasional bitchiness, which was turned against Powell. Enoch, he told visiting academic David Butler in June 1965, 'talked utter balls' when it came to economics in general and incomes policy in particular.[33]

Maudling hoped that, if the Conservatives won the general election in 1964, it would become easier to reach agreement on an incomes policy with a fresh mandate and at least four years before the next Labour government could make a better offer. He wrote to Douglas-Home in August 1964 that he wanted to 'announce that as soon as the Election is over we intend to call a National Conference of representatives of Government, employers and Unions with the object of achieving agreement on the principles of an incomes policy and on a system to carry it out in practice'.[34] Maudling wanted to make the announcement as soon as possible, to show that 'we are determined to treat this as the major economic problem to be tackled after the Election and that if management and unions do not cooperate the only alternative will have to be a holding back of economic expansion'. There was scepticism from some in the government, such as Heath; Douglas-Home appeared prepared to go along with Maudling's idea but it was not made a major element of the 1964 election campaign. The National Conference – an idea that later featured in Labour economic policy – was another of the might-have-beens of Maudling's Chancellorship. All one can really say is that it stood a better chance of success than his pre-election attempts at agreeing an incomes policy, and that if successful it could have helped keep the growth policy on the road; but it would also have been a risk to hold such a conference during the time of greatest strain for sterling. Bumps in the road are inevitable in such enterprises, and each one might have led to the markets taking fright and causing a sterling crisis.

While incomes policy was ultimately outside Maudling's control, unless he changed course and introduced a statutory policy, public spending was not. Perhaps thinking about the two should have been integrated – if Maudling had talked to the unions about the benefits that would flow to their members from his increases in public spending, perhaps they might have been more willing to give a little on wages. It would hardly have involved Maudling in any additional public spending, as his existing strategy was to turn on the taps to the maximum extent. The rationale was no longer pump-priming; in summer 1963 Reggie concluded that there need be no more public spending projects approved specifically for this purpose as the private sector was already taking up the slack. What it amounted to was a significant shift of resources towards the public sector, driven by Maudling's own social priorities. Maudling's policies, if they had been introduced by a Labour

Chancellor, would surely have been denounced as socialist profligacy by the Tory press, and even the international bankers.

Within the Treasury, the Public Expenditure Survey Committee (PESC) system had been working away on the prospects for spending in the period between 1963/4 and 1967/8. Maudling persuaded the Cabinet on 12 November 1963 that for the first time the results of the PESC study should be published,[35] and this was duly done in a White Paper in December 1963. It was an attempt to inject a greater element of realism and rationality into the debate than had been apparent previously. Maudling hoped to show that criticisms of the government's policy – on the one hand for being inadequate and on the other for being spendthrift – were wide of the mark. He was broadly successful in showing that a higher level of overall spending was not practicable in the circumstances of 1964, and this did have the effect of making political discussion of the matter more realistic.[36] The most coherent criticism, that it was more than could be afforded, still remained. Maudling's Shadow, James Callaghan, said on 9 November that the existing plans: 'will be the biggest spending spree by any Government in peacetime; and yet two years ago they were unable to find another sixpence for the nurses. If they carry out this programme without the capacity to pay we shall be in for a period of galloping inflation.'[37]

The December White Paper's plans were for a 17.5 per cent increase in public spending at constant prices between 1963/4 and 1967/8. While the PESC projections were affordable with 4 per cent growth over the period until 1968, any shortfall would cause severe problems. PESC could not publicly assume less than 4 per cent, for obvious reasons, but a more conservative estimate was still considered realistic among senior Treasury officials. According to Sir Richard Clarke, in retrospect: 'The increase of expenditure was put at about £1,900 million [over £20 billion on current price levels], which was probably about £500 million more than could readily be accommodated by the national economy on a realistic estimate of the prospective growth of resources.'[38]

In April 1964 Maudling reported to the Cabinet that since the White Paper additional public spending commitments had been made and that it would be necessary to raise another £300–400 million in taxation by 1967.[39] Some of it he had approved, but other things – such as a fifth Polaris submarine – resulted from defeats in Cabinet. His colleagues suggested higher indirect taxes and that 'further consideration' might have to be given to defence expenditure, which was high and rising, and it was noted that the 'abandonment of some of our major overseas commitments' was the only way of saving large sums of money. Even if the 4 per cent growth target was accomplished and public spending growth restricted to the original plan, this would mean an increase in the public share of GNP from 40 per cent to 41.5 per cent; it had been 36 per cent in 1947 under Labour, when the Conservatives had complained that it was unsustainably high. If, Maudling did not remind the Cabinet, growth fell short while spending continued to rise, the share of GNP would rise even higher. Sir Donald MacDougall at the NEDC watched with 'amazement and then horror, as the Government under Sir Alec Douglas-Home made one announcement after another of increased public spending plans'. These were well above what the NEDC thought could be afforded even with 4 per cent economic growth.[40]

The spending spree of 1963–4 was partly a bid to buy electoral popularity and leave Labour with little room for manoeuvre, and arose in part from Reggie's inability to say 'No' and thereby displease people. By 1964 his colleagues in spending departments had grown wise to the fact that they would be more likely to get what they wanted from Reggie than his more austere Financial Secretary, John Boyd-Carpenter.[41] But it was also because Reggie believed that private affluence and public squalor did not necessarily go together, and that there was something to be proud of in all the new schools, hospitals and roads that were springing up all over Britain in the mid-1960s.

Alongside the public spending boom, the general economic situation was changing rapidly. There were still some concerns lingering in the Treasury about slow growth as 1963 ended, but as 1964 began it became clear that the economy was roaring ahead and that there might have to be some sort of restrictive action during 1964. By February economic commentators started to talk in terms of restraint. During the 1964 Budget planning it was apparent that unemployment was falling much faster than anticipated and that consumer spending was sucking in imports at an alarming rate. Maudling's first touch on the brakes of the economy came on 27 February, when he raised Bank Rate from 4 per cent to 5 per cent. It had been a particularly difficult rise to organise, given sensitivities over prices and incomes, the commercial interests of the banks and even the need for meetings between Douglas-Home and US President Johnson to discuss monetary policy. It took three months to clear the rise with all concerned.[42] The rise attracted little public criticism, partly because of a behind-the-scenes deal with Harold Wilson. Wilson was threatening to allege publicly that the Bank of England was 'cooking the books', which at this stage they were not. Maudling and Home told him that there was nothing funny going on, and offered to let up on criticising Labour policies as a potential threat to sterling if he would go easy on the forthcoming Bank Rate decision.[43]

Politics was unavoidable in the planning of the 1964 Budget. Preparations became tied up with election timing to the extent that in a budget meeting in mid-February, civil servants and all, 'we drifted by degrees into discussing merits of different election dates while protesting that our only concern was with regulation of demand'.[44] One possibility was for an April or May election preceded by a short, caretaker budget which would not change the level of taxation and leave more substantive matters until afterwards. The other was to have a full budget and the election in June or October. The budget date itself was determined with reference to the elections for the new Greater London Council (GLC) that were to take place on 9 April. Reggie opposed a budget before the GLC elections mainly because it would box the government into making a decision on the general election before knowing what the GLC vote would reveal about the state of public opinion. He also worried that 'immediate political pressures would be bound to influence the Budget judgements' if the Budget were to go ahead on the expected date of 7 April. Maudling was not such a purely political Chancellor that he did not see the risks of local election jitters watering down whatever mild restrictive measures he wanted to introduce.[45] He managed to get the Budget delayed by a week.

By the start of April Maudling still had two draft budgets, one 'long' and one 'short', although the short budget was now at twelve clauses, only six clauses shorter than the 'long' version. Maudling wondered whether the six extra clauses were worth bothering with anyway, and ministers' opinions moved towards the same budget for June or October. Number 10 asked the Treasury to prepare a 'crash operation' budget, whose contents would be limited to giving the government powers to continue collecting taxes at the current rates. This was a contingency plan, just in case the Conservatives did unexpectedly well in the GLC elections and there was an opportunity for a snap May election.[46]

Maudling's opinion about election timing, often and forcefully expressed, was that the election should come in June. In January 1964 he had started briefing contacts in the press that the election should come soon.[47] In March he told ministers that 'the Government has now ceased to govern' because of electioneering. He complained that it had lost control of public expenditure – which was to a considerable extent his own fault – but the truth of his criticism was widely acknowledged in Whitehall. Tim Bligh, the Prime Minister's loyal Private Secretary – soon to depart and possibly speaking more frankly than usual – added that foreign affairs, the Commonwealth, defence, nuclear power, decimal currency and above all the balance of payments were also subjects where the government had ceased to make decisions.[48] Maudling also feared that he could not guarantee that the economy would continue to be doing well, a sign that his confidence in the economic Experiment was less complete than he claimed afterwards. He had told John Junor in January that this uncertainty was part of the case for an early election.[49] In June he told election analyst David Butler that 'as far as the economy is concerned, he still didn't know whether there would be serious trouble in the autumn . . . He was far from clear what electoral impact an economic crisis would have and suggested jocularly that perhaps he should ask his colleagues whether they wanted a crisis or not. Certainly he didn't want one from his point of view.'[50]

Maudling might have found more takers among his colleagues for an economic crisis than an early election. Labour had a double-figure lead in the polls and would almost certainly have won a June 1964 election handsomely.

Reggie's argument for an early election in 1964 seems to show that in his mind the prospect of a Labour victory was less alarming than another four months of sleepwalking Conservative government. Like Stafford Cripps in 1949, Maudling found few takers among his Cabinet colleagues for the risky path of fiscal and electoral rectitude. Most of them preferred to carry on until October in the hope that things would improve, particularly if Maudling's economic recovery gathered even more strength. On 7 April, before the GLC polls closed to limit allegations of running scared, the Prime Minister announced that the election would not come in June. When the votes were counted, Labour had won an unexpectedly large majority on the GLC.

Maudling's second Budget, announced on 14 April, was moderately restrictive. Of all the budgets under the Conservative years from 1951 to 1964, it was the largest set of tax increases introduced in a normal spring budget. The increases totalled £100 million, so Maudling was taking back a bit over a third of his generosity the previous year, and he was acting precisely in line with what his Permanent Secretary, William Armstrong, had recommended during the budget planning meetings, although what Armstrong said was coloured by his knowledge of the maximum restriction Reggie was prepared to contemplate.[51] Some independent commentators talked in terms of a £200 million touch on the brakes being required,[52] and criticised the Budget for leniency.[53] All in the Treasury were aware that it would probably not be the last tax-raising budget if the government intended to stick to its public spending plans.

The burden of the new taxes fell most on excise duties, with beer, spirit and cigarette duties all being increased significantly. It was the opposite of what is normally perceived as an electioneering budget, in that the pain was inflicted in a way that probably maximised populist grumbling. 'Maudling's small beer' complained the Daily Mail. The budget speech itself was dull and had several passages of such numbing tedium that at one point the commentator on the budget radio broadcast announced, 'We have run into another dead period and I am going to ask for some music.'[54] While Maudling's delivery was poor, the measures he was announcing were extremely unexciting, being dismissed even in the Economist as 'this fag-end of a budget at what looks like the fag-end of a decade and a half of Tory rule'.[55] He could have done with saving a gimmick or two over from 1963. He ducked the possibility of introducing a betting tax for largely technical reasons.[56] There had been inconclusive Treasury efforts to investigate the subject, and officials who had been sent abroad to study the subject came back with no particularly useful ideas other than a system for winning at roulette.[57]

There were encouraging words from some quarters. George Woodcock of the TUC, although he made a pro forma criticism of the details of how it was done, thought that Maudling's attitude was basically right, having resisted an electioneering, gimmicky budget and also having refused to revert to 'stop-go' by cutting back in traditional Tory fashion. 'A hundred millions is just, in my view, about right,' as an overall tax increase.[58] It is hard to find significant fault with the 1964 Budget's overall stance, particularly given that the Treasury envisaged the 'regulator' powers allowing the Chancellor to adjust taxes between budgets being used to damp down demand if necessary. For an election-year budget from a Conservative government, it was at the responsible end of the spectrum.

Maudling's big story for the Budget was that it was about the transition from the unsustainably rapid – about 6 per cent – growth that had been raging for the last two or three quarters, to a more sustainable growth pattern of 4 per cent for the next few years. Whether 4 per cent itself was sustainable was a question almost as unmentionable in polite company – or Maudling's company at any rate – as devaluation became under Labour in 1964–7. The weak point was the balance of payments; as consumer demand grew so did imports, and therefore an excess of supply over demand for pounds at the current exchange rate. The hope was that, boosted by the supply side measures overseen through the NEDC and the Board of Trade, exports would rise, but in part this was a function of world demand. Maudling had tried to stimulate the growth of world trade through his IMF Plan, but the matter was essentially outside his control. British exports picked up only sluggishly in 1963–4, and the balance of payments deficit grew. A continuing deficit not only weakened the currency directly, but it also created expectations that a devaluation might be on the way, and therefore encouraged investors to sell pounds at the current fixed price while they could. To counter this, the government had several weapons – Bank of England intervention, to stabilise the pound (which could work as long as there were gold or foreign currency reserves available to buy sterling); attracting capital by raising interest rates; and the most effective but unreliable, manipulating market psychology to instil confidence. Further, economic thinking in 1964 was that attempts to respond to every fluctuation in the balance of payments had on balance been destabilising, and that pursuing a consistent policy was a better approach than panicking at the first signs of a big deficit.[59] Maudling's calculation was that exports would pick up at some stage within the next year or two, and that in the meantime the deficit would not get out of control and confidence could be maintained.

At the beginning of 1964 there were some concerns about the balance of payments, but they were relatively mild. In February Cairncross advised that 'we do not foresee the kind of large deficit on current account which we suffered in 1960; but we may be mistaken'.[60] From this point on, the forecasts got worse and worse. By June Cairncross was talking in terms of a £600 million deficit in 1964 and another £300 million deficit in 1965, with these figures potentially subject to revision.[61] Some even worse figures were circulating in the Treasury. In March 1964 Cairncross wrote in a covering note to Ian Bancroft in the Private Office:

the obvious danger point, as the Report brings out, is the balance of payments. The deficit in prospect for 1964/65 is over £800 million. The public has no inkling of this, partly because outside commentators do not look so far ahead and partly because the very high long-term capital outflow in prospect is not yet known . . . there is a serious danger that even in 1966 the balance of payments will remain in deficit.[62]

The documents given to the incoming Wilson government were therefore not the first time the figure of £800 million had appeared in official advice, but it is quite possible that Maudling was right to claim as he later did that he never saw such a figure, as this mention was a one-off in a note exchanged between officials; the normal figure, which was used by Cairncross as late as 30 September, was £600 million. In July Cairncross noted that the forecasts of the balance of payments displayed a tendency to 'wag alarmingly', with different figures coming in even during the same day.[63] Published forecasts and those supplied to international organisations were done on a 'highly optimistic' basis, with imaginative figures in the region of £300–450 million.[64]

The changing forecasts in the first half of 1964 showed two linked problems – that the anticipated worst point of the deficit would be much more severe than Maudling had hoped, and, more destructively for the Experiment, that the deficit would persist for longer. If it was seen to be a structural deficit (as indeed it was) rather than a temporary one, the rationale for devaluation, and the pressure in the markets, would be all the stronger.

However, there was no great pressure on the pound in the first half of 1964, and international bankers seemed to have no great concerns about the situation in Britain, even though Lord Cromer was starting to worry about 'the prospect of deficits far larger than we can manage without loss of solvency and of independence'.[65] Treasury civil servants were astonished that the Bank of England official reserves held up so well over much of the summer despite the expanding deficit. They had wondered for some time how long this excess of confidence could last. In July Cairncross wrote in his diary:

Where anything we did used to be travestied and misrepresented now the Press takes everything in the light thrown on it by the Treasury and loses all sense of proportion. It looks as if we shall have to wait till end of September for real denouement with issue of Q2 figures. But perhaps gold losses will be severe before then. It is extraordinary that reserves have risen over past six months while deficit has been of the order of £600m.[66]

Market psychology was all that was keeping the reserves, and therefore sterling, steady as the summer of 1964 began. The fact that the conjuring trick was successful for so long had much to do with Maudling's own ability to communicate a sense of optimism and confidence, but it could not last for ever. Even in January, Cairncross had thought a severe loss of reserves over the summer was possible even without a full-scale crisis,[67] and this is duly what happened. The confidence the markets had placed in sterling had begun to sag and the Bank of England was intervening steadily to prop up the pound at its fixed international value. The monthly figures for the reserves gave an indication of how much pressure the pound was coming under, and from June onwards these particular books were being cooked. The first steps were to increase forward sales of sterling, and then to conceal a $15 million exchange loss, consequent on buying Polaris, which could be done using an agreed swap facility that was not disclosed in the public figures.[68]

After Maudling's advice about election timing was turned down he became more and more slapdash and inclined to take risks with the economy. Maudling's last few months at the Treasury were not his best. He was there only reluctantly, having given his advice on election timing and seen it overruled, and did not expect the Conservatives to win when it came. He had started to become fatalistic and even flippant; in contrast to his hard line on pay settlements at the Board of Trade in 1959–61 he was now one of the ministers most inclined to settle the railway pay claim on the union's terms. He was also seeing the Experiment move into its period of greatest strain; in May he asked the chairmen of the nationalised industries to make sure that their investment plans did not peak all at once.[69] A general sense developed within the Treasury during summer 1964 that reality would have to be faced after the election, whoever won.[70]

There was only one specific decision where Maudling went against official advice in order to relax policy during 1964, and that came in the summer as the election approached and the Labour lead in the opinion polls shrank. Maudling had wondered in May whether a further tightening of monetary policy was required, and in discussions in early June he agreed that he would issue a call to the banks for special deposits (whose removal had been Maudling's first reflationary step in 1962) on 26 June, but in mid-June Reggie changed his mind and decided not to make the call. During July a further rise in Bank Rate was mooted instead within the Treasury, but in the end Reggie decided to do nothing because he had interpreted industrial production and GDP figures as saying that growth had stalled; on seeing some figures that summer he quipped, 'I see; inflation without expansion, eh?'[71] in contrast to the promise of 'expansion without inflation' in his 1963 Budget. He would have been wiser to trust the evidence of his own eyes, which indicated that the economy was far from stuck.[72] Maudling was reluctant to do anything to undermine the 4 per cent growth policy, and certainly not before the election.

Meanwhile, other contingency plans were being prepared. Direct action against imports was the favourite in the Maudling Treasury, as it would not interfere too much with the growth of domestic demand, unlike raising interest rates or other restrictive action. There were two possible avenues – an import surcharge, which breached GATT and EFTA rules but would be likely to have an effect, and import quotas that were allowed but regarded as less effective. From March 1964 onwards, studies were going on within the Treasury to examine how import controls of one sort or another might be implemented.[73] It would have tested Maudling's powers of persuasion to introduce them, as he was preparing to do if re-elected in 1964, without causing a crisis of confidence. *In extremis*, there was the possibility of floating the pound.

In September, Reggie travelled again to the annual IMF and World Bank meetings, which were in Tokyo that year. Eric Roll, part of the British Treasury team, was very worried at this stage by the financial prospects, but admired Maudling's 'assurance, good humour and skill' at this meeting. It was vital for Maudling to keep up a good front, because any sign that he was having doubts risked cracking the increasingly thin ice on which the pound was skating.[74] At the same time, back in Britain, the long-awaited election campaign finally began when Douglas-Home visited the Queen at Balmoral and confirmed what everybody already knew, that polling day would be 15 October.

Beryl and Caroline had come with Reggie to Tokyo, but while Reggie flew straight back to London the two women took a circuitous route home. They flew to Hong Kong, travelled around China and then took the Trans-Siberian Railway from Irkutsk to Moscow. Beryl flew back from Moscow to be with her husband during the general election, although she missed his adoption meeting, while Caroline stayed in Russia in her capacity as 'travelling teenager' reporting for the *Daily Mail*.[75] His national responsibilities meant that Reggie took Barnet rather for granted in 1964, leaving the running of the campaign to his strong local Conservative organisation and to Arthur Fawcett in particular. Reggie attracted some adverse publicity for refusing to attend a joint debate involving the other candidates.[76] His adoption meeting was a celebration of his high profile, his chairman, Stanley Head, introducing him with the comment that had it not been for the disclaiming of peerages, 'Mrs Maudling's laundry bills would now be going to Number 10 instead of Number 11 Downing Street'.[77] Reggie's adoption speech centred on the economy: 'I think it can be fairly claimed that while the economy is very heavily loaded there are not the acute bottlenecks and widespread labour shortages there have been on previous occasions. In other words, though the economy is running full out, there are not yet signs of overheating.'[78] The next stage would be steady growth of 4 per cent based on an incomes policy negotiated between government, employers and trade unions. 'There is no doubt whatever that success lies within our grasp if we have the energy and the determination and the self-restraint to achieve it.' Many of his 1964 speeches followed the same general lines. The Liberals, fighting the seat for the first time since 1951, attacked him for his 'do-nothing' attitude towards Europe and the economy: a 'great big cloud that was about to burst over our heads in the autumn'.[79] But the Liberals had little realistic hope of winning Barnet – their vote had receded since the 1962–3 high tide and the

Conservatives had performed unusually well in the Barnet area in the 1964
GLC elections. Their attentions in the area were concentrated on Finchley,
where the incumbent was a junior minister called Margaret Thatcher, but
these also proved in vain. The Labour campaign in Barnet was also, given the
size of Maudling's majority in 1959, pretty pro forma and Maudling's success
in his own constituency was never really in doubt.

The national Conservative election campaign was based around three
principal speakers. Alec Douglas-Home made a speaking tour of the country,
while Reggie Maudling and Edward Heath took the press conferences and
most of the television appearances respectively. Election press conferences
were an innovation of Morgan Phillips, the Labour General Secretary, in the
1959 campaign, but even as early as 1964 they were a fixed part of
campaigning routine. Taking the press conferences required good relations
with journalists, a quick mind and the ability to talk in an interesting way
without making gaffes or giving much away. Maudling was basically a good
choice for the role. He overcame his nervousness and dislike of partisan
electioneering[80] and handled most of the daily press conferences, earning
admiration from Richard West in the *New Statesman*: 'Thank goodness the
Tories did not choose Maudling. With luck and a good summer – the
government has enjoyed both these things – he might be a serious threat to
Labour. Affable, intelligent and likeable, his press conferences have been a
success and should establish his claim to the leadership of the opposition.'[81]

Maudling's cheerful, expansive manner suited the mood of optimism and
progress the Tory campaign was trying to communicate. The title of their
manifesto, 'Prosperity with a Purpose', was itself a very Reggie-ish phrase. The
platform was decorated with images of prosperity and public investment and
slogans boldly proclaiming 'UP with even more new schools', 'UP with more
houses', 'Keep Britain booming'. As Chancellors do, Maudling felt
uncomfortable with some of these slogans; his successor and fellow optimist
Ken Clarke disliked many proposed advertisements proclaiming Conservative
economic success in 1997. Maudling's first press conference on Monday
28 September put the heat on Labour's deputy leader, George Brown, by asking
if his talk about reducing mortgages to 3 per cent was a promise and if so
what it would cost. On Wednesday he scored one of the best-judged responses
of this eventful campaign. Harold Wilson, at the Labour press conference, had
commented on a strike at an important firm in the motor industry, the Hardy
Spicer propeller company. He said that it was strange that there seemed to be
strikes in sensitive firms at every election – it was British Oxygen in 1955 and
1959 – and that Labour would hold an inquiry to see whether these were
politically motivated. Maudling chortled when the remark was put to him:
'I must say that's a rum one – Tory shop stewards going round sabotaging
Mr Wilson's election! Really!'[82] He succeeded, briefly, in making the apparently
dynamic Labour leader a figure of ridicule, and returned to the issue the next
day saying, 'it takes a worried man to sing a foolish song'.[83]

However, despite his impression of confidence Maudling was also a worried man. He was struggling to contain the growing economic difficulties revealed by the figures coming in to the Treasury. The Treasury issued the balance of payments figures for the second quarter of 1964 on Wednesday 30 September, showing a large deficit that contradicted Maudling's assurances in the early summer that it would be better than in the first quarter. Wilson was rattled by the Hardy Spicer affair, but this was only a superficial reflection of his fear that the election was slipping away. That morning the NOP poll had showed the Conservatives 2.9 per cent in the lead, which would be enough to return them to power with a comfortable majority. Not only would Wilson not be Prime Minister, he would probably not have long as leader of the opposition; the Gaitskellites were waiting to launch a coup against him if he failed. In discussions with his economic advisers that morning Wilson decided to abandon Labour's policy of not talking up the risks to the economy. Callaghan had argued that they would win anyway, and that causing alarm would make his job as Labour Chancellor much harder. In his speech at Norwich that evening Wilson launched a harsh attack on the Conservatives' economic management, comparing Douglas-Home to John Bloom, the Rolls Razor boss whose corporate collapse was in the news in 1964, and comparing the situation to 1961 when 'stop' followed 'go'. Wilson's speech was followed up by a still more outspoken broadcast by George Brown on Friday evening which warned: 'This country is lurching towards the biggest economic crisis since the war. If the present trend continues it will mean that our jobs, our wages, our hire purchase agreements, our mortgage rates are all in jeopardy.'[84] Even a relatively friendly account of Wilson's election recorded that the Norwich speech 'created just those long-term difficulties that Callaghan had feared. The drain of British gold reserves really began from the time of the speech in which Wilson exposed the desperate plight of the economy.'[85]

However unattractive the cynicism of Wilson's attack may have been, it cannot do all the work required of it by defences of Maudling's Chancellorship.[86] To expect a tacit truce on such a central issue to last through a close election campaign, in which announcements like that on September 30 took place, was unrealistic. It also took a lot of cheek for the Conservatives to criticise Wilson, as they had won the 1951 election with alarmist talk about economic crisis. A Tory 'talking points' bulletin said in 1952 that 'When the Conservatives won last October they found things much worse than expected and far worse than the Socialists had ever told the country. The nation was heading for bankruptcy. We were over-spending abroad at the rate of over £800 million a year.'[87] Even the numbers were the same.

The Bank's reserves had actually started draining well before Wilson spoke, although the government managed to conceal the extent of the losses. The problem revealed by the September figures was acute. There had been something of the order of $200 million in short-term inter-Central Bank credits to the Bank of England during September, which had protected sterling from the growing pressures on the financial markets. The fact that these alarming figures came in during the election campaign made the matter even more sensitive. If the extent of the losses were to become known it would have blown a large hole in the Conservative election campaign, which naturally worried Maudling and Douglas-Home. There were also risks to sterling from revealing the true figures in the highly charged environment of an election campaign. The Governor of the Bank of England was extremely concerned. He and Maudling agreed in the last days of September that the announcement would conceal the true losses. Reggie took the trouble a few days later to write a letter to Cromer, making sure that his version of events was on the record and making clear that the initiative for the decision on the reserves announcement came from Cromer: 'advice you gave me orally that it would not be in the best interest of sterling to publish either the amount of the short-term Central Bank facilities used to date or the true loss in the month of September, and as you know the reserves announcement made last Friday was framed on that basis'. Cromer was still extremely anxious and asked if he could give Harold Wilson a private briefing about the problem. Maudling refused Cromer's formal request to inform Wilson, and just when they were wondering about what to do they received word that Wilson had said to a Labour press conference that it was not customary for short-term loans to be disclosed. This removed the last doubts and the figures were published in cooked form on the afternoon of Friday 1 October.[88]

There was some contemporary press comment about the obscurity of the announcement, with *The Times* business section observing that 'the fact that the monetary authorities refuse to indicate the amount [of short-term credit] involved robs the published exchange reserve of any real value'.[89] Press estimates of the short-term credit facility used up were £40–50 million, while the real figure was half as much again. On 2 October increased credits from overseas central bankers became available, which halted the immediate drain on reserves. The short-term credits not reflected in the September figures got the pound, and Maudling, through the election.

Maudling had started the election with an extra burst of energy and enthusiasm, but by the end of the first week he was tired and put under strain by his efforts to keep a lid on the economic situation.[90] He was good at the morning press conferences but he was not exactly willing or able to operate a 24-hour news service. Nigel Lawson, then a journalist who was offering some publicity advice, realised that he was not the man to cap a Wilson-generated headline after the first editions at 10.30p.m.[91] The 1964 election was a particularly rowdy and passionate campaign, and Maudling felt the rough edge of it when he was forced to abandon his speech to a London meeting on 29 September. He did not thrive on this sort of thing, however well he was suited to the press conferences.

The middle of the 1964 campaign saw the momentum with Labour, who had gone significantly ahead in most polls. Leading Conservatives had made a series of gaffes, including Douglas-Home talking about pensions as 'donations', a memorable explosion from Quintin Hogg about 'adulterers', and Rab Butler saying that it was a close election but things were unlikely to slip the Tories' way. Maudling, although he had been slow off the mark on several occasions, had not blundered at all. His 'defensive batsmanship' was noted by the *Economist* as one of the most impressive features of the campaign.[92]

Shaking off his mid-campaign lassitude Maudling returned to attacking form in the final week with his long-promised assault on Labour's taxation policy finally being launched on Tuesday 13 October. Maudling estimated that Labour's plans would necessitate a range of tax increases, including 9*d* on income tax, 6*s* a week on national insurance plus duty increases on petrol, drink and cigarettes. It was the first time an exercise like this had been attempted, and there were misgivings within the Treasury and the Cabinet Office over whether it was appropriate.[93] The precedent stuck, and 'costings' of opposition plans became an element in several future election campaigns, particularly 1987 and 1992 (and 2001, when the boot was on the other foot and Labour made play with the spending cuts that would follow from Tory tax plans). At least Maudling's costings had the unusual distinction of being relatively accurate. Callaghan's November Budget did raise income tax, if only by 6*d*, and put 6*d* on petrol as Maudling predicted. It was not as dramatic a claim as hyperbolic estimates of national ruin offered in other campaigns, but for that reason it was maybe more effective.

Maudling's discovery of this low-powered tax bombshell was part of a good last week for the Tories. Wilson had decamped to Liverpool and was taken out of the national campaign; unofficial strikes broke out on the London underground and Alec Douglas-Home delivered a strong eve-of-poll broadcast. Forecasts of a Labour landslide receded and all that could be said on election morning was that it would be close. Reggie spent a large part of the day at the Treasury, and in the evening did the rounds of the television studios, seeming less than distraught at the initial results, which seemed to indicate that Labour would win with a comfortable majority. He commented several times with a smile that 'Britain is a Conservative country that occasionally votes Labour'. At midnight he went up to Barnet's Drill Hall for his own count. He was returned on a minority vote in Barnet for the first time. Reggie suffered a slightly above average swing[94] in his own constituency as a large chunk of his vote floated off to the Liberals, but Labour had made little headway. He and the other candidates confined themselves to formal words of thanks to the returning officer and his staff.[95]

Reggie was still Chancellor for a few hours on Friday 16 October. Clear-headed if a little tired after the parties and excitements of election night, and still following the election returns, he stayed at Number 11 for most of the morning although he had originally intended to go and 'lie low' in the country. Alec Douglas-Home rang a couple of times from next door. The first occasion was to ask him whether they should announce an increase in Bank Rate principally in the light of the ousting of Krushchev, but the economic situation in Britain and the uncertainty caused by the still to be finalised election result were in the background. Maudling and Douglas-Home decided that it could only be done with the agreement of Harold Wilson who was on a train somewhere between Liverpool and London and due to arrive at around 12.45p.m. The delay allowed William Armstrong to persuade the Tory ministers that the financial markets seemed calm and a panic measure might exacerbate the situation.[96]

Electorate		65,493		
Turnout			81.6	
Reginald Maudling	Conservative	25,537	47.8	−14.9
David Levy	Labour	17,024	31.9	−5.4
Hugh Tinker	Liberal	10,179	19.0	
Patrick Figgis	Independent	706	1.3	
Conservative majority		8,513	15.9	

The next call from the Prime Minister was mainly social. He invited all the ministers still in London to come to Number 10 for a midday drink to assess the situation. The talk was mostly of the mechanics of how they would resign and when Douglas-Home would go to the Palace, but Elizabeth Douglas-Home came in and said that it might not all be over;[97] there was a brief moment when Labour's projected majority disappeared. It did not last and Labour's narrow victory was confirmed to the ministers and to Harold Wilson, pacing the floor at Transport House after his nerve-fraying train journey. The last ministerial meeting of the Conservative government broke up and Reggie went back to Number 11 to pack. He had ordered a removal van to come to the back of Number 11 and later in the afternoon 'struggling across the garden carrying a packing-case full of the usual debris of domestic life, such as ageing toys, and half-empty bottles of ketchup' saw the beaming visage of Tommy Balogh, Wilson's new Economic Adviser, looking at him from a window of Number 10.[98]

Maudling called in at the Treasury to say goodbye to his officials. He had a contemplative conversation with William Armstrong and Alec Cairncross about his Chancellorship. Cairncross was particularly sympathetic:

I said that the truth was that expansion had involved grave risks, bigger than we had realised, and that in the circumstances it had been hard not to take the risks. Reggie agreed that he couldn't have followed a non-expansionary course and that the trouble lay not so much in economic gimmicks as deep-set public attitudes.[99]

Armstrong was a bit more critical, even though he had supported Maudling fairly consistently while he was in office. After the election Armstrong reflected that public expenditure control had been too lax and that Maudling should have taken action on special deposits over the summer, and (although he spared Maudling's feelings by not mentioning it to him) the 4 per cent growth target 'illusion'. Maudling was clearly already worried about the damage a reputation for irresponsibility might do to his future career and was anxious to get the officials to confirm that he had taken all the restrictive action he had been told was advisable – even though this was not exactly the truth.

As Maudling was clearing out the private flat upstairs at Number 11, his Labour successor Jim Callaghan was moving into the official rooms downstairs. Maudling liked Callaghan, and in all seriousness he was sympathetic to the problems he had bequeathed to his successor. He called in, suits piled over his arm, at the Chancellor's study to find Callaghan reading through the intimidating bundle of briefing papers he had been handed as soon as he stepped through the interconnecting door from Number 10. Maudling beamed and quipped, 'Sorry, old cock, to leave it in this shape. I suggested to Alec this morning that perhaps we should put up the bank rate but he thought he ought to leave it all to you.'[100] Reggie took his leave and ambled across the lawn at the back of Downing Street towards the removal vans. So ended the Maudling experiment.

Chapter 14

AFTER THE EXPERIMENT, OCTOBER 1964–JULY 1965

Maudling's reputation as Chancellor has been associated with economic irresponsibility, electoral manipulation and general risk-taking ever since 1964, in the rough world of politics and the more refined domain of economic history. Although Harold Wilson hoped to tar the Conservative Party in general with a reputation for economic incompetence, the damage was done mostly to Maudling personally. Maudling's bad relations with Lord Cromer harmed his chances in the Tory leadership election in 1965. The next Chancellor to approach an election after a full term, Roy Jenkins in 1970, found that Treasury civil servants suffered from '1964 guilt' and were determined to put up more resistance than William Armstrong had done to Maudling's drive for expansion.[1] Reggie's history prevented a return to the Treasury after the death of Macleod in 1970. As late as 1997 Tony Blair felt it worthwhile in an election speech to summon up Maudling's ghost as a representative of Tory economic incompetence. Mervyn King, now Governor of the Bank of England, expressed an official view in his 1996 ESRC Lecture that 'it is impossible to read Reginald Maudling's budget speeches of 1963 and 1964 without a feeling of impending doom'.[2]

Edmund Dell, in his influential work *The Chancellors*, in which Chancellors from Dalton to Major are measured up and found to be less austere and less economically literate than Mr Dell, makes a characteristically direct and persuasive assessment of Maudling's term of office:

> The idea of breakthrough by precipitate expansion was one that only businessmen, politicians in a hole, and their friends in the economics profession could possibly claim to believe. There was also, in Maudling's attitude, an element of carefree, romantic, cavalier defiance. If the world insisted on confining the British economy within a strait-jacket entitled the balance of payments, he would show that, like Houdini, he could break free.[3]

The case against Maudling is easily made. As Chancellor, as in other aspects of his life, Reggie was inclined to the soft option and to the idea that increasing prosperity was simply a matter of willpower rather than working with real resources within real constraints. Even worse, it is easy to accuse Maudling, as a politician with more than a trace of cynicism in his nature, of stoking up a monstrous pre-election boom, putting his career and his party loyalty before his public duty: 'criminal negligence', Ben Pimlott calls it in his biography of Harold Wilson.[4] Even in November 1963, Reggie was aware that it might not look good for his reputation. Maudling's Chief Economic Adviser, Alec Cairncross, recorded in a diary entry that Reggie 'was rather amused at way everything shaping for a splendid bit of expansion next spring followed by election and then efforts by Callaghan and Co. to cope with exchange crisis. Said nobody would believe we hadn't planned it.'[5] However, the accusation that Maudling was a particularly political Chancellor, who deliberately stoked a boom that would either win the Tories the election or leave Labour with an awful mess, cannot be sustained. Jim Callaghan, who would have the most reason to accuse Maudling, does not: 'He hoped to make a breakthrough with higher productivity based on increased investment . . . He genuinely believed it was worth a try, and I don't accuse him of concealing anything in his 1963 Budget.' It is further belied by the fact that he was the leading advocate of an early election, which in 1964 amounted to throwing in the towel and letting Labour take over before things had got too far out of hand. He was realistic enough to know that the Tories' chances of winning were slim. David Butler, who saw him in June 1964, found him 'affable, relaxed and forthcoming. He seemed not particularly optimistic about the outcome of the election but not much to care.'[6] It was hardly the attitude of a man desperate to win by hook or by crook.

Maudling did not go much beyond his official advice; the only outright failure to do something he was advised to do came with special deposits in summer 1964. His judgements about the overall thrust of the two budgets – relaxation in 1963 and a modest tightening in 1964 – were in line with what was considered prudent on both occasions. He was not, despite his reputation, a Chancellor to take risks by defying his advisers or the broad outline of economic thinking at the time.

Dell acknowledges that Maudling has a strong defence in what, after Macmillan, is known as 'Last Year's Bradshaw'. Macmillan likened running the economy on the official statistics available to attempting to plan a train journey using the previous year's railway timetables. Maudling suffered worse than most Chancellors from uncertainty about exactly where the economy was in the cycle. There appeared to be a serious risk of Britain going into recession during his first months in office, and he was criticised for taking too long to respond to rising unemployment and stagnant output. Even at the time of the 1963 Budget, as well as the official statistics being last year's Bradshaw, Maudling was working from a particularly smudged edition. Nobody knew whether the trend in employment and output was up or down, or how strong any trend might be. Even after the Budget, when the economy was starting to roar ahead, Reggie was ill-served by Treasury forecasters, who failed to take much account of the likely impact of faster growth on the balance of payments ('an extraordinary misjudgement' admitted Alec Cairncross).[7] In the circumstances, his judgement was not irresponsible. Nor was what he did in the 1964 Budget, when it was reasonably clear that the economy was growing too fast. Where he can be validly criticised is in not following the 1964 Budget with some stronger counter-inflationary measures, but it would have taken a rare Chancellor to bludgeon his colleagues into such rectitude in an election year. Maudling did, to give him his due, recognise the dangers and ask for the election to be got out of the way as soon as possible.

The personal case against Maudling as Chancellor is therefore facile, rather than easy. A more sophisticated indictment of Maudling, such as that made by Cairncross and endorsed by Mervyn King, recognises that he was not uniquely culpable but argues that the current ideas of his time were misguided. The 1964 election was no turning point in economic policy; that had come during the course of Selwyn Lloyd's term of office and was developed further by Maudling, and the basic framework of Maudling's policies survived intact under Wilson and Callaghan. The early 1960s were the high point of faith in the view that the economy could be steered, in that policy makers could take actions that had a fairly predictable effect on the economy. Maudling's policies were based on these general assumptions. To criticise Maudling for failing to break with them is anachronistic, and also mistakes the nature of the man; Maudling's approach, which made him such a capable politician, was always to work from the existing course, accommodating new ideas and potential challenges by modifying assumptions and looking at things from new angles.

There is a considerable amount to be said for criticism of the policy environment Maudling accepted, particularly in analysing the failure of the framework Maudling (and his immediate predecessor and successor) tried to create to foster economic growth. Cairncross concluded that 'The more firmly unrealistic expectations of faster growth took root, the greater the inflationary pressure both in the form of excessive wage settlements and in the tendency for governments to let expansion proceed unchecked and overheat the economy'.[8]

The NEDC and Maudling lacked a satisfactory set of intellectual foundations for the 4 per cent project. What, after all, determined growth? To Reggie, it was in principle relatively simple, amounting to technology and psychology. Advanced technology was a 1960s panacea, and there is no doubt that technological advance is an important factor in spurring economic growth. At least the government could do something about technology, by shovelling tax incentives at investment and funding as much scientific research as possible, a process that had started well before the 1963 Robbins Report. However, the transmission mechanism from technology to growth is much more complex than Maudling and others believed in the early 1960s.

Perhaps Reggie's 1950s experience in the aviation sector, where development was a bargained arrangement between very small numbers of suppliers and purchasers, was a poor training ground for creating policy that would try to influence millions of interlocking, small-scale decisions to produce a better outcome.

More difficult for government to achieve was what Maudling always emphasised, a psychological change in terms of will and attitudes to work. In his memoirs Reggie quoted, with some fondness, TUC General Secretary George Woodcock as having said to him, 'Well, Reggie, I have come to the conclusion that if achieving greater productivity means getting up half an hour earlier in the morning, I am against it.'[9] Maudling did not blame the unions entirely for this attitude, which he said was a general English one at the time, and although he would not admit it, was one he basically applied to his own life. Reggie was an unconvincing advocate of self-denial and buckling down to hard work as Chancellor, and even more implausible in his later exhortations along these lines. But a less radical project in political economy, still with a psychological dimension, was to change expectations. If everyone behaved as if the economy was going to grow by 4 per cent, made their own output decisions accordingly and trusted others to do the same – then, by its bootstraps, the economy would haul itself up to a growth rate of 4 per cent.

The idea of a growth target, evolved from consultations with industry rather than internal Treasury assumptions, carried over into the Labour government, just as Maudling had inherited and developed it from Selwyn Lloyd's term of office. So did the hope that stating a target, albeit in a more elaborated form in the 1965 National Plan, would help in and of itself in producing better economic performance. The theory was that an expansionist policy would, if pursued with enough clarity and consistency, do more than create a temporary boom, but itself raise the long-term growth potential of the economy. Higher expectations of growth would lead, in a virtuous circle, to higher capital investment by industry, a renewal of productive capacity and therefore the ability to achieve higher growth.

Even at the time, economists within the Treasury were extremely sceptical, with Alec Cairncross estimating the long-term growth potential of the British economy at 3.5 per cent at the outside and William Armstrong flatly calling the 4 per cent target an illusion. Politically, Maudling had made it impossible for Labour to promise any less, even though it was becoming increasingly apparent in 1965–6 that the original target had been unrealistic. The British policies acknowledged French indicative planning as an inspiration, but the British were trying to do more with less – lever the economy up to a faster level of growth, as opposed to sustaining an existing rapid rate of growth in France, by using less intrusive tools than their French counterparts.

There were two obvious risks, even if the theory is to be accepted. One was simply that investment, and the resulting improvement in productivity, takes a while to arrive and that it is far from guaranteed that the policy will not come unstuck because of its effects on the balance of payments, the value of the currency and inflation in the meantime. The other risk is that the policy runs into capacity constraints at an early stage. Booms affect different industries and regions in different ways, and an expansion strong enough to lift Scotland and shipbuilding would probably by then have more than soaked up spare capacity in south-east England and the construction industry, causing shortages and inflation. Maudling was well aware of both dangers; the balance of payments he hoped to finesse his way around with central bank loans, fudged figures and if necessary an import surcharge until exports picked up and the problem went away by itself. The answer to the latter problem Maudling always sought in an incomes policy by which wages in inflationary sectors could be held down by consent.

In a perverse demonstration of the power of expectations, the Labour government after July 1966 in fact managed to conduct the Maudling experiment in reverse. By first declaring a growth target in the National Plan, and then sacrificing it to get over a short-term financial crisis, the Wilson government discredited the assumptions that underpinned growth policies like Maudling's. Why should an expansion phase, no matter how much it was backed up by declarations about planning, strategy, and consistency, result in higher private investment if it was liable to be reversed when the winds changed? The July 1966 measures queered the pitch for any future repetition of the Maudling experiment.

Maudling, once converted to the idea of an incomes policy in the late 1950s, remained a strong advocate for the rest of his life. Control of the growth of incomes was a logical part of an overall programme for expansion. Maudling's quest for an incomes policy reflected his view that economic problems were basically political ones. The priority was to stop inflation; the most threatening cause of inflation at the time was the tendency for earnings to rise faster than output. From Maudling's point of view, that the supply of labour was under the control of a monopoly supplier need not automatically have bad consequences. Earnings were, by and large, determined by social institutions, namely unions and management, and the government as the leading social institution could, as long as there was goodwill all round, combat an economic threat using political techniques.

The problem in the circumstances of 1962–4 was the lack of goodwill, resulting from the clumsiness with which the pay pause had been introduced in 1961; the TUC resented the lack of consultation and the lack at that stage of similar measures affecting profits and prices. The NEDC and, particularly, NIC were hobbled by the refusal of the unions to participate wholeheartedly in consensus institutions. Their structure was not conducive to such partnership, and in any case from 1962 to 1964 they could look ahead to a better deal from a future Labour government rather than settle with a sinking Tory administration. Woodcock regretted this in retrospect, telling a seminar in June 1972 that he had found it 'easier and more congenial to work with

Reginald Maudling than his Labour successors' who came in with preconceived ideas when they took over in 1964.[10]

A more general problem with incomes policy was analogous to the one that deterred Reggie from doing much about tax reform. The most effective incomes policies were the ones that were most easily understood – the flat rate policy of 1975 being the best of all, and next best being a percentage limit. However, by their nature such simple policies could only be kept going for a few years at most because of the number of anomalies and hard cases that would be thrown up. A longer-term policy would need procedures for reviewing exceptions, or a more flexible rule – in which case it became easy for it to be subverted. Future attempts became bogged down in complex discussions of norms, comparability and relativities, and in the end were destroyed by workers who found themselves in particularly powerful market positions. The hope for the Maudling policy is that it might have been enough to manage the transition to a higher level of growth, at which point there would be sufficient goodwill to continue to use it as a counter-inflationary policy.

Maudling's Chancellorship illustrates some other facets of his character and the nature of British politics at the time. During the early 1960s, bishops and leader-writers for the more elevated sort of newspaper liked to make disapproving comments about the erosion of morality and purpose which went with increasing prosperity. There was an instinct, usually expressed on the left but found at all points on the political spectrum, that there was something unseemly about the consumer society and 'vulgar affluence'. Maudling would have none of this. In his 1963 conference speech he talked about the great things that affluence could enable society to achieve – the relief of poverty, the beautification of the urban environment, the fine public services that could be afforded. Maudling celebrated the fact that in the late 1950s and early 1960s, and of course in his time as Chancellor, ordinary people had access to consumer goods such as televisions, household appliances and cars. Sensitively, for a man who had not known material deprivation, he had an instinct for what a difference this made, at a time when some in the Labour Party were still talking as if there was socialist virtue in doing washing by hand rather than putting it in a machine. There is nothing uplifting about drudgery and poverty, and Maudling had a sense not only for the pleasure and freedom that affluence could bring, but also the noble purposes to which it could be applied.

Maudling was trying to speak to that early 1960s feeling of idealism, practicality and confidence that coalesced around John Kennedy in the United States, despite Kennedy's own devious political career and chronic self-indulgence. But Reggie was a far inferior orator, and despite being the same age he communicated ease while Kennedy seemed energetic. Maudling's talk about ideals as Chancellor was not just waffle. He took significant measures towards social equality, and for the most part the large additional spending he authorised was public money well used. Investment in new schools, roads, hospitals, fitted with his view of public affluence flowing from private affluence. Britain could afford to build a new generation of schools and hospitals, and Maudling felt that it should. Maudling even did something for foreign aid, which rose in dollar terms by nearly 15 per cent between 1962 and 1964.[11] There was no political benefit in Britain from being generous to foreigners. Britain could afford to expand access to higher education, and indeed did so with Maudling holding the purse strings. When Maudling made a tax concession, he did it in the most expansionary and egalitarian way he could: he did not accept that 'incentives' only applied to the rich. He knew that it would be impossible to make further large tax cuts after 1963 because of the public spending commitments, and said so publicly to the disappointment of many Conservatives. He may have taken chances with the balance of payments, but he was responsible in his attitude to government finance.

While one would not wish to defend Maudling's Chancellorship in every detail – and certainly not the demob-happy last few months – it does not deserve the bad reputation that still clings to it. He was no tax reformer like his successor, Jim Callaghan, and no great administrative innovator like his predecessor, Selwyn Lloyd – nor such a capable pilot through choppy waters as Roy Jenkins or Denis Healey – so one cannot claim greatness for his time at the Treasury. Had his experiment worked, maybe he would be hailed as the miracle-working Erhard of Britain; it was a gamble he took with his reputation, and lost. Even so, Maudling managed to bring an alarming recession quickly to an end in 1962–3; he was a constructive and popular international financial statesman; and his legacy of schools and hospitals is still with us. It was not a bad record.

Maudling's sense of responsibility made him uncomfortable and inhibited in his role as Shadow Chancellor, to which Alec Douglas-Home formally appointed him a couple of weeks after the election, together with a more loosely defined role as 'coordinator of domestic affairs'. Some had expected him to be formally designated a deputy leader, but he was not.[12] Maudling knew that at some point his policies would generate a large deficit, which would somehow have to be bridged, before the deficit started falling as domestic output rose. Maudling had prepared two possible measures to deal with the deficit: temporary import quotas (which were then compatible with the rules of GATT) and an import surcharge (which was flagrantly against GATT and EFTA rules, but which had been used by Canada in 1962 with apparent success). Before he lost office, Maudling tended to favour the surcharge as being more useful because of its dampening effect on domestic demand, particularly for imports. When the Labour government announced a 15 per cent import surcharge on 26 October, Reggie was intellectually honest enough to acknowledge that there was some continuity in policy. He commented, amused, in an economic debate in November 1964 that 'I must say that a great deal of what the Government say we would agree with. They seem to echo not only our words but our actions. Indeed, I seemed to recollect a certain number of passages of my own about incomes policy in the First Secretary of State's [George Brown's] speech today.'[13] Although not in that parliamentary speech, he commented, on the import surcharge, that the government had inherited both his problems and his solutions.[14]

However, the White Paper that announced the surcharge also announced that the deficit was much worse than anyone had believed, and this was the first occasion on which the dramatic figure of an £800 million deficit was published. There was a quality of cognitive dissonance to the White Paper; on the one hand, the problem was worse than anyone had believed, on the other, no devaluation or deflationary policy was necessary. Something had to give. Confidence in sterling had been held up for much of 1964 by irrational factors, and had been strained during the summer and the election, and it could have given way at any time. The November Budget heightened the sense that the government was going ahead with its aims, of which conservative foreign bankers disapproved, regardless of the balance of payments crisis, and City sourness was increased by the trailing of a new Capital Gains Tax in the Chancellor's speech.[15] It was hardly Wilson's fault that he was operating in the face of political prejudice, and that he was therefore unable to take the risks that Maudling had done. Pressure on sterling increased, Bank Rate increased from 5 per cent to 7 per cent on 23 November but did nothing to ease the situation. Maudling changed his tune as the crisis progressed, claiming on 23 November that the Bank Rate rise was caused by the government's actions, while Callaghan retorted that Maudling should have a bad conscience for having failed to take action over the summer.[16] He did not publicise the fact that Maudling had considered raising Bank Rate on the day after the election.

When the interest rate rise failed to stem the outflow, Lord Cromer went to Wilson and more or less demanded the abandonment of the government's programme to satisfy the financial markets; Wilson refused and threatened to float the pound and call a 'who governs' election. Cromer went away and managed to raise the astonishing sum of $3 billion in credits from other central bankers. When Alec Douglas-Home and Reggie Maudling turned up in Downing Street the next day, offering to support a coalition government, Wilson was able to send them packing. The crisis was over, but so was the hope that 1964–5 could be negotiated without a 'stop' phase.[17] The crisis and the government's response sealed the fate of the Maudling experiment.

Maudling blamed the Labour government for panicking. He claimed that the new government's policies were to blame for the sterling crisis and the resulting economic damage: 'They arose from those follies and from nothing else. The situation occurred for one reason – because they lost their nerve and because they were determined to make everything look as black as possible to suit their own party interests.'[18] Maudling was always wistful about his great unfinished experiment, seeing it for the rest of his life as a tragic lost opportunity,[19] and unusually for him could occasionally sound bitter about Wilson for terminating it and 'dining out for seven years on the £800 million deficit'.[20] His criticism of Wilson and Callaghan is not entirely fair. They were genuinely disturbed to be handed such bad figures when they came to power. It was not unnatural to be alarmed when confronted by the Governor of the Bank of England talking in apocalyptic terms. While the rushed White Paper did strike the wrong note, confidence in sterling could have collapsed at any time. It was the old political joke 'The previous government brought us to the edge of an economic precipice – since then we have taken a great step forward' made real. How might Maudling have explained away an import surcharge, which was certainly an option he was actively considering, without causing talk of a crisis and a loss of confidence? Could Maudling have hung on through 1965 as the balance of payments deficit fell back from its freak level of 1964 but still remained worryingly adverse? The window of opportunity for his policy to achieve a lasting improvement in Britain's economic performance was narrower than Maudling imagined, but it was not non-existent as Edmund Dell appeared to believe. If a re-elected Tory government had managed to get through the winter of 1964–5 without having to change course it would have been a miraculously successful confidence trick; but this is not to say that it should not have been tried, or might not have worked.

Maudling's spell as Shadow Chancellor was brief. Rab Butler resigned from the House of Commons in February 1965, having been appointed Master of Trinity College, Cambridge, by Harold Wilson. The departure of one eternal deputy opened the way for another to emerge. Alec Douglas-Home nominated Maudling as his deputy leader and Shadow Foreign Secretary. While denying that Maudling was his designated successor, Douglas-Home did say that the appointment would broaden his outlook, a remark that indicates that Maudling's career development was still a priority for the leaders of the Conservative Party.[21]

Maudling's spell shadowing Foreign Affairs was notable as the time when he finally reconciled himself to joining the European Community. He was still talking about bringing EFTA and the EEC closer together, but he also recognised that in fact the Treaty of Rome had proved to have been much more adaptable and acceptable than he had thought in 1957–61. Maudling summed up Conservative European policy in March 1965: 'Our basic policy remains to secure entry into the European Common Market on acceptable terms. This clearly cannot be achieved for some time to come. In the meanwhile our political objective must be to show ourselves to be more progressive and positive than the Government in our attitude to European unity.' Further, he was willing to think in terms of 'preparing the ground for the united Europe of the future'.[22] Maudling's commitment was not wholehearted, as he still saw the French veto as barring the way to British entry in the immediate future, and was worried about the possibility that Wilson could win popularity by playing the Euro-sceptic. But Reggie's conversion marginalised the Conservative anti-European tendency, which was now confined to the backbenches and lacked a plausible leader. Maudling's new position enabled the Conservatives to unite, for all intents and purposes, as the European party. While Heath pursued the project with more determination than Maudling would have done if he had become leader, the essential transformation of the Tories from the party of Empire and Commonwealth to a pro-European position had been completed in early 1965 under Alec Douglas-Home.

Maudling performed dutifully if not particularly prominently as Shadow Foreign Secretary.[23] He spoke for the party in foreign affairs debates in April and July 1965, gently sparring with Wilson on the first occasion, and sounding more abrasive about Wilson's attempts to mediate in Vietnam in July; no doubt the speculation about a Tory leadership contest encouraged him to make an effort and please his own side.[24] Given that Alec Douglas-Home took a particular interest in the subject of foreign policy, and had the prestige of a former Prime Minister, there was little opportunity for Maudling to shine. Nor did he wish to cut much of a dash in party politics, as he adhered firmly to his idea, as expressed to the Chief Whip in 1950, that foreign policy should not be a matter of partisan debate. He went on several foreign trips, often also with a business component – to New York in February, and to Moscow at the end of June for long talks with Kosygin. The issues of the moment were the escalation in the Vietnam war, and the situation in Rhodesia. The Central African Federation having been dissolved, and Northern Rhodesia (Zambia) and Nyasaland (Malawi) achieving independence, Southern Rhodesia was the only outstanding British colonial issue in Africa. It had become even more intractable in May 1965, when Ian Smith's Rhodesian Front party won a large majority in parliamentary elections. Maudling called Rhodesia 'Britain's own problem and we must proceed to majority rule as soon as we can',[25] but in November 1965 it was taken out of the familiar post-colonial process when the Smith regime unilaterally declared independence.

Maudling was on sharper party-political form when he spoke as deputy leader, for instance at Manchester on 10 April when he blamed higher interest rates, taxes and inflation on the Labour government. As time went on, and in fairness he suffered more criticism for the state of Britain's economy, he was more inclined to lash out at the government as incompetent and to blame decisions taken since the election for all the problems.

On 16 October 1964 Reggie's salary fell from £5,000 to £1,750. He had been thinking about what to do with his personal finances once out of government for at least two years. In November 1962 he had told *Guardian* editor Alastair Hetherington that 'he knew very well that the minute he was out of office he'd be looking for the fattest directorship he could find: he would need the money'.[26] Maudling's candidly avaricious remark to Hetherington was not the only indication that he had been dwelling on the material consequences of losing office in 1962–4. He told the local paper, though not for attribution, that he was not too worried about the financial implications of losing office: he was almost bound to be snapped up by businesses and would probably be better off for not being Chancellor.[27] Reggie had spent so long in ministerial office – he went in at the age of 35 and left at the age of 47, and before that had been a civil servant and a political researcher – that he had grown worried and dissatisfied with his financial lot, even with Lloyd's. The early start to Reggie's ministerial career had cut off the classical Tory career path before then – to make a pile of money in the City or industry and then use that position to pursue a political career. Reggie was one of the first to pursue the modern path, of using political prominence as a means of securing high-paid jobs while out of office. Reggie's early marriage had closed off another possibility, of marrying money – Beryl's family were not as well off as Maudling's own. But Reggie was anxious to be taken seriously as a Tory grandee, and lacking inherited wealth he felt obliged to go out and earn enough to hold his head up among the upper classes. Men like Heath and Powell came from modest backgrounds and were subject to some of the same social pressures, but lacked Reggie's sensitivity. Snubs mattered less to a driven intellectual such as Powell, or a stubbornly independent man like Heath, than they did to someone like Maudling.

Reggie was driven by the fear that he would be unable to provide for his family, who were increasingly demanding and tended to expect him to provide a luxurious living. His mother-in-law, Florence Laverick, told him, 'You've done all this work and got nothing out of it,' and bluntly expected him to go out and earn heaps of money.[28] After the election, the *Daily Mail* asked displaced Tory ministers what they would do now they had lost power. There was particular sympathy for Reggie, 'with four children to keep in Mod gear', who was vague about what he wanted to do but said he would not 'go back to the Bar' but do 'some sort of business'. 'I hope he doesn't launch out into anything foolish,' quipped the paper's gossip columnist.[29]

Reggie's first move into business was hardly foolish. On 16 November he announced that he had joined the board of the merchant bankers Kleinwort Benson as a full-time executive director. Ernest Kleinwort told a *Daily Mail* interviewer that 'whatever else he may do, we are his spiritual home and here he sits for most of the time'. Every Tuesday morning Maudling attended Kleinwort Benson's banking committee; his particular role was to work in the bank's international finance department, granting credit to facilitate international trade, although he also gave general economic advice.[30] He was paid over £10,000 a year (the equivalent of a six-figure salary), which made Kleinwort Benson his principal source of income. It was a considerable sum, but not out of line with what full-time directors of banks were paid at the time.

Kleinwort Benson does not appear proud of the Maudling connection; his name surprisingly does not appear in the authorised history of the firm.[31] But he was part of the story of several of the good years of the merchant bank, in which its activities branched out and its position was greatly strengthened in overseas markets. With the help of Maudling's strong connections, it consolidated its position in Scandinavia, and also moved into East-West trade and the Middle East, areas where Maudling had something to contribute.[32] Maudling's friend, and PPS 1970–2, Clive Bossom criticised the bank for exposing Reggie to some bad businesses,[33] but in the case of Poulson and the Real Estate Fund this was not correct – Cyril Kleinwort was ignorant about one and horrified about the other when he found out. However, sending Reggie into the Middle East with a roving brief to generate business did turn out to have ominous consequences.

Following the Kleinwort appointment Maudling was criticised for taking on such a demanding job, and letters appeared in the *Barnet Press* complaining that Maudling was a part-time MP.[34] He did not seem bothered by the criticism, and joined the board of Dunlop rubber as a non-executive director, then on 16 January 1965 joined the board of Associated Electrical Industries. Towards the end of January 1965 Reggie joined the board of Shipping Industrial Holdings (SIH), run by Sandy Glen. He was spreading himself thinly, but perhaps because of his friendship with Glen he made an effort for this one. Reggie was appreciated for his ability, found in the best barristers and generalist civil servants and ministers, to see very quickly what the essential issues were. According to Glen: 'He had the ability to ask the crunch question, get to the key point. He had a first rate mind. He made a great contribution to the companies. He was well-prepared; he had always done his homework and when he spoke he made strong, well-judged points.'[35] SIH was the last of his early spree of directorships, all of which were entirely reputable. The problem at this point was that his earnings were taking him to the highest tax bracket, and depending on quite what category each payment belonged to he was probably paying 91 per cent tax on any further earnings once he had reached the top band. The options here, if he wanted to accumulate still more money, became less attractive. One possibility would be to take sinecure directorships which entailed no work, because while splitting the proceeds of some hard work £90 for oneself to £910 for the Revenue is not attractive, getting £90 for having lunch once in a while, while £910 supports public services, is almost a pleasant way of doing one's duty. Reggie did a certain amount of this, which is a slow way of getting very rich. Another option is to seek employment with people who are willing to bend the rules, and make payment through channels that avoid taxation at such a high level. The problem of this approach was that the people who were most accommodating about this tended to take a cavalier attitude to even more important aspects of business ethics. Maudling's first involvement in this sort of thing came with an apparently clever tax avoidance wheeze.

The removal vans from 11 Downing Street had taken the Maudling family's effects to Essendon or to Chester Street. The Maudlings had sublet Chester Street during their year in Downing Street, latterly to some drama students, who were rather embarrassingly evicted at the behest of the Grosvenor Estate just before the October election. There was nothing shabby about the rented Chester Street flat, but Reggie and Beryl now wanted something bigger and better and thanks to Reggie's directorships they could just about afford to buy a grandiose house at 27 Chester Square, the other side of Eaton Square and a bit closer to Victoria.

While there was something happy about Chester Street, and Bedwell Lodge had a split personality, there was always a rather decadent feel to Chester Square. It was a beautiful house, a large early Victorian building with a south-facing balcony overlooking the gardens of one of London's most attractive squares. The balcony was a calm and peaceful spot where Reggie would, weather permitting, go through his post in the morning after taking William to school. Shortly after they moved in, Kleinwort Benson paid for the reconstruction of the ground-floor rooms so that they could serve as a self-contained space for receptions and parties.[36] This was presumably in the expectation that Maudling would host client events, but even so it was a private benefit paid in a slightly devious fashion. The main family rooms were, as is usual in houses of that vintage, on the first floor, and it was there that Beryl's tastes were allowed to run riot. In the drawing room there was a brown sofa of staggering dimensions, scattered with brightly coloured cushions, and behind it an enormous Chippendale mirror encrusted with curlicues of gilt; either side were two gold-coloured, pineapple-shaped lamps. The house was cluttered with antiques and knick-knacks, some gifts and souvenirs from Reggie's travels (such as the drinking horns from their 1961 trip to the USSR), and some bought from antique and junk shops, of which Beryl in particular was a devotee.[37] In time, valuable gifts from the Middle East started to appear in the living rooms. The Maudlings also filled spare corners with flowering plants. On the landing, behind a mirrored door guarded by two unnervingly realistic-looking stone Siamese cats, was an office where he installed his personal secretary. The house at 27 Chester Square was cluttered, even untidy; colourful, even florid, and despite its grandeur it was a comfortable place to live.[38] It was beautiful, but it was too much. The Chester Square period of Reggie's life was imbued with excess, and the house epitomised this quality. Chester Square ran Reggie to the limits of his financial capacity. In March 1964 the annual cost in terms of ground rent, rates and maintenance was estimated at £2,250 for the previous year, and at least £2,400 for the following.[39] This ate up the bulk of Reggie's parliamentary salary of £3,250 in itself, even before the mortgage costs, furnishing, heating and living costs are considered.

The purchase of the house had itself created a financial problem, in that now he had two residences there would be (as of the 1965 Finance Act) Capital Gains Tax implications on the sale of one of them, which created the potential for a large tax bill if his circumstances changed. The solution came courtesy of Eric Miller, a director of Peachey Property and numerous subsidiaries. Maudling and Miller had met at some stage while he was Chancellor, at least according to Reggie's recollection in the late 1970s[40] and got on well socially; Miller was an accomplished businessman with a reckless line in generosity, particularly to the politically interesting. Miller enjoyed playing the tycoon with his friends, although, as it happened, a lot of the money he was spraying around had been improperly diverted from the accounts of the Peachey group. People who received his gifts were, for the most part, not aware of Miller's criminality, and merely assumed that his excesses demonstrated how nouveau riche property developers were supposed to behave. Some people found Miller vulgar, charmless and sinister, although others found his company nearly irresistible, including in different ways both Harold Wilson's powerful Political Secretary, Marcia Williams, and Reginald Maudling. Miller even became something of a Maudling family friend; Edward Maudling remembers going to Kent for fishing trips with Miller.[41] Miller offered Reggie a directorship of the firm in 1965 but given all his other earnings and commitments Maudling decided not to accept, instead becoming a consultant to Peachey. According to an official report, 'he began his advisory work with Peachey in 1965, on the basis that some form of emolument would be arranged later'. He worked on this basis for about two years, usually giving his advice in a social context while being entertained at Peachey's expense at Miller's Edgware Road flat or in the Churchill Hotel, which Miller used as a base. This unusual and flexible consultancy arrangement was only formalised a couple of years later, when Miller had become chairman of Peachey.[42]

The form of remuneration, and assistance for Maudling's taxation problems, which Miller devised in 1967 was for Peachey to purchase the freehold of Bedwell Lodge, for which it paid £3,000, much less than the market value of the property, and in return the Maudlings (specifically Beryl Maudling, in whose name the house was registered) were granted a seventy-year lease for the property at a cost of £100 per annum. Peachey would undertake various improvements, including the installation of central heating. Reggie would contract to offer advice to Peachey. According to Reggie in 1977 when the deal was unwound, the arrangement was 'in lieu of salary . . . it suited me and was acceptable to the Inland Revenue'. According to Maudling, his standard consultancy fee was £5,000 a year, paid through a small family firm, and the leaseback deal was essentially equivalent to a five-year consultancy agreement at that rate.[43] Maudling denied that it was a CGT evasion scheme, but later admitted that the Revenue did query the arrangement and he 'had to give in, in the end'.[44]

The details of the arrangement are obscure, and according to Lord Mais, Miller's successor at Peachey in 1977, documents relating to the transaction were destroyed at some time during Miller's chairmanship. What is known about the leaseback is basically from Lord Mais's statements when he appealed to Maudling to unwind the deal, Maudling's statements to the *Daily*

Mail in 1977 and Maudling's evidence to the Department of Trade Inspectors who looked into Peachey after Miller's fall. The inspectors accepted that Maudling had performed advisory services for the company in 1965–70 for which £5,000 was not excessive payment. But in the light of the arrangements he made later with Poulson and the inadequate documentation in that case, it is possible that this does not reflect the whole story of the leaseback deal. It certainly seems strange to imagine that Maudling acted for Peachey effectively for nothing from 1965 to 1967.[45]

Still, in 1965 the Miller leaseback scheme was in the future, and there was no reason to question Maudling's judgement or honesty in the business connections he had made up to this point. But the alacrity with which he had plunged into business activity had caused raised eyebrows, and called into question how much commitment he had to political affairs. Maudling was, on the basis of conversations with Labour leaders, expecting an election in 1966, and felt he had time to play the long game. After the 1964 election, Maudling was in a difficult position; he privately admitted at the time that his line of criticism on economic affairs was not effective propaganda, although he was confident about it intellectually.[46] His record, and his early admission that Callaghan had inherited his problems and his remedies, inhibited his ability to make capital from the Labour government's problems. The switch away from economics towards foreign policy, while it was better for him in terms of political experience and combining business trips with political talks, also took him out of the limelight. When Tories gathered to speculate about who would take over the leadership after Alec Douglas-Home, Maudling was still the favoured candidate, although he did not have the same degree of dominance as he had enjoyed in June 1963, or indeed immediately after the 1964 election. When Douglas-Home surprised the party by calling a leadership election at the end of July 1965, Maudling had every reason to expect that his hour had come.

Chapter 15

THE TURNING POINT, JULY 1965

n oft-repeated and inaccurate cliché about the Conservative Party is that loyalty is its secret weapon. For a start, Tories will not shut up about it, so that it is hardly secret; it is also in short supply when the party leader is in any kind of trouble. Conservative Party leadership elections have developed a particularly piquant flavour over the years, of backstabbing and bitchiness of a high order. The 1965 leadership election in which Reggie Maudling was narrowly defeated by Edward Heath was no exception.

Harold Wilson lit the fuse on 26 June 1965 by announcing that there would be no general election in 1965. The Conservatives had previously been constrained by the fear that Wilson would capitalise on any disunity by calling an election, and now knew that if they changed leader the new man would have several months and a party conference to establish a new course. Murmuring on the backbenches began, and at the 1922 Committee meeting on 5 July there were calls from some MPs, mainly but not exclusively from supporters of Edward Heath, to open the issue of the leadership.

Sir Alec became more uncertain about his position as July wore on, despite several public statements of his determination to carry on, and the whispering increased in volume. On 18 July he was distressed to read William Rees-Mogg in the *Sunday Times* saying that it was the right time for a change in the leadership, and being a gentlemanly sort he was unable to ignore this wayward prophet. He also read the polls and was appalled to discover that he was regarded as less honest than Harold Wilson, although consoled by the equally strange finding that he was seen as being pretty much as intelligent. He resigned on Thursday 22 July, telling Maudling and Heath and a couple of other key figures in the morning before addressing the 1922 Committee in the evening.

The 1965 contest was the first democratic leadership election in the party's history, as the party had agreed new rules in February 1965 to prevent a repetition of the embarrassing fiasco of 1963 and the subsequent recriminations – although the party discovered in 2003 that the old system of having a leader 'emerge' had something to be said for it. In July 1965, for the first time, there would be a secret ballot in which all Tory MPs would have a vote, and a brief period between formal nominations and the election to allow a short, sharp campaign. A strict timetable was laid down for the process. The leadership election, from the resignation of the previous leader to a clean and decisive result, was compressed into less than a week.

From the beginning of the contest Maudling was seen as the leading candidate, the heir apparent. He was effectively the deputy leader to Douglas-Home, he was experienced in senior office, he was popular among the electorate and widely liked in Parliament. Two other candidates emerged to fight Maudling for the party leadership – Edward Heath and Enoch Powell. There had been speculation that others would stand, with Peter Thorneycroft and Quintin Hogg giving up quickly after finding negligible levels of support. More seriously, Christopher Soames was dissuaded by Harold Macmillan, and Iain Macleod realised that there were still too many Tories who profoundly distrusted him for him to consider running.

The Powell campaign can be dealt with rapidly. The Enoch Powell of 1965 was not the famous demagogue who burst into anti-immigration politics in 1968. 'Powellism' then was free market economics, and Powell himself was an enigmatic and austere personality who cut a strange figure as a potential leader. Powell's support was limited to personal friends like Edith Pitt and devotees of classical economics like John Biffen and Nicholas Ridley. Powell called his derisory vote of fifteen as being a 'calling card' but in the short term it weakened his claim to speak for a substantial body of Tory opinion. Like Barry Goldwater, the purist right-winger who was overwhelmingly defeated in the November 1964 US presidential election, Powell had offered 'a choice, not an echo'. Also like Goldwater, he could look back from the 1980s and justifiably claim that his ideas had proved stronger within his party than those of his moderate opponents. The effect of his intervention in 1965 is unclear – Reggie's supporters claimed that the Powell vote would otherwise have been theirs and resulted in a virtual tie, but there is no way of checking.

The choice between Heath and Maudling (or 'Reggie and Ted' – it was an intimate sort of election) was hardly an ideological one. The biggest difference between them was over Europe, where Reggie's recent conditional conversion contrasted with Ted's wholehearted support for British entry to the EEC. Europe, however, played next to no part in the contest. Ted was also perceived as being rather more free market on economics because of Reggie's consistent support for incomes policy, although Ted was far from dogmatically opposed. They had been agreed on the abolition of Resale Price Maintenance in 1964, and it is impossible to identify either man with previously existing ideological or personal factions. Reggie, hitherto a Butler man, had the support of many of those who had opposed him in 1963, but Ted was backed by Macmillan and Macleod; Powell had been a passionate Rab supporter in 1963 but now stood for a break with his style of politics. All three candidates had been 'One Nation' members.

The main difference between Reggie and Ted was in temperament. Reggie was almost impossible to dislike, a claim nobody has ever made for Ted. But the virtue of likeability was out of fashion in 1965, when many

Conservatives yearned for an abrasive, tough leader who would take the fight to Harold Wilson. The Conservatives have always been happier with consensus politics when they are in charge of steering the government. The worry about electing Reggie was that he would drift along amiably and allow Wilson to get away with too much, and that his image as a slow, comfortable sort of man would suffer by comparison with Wilson's apparent dynamism. Heath was a moderniser, although in 1965 few realised quite how radical his instincts about the modernisation of Britain actually were, while Maudling was more of a steady-as-she-goes Tory. 'Heath really is a positive force – a leader – while dear Reggie, though very intelligent, does like a good lunch and parties that go on late into the night,' was how newspaper proprietor Cecil King saw the situation.[1]

Heath's merits had been recently displayed through leading the parliamentary opposition to Labour's 1965 Finance Bill. Callaghan's Budget, presented on 6 April 1965, was one of the most complex tax-reforming measures ever presented, with new regimes for the taxation of capital gains and corporate profits, an insanely complicated tax intended to curb land speculation and curbs on allowable expenses such as business entertainment. Callaghan, unlike Maudling, was trying to be a reforming Chancellor. The Bill was strongly opposed by many City and business interests, and, given the small government majority in the Commons, the Labour Chief Whip, Ted Short, thought it was 'sheer idiocy' to try to force it through.[2] The Finance Bill was a target for a masterful parliamentary campaign, in which Heath and his junior spokesmen managed to embarrass the government and rally Conservative spirits after the disappointment of electoral defeat. Stratton Mills, the moderate Unionist MP for North Belfast, one of Heath's lieutenants in the Finance Bill campaign, was one of a significant number of MPs who decided to support Ted after witnessing him in action:

> After seeing Ted I was much more impressed by his style and approach, his energy, than with Reggie. Reggie went down in my estimation while Ted went up. Ted said that the government had 600,000 civil servants to tell Callaghan what to say, while we only had ourselves and a small group of backbenchers, but if we can win the argument, even if we don't win the vote, we can demoralise the government. He put it very graphically. If Reggie had been handling that Finance Bill it would have been totally different. Callaghan ended up totally demoralised at what he had brought in.[3]

Callaghan would dissent from this, but the spring and early summer of 1965 were a gruelling experience for Labour MPs, who were frequently kept up past midnight during the long sittings.[4] Except for two minor clauses, the line held, but by the end of the Finance Bill battle Labour MPs were exhausted and run ragged, while the Tories were in the mood to celebrate. Edward Heath threw a party in his Albany flat to celebrate the success of the Tory parliamentary campaign, and eighty Tory MPs attended.[5] Only a day later, Alec Douglas-Home announced that he was going to resign as leader.

While Heath had been rallying the troops, Maudling had been less prominent. His move to foreign affairs was a tactical mistake, as the Leader of the Opposition tends to make the most important foreign policy speeches rather than the Shadow Foreign Secretary. Maudling compounded the problem by too obviously chasing directorships over the winter and giving the impression that his interest was waning. MPs could only look back and contrast what Heath had been able to achieve on the Finance Bill to the likely progress of events under Maudling. Up to a point, this was a high valuation to put on some rather absurd Westminster games that barely altered the Finance Bill, but such things are important in politics.

There was another fundamental problem to the Maudling campaign. Maudling had hoped to run as the establishment candidate, the natural choice for the succession, but when the campaign started this turned out to be a fatally flawed approach. The party's grandees unexpectedly favoured Heath. Harold Macmillan recorded in his diary after the result that 'I feel sure that Ted is the best choice. He is a stronger character than Maudling',[6] and gave discreet support in the campaign. Rab Butler, Lord Margadale (formerly John Morrison of the 1922 Committee) and Lord Aldington all preferred Heath, and the Tory peers also seemed to be heavily aligned in Ted's favour.[7] Alec Douglas-Home, though deeply hurt by the circumstances of his resignation and assumed by the Maudling camp to have been one of their supporters, kept his counsel during the campaign. It is not clear for whom the former leader voted; a fog of ambiguity and double-talk about his intentions descended even during the campaign.[8] His biographer records him as having voted for Heath, though in a conversation in 1967 he said that he favoured Reggie on the grounds that lazy men came off better in a crisis.[9] Reggie, in retrospect, felt that Douglas-Home's attitude had damaged him: 'It was Alec who did for me,' he said ruefully to his friend Michael Rice.[10] It was another illustration of Home's remarkable ability to seem simple and straightforward while being as devious an operator as any on the Tory front bench.

The Maudling campaign team therefore had to shore up the shallow initial support that came to Reggie because of his credentials as the front runner. They utterly failed to achieve this strategic objective. A large part of this failure was because of the amateurish efforts of his campaigners. Philip Goodhart, a member of that team, called it 'the worst organised leadership campaign in Conservative history: a total shambles'.[11] In fairness, Maudling himself, for his own refined reasons, failed to give a lead to campaign organisation, and organising an internal election like this was new territory for the Conservatives, but most of Maudling's men failed to recognise what had to be done. The idea of canvassing and recording voting intentions was a new and highly suspect one for some of his traditionalist supporters. They were not very good at it.

When news of Douglas-Home's resignation percolated around Westminster the supporters of each potential candidate started to meet. Patrick Wall sprang into action on Maudling's behalf and summoned a meeting of likely Maudlingites at William Clark's house near the House of Commons for nine that evening. Reggie met the group, consisting mainly of right-wing backbenchers such as Wall himself and Stephen Hastings,[12] although he and his supporters failed to capitalise on the quick start. After the initial meeting on the evening of 22 July, the campaign did not meet again collectively. There was no campaign manager. According to Robert Carr, 'We didn't really work as an organised team, with things now taken for granted like assigning the task of talking to particular people between us.'[13] This failure to organise the campaign allowed the inexperience and overenthusiasm of his supporters to shine through. The Maudling campaign did not grasp that persuasion was more effective when carried out by friends of the targets, rather than through peremptory questioning of anyone who happened to be around. One Maudling supporter, Captain Sir Henry Kerby, described his canvassing technique as follows: 'One sees chaps all over the place, in the chamber or in the lavatory, and one says, "Heath seems to have succeeded in his aim to stab the party in the back, the saboteur." Then one sees how the land lies.'[14] Robert Carr was one of the few senior liberal Tories to campaign for Maudling, but his diffidence in approaching people and arguing Reggie's case meant that he could not undo the damage done by the blundering of Kerby and his ilk. The campaign's intelligence system was woeful. Few records were kept at the time, but a canvass list did survive in Patrick Wall's meticulous filing system. Many MPs who did not support Maudling when it came to the vote are listed as being for Reggie (the Powell vote in particular was disastrously badly recorded). The record was so inaccurate that among Maudling's 123 listed supporters was George Thomson, who was in the Labour government as Minister of State at the Foreign Office.[15]

By contrast the Heath campaign was disciplined and effective. It was organised by Peter Walker and at its core were a group of young veterans of the Whips' Office. Walker ran the campaign out of his house in Gayfere Street in Westminster, and allocated each of the campaign team a list of MPs either to approach or ask someone else to sound out. Two MPs whose excessive enthusiasm for Heath was likely to alienate potential supporters were asked to stay away from Westminster during the campaign.[16] In a contest where knowledge of the individual peculiarities of each MP was important in determining how to make an approach, the Heath team had the valuable advantage of professionalism. They knew how to count and deliver votes, and the Maudling forces simply did not.

Maudling's support trickled away during the campaign. A lot of his young, progressive backers in 1963, such as Jim Prior, had become disenchanted before the campaign began and gravitated towards Heath. Prior had come to the conclusion that 'Reggie was a very agreeable man, and I was very fond of him, but he wasn't the stuff of which Prime Ministers were made'.[17] Heath also had the support of most of the young Bow Group entrants of 1964 such as Geoffrey Howe and Patrick Jenkin.[18] Even some of those invited to Patrick Wall and William Clark's soirée on the first night of the campaign ended up voting for other candidates, including Bernard Braine (Powell) and Margaret Thatcher, who was persuaded late in the campaign by Keith Joseph to switch her support to Ted Heath on the grounds that 'Ted has a passion to get Britain right'.[19]

The most wounding defection was that of Iain Macleod. The Maudling campaign had taken his support for granted on the grounds of his friendship with Reggie and their generally similar political outlook, but Macleod was never one to let sentimentality affect his actions. He dithered as to whom to support but eventually came down on Ted's side. According to his former PPS Charles Longbottom, the progressive Tory MP for York from 1959 to 1966: 'Macleod did not support him because he was worried about the idle side to Reggie's character. Reggie didn't discipline himself. Iain felt that Ted was more organised and a better prospect for taking on a job which needs a very disciplined approach.'[20] Macleod's economic thinking had also been shifting away from Maudling's corporatist approach, and he was willing by 1965 to concede in private that there was something to be said for Enoch Powell's free market heresies. But Macleod did not tell Maudling to his face why he had switched support, and Reggie was always puzzled by his behaviour.[21] Macleod had a devoted band of supporters but he did not give a firm indication to them of how he was voting; nevertheless, his lack of enthusiasm for Reggie did come across and most of them ended up voting for Ted. One exception was Longbottom, who was persuaded that Reggie's attractive human qualities would go over well with the electorate.

The voters who did support Reggie in 1965 were a disparate bunch, suggesting the incoherent nature of his appeal. He did collect a few aristocrats and Scots as the legitimist candidate, but there were fewer than expected who backed him out of distaste for the involvement of Heath supporters in overthrowing Alec Douglas-Home. Maudling could not even claim the support of the former leader. Reggie won some support among the 'knights of the shires', but more among right-wingers who had got to know him while he was Colonial Secretary. Although they knew that he did not agree with their views, they appreciated the courtesy and respect with which Reggie had treated them, and regarded him as a gentleman. The side of Reggie that loved traditional Englishness – clubs, public schools, green fields, village pubs, good manners – could communicate well with old-style Tories, and they in turn felt that his heart was in the right place.

The Reggie vote was also to some extent an anti-Ted vote, in that those MPs who had been bruised by Heath's legendary rudeness and abruptness naturally rallied behind Maudling. Sir John Rodgers, a One Nation founder, fell into this category. One other category of supporter seems notable –

Maudling seems to have had the backing of several MPs who sailed close to the wind in their financial affairs, namely Freddie Bennett, John Cordle, Richard Reader Harris and Stephen McAdden. The prominence of Bennett as a Maudling supporter did not inspire confidence in many waverers. At lunch a little after the leadership election when Peter Walker and Reggie compared notes, they found that forty-five MPs had pledged support to both sides,[22] so it is difficult to establish with any certainty who voted which way, and why.

The short campaign did not go according to plan. Maudling had tried to avoid some bad publicity by cancelling a cricket weekend with Edward du Cann in Somerset, fearing that a country weekend was not what his image needed. He was also worried about the press taking pictures of him in undignified contortions at the wicket. Heath for once seemed more relaxed, keeping an engagement at Glyndebourne (to see the eerily appropriate *Macbeth*) and staying with his father at Broadstairs. Maudling had tried to eliminate the negatives, but Heath still had the best of the weekend. When MPs returned to Westminster on Monday the story was going around that Maudling was an atheist, which in those days when the Tory party was more attached to the established Church was a damaging allegation. William Teeling, the right-wing MP for Brighton Pavilion and a staunch Maudling supporter, rang him up and asked for his authority to put out a denial. 'He replied: "Of course," and added a little bitterly: "My wife and I went to church on Sunday here in Chester Square. It's funny that nobody bothered to find out and that all the photographers were at the church to which Heath went!"'[23]

This was an entirely characteristic Reggie blunder. He and Beryl had bothered to stay in London rather than retreat to Essendon, and had even gone to the trouble of attending church although he had failed to let the press or television know about it. It was an ineffective attempt to counter the basically accurate charge that he didn't believe in God. Reggie was not an atheist, more a sceptical agnostic whose philosophy was based on rationalist writings. Although he was willing to observe Church of England niceties from time to time and have his children baptised, he had made a point of having a civil wedding and his daughter Caroline felt that 'he had no religious beliefs'.[24] He made one exception to the general rule. When he was being driven to Heathrow airport, he and Beryl would ask to stop at a church on the A4 for a couple of minutes of quiet contemplation.[25]

Ted may have had the religious vote, but Reggie still had the advantage of being a family man. Ted rather desperately borrowed some friends' children, but Reggie did have what appeared to be a perfect happy family and a thoroughly suitable hostess for Number 10 in Beryl. It seems unlikely that her developing personality flaws, notably her heavy drinking and her pushiness, counted much against Reggie. Most Conservative MPs then regarded her as a graceful, lively and pleasant adornment to Reggie and she was quite popular among Tory wives.[26] If she drank a bit too much, she was nowhere near as bad as Dorothy Macmillan, and Beryl also had the advantage that she was faithful and emotionally supportive. Some of Maudling's supporters were not above drawing the contrast with Heath's bachelordom, and the candidate himself took care to be photographed with the family, but there was no rumour campaign against Heath. If anything the family issue might have told in Heath's favour, as he seemed to receive solid support from what Gerald Kaufman delicately referred to as the bachelor vote, 'a strangely neglected but nevertheless substantial vote'.[27]

Another problem for Maudling was feeling in the constituency parties, which was communicated to MPs through informal conversations and soundings over the weekend of the campaign. Heath was more popular among Conservative activists, who rated him as more likely to be a decisive and effective leader than Maudling. Significantly, the Conservative association in the safe West Midland seat of Solihull reported that people had been calling the office all morning in support of Heath, and 'Nobody has actually rung up to back Maudling. They like him, but they don't want him.'[28] Among the general public, however, Maudling was the definite leader, with 44 per cent support to 28 per cent for Heath and only 3 per cent for Powell, according to NOP in the *Daily Mail*. Among Conservative voters, Maudling's advantage was even greater, with 48 per cent supporting him. The public's estimation of Maudling's positive qualities was very high, with a 41–16 lead on who is 'most in touch with ordinary people' and 42–28 on 'most progressive and up to date'. The only comparison on which Heath had an advantage was 'toughest', although this was only a 30–29 lead over Maudling.[29] Heath was annoyed, telling Peter Walker, 'these polls are certainly bloody. I really don't believe anybody thinks I have less energy than Reggie.'[30] However, the balance of press opinion favoured Heath, with the *Daily Mail* and *The Times* adding influential endorsements. Maudling particularly resented the *Mail* proprietor, Lord Rothermere, for suggesting that his victory would destabilise the pound, but behind Rothermere and some other press coverage was the hand of Lord Cromer, Governor of the Bank of England. On 23 July Cromer called Cecil King, who owned the *Mirror*, 'to say that the foreign bankers regard Maudling as the architect of our present financial misfortunes and that, therefore, if he is chosen as Leader the effect on the pound will be bad'.[31] It was an outrageously improper intervention by a supposed public servant in the affairs of an opposition party. The combined effect of the newspaper endorsements and the negative opinion propagated in City circles by Cromer may well have been enough for a few Tory MPs to have changed sides – if more than one did so, this accounted entirely for Heath's overall majority. Maudling's economic policy had brought the Conservatives so close to a victory which he, and many others, believed impossible in October 1964 – but there is no gratitude in politics or finance.

On the morning of the poll, 27 July, Maudling was still, as he had been throughout the campaign, narrowly the bookies' favourite.[32] Reggie was confident of victory as voting began. His team had assured him of enough support for an overall majority on the first ballot, if not perhaps the 15 per cent lead over Heath that was needed formally to conclude the election there and then. However, he was fortified by an agreement with Ted that if either candidate won an overall majority on the first ballot, the loser would pull out and endorse the winner.[33] He wandered amiably around Westminster in the morning, popping into the Smoking Room to encourage his supporters to get to the polls, and asking Heath supporter Stratton Mills how it was all going. Mills could not bear to tell him what he knew, that Heath was going to win.[34] When most of the votes had been cast, Maudling characteristically headed off to the City for lunch at Kleinwort Benson.

At 2.15p.m. Sir William Anstruther-Gray, the chairman of the 1922 Committee, announced the result to waiting MPs and journalists. The figures were: Edward Heath 150, Reginald Maudling 133, Enoch Powell 15. It was a genuine surprise to all concerned, except for Heath's number takers and readers of the *Western Morning News*, the only paper to call the result correctly. Robert Carr was Maudling's representative at the count, and had to telephone the candidate with the bad news. Reggie seemed at first to take it quite well, telling Carr immediately that Heath's two-vote overall majority was decisive and that he had no intention of contesting a second round. Maudling's decision was not publicly announced immediately because some of his supporters still hoped to persuade him to stay in the fight – William Teeling begged him, and according to a contemporary report a former Cabinet minister was seen pleading tearfully with Reggie.[35] None of it worked: 'I'm still game, but I don't think it's worth it,' Reggie told supporters.[36] When Reggie returned to Westminster a couple of hours later he publicly conceded the election. Edward Heath was acclaimed as the new Conservative leader. 'Well, it's a world full of surprises,' Reggie told journalists, anticipating what Margaret Thatcher said twenty-five years later in similar circumstances.

A significant proportion of Maudling voters and even campaign members such as Philip Goodhart felt in retrospect that the party had chosen wisely. Reggie said himself in his memoirs that 'I think the Party were probably right'.[37] However, this was not the immediate reaction in the second half of 1965. Heath quickly disappointed his supporters with a poor showing in a much-hyped censure motion on the Labour government on 2 August, a few days after his leadership victory, while Maudling made what even the *Daily Mirror* acknowledged as 'a brilliant, forceful speech' in the same debate.[38] Reggie, as he sometimes did, performed best when it made the least difference, as if to prove to himself and his colleagues that he could still dazzle when he put his mind to it. It can be seen as a passive-aggressive way of telling the Tories that they had got him, and Heath, wrong the previous week, and that if they had assessed his abilities properly they would have realised that he could give them incisive opposition. There was a constant undercurrent of discontent with Heath's leadership over the next few years, even when the

Tories were doing extremely well as in 1967–9, which owed its origin to the sense that the party had been sold a false bill of goods in the July 1965 election. Heath failed to inspire the public or offer a convincing alternative course, and his parliamentary performances of which so much was expected were limp; Wilson would usually get the better of him. But whatever the discontents with Heath, few saw 'Come back Reggie, all is forgiven' as the solution for very long.

Rather like Michael Portillo in 2001, Reggie Maudling was unwilling to stoop to conquer in 1965. He was ambitious and very much wanted to lead, but he wanted the party leadership on his own terms, and was not going to cajole and twist arms to engineer a victory. He would have been happy enough to be invited to be leader, but was not going to spoil the prize by striving for it. 'Had I fought for the leadership as a matter of personal ambition, had I seized it as a result of some campaign or stratagem, the weight of subsequent responsibility would have been infinitely multiplied.'[39] He wanted the party to recognise its true nature in him, and come to him of its own volition. It was a very Hegelian approach to running a leadership election campaign. There is something reminiscent of the attitude of the bridegroom about Maudling and the Tory party, in that true, free consent is essential and that to use trickery invalidates the whole exercise. Maudling loved, and thought he knew, the Tory party, and also thought that it knew and loved him. While it was honourable of Maudling to seek an unforced mandate, it also maximised the psychological impact of defeat. What if the party knew him, and had affection for him, but did not love him?

The problem with Maudling's approach was that, to some extent, the leadership campaign was itself a demonstration of how the candidates would respond to electoral opportunity, and Heath's professional and determined approach promised tough opposition and an aggressive election campaign when the time came. Maudling's failure to sustain his initial advantages, and put himself before his public, gave the impression that his style of opposition was lazy and complacent. He reminded them of his failure in 1963. The subtlety of what he was trying to do was lost on many Tories, even some of the most sympathetic and intelligent among them. Lord Butler wrote privately a few days after the election: 'I personally think the Party's instinct was right, in that if it were going to have a change which took many by surprise, it was really better to go for the more forceful of the two contenders, otherwise there would be no change at all.'[40] Lord Carrington, who liked Reggie, could not support him, on the grounds that he did not seem to care enough about it.[41]

Having won without the need to pay any debts, Maudling would have been free to make the party in his own image, much as Heath did in 1965–75. When Heath conducted the Tory orchestra, it played discordant, modern music, while under Maudling it would have played a more comforting, traditional tune: Elgar rather than Stockhausen. Maudling may not have had the energy and determination it took Heath to get Britain into Europe, but he would have been unlikely, had he been leading the party, to have got into such trouble with the trade unions. He might have been able to take more advantage of Labour's estrangement from the unions in 1969 after 'In Place of Strife'. If anyone had what it took to organise a corporatist, tripartite settlement in Britain, it was Maudling, and he may have been successful in this for good or ill had he become Prime Minister. He would have tried to run it alongside floating the pound and headlong expansion of the economy, so a Maudling government in the early 1970s would surely have been an inflationary business, even if not as crisis-ridden as Heath's. The question is whether it was Heath's dogged determination that won the Conservatives the 1970 election. Maudling's personal standing with the electorate was much higher than Heath's, so he would not have had to overcome the negative feelings that Heath did; but he would also have been less convincing at demolishing Wilson's modernising image in 1970. While vagueness is necessary when describing the effect on the Tory party of the election going the other way, one can be definite about its effect on Maudling. Had Maudling become leader, he would have been equal to the task. He was an able and intelligent man who, when it was necessary, could perform at a high level and knuckle under to the burdens of a job. There is no reason to believe that party leader Maudling would have been different from Chancellor Maudling – hard-working, caring, thoughtful, intelligent, open-minded and engaged with what he was doing, but still retaining his perspective and sense of humour. While defeat brought out the worst in Reggie Maudling – greed, despair, dissolution, laziness, cynicism, self-indulgence, even dishonesty – victory could well have brought out the best. Maudling at his best was a man of such admirable qualities that it was a national as well as a personal tragedy that the world would see so little of them after 1965, and it was a true tragedy in the sense that his defeat came as a result of the flaws in his own character.

As the afternoon of 27 July 1965 wore on, Reggie realised the scale of the defeat he had suffered. He sat morosely, alone in the Smoking Room. His paralysed misery left a vivid, lifelong impression on several MPs, such as Edward Boyle; his colleagues were shocked to see the bluff, agreeable Reggie reduced to such a state. His public emotional bleeding was surely about showing them how deeply their personal rejection had hurt him. It was, to Reggie, as if he had been jilted at the altar. In the evening Reggie did not even have the comfort of Beryl's shoulder to cry on, having insisted that she go on ahead to the family holiday with Yugoslav shipping magnate Vane Ivanovic in Majorca.[42] Nearly everyone who knew him thought that he was never the same man again after the trauma of his defeat. To his daughter Caroline, who saw him come back to Chester Square in a visibly shaken condition, it had the impact of 'a seismic change in his life'.[43]

Two futures had stretched before Reggie Maudling on that July day in 1965. One led via the leadership of his party to Number 10. The other led to disappointment, disgrace and an early death.

Chapter 16

BLURRING THE BOUNDARIES, JULY 1965–FEBRUARY 1967

Reggie Maudling was never really the same again after his shattering – for once the word is appropriate – defeat in the leadership election. To lose a personal popularity contest to Ted Heath was humiliation indeed, particularly for a man like Reggie who needed to be loved. After the defeat many of the problematic, flawed aspects of Maudling's character emerged in sharper relief, as if he could no longer summon up the determination to keep them in check. Notable among these was excessive drinking. By 1966 he was starting each working day sipping slowly on brandy and black coffee as he went through the post and the papers, and he was also partial to gin and tonic in the morning.[1] He would then have wine and possibly some spirits over lunch, and later on in the evening would usually have more alcohol at parties or over dinner. His consumption, always heavy, was escalating. While in ministerial office between 1952 and 1964 he had not tended to drink in the mornings and his colleagues and, more importantly, his civil servants in the various Private Offices, did not believe that his performance in office was affected by his intake. The structured nature of ministerial life tended to impose demands that prevented Maudling from doing what he liked. But out of office in the mid-1960s Reggie could not be bothered *not* to drink whenever he felt like it.

Alcoholism comes in many varieties. The classic stereotype is of a hopeless, inadequate, embarrassing drunk, but the reality is that many alcoholics are super-competent people who even with a self-imposed handicap are capable of functioning at a high level. Reggie fitted fairly obviously into the category of the 'self-indulgent alcoholic'.[2] He had always enjoyed drink and its effects, and he came increasingly to rely on it as a means of reducing his frustration, passing the time and achieving reliable gratification in an unpredictable world that had started to turn hostile. 'Of all the alcoholics,' states one study, 'the self-indulgent is most likely to drift into alcoholism without realising it, and to take to drink like a voluptuary.'[3] There was, until near the end, a sensuous enjoyment to Maudling's drinking; he cared about the quality of what he drank, and the pleasure of good food and lots of it never palled for Reggie.

Reggie was not an ugly drunk; he did not drink to release a beast within, because his personality was essentially benign. A friend who whiled away an afternoon drinking with him recalls him on the way home from the session just beaming beatifically, lumbering silently through the fog. Even this was an unusually apparent indication that he was drunk, for Reggie could drink very large amounts, until late on in his life, without becoming what most people would recognise as drunk. Reggie was not a binge drinker; he just bathed his life in the stuff, from morning to night, and while he was only rarely obviously intoxicated, neither did he have many moments of stone-cold sobriety from this point onwards in his life. Maudling was a different sort of drinker from the most famous parliamentary alcoholic of the period, Labour's George Brown. Brown drank heavily and steadily and was prone to behave boorishly and become 'tired and emotional' under the influence. George Brown drinking stories are amusing.[4] There are no amusing Maudling drinking stories, except the ones he told himself, because even when he was drinking truly enormous quantities he hardly ever lost control.

Even so, Reggie – although for various reasons his friends would not recognise the description – was, or was a long way along the process of becoming, an alcoholic in the later 1960s. It was starting to corrode his personality and blur his moral boundaries, and to generate confusion and dissolution in his previously fairly disciplined private and business life. Reggie proudly displayed at Chester Square a horoscope that said that he was 'wonderfully indulgent to his wife and children'.[5] This was one way of putting it. What was essentially a virtue was by the mid-1960s becoming a flaw that was damaging Reggie and those around him. The darker undertones of the relationship between Reggie and Beryl were becoming stronger after their ejection from Downing Street and Reggie's defeat in the leadership election. Beryl had always spurred Reggie on in his career, inspired him to go further and higher, but after July 1965 further progress in his political career had been halted, at least for a few years. But her ambition was still burning. Beryl insisted that they should entertain frequently at home, and the guests were normally her choice. The Maudlings did not run a political salon at Chester Square; a friend remembers 'they had rather embarrassing dinner parties there, with some very odd people. Rather dreadful people – nouveaux riches, showbiz people.'[6] As a good friend said, with sadness and without malice:

She wanted the good life and the bright lights, and Reggie was not strong enough to stand up to her . . . She got insatiably greedy for the good things in life. There was constant pressure at home for money, for something more. She never let up. He was working very hard and they were going to every party. He was a tough, big man but that would take it out of anyone. It sapped his strength.[7]

When Beryl's wishes were frustrated she would throw a tantrum like a spoiled child. Reggie's secretary in the mid-1960s, Alex Saville, once saw her stamping her foot at Reggie.[8] Another friend drove back with them from Germany after a week's holiday and as they were passing through Kent on the last leg of their trip 'Beryl saw an antique shop and said she wanted to stop so that she could buy something. The rest of us didn't really want to stop and said so, but she went into a complete fury. She had a temper. She got her way. This was a bit of an eye-opening experience.'[9] Beryl's tantrums were directed exclusively against Reggie; to others the charming, sweet side of her nature remained intact, although she had adopted something of the demeanour of the lady of the manor to some people.

Beryl was an ornament to Reggie, in the best and worst senses of the word. She was pretty, charming, a gracious hostess, glamorous and pleasant company at parties, took an interest in the arts and was generous with her time to charities such as the Westminster Hospital appeal – but she was also decorative rather than practical. She had become accustomed to having everything done for her. The duties of Reggie's secretaries extended to ferrying her around town to the hairdresser and the masseuse and picking up the younger boys from school. 'Could you just . . .' was usually the prelude to some such request. Alex Saville did not mind because Beryl was so polite about it, but it had grated on her predecessor.[10] Upkeep of Chester Square involved a retinue of domestic staff – a cleaner, an au pair, a nanny, a cook and a butler – when they were entertaining. The most appalling job in the Maudling household fell to Josephine, a cockney lady who came in to do the cleaning. 'Nobody in that house cleaned up after themselves,' according to Alex Saville. It was not unusual for Josephine to arrive in the morning and have to clear up dog mess produced by the large, shambling Great Dane that wandered around the house. 'Easy day today, Alex,' she would say when Reggie and Beryl were off on a foreign trip.

'It was at Chester Square that things were going wrong. There was too much booze, too many trips abroad,' remembered Sandy Glen.[11] The Maudling household was degenerating into a miasma of drink and general chaos. It was an unsettling place to try to grow up in. The younger boys were brought up, until Willie went away to boarding school, by a nanny, Miss Portess, whom Edward (Eddie) remembers as 'a little old lady, an old-fashioned nanny'.[12] But Miss Portess was 'not young enough or shrewd enough'[13] to have much effect in the dysfunctional conditions of Chester Square. It was as parents that the Maudlings' dissolution was most harmful and tragic. The Maudlings were ultra-permissive parents. Partly, this was an understandable reaction to the lack of love and tolerance in Reggie's own childhood, partly Reggie's own libertarian instincts, partly also Reggie and Beryl's mutual absorption – and partly also outright neglect.

The positive side of the Maudling household was that Reggie was immensely generous and kind to his children. Reggie denied Caroline very little, and she in particular adored animals – she rode, and also acquired a menagerie of dogs and cats that wandered around contributing to the general atmosphere of cosy disorder. Reggie could also treat the children with considerable respect for their intelligence; Edward remembers him emphasising the value of intellectual integrity, saying that one should not do things in which one does not believe simply for form's sake. Reggie supported Edward's (successful) argument with his school that as a non-believer he should not have to attend religious services.[14] He was very slow to anger. But the regime of generosity, indulgence and attempting to treat the children as small adults was no substitute for his time, his affection and his guidance. His indulgence was more than material kindness to the children; it was also a failure to set boundaries of behaviour, which became progressively worse with each child as Reggie's own boundaries were washed away. A common alcoholic behaviour pattern is to encourage others around one to drink as well, and the Maudlings were free with their alcohol not only with members of the domestic staff (who rather appreciated it) but also with the children. Sandy Glen remembered that 'They would be introduced to wine and cocktails at a very young age. I tried having a word with Beryl about the children and drink, but she completely refused to listen.'[15]

Glen, and also Freddie and Elizabeth Erroll, who were close friends, had a go at saying that the children needed more discipline in general, but to no effect. Reggie and Beryl simply had no idea about how to raise children. 'He was busy and didn't understand and she just didn't understand,' thought Alex Saville sadly. Eddie was a boisterous child, and when neighbours complained that he was being a nuisance kicking a ball around the square, Reggie took the neighbours to task in florid language ('scrimshanking fuddy-duddies!') rather than telling Edward to stop. Willie, their youngest son, was the worst casualty of his parents' regime of excess and neglect. He was a sensitive little boy with translucent, fragile good looks and an intelligence that was so far above average that he found it difficult to understand ordinary problems or form relationships with people. His parents did not really know what to make of him, and left some who knew the family with the impression that they did not treat him fairly, and not as generously as his siblings.

Although Reggie loved his family very much, they rarely did anything together as a unit, birthdays would slip by without the sort of fuss children appreciate – Beryl was never someone to bake a cake – and the older children would often eat by themselves, upstairs, out of tins. There was, even then, a sense of tragedy in the making about the Maudling family. The pressure on Reggie to generate money was unrelenting, and with his own standards gradually deteriorating, the elements were in place for the depressing series of events that took place in the last thirteen years of his life.

At the end of October 1965 Maudling went on Kleinwort Benson business to the Middle East. The merchant bank was interested in expanding into the region, having previously done little there, and it seemed exactly the right sort of mission for Maudling. The tour first took him and his travelling companions to Beirut, one of the two principal commercial centres of the Middle East, where he had arranged to meet his old friend Michael Rice. Rice had abandoned any thoughts of a political career in the mid-1950s and had moved into the developing world of political public relations (PR), numbering among his clients the Egyptian government under Colonel Nasser and the emirate of Abu Dhabi on the Persian Gulf. The 1965 Kleinwort Benson trip took Maudling from Beirut to Abu Dhabi and neighbouring Dubai. These small emirates were then poor and primitive places, ruled by tribal sheikhs and apparently barely touched by the nineteenth century, let alone the twentieth. There was a semi-colonial system whereby the British provided defence for the Gulf states and put in place a system of Political Agents, foreign office diplomats who guided local affairs and advised the Rulers, often in the most patronising fashion.

However, the Gulf states were on the verge of momentous change. Abu Dhabi was a sandy wasteland until a sudden, massive oil find at the very end of the 1950s. Its traditionally minded rulers feared the destruction of the desert way of life. The oil was discovered during the rule of Sheikh Shakhbut, who was horrified and bewildered by the scale of what was happening and tried to stop as much of the progress and exploration as he could. His policy – allegedly a literal one – of stashing banknotes under the bed until termites came and ate them aroused powerful opposition. The British organised a coup against him in 1966. They installed Shakhbut's brother Zayed, who was himself also a traditional Bedouin leader of simple personal tastes but favoured rapid modernisation of his country. Zayed instantly became one of the richest men on earth. According to Abu Dhabi custom and law, the land and resources of the emirate are the personal property of the Ruler for him to use and dispose of as he wishes. Michael Rice and the British Political Agent, Archie Lamb, were able to make introductions in Abu Dhabi, including arranging a meeting with Zayed, not then the Ruler but clearly a coming man. Zayed was puzzled, and did not understand who Maudling was or what he wanted; when Lamb told him that Reggie had been the minister in charge of finance, Zayed said that in that case he must be very rich and in that case why was he interested in Abu Dhabi's money?[16] But the door had been opened, and it was a useful business visit.

The stop in Dubai was less felicitous for Kleinwort Benson, but it was extremely significant for Reggie Maudling. The bank party climbed down the steps from the plane to be greeted by a beaming Evi Hambro, who had long since sewn up merchant banking business in Dubai for Simon Montagu.[17] Dubai was a more sophisticated emirate than Abu Dhabi, if oddly insubstantial and rootless. It was a centre for gold smuggling, with bars ferried across to India and Pakistan in purpose-built dhows; in 1970 the emirate imported 259 tons of gold, little of which remained to gild its palaces.[18] Even before the scale of Dubai's oil wealth was apparent, its Ruler, Sheikh Rashid, had the vision of establishing Dubai as a trading centre, a kind of Hong Kong of the Middle East, and astonishing economic growth was taking place. The Dubai Political Agent, Julian Bullard, described him in 1970 as 'the merchant prince with the happy knack of picking the right horses, briskly disposing of business with a wave of his little pipe in one hand and a lighted match in the other, reading my thoughts far in advance and barking out his instant decisions'.[19] Rashid, like Zayed, was a remarkable man, whose achievement in using oil revenues to promote peace and prosperity has been all too rare.

Rashid had two principal advisers, Easa Al-Gurg and the more buccaneering Mohammed Mahdi Al-Tajir. Tajir was a flamboyant citizen of the world who spent almost all his time in the first-class compartments of aircraft going from meeting to meeting. When Edward Maudling asked him how long he was staying in Britain for Anthony Eden's memorial service in 1977, Tajir smiled and told him that he was around for about four hours. Tajir was an elegant, thoroughly Westernised Bahraini, who started off as a port official but had served since the early 1960s as general adviser to Sheikh Rashid. He shared the trading, modernising vision of the Sheikh and did a great deal to create the present prosperous and harmonious societies that are Dubai and the United Arab Emirates. Rashid, Tajir and Gurg between them managed a rare feat, of moving a country rapidly from Third World to First, from backwater to communications hub, to one of the most cosmopolitan, mixed places on earth – all the while preserving many of the best Arab traditions. There is much to admire in the history of the Gulf states during the period that Maudling was involved. The leaders of the emirates presided over astonishing changes over a very short period, and absorbed a wave of immigration that saw the Gulf Arabs becoming minorities in their own countries. They did so in conditions of social peace, and although the UAE and its constituent states are not democracies in the Western sense there is a reasonable degree of freedom of expression and the rulers have remained accessible to their people through the majlis. The rulers have used their wealth wisely for the most part. Social conditions – health, education, infrastructure, housing – have been transformed for the better. Politically, the rulers of the emirates – particularly Rashid and Zayed – made sacrifices of sovereignty and money in the interests of creating a stable federation. Given the collapse of other attempts to form post-colonial federations, this is a tribute to the far-sightedness of the Arab rulers. In all that follows, it should be recalled that there were achievements to be proud of in the development of Dubai.

However, there was a less attractive side to Middle East business culture at the time, which has persisted to varying degrees since. It was customary to pay commissions on deals to interests associated with the minister and his family. According to Michael Rice, who knew the area well:

Each minister was a kind of fundholder. He had a retinue of dependants, who looked to him for help with sending children to school and university, medical treatment abroad and the like. The minister needed to keep his people happy, or else he wouldn't be a minister for very long. It is Islamic custom that one's first responsibility is to one's family, who represent a large group in the Arab world, and after that to ensure that one's servants or slaves are provided for. Then come more general duties. The system was a long-established fact of life in these societies. In a subsistence economy you need to grab money where you can find it. When the oil came the same practices became part of the national economy.[20]

The importance of such practices has diminished over time in the UAE, but they were central to life in Dubai at the time. Mahdi Tajir was an essential contact for anyone doing large-scale business in Dubai and extracted hefty commissions from nearly every deal in the emirate. He had power to start or stop any project in Dubai, and Rashid deferred to him on many business matters. Tajir started off as a port authority official in a Third World country and became one of the richest men in the world, arguably the world's only billionaire civil servant.[21] 'If you want to do business or get a contract, add 5 to 20 per cent for Mahdi and it will happen. Otherwise, save yourself a trip,' was the advice of one banker about Dubai in the 1980s.[22] Tajir showed the Kleinwort party around on that first stop,[23] and after it he stayed in touch with Maudling and became a friend and business partner. It was a close alliance that was to take Maudling into some very dangerous territory.

Maudling kept a low public profile for the remainder of 1965, concentrating on his business activities and leaving Heath to make the running. It was Heath, in his conference speech and thereafter, who took the main public part in attempting to refute Labour charges that the Conservatives had left the economy in a mess in October 1964. Maudling's most prominent political contribution was to wage a semi-public campaign to persuade the Conservatives to keep an incomes policy, while Powell and Macleod were unconvinced.[24] But Reggie's cause was in retreat and the 1966 Tory manifesto was much cooler about incomes policy than the party had been in 1964.

Reggie slipped quite quickly into a different role in Tory politics, that of wise counsellor. Reggie's secretary of 1966–8, Alex Saville, remembers that 'Edward Heath would call often – not quite daily, but very frequently. He was very dependent on Reggie. He asked him for advice and Reggie was often reassuring Ted, saying not to worry about things.' Enoch Powell used to ring periodically with concerns political and neurotic, as he had in the 1940s; on one memorable occasion he said he couldn't leave his house because 'they' (presumably journalists) had him surrounded. Reggie's reputation for sound judgement was if anything enhanced by his distance from the political fray. Colleagues could rely on him for dispassionate advice, unclouded by partisan emotion or personal calculation, and he could give it fluently and quickly. 'Go and see what Reggie thinks' was part of the process of assessing a potential course of action.[25] Reggie was a solid, stabilising presence in the inner councils of the Conservative Party. In his political life as well as his personal life, he was a bearer of the burdens of others.

When the politicians returned from their holidays in autumn 1965, the political mood had changed. Labour's standing in the opinion polls was consistently strong from then onwards. With a majority of only two at that stage, and several Labour MPs in poor health or unreliable, Wilson was looking for an opportunity to call an election. A key test was the January 1966 Hull North by-election, in a seat Labour had gained in 1964 and where the Tories seemed to be running a strong campaign. Hull North was a Labour triumph, with a considerably increased majority, and after it there was constant speculation about an imminent election. While Maudling was on another trip to the Middle East at the end of February 1966, news came through that Harold Wilson had decided to call an election for 31 March.

The 1966 election was a disappointing business for Maudling. He was the most prominent Conservative speaker after Heath, although the 1966 campaign was a presidential affair in which more than half the party's media coverage went to the leader.[26] The original plan of campaign had been for Heath to take the high road and his lieutenants, Maudling and Macleod, to launch most of the attacks on Harold Wilson, but Maudling failed to follow the plan: 'Reggie is just not good at that sort of thing,' lamented Heath.[27] Maudling would have also preferred to do more television and less touring, but the overall campaign plan sent him around the country. He did not make much effort to ensure publicity for his speeches, as he disliked having to do handouts for local and travelling journalists[28] because he preferred to extemporise on the basis of a few scribbled notes. Whether it was Newcastle on 15 March, or Great Yarmouth on 25 March, he gave variations on one of two stump speeches, concerning either economic policy or the European Common Market.

The national contest in 1966 lacked drama, and suffered particularly in comparison with the exciting election of 1964. A Labour victory was expected throughout the campaign, there were no notable blunders by either side and no extraneous international events that disrupted the campaign. In Barnet, the campaign was also thoroughly routine. Even with Labour riding high nationally, it was still the longest of long shots and Edward Heath's Bexley seat looked a more likely bet for a humiliating surprise for the Tories. Reggie, trusting his agent and the organisation once again, cruised through on automatic. The Barnet result was pretty much in line with the national average. Other than his defeat at Heston in 1945, it was the smallest majority in Maudling's political career. However, Reggie's own victory was never really in doubt, and neither was the national result. Wilson had timed the 1966 election to perfection and improved Labour's majority to ninety-seven seats.

Electorate		65,487		
Turnout			80.5	
Reginald Maudling	Conservative	24,833	47.1	−0.7
Geoffrey Hickman	Labour	19,347	36.7	+4.8
Hugh Tinker	Liberal	8,539	16.2	−2.8
Conservative majority		5,486	10.4	

Reggie did the rounds of the television studios on the Friday to make the best of the Conservatives' severe defeat, bemoaning the fact that he had to miss a Shipping Industrial Holdings board meeting: 'they do such a jolly good lunch!' After the election Reggie was even more at a loose end, dissatisfied and looking for distraction, than he had been after July 1965. The Tories were in for a long haul of opposition, while previously they had hoped for a rapid restoration. Political life presented a vista of boredom and frustration. One pleasant possibility that presented itself in 1966 came from Jim Callaghan, who sounded Reggie out about whether he wanted to become Governor of the Bank of England.[29] It would have been a sensible proposition in many ways, although Reggie's unorthodox views about the power of the City and his own financial policy would have made him a highly controversial choice. Cromer for one would have been apoplectic. Unfortunately for Reggie, he did not pursue the governorship, but instead decided to increase his business activities. The costs of running Chester Square, Beryl and the family as a whole were enormous. While up to this point he had been expert in staying just the right side of the line in his financial affairs, finding loopholes rather than breaking the rules, Maudling's general weakening of will and erosion of boundaries was soon to have disastrous consequences for his business life.

Not long after the election a Labour MP called Albert Roberts approached Maudling in the House of Commons and mentioned a successful architect and builder called John Poulson, who had dealings in Roberts's Normanton constituency, who wanted to talk to him. Poulson, added Roberts, had been a close colleague of the recently deceased National Liberal MP for Holland-with-Boston, Sir Herbert Butcher, who had resigned from government office in the early 1950s to pursue wealth and happiness in business. Maudling murmured that he would indeed be prepared to meet Poulson, remembering the architect from the 1961 National Liberal dinner, and Roberts reported back this approval. On 10 June Poulson wrote to Maudling, offering a couple of dates when he would be at his London base in the Dorchester Hotel and inviting Reggie for lunch. Reggie accepted, thinking that the worst that could come of the meeting would be a decent free lunch at the Dorchester. The deal was done on 4 July, Poulson's mind fogged by sleeping pills and Maudling drinking steadily; Maudling would accept a position as chairman of Construction Promotion (CP), one of Poulson's firms, provided that it was an export-only company.[30]

Anthony Eden visits Reggie's campaign headquarters in Barnet, 1950. Arthur
Fawcett stands to the right of Maudling. *(Collection of Trudi Fawcett Kotrosa)*

Reggie as a keen young junior minister, 1952 *(PA Photographs)*

A devoted couple: Beryl and Reginald Maudling, *c.* 1950. *(Collection of Trudi Fawcett Kotrosa)*

The Maudling family, 1959. *From left to right*: Caroline, Reggie, William, Beryl, Martin (rear), Edward (front). *(Collection of Trudi Fawcett Kotrosa)*

Right: Beryl and Reggie leaving their home at Chester Street, April 1963. *(Associated Press)*

Below: Reggie playing monopoly with William and Edward before the 1964 Budget. *(PA Photographs)*

Maudling and Macleod, 1961: friends, rivals and liberators of the colonies. *(Associated Press)*

Reggie during the 1963 leadership contest, pensive amid the crowds. *(Associated Press)*

Reggie – and sterling – under strain, 1964. *(Associated Press)*

Reggie in ebullient mood at a Conservative press conference, on the eve of the election he nearly won for them as Chancellor, 1964. *(Associated Press)*

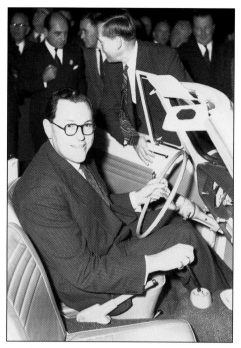

Reggie promoting the British motor industry as President of the Board of Trade, 1960. *(Associated Press)*

Martin and Caroline Maudling, 1964: the family added some youth and glamour to Downing Street. *(Associated Press)*

Sheikh Zayed of Abu Dhabi on a visit to London in the late 1960s. *(Associated Press)*

Reggie wine tasting at the Savoy, 1971. *(Associated Press)*

Beryl hits the jackpot, 1967. *(Associated Press)*

Bewildered in Belfast, shortly before he denounced Northern Ireland as 'a bloody awful country', 1970. *(Hulton Getty)*

John Garlick Llewellyn Poulson – architect of Maudling's downfall. *(Hulton Getty)*

Maudling, uncomfortable as Thatcher's Shadow Foreign Secretary, 1975. *(Associated Press)*

Beryl and Reggie, together through all adversity, 1974 *(PA Photographs)*

Maudling and Poulson were an incongruous couple. The architect took pride in his self-image as a bluntly spoken Yorkshireman and had a blustering, hectoring manner about him that could alienate potential allies. Poulson was a conspicuously pious Methodist and – financial affairs aside – was a strict, narrow-minded moralist. Maudling was an increasingly hedonistic man of the world. What united them, and some of Poulson's other allies, was a broad, fuzzy vision of big ideas and a certain cynicism about how one achieved them. Poulson, for all his appearance of practical no-nonsense business sense, was a world-class dreamer whose finest buildings were the castles in the air he conjured into virtual existence. Dr Ken Williams, like Maudling a much more sophisticated and intelligent man than Poulson, felt that Poulson was 'charismatic in an indefinable way. He had ability and solutions to important problems. I became close to Poulson and I enjoyed his company, despite him being a difficult bastard at times.'[31] T. Dan Smith, the Labour ex-leader of Newcastle council and Poulson's main local government contact in Britain, also had a strange charisma, a sense of vision and purpose about him that was never quite reflected in reality.[32] Like an aurora, the vision of Poulson, Williams and Smith lit up the sky but had an elusive, insubstantial quality that was difficult to pin down, and impossible to describe adequately to someone who had not seen it.

Poulson argued that he was on to an important new technique that could make a difference and provide an attractive commercial model. By grouping architectural, engineering and equipment expertise in his new company, International Technical and Constructional Services (ITCS), Poulson was able to offer integrated, all-encompassing designs for new buildings, particularly hospitals. His new venture was a genuinely exciting idea, at least on paper. Poulson himself seemed a dynamic force who had built up one of the largest architectural practices in Europe from his base in Yorkshire. The proposition Poulson put to Maudling in June 1966 seemed to have considerable merit. Construction Promotion and ITCS, which Poulson was in the process of establishing, existed for the purpose of furthering Poulson's business abroad. Contracts they secured would generate exports, of professional architectural services, civil engineering and building work, and if the businesses were successful they could contribute to improving Britain's balance of payments. Maudling had always been keen on promoting exports, and his time at the Board of Trade had been largely spent in this cause. It was not unreasonable for him to believe that with Poulson, as with Kleinwort Benson, his private interests were not inconsistent with the interests of the economy. His motives were not entirely selfish and greedy and his defensive bluster when Poulson was exposed, about doing something for the balance of payments, was not dishonest. Poulson also talked a very good game of doing something good in the world, providing modern hospitals to countries where there was a desperate need for good health care. Maudling was receptive to this appeal; he had after all tried to convince a sceptical Tory conference in 1963 that overseas development was one of the great purposes of the age. In joining Poulson, Maudling was no more blameworthy than Jim Callaghan or Jimmy Carter whose genuine concerns for Third World issues led them into association with the Bank of Credit and Commerce International, which had put up a façade of idealism to disguise the truth of its corruption.

There is, therefore, a strong case to be made in Maudling's defence for linking up with Poulson. Reggie himself tended to spoil it by overdoing it. He told a House of Commons inquiry in 1977: 'When he approached me I took a bank reference from his bankers. I took a reference from a leading credit advisory organisation. I spoke to several Government Departments. I spoke to several very prominent businessmen who worked with him. Not one of them produced any criticism of him at all.'[33] Maudling's checks were a lot less methodical than he claimed. He may well have spoken to 'government departments' in the shape of his former Treasury Principal Private Secretary, Ian Bancroft, whom he did consult about his business appointments,[34] and conceivably top people at the Board of Trade. The Ministry of Transport had recent dealings with Poulson, and could have told him that his design for a flyover in Barking had won a prize but needed some modifications before it was usable.[35] As various trials in 1972–5 proved, there was no shortage of people in Whitehall willing to give Poulson a positive reference for entirely personal reasons. Quite what Maudling could have achieved with these enquiries, beyond establishing that Poulson was indeed a reasonably successful and (at least in 1966) solvent contractor, is doubtful. Maudling's enquiries among business contacts were perfunctory at best, assuming they took place at all. Neither Sandy Glen nor Cyril Kleinwort was approached for their opinion, much to their puzzlement: 'Reggie never asked me,' complained Kleinwort.[36]

Above all, Reggie neglected to ask the Royal Institute of British Architects (RIBA), who would have certainly raised questions about Poulson's conduct. Poulson was only a licentiate rather than a fully qualified architect and his abilities were not highly regarded by his peers: one commented that 'Poulson couldn't design a brick shithouse'. The success of his practice depended on his employment of several genuinely talented and honest architects, to whom he gave generous rates of pay in order that they would put up with his rudeness and bullying in the office. The professional rules then in force prohibited architects from controlling building and civil engineering companies, but this is precisely what Poulson was doing through the front companies to which he recruited Maudling. The shareholding was usually in the name of Poulson's wife, and Poulson not only attended and organised all their board meetings but also actively directed the companies' affairs. It was these relationships that led RIBA, in a classic case of shutting the stable door after the horse had bolted, to disbar Poulson once he had gone bankrupt in 1972.[37] At that time, the *Architect's Journal* commented that 'If Maudling has been reported correctly, he has suggested that the main function of ITCS was to tout for Poulson. If so, the position is extraordinary. The former Home Secretary says that he was in charge of a company which sold professional services; yet had the nature of his alleged activities been known, Poulson would probably have lost his professional status.'[38] Maudling was, reported Poulson, 'amused' to note that press coverage of the foundation of ITCS did not make any connection with Poulson.[39] Like tax avoidance, Maudling's work for companies set up on this basis was not illegal, or even particularly unethical, but it did, of itself, involve a departure from the strictest standards of honesty.

Poulson, as well as flagrantly breaching professional standards, was also, if not a total stranger to legal, financial and moral principles then a man who recognised them only in passing from the other side of the street. By 1966 he, with the cooperation of T. Dan Smith and his network of cronies, had won contracts throughout the public sector in Britain by means that had become unabashedly corrupt.[40] Maudling could join Poulson on the high road of exports, hospitals and vision, but the real question about his relationship with Poulson was how far he travelled along the low road of 'consultants', 'commission', corruption and bribery. Reggie's version, which he insisted on as late as the Commons inquiry in 1977, was that of the three Poulson companies in which he had positions, 'I am not aware of any irregularities ever taking place in any of them'.[41] He claimed that the first time he had heard of any irregularities at all was in the newspaper coverage of Poulson's bankruptcy hearings in 1972. The general consensus among parliamentarians about Maudling's business involvements was that he displayed bad judgement in being taken in by crooks like Poulson. If pushed, his colleagues would admit that he was greedy for cash and was less than diligent about checking up where it came from. Journalists who investigated him in the 1970s believed that he had behaved corruptly in accepting money through devious channels for acting unethically on Poulson's behalf. The bankruptcy investigators came to believe that the truth was even worse – that he was deeply implicated in corruption and possibly major fraud at Poulson's expense rather than for his benefit.

Poulson, at the time he met Maudling, was an accomplished manipulator. He had an uncanny knack of identifying and working on people's weak points, of seeing a man's dream and turning it into a nightmare. He understood the desire of greedy small-time Labour councillors to go on 'fact-finding visits' to warm countries, and the pretensions of corrupt civil servant George Pottinger to be a man of culture and sophistication. Reginald Maudling, when Poulson approached him, had his own weak points. These were his wounded pride, his need for money, his adoration of Beryl and his responsibility for his family. Poulson approached him at a particularly worrying time in his life, when Martin had just come down from Oxford without a degree to show for his time there and without much by way of a job in prospect, and when the Adeline Genée Theatre had lurched into yet another crisis. Builders were asking, increasingly urgently, to see their fees for the job which had gone grossly over budget. Reggie needed indirect, non-taxed benefits to help him solve these family problems, and maintain Chester Square in the appropriate style, and Poulson had a flexible attitude to arranging these. The architect provided an immediate solution to the Martin problem. At Reggie's request, Martin was taken on to the board of Poulson's Open System Building (OSB) company, despite a lack of any prior business management experience, and by April 1967 had been paid £1,000 in directors' fees.[42] Martin, as well as Reggie, was drawn deeper and deeper into Poulson's enterprises over the next few years, becoming an employee as well as a director of OSB and ITCS.

The Adeline Genée problem was also brought under control thanks to Poulson. In October 1966 he signed a covenant to the effect that he would give £5,000 (£1 in 1967 is worth approximately £10 now, hence a contemporary equivalent would be £50,000) a year for seven years to the Trust that was overseeing the construction and maintenance of the theatre. This was an astronomical commitment for an already overstretched enterprise, and because of the law on covenants was not subject to Maudling's continuing participation in the Poulson organisation – Poulson was obliged to pay regardless. Poulson, for all his penny-pinching on minor matters, was incompetent at managing large sums of money and protecting his own interests, and the 1966 covenant was an example of this weakness. Poulson seems to have meant to give the theatre £5,000 gross per year, but in the event the payments were made net – which meant that Poulson had to convey a further £3,510 through the tax system. It was also an early example of the fog that shrouds what exactly was going on between Maudling and Poulson. The £5,000 sum was identical to the previous Construction Promotion chairman Sir Herbert Butcher's salary and the sum initially discussed for his own salary, but was replaced by a rather smaller £500 per year when Maudling took over at CP. According to Poulson, the £5,000 covenant was in lieu of Maudling's salary but Maudling himself denied this; the tax treatment of the Genée payments was a particularly involved matter and caused no end of trouble later, but for the moment the theatre problem was solved – although the Trust was told not to publicise the donation.[43] The Trust could pay off some bills and prepare for a grand opening, and start to think about what would appear on its huge purpose-built ballet stage.

This was what Poulson offered Maudling. On Poulson's side, Maudling's reputation was an advantage in opening doors. According to Poulson, much later, 'I had been to various parts of the world and I chose Mr Maudling after enquiring from a number of leading men in these various parts who they respected most and it was him.'[44] This came as a surprise to Poulson, who had expected his contacts to name Alec Douglas-Home, but Reggie's time as Chancellor had clearly won him widespread admiration for his international financial knowledge and his charm. With the recruitment of Maudling, the

Pontefract architect had levered himself up into another league of international business activity. It was a boost to Poulson's already substantial ego. Poulson was keenly interested in politics, and sponsored the remnant of the National Liberal Party as a vehicle for meeting senior Conservative politicians. Now he was forming a close business relationship with the deputy leader of the party, an impressive connection by any standards.

Poulson would frequently use Maudling's name to impress or intimidate employees and business associates. It helped in his game of one-upmanship with Harry Vincent of the Bovis construction company, with whom Poulson had once had a close association. That alliance had ended, as Poulson's alliances often did, in acrimony generated in large part by Poulson's rudeness. Bovis was the family firm of former Cabinet Minister Keith Joseph, and this rankled with Poulson when Vincent mentioned it. Now Poulson had an answer. 'Let it be known that Poulson and Maudling are great friends and get on well together and go on several trips abroad, the next to Teheran,' Poulson instructed an employee due to have contacts with Bovis in October 1966.[45]

The trips abroad increased in number with the establishment of ITCS. In theory, it was the most elaborated form of Poulson's package-deal concept of architectural services, and it might have been a good idea under other circumstances. ITCS would serve as an umbrella organisation for large-scale construction projects, particularly of hospitals. The Poulson practice would design the buildings, in cooperation with the scientific expertise of the Vickers Medical organisation under Kenneth Williams. Williams was a brilliant, wayward man, multiply qualified as a scientific and medical doctor, with a restless intellect that pondered the social effects of technology and saw in Poulson's propositions a means of using professional and technological progress to bring social benefits.[46] Poulson and Williams believed, with some reason, that the divide between architecture, civil engineering and technical equipping was obsolete and inefficient. Maudling's role in the operation was to be a public ambassador for the firm and the concept, and in the background was his directorship of Kleinwort Benson, which, or so the plan went, would help provide finance for major capital projects. The package deal concept could therefore be expanded even further to include arranging loans to cover the construction works.

This being a Poulson operation, the high ideals were to be impeded at every step by incompetence and corruption and never amounted to much in reality. The ITCS concept in practice was much less appealing than in theory. It was more expensive for the client, and Mr Justice Waller, the intelligent and thoughtful judge at Poulson's trial in 1973–4, after a long time with the evidence, found the role and purpose of ITCS very difficult to understand. There was something shadowy and insubstantial about the company from the very beginning. Almost from the start, it was later alleged, the company was hopelessly insolvent[47] and during its short life it mutated into something quite different from its original intention, be that as a front for Poulson or a vehicle for something more idealistic. The first meeting of the ITCS board was farcical, which was a fair indication of how the company would continue to operate. Ken Williams recalls:

> I met Maudling at the first board meeting of ITCS. It was not an auspicious start. The meeting was in the morning and Reggie may have had a drink. When we were introduced Reggie groaned 'Not another fucking bloody scientist!' A little later on I started calling him Reggie on the grounds that we were on first name terms after that introduction.[48]

Poulson presented a wonderful series of projects that were in the pipeline: schools, ports, airports, seaside resorts from Mexico to Lebanon, including a package deal, if Poulson could be taken at face value, to build virtually an entire infrastructure for Libya. Hardly any of this ever got further than Poulson's ever-productive drawing board. Other failures of the first board meetings of ITCS were that they never actually got round to deciding how directors should be paid, nor to working out what relationship the company had with the other parts of the Poulson empire. At first it was not important – ITCS, OSB, CP, J.G.L. Poulson, and the evocatively named Ropergate which Poulson and Sir Herbert Butcher had incorporated as a service company – it was all 'Poulson'. According to the trustee's investigations after Poulson went bankrupt: 'we know that practically all the cost of ITCS was met out of the Ropergate account – very large sums . . . All over the world, in Beirut, in Mexico, in Nigeria and Peru, it is always out of the Ropergate bank that the money comes.'[49] There was nothing on paper, or at least nothing that survived Poulson's crash, that specified the financial arrangements governing ITCS. In the end, this would have dire implications for Poulson, but these accountancy questions seemed mere quibbles at the start of the ITCS adventure.

After the foundation of ITCS, CP was confined to Spain and Portugal and their African colonies, while the new company took on the rest of the world. The status of existing overseas projects negotiated by Poulson was another matter left vague when ITCS was founded. Notable among these overseas projects was Malta. Construction Promotion had already made progress in Malta, independent since 1964 under the process Maudling had started as Colonial Secretary and Duncan Sandys had seen through to completion. Malta's economic dependence on the naval shipyards had produced huge problems in the negotiations, as it could be argued with justice that 'no nation is truly independent as long as its economy remains dependent on the military expenditure of another country'.[50] The solution was a financial agreement with Britain in which the rundown of the docks would be cushioned by development aid to give the place modern civilian infrastructure and an economy that was no longer dependent on the British navy. The sum of £50 million would be available over the next ten years. Quite what would be done with the money was a divisive issue within Malta. The principal argument was over the outlying island of Gozo, whose population only amounted to 30,000 and who had long felt neglected by mainlanders. Public services on the island were poor and its hospital was particularly primitive. Shortly before the first post-independence elections in March 1966, the Nationalist Party government reversed its previous policy of concentrating development on the mainland and announced that Gozo would get a new hospital. The Gozo hospital therefore started out as an electoral bribe, a Maltese version of the Humber Bridge that Harold Wilson was using at the same time to woo the electors of Hull. The decision did the trick and the party returned to power, with its traditionally strong support in Gozo holding firm. The election out of the way, the Maltese now had to build the hospital.

Designing and building the Gozo hospital was too big a job for indigenous Maltese firms, and the process had to be put out to foreign contracts. Initially, the Maltese tried to do it properly and asked RIBA and the British Crown Agents for advice on suitable contractors to conduct a study. Lists came back, from which the name J.G.L. Poulson was absent. This was not much of a surprise, as Poulson had not been known for his overseas work, but the architect's CP business partner Leslie Pollard had drawn the possibilities of the island to his attention and Poulson did not give up easily. He recruited Labour MP Albert Roberts, who had already been working for him in Spain and Portugal, to bang the drum in Whitehall and press Poulson's claim with the Maltese Minister of Public Works, Carmelo Caruana. Meanwhile, he had also teamed up with Maltese building supplies contractor John Abela, who was promoting his interests on the island. None of this seemed to be doing much good, but in October 1966 Carmelo Caruana changed his mind and Poulson was suddenly being considered.

For Poulson, Caruana's decision was the first fruits of the association with Maudling, who had on Poulson's instructions written several letters in October 1966 as soon as the Genée covenant was arranged.[51] Abela reported to Poulson on the reaction to the Maudling letters: 'I can assure you that the impression of his signature has greatly influenced one and all.' Maudling was taken very seriously in Malta, and the prospect was there of him returning to high office at some time in the future. Caruana ordered the Maltese High Commission in London to look into Poulson. Although the reply was not entirely encouraging, Poulson was certainly now in the game, and in November Poulson arranged with John Abela that £5,000 should be paid over to the Nationalist Party's Press Fund as a sweetener.[52]

Poulson was using pressure to get the Gozo contract through as many channels as he could, and the deployment of Maudling was one part of this process – as was Abela's disbursement of cash in Malta. The Gozo operation was a coordinated pressure campaign, but it was Poulson who was responsible for the overall plan rather than Maudling. Although some Scotland Yard detectives in 1973–5 believed that they could tie Maudling to the Abela bribe, counsel for the Director of Public Prosecutions dismissed this possibility. Poulson's relationship with Abela had hidden depths; Abela hoped to gain contracts for his own business once the main contract went through, and both Poulson and Caruana were hoping for kickbacks from this operation. Ken Williams, who arranged the £5,000 payment via Vickers Medical, disputes that it was a bribe:

> Abela worked extraordinarily hard for us, I mean the number of trips he made to London and we didn't pay any of that, and he came once and said, 'look, my expenses are getting out of hand, my cash flow's going pretty negative.' . . . So we paid him £5,000 commission in advance. That's all it was. Now where it went to, we didn't want to know.[53]

When Williams was prosecuted over this in the early 1980s, the case collapsed on the first day; Williams also claims that some of the documents in the case were forged. A case against Abela in Malta in 1975 only reached the committal stage and was shelved – he was neither cleared nor found guilty. But the Abela payment adds to the impression that the Gozo project was not a particularly admirable enterprise.

Contracts for such large projects are agreed in many separate stages – from agreement in principle to a detailed contract, to receiving payment for work done can be a long road. The Poulson team, including Maudling, needed to remain on the case, consolidating and pushing, for practically the next two years. Poulson travelled to Malta in November 1966, and although he came back without a detailed contract, he was optimistic enough to order his architects to start design work for the project. Another visit followed in January 1967, which was notable in that it attracted some local media attention, with the *Times of Malta* interviewing Maudling about business and political matters. He made it clear that Gozo hospital was not the end of the ambitions of ITCS in Malta, and that he was hoping for civil engineering contracts for harbour and industrial developments.[54] The visit was a success, Poulson writing to Maudling when they returned that it was 'a wonderful visit to Malta. I am certain we have cemented our position there and acquired a good deal more work. It was good of you to spare the time to go with me and make such an excellent contribution.'[55] But it was far from the end of the tangled tale of the Gozo contract, as the scale of the enterprise was such that the Maltese government had to seek aid for it from the British Overseas Development ministry, and it therefore acquired a British official dimension.

During late 1966 and early 1967, the same period as the bid for the Gozo contract, British government relations with Malta were under review. The Labour government was looking for economies in overseas military expenditure, which would help both the budget and the balance of payments, and the Malta commitment was vulnerable. But given that British defence spending was such a large part of the Maltese economy, it was feared that the blow from any cuts would prove disastrous unless more aid was offered to cushion the impact on the island. Malta also had a hold on the emotions of some on the Tory right, such as Freddie Bennett and Patrick Wall, who admired its gallantry during the Second World War and felt that Britain owed Malta a debt of gratitude.

On 2 February 1967 there was a House of Commons debate about Malta, in which Reggie spoke as the leading Conservative spokesman on Commonwealth affairs and overseas development. He was in an unusually cross mood, lashing the minister's speech in the debate as 'totally and pathetically inadequate. She demonstrated that the Government have no understanding whatever of the problems facing the people of Malta, the feelings of the people of Malta, and the real dangers for our national conscience that arise from the situation.' From another MP this might have been dismissed as synthetic indignation, but Maudling was not a ranter by nature and MPs who spoke after him, such as Tom Driberg and Denis Healey, the Defence Secretary, commented on his militant tone. As the speech went on, he calmed down a bit but he was highly critical of the government for breach of faith with Malta and over the economic consequences of military cuts.[56] When Reggie sat down at the end of this apparently routine parliamentary engagement, he could hardly have imagined that it would end up being one of the most famous, and certainly the most notorious, of all the speeches he ever made.

Chapter 17

DEATH OF AN IDEALIST,[1] 1967

The three-year period from the founding of ITCS until early 1970 is the most convoluted, obscure yet important period of Reggie's life. He was at once the deputy leader of the opposition in Britain, a full-time executive director of a major merchant bank, intimately involved in the workings of ITCS doing business across the world, a non-executive director of a large number of other firms, Poulson and non-Poulson alike, financial adviser to an Arab Ruler, and involved with Mahdi Tajir in complex machinations in the Middle East. He was head of a large, demanding family who were going through their own problems and perplexities at the time. Each of these roles blurred into the others. His business and political lives complemented and interfered with each other. His family and business lives became tragically entwined. His activities in the Persian Gulf came under a dizzying number of headings. Throughout it all, Reggie carried it off with the appearance of nonchalant goodwill, but under the surface the strain was telling; he was drinking too much and he was getting things increasingly wrong. During this time out of office he lost his ethical moorings, and drifted far out into corruption.

Malta was quite a gentle introduction to misconduct, but corruption is an insidious business; people rarely plunge in at the deep end. Maudling's 2 February 1967 speech in Parliament transgressed at the margins rather than at its core; it was primarily concerned with defence policy although it did stray into the economic implications of the rundown of the British military presence, arguing that it would 'impose on Malta sacrifices greater than we can justifiably ask the Maltese to bear', and drawing particular attention to the unacceptably high levels of unemployment that would result. It made the case for more aid by implication rather than directly, and the angry beginning of the speech was at the prospect of the withdrawal of existing aid.[2] More questionable was his intervention on 30 January, in which he claimed 'on this side of the House we feel very great concern about the damage to the economy of Malta and, in particular, about the feelings of the Maltese that they have been let down by the British government'.[3] The feelings of the Maltese, and the state of the island's economy, were of more interest to some Tory MPs than others.

To Maudling's critics in the 1970s, his actions over Malta were clear evidence of corrupt conduct. According to Ray Fitzwalter, who first broke the Poulson story: 'There were at least five specific occasions on which there was a provable sequence of events showing that he was guilty. He was jointly engaged in the projects with Poulson. Poulson asks him to do underhand things to further the cause. Maudling does it. The effect follows. Then there is reward and congratulation flowing from Poulson to Maudling. The evidence was all there. It passed the tests for corruption of being a pecuniary interest, and being underhand.'[4] The House of Commons Select Committee in 1977 endorsed much of this analysis but drew back from alleging corruption, instead commenting on the 'close chronological interlocking of actions by Mr Poulson on behalf of the Theatre Trust and actions by Mr Maudling in the House and contacts with the Maltese Government and senior British officials which were to the benefit of Mr Poulson'. Even under the rather vague rules of parliamentary conduct prevailing in 1967, this was below the standards expected.

In defending himself, Reggie attempted to argue that the debate had no relation to the Gozo hospital project, and recruited Lord Maybray-King, who had been Speaker in 1967, to support him. Maybray-King wrote to Maudling in 1975 that as far as he was concerned it was a defence debate and that he was in the clear; the House of Commons Select Committee disagreed with this interpretation and said so. The evidence that the debate was relevant to British aid to Malta is conclusive. Judith Hart, the Minister of State for Commonwealth Affairs who opened the debate, spent about a third of her speech talking about aid to Malta, which she pointed out was running at £18 per head compared to 1s 4d to India, and dealt head-on with the relationship between the defence policy changes and aid:

> Nevertheless, it had been suggested that to compensate for the run-down we should offer an even higher level of development aid, particularly during the next two years. This may seem an obviously attractive solution, but let us be clear. On the one hand, at present we could give further aid to Malta only by depriving some other nation. That is one factor. The other is that the Malta Government have themselves said that they could not absorb further financial aid quickly enough to counteract the effects of the run-down.[5]

Although Maudling did not mention hospitals, and was not particularly concentrating on aid questions, his attack on Hart was part of an effort to force the government to reconsider its policy towards Malta, and do so in a way that would be more generous to the island – and therefore benefit contractors for infrastructure projects. Maudling's emotional pitch was no doubt raised by his recent visit to Malta, and his indignation was probably mostly genuine. While he felt that he could argue his case on Malta on sound public policy grounds, the information that he was hoping to win contracts such as the Gozo hospital would have been relevant to assessing his argument. There was a personal interest it would have been better to declare.

Overlapping with the Malta issue was the unsteady progress of the prime beneficiary of the Poulson connection, the Adeline Genée Theatre. At the end of January 1967, just before the Malta visit, the theatre was ready to open its doors at last. It did so in some style, with a gala opening performance attended by Adeline Genée herself, who spoke briefly, Princess Margaret and Lord Snowdon, and of course the Maudlings. Guests saw Margot Fonteyn dance on the enormous, purpose-built ballet stage in the 330-seat theatre on the rural fringe of East Grinstead. The 'Little Glyndebourne for Ballet' had become a reality after all the cost overruns and building hiccups.[6] However, after the glorious opening night the theatre was once again in financial trouble. It was an expensive concern to keep going – over £1,000 a week according to Michael Rice, who against his better judgement had been brought in to chair the theatre's board.[7] The problem was that it was structurally almost incapable of making enough money to pay its way. It had to charge ticket prices similar to London's West End theatres, despite its inconvenient location, and be virtually full (despite the avant-garde nature of its early productions and the competition of other theatres in Sussex and Surrey). Being financially unviable is not necessarily a fatal flaw in arts projects, as long as public subsidy can be arranged, but despite the Genée Theatre's influential supporters this proved hard to find. The Arts Council turned down a grant proposal in 1966, despite efforts to pull strings through Lord Goodman and Edward Boyle, and was similarly reluctant when asked again in March 1967.

Even though the problems of operating the theatre were severe, the Poulson covenant had enabled the Adeline Genée Trust to cover the debts run up during construction, or so everyone thought initially. The best solution for the Trust was to take out a bank loan and pay off the creditors on the strength of the future income stream from the covenant, but the bank did not accept a covenant made out by Poulson's Construction Promotion company as adequate security, and insisted that the covenant be drawn on Poulson's Ropergate firm and personally guaranteed by the architect. While the covenant was rearranged, Maudling personally guaranteed a £20,000 loan from Kleinwort Benson to the Trust in order to clear the construction bills, so if somehow the Poulson arrangement collapsed he was in a very disadvantageous position. Maudling was sure that this would not happen, but the sooner Poulson arranged a new covenant that would release Maudling from the loan guarantee the better. In the meantime, Beryl had appealed to Lord Goodman for Arts Council funds to plug some of the gap:

We have collected, in cash and covenants, practically the whole cost of building the theatre, but as the covenanted money is not all immediately available, we are forced to borrow on the security of the covenants. If it were possible for the Arts Council to grant us £10,000 towards the cost of the building, this would release money from the Trust Fund which we could use to help us get on our feet with the Productions side.[8]

Goodman was puzzled, because at a meeting the previous day Beryl had not asked for anything towards the building costs – the suggestion sounds like a scheme of Reggie's to relieve the financial pressure. Goodman was having none of it, and told Beryl to try harder to persuade the local authorities in Surrey and Sussex to stump up grant support.[9] Few seemed willing to do so, but the search for support for its running costs had effects. The concept of the Theatre was having to change – from being a Glyndebourne for ballet, located in East Grinstead and not for East Grinstead, it was now apparently intended to develop it as a local arts centre serving, among other places, 'the big industrial development of Crawley New Town'.[10] There was no real alternative to Poulson on the horizon.

Maudling sent a revised covenant form to Poulson in February 1967, shortly after they returned from the Malta visit, but the new arrangement was not sealed until July. Much was made when the matter became public of a reference to a business trip to Liberia in the letter enclosing the revised covenant, suggesting that this meant that Maudling's presence in Liberia was conditional on the covenant being arranged before they flew out. However, Maudling's 1973 explanation that this was a matter of convenience – that while in Liberia they would not be able to do much about it, and that it was best to get the paperwork done quickly – is convincing.[11]

Other aspects of Maudling's version of the origins of the covenant are less acceptable. He claimed to the 1973 bankruptcy hearing that it had been arranged prior to his joining ITCS, which was true as far as it went, but neglected to mention that ITCS did not exist as such in October 1966 and the covenant was concurrent with his joining Construction Promotion. Poulson's secretary, who dealt with the February 1967 letter enclosing the new covenant form, noted concerning the Adeline Genée payment 'This is really for Mr Maudling'.[12] The rewritten covenant meant that Poulson was liable for another year's payments. The covenant, despite Maudling's later protestations, does look entirely as if it was part of an agreement to secure his services for Poulson companies. That the second covenant relieved Maudling of the worry of the loan guarantee is incidental. Given that pleasing Beryl was a large part of the motivation for Reggie's income-generating activities at the time, the theatre covenant was a clever and tax-efficient way to accomplish this. That it was actually against company law because Ropergate's objectives did not cover charitable donations to unrelated companies did not emerge until later.[13] When the transaction became public in 1972 Maudling was indignant, and referred repeatedly to it as support for a charity. This is legally what it was, but a stage for putting on pantomimes

located some way outside the town centre of East Grinstead is not exactly on
a par with Oxfam. While it did exist to promote the arts, it was hardly the
most deserving or efficient charity even in that sector. It could not attract
support from the Arts Council or local authorities, or paying audiences, in
sufficient measure to be viable, and its achievements for the general good of
society were limited.

Poulson was delighted that Maudling had thrown himself so powerfully
into the Malta lobbying operation in late 1966 and early 1967 and decided
that money was no object when it came to securing his services. Poulson was
always generous with his employees, paying above the normal rates in an
effort to secure their loyalty, and Maudling was no different in principle. It
was a considerable coup for the Yorkshire architect to have such a prominent
figure on his side, not just a name on headed notepaper but acting
energetically on his behalf; it fed his vanity and offered the opportunity of
hitting the really big time as an industrialist. Poulson turned the taps on as
hard as he could for Maudling during 1967, with the Adeline Genée
covenant, employment of Martin, free transfers of shares to the Maudling
children,[14] and directors' fees, which for ITCS were paid at £9,500 per
annum. Including income tax recoveries for the payments to the Trust,
Poulson's accountant Vivian Baker totalled the 1967–8 cost to Poulson of
employing Reginald Maudling as £25,531 17s 6d – and this did not include
costs relating to Martin. In a letter to Poulson after this account was
presented, Reggie wrote:

My dear John,
    The account Baker sent me set out very graphically the total cost to you
of the Maudling family and their interests. It certainly is colossal. I only
hope you think it is worth while; never hesitate to tell me if you have
doubts.
    Take care of yourself: you've been going at a hell of a pace for a long
time. When do you get a holiday?
    Reginald Maudling.
    No reply please.[15]

For most of 1967 Maudling, as far as he was concerned, was worth his
'colossal' cost, although doubts started to creep in later in the year. During
much of 1967 there was a delicate game between Maudling and Poulson
about how far each of them could go, and how far each of them could let the
other man see them go. Poulson was certainly keeping some of his activities
from Maudling, particularly the full extent of his relationship with T. Dan
Smith and corruption in local government ('The [OSB] directors are not
aware of our financial arrangements, of course – only me – and there are
other things they are not aware of'[16]), and also some questionable foreign
exchange transactions. Poulson knew that there was a limit to what

Maudling would be prepared to connive at, although he did try to push the boundaries back as time went on. A particular example of this came in February 1967, when his secretary wrote to Maudling that:

> A personal friend of Mr Poulson's – a Mr. A.J. Merritt, Principal Regional Officer at the Ministry of Health, Leeds – who has been extremely helpful to the firm in that capacity, is retiring at the end of this year and wishes to make a sea voyage in January/February 1968. He has already written requesting information and received the enclosed letter. Mr Poulson wonders if your travel agent would be able to do anything to assist in this connection.[17]

Maudling did as Poulson asked and booked a cruise, through Clarkson's travel agents, for the civil servant, the cost of which was then met by the Poulson organisation and written off against tax as a business expense. It is hard to imagine what Maudling thought he was doing. Did Poulson not have his own travel agents? The truth was that he did, but both of them had become so exasperated with his failure to pay his bills that they had refused to offer him further account facilities. Why should the deputy leader of the Conservative Party concern himself with such matters as booking a holiday for a regional civil servant, even an 'extremely helpful' one? It does not take an unnaturally suspicious mind to ask how someone in Jack Merritt's position might have been helpful to a building firm in his official capacity, and why Poulson was making his holiday dreams come true. Merritt was found guilty of corruption in 1975 for his relationship with Poulson, which involved many gifts and many NHS contracts in the Leeds area for the architect.

Maudling, on his side of the bargain, also had to discover quite how remunerative the Poulson connection might be, and what he could get out of it, and he quickly discovered that Poulson was reckless about what was spent from the company account. Merritt was not the only one to be travelling at Poulson's expense; one of the most ludicrously excessive episodes of the Poulson affair was in March 1967 with the grand trip to Mexico.

Poulson's Mexican venture was a comic overture to the failure of his efforts to play the international businessman. He first visited Mexico in December 1966 and it seemed to be an ideal client for the sort of hospital projects he had been working on with Williams and Vickers. The scale of the developments he envisaged was vast, particularly the 'Reforma' project in Mexico City. Along the usual Poulson lines, enormous design models were prepared, and an influential local figure was recruited. Eduardo Echeverria was an architect who was the son of a politically connected doctor who later became President of Mexico.[18] ITCS opened a flashy office in Mexico City at the cost of £18,000, and Poulson professed horror at what he saw when he first visited: 'I nearly had a heart attack. I have never seen such luxuriously furnished premises in my life. ITCS London was bad enough, but this was even more so.'[19] Reggie and Beryl Maudling, and Ken Williams, accompanied Poulson on his next visit in March 1967.

The Foreign Office only found out about Maudling's trip late in February, but once they did British diplomatic facilities were placed at Maudling's disposal and the ambassador offered him and Beryl official hospitality. Maudling declined this offer, telling the diplomats that 'as we are travelling with business associates I think we should stay at the hotel with them'. The Embassy sprang into action and arranged a dinner and a series of meetings with prominent politicians and officials in Mexico. Maudling asked to meet the minister of housing but was told that no such post existed in Mexico; the mayor of Mexico City was an acceptable substitute. The official part of the trip was concentrated after his arrival, from 17 to 22 March. Most of the arrangements for the trip, other than the official engagements, were made by local Vickers staff,[20] as part of the arrangement between Vickers Medical and ITCS about hospital projects. While he was out there, Reggie also conducted some business for Kleinwort Benson, who were interested in financing a new sewerage system in Mexico City.

Travel with Poulson had its compensations. After the official engagements, the Poulson party decamped to Acapulco for a week of high living. His secretary told a court, when asked whether a trip she went on was business or holiday, 'We did have a good time – well, it was a bit of both.'[21] Ken Williams fondly remembers the Mexican jaunt: 'A good time was had by all and we spent a lot of money – mostly John Poulson's. Within days Maudling had become part of Mexican society . . . Old Reggie was always badly dressed. He would drive down to the swimming pool in tatty swimwear, which was a sight to behold.'[22] ITCS – i.e. Ropergate, i.e. Poulson – picked up the tab for this expensive holiday week tacked onto a business trip. It was ratified retrospectively at the next board meeting in April that spouses could accompany directors, with specific reference to Beryl Maudling.[23] Maudling's incidental expenses for this trip were met without question, and without notification to the Revenue, by Poulson – even though his claim was a tatty, undated and partly illegible scrap of paper with entries like 'travel & like – 100', 'flowers and presents – 100' and 'meals and [illegible] – 350'.[24] Except for the tatty trunks, Poulson saw Maudling to considerable advantage in the Mexican trip – working hard and playing hard, deploying his political connections to advantage by arranging meetings and interviews through the Embassy, opening doors, winning people over with his charm, and in the background the promise of finance through Kleinwort Benson.

Poulson's relationships with people frequently went through a cycle of initial excessive optimism, then blind adoration and eventually disillusion and scathing, bitter hatred. In summer 1967 Poulson was growing disillusioned with Dan Smith and believed that the Labour politician was sitting back and collecting his £15 per unit rake-off from local authority housing developments without doing as much work as he should.[25] Part of the problem was that the Conservatives were doing increasingly well in local elections, and Poulson and Smith's cronies had lost power in many local authorities, such as Bradford, in the municipal elections of April and May 1967. With every Labour loss Dan Smith became less important, and his role in the toothless Regional Planning Council was no substitute. A particular blow for Smith was the fall to the Conservatives of the newly created borough of Teesside, in an area in which he had previously been influential. As well as losing members of his network, there was a general loss of opportunity for Poulson in that the new Conservative councillors were less inclined to spend large amounts of money on housing redevelopments than their Labour predecessors. What Poulson needed was a Tory Dan Smith to organise the inexperienced new Tory rulers of town halls across Britain. He may have hoped that Maudling was going to fit the bill, and berated Smith in July 1967, two days after he gave a downbeat report to the OSB board meeting at which Reggie joined the board, telling him brusquely that 'some of the Directors to OSB are not satisfied and particularly the new one . . . I would go so far as to say that I am sure Mr Maudling could have submitted better figures than yours,' about prospects for OSB.[26] Maudling could, he hoped, work at two levels – on Tory councillors and with central government as he did over aid for Malta.

However, Maudling's activities in the domestic field for Poulson were a disappointment to the architect. While Maudling promised Poulson on a couple of occasions to promote OSB to Tory councillors, little came of these activities and it is doubtful that he did anything discreditable himself in pursuing contracts for OSB beyond pushing rather feebly for it to be considered. His hope of helping in Birmingham, which he announced to his first OSB board meeting in July 1967, was naive, because the local firm of Bryant's had already sewn up the city with a corrupt network of their own. Maudling was not particularly interested in system-building and the prospect of a free trip to an out-of-season seaside resort for a housing conference held little appeal for him. Dan Smith tried to encourage him in 1967 to use his influence on several boroughs to gain support for OSB and Poulson in London, commenting that his assistance 'would be very useful indeed' in places such as Croydon, Westminster and Brent. Then there was his constituency: 'he intends to introduce Barnett Corporation [sic] to OSB,' it was noted in September 1967.[27] Reggie talked about Bradford as well. Poulson wrote in February 1968, 'Bradford looks like coming to life. We sent off details to them the other day and Mr Maudling has written personally to the Vice-Chairman of the Housing Department whom he knows.'[28] The Bradford councillor concerned, John Brennan, told a House of Commons committee in 1977 that Maudling did advocate Poulson's cause, but that he was open about the fact that he had an interest in the company and his story showed that Maudling was quite easily fobbed off.[29] Martin, who had joined the board in January 1967, was no substitute for Dan Smith either – he proved unable to make headway in places such as Teesside; his 'contacts' failed to come through.[30] Arthur Pearson, the Tory housing chief in Teesside, brushed off attempts to lobby him by telling all prospective contractors that they would have to get on the tender list and that firms would be treated on an equal footing.[31]

Reggie may also have tried to lobby for OSB in Whitehall. A cryptic Poulson letter in June 1967 to Sir Bernard Kenyon, OSB director and clerk to the West Riding County Council, states: 'I am arranging for a letter from Mr Maudling to the Minister to be handed to you after I have heard where you wish this to be done. I certainly don't intend it to be left at [the Poulson offices in] Buckingham Gate; they would steam it open – and that isn't being funny. There is nobody I trust there.'[32] The minister in question was presumably Maudling's fellow Old Taylorian, Anthony Greenwood, then Minister of Housing and Local Government.

Reggie's political life during the first half of 1967 was fairly placid. He was more inclined than he had been in government to favour entry to the EEC, telling American diplomats in January that 'he saw no substantial reasons why Britain should not be admitted to membership in the EEC', and envisaged Europe as 'an association which should use its increased strength to participate more vigorously in other markets, particularly in trading with North America'.[33] However, he opposed the idea that Europe should speak with one voice in foreign affairs; his view of Europe was still mainly in terms of economic cooperation rather than political unity, although he had no problem in expressing the Heath-led Conservative Party view, which was strongly in favour of entry to the Community. In May he appeared with George Brown at a conference about the Labour government's application to try again to join the EEC. However, the Labour government's attempt encountered the same obstacle that had impeded Reggie himself in 1958 and prevented British entry in 1963 – French President De Gaulle still opposed it and vetoed the proposal in November 1967.

The other running foreign policy story with which Reggie was involved was Rhodesia. Unilateral independence (UDI) in November 1965 under the minority regime of Ian Smith was followed by several inconclusive rounds of talks between the British government and what was now considered an illegal regime. Britain, and the Wilson government in particular, wanted an acceptable, non-racial constitution that would produce majority rule in the former territory before it recognised independence. If there was a deal, or the Rhodesian government put itself under the authority of the crown once again, then sanctions imposed in November 1965 would be lifted, and constitutional talks could restart. But as time wore on, the Smith regime discovered that thanks to its allies in Portugal – that controlled Mozambique and therefore Rhodesian access to the sea – and South Africa, and also the duplicity of British and French oil companies, sanctions were ineffective and there seemed no pressing reason from Smith's point of view to settle.

Maudling as Shadow Commonwealth Secretary had a delicate task. The white Rhodesians had considerable support on the Tory right, for crude 'kith and kin' racial reasons, but some Cold Warriors also convinced themselves that the white regimes in southern Africa were an important bulwark against communism. There were some on the Tory left such as Macleod and Boyle who were deeply committed to majority rule and racial equality and strongly opposed Smith. There were others who took a legitimist view about the proper procedure for decolonisation and disliked UDI. Maudling's own view, as a former Colonial Secretary, tended towards legitimism, and a desire to preserve party unity. This was a difficult job, and on several occasions Conservative MPs split three ways in parliamentary votes. Reggie flew out to Rhodesia and South Africa at the end of September 1966 essentially for a fact-finding visit rather than to launch any particular new proposals, and came back with the 'strong impression that the gap can be bridged . . . if there is enough determination and enough courage on both sides'.[34] There was not. But the gap within the Conservative Party was more easily bridged, and in a conference speech in October 1966 Maudling managed to create something that seemed like Tory unity on Rhodesia by stroking the party's ego: 'This great conference, by speaking loud and clear with one voice in the name of common sense and common humanity, may halt a situation now moving rapidly towards disaster.'[35] It was one of his more effective conference performances, but it was a piece of short-term party management.

Reggie's close relations with Labour ministers, who regarded him as one of the most responsible opposition figures, were deployed in summer 1967 in a tour of the Middle East, which was the occasion for a close entanglement of his business and political roles. At this stage, however, he was still just about able to keep them apart. In June 1967, after years of tension and aggressive speeches that were winding up to crisis point throughout May, war broke out in the Middle East. Israel, under threat from her neighbours, launched a devastating attack on Egypt and Syria, destroying the Arab air force and sweeping into Sinai, the West Bank and the Golan Heights. Within six days, the war was over. The Israeli success was a devastating blow to the secular Arab nationalism of Nasser, and a humiliation for the Arab world in general. The sinister ambition of some on the Arab side in the war, voiced on radio broadcasts, to complete Hitler's work and 'drive the Jews into the sea' meant that there was little sympathy for their cause. The British government, under Wilson who was always sympathetic to Israel, was falsely accused in the Arab world of aiding the Israeli attack, and for a time oil supplies were cut off. For Britain, the backwash from the short war was the destabilisation of the economy, particularly the ever-fragile balance of payments, and a diplomatic rift with the Arab world. During July Labour ministers approached Reggie and asked him to go on a semi-official fence-mending tour of the Middle East. An official cable to embassies stated:

For your information Mr Maudling is making his trip primarily in response to a suggestion by ministers that a senior Privy Councillor from the Opposition should pay a visit to some of the quote moderate unquote Arab countries with a view to balancing the numerous visits which MPs, including Mr Selwyn Lloyd, have recently been making to Israel.[36]

Reggie's itinerary was worked out with reference to the embassies' requirements, and British interests of state were uppermost in his mind during this trip. He provided elegantly written notes of his conversations with the Arab rulers to the Foreign Office. In Jordan on 3 August, Reggie had an interview with King Hussein, who 'seemed absolutely shattered by recent events and in a very emotional condition. His reception was most cordial and he stressed how much help he needed from all his friends.' Reggie encouraged him to visit Moscow to consolidate relations there, and reported that Jordan needed defence equipment and wanted Iraqi and Syrian troops out of the country.[37] Reggie's visit to Jordan, reported back in detail to British diplomats, was a valuable boost to King Hussein and may have had some effect in consolidating Western influence in the country. Reggie also stopped a couple of times in Beirut. It was mainly an official visit, which was rated a great success by British officials:

> Mr Maudling's visit to the Lebanon was a great success. He told us when he was coming and what he wanted to do; he consulted the Embassy on every point, and he staunchly and energetically supported the policy of Her Majesty's Government . . . [we are] extremely grateful to him for having submitted himself to such an arduous programme.[38]

Reggie handled himself well in a television interview for Tele Orient and spoke with what the British chargé called 'quiet authority' and stressed that there was no difference on Middle East policy between the government and the Conservatives. There was some media coverage in Beirut to the effect that Maudling was on a peace mission for an overall Middle Eastern settlement. When he returned to London he announced his own suggestions to solve the Arab-Israeli problem. These were as follows:

1. Withdrawal by Israel from the territories recently occupied.
2. In exchange for withdrawal, there should be effective guarantees against further aggression, and proper legal rights for Israel as a member state of the United Nations without being subject to any discrimination.
3. A resolute effort to solve the refugee problem permanently, with a lead from the World Bank.
4. Appropriate recognition of the unique religious status of Jerusalem.
5. Special attention to the serious and urgent needs of Jordan.[39]

It was a sensible and moderate set of proposals, although, as critics commented, it offered more concrete satisfaction to the Arab side than the Israelis. It anticipated in some aspects the Camp David accords between Israel and Egypt in the late 1970s, and Maudling's pinpointing of the problems of refugees and Jordan was insightful. Out of the misery of the Palestinian camps came terrorism, and three years later Jordan was convulsed by civil war. Some serious money spent by the 'world community' in 1967 as Maudling suggested would have been amply repaid.

However, there was also business for Maudling to do during the Middle East trip. Beirut in the late 1960s was a congested, prosperous and chaotic city with a truly Levantine trading mentality; commercially, the atmosphere was little short of 'anything goes'. It was a low-tax, low-regulation financial centre with strict bank secrecy laws and an extreme case of private affluence and public squalor,[40] but it was the commercial, financial, media, transport and diplomatic capital of most of the Middle East and therefore a logical place to establish the regional office of Poulson and ITCS. Poulson had been first introduced to Beirut business in about 1965 and an ITCS local director for the Middle East was appointed in 1967. The choice was Costandi (usually known as Costa) Nasser, who had been employed as an engineer by Poulson since 1965.[41] Nasser was a Jordanian Christian based in Beirut. He was a smooth agent and go-between, well educated and fluent in Arabic, English and French, with valuable connections such as Sheikh Khalifa, the son of the Ruler of the oil-rich emirate of Abu Dhabi. In 1967 Costa Nasser was an enthusiastic, ambitious civil engineer; by 1973 he had become a wealthy man thanks to his service for Poulson and, above all, himself. He and Maudling struck up a strong friendship almost immediately, a friendship that survived the collapse of the Poulson empire and remained strong enough for Maudling to protect Nasser when he was under investigation in the 1970s. As Nasser wrote to Poulson:

> To day I met Mr Maudling for 50 minutes, I do not know how to thank you for he took me in his confidence from the beginning and treated me as if he knew me for years. We are meeting in Abu Dhabi and Dubai and eventually are coming back on the same plane. Tonight he is on television and really his visit was very much appreciated.[42]

With the meeting between Nasser and Maudling, ITCS and the Poulson affair in general took on a new dimension. The dark secret of ITCS, at least according to the bankruptcy investigators in the 1970s, was that it was itself a commission-gathering vehicle that generated between £300,000 and £800,000 in untraceable money in the Middle East. The bankruptcy investigators managed to find 'proof positive' that commissions were paid by several suppliers to ITCS, mostly through the Middle East office and Costa Nasser.

When we were first instructed in the Poulson Bankruptcy we were told, in the strictest confidence by various parties with whom we were in dialogue, that Mr Poulson and/or his companies had very large sums of money deposited abroad, particularly in the Middle East. At least one individual, together with others directly or indirectly associated with him, was able to give us most positive information as to how in practice these monies had been secretly accumulated.

The estimates as to the amount actually held abroad varied between £300,000 and £800,000 and these monies were made up of secret commissions paid by suppliers to various of Poulson's projects in consideration of Poulson and his associates procuring acceptance of their tenders etc, and these commissions varied from 10% to 30%.

The writer was introduced to various individuals who gave us proof positive of the payment of these commissions and who, in some instances, actually handed over their files with all the secret information therein. Now it is true that the total commissions we were able to identify were under £20,000 and there is no chance of us recovering more than £11,000. Nevertheless we had the clearest possible evidence that commissions were paid, that some at least were paid abroad and that the commissions we were able to identify were simply an example of the whole. Indeed, we were informed by one contractor that with very rare exceptions every contractor will have paid a commission. We know that the rate was between 10% and 30% and it would follow then that there were sums of between £300,000 to £800,000 which remain unaccounted for.[43]

Some evidence about commission-taking is available in Poulson papers that were first released in August 2003 and which tend to confirm the picture of commission payments taking place on a routine basis into the Beirut office. Nasser's methods were quickly the subject of a pained letter from Donald Jowett, Poulson's architectural consultant in Beirut, to Poulson in Pontefract:

I am writing to you further to my letter of the 6th of September in which I commented upon the practice of Mr Nasser acting as selling agent for building equipment suppliers. I have discussed the situation with him and he tells me that he has your full authorization to this course of action, and that he intends to obtain the maximum amount of commission from all suppliers of equipment to projects built under the supervision of this practice in the Middle East. Furthermore I am lead [sic] to understand that he will be responsible for the nomination of all suppliers and not myself or my successor.

I am sure that I need not remind you that this constitutes grossly unethical behaviour and is entirely contrary to the standards laid down by the Royal Institute of British Architects.[44]

Nasser told Poulson when he was asked about Jowett's allegations that 'ITCS is a commercial firm and if it receives commission I do not see what this has to do with J.G.L. Poulson [the architectural practice] or Mr Jowett'.[45] Jowett left Beirut that autumn, Poulson's insult that he was behaving like an immature little boy ringing in his ears. Nasser also offered Poulson his services in international financial chicanery that September:

Thus, if you agree I will present the invoices on ITCS paper and I would like to have your instructions on whether to remit the whole amount to the UK or retain part in Beirut. If I may mention a point with this connection, France is now a free currency area with no restrictions at all and we could, if you wish, open an account for you there with the Chase Manhattan Bank in either dollars, sterling or francs.[46]

Poulson, wary of breaching conditions given to the Bank of England exchange control department, demurred, writing with no little irony to Beirut: 'Thank you very much, Costa. I appreciate you wishing to save me the high rate of British taxation, but at the same time I don't wish to be resident anywhere other than at 'Manasseh' – and by that I mean at Her Majesty's expense somewhere!'[47] The Poulson trustee in bankruptcy alleged that, 'in the files of correspondence of Mr Poulson there are many references to the taking of commissions but there is no record of the receipt thereof in the books of the Companies or of Mr Poulson'.[48] In a memo to Poulson in December 1967 Nasser pointed out that it could be embarrassing to handle 'the recommendation and supply of every form of equipment connected with the building industry' under the same heading as the other ITCS services because 'it involves receiving commissions' and proposed setting up a separate company to receive the commissions.[49]

The bankruptcy investigators managed to follow the money trail on a few transactions, thanks to co-operation from suppliers who had made commission deals with ITCS. One firm had arranged to pay 10 per cent, but the trustee in bankruptcy noted, 'commission in the sum of £1,527 30s was paid at the direction of Mr Nasser not to ITCS but to one Karim Azouro of Zurich . . . My Solicitors have been informed that if Karim Azouro is in fact Mr Karem Azouri then he is a dealer in documents used to facilitate improper dealings in arms.'[50] On the documentation currently available, it is questionable as to whether the solicitors' sources were reliable. The 'Azouro' payment ended up in an account in a Swiss bank – Roberto Calvi's Banca del Gottardo in Lugano, no less, which later assisted Maudling in forming a Liechtenstein company. Maudling's international financial dealings show a certain interest in tax havens, loopholes and bank secrecy, which suggests there might be more to his brushes with people like Calvi than meets the eye.

The bankruptcy investigators found the Azouri/Azouro business worrying and ultimately frustrating for lack of substantive evidence about the man's

activities and what might have been the purpose of the payment. They had
their theories and discussed the matter inconclusively with the Foreign Office.
There was the odd crumb of other evidence in the files, which they agreed to
pass on to MI6, concerning arms, the Middle East and Fatah, the principal
militant Palestinian organisation.[51] Reginald and Martin Maudling had
allowed Nasser considerable freedom over the money flowing through Beirut.
This in itself was irresponsible, in that Reggie was aware that Nasser was a
patriotic Arab and felt extremely strongly about the plight of the
Palestinians.[52]

Maudling may well not have been aware of all that had been going on,
but it is implausible to suppose that he knew nothing about the commission
business. There is evidence in the files in the form of a letter from Nasser to
Maudling over subcontracts on Dubai airport that Nasser was not bashful in
mentioning commission arrangements to Reggie, at least by early 1968.
Nasser and Maudling corresponded in 1969 about setting up a subsidiary
company under Abu Dhabi corporate law, which seems like a revival of the
December 1967 scheme to set up a commission-only business. In September
1969 Reggie ensured that 'salaries, commissions and so forth' were paid
directly to Martin in Abu Dhabi. Calvi's Swiss bank was also involved in
setting up a Liechtenstein offshore company to deal with the Middle East
business of the London company. Poulson professed to know nothing about
that.[53] ITCS in the Middle East was a dark business, that brought Reggie
into close contact with dubious offshore finance and secret commission
payments, and which was only to grow deeper over the next couple of
years.

While Poulson shielded Maudling from knowledge about some of what was
going on in Britain, like the depth of the relationship with Dan Smith and the
local authority corruption, he seems not to have done so in the Middle East.
As well as the 'green light' letter instructing Maudling to bribe Tajir, there are
references in letters to Nasser and other employees that when talking to
Maudling 'give him all the details' or that he 'is most anxious to know what is
happening so please make your report very full'.[54]

Maudling's public-spirited summer 1967 trip to the Middle East raised
troubling questions of a different sort about the relationship between business
and politics. He was representing the potential future Tory government of
Britain, and also in a vague and deniable way the existing Labour
government. The British were still in the business of putting Rulers on – and
taking them off – thrones, in Abu Dhabi in 1966 and Oman in 1970, and
ran the intelligence services of the Gulf states. The Rulers had powerful
incentives to keep Maudling happy. When he came, as well as talking politics
he was also representing ITCS and sometimes Kleinwort Benson in his
discussions with Middle Eastern Rulers. The potential for conflict of interest in
such circumstances is obvious. Before he arrived in Abu Dhabi the Bank of
England cabled the British authorities there saying that 'in their view

Mr Maudling's commercial interests in Abu Dhabi make it undesirable that he should be briefed to speak to the Ruler about Investment Board matters'.[55] The Investment Board was an institution intended to protect Abu Dhabi from being fleeced by all and sundry piling in to take advantage of Abu Dhabi's surplus of investment funds.[56] But Maudling's political status enabled him to gain direct access for his other business activities.

The Maudling visit and the travels of Costa Nasser around the Middle East had raised Poulson's ambitions in the region to grandiose proportions. Reggie came back from the Gulf part of his August 1967 Middle East trip with a potentially extremely lucrative deal for Poulson. During his meeting with Sheikh Zayed, the Ruler had given Reggie and ITCS the commission for a hotel development in Al-Ain, the second town of the emirate located inland near the Buraimi oasis.[57] There were other developments on offer in Abu Dhabi city, and prospects in Dubai and Iran trailed by Mahdi Tajir and Sheikh Rashid including a new airport terminal. A few months later Reggie led Poulson to believe that the airport was given to him for political or personal reasons because Tajir wanted to please him.[58] While this entanglement of political and business activities overseas was not unique to Maudling,[59] it was developing into a pattern.

Another sign of Maudling's failing sense of what he ought to be doing was that his successful Middle East trip (during which he had done some genuine good work for Britain alongside his commercial activities) was followed, like Malta, with a reward and the deepening of the relationship with Poulson. At the start of September 1967 Maudling wrote to Poulson with four bills of expenses, asking Poulson, 'I don't know whether you think these various claims are legitimate from the tax point of view. The entertainment is all foreign customers, Legerrotto, Mahdi Tajir etc. The luggage and clothes were needed for Mexico and the Middle East. If you have any doubts, let us discuss.' A lightweight suit may have been desirable and legitimate for the fierce heat of the Middle East in August, and Reggie made this point to the Select Committee in 1977, but it was far from his first visit to the region. His luggage, and entertainment expenses for his friend Tajir, seem very questionable. Reggie's speculative bid for reimbursement, which he does seem to acknowledge might be pushing the boundaries of what was acceptable, met no resistance: 'Yes, pay,' was Poulson's instruction. When questioned about this later, Poulson floundered:

Q. Why should you pay for Mr Maudling to have luggage and clothes?
A. Well, sir, I understand that when one is equipping people to go out to these various places it is the usual practice.
Q. Did Mr Maudling not possess clothing, or luggage?
A. I don't know, I wouldn't know.
Q. Why should you give a gentleman of his standing to whom you had just conveyed an enormous sum –

A. For the simple reason he asked for it, I suppose, sir.

   .   .   .

Q. But Mr Maudling was just, as I understand it, flying to see a Sheikh or something. Do you mean you had to buy him a suit of clothes to go in?

A. Can I talk without this being recorded and I will tell you then.

What Poulson had to say about why he bought Maudling a suit on expenses was not recorded, even on the transcript of the private examination in bankruptcy[60]. In 1974 DTI Inspectors found that the treatment of Maudling's expenses could well have been illegal and in any case lacked the appropriate Inland Revenue form.[61]

In September the social relationship between Maudling and Poulson became closer, Poulson describing in a letter a visit from Maudling to his house when they had a swim in the pool and 'a jolly good talk'.[62] During September Reggie went on to propose further steps he could take for OSB, and in early October he asked Poulson for an advance on his ITCS salary of £2,000 (modern equivalent is about £20,000). This was given, in circumstances which are very difficult to get to the bottom of, but which give a most shifty and unsatisfactory impression. It was listed in the Poulson books in spring 1968 as part of his fees, but Maudling wrote to Poulson's accountant a little later saying that it went to the Adeline Genée Theatre. Maudling contradicted himself in his examination over the Poulson bankruptcy in July 1973 on this point:

Q. Now, in whose favour do you think this cheque was drawn?

A. If it was drawn in my favour, which it may well have been, I then made a cheque out myself for the same amount and gave it to the theatre.

Q. Well then, you would have received £2,000?

A. Not necessarily; not necessarily. This is a matter no doubt between me and the Inland Revenue. It is nothing to do with me and Poulson's creditors. I am perfectly entitled to receive that if I want to.

Q. I must tell you, Mr Maudling, that the Trustee and Liquidator of Mr Poulson and his companies have acquired the share capital in ITCS and we are, therefore, entitled to an account of its directors' dealings.

A. Yes. Well, I can tell you what happened to the £2,000. It went to the theatre.

Q. If, in fact, you were paid the £2,000, then that was a payment to yourself?

A. Yes.

Q. I suppose a cheque in your favour?

A. Yes.

Q. Well then, you received it. You then chose to bestow it on the theatre, as you might have bestowed it on anything – a boys' club, overseas mission?

A. Yes.

Q. Why do you say that was not a payment to yourself?

A. I don't quite see, I am afraid, what relevance this is, because I was entitled to receive such a payment. If I had been paid that, I was entitled to be paid it. I don't see the point of this. I was entitled to be paid for a job, surely?

Q. You have actually said here and in the newspapers, and in the correspondence that you never received a penny from this company?

A. That is right.

Q. Well now, if, in fact, you received a sum of £2,000 on the 6th October 1967, then that statement would need to be corrected?

A. If I may say so, that would be the height of pedantry. The point is, where the money went. It went to the theatre, it was intended for the theatre. If the cheque was made out in my name it was an error; it should have been made out in the name of not the theatre, the production company.

Q. In what capacity was it paid to you as your fee?

A. No, it wasn't paid to me as my fee.

Q. Are you suggesting that you as Chairman of the company procured ITCS to pay a sum of £2,000 to the theatre company?

A. No, ITCS did not pay it, Poulson did.

Q. It was a Ropergate cheque, surely?

A. Yes, it was a charitable donation, a supplementary thing to the Theatre Trust.[63]

Maudling seems to have left the Trust and his own accounts in the dark about the nature of the transaction. In 1974 he was interviewed at length by tax inspectors over this payment, which it is hard to see other than as fraud. His tax returns painted a consistent picture of no remuneration from Poulson in 1967 and 1968. If it was paid to him as entitled, and then bestowed according to his wishes to a third party of his choice, it was surely taxable income. Within the hour in the bankruptcy inquiry, and when interviewed by the House of Commons Select Committee in 1977 Reggie's recollection of the event was different; Poulson, he said, volunteered that it would be offered in addition to the salary, not substituting for it, and that it was a present to 'come out of his charitable funds'.[64] If Poulson did this, it was fraudulent, as the theatre production company was separate from the Trust and not itself a charity;[65] in any case it was an incredibly tax-inefficient way of conveying money, in contrast to the (eventually) well-organised covenant to the Trust. Conveniently, Maudling's testimony to the bankruptcy hearing was to the effect that it was paid as according to his entitlement, which would mean that it was not recoverable for Poulson's creditors; while to the tax authorities he claimed it was not earnings, and therefore not taxable.[66] It was a shabby business.

The £2,000 does not seem to have made much difference to the fortunes of the production company in any case. By the end of November 1967 it had to announce that the theatre would temporarily close and various contracts were cancelled.[67] In March 1968 the production company went into liquidation and the theatre stood empty for a while before a theatre impresario, Myles Byrne, reopened it in 1970 and managed to keep it going until 1979. The Adeline Genée Theatre's days as a centre for British ballet were short and troubled. Michael Rice, who resigned from the board after an unhappy time there, summed up: 'It was a disaster from beginning to end and started to get some very bad publicity. The whole thing had lacked sound professional advice – they probably felt they didn't need it. The intention was obviously immaculate, but the execution was a disaster.'[68]

As well as the highly questionable £2,000 payment, the minutes of an October 1967 OSB board meeting, at which both Reggie and Martin Maudling were present, record that a dubious proposition was discussed. A quantity surveyor had approached the company and claimed that he could get them a contract for 900 housing units in Basildon New Town in Essex if he could have a job as their man in London; Poulson refused to countenance this but was prepared to offer the man a commission ('nothing else') on each sale if he helped them.[69] There is no record of any dissent about this business approach. This was Martin's last meeting for a while, because shortly after this he emigrated to Australia – although he remained on the board of the company. He did not stay long, and returned to Britain in spring 1968, although he had acquired a glamorous Australian fiancée during his brief stay. They were married in Sydney in January 1969. Her engagement ring was made with a large diamond that Martin had smuggled back from a trip to South Africa stitched in his underpants,[70] and the couple enjoyed some spectacular gifts, including some high-value items from two businessmen in Dubai. Beryl Maudling, via the Poulson organisation, looked into their identities (Mahdi Tajir's brother and his assistant) with a view to giving them an appropriate present in return.[71] Reggie bought his son and new daughter-in-law a town house in west London.[72] Despite all this, the marriage was short-lived.

After the successes of the winter of 1966–7, the Malta hospital project had become bogged down in autumn 1967. Design and consulting work was under way, but there was still no official word from the Maltese government about the appointment of consultants to oversee the project and the method of financing that would be used. Poulson told John Abela in May 1967: 'The best thing is if you can see the Prime Minister or his brother and remind him that he said to Mr Maudling "what can I do for you?" and here is the opportunity for him to do something. This was after his visit to London for the negotiations.'[73] In June an alarmed John Abela telephoned the Poulson office. It was reported to Poulson that their agent 'feels that something "very tricky" is going on behind his back. He then went on to say that he had just received a cable from his brother in Malta from which he learnt that for various reasons which he could not discuss over the telephone they were in desperate need of some money in Malta,' and asked whether Poulson would buy 20 per cent of their shareholding in Malta Cement for £8,000 immediately.[74] Maudling wrote to the Prime Minister, Giorgio Borg Olivier, in July 1967 to chase up progress. Despite all this, there had been no further advance by October 1967, when Maudling again wrote to Borg Olivier. A few days later, the Maltese announced that the Poulson firm had been appointed consultants to the project.[75] A further issue, as Maudling then wrote to Borg Olivier, and the British High Commissioner in Valletta, Geofroy Tory, to point out, was that the Queen was due to lay the foundation stone for the new hospital on 16 November, and that:

> She will be doing so before any steps have been taken on negotiating the contract to build, equip and commission the hospital. Indeed I am told that the instructions to the consultant are that the project shall be subject to international tender. You will realise that using such a tendering procedure would cause a further major delay, and so the hospital could not be completed by May 1970. Also, and this is exceedingly important, it should certainly produce an embarrassing situation if a project where Her Majesty had taken the first major step forward, was, six months later, advertised internationally as a tender for contract. May I respectfully suggest that a way out of this situation would be to instruct your consultants, before November 16th, to negotiate with reputable international firms to carry out the total project, including building, equipping and commissioning.[76]

This rather crude steer towards ITCS, and the even cruder pressure applied by referring to the royal visit, did not prove successful – in large part because British Overseas Development grants required competitive tendering. Another reason was that the Maltese government was becoming more sensitive about its image, as rumours had started to circulate that there was widespread corruption in land transactions and development; one Tourist Board member was apparently known as the '10 per cent man'. The Nationalists had no desire to be labelled the party of corruption, and even Borg Olivier privately conceded that there should be an inquiry.[77] Although the Gozo hospital was one of the biggest contracts J.G.L. Poulson obtained, there was no role in the project for ITCS. The royal visit went ahead as planned, although Prince Philip in his customary way did ask who was going to pay for all this. The answer was not to come for a few more months, but it was the British taxpayer through the Ministry of Overseas Development.[78]

John Poulson attended the royal unveiling of the Gozo hospital foundation stone, but Reggie was on the other side of the world. He called in at Fiji, Australia and New Zealand. After a couple of days on the Pacific island he arrived in Sydney on 11 November and had a round of social, business and political engagements during which, 'when asked about the prospects for devaluation he answered categorically that he was sure the Government would not do it'.[79] Reggie arrived in New Zealand on the evening of Saturday 18 November, and woke up next morning to hear that sterling, under pressure on the financial markets for so long, would be devalued from US$2.80 to $2.40.

Devaluation was an abject moment for Wilson's Labour government, forced to abandon the policy on which it had staked so much since October 1964. Wilson made matters worse with a patronising and shifty television broadcast in which he claimed that 'the pound in your pocket' had not been devalued. Jim Callaghan had been humiliated and was forced to switch places with Roy Jenkins and take over the Home Office. Labour's poll rating sank, and the government was plunged into a two-year ordeal of unpopularity, broken promises, plots and paranoia on a scale otherwise unknown before the similar travails of the Major government after Black Wednesday in 1992.

Although in party political terms devaluation was a boon for the Conservatives, it brought Maudling nothing but problems. He realised that as well as discrediting Labour's economic policy, it also reflected badly on his own stewardship of the economy in 1962–4. Labour's best attack, as it had been ever since the election, was to blame Britain's economic problems on the Maudling boom. Reggie ended up bearing the brunt of the counter-attack and resented it as bitterly as he resented any political attack. There was a tetchy exchange of letters with Wilson in the days after devaluation, in which Reggie objected to his statement that the Tories had considered devaluing in 1964. The truth of the matter was ambiguous; Reggie argued that a floating rate, which he had indeed considered, 'is of course a different matter from devaluation', which is technically true but misses the point that any float in the circumstances would have been downwards. Wilson, for his part, had assumed that the options presented to Labour on taking office had been the same as those Maudling had considered before the election, but in fact William Armstrong had taken the decision himself to offer up the possibility of devaluation.[80]

Reggie also had personal reasons for resenting devaluation. As well as his public embarrassment in the antipodes, the decision had made a fool of him in front of his business associates in the Middle East. During his July and August 1967 trip he had made cast-iron assurances that the pound would not be devalued, in Kuwait and elsewhere, which had been noted and welcomed by the Gulf Rulers and Arab holders of sterling.[81] He had done the right, patriotic thing as he saw it, but had been made to look ridiculous and received considerable political abuse. It was a further reason for him to have a jaundiced opinion of the political game and concentrate instead on business, which was taking on a steadily grubbier tinge. Poulson now felt able to write to him in explicit terms, saying in late November that a Lebanese politician,

Sheikh Khalil el-Khouri, 'is prepared to do anything for us, but he wants paying and ITCS can make the arrangements'.[82]

The year 1967 had seen a steady deepening of Maudling's relationship with Poulson and, in parallel, his Middle Eastern entanglements grow more complex. His financial affairs had grown more obscure as well, with the Adeline Genée covenant at the start of the year, and the Bedwell Lodge leaseback seeming almost straightforward compared to the £2,000 payment in October, let alone any involvement with offshore ITCS commission funds. But 1967 was only another step downwards in Maudling's moral breakdown, and it was followed by more and worse.

Chapter 18

'WHATEVER YOU ARRANGE, REGGIE, WILL BE ALRIGHT BY ME', 1968

During the 1970s, criticism of Maudling's foreign activities for Poulson tended to concentrate on Malta. The reasons, according to Ray Fitzwalter, who covered the story, were understandable:

It was the most tangible case. We got a long way in Gozo because it was a former British colony that still had strong links with Britain, it had a recognisable structure of ministries and politicians, it involved a grant from the British Overseas Development ministry so that documents could be obtained from Britain and there was lots in Hansard. And, unlike many of Poulson's schemes, it was seen through and actually got built.[1]

With more of the Poulson archive now open, the outline of what was going on in the Persian Gulf in the late 1960s has become clearer. The presence of the Political Agents in the Trucial States also means that there are reasonable official sources giving a perspective on events. Although little got built, the attempted Poulson incursion into Dubai is instructive about Maudling's true role both in the Poulson organisation and operating on his own account. As 1967 ended, Maudling threw himself more than ever into business activity in the Persian Gulf emirates. He was already involved in business in Dubai with Mahdi Tajir, in circumstances that seem to indicate that he had set himself up in a small way as a commission agent. Costa Nasser reported to Poulson in April 1968: 'Mr Maudling said to me that, in fact, it was he who introduced Mahdi to Costains and that is how the harbour deal was made and, I think, as a result of this, both Mahdi and Costains must owe a lot to Mr Maudling.'[2] Gratitude in these circumstances is a tangible commodity. According to Poulson in his 1974 police interview, the connection was made via Albert Costain, the Conservative MP for Folkestone (1959–83) and from 1966 to 1969 the Chairman of the Costain Group.[3] A deepwater harbour was an ambition for some time of Sheikh Rashid, and Maudling's involvement pre-dated his Poulson connection. In May 1966 Maudling had, wearing his Kleinwort hat, expressed interest in financing it but asked Mahdi Tajir – who, inevitably, was running the project – to go for a British construction contractor.[4] Agreement was concluded in October 1967, with a clause in the contract between the consulting engineer (Halcrow's) and Costain construction to the effect that if the deal collapsed through no fault of Costain during the first year, 3.5 per cent of the cost of the contract would be certified as already done and duly paid for. This provision, amounting to perhaps £6 million at 1969 prices (£60 million now), was – although it could not be stated in open session during the negotiations – to cover commission paid to Mahdi Tajir.[5] Also involved in the harbour deal, on a much smaller scale, was the Costain agent in Dubai, none other than Mohamed Fayed. One of Tajir's minor claims to fame, according to Fayed's biographer, Tom Bower, is that it was he who put the 'Al' in 'Mohamed Al-Fayed' – the honorific was invented at his suggestion in around 1970 to give Fayed some bogus aristocratic credentials.[6]

The deepwater harbour, it must be said, became important to Dubai's trade despite the scepticism of the British about whether it was too grandiose for a small emirate; in fact, it had to be enlarged within a few years. It was the first of a number of large construction projects in Dubai that equipped the emirate with the infrastructure of a modern state, and with which Tajir was deeply involved. There followed a succession of deals over the next few years in which Tajir allocated contracts to Costain's and from which he profited handsomely; in January 1968 the British Political Agent noted that some Dubai merchants were opposed to Tajir and distrusted the way in which he was now operating.[7] By 1970, Neville Allen of Halcrow's, an engineering firm with traditional links in Dubai, was furious and spoke of leaving for ever and telling Rashid 'everything he knows about Mehdi Tajir'. British officials commented that Tajir's enemies were saying that his intention is 'to launch as many projects as he can within the next year or so, pocket his commissions on all of these and then decamp to Europe or the United States where he already has substantial investments'.[8] By 1970, after considerable public service, Tajir had become an unpopular figure in Dubai because of this alleged commission-taking spree which meant that even if there was revolution or instability around the Gulf he was personally financially secure.

The infrastructure projects included an extension to Dubai's now unacceptably primitive airport terminal buildings. Again, this was a far-sighted thing for Rashid and Tajir to invest in: Dubai is now an international aviation hub, with, in fine Dubai pragmatic style, an exceptional duty-free shop. Tajir had first instructed a firm called Page and Broughton to prepare plans in 1966, but he lost patience with them and in 1967 he asked Maudling whether he would submit designs for an expanded airport.[9] This was referred on to Poulson, whose firm did the designs, but they heard little out of Dubai for the rest of 1967. Costa Nasser complained in October that 'I have had several telephone conversations with Mr Tajir but without any tangible results'.[10] On 19 December, he wrote to Maudling:

Concerning Dubai I am finding it extremely difficult to get hold of Mahdi and Sheikh Rashid would not take a decision without him. He is now in London and we are very keen on getting the Airport Terminal Building and Sheikh Rashid's Building. I have heard that Mahdi has made the remark that our airport design was a copy of the Dahran [sic] Airport. This is certainly not true and it is the design that has been made by Page and Broughton that is an exact copy of the Dahran Airport.

I have a feeling that Mahdi requires a particular favour from us before giving us the green light and this particular favour may be based on offering him the complete hotel design either for a very low fee or for free. I should be very grateful if you can indicate to me the best course to follow in dealing with Mahdi.[11]

Poulson, on seeing a copy of this letter he was sent, then wrote to Maudling on 21 December: 'You will notice in your letter from Costa that he mentions Mahdi requiring a particular favour from us before giving the green light. Whatever you arrange, Reggie, will be alright by me. The thing is that we want this work. If somebody will just pay us for it we will certainly do it.'[12] Reggie then offered Tajir, who was in London over the Christmas period, the bribe as suggested, but it was turned down. Poulson wrote to Nasser on New Year's Day 1968:

He has apparently offered Mr Maudling the management of the Building Contract side of it, but this isn't any good to us. I am seeing Mr Maudling this afternoon and telling him we don't accept this without the design. He is seeing Mahdi at night. When Mr Maudling suggested that we might do the hotel and casino for next to nothing in the way of fees, I understand Mahdi was most indignant he wanted Mr Maudling to have the work and pay us the full fees! Mr Maudling said Costa must be misinformed about Mahdi, but I said Costa wasn't he was trying to impress Mr Maudling![13]

When asked privately about this in 1973, Maudling denied offering the bribe, although he was confronted only with the two earlier letters and not this last one.[14] But the three interlocking letters clearly demonstrate a conspiracy between Poulson, Maudling and Nasser to corrupt Tajir – to offer a private favour to influence his judgement as a public official in Dubai. That it was not, for whatever reason, accepted, is almost immaterial. Tajir's hotel and casino project – in Bandar Abbas, Iran – did not get very far, and turned out to be another dead loss for Poulson, with Tajir owing the architect £4,042 6s for the design work which was certainly not recovered before Poulson went bankrupt.[15]

Then British politics intruded on the Dubai projects. Public spending cuts were a consequence of the November 1967 decision to devalue, and British commitments abroad were the most vulnerable to cuts because they were costly in terms of public spending and a drain on the balance of payments. As early as 1963, Maudling himself as Chancellor had envisaged scrapping this expensive commitment.[16] The Defence Secretary, Denis Healey, had been planning for the rundown of military outposts 'East of Suez' and with the 1967 application to join Europe, the Labour government signalled a reorientation in policy that would see Britain pulling out of Singapore and cutting the military deployment in the Persian Gulf. Devaluation accelerated the withdrawal and on 16 January 1968 Harold Wilson announced that British forces would pull out of the Trucial States by the end of 1971. Rather unusually for a detailed foreign and defence policy decision of this kind, the Persian Gulf became a divisive issue between the two main parties in Britain and Maudling, in the early stages, was in the thick of it at the same time as he was bidding to build the Dubai airport and other buildings. After Wilson's announcement there was a public expenditure debate, and for the most part Maudling's contribution to it was about economic policy, but he did also mention the Persian Gulf and his personal feeling of betrayal, having constantly assured people there that the British would not devalue or pull out. 'I proved a very bad adviser. I shall not rely again on the word of this Government when giving advice.'[17] Having misled the Rulers[18] for the best of reasons, and to his credit worked hard in what he saw as the British national interest, Maudling was now going to reassure them that they could rely on him.

The 18 January speech was the start of a consistent and rather energetic campaign of parliamentary questions and speeches Maudling waged over withdrawal from the Gulf. He was particularly active just before and just after his February 1968 visit to Dubai, Abu Dhabi and Kuwait.[19] Many of his questions aimed at finding out how much the government believed the commitment cost, something that interested the Rulers in framing offers to cover the costs. Reggie spoke in the foreign affairs debate on 25 January, concentrating mainly on the Gulf. In his speech Maudling made what amounted to a partial declaration of interest, although it was couched in terms of how authoritatively he could speak on Gulf issues: 'As honourable Members know, I have paid many visits to the Gulf and to the Middle East recently, largely engaged in trying to sell British financial and other services.'[20]

It is significant that Reggie chose to stress his work for Kleinwort Benson rather than the 'other services' he was trying to sell; even civil servants at the Foreign Office advising a minister due to meet Maudling in January 1968 did not seem to be aware of ITCS or Poulson. Maudling's failure to be open about his role suggests that there was something suspect about it. The ministry knew that Sheikh Rashid had already invited Reggie to become his 'Financial Director',[21] but the House of Commons did not, and Reggie did not trouble to tell them. MPs would have been entitled to take a different view of his speeches on East of Suez if the real scale of obligations involved with the airport, the discussion of bribing Tajir and his personal employment by Rashid had been known. It was not so much that the continuing presence of British forces in the Gulf would have directly benefited the airport contract, but that he was using parliamentary speeches to promote his interests by impressing the Gulf Rulers, and their interests by eliciting information they wanted and speaking on their behalf. No doubt Reggie genuinely believed what he was saying, but that is not much of a defence to such a conflict of interest, and his backhanded declaration almost makes it worse because of its devious incompleteness. It was a repeat, for higher stakes, of his behaviour a year earlier over Malta, and altogether a sorry moment in his parliamentary career.

Reggie went on to criticise Healey for rejecting Zayed's offer to contribute to Britain's costs if the military presence was maintained. Healey had rudely rejected this offer, telling Robin Day in an interview on 22 January: 'I don't very much like the idea of being a sort of white slaver for Arab sheikhs . . . it would be a very great mistake if we allowed ourselves to become mercenaries for people who would like to have a few British troops around.' The remark went down extremely badly in the emirates, and Healey was obliged to apologise.[22] Reggie added to the criticism. Speaking from personal knowledge, he revealed that, far from the government's version that the Rulers had offered to contribute to costs only after the decision, 'the fact is that the Government were offered substantial financial assistance by at least one of the Gulf Rulers towards meeting the cost of defence, and the Government have been aware of this for many months.'[23] This came as a surprise to the British Political Agents in the Gulf, who looked up the record of Maudling's August visit and found that he had indeed mentioned that Zayed had offered secret funding for the British military presence if it could be continued. It had been misfiled under 'Arab/Israeli' and did not reach ministers at the time.[24] Maudling pledged that unless Labour had made it completely impossible to reverse the decision to withdraw, 'reverse it we shall' when the Conservatives returned to power.

Reggie's parliamentary activities and his firm commitment to reverse the East of Suez policy were a positive background to business on his next visit to the area, which had been in the works for some time, but the final arrangements were made at the invitation of Sheikh Rashid in mid-January after he had been informed about the British government's intentions. Maudling told Poulson that he would not initiate any discussions on business in Dubai, because the meeting was in connection with the political situation, but much business seems to have been talked when it came to it; he was prepared to mix business and politics if this arose from Tajir or the Sheikh, as he surely knew it would. Poulson was conscious that Maudling's activities in the Gulf were a sensitive area, telling Costa Nasser:

> Please keep this [Maudling's] itinerary entirely to yourself – suggest you keep this letter at home. If it is mentioned to the Press we shall have all sorts of embarrassments for ourselves and Mr Maudling. Whenever I

mention him in future in such matters, you must always take the utmost precautions – however I know you appreciate this.[25]

In the light of this, it is surprising that the paper trail is so extensive and revealing, even if there are hints of deeper and murkier matters that could not be expressed directly. Reggie flew out on 3 February, a little over a week after his Commons speech and only days after further parliamentary questions. Nasser joined his plane when it stopped off briefly in Beirut.

During this trip Maudling and Poulson started to attract some critical official attention because of the unscrupulous behaviour of ITCS. Maudling's friend Michael Rice, who knew his way around the Gulf states, had heard derogatory information about Poulson, and passed it on to Maudling,[26] and it could hardly escape the notice of the British intelligence network in the area. Ethical shortcomings were not a fatal flaw in firms operating in the Gulf, as long as they were technically competent and did not behave in an embarrassing manner. There was, in some circumstances, even an official nod and wink towards corruption in procuring contracts. Some firms were quicker to catch on than others. Two British firms were waiting patiently for news about progress with tenders on an airstrip in Saudi Arabia and complained to the British consulate that they 'to put it mildly, have serious doubts about any objective assessment of bids taking place but are nevertheless patiently waiting developments at the Saudi end'. 'Why patiently?' was the Foreign Office reaction, 'They ought to be actively bribing people in the right places.'[27]

When bribery overlapped with politics, tolerance went even further. There are always a certain number of British Members of Parliament who are out to make a fast buck, and in the 1960s Arabia was a new field of action. Veteran parliamentary commentator Andrew Roth put it well: 'There was a certain sort of Tory MP whose eyes would light up at the very mention of the Middle East. They would have visions of consultancies, riches and gold bars. Any of the ones on the make in the 1960s and 1970s would regard it as a pot of gold to be tapped.'[28] Jonathan Aitken became deeply involved with Saudi royalty and business, but it was not only Conservatives who were on the make. Margaret Mackay, the eccentric Labour MP for Clapham from 1964 to 1970, was passionate about the Arab cause but mixed her devotion with outright corruption. She sponsored an informal trade mission to Saudi Arabia in February 1967, which she portrayed as official, and used the visit as a fund-raiser. She attempted to extort a secret £100 per month 'public relations consultancy' plus 1 per cent commission on any deals done from the firms as a result of the visit. The approach was so crude that three firms reported the corrupt offer to British diplomats – the other firm involved, the officials concluded, must have paid up. While some among the officials wanted Mackay prosecuted, the evidence was left on file and an embarrassing trial averted.[29] Undaunted, Mackay continued her efforts in the Middle East and persuaded the Sheikh of Abu Dhabi to give her a fund of £100,000 (current value: £1million) to spend on promoting the Arab cause in London, which seemed to involve her spending the money as she saw fit.[30] The Foreign Office tolerated Mackay because she was a channel for political communication with radical as well as conservative Arab Rulers.[31] Given that a minnow like Mackay was given such latitude, it is hardly surprising that Maudling, who was much more useful and responsible than Mackay, and undertook sensitive missions like the August 1967 tour in a semi-governmental role, got away with his behaviour.

The problem that attracted some official concern in February 1968 was not so much with bribery, although too much of it was bad for business all round, but with the prospect of a public argument between two British firms. Page and Broughton had complained loudly to the local British authorities as they saw the contract for the airport slipping away to the Poulson–Maudling operation. Page was suspicious that Poulson had stolen his firm's plans.[32] Roberts, the Political Agent, stepped in as an honest broker and told Page and Broughton that he would be prepared to ask Rashid to settle but

> advised them to try to see Mr Maudling while he was in Kuwait and put their case to him. This they have agreed to do. My suggestion that they consult Mr Maudling was made both because it was the obvious immediate action and because I thought that they would get a fairer deal in this way than by trying to negotiate with the other members of ITCS concerned, namely Poulson and Mehdi Tajir . . . Page is of course fully aware that ITCS is little more than a front organization to enable Poulson to solicit for business, which, as an architect, he is not entitled to do under British professional practice. ITCS is alleged to have submitted an alternative design to Sheikh Rashid which is supposed to be cheaper and better. This does not of course explain why Poulson should be so anxious to obtain Page's drawings.
>
> My only concern in all this is to ensure that Page and Broughton receive fair compensation for the quite considerable work that they have put into this project so far. Page himself would like in some way to be associated with the scheme; but Mr Maudling has told me that it would not be 'ethical' for Poulson to work in association with an unqualified architect.[33]

This last was an outrageous comment, as Poulson himself was only a licentiate rather than a fully qualified architect and ITCS was acknowledged to be a means of getting around the rules of the architectural profession. Broughton was in fact on the RIBA register. The note by Roberts is also interesting because of its assumption, presumably as a result of Maudling's obviously close relationship with him, that Tajir was himself a stakeholder in ITCS.

After Abu Dhabi, Maudling travelled up with Poulson to Kuwait.[34] What happened there on 8 February 1968 is some of the dark matter of the Maudling story. According to Poulson, interviewed by the police in February

1974, Maudling turned up in high spirits. Reggie had been invited to a reception at the American Embassy and was wryly complaining that it was going to be a 'dry' do with no alcohol, in deference to Islamic custom:

> He says 'We'll never get any drink here.' I said 'I will' and I went downstairs and I saw the head porter and we managed to get a couple of bottles of whisky and I walked upstairs with them and they were absolutely over the hills, he and his wife, and after drinking a bit then he produced some jewels, and showed us them, they were uncut stones.
>
> Q. Yes, you actually saw them Mr Poulson?
> A. Yes, and so did Williams.
> Q. How many, any idea?
> A. I would, from memory, I would say twenty.
> Q. Twenty uncut stones?
> A. Yes, they were large, chiefly diamonds . . . these were in a velvet cloth and he put them on his bed and we saw them and in my mind there was no question as to where they had come from, because that trip we hadn't been, Williams and I hadn't been to Dubai, we'd met him in Abu Dhabi and he'd come on from Dubai.[35]

Poulson was sure they had come either from Tajir or from Sheikh Rashid himself. This allegation, unlike some of Poulson's other tales, has something of a ring of truth to it. Poulson was not the only source for the allegation; another witness seems to have told Superintendent Etheridge a story about jewels before he talked to Poulson. In September 1967, not long before the alleged incident, the Chester Square house had been burgled and several thousand pounds' worth of Beryl's jewellery had disappeared.[36] It is not stretching credibility too far to imagine that a rich and generous Arab, with whom Reggie was on close terms, might have commiserated with his loss and offered such extravagant help, and would not necessarily have been doing anything wrong in offering it. There is no reason to suppose that Maudling would have had moral problems with accepting, as it is indisputable that he accepted valuable gifts from the Middle East; 'a pearl in an oyster from the Persian Gulf, a much decorated Kuwaiti chest' among them.[37] If the incident with the uncut jewels took place, it was not actually a criminal offence, no matter how dubious the circumstances. The problem as far as British law was concerned would have been Maudling's evasion of customs duty and perhaps taxation offences when he brought the stones back to Britain. Poulson noted when they returned from foreign trips that Maudling would go through a special customs channel for VIPs and was not subject to the same sort of inspections as ordinary passengers.[38]

Poulson, not a sturdy drinker, was out of action the next day and still complaining of 'bad food in Kuwait' the next week. Perhaps the sight of

Reggie, drunkenly revelling in the valuable gifts he had received, was too much for Poulson's tender stomach and fickle conscience. Even if Poulson's jewels tale was exaggerated, there were certainly many other lavish gifts, some cash subventions, and his shadowy role as financial adviser to Sheikh Rashid. The relationship between underhand financial reward and Maudling's parliamentary actions is even clearer in the case of Dubai than it was with Malta. It was, and there is unfortunately nothing else one can call it, a pattern of corruption. However much Maudling believed in his own mind that he was not compromised, the pattern of the evidence against him is devastating.

As Maudling left the Persian Gulf, other British diplomats tried to work out what he had been up to.[39] Archie Lamb, the Abu Dhabi Political Agent, who was less familiar with the ins and outs of ITCS than his counterpart in Dubai, minuted on 8 February to his superior Stewart Crawford in Bahrain that far from being a political visit:

Mr Maudling appeared to be more interested, during his visit to Abu Dhabi, in furthering the interests of a firm of architects and consultants with whom he is associated . . . but all the architects and consultants already established or visiting Abu Dhabi are rather critical of Mr Maudling's chief associate, a Mr J.G.L. Poulson of Pontefract who apparently sails very close to the wind in his ethics. Both Maudling and Poulson are also associated with ITCS of Beirut . . . Maudling will almost certainly look to the Political Agency for commercial support for a British venture in Abu Dhabi and I think we should know precisely whom we are being called upon to support.[40]

For Poulson's methods to stand out as particularly malodorous among contractors operating in the Middle East was revealing of his crudity as much as his corruption, although as a new entrant he had to offer more to overcome the existing relationships of contracts and commission payments. In Abu Dhabi the technique had been for Costa Nasser to agree to take a smaller than normal professional fee (5 per cent) in order to get the business, and then – as far as one can tell – recouping the damage in under-the-counter ways such as extracting commission from suppliers. There is a particular delicacy about diplomatic language, particularly as honed to a rare degree of refinement by the Political Agencies the British installed in the small states of the Persian Gulf. Lamb's letter was interesting in its open acknowledgement of Poulson's unsavoury reputation, and in the impression he had received that ITCS was a Beirut company. The Political Agent was accustomed to providing translation and advice for visiting British figures, but on this occasion Maudling dispensed with his services and conducted business via Costa Nasser instead.[41]

The very first British official inquiry into Poulson was prompted by Archie Lamb's letter but it was not taken up with much enthusiasm; the Board of Trade in London were asked if there was anything on file, and gentle questioning pursued Maudling up the Persian Gulf. It was easy for British officials who were so inclined to dismiss fears about Poulson as being rumours spread by jealous business rivals.[42] The reply from Kuwait was particularly revealing about official attitudes to what was happening: 'I shall be writing separately about Mr Poulston's [sic] visit, from which we have high hopes. He impressed me as a rough tough old Yorkshireman – and probably just the sort of chap we need out here to tackle our far from scrupulous competitors.'[43] The British diplomats considered sabotaging the ITCS operation in the Gulf by advising the Rulers against it, if they decided that it was not a competent organisation to undertake hospital contracts.[44] However, the presence of Ken Williams and Vickers (plus Maudling for finance and Poulson for architecture) reassured them that whatever the problems with the ethics of ITCS it could deliver, and no official edict went out. The involvement of Maudling in some free-floating, personal role in the Gulf was a matter of delicacy as far as officials were concerned: 'You will understand that as Mr Maudling in his relationships with ITCS and Mehdi Tajir seems to be operating personally rather than directly for Kleinwort Benson it is difficult for me to make any direct approach.'[45] However, the doubts of the British diplomats were later communicated informally. Maudling, in conversation with a Board of Trade official in June 1968, admitted that he was well aware of the widespread doubts about Poulson's 'professional ethics'.[46]

When Maudling returned from the Gulf trip, he continued to speak in strong terms in Parliament about Gulf withdrawal, while ITCS tried to organise contractors and subcontractors for building and equipping the airport. Discussions were opened with the British electronics and aviation firm of Plessey. In early March 1968 Maudling was due to meet their representative, and Nasser wrote to him to inform him about discussions: 'It is worthy here that when quoting Plessey should allow a percentage for the main contractor somewhere between 5% and 10%. Also depending on how we propose to be paid a certain percentage would be required for us.'[47] This rather opaque suggestion can bear several readings. Poulson, in a later letter, was under the impression that Plessey themselves would be the main contractor, in order that the project could attract British Export Credit Guarantee Department approval.[48] But the vague bandying around of percentages and the possibility that there was more than one way of arranging payment to ITCS suggest that Maudling enjoyed a familiarity with commissions and unorthodox financing.

The Dubai airport contract seemed to have been sealed at last on 15 April, when Tajir wrote to Maudling on behalf of the government of Dubai that the desire of the Ruler was 'to appoint your firm as consultants for the Dubai hospital and the Dubai terminal buildings';[49] the hospital was a new addition to the project. For a moment things looked very rosy for Poulson and ITCS in Dubai, but there was a quick and mysterious about-turn. Costa Nasser wrote a strange letter to Maudling dated two days later:

I have pleasure in enclosing a photocopy of Mahdi's letter to you which I obtained from him on Easter Sunday.

He told me that we have lost the airport and asked me whether we could finance the hospital, he also said that Costains will finance the airport.[50]

Nasser went on to say that ITCS were principally consultants and pressed Tajir to consider them on this basis. Tajir eventually agreed that he should meet Maudling and Costain executives soon for a meeting with regard to the airport. According to Reggie's private 1973 recollection of the end of the Poulson involvement in the airport, he received a wire saying:

'Sorry, chum, the airport building is out' because, in fact they preferred the design done by Page and Broughton. And subsequently Mahdi came to see me and said, 'We don't like Poulson very much. You can have the hospital thing for ITCS if you drop Poulson,' and I said 'No.' So we did neither. Bernard Sunley did one and Costain's did the other.[51]

This does seem to go some way to explain Poulson's failure in Dubai. Maudling would be offered contracts for 'his' firm, but when Poulson stepped from the shadows the Arab clients became a lot less keen. Poulson was precisely that sort of Western businessman known to the Arabs as 'fellaheen' – a crude operator with bad manners whose word could not be trusted.[52] Maudling, on the other hand, was a man with the possibility of power, and an easy manner about him that enabled him to work well in the Arab world. To the uninitiated, doing business in the Arab world seems to involve a great deal of wasted time and chitchat over mint tea on the way to a deal, but to the more subtly minded, polite and flexible it holds few unpleasant surprises. In 1973 Maudling spoke rather blandly about the Dubai airport incident, but it must have been the start of the realisation that working for Poulson in the Middle East was not going to produce untold riches, no matter how many lightweight suits he could claim on expenses, and he should look elsewhere. What exactly went on in April 1968 over the airport contract is far from clear, particularly why Tajir should send two such contradictory statements within a couple of days, and why Nasser should apparently unconcernedly forward them both under the same cover to Maudling.

By the end of April Poulson was becoming increasingly suspicious of what was going on in Dubai. Poulson was livid with Tajir for his duplicity and blamed him for the loss of nearly all the Dubai business in which he had vested such high hopes. In October 1968 he wrote to Nasser: 'Costa, a lot of money has been invested in the Middle East, a lot has been lost in Dubai. Some of it could be got back if Raschid abdicates (let us hope that he and Mahdi have an early death); such scoundrels ought not to be allowed to live.'[53] Even by Poulson's vituperative standards, these were harsh words. In November 1968 the airport contract was publicly announced, with Page and

Broughton credited with the design work and Costain's doing the construction. The Poulson designs for the airport, other Dubai buildings and Tajir's Bandar Abbas complex all had to be junked.[54] Poulson brooded over his failure and in September 1969, when he was in dire financial trouble, decided that he should bill ITCS a grossly excessive £70,000 for the Dubai projects; in a rare attack of professional ethics, Poulson had remembered that architects are not allowed to do speculative work.[55] Poulson hoped that this would put pressure on Maudling to pursue the claim. Even in November 1970 he wrote, 'I shall never be able to understand why he [Maudling] never collected the £70,000 from Sheikh Raschid and Mahdi Tajir. The instructions for the work were given to my staff, not me, who did the work and should have been paid.'[56] If Poulson never understood that, he understood very little indeed. Even in summer 1968 he should have started to wonder whether Maudling and Nasser had his interests at heart, given that Maudling in particular continued to be deeply involved in Dubai even though the place had turned out a dead loss from the Poulson point of view. Maudling's relationship with the 'scoundrels' on whom Poulson wished an early death was always worth more to him than the Poulson connection itself.

Although Dubai had been a disappointment for Poulson, there was still work to be done in neighbouring Abu Dhabi, where the construction boom was if anything even more frenetic than in Dubai. The British Political Agent remarked that the first anniversary celebrations in Abu Dhabi in August 1967 were a vulgar showcase for the excesses of the construction companies, one of which brought a jet aircraft down the runway they were building, and another put up a 'truncated green Cleopatra's Needle erected at the main crossroads, which was pungently but unrepeatably described by Mr Maudling on his visit shortly afterwards'.[57] The contracts offered to Maudling during that visit had not proved to be so many mirages in the desert. The hotel at Al-Ain was joined by a large, modern palace for Sheikh Khalifa, Zayed's son, and there were office blocks and a hospital on offer in Abu Dhabi city. 'All the work in the Persian Gulf has come about as a result of Mr Maudling,' Poulson wrote to Bernard Kenyon in June 1968.[58]

Abu Dhabi was an exceptionally rare success for ITCS, which in its shadowy existence achieved remarkably little. According to Ken Williams, ITCS was all about political fixes. According to the bankruptcy investigators, it was all about corruption. The failed projects, in Mexico and Dubai, have a strong whiff of political manipulation about them – Echeverria became President, Tajir became one of the richest men in the world, protected by diplomatic immunity. A semi-successful project, the King Faisal Hospital in Riyadh, became a baroque technological showcase, although this was long after Poulson lost control and Ken Williams formed his own partnership with Faisal. The apparently successful projects in Abu Dhabi (and Nigeria), which resulted in Poulson putting up buildings, reveal the true nature of the Poulson formula.

The Al-Ain hotel is a particularly piquant example. The hotel was designed with specific suppliers in mind, who had paid for the privilege with commissions. The kitchens were measured out to a specification that fitted exactly with the preferred bidder's standard sizes, enabling that contractor to offer a highly competitive bid. The benefits from the set-up would be split between the contractor and the principals of the commissioning agency, ITCS. The decor of the rooms would similarly be chosen with particular suppliers' furnishings in mind: the lifts, the desks, and any other facility the main contractor could think of. Hotels in places such as Abu Dhabi are separately owned and managed, and the relationship between the ultimate owner and the global franchise is another point at which untraceable money can be generated. Asked about a falling out between another partner and Martin Maudling, Poulson told the bankruptcy inquiry in 1973 that 'he wanted to get rid of Hilton and bring in Sheraton; there looked to be some funny business going on'.[59] Khalifa's palace, a larger project, was similarly structured to generate commissions and kickbacks, and the Poulson bankruptcy inquiry made considerable progress in tracking down the commissions on the two large Abu Dhabi contracts. The Abu Dhabi contracts outlived the Poulson–Maudling connection. The cranes were moving on the desert skyline in the early 1970s at the Buraimi oasis, and Sheikh Khalifa was a reliable and honourable payer when accounts fell due, which made the projects particularly valuable. The stream of income from Abu Dhabi went through the Poulson organisation until mid-1969, when Poulson's financial difficulties led Reggie Maudling to assume control of the flow of payments. Costa Nasser and Martin Maudling were involved in administering the projects, paying the locally employed building workers and deciding subcontracts. It was from these that commission payments ended up in the hands of Nasser family interests and the mysterious Karim Azouri.

The Poulson formula was also applied in West Africa, whose business culture ran along lines that Poulson found very familiar. In 1969 the British High Commissions and Embassies in West Africa held a sort of competition among themselves as to which country was most corrupt. Nigeria was the winner, but Liberia was quite a strong runner as well: 'Corruption in Liberia is part of the fabric of society, though certainly no worse than it is in Ghana, a complication in estimating its extent is that it is an acceptable practice here for ministers and officials to run private businesses on the side.'[60] Poulson's main parliamentary associate on West African issues was John Cordle, Conservative MP for Bournemouth East and Christchurch, and Albert Roberts had also been helpful with the Portuguese who controlled Angola, but in the late 1960s ITCS and therefore Maudling started to come into the picture. In Liberia, which he had visited with Poulson in February 1967 as a guest of President Tubman, there was the prospect of an enormous town expansion and harbour development, but despite employing Tubman's son in the

London office, and making regular payments to the President's financial adviser as a 'consultant', there was nothing in that country for him.

There were better pickings in Nigeria, or so it seemed. Poulson knew the Lord Chief Justice of Nigeria, Ade Ademola, because his children went to Queenswood school with Poulson's two daughters. Ademola and Maudling between them could open many doors in Nigeria, and there followed architectural contracts for the law school in Lagos, two large hospitals in provincial cities and some smaller contracts. A local official, Mr Audifferen, was put on the payroll – as in Liberia it seems to have been an accepted practice in Nigeria at the time for people to combine public office with private business. Maudling and Audifferen were both members of the board of Construction Promotion (Africa) Ltd.[61] Poulson, normally an utter hypocrite, claimed to his solicitor in 1970 that 'there hasn't been a penny bribe as far as I am concerned' but accused his partners of bribing a Nigerian official.[62] Things were going well until civil war broke out in Nigeria in July 1967 and a secessionist 'Biafra' government was set up in the eastern area; the Nigerians had more on their minds than architectural contracts for the rest of the 1960s and the country became another headache for Poulson.

War in Nigeria was also a political issue in Britain, with very strong feelings being aroused particularly among the supporters of Biafra. The British government was in an awkward position, because to support splitting up one African state could destabilise the entire continent as there was potential for secessionist movements in many areas, and continued to supply small and medium weaponry to the Nigerian federal forces. It fell to Maudling to speak for the Conservative Party on the matter, and he did so with his usual caution and diplomacy:

> Everyone is very tempted, visiting one side or the other and listening to the spokesmen of one side or the other, to take sides. This is the most dangerous attitude for hon. Members to adopt. In this conflict there is much of the element of true tragedy. It is not a conflict of right and wrong, but one of right and right.[63]

Maudling's moderation on Nigeria frustrated John Poulson, who muttered that Maudling was 'anti-Nigerian'. It was in Poulson's interests to see the Nigerian federal forces win as quickly as possible. John Cordle had spoken in summer 1967 urging that the British government should supply aircraft and bombs to the Nigerians, but in conversation with the Commonwealth Secretary, George Thomson, Maudling deprecated Cordle's attitude.

Maudling held periodic meetings with Thomson about Nigeria, and in their discussions often complained about the pressure he was under from his party, particularly from supporters of Biafra, to take a hard line and condemn the Labour government's policy. Maudling always tried to keep the issue out of British politics as far as possible; in March 1968 he and Thomson agreed that a Commons debate would do more harm than good. Maudling was told on confidential terms about British efforts to sponsor secret 'talks about talks' and was able to go back to his party and tell them that he was satisfied that the government was doing all it could to help the situation. He offered to go to Nigeria where, he told Thomson, he was 'connected with a small company of consultants who had an office in Lagos and he could if necessary make an excuse to visit them'.[64]

Those consultants' contracts in Nigeria outside the war zone should in theory have been progressing despite the situation, but the war slowed everything down and diverted resources, and Poulson started to turn his attention much more to the Middle East than Africa. The Lagos office was kept open, and Audifferen on the staff, but there was little to show for the operation except a rather embarrassing incident involving Maudling. As Poulson wrote to a colleague at the end of August 1968:

PS Audifferen wrote me a letter on 26th July which arrived here on 30th when I was on holiday asking if I would let a Mr. Guobadia have £300 here in London if this chap paid it into our account in Lagos. Miss McLeod handled this with Mr Maudling but telexed Audifferen asking for confirmation that the £300 had, in fact, been paid into our Lagos Bank. We have never heard a word from him. Perhaps you will clarify this please.[65]

Reggie, a former Chancellor of the Exchequer, seems to have fallen for an early version of the infamous Nigerian '419' swindle, although even if the transaction was what it purported to be it was an obvious exchange-control violation committed on behalf of a mysterious third party. The Nigerian war did not end until early 1970, when the federal forces overran Biafra, but it was too late for Poulson, who had lost control of his companies by that stage. However, there was still money to be recovered from the Lagos contract and design work for his successors, ITCS – and Maudling. When the bills were finally acknowledged by the Nigerian clients in July 1970, it led to one of the most squalid episodes in the entire story (see Chapter 22).

During 1968 Maudling's involvement in the Gozo hospital contract came to a successful conclusion. In April he saw Sir Andrew Cohen, the Permanent Secretary of the Ministry of Overseas Development, whom he had known at the Colonial Office, to ask for help because Poulson had still not received his fees from Malta. They found the Maltese refusing to pay until they had received the Overseas Development grant from the British government. This went through with unusual haste and was approved by the minister, Reg Prentice, in June 1968 although the public announcement was not made until July. Poulson was desperate for the cash, as he was being pressed by the Inland Revenue for payment of a large tax bill and was depending on the Malta revenue for funds to pay them and also fund some further lunatic expansion plans. Poulson sent Martin Maudling out to Malta in July and told him to stay there until the Maltese paid up; he came back a few days later with a cheque for £56,000, which had come effectively from the British government via the Maltese government. Once this barrier had been broken, Poulson was able to secure payment for revised estimates – his books in May 1968 put Gozo costs at £65,100 already – and in total received £190,000.[66] The arrival of the money from Malta took the pressure off Poulson – his solicitor had just been pleading with him to 'turn off the taps . . . I know nothing of ITCS but I am inclined to think that it must owe you a lot of money and that unless you take radical steps to stop this expenditure, the situation must get worse and end in disaster. Turn off the taps, for the sake of yourself, your wife, family and staff.'[67] Receipt of the Gozo money meant that Poulson could continue to fund ITCS and refuse to face reality for a little longer. He waved Maudling off on holiday in summer 1968 cheerily, 'I came to the conclusion that if I didn't bring somebody like you into it I was going to be played around with for the next month or two. May I take this opportunity of wishing you a jolly good rest in Majorca, with plenty of sunshine and swimming.'[68]

The building of the hospital was slow, and there was little progress by the end of 1969, when Poulson started to become concerned about the risk of the project being cancelled. An election was due in Malta in 1971 and the Nationalists were expecting to lose to Dom Mintoff's Labour Party. A 'senior minister in the Maltese government' opened discussions with Poulson to become a 'major consultant' on up to £1,000 a month as soon as he was out of office;[69] the hope for Poulson was that the Nationalists would accelerate construction so that a Labour government could not unwind the lucrative arrangements. In 1970 Mintoff told Richard Crossman that the Maltese were wasting British aid, and named the Gozo hospital as a specific example.[70] When Labour won the election the plans were scaled down but it was too late to start again, and the hospital eventually opened in 1975.

The year 1968 was an exhausting one for Maudling. He was constantly travelling, for Poulson, Kleinwort Benson and other business interests as well as in his party political capacity; he would, even if not on some sort of unofficial British government mission as he was in the Middle East in 1967 and Nigeria in 1968, often be working in three or four causes at the same time. It was a recipe for confusion and conflicts of interest, even had he not been drinking as much as he was by this time. Conservative disquiet about his commitment to politics was also increasing. In early 1968 a well-informed Conservative official told David Butler that there were 'demands for Reggie to get his finger out'.[71] As Shadow Commonwealth spokesman he seemed to be spending most of his time damping down Conservative opinion on issues such as Nigeria and Rhodesia at the behest of the Labour government, rather than mounting a partisan onslaught.

The months between March and May 1968 were extremely turbulent in British politics. In early March, not so much because of sterling's own weakness but as a by-product of the falling confidence that the dollar value of gold would be maintained, the Bank of England's reserves showed a worrying decline and between 12 and 14 March the new sterling parity came under intense pressure. A second devaluation would have been the ruination of the Labour government. On 16 March Maudling made what he called a 'solemn proposal' to the Labour government that the Conservatives would support emergency measures on condition of an early election. This was a less than generous offer, which the government unsurprisingly turned down; it was revealing of a strand of Maudling's politics that believed there was something aberrant in a situation when the Conservatives were not in power, and the solution for any crisis that hit a non-Tory government was for the Tories, in coalition or through an election, to be installed in power. But at the Tory Central Council meeting in Bath that weekend he 'sounded the only restraining note' to a jubilant occasion hoping for a return to government within weeks, warning that the Tories should support measures in the national interest and hinting that they should not shut the door on incomes policy as a solution to the increasingly evident inflationary potential in the British economy.[72] Reggie put it more bluntly in an interview for the financial magazine *The Banker*, saying that 'an effective incomes policy is feasible. And if it isn't, we are all down the drain.'[73] Maudling now found himself isolated – Iain Macleod as Shadow Chancellor was increasingly sympathetic to Enoch Powell's free market hostility to intervening in pay settlements.

However, even if his economic ideas were starting to be taken more seriously, this did not mean that Powell was a more popular figure in the Shadow Cabinet than Maudling. Maudling, and others, had been complaining since just before the 1966 election about Powell's tendency to make political pronouncements outside his area of responsibility, which was defence, without consulting the relevant shadow ministers. In September 1967 Maudling was given a general, vague brief to coordinate domestic policy, and when Powell spoke on 20 April 1968 in lurid terms about the future of race relations in Britain, talking of seeing 'The River Tiber foaming with much blood', Maudling was livid. Ken Williams remembered being woken up by a telephone call the morning after, and Maudling starting a furious rant against 'that fucker Enoch Powell' and his 'awful speech in Birmingham'.[74] It was not only Powell's indiscipline as a Shadow Cabinet member that angered Maudling, but also what he said and the way he said it. Reggie believed in racial equality, and disliked demagoguery in all its forms. It was a parting of the ways for the two old comrades of the Secretariat. As Home Secretary, receiving a note on some of Powell's questions to the department on immigration one Friday, Reggie sighed with nonchalant disgust, 'What a mighty brain is here o'erthrown', and walked straight out to his shooting weekend.[75]

A few days after Powell's 'rivers of blood' speech it fell to Maudling, and Quintin Hogg, to speak on the Second Reading of the Race Relations Bill, which aimed to outlaw discrimination in employment and housing but was in fact too cautiously drafted to have a dramatic effect and served mainly as a symbolic demonstration that discrimination was unacceptable. Maudling steered a careful course in speaking, as the Tories were split three ways. Some were willing to support the Bill warts and all; Maudling, and the Conservative front bench, disapproved of discrimination but had reservations about the details of the Bill, while some backbench Tory MPs – now including Enoch Powell – disapproved of the entire principle of banning discrimination. Maudling followed the unlovely right-wing Birmingham Tory MP Harold Gurden, and had to distance himself from the contents of that speech.[76] Maudling's own speech was not one of his finer Commons speeches, but in its very dullness it applied some balm to an inflamed situation.

When Heath fired Powell, Maudling was appointed in his place until November 1968 as Shadow Defence Secretary, which was a less vague role that required rather more parliamentary work than the Commonwealth – Reggie was back among the arcane details of forces pensions and the organisation of the voluntary reserve, in a subject for which he had little great interest. But defence meant that he was still directly involved in the East of Suez question, and therefore speaking on issues concerning the Persian Gulf.

The Conservative policy on reversing British withdrawal from the Gulf, so long as the Rulers still wanted troops there, was a complicating factor in the discussions between the Rulers about future political arrangements. According to a Foreign Office minute: 'The danger is that such a statement may lull the Shaikhs into complacency and inactivity: and they will find by 1971 that they have been deluding themselves.' The Foreign Office response was a most unusual campaign to persuade the British official opposition to change its policy:

I recommend so far as the Gulf is concerned that Foreign Office Ministers and officials should take every suitable occasion that may present itself in private conversation with front bench Conservative Members of Parliament, or other Conservative MPs with an active and responsible interest in foreign affairs, to point out the dangers inherent in such pronouncements.[77]

Alec Douglas-Home, as chief foreign affairs spokesman, took the leading role in Conservative statements on the Gulf, and his assistant Miles Hudson prepared a research paper in 1969 arguing for staying East of Suez. Heath, particularly after a 1969 visit to the area, was particularly insistent that he would reverse the withdrawal. One diplomat recorded in April 1969 that they had warned Heath about the risks of encouraging wishful thinking among the sheikhs and accepting assurances that might not turn out to be possible, that Heath 'Was over-emphatic in rejecting such warnings. His tour will clearly have strengthened his preconceptions. He told Sir William

Luce that he knew what the Arabs thought. That is so presumptuous a
statement for anyone to make about Arabs that, in context, it is positively
alarming.'[78] Maudling himself, after his initial flurry of activity in early
1968, was not a prominent public protagonist of the cause of staying,
although undoubtedly an influence on the policy. His own attitude to the
question seems to have been mutable, at times giving the impression that he
was not 100 per cent committed to the idea, but at other times seeming
adamant. His subtler attitude reflected a deeper knowledge of the region,
but perhaps also his own interests.

After British withdrawal, the emirates would have to make their own
defence and foreign policy arrangements, and given their small size logic
suggested that they should form some sort of federal arrangement among
themselves. While this logic was accepted and a very loose regional forum
called the Union of Arab Emirates was formed in February 1968, an actual
federation only emerged after extremely complicated and devious political
manoeuvrings. The main issues were which states would join the federation
(Bahrain and Qatar in the end did not), the relations between member states
– essentially the degree of dominance Abu Dhabi, with its wealth and larger
population, would exercise – and its relations with the larger neighbouring
states of Saudi Arabia and Iran, both of whom had territorial claims and
relationships of various sorts with figures in the internal politics of the
emirates. Machiavelli would have been on familiar ground, with the
squabbling emirates rather resembling medieval Italian city-states led with
varying degrees of low cunning and wisdom by autocratic princes, and a
distinct Florentine tinge to advisers such as Mahdi Tajir. Tajir was accused at
various times in the negotiations of 1968–71 of being in the pay of at least
three of the disputant parties,[79] and he and Maudling were clearly in 1968
deeply in partnership.

The Maudling–Tajir partnership was demonstrated to the British
government in a rather unexpected fashion in summer 1968. In the
backwash from devaluation the Treasury acted against the sterling balances,
which had been one of the technical factors Maudling and Callaghan had
worried about as Chancellors in undermining the pound. The strategy in
1968 was to reach agreement with large-scale foreign holders of sterling and
ask them not to run up sterling balances any larger than those they already
had. Dubai was a significant holder of sterling balances, and a particularly
porous frontier of exchange control given the local tradition of gold
smuggling. When in July 1968 the Foreign Office asked the Dubai mission in
London for talks, they were surprised to receive a telephone call from none
other than Reggie Maudling, who announced that he was Sheikh Rashid's
financial adviser and he would be conducting the negotiations. There was a
perceptible raising of a Whitehall eyebrow: 'presumably we can make no
objection to [Rashid's] choice of financial adviser.'[80] Reggie then disappeared
for a few weeks abroad and came back in the middle of August.

Maudling was in an exceptionally odd position because of his simultaneous role as adviser to a foreign ruler and as a leading opposition spokesman in parliament. The sterling balance negotiations and dealings with the Bank for International Settlements in Basle were secret government business that had not been disclosed to backbenchers or the opposition. Maudling's position was referred all the way to Chancellor Roy Jenkins, who approved it on condition that there was a binding agreement that Reggie would have to refrain from using anything he discovered in his professional capacity in public or parliamentary discussion. Reggie was brought in on 15 August to see the Chief Secretary, John Diamond, to discuss terms and was willing to accept the Treasury's terms. Jenkins explicitly said that he trusted Reggie to honour the agreement.[81]

When the talks took place, the Dubai delegation consisted of Maudling and Mahdi Tajir, who had been given a broad brief by Sheikh Rashid to cooperate with the British government. The actual discussions were over quickly, on 22 August, and agreement was easily reached. Maudling did indeed honour the agreement with the Treasury, and refrained from using his inside knowledge to any political advantage; but it is difficult to see how he could have done, given that if he had broken the agreement the Labour government could have made his life very difficult by exposing his relationship with Dubai.

Maudling also saw Sheikh Zayed the next month during the Ruler's visit to London. Quite what happened during this trip is not clear. In his memoirs, *The Price*, John Poulson alleged serious, outright corruption against Maudling that came to light during this period. Poulson's book was withdrawn almost immediately after publication in 1981 because it contained numerous libels and inaccuracies against people who were still alive and ready to sue. Poulson's mental state after prison was shaky and he was inclined to bitter tirades against people he felt had done him wrong, including Reginald Maudling. According to the disgraced architect in 1981, Sheikh Zayed, holed up at the Selsdon Park Hotel in September 1968, had ranted angrily about Maudling, 'An agent known to me has paid a sum of a million pounds into your Mr Maudling's account, no doubt into one of those convenient affairs in Switzerland where a number suffices for a name.' The bribe was supposedly for his services to promote the interests of Dubai during the UAE federation talks. Poulson, by his account, defended Maudling but then summoned him to Selsdon Park to hear what was being said about him and after 20 minutes with the Sheikh, 'Whatever it was that Zaid had said to him had put years on him. He was pale and exhausted, a shadow of the relaxed, pleasure-seeking statesman I had ushered in less than half an hour before.'[82]

Poulson's version in *The Price* is embroidered after years in prison. The version he gave to the police in February 1974 of this encounter at Selsdon Park is similar in many ways, but during an interview when he was anxious to get Maudling into trouble, and the police had warned him that they wanted to hear any allegations against Maudling then rather than later, he did not mention any allegation from Zayed that Maudling had been directly bribed, nor did he claim that Maudling seemed unduly perturbed after the encounter with the Sheikh. What he did have to say was less drastic and incriminating but probably more credible, although there is no independent evidence beyond the fact that Zayed was in London and it would have been unusual had Maudling not tried to see him. According to Poulson's testimony, Zayed had exploded in fury against Mahdi Tajir and produced a photostat of a cheque that was part of a £3 million payment to Tajir to switch his allegiance towards Abu Dhabi. Poulson said to the police that Zayed alleged: 'Mahdi Tajir had told him [Zayed] . . . that Mr Maudling, he [Tajir] could get him [Maudling] to do anything.'[83] Poulson put this in a less convoluted fashion to the bankruptcy inquiry in July 1973, that according to Zayed, 'Mahdi Tajir had given him the opinion that Mr Maudling was very much under his, Mahdi Tajir's, thumb'.[84]

Although Poulson seemed to be suggesting that some of the money Zayed had given Tajir had been passed on to Maudling, there is no direct allegation of bribery and Poulson avoided making it in the police interview or in his private evidence to the bankruptcy inquiry. The extended version of this story told in *The Price* can be dismissed. To have taken a massive cut of a bribe to change his view on a political issue is surely a step too far, even for someone in the sad condition of Maudling in 1968. Malicious rumours are common currency in Gulf business circles, and Poulson's mental state in prison and immediately afterwards was questionable. 'Follow the money', Deep Throat told Woodward and Bernstein. With the Arab money question one is not sure whether there really was any money to start with and any number of places where it could have gone if it existed. As Maudling wrote of Poulson, one would have to see the tax returns and the bank details – including an unknown Swiss bank – to know if there was really anything wrong. It seems much more likely that Maudling was given the occasional crumb from the table rather than a massive bribe.

But it is hardly an exculpation of Maudling, as the charge that he was unduly under the influence of Tajir is backed up by plenty of evidence from other sources. There were very strong social and business links, and payments did take place. He did take an interest in the federation talks, in a very ambiguous way in which business, his political affiliations with Rashid and his ability to act as an unofficial British envoy all collided. After a June 1968 visit Maudling tried to persuade the British government to hurry the talks on their way by taking an initiative; this was an approach he had used in decolonisation talks but on this occasion the Foreign Office felt there were hidden dangers in the idea and dissuaded him from pursuing it.[85] There are shadowy indications that Maudling was involved in local attempts at fixing matters, such as the fact that Zayed thought it worthwhile asking Maudling to press the Sultan of Oman to create employment for Omanis because he feared discontent and revolution in the Gulf, and an opaque reference in a letter from Poulson to Costa Nasser in January 1969: 'Have reported to Mr Maudling about the British Government's interference in your friend Feisal's adjoining Trucial State. You might write to Mr Maudling a personal note about this. I think it would be very useful. Give him all the details.'[86]

While he personally was doing well in the Gulf, Maudling was starting to worry about the implications of Poulson's incompetence and corruption for the stability of the whole business. In April 1968 Maudling turned his attention to the tax problems of Open System Building, the domestic company. It was running up 'general costs' at a frightening rate – £42,512 as of May 1968 not including various project-specific items. Like ITCS, the company was a bucket with a hole in the bottom, which had to be kept topped up with funds from Ropergate. Maudling had an idea about a more sustainable arrangement. Poulson wrote to his accountant that:

Mr Maudling has asked for the following points to be incorporated in the Minutes in the interests of J.G.L. Poulson. He seems to be the only person interested in paying me anything.

1. The outstanding debt of OSB to Ropergate Services Ltd of £32,000 must be paid off at once.
2. The sum, possibly £200,000, which I have spent on behalf of OSB to be paid off as money available.
3. A sum of £200,000 representing the value of the OSB design which I have made available to the company.

Mr Maudling points out that the second item will be a revenue item for OSB and therefore deductible [sic] from their profits, but really a very large portion of it would be tax. With regard to item No3, the Royalty Agreement is what they would purchase for the £200,000. Mr Maudling states that he sees no reason why the Company should not seek to terminate the Agreement for a capital sum such as the £200,000 and the capital sum would be a revenue item for the purposes of OSB taxation and a capital receipt for me.[87]

Maudling's tax planning advice was ignored, but the letter is interesting in its acknowledgement that OSB was indebted to Ropergate, which was a matter of dispute later in the analogous case of ITCS. Even though it was less crucial than ITCS, OSB was still an important part of his connection with Poulson. Maudling was evasive about OSB when the Poulson scandal broke; his director's fees from OSB falsified his claims – arguably technically true of ITCS – of not having taken any remuneration from Poulson. It was also the first aspect of his business life to attract the attention of the police, because of the activities of Sidney Sporle, a crony of Dan Smith who was the firm's consultant in the London borough of Wandsworth.

The Wandsworth affair centred on Sporle, who dominated the controlling Labour group on Battersea council and then, when the two were amalgamated in 1965, Wandsworth as well. Sporle was bullying and dishonest and took full advantage when it came to demolishing the borough's dingy terraces and replacing them with system-built flats. Sporle's undoing came in July 1968 when Wandsworth's new Town Clerk, Barry Payton, made a statement to the police about irregularities he had discovered. Payton's reward from the newly elected Conservative majority on the council was dismissal – nominally Sporle's political opponents, the Tories had no interest in upsetting cosy relationships in a borough where much business was sealed with a Masonic handshake. But Payton had started a police investigation that could not be stopped so easily; the officers concerned said to Dan Smith that they would put 'love' into the Wandsworth case, and they took the proverbial crowbar to Sporle's bank accounts and when they looked at them there was a pattern of blatant corruption. Sporle had taken money from builders and engineers in exchange for contracts on Wandsworth's new estates. Sporle had also linked up with Dan Smith, who had been given a Wandsworth council public relations contract and employed Sporle as a consultant to OSB, for whom he wrote reports on progress in selling their system-built designs.

The Wandsworth police naturally looked around Sporle to the firms that had been giving him money, and hauled in Dan Smith and others for questioning. Maudling followed the case with some attention, at least according to Dan Smith, who recalled in his unpublished memoirs that in November 1968:

Within days of my questioning by Superintendent Mees, I attended a private meeting in London with Reginald Maudling MP. He questioned me first about my Poulson connection and indicated that 'all was not financially well'. He then asked about my position in the Wandsworth Public Relations contract remarking, 'that he had heard on the grapevine that I had problems.' I told Maudling the details of my relationship with Poulson of which he was unaware . . . I told him that my association with Poulson would not last much longer.[88]

The scuttle of rats leaving a sinking ship had started to become audible. In 1969 Maudling acted much more ruthlessly and effectively than Dan Smith to protect his own interests as Poulson went down.

Chapter 19

'A LITTLE POT OF MONEY',
1969–1970

R eggie at last acquired the use of a swimming pool at Bedwell Lodge, his Hertfordshire country house, in early 1969. He always liked swimming and had wanted for some time to have one at home so that he could take a regular dip before breakfast. Beryl was also very keen on the idea and would nag him to do something about it.[1] The swimming pool was an emblem of this stage of Maudling's career. The original idea had not been without some merit (and indeed, the Maudlings did frequently use and enjoy the pool), but it did have a showy, excessive quality. 'It must have cost a bomb,' exclaimed Sandy Glen when he first saw it, and Reggie told him that Poulson had done a lot of the work.[2] Despite its splendid appearance, it was a bit of a botched job. It was finished months late and it was always going wrong; Reggie often had to call in engineers, or get more chlorine to keep it working.[3] The saga of the pool illustrates the farcical and sad sides to the Poulson affair – the sheer incompetence of John Poulson and the inability of Maudling to obtain a good price when he chose to sell his soul.

The pool was, in fine late 1960s style, purple and kidney-shaped; and the original designs provided for a sophisticated heating system and even a changing pavilion next to it. It was supposed to be a free ride for the Maudlings; the design work was done by the Poulson organisation and the bills were sent to the freeholder, Eric Miller. However, the financial arrangements were chaotic; the paper trail left by the construction of the pool demonstrates utter confusion and obfuscation about who was doing what, with the Poulson employee involved being under the clear impression that Reggie was the client and would be billed in the normal fashion for it but this clearly not being the case. The Poulson practice records put it in a category of 'Non Fee Earning' jobs, most of which were either somehow charitable (for buildings at Poulson's daughters' school, Queenswood, and various Methodist projects) or internal to the Poulson organisation. By May 1968 it had cost Poulson £472 10s 4d, which in itself was a substantial financial contribution.[4] At one stage Beryl appears to have paid £233 as deposit for the pool, but in October 1968 Poulson paid this amount to some solicitors with instructions that they send the same amount to Beryl. Why this circuitous payment took place is not clear.[5] The swimming pool was a crooked, underhand benefit paid to avoid taxation and public accountability. It was in the same category as Poulson's corrupt provision of houses to people like George Pottinger and the distribution of cash and holidays to councillors across the North of England, and Maudling was never comfortable and open about the pool. Despite being reminded about it almost every weekend when he took a dip, he did not volunteer that he had taken this benefit from Poulson, and it took over two years and arbitration for Poulson's creditors to extract payment from Maudling.

The turbulence was far from confined to the chlorinated waters of the Essendon swimming pool in late 1968 and early 1969. Poulson had been in increasing financial difficulties since the start of 1968, when the Inland Revenue took action against him because of vast and accumulating tax liabilities. Two large cheques Poulson wrote to the Revenue, in February and June 1968, bounced, but they were slow to take action against him and Poulson seemed, for a long time, undaunted. A judgement against him in November 1968 for over £200,000, including nearly £50,000 of PAYE deductions that had not been passed on, was met with a promise of funds from lavish contracts around the corner.[6] Poulson was leaking money all over the place, to OSB, to his under-the-counter network of consultants, and above all to ITCS. Poulson's solicitor had pleaded with him, on the basis of personal friendship as well as professional survival, to 'turn off the taps' in 1968, but the taps kept flowing into 1969. John Poulson was not coping well with his business problems. He was increasingly unable to concentrate on matters and suffered from mood swings,[7] and became more unpleasant to be around in the office than ever. Poulson became increasingly unrealistic about what he could achieve. He hoped for a vast series of contracts from Libya, and developed the worrying habits of attempting to enter spending into the books as an asset, and adding zeroes to estimated revenues from future projects.

The last dribbles from the Poulson taps came with the end of year accounts in spring 1969. However, the Adeline Genée covenant was paid, and there was also the complicated issue of Maudling's personal remuneration. The belated 1969 accounts noted that directors' fees in previous accounts had not been voted in General Meeting. In March 1969 Maudling wrote to Poulson's accountant Vivian Baker:

My fee for 1967/68 is still outstanding in the form of a loan, and it is important for tax purposes that I should receive my fee for that year, rather than for 1968/69. My proposal, therefore, is that I should receive the 1967/68 fee, and I will then waive my right to a fee for 1968/69. Nor do I wish to receive any fee for 1966/67. It follows that the single payment of £9,500 gross will completely cover all my claims to fees so far as International Technical and Constructional Services is concerned, though I would like to discuss with Mr Poulson the future position as regards our Middle East subsidiary.[8]

The main point of the letter was the peculiarly flexible attitude to fees. Within a month, he had asked Baker not to proceed with this proposed arrangement and instead left the fees to be paid by Poulson as and when possible. This request was related to Maudling's own tax position. At different[9] times the fees were supposed to have been paid, waived, paid and then loaned back to the company, and in the earlier years the position was still vague after supposedly full accounts had been filed.

The treatment of Maudling's remuneration is a particularly opaque business. Maudling claimed that there was an agreement between him and ITCS that his remuneration would be deferred until ITCS was a profitable and steady concern, but when Maudling's tax returns were audited in 1974 the inspector noted that with regard to deferred payments 'no independent evidence of the agreement was now available'.[10] Although it is far from clear, it appears that this alleged agreement was only thought up after Poulson's affairs reached a real crisis in June 1969, and given the vagueness of where exactly ITCS would get its money from, and whether its profitability was intrinsic to its own efforts or a consequence of how the internal accounts of the Poulson group were arranged, it would make little sense to defer fees in anticipation of future profitability if this might well never arise. In 1973, when questioned about whether ITCS was intended to run on a no loss, no profit relationship with Poulson, Maudling answered, 'Certainly a no loss relationship; I don't know about profits, but certainly no loss. Obviously there would be a no loss relationship because the whole point was if we had a loss we had no income against which to set it whereas Poulson had.'[11] Thomas Sweetman, who was involved in clearing up the mess, was under the impression that it was not intended to make a profit at all. But if there was no profit, the family shareholding in this firm without capital was worthless and the company would never have the money to pay the directors' fees. A clue to this mystery lies in Maudling's reference to the Middle East subsidiary.

Reality had started to catch up with Poulson after the appointment – on a lavish salary of £15,000 and fringe benefits – of former civil servant George Wilson as his administrator in December 1968. In April 1969, concerned about the financial position, Wilson called in London accountants Cooper Brothers to do a study of the cash flow. In June Wilson, and the accountant Vivian Baker, reported that Poulson was insolvent to the tune of approximately £100,000.[12] There is little doubt that from this point onwards the Poulson operation, and therefore Maudling, was trading while insolvent.[13] More bad news came with a legal action by a former partner, Peter Harvey, to reclaim some money Poulson owed him. The crisis brought in a more effective manager of the problem in the shape of John King, an industrialist whose sale of his share of the Pollard Ball Bearing firm at the start of 1969 as part of the Labour government's reorganisation of the industry had made him a rich man. John King – now Lord King of Wartnaby – is reticent to the point of aggression about personal publicity,[14] and even hostile books such as

Martyn Gregory's *Dirty Tricks*, which concerns the corporate misconduct of British Airways, do not mention the Poulson connection.[15] Those consulting his entry in *Who's Who* for a mention of his involvement with Poulson, or even his date of birth, will go away disappointed.[16] But before the Poulson affair he was a successful although obscure industrialist, with a business reputation for toughness; afterwards he was a power in the land. His first wife, who died in 1969, had made him promise to look after her sister – who was none other than John Poulson's wife Cynthia. This family connection brought King into the affair in June 1969 when Cynthia and John Poulson called for his assistance on learning about the disastrous condition of the Poulson finances.[17] King, and solicitor Nigel Grimwood of Clifford Turner, whom he called in to assist in the reorganisation, became increasingly important in the Poulson business as it struggled for survival.

Poulson was not the only crisis in Maudling's business life at the time. The first public embarrassment over Maudling's finances did not involve Poulson or the Middle East, but was over a concern known as the Real Estate Fund of America (REFA).[18] The importance of the REFA affair was not so much in the depth of trouble Maudling was in, but as the first large shadow over his reputation for competence and judgement in his business dealings. It was a prelude to the more searching enquiries into Poulson, and had it not been for Maudling's relationship with REFA's controller, the outlandish fraudster Jerome Hoffman, Poulson might have been written off as an aberration rather than a pattern. To paraphrase Lady Bracknell, to be involved with one criminal businessman may be regarded as a misfortune, to be involved with two looks like carelessness.

While the Bracknell aristocratic title was an invention of Oscar Wilde, Brentford, a few miles down the M4, does have a peerage, and it was through Lord Brentford that Maudling encountered Hoffman. The Brentford title belonged to the Joynson-Hicks family, who mixed Conservative politics with law. Lord Brentford had served in government alongside Maudling in the 1950s, and the legal firm also worked on behalf of Cynthia Poulson. The Joynson-Hicks firm had done some work for Hoffman, and when Hoffman decided to set up an international investment operation he looked to his prestigious British political and legal connections to launch himself into business. In December 1968, on the recommendation of Brentford, Maudling agreed to join the board of the Real Estate Fund of America.

Tajir, Miller, Poulson – and, above all, Maudling – all had some personal qualities that raised them beyond the sum total of their business dealings. Jerome Hoffman had not, although at least he knew what he was. His self-description, 'I'm a promoter – I may not be an honest guy or a virgin of goodness', places him very accurately. He was a salesman above all, with irrepressible self-confidence, a thick skin, off-putting personal mannerisms and a disregard for the truth so blatant it was almost funny – to take a small example, his short-lived puff magazine *Fund Forum* claimed that its September

1969 issue was 'No. 1904'.[19] In the mid-1960s he set up a mortgage scheme in New York which a prosecutor branded 'reckless, improvident and fraudulent', and as part of a plea-bargain on an injunction concerning this scheme he agreed not to engage in share dealing in New York. Hoffman's name being mud in New York financial circles, he looked elsewhere for his next venture, to the magical world of the offshore investment trust.

The offshore market leader was Bernie Cornfeld's Investors Overseas Services (IOS), which had grown steadily from an investment fund marketed among American servicemen in Europe in the late 1950s. As the authors of a book on IOS put it, 'The essence of offshoreness lies in turning an enormous number of loopholes into a viable, but unregulated corporate structure.' Most bodies of company law have anomalies, and it is in the nature of international legal arrangements that some things are legal in some jurisdictions but not in others. Regulations vary in stringency and the degree to which they are enforced. The offshore operator can pick and choose which bits of the 'group' are established in which jurisdiction, and for added protection can use companies incorporated in places like Liechtenstein where reporting requirements are minimal. Revenues can be reported where the burden of tax is lowest.[20]

The 'investment trust' part of the offshore concept is a simpler principle. If one invests in a single company, one is at the mercy of that company's idiosyncrasies – even though it is in a growing industry it may be a poor investment because of bad luck or bad management. It is safer to invest in several companies, but it is difficult for individuals with only small amounts of money to do this satisfactorily. The solution is for many investors to pool their resources into a mutual fund, which is then invested on their behalf. The firm operating the fund can then charge a management fee for providing this service. There are a number of possible refinements, but this is the basic idea. An offshore investment trust, if it works properly, should enable investors to reap the benefits of its flexible, deregulated, untaxed investment operation. But the problem is that by their nature offshore operations lack transparency, and are potent vehicles for their managers to pass money around between tax-haven companies creaming off a little at each stage, use the money to fund projects in which they have personal interests, and all manner of financial irregularities. A dodgy investment fund bears a distant family relationship to the classic three-card monte con – the money switches back and forward between companies with similar names registered in different tax havens, and somehow it's never under the card that the investor expects.

REFA was a particularly egregious example of a bad offshore investment trust. Separate Sales and Management companies were registered in the permissive corporate climate of Liberia, although some inactive companies also seem to have been registered in the Bahamas, which generated confusion for Maudling in particular.[21] It had offices in London but was controlled from Bermuda. It purported to invest in construction and property ownership in the United States, but only did so on the smallest of scales despite considerable amounts of investment in the fund. The Sales company paid out commissions to salesmen and took its share, but the real money was made in the Management company which took a cut of 6–7 per cent for processing the funds. Maudling never received any money as such for his involvement with REFA. A salary of £3,000 was offered but never paid. He was remunerated in the form of shares and share options, which Hoffman gave him free. He was potentially the second largest shareholder in REFA's Management company if he had taken up the options, and therefore closer to the heart of the fund than the other names Hoffman freely bandied about such as Paul-Henri Spaak and ex-Mayor Robert Wagner of New York. Reggie's interest in REFA, with its abstruse and dishonest corporate structure, is a mark of his ethical decline from the early 1950s when he had spoken eloquently against artificial tax avoidance schemes: 'I am sure that everyone in the House will thoroughly deprecate the use of a dissolution of a company and a re-forming of a company by a change that is purely nominal for the sole and only purpose of avoiding taxation. I am sure we all agree that that is thoroughly to be deprecated.'[22]

Maudling and Hoffman launched the Real Estate Fund at a press conference in London on 16 May 1969. Hoffman constantly praised Maudling as a 'busy, active President' of the company but there is a significant conflict of evidence about how accurate this description was. Maudling, in an affidavit signed in February 1972, gave the impression that he did little more than lend his name to Hoffman's concern, but other directors and employees interviewed by Michael Gillard, and letters Maudling signed, gave a different impression.[23] While Hoffman undoubtedly ran the day-to-day operations of the firm, Maudling was certainly energetically engaged in promoting REFA to his high-level contacts in June 1969. One such was Guido Carli, who was now President of the Italian central bank and had known Maudling well during the abortive European FTA negotiations in the late 1950s. Italy was a rare jurisdiction in which REFA sales were legal, and Hoffman was planning to set up an Italian fund in 1970. Another was Johan Melander, managing director of Den Norske Creditbank, whom Maudling had also encountered through the FTA; Melander had done the preparatory work on the OEEC before Maudling came in.[24] The Norwegian bank, after an approach from Maudling, was the largest institutional investor in REFA, to the tune of £200,000. After Maudling's resignation from REFA in July 1969, Melander lost confidence in the fund and attempted to hold Hoffman to the fund's promise that investors could redeem their money at any time. Hoffman stalled for months, and the Norwegians never saw £140,000 of their investment again.[25] As well as being dishonestly promoted, REFA also suffered from a structural problem, that its investments were essentially illiquid – it was borrowing short, by promising to redeem investors' money at any time, and lending long in the US property market. To pay withdrawing investors like Melander it needed to do so with money from new investors – as with the classic Ponzi scam.

Maudling also had high hopes of doing Real Estate Fund business in the Middle East. He sent Poulson and Williams to Saudi Arabia with packages of promotional material for Hoffman's offshore scam for a member of the Juffali family, a prominent Saudi business dynasty. Overcome with curiosity, Poulson and Williams opened the packages during the flight out and were horrified at what they saw. Even Williams, not particularly experienced in business or finance, could see through the flimflam and realised that REFA was a dubious outfit and that having anything to do with promoting it in Saudi Arabia could be disastrous for their chances of doing business. They threw the brochures away and reported back to Maudling that Juffali was out of favour and that they were unable to see him.[26] A further attempt to link REFA into the Middle East was allegedly made in April 1970, when it was proposed that REFA should invest in the National Bank of Dubai, a concern run by English banker David Mak. Like nearly everything to do with REFA, it came to nothing.[27]

While Poulson in 1966 seemed like a solid enough business, Maudling's newer associate, Hoffman, did not withstand even some fairly brief enquiries. Charles Raw of the *Sunday Times* had rapidly discovered that Hoffman had been banned by an injunction from share trading in New York; Raw interviewed Maudling about this on 20 June. While he was surprised when Raw told him about the injunction, he did not seem to enquire any further into Hoffman and remained on the REFA board, even after the *Sunday Times* published a critical story on 22 June.[28] He may have been preoccupied with the crisis in Poulson's affairs during this time, but the initial story had broken the dam and investigations by the BBC *Money Programme* and *The Times* followed, with further revelations of what Hoffman had done to earn his ban on share dealing. Maudling also came under pressure from Kleinworts, who did not want even an indirect link between them and a sleazy operator like Hoffman, and according to Sir Cyril Kleinwort, when Reggie was confronted he agreed to resign from REFA. On 18 July (not an auspicious date in the Maudling calendar), Reggie handed *The Times* reporter Oliver Marriott a personal statement announcing his resignation from the Presidency of the Management company and the board of Sales.

Reggie's resignation statement purported to be unconnected with the doubts uncovered by the New York injunction, and he continued to express confidence in REFA as 'a good and sound investment',[29] and indirectly in Hoffman as well. His grounds for resignation were given as arising from his own personal circumstances. His Presidency of the Fund would require detailed, day-to-day checks on its operations and 'this, I am afraid, I just have not the time to do'. He went on: 'As the election draws nearer I am finding I need more and more time for my political work, particularly in connection with party policy.' The sudden abandonment of active involvement with REFA came as a considerable surprise to REFA management and the British Embassy in Lebanon, who had been expecting Maudling to host a reception in Beirut to promote the fund on 4 August.[30]

Maudling's commendation of REFA as 'a good and sound investment' was very useful to Hoffman, and frequently repeated on REFA literature in the months that followed. Reggie's connection with REFA was not severed by his resignations, and he continued to hold shares in it and support it as an investment, even increasing his share in a rights issue in February 1970. There was no market in private REFA shares, so even if he had wanted to he could not sell them, and they remained embarrassingly on his portfolio until he legally renounced them in October 1970 not long before the fund finally crashed. Maudling attended and was photographed at its Christmas party in December 1969, even after the failure of Hoffman to refund Melander's money should have caused severe worries. There were other meetings between Maudling and Hoffman in the first half of 1970. Maudling also tried in March 1970 to put Hoffman in touch with Costa Nasser concerning the Londonderry House Hotel in London, which was temporarily owned by a Lebanese state bank. Hoffman was interested in buying it, and if the deal had come off, according to Gillard, there may have been a 'considerable' commission for Martin Maudling.[31] The Londonderry House Hotel also crops up in the later stages of the Poulson affair as a potential source of commission deals. In July 1970 the hotel was sold to a British group. This connection made by Maudling does have the appearance of self-interested involvement in a knowingly underhand operation, which casts his protestations of complete innocence in the REFA affair into some doubt.

In October 1970 REFA, now under the name International Investors' Group, started to go under – the whole offshore sector was tottering in late 1970 – and the next month it was kicked out of Bermuda and then Italy. DTI and Fraud Squad inquiries began in Britain. Most of the traceable money invested in REFA had been dissipated on office expenses, commissions and charges, but some had simply disappeared. In November in Rome, Hoffman announced, 'if things get worse, Abboud [his Lebanese assistant] and me are going to take the money and run, and you guys can look after yourselves'.[32] Hoffman was detained at Brindisi ferry port, in charge of a vanload of documents he was trying to take out of Italy.

The question, which is still baffling even knowing the fuller story of the Poulson affair, is why on earth Maudling had anything to do with Jerry Hoffman – why did he succumb to the disastrous 'REFA madness'? How could anyone think this was a good idea? In a perverse way, the REFA affair is evidence for the view of Maudling as naive rather than truly crooked. In the 1976 DTI inquiry report into London and County Securities, a secondary bank Liberal leader Jeremy Thorpe had joined and which subsequently crashed amid allegations of fraud, the inspectors warned politicians that Thorpe's involvement was a cautionary tale for any leading politician. For unless he is properly informed of the affairs of the company he joins, he cannot make his own judgement on the propriety of its transactions; and he is liable to be reminded, as Mr Thorpe must have been, that his reputation is not only his most marketable, but his most vulnerable commodity.[33]

Maudling was so desperate for money in 1968–9 that he was willing to sell his reputation for just the chance of a fortune. A crucial element of the solution to the puzzle of Maudling's involvement with Hoffman must be in the partial flotation of IOS in November 1968. Some blocks of shares in an IOS management company registered in Canada were marketed at $12.50, started trading at $75 and by March 1969 were worth $180.[34] The shares had mostly originally been acquired for nominal sums or as remuneration, and the capacity for capital gains for people who had bought into an offshore fund at the ground floor seemed nearly limitless. The principal IOS flotation was due later in 1969. In May 1969 another fund, GRAMCO, performed the same financial alchemy. According to John Poulson, Maudling boasted that REFA could make him 'not just a millionaire but a billionaire', and on the basis of the IOS multiples this seemed an acceptable level of hyperbole – he could think about sums in the tens of millions if it all came off.

That it was a swindle need not have been a complete deterrent for Reggie. Its client base had, to a considerable degree, that combination of greed and fear that attracts people to swindlers. A lot of the money invested in REFA had a rather grubby tinge, and to Reggie there was no real reason why these ill-gotten funds should not be separated from their owners. REFA's prime marketing effort was to attract flight capital from Third World countries, from the ordinary well-off classes evading exchange controls to the recipients of bribes looking for an untraceable way of banking them. A fair indicator of what was going on was the admission by the regional sales director that REFA Latin America sales division covered twenty-nine countries, but was legal in only two; the money invested in Brazil was taken across a border river to Paraguay in canoes.[35]

There were certainly millions to be made defrauding the new rich of the Gulf, and the frightened rich of many Third World countries, in the 1970s. Hoffman's outfit was too bizarre to survive for long but a more sophisticated operator, Pakistani banker Agha Hasan Abedi, already had his claws dug into Abu Dhabi and the Arab ultra-rich. His Bank of Credit and Commerce International (BCCI) was founded with the backing of Sheikh Zayed in 1972, shortly after the UAE was formed. BCCI came to specialise in flight capital, money laundering and fraud and was shut down by banking regulators in 1991. Some of BCCI's techniques were the same as Hoffman's. Its corporate structure was so complicated that it was difficult to show that it was subject to the corporate governance and investor protection laws of any country on earth. It concealed its true nature with a veneer of pseudo-ethical concern and gathered respectable front men in countries in which it operated. Jimmy Carter and Lord Callaghan innocently lent the operation respectability, and Freddie Bennett also gave the dubious benefit of his reputation to the concern. There was also, by the late 1960s and early 1970s, an increasingly strong whiff of organised crime about the offshore sector. Hoffman's path had crossed that of New York Mob interests before he founded REFA, and after the fall of Bernie Cornfeld in 1970 IOS fell into the hands of Robert Vesco, an apparently unremarkable financial adviser who, on the quiet, was a criminal genius. During the 1970s and 1980s Vesco walked off with most of the IOS investment pool, contributed lavishly to Richard Nixon's 1972 campaign, entered the drug trade and ended up in exile in Cuba.[36]

REFA was predominantly a story for the City pages, and as of 1969 the fund was still a going concern, so it did not seem a particularly serious cloud over Maudling's public image. Still, it was proper to ask whether it was wise of him to get involved in the first place, bow out of an active role only a couple of months after launching the fund, and continue to recommend it as an investment despite the serious questions about Hoffman's record in New York. The political columnist Alan Watkins asked these questions in the *Sunday Mirror* and received a letter from Maudling's solicitors. This came as something of a surprise, as Reggie was not known as a professional litigant, an unpleasant and thankfully small category of public figures. The *Mirror* executives settled immediately and deferentially, with a payment of £500 before Watkins was even interviewed and asked whether he believed the article to be defensible. Reggie's connections with the senior managements of newspapers were extremely good, consolidated by frequent lunches and social engagements, and the *Mirror* was no exception. Hugh Cudlipp and the *Mirror*'s legal counsel Ellis Birk were both personal friends, and Cudlipp rushed round to Chester Square as soon as he found out about the legal threat. Reggie's first attempt at halting damaging publicity by legal threats and string-pulling had worked, and given him confidence that any story reflecting adversely on his personal integrity would be similarly easily squashed.[37]

However, *Private Eye* had become steadily more involved in serious investigative journalism, with the expertise of Michael Gillard in City affairs and the reporting skills of Paul Foot adding depth to its coverage in the late 1960s and early 1970s. The *Eye* did not leave REFA alone, and 'Tales of Hoffman' became a regular feature in the back pages of the journal from 1969 onwards, complete with references to its 'First President', Reginald Maudling. Reggie was flagged from then on as someone who had been involved in one dodgy business and was therefore open to question in his other financial relationships. His offhand comment about REFA in August 1969, that he was hoping to build up 'a little pot of money' for his old age, was duly noted, and when his name came up after Paul Foot had started to look into Poulson it was interesting to say the least. However, the theory advanced by some of Maudling's supporters that he was the target of a vendetta by Foot and others because of his actions in the controversial Rudi Dutschke case as Home Secretary lacks substance. The first 'Tales of Hoffman' piece pre-dated the Dutschke affair by over a year, and while Foot had strong and openly proclaimed socialist views this was not the same for Gillard. There was a certain amount that was unattractive about *Private Eye* in the 1970s, but the *Eye* was doing a job that the mainstream press, for reasons of laziness, sympathy for Maudling or traditionalism, was failing to do.

While he had been promoting REFA in June 1969, Maudling had also been insulating the most viable aspects of ITCS from the developing Poulson fiasco. A particular concern for him was the position in the Arab emirates, where at last the British authorities had recently started giving Poulson a seat at the top table and recognising him as an important contractor.[38] The palace for Sheikh Khalifa and the hotel development at Al-Ain in Abu Dhabi were under way and money was starting to flow from these contracts in 1969. Poulson had been complaining for some time that he had only the weakest control over the Abu Dhabi contracts, telexing Nasser in November 1968 to complain that he had paid someone with money 'which we didn't know about in Abu Dhabi' and that Nasser seemed reluctant to allow ITCS directors to see what was going on there.[39] The bankruptcy investigators concluded from other papers that 'Sheikh Khalifa had been extensively cheated over building costs'.[40] In January 1969 Ken Williams wrote to Nasser to complain about his failure to remit £11,000 back from Abu Dhabi to Britain: 'You cannot play around with the Bank of England like this and, of course, you are putting ITCS and J.G.L. Poulson in a very unsatisfactory position, as their statements must in all cases be carried out. Mr Maudling would be horrified if he knew of this.'[41]

However, in June Maudling was actively promoting the autonomy of the Abu Dhabi operation. He wrote to Nasser on 10 June that 'I was glad to hear that you have now arranged the incorporation of our Middle East subsidiary under the law of Abu Dhabi',[42] and his reference in March in his letter to Baker suggests that while he was willing to waive or defer fees from the main part of ITCS he was still interested in the Middle East subsidiary as an income-generating operation for himself. In the June rearrangements he took a keen interest in the Middle East operations. Funds received from the Abu Dhabi contracts would in future be paid into a bank account in Abu Dhabi and transferred to an ITCS account in London rather than going into a Poulson account; Maudling then told Baker that he would reimburse Poulson from the ITCS London account. Poulson appears not to have been paid all his fees on the Abu Dhabi work following Maudling's new policy of intercepting the fees and channelling them through ITCS. This policy, inaugurated in mid-June 1969, seems to have been intended to plug the hole in the company's books and enable semi-respectable accounts to be filed that did not show

ITCS to be insolvent. As Maudling said in 1973, the reason for the diversion was 'that he [Poulson] was getting into serious trouble. I was not going to have my company having creditors, so I insisted on getting the money myself so that I could pay my creditors first and pass it on.'[43] As Maudling wrote to Baker at the time, 'Now there is some prospect of reducing the outstanding losses of this company, I want to separate its management and accounting from any other concern and put it on a normal business basis.'[44] Maudling told the bankruptcy investigation in 1973 that 'I said, "send any money they don't need for local expenditure back here and we will pass it on to Poulson." We may have kept a small reserve to meet our own creditors, but I don't know.'[45]

In other words, the purpose was to salvage ITCS from the Poulson implosion, but in practice – according to Hunter – this meant appropriating £111,000 of Poulson's fees when the architect was off-balance. At a highly informal 'board meeting' on 12 August a resolution was passed that gave Reginald and Martin Maudling control over the London bank account.[46] Further, on 10 September Maudling wrote to Nasser asking for monthly statements of the Abu Dhabi account, and for the administration of the Abu Dhabi account to be transferred to London. From the local account in Abu Dhabi, Nasser's pay would be the first charge but after that 'Martin Maudling to be given salaries, commissions, and so forth'.[47] No remuneration for Martin Maudling went through the books of ITCS London between February 1970 and September 1971, an anomaly that attracted the interest of DTI Inspectors.[48]

Until the rearrangement in June 1969 ('Of course, the whole thing was just a piece of carpentry, Mr Poulson?' suggested Muir Hunter at the 1973 bankruptcy hearing), the operating costs of ITCS had all come from the Ropergate bank account, and as Maudling says in his letter to Baker in June 1969 the company was running a large accumulated loss which eventually reached £157,000. Whether this money was effectively a gift, or a properly accounted debt was in dispute. Maudling wrote to Poulson on 5 July 1968 asking whether these payments were to be 'recorded as a loan of working capital or as payments made on behalf of ITCS'. A conflict of interest, and evidence, emerges at this point. Poulson testified that they were loans. Maudling that they were expenses carried out on behalf of Poulson by ITCS and therefore not a debt.[49] Poulson's creditors would have a claim on it unless the debt could be made to disappear. The most elegant way of making the ITCS debt to Poulson vanish was to establish a corresponding debt from Poulson to ITCS, to cancel it out and square off the accounts, and validate the retention of the Abu Dhabi funds.

There was some sort of understanding that ITCS would reap some benefit from projects that it obtained for Poulson but beyond that it was extremely vague. Poulson ludicrously claimed that ITCS would generate money from arranging finance on projects, while Maudling claimed that there was an agreement that ITCS should be allocated a share of the fees coming in from overseas projects. There was no paperwork that conclusively demonstrated either point of view, and it was never made clear even when both companies passed into the hands of the liquidators. ITCS was eventually wound up in August 1973 although the dispute with Poulson's Ropergate company meant that it was liquidated only in 1995, an extraordinarily long liquidation process by any standards.

The Open System Building accounts indirectly undermine Maudling's version of the relationship between the companies. Maudling, in bankruptcy testimony, claimed that only 'a bunch of cretins'[50] could organise a company on the basis that Poulson claimed that ITCS was set up; that it would be a loss-making subsidiary of a profitable parent company. But OSB was precisely and unambiguously that, and Reggie served on its board for two years. The bankruptcy investigators seemed to treat both versions with considerable scepticism, and they do look like cover stories that were organised to avoid investigation of the stream of income from commissions on subcontracts.

During the bankruptcy hearings Maudling consistently claimed that the ITCS share had been fixed at 20 per cent, but there is no evidence dating before the first signs of the fall of the house of Poulson in June 1969 to this effect.[51] The 20 per cent of fees arrangement seems to have become fixed at some point during 1970, having been back-calculated to cancel out the Ropergate payments to ITCS. 'Mr Maudling starts re-arranging the figures in ITCS accounts so as to produce a commission for the company of 20%,' was how Muir Hunter read the situation in 1973.[52] Even so, the 20 per cent was not quite enough to cancel the indebtedness to Poulson, and in 1970 and 1971 the ITCS take was raised to 25 or even 33 per cent to balance the books. In relation to Abu Dhabi, it seems to have been nearer 70 per cent, even assuming a £42,000 payment entered into the books as being for Poulson was actually passed on, which is not completely clear. Maudling explained in 1973 that the take from Abu Dhabi 'brings in the Riyadh hospital, the Gozo, and so on'.[53] Reggie and Martin Maudling took an active interest in this imaginative accounting. It did the trick, as long as revenue from projects such as the Gozo hospital was included – and the ITCS claim to any share of this unusually productive cash-generating project was highly questionable. It also displayed ethics reminiscent of the vulture, in that through this rearrangement ITCS ensured that it had grabbed what Maudling thought was its share as soon as Poulson looked like going down. Other creditors had a less pleasant experience.

At least two separate versions of the vexed 1968 accounts of ITCS were produced, and it became clear in the private bankruptcy hearings that Maudling had approved and then disposed of the first version between June 1969 and July 1970.[54] It took until February 1972 to produce some very sketchy agreed accounts, which were given a heavily qualified audit. The directors at that time found that owing to 'inadequate documentation and to conflicting opinions' it was impossible to be precise about what had gone on in the company in the late 1960s. The accountants then thought that the problems of the company 'are of such a serious nature as to preclude us from certifying that the accounts set out above give a true and fair view of the state of affairs'.[55] A first draft of 1970 accounts was prepared but a final version was never submitted.

The back-calculation of the ITCS accounts seemed a smart move, but in the opinion of counsel to the Director of Public Prosecutions in 1974 the rearrangement of the ITCS accounts involved offences of conspiracy, larceny and theft and, in the event, anyone who had not been a Privy Councillor would have been prosecuted for them. Maudling was ignoring company law because it was inconvenient, as he had previously ignored the rules on ministerial interests. He had no doubt convinced himself that as there was no particularly dishonest intent, he was in the clear, but his sense of what was honest and dishonest had been blurred by alcohol and by exposure to men like Miller, Poulson and Hoffman, not to mention the flexible morality of business in the Gulf.

In September 1969 Poulson counterclaimed that ITCS owed him £70,000 for design work in Dubai connected with a hospital, a hotel development and the infamous airport terminal. Maudling flatly refused to acknowledge this as a legitimate debt from ITCS to Poulson. But Poulson was, in the breach, honouring the rules of his profession; as the *Architect's Journal* commented in 1972 he 'would have acted unprofessionally in not submitting a fee as that would have implied that he was doing speculative work'.[56] While ITCS was essentially fronting for Poulson, the claim that the professional practice was owed something for Dubai is technically at least as defensible as the claim that Maudling could do what he did with the Abu Dhabi funds. The dispute culminated in an acrimonious meeting in September 1969 between Maudling, Poulson and solicitor Nigel Grimwood, at which, according to Poulson, 'We arrived at 4pm and Maudling was in his shirt sleeves and drunk. Grimwood was very belligerent and abused Maudling. Consequently as a result of the atmosphere we left and the matter of the £70,000 has never been raised again with Maudling.' Neither Maudling nor Grimwood recognised this version of events; Grimwood denied being abusive.[57] In November 1969 Poulson's executive officers concluded that 'we consider no useful purpose would be served in attempting to recover the amounts which we could possibly claim against various clients there'.[58]

With the situation deteriorating, Reggie and Martin Maudling resigned from the board of Open System Building at its meeting on 14 October. OSB was an unsuccessful building company and it became even less successful as time went on. In 1969 it signed contracts for only forty-three houses. Reggie explained at the time that he was too busy to keep attending board meetings. Martin's resignation was ostensibly for the same reason, but given that he had stayed on the board despite living in Australia back in the winter of

1967–8 this seems unlikely. Later Reggie told investigators that, given that OSB's work was mainly in the north and he was based in London, he felt unable to keep himself sufficiently informed about the company and its activities to stay on. The looming legal problems of Dan Smith in the south London borough of Wandsworth cannot have helped, and nor could its developing financial problems. It was deeply in debt, another misbegotten, overambitious and under-capitalised Poulson venture. When Billy Sales, a Coal Board official of considerable intelligence whom Poulson had corrupted, took over as Chairman in summer 1969, he discovered its financial position from Martin Maudling:

> The detailed arrangements concerning the financial aspects of the Company were unknown to me though I had gathered from a memorandum prepared by Martin Maudling and indications by other Directors that the Company was in effect a Sales organisation and that its income was derived from the royalty fees on the houses sold. To the extent that the fees received did not meet the outgoings of the company, funds were supplied by Ropergate Services Limited. I understood that there was no difficulty concerning the supply of those funds, though it was clear to me that the Company would be in a state of growing indebtedness to Ropergate Services Limited until such time as OSB Ltd became viable.[59]

OSB was sinking, and dependent on Poulson's continued viability, which Maudling well knew by October 1969 was a weak basis for a company. DTI Inspectors reported in 1973 that there were possible criminal charges against Maudling for trading while insolvent.[60] Maudling got out when he could, although his relationship with ITCS was much more involved. In November 1969 Poulson's position went from bad to worse. During 1968–9 he had recruited competent managers in George Wilson and Billy Sales, albeit at high salaries, but it was too late to turn things around. Poulson had tried to ignore the problems that had been revealed over the summer, but in November 1969 Wilson came to him with an alarming memorandum, backed up by Vivian Baker, the accountant who had tried to inject some realism into the Poulson operation, and Alistair McCowan, Poulson's chief civil engineer. The report, and a further document from Coopers' in December 1969, recommended various cuts, including the termination forthwith of payments to 'consultants' (quotation marks in original) and provision of benefits to non-employees.[61]

The dying Poulson empire – Poulson claimed that he had lost effective control over the companies by now – did make several cuts, including an agreement between Maudling and Grimwood on the cancellation of the Adeline Genée covenant in late 1969,[62] but it was too little, too late. On the last day of the 1960s, John Poulson was called by some business partners to a meeting at the Queen's Hotel in Leeds. He arrived expecting a New Year party but in fact Poulson stumbled into a business meeting attended by solicitors who gave him documents and urged him to sign them. John King had set up a company, Inter Planning and Design (IPD) just before Christmas as a vehicle to buy out the Poulson practice; the architect himself would remain on the books as a consultant and was given promises of fees and an eventual lump sum payment – very little of which materialised. Poulson was reluctant and would not sign until he had received clearance from Grimwood, who was at a party and unavailable until 3a.m. Grimwood advised Poulson to sign, and control over his practice passed to IPD. The details were formalised in agreements dated March 1970.

Like many aspects of the Poulson affair the IPD takeover is ambiguous. On one level, while unsentimentally executed with a lack of festive spirit, it was a sensible business salvage operation. Poulson was manifestly incapable by that stage of dealing with the situation, and if the whole practice went down there would be unfinished projects in Britain and abroad, further losses and a disastrous outcome for clients, staff and creditors. IPD was in a better position to raise funds, including £30,000 in soft loans from the McAlpine construction concern, to keep things going.[63] Another way of looking at IPD was as a mechanism to keep Poulson's assets at least temporarily out of reach of his creditors and any possible trustee in bankruptcy. The controllers of IPD would then be in a position to oversee the distribution of assets on Poulson's behalf at their discretion.[64] When summoned to a private bankruptcy hearing in July 1972, John King replied to Muir Hunter as follows:

Q. Well, the people for whom this trust was created, as I understand you, is the creditors of Poulson, and what have you done for them?
A. What have we done for them?
Q. Yes.
A. Nothing yet.
Q. No.
A. The only thing we can do for them is to pay them.
Q. So for two years you have kept the creditors of Poulson, collectively, out of the assets of Poulson, have you not?
A. It's certainly not my intention. If that's what it boils down to; I don't know. I know what we have been trying to do, and that is to see that his creditors are paid, and that's the object of the exercise.[65]

King gave the impression of being a reluctant witness, who would not even volunteer his middle name until specifically asked and professed ignorance of the details of the transactions, claiming that he had signed what the lawyers had put in front of him.[66] Hunter lost his temper with King at the hearing, shouting, 'What is the Court to make, Mr King, of a person in your position who pretends he does not know a single thing about the collection of £160,000 worth of creditors' money? You tell me what we are to do with you?'[67] The bankruptcy investigators were far from satisfied that the IPD arrangement was legitimate, the Registrar commenting in August 1972 that the March 1970 agreement 'so far as I can tell at this stage attempted to put the assets of the bankrupt out of the reach of his creditors. The propriety of that deed and the way it would work to pay the creditors has not in my view been properly or satisfactorily explained.'[68] In the end no action was taken against any of the IPD principals, although there was a voluntary financial settlement in 1973. The legal work on the conversion itself became a matter of dispute and the bankruptcy trustees later recovered £2,000 under statutory provisions from Grimwood's firm Clifford Turner. However, Maudling was happy enough with the running of IPD and the business relationship between King and Maudling rapidly developed a social side: Maudling was a guest at King's second, high society, wedding in 1970.

Other loose ends were being tidied up. Reggie and Martin Maudling renounced any claim to unpaid directors' fees and other assets from Poulson in April 1970; Maudling was technically owed something of the order of £30,000 but it was completely irrecoverable and, given the scale of the diversions of cash from Abu Dhabi and Nigeria, would have been pushing his luck to insist on repayment. In May 1970 Poulson was prevailed upon to sign away his remaining claims against Maudling, some of which, like the Dubai design work, were quite substantial. Poulson hardly knew what he was doing at that time, and by his own admission he was suicidally depressed during that month. The May 1970 agreement was clearly made under duress, although it was a significant complicating factor when it came to unravelling the Poulson financial position after his personal bankruptcy in 1972. In November Poulson wrote to Bernard Kenyon, who had been a director of his companies:

I signed a letter, the validity of which you never agreed, giving Maudling exemption from any debts, but I shall never be able to understand why he never collected the £70,000 from Sheikh Raschid and Mahdi Tajir. The instructions for the work were given to my staff, not me, who did the work and should have been paid . . . On top of the £70,000 from ITCS you are well aware that there is a further £230,000 accumulated losses. You resigned because you didn't agree with the way Maudling was carrying on spending all this money and not having any return for it.[69]

Maudling was still much involved in the affairs of the Gulf, despite the collapse of his partner Poulson, thanks to his continuing strong ties with Mahdi Tajir. The Maudlings made a jokey public allusion to their dependence on the Arabs at a grand society event, Antonia Fraser's Field of the Cloth of Gold Ball in January 1970. Roy Strong recorded in his diary that 'the Reginald Maudlings, never ones to miss a party, appeared for some inexplicable reason dressed as Arabs'.[70] Business was still mixed with politics.

The official Conservative line even in October 1969, despite the mandarins' campaign to persuade them to change their minds, was that 'the federation appears at this moment to have little chance of an effective future',[71] and that they would keep the troops in the Gulf. A diplomat who sat next to Reggie at a lunch in February 1970 reported that:

> Incidentally, Mr Maudling said that if the Conservative Party won the election they fully intended, so far as he was at present aware, to put the clock back as regards withdrawal. He thought that the first step after a successful election would be to send an emissary to the Gulf to discuss new treaties with the Shaikhs or with the Union if it had come into operation under which some British troops would be retained in the Gulf area. He was vague about this because, as he said, it would be necessary to 'study the papers'.[72]

But when the Conservatives came to power in June 1970 the Arabian Department line in favour of withdrawal stuck, even though it was still possible to remain; by autumn 1970 advocates of a continued British military role in the Gulf, such as Patrick Wall, were disenchanted that nothing had been done and the clock was still ticking.[73] The Heath government turned over the withdrawal question to a mission by the experienced Arabist diplomat Sir William Luce, and it was no surprise when Luce confirmed that it would be better to go ahead with the pull-out. The federation talks, after their earlier uncertainties, went well and as the British forces withdrew in 1971 the United Arab Emirates (UAE) became a fully independent, federal state under the presidency of Sheikh Zayed of Abu Dhabi. The seven Trucial States joined; Bahrain and Qatar became small independent emirates. In contrast to post-colonial federations in Africa and the Caribbean, the UAE federation was stable and durable, and Zayed proved an astute leader who, despite the imbalance of wealth, was willing to share power. An important gesture came in 1972 when the new UAE established its diplomatic missions around the world and the London posting was given to the power behind the throne of Dubai, Mahdi Tajir, on a part-time basis that allowed him to continue his numerous profitable lines of business.

Just as his business was collapsing, John Poulson and his cronies had started to attract some official and unofficial investigation, from a multitude of directions. The first threat, which Poulson managed to dodge, came from two police investigations in the late 1960s that impinged on the Poulson–Smith network. In both cases Poulson managed to escape detailed scrutiny and his name came up as a puzzling loose end, but the web had started to unravel. One of the cases was a corruption investigation in Bradford, with which Maudling had absolutely no connection but which ultimately drew serious journalistic attention to Poulson. There had been a series of corrupt transactions, expenses fiddles and freeloading at the expense of municipal contractors at the City Architect's department and at a trial in Leeds in 1969 four officials were sentenced. The City Architect himself was dismissed without notice by the council in March 1970 after a District Auditor's report made the scale of his corruption clear, although the Bradford police request to the Director of Public Prosecutions that there should be further charges was refused; the resolution of this matter had to wait a further six years. The council clean-up instituted by Bradford's short-lived Tory administration included blacklisting firms that had been found to have been involved in corruption. The boycotted firms, with some justice, felt that they had been penalised while other guilty firms had got away with it. Ray Fitzwalter, a reporter for the *Bradford Telegraph and Argus* who was covering the corruption cases, heard their grumbling about the big shot from Pontefract, John Poulson, and decided to investigate. The result was an intriguing article in the local paper and in April 1970 a *Private Eye* piece by Paul Foot, 'The Slicker of Wakefield, by Oliver T. Dan Goldsmith' which hinted at Poulson's political connections. Fitzwalter remained on the Poulson story, on and off, for most of the next decade. His tenacity ultimately led Maudling to blunder into a disastrous legal labyrinth when he sued the reporter for libel in 1974.

The other corruption case was Wandsworth, where the police investigation that started in 1968 was drawing to a close in late 1969. The case against Sporle on the basis of his relationship with the housing contractors was so clear that the police naturally focused on this when they investigated him. The chief investigating officer, Superintendent Mees, reported that what he found in Wandsworth indicated that 'Sporle had so many irons in so many fires that the whole conception of honest local government becomes a farce'.[74] Sporle's relationship with T. Dan Smith was regarded as a corrupt bargain, but the Wandsworth police missed its full significance. The police evidence was submitted to counsel to the Director of Public Prosecutions, K. Richardson.[75] In his report submitted on 28 November 1969, the barrister found that the picture it presented was so alarming that the best course of action would be to set up a full-scale judicial inquiry into local government corruption. Richardson's findings – which if acted upon would have broken the Poulson affair wide open three years early – were brushed aside.

The Labour Attorney General, Elwyn Jones, refused a public inquiry on the grounds that a 1966 review of the procedures for tribunals of inquiry had ruled that they should not be used for minor or local matters 'but always confined to matters of vital public importance concerning which there is something in the nature of a nation-wide crisis of confidence'. Richardson could not say so, but he obviously believed that this argument was nonsense and stated in a further opinion that the evidence that had come up in the closing stages of the police enquiry proved that it was not a purely local problem. One of the witnesses testified that an influential councillor in Scotland had indicated that his firm would have a good chance of a large contract if it provided him with a new Rover 2000 car.[76] There were strands connecting the Wandsworth case, through Dan Smith and his confusing corporate web, with councils in the Midlands and the North. If they had but known, there was a link to Bradford, in that one of the suspect contractors in Wandsworth had also obtained contracts by dubious methods there.

Unknown to Richardson, increasingly clear confirmation that corruption in local government was not confined to Bradford and Wandsworth was coming in to central government in 1969 and 1970. In late 1969 or early 1970 Alice Bacon, a redoubtable Leeds Labour MP, had become suspicious about corruption in local authorities in the West Riding and approached Harold Wilson, who asked her to prepare a memorandum on the subject. Bacon was a bit reluctant to get too involved, as she was a Home Office Minister of State, and nothing had come of this inquiry by the time of the 1970 General Election. According to Wilson, Bacon had discovered that Poulson was one of the guilty parties, and that Maudling was connected with him.[77]

There was also a more substantial, formal warning. District auditors, responsible for checking that local government expenditure was made according to the law, had become suspicious and as well as the special inquiry in Bradford other problems had come to their notice. The same names kept coming up – John Poulson, T. Dan Smith and Andy Cunningham, the power broker in County Durham. The outcome was that early in 1970 the Chief Inspector of Audit submitted what a later official inquiry called:

> A dossier which he had compiled of detailed and disturbing information about certain relations existing between Mr Poulson, Mr Smith, Mr Cunningham and other individuals. This dossier (which we have seen) was considered over a period of some nine months within the Department of the Director of Public Prosecutions in consultation with the audit inspectorate and the police.[78]

The widespread nature of local authority corruption was not Richardson's only argument for a public inquiry in the light of the Wandsworth affair. He wrote that the Wandsworth affair was sufficiently complicated and the corruption law written in such a way that it might be possible for the defendants to argue for separate trials, which would make it hard for the prosecution to demonstrate the system of corruption that Sporle had organised. The charges against Dan Smith were a particular worry and Richardson advised that these were the most tenuous parts of the proposed charge sheet, and so it proved when it came to court, although Richardson stopped short of arguing that it was inadvisable to charge Smith. The most important aspects of the case, namely what Inspector Mees called the 'web of intrigue' spun by Dan Smith and the insight into systematic local corruption, were precisely what was lost in the process of drawing up criminal charges, although they would have been thoroughly explored had there been an inquiry.

The Labour government's decision not to call an inquiry into local corruption in 1969 or 1970 was disgraceful given the weight of evidence and rumour that had accumulated. Some of the reason must have been a failure of coordination – that nobody had an overall view of the scraps of information that were raining in from all directions. But there were also political fears that an uprooting of council corruption would involve disgrace for many Labour councillors and bring the party into general disrepute. There was an additional complication with Smith and Cunningham, who were important figures in the national party; Smith also had undertaken public relations work for the Labour Party in the north during the 1964 and 1966 elections. There were wider, vaguer fears that others might be brought down. Bob Mellish (Minister of Public Buildings and Works 1967–9 and Chief Whip from April 1969) was cut from the same cloth as Sidney Sporle – a bullying machine politician who dominated a decaying south London inner-city borough full of system-built housing. Mellish, who was never keen on putting housing estate contracts out to open tender, knew Sporle quite well, and Harold Wilson at least believed (possibly wrongly) that Mellish had been involved in the Poulson scandal.[79] Tony Greenwood, the Minister of Housing, frankly told his civil servants that when MPs asked to see him to talk about Wandsworth that he 'wants to find an excuse not to', and the prosecutors were approached to try to find such a pretext.[80] Another person who would be tarnished by the fall of Smith would be Ted Short, the Education Secretary, who had done business with Dan, and as MP for Newcastle Central was a political ally. Maudling was protected from Poulson fallout in 1969–70 as a corollary of Labour's self-preservation instincts.

The Wandsworth affair therefore passed off relatively quietly. Smith's network of companies had confused the police. The subject of Open System Building came up, but Sporle had actually been paid through an account called Dansmith PR and the police did not know how OSB featured in the case except through some sort of relationship with Dansmith PR and the building methods Smith was promoting. They did go to the trouble of compiling a list of directors of the firm, which included Reginald and Martin Maudling, but did not follow the trail any further. The charges against Smith were brought from the wrong end of the telescope – the police thought that the consultancy payments to Sporle had been a sweetener for a £5,000 a year PR contract, rather than the PR contract being a kickback paid by Wandsworth to Smith for bringing Sporle into his network. The PR contract was dubious but not a swindle – Smith did do some work for it and produced material promoting Wandsworth's local services. Smith for his part was incredulous that he could be prosecuted for this and came to believe that it was a stitch-up. John Poulson's name came up as having had dealings in Wandsworth, but he was a relatively small player there. The 'Slicker of Wakefield' article did not go completely unnoticed. The prosecutors in the

Wandsworth case included it in the case file although not for the reasons Foot and Fitzwalter might have hoped. It was read to see if its authors could be prosecuted for contempt of court,[81] and its contents were not followed up – the priority was now to seal the case against Sporle and Smith, not to cast the net still wider.

Reggie was, understandably, tired and depressed in autumn 1969. It had been a tough year, with only a week of proper holiday, and his general exhaustion had been compounded by the growing realisation that his business links with Poulson and Hoffman had produced embarrassment rather than the wealth for which he had hoped. They were a source of anxiety and fear at the prospect that there would be investigations and a public scandal, and his hasty resignations from REFA and Open System Building could not insulate him completely. His basic financial problems remained unsolved despite the many directorships he still had in reputable concerns, his consultancy for Eric Miller and the occasional subvention from Mahdi Tajir.

Reggie's political career had been stagnant, with his public profile remaining low and the mood in the Conservative Party turning against his pet cause of incomes policy and his consensual style.

Reggie and Beryl also had family worries during 1968 and 1969. Caroline had been pursuing a repertory acting career, making friends and enjoying herself, but at the end of 1968 she found herself pregnant as a result of a relationship that had run its course. After the breakup, she had flown to Kenya for a holiday and when she discovered that she was expecting a child she stayed in Kenya and kept her secret to herself. When the baby was born in May 1969, Caroline screwed up her courage and returned to London to face her parents, who had been bewildered by her long stay in Kenya. She need not have worried. Both Reggie and Beryl were 'wonderful and full of understanding', and although Beryl did feel that Caroline should marry the father they supported her completely. Then Caroline went on a two-week holiday to South Africa and met Anton Thompson, with whom she had a whirlwind romance that resulted in a quick marriage that was celebrated on 12 September. Thompson was smitten by 'the fascinating aura of her personality, her beauty, her courage, her honesty and above all her love and compassion for mankind', and was welcomed into the family.[82]

Reggie was forthright in supporting Caroline, telling the *Express*, 'I can't understand all this fuss. We have a daughter of whom we are very proud and our greatest desire is that she is happy.' Both Reggie and Beryl were caring and loving grandparents. Beryl was shortly going out to South Africa to see Anton Thompson and Caroline, who had thrown herself into anti-apartheid drama projects.[83]

The lead that Reggie set was followed for the most part in the press. When the story broke in the British press a bit over a week after Caroline's marriage, it received lavish coverage in the tabloids, and a little in the

Telegraph as well. Concern was expressed by the National Campaign for Civil Liberties about the apparent invasion of privacy, but Caroline herself seemed happy enough to give interviews[84] and the tone of most of the coverage was friendly to her and the Maudlings, celebrating it as a good old-fashioned romantic drama with a happy ending. The London *Evening News* commented that 'How splendidly Mr and Mrs Maudling have faced a test that is a nightmare to many a parent. How different their love and loyalty from the attitude, still common, of "Go, and never darken my doors again." They make it quite clear that they are proud of their daughter and delighted with their first grandchild. Long may they all live to bring each other such family joy.'[85] Predictably, the only sour note came from Jean Rook, who sneered at Caroline and offered crocodile tears for the Maudlings. 'And how the hell is Beryl supposed to explain this one to the Barnet Mothers' Union?'[86] Times had changed, and many of the ladies of Barnet admired Reggie and Beryl's display of true family values more than the loveless moralistic posturing of people like Rook.

The birth of Reggie's grandchild was a private event with some public consequences. Reggie thought that any question about its effect on his career was 'a damn silly question . . . The world is changing and mainly for the better I think. We do not comment on our children's affairs. All we are concerned about is their happiness.'[87] Reggie's acceptance, not only of Caroline's life but also the social changes her recent experiences represented, was genuine. He deserves an approving note in the history of the liberalisation of British society for his treatment – which contrasted with the traditional concealment and shame that only ten years previously most Tories would have regarded such a saga in their families.

Reggie was never a traditionalist about so-called moral issues, as his advocacy of freer divorce in 1951 demonstrated. His own experience of bringing up children in the 1960s broadened his outlook even further, and his welcome for the social changes of the 1960s came from the heart and prefigured his liberal policies at the Home Office. However, most of the time he was less a liberalising crusader than a relaxed permissive, and his failure to record a vote in most of the key Commons divisions on social reforms in 1966–70 does not show a burning libertarian concern. There was sometimes a touch of selfish indifference. Reforming Labour MP Leo Abse was rather shocked when he struck up a conversation with Maudling one rainy night waiting for a taxi under the canopy at the House of Commons. Abortion was the issue of the moment. According to Abse:

> It was not so much what he said as the way he said it, there seemed to be a coarseness, a lack of sensibility. I was trying to steer some sort of reconciling path on the issue. I felt it was a deep, serious issue, a moral dilemma, a conflict between respecting life and respecting rights. Maudling's comments seemed to be insensitive to the seriousness of the

matter of abortion. The remarks he made were something along the lines of 'why can't a woman be allowed to get rid of it?' It was an unpleasant, coarse, insouciant response to something sacred which was so out of keeping with my image of Maudling.[88]

Maudling's declining powers and increasingly undisciplined lifestyle did not go unnoticed among his colleagues. His prospects of succeeding to the leadership should Heath fall were becoming more and more remote thanks to REFA and some traditionalist worries about his family life. 'Reginald Maudling, though still nominally Deputy Leader, has as little chance of becoming Leader as George Brown of becoming Prime Minister in place of Mr Wilson,'[89] wrote Andrew Roth. By the mysterious process by which political generations are designated, he had gone straight from being seen as a bit young for the top job to being seen as too old.[90] His drinking was becoming a subject of gossip within political circles; for instance Robin Day commented to Cecil King in October 1969 that 'Maudling is bone-lazy and quite useless after lunch'.[91] The only thing that amused Reggie about his changing image was his adoption as a kind of mascot by the surreal comedy programme *Monty Python's Flying Circus*. It might be a sign pointing to 'Reginald Maudling's Naughty Bits' one week, or a gratuitous mention of his name in a strange context the next, but he was not one to take offence at this unlikely form of celebrity.

Reggie was reluctantly obliged to take a more active role in politics – his claims to be doing more in this respect when he resigned from REFA and OSB were not incorrect, although he was not completely inactive in 1967–8 either as he was President of the National Union of Conservative and Unionist Associations, presiding at the 1968 conference, and involved in reaching agreement with the Wilson government on the vexed issue of Lords reform. But in 1969 he became more involved in the Advisory Committee on Policy, and was also guarding his position in the Shadow Cabinet in the hope of being made Chancellor. This had the unintended effect of launching the political career of Margaret Thatcher. Much to Maudling's regret, the strongly pro-comprehensive Shadow Education Secretary, Edward Boyle, resigned, and Heath's original plan had been to move Keith Joseph into Education and then give Maudling Joseph's old job at Industry. Reggie strongly objected to the idea, and it is difficult to imagine a less suitable post for him, because he hoped that if he remained without portfolio he would be well placed for a switch into the Treasury after the election. Maudling's resistance was successful – but Heath needed another person to shadow Education. The choice was Margaret Thatcher.[92]

Maudling could not have guessed the consequences at that point, but even so his political career, as with his business activities, was not a source of much pleasure. At a particularly low point in October, he wrote to his Barnet agent that: 'Conferences always do depress me and Brighton was no exception. The voice of reason was completely stifled . . . Anyway, your letter did much to cheer me up. Your steady support and confidence is something I value very deeply. I'll certainly carry on on the same lines. One cannot change one's nature or style.'[93] His lassitude and sloppiness were apparent to visiting academics David Butler and Michael Pinto-Duschinsky in November, as was his cynicism. The Conservative Party in opposition under Heath had undertaken an extraordinarily detailed and painstaking policy review, with myriad committees holding earnest discussions on subjects such as pensions, industrial relations and the scope of the public sector. In many ways it was an impressive and open-minded exercise. Reggie was involved in an overall coordinating role during this work, particularly after November 1968 when he took over some work in this connection previously carried out by Heath, but he had doubts about the wisdom of the general approach. He felt that a party could not really do policy formation without the civil service, and that it would be better to offer just a few broad emphases; however, he said in 1968, 'Ted was very keen on policy and a lot of hard work was being done.'[94] In 1969 he felt that he had made some progress on avoiding specific commitments, telling Butler that 'We have come out with a glorious set of platitudes and have avoided having a detailed set of economic policies. All our policies amount to is 1. Cut down the size of government. 2. Reform taxation. 3. Reform social services. 4. Reform industrial relations. That is all. Nobody understands about things like pensions.'[95]

In his relationship with the Research Department and its efforts, Reggie did not attend policy group meetings and avoided setting up any new ones, but chased progress on the ones that lagged behind. He also stopped some more radical suggestions that emerged from discussions on the public sector, prompted by Nicholas Ridley. 'People are much more sensible about denationalisation than they were before.' Reggie told eager Tory researchers that denationalising the telephones was not on, and that while hiving off one or two commercial branches of the government and introducing more competition in steel was fine, a 'shopping list' approach was not.[96] But other than these specific interventions, he took no interest in proceedings on policy.[97]

By the beginning of 1970 election timing was starting to become a factor in political calculations. Labour had clearly come through the worst by the conference season in 1969 and the real fight was on. The Conservative Shadow Cabinet convened on the last day of January 1970 at the Selsdon Park Hotel for a weekend conference to plan their manifesto and their approach to the election. Maudling did not play much of a part in the discussions, attending most sessions but saying very little. He found few allies during the economic policy debate at Selsdon for his case for an incomes policy – only Peter Walker and Edward Boyle supported him. By 1969–70 the Labour government had given up attempting to enforce its general incomes policy and, given that the substitute policy embodied in *In Place of Strife* had also collapsed, there was no defence against wage-push inflation that was delivering higher incomes in 1970 but storing up inflationary problems for the future. Macleod claimed at Selsdon that the short-term answer to the problem of wages amounted to 'arm twisting and standing firm in the public sector'. Reggie plaintively said during the debate on controlling prices:

> We are left with little to say about what we are doing. Have not got a simple answer . . . Is going to be very big gap to fill in our policy.
> Barber: Can it be filled?
> Maudling: No.[98]

Reggie was absolutely right, and the Conservatives' 1970 policy had no solution to the problem of wage inflation. It was the Heath government's fatal flaw. But, short of engineering a return to the Treasury, there was nothing Reggie felt he could do to avert what he saw as a fiasco in the making. He had agreed a non-aggression pact on incomes policy with Iain Macleod before the 1969 party conference, and had no real determination to cause a fuss at Selsdon, although he was still openly making his case in public, as in a *Spectator* article in April 1970.[99] Despite Selsdon's show of unity, Maudling was out on a limb. His lack of appetite for current politics communicated itself to observers. Reggie told Cecil King in March that 'If events are to be turbulent in the period when his party is in office he will seek an Embassy or the F.O.! He thought that if the Tories get in with a sufficient majority, they may well tackle the unions seriously.'[100] To talk about an Embassy, even idly, at a time when his party was on the verge of returning to power, does betoken a lack of commitment.

Labour's position in the opinion polls suddenly improved in May 1970, and with this shift the whole atmosphere of politics changed. The Tories had been regarded for most of 1967–9 as nearly certain winners of the next election, but from autumn 1969 'if we win' started to replace 'when we win'.[101] But suddenly it was almost 'when we lose'. Reggie Maudling, even at the worst point for the Wilson government in October 1968, was still stressing that Labour could still win when the election came round in 1970, once the economic benefits of the 1967 devaluation had worked their way through the system.[102] The warm, sunny May of 1970, with earnings rising much faster than prices, the balance of payments coming right and England progressing well in the football World Cup, seemed a good time for Labour to win an election. Wilson went to the country with an exceptionally complacent and vacuous manifesto called 'Now Britain's strong let's make her great to live in', and spent most of the campaign pottering around the Downing Street garden. The task of the Conservatives in the election was to puncture the mood of national optimism, a task to which the more brutal partisans like Heath and Macleod took with relish but Maudling found distasteful and almost certainly doomed to fail.

Reggie appeared on the second of the five Conservative party political broadcasts. Most of the broadcasts were extremely negative, and indeed the first one introduced vox pop grumbling and even vulgar abuse to British broadcast politics. For the most part the Tories took the low road in 1970, but Maudling was an exception in putting an idealistic case – Conservative competence meant higher growth than Labour had achieved, and therefore more ability to show compassion for the poor and ill.

Maudling's broadcast was poorly received by some party faithful, who complained that it was too 'gentlemanly'; they preferred the knocking tactics of Heath and Macleod.[103] He undertook the usual round of speaking and newspaper article writing, talking economics opposite Roy Jenkins on television, for instance, but had slipped to third in prominence in the Conservative campaign after his two leadership rivals from 1965 – Heath, and more surprisingly Enoch Powell. Powell stumped the country with speeches that recalled his 1968 outburst about rivers of blood, and verged on paranoia in their vision of sinister forces out to destroy the British nation. Thanks to a hysterical counter-attack from Tony Benn, which compared Powell's Wolverhampton to Hitler's Dachau, Powell won some sympathy even from the centre ground. Powell's purposes were obscure. Many thought he was staking out a claim for the Tory leadership after an election defeat, but a side effect of his speeches was to attract support for Heath's Tories, or at least cause working-class voters to think again before voting Labour. Then a series of bad news stories struck Wilson in the last week – England were knocked out of the World Cup, and the monthly balance of payments figures showed a freak deficit. The warnings of the Conservatives that there was a crisis on the way as soon as the election was over gained credence among the electorate, and the recently rediscovered enthusiasm of Labour supporters waned.

Even though he had his doubts about the national outcome ('in defeat, defiance!' he said in Churchillian fashion before the poll to Heath's young aide Douglas Hurd),[104] Reggie was confident that Barnet would return him again – Labour would have to do considerably better than they did in 1966, itself a good election for the party, to unseat Maudling, and once the constituency boundaries were reviewed the seat would become even safer. The new Barnet Liberal candidate John Henchley attacked Maudling's vulnerable constituency record: 'Maudling spends too much time in the City and too little among his constituents,' and promised to be a full-time MP.[105] Maudling's appearances in Barnet had become more and more infrequent and perfunctory over the years and this was an obvious line of criticism. However, it did the Liberals no good; their vote slipped back and they ended up losing their deposit. Even so, the swing to the Tories in Barnet was rather less than nationally, a sign that Maudling's local strength was past its peak. By the time Barnet declared, it was clear that the Tories had achieved a surprising success.

Electorate		71,828		
Turnout			71.5	
Reginald Maudling	Conservative	26,845	52.3	+5.2
Joan Baker	Labour	18,166	35.4	−1.3
John Henchley	Liberal	6,329	12.3	−3.9
Conservative majority		8,679	16.9	

There is still a psephological argument over what happened in 1970 – whether the polls had been wrong and the Tories had been ahead all along, or whether there had been a late swing to the Tories. Reggie himself believed in late swing: 'the big shift to us came in the last few days of the election campaign. I had expected a swing to us but this was bigger than I had anticipated.'[106] Reggie was noted as looking 'pensive' on election night as the Tory victory unfolded.[107] Edward Heath had triumphed, and his new Conservative government had a parliamentary majority of thirty, enough to see it through a full term. Rather than face a delegation of Lord Carrington, Alec Douglas-Home and Reggie Maudling, assuming the role for this purpose of the men in grey suits (although none of these grandees would have been clad in something so middle-management) to ask politely for his resignation, Heath had to work out which Cabinet offices to give them.

One of the first announcements to be made was that Reginald Maudling had been appointed Home Secretary. Jim Callaghan, who also held office both as Chancellor and Home Secretary, had told him in 1968 that the Home Office was greatly to be preferred to the Treasury: 'If you wanted something done you could get it done whereas in the Treasury if you wanted the economy to go somewhere it never did.'[108] But Reggie still hankered after a return as Chancellor. Home Secretary came as rather a surprise; Quintin Hogg had been the Shadow Home Secretary and had expected to be given the job for real, but in the event Heath decided to return Hogg to the House of Lords as Lord Chancellor, thereby recreating 'Lord Hailsham' who had lapsed from existence during the 1963 leadership crisis.

For reasons, one can do little better than to quote the words of a US Embassy cable about the new government: that while Hogg had legal expertise he was 'a person of mercurial temperament whose emotional ups and downs have been embarrassing on occasion' and a 'poor administrator' unsuitable for a big department of state, 'particularly one as potentially explosive politically as the Home Office'.[109] There was also the need to recognise Maudling's seniority by giving him one of the three great offices of state (as Chancellor of the Exchequer, Foreign Secretary and Home Secretary are quaintly but usefully known to political journalists).[110]

The appointment of Mr Maudling as Home Secretary has been on the cards ever since the germination of the idea of moving Hogg. Maudling would have preferred to be Foreign Secretary, but it has long been understood that

Sir Alec should have that post if he wanted it. Maudling would also have liked to go back to the Treasury, but his performance in that position during the last years of the Macmillan government became such a political liability subsequently for the Conservatives that there was no question of his returning. In these circumstances Maudling, above all a realistic man who would not do anything to strain the unity of the party leadership, gracefully assented to being Home Secretary. The presence of Maudling, with his tremendous intellectual capacity and proven ability, at the Home Office should add strength to the government on a vital domestic front.[111]

Maudling did add these qualities to the government, but he carried with him the fatal flaws that had become so prominent in the previous five years. They did not stop him being, for the most part, a decent Home Secretary and a stabilising influence on the government, but they were seen to disastrous effect in one of his side responsibilities. In 1970 the Home Office was the ministry with responsibility for Northern Ireland. Reggie's troubles became part of everyone's Troubles.

Chapter 20

'A BLOODY AWFUL COUNTRY':
NORTHERN IRELAND, 1970–1972

The political situation in Northern Ireland was worrying but not completely hopeless when Maudling took charge in June 1970. Looking back from outside the province over thirty years of suffering, episodes in the conflict seem to blend into a continuous roll-call of atrocity and murder with only particularly appalling incidents – Bloody Sunday, the Shankill Butchers, the Enniskillen and Omagh bombs – having a strong hold on memory. It was not like that from the beginning. At the time of the 1970 election, nobody had been killed in political violence in the province since October 1969. No British soldiers had been killed before February 1971. The first car bombs were planted at the end of 1971. The first fatal bomb attack in England in the conflict was in February 1972. All these steps downwards towards the abyss took place during Maudling's term as Home Secretary.

Brian Faulkner, after the fall of the power-sharing executive he led, said in July 1974 that 'you can do three things in Irish politics – the right thing, the wrong thing or nothing at all. I have always thought it is better to do the wrong thing than nothing at all.'[1] Maudling was temperamentally incapable of understanding what Faulkner was driving at; indeed, he sometimes had to be convinced that doing the *right* thing was better than doing nothing at all. By the time he handed over to Whitelaw in March 1972 fatalities were running at around one a day, the Provisional Irish Republican Army (IRA) had turned into a lethal adversary of the British army in what Maudling had called 'a state of war', and leading Unionist politicians were addressing fascist rallies with bloodthirsty talk of being ready to 'liquidate the enemy'. Even if it had not been the case when he first flew over in July 1970, Northern Ireland had certainly become a 'bloody awful country', to use Maudling's own infelicitous phrase, when he gratefully gave up his role as minister answerable for the province.

The 'Troubles' were, depending on one's definition, around a year old in June 1970, although the history of the province before that was a shabby tale of sectarianism and prejudice. Northern Ireland was founded in 1920 when the Government of Ireland Act divided the island into two parts with devolved institutions under overall British authority. While this was a dead letter in the south, and was replaced in 1922 by effective independence in the form of a 'Free State', the 1920 arrangements were still basically in force in 1970 in the northern six counties of Ireland. A Northern Ireland parliament, with similar responsibilities to those of the post-1999 Scottish parliament, sat in Stormont to the east of Belfast. The leader of the executive was styled as 'Prime Minister'. Stormont was described by its first Prime Minister, Lord Craigavon, as 'a Protestant parliament for a Protestant people'. A single party, the Ulster Unionist Party, had controlled the government of the province continuously since 1920, a record of electoral success that would be more impressive if it was based on more than mere sectarian voting patterns. Attempts to found other Protestant or non-denominational parties, as with the Labour Party in the 1930s, were seen off by appeals to the 'Orange card'. Politics in Stormont was contested between a permanent Unionist majority and a powerless minority of more or less nationalist MPs elected from Catholic areas.

Tocqueville wrote that 'le moment le plus dangereux pour un mauvais gouvernement est d'ordinaire celui où il commence à se reformer' (the most dangerous moment for a bad government is usually when it starts to reform itself).[2] This process began in Northern Ireland in 1963, with the election of Terence O'Neill as Unionist leader and Prime Minister. Previously Minister of Finance, his main concern was the decay of the economy in Northern Ireland, heavily dependent on declining textiles and heavy industry. The economic plan was to encourage the establishment of new manufacturing industries in the province to replace the old industries. Economic progress, it was hoped, would remove some of the sectarian divisions in society and put the union with Britain on a secure footing. O'Neill certainly did not believe that there was anything fundamentally wrong with Northern Ireland, but made some gestures towards better relations with the Irish Republic and respect towards Catholic faith. He did not want to dismantle the unionist state and had only limited objectives on civil rights issues, although he was willing to reform the franchise for local elections which was a particularly sore nationalist grievance.

Maudling would have found Northern Ireland more congenial if he had been dealing with O'Neill, a cool and rational politician with similar ideas about the economy who was not out of place in the Conservative Party of Heath and Maudling. Jim Callaghan thought that 'O'Neill would have made an excellent Prime Minister in the Conservative tradition in easier times'.[3] However, O'Neill's extremely limited opening to modernity aroused anger and fear among traditionalist Unionists and between 1966 and Maudling's arrival in power in 1970 everything changed.

The opposition to O'Neill among Protestants was not an attractive phenomenon. Some of it was simple sectarian bigotry – when Belfast's Lord Mayor flew the city's flag at half mast in sympathy for the death of Pope John XXIII in 1963 a previously little-known Presbyterian minister called Ian Paisley led a thousand Protestants in protest at 'lying eulogies now being paid to the Roman anti-Christ'. Protestants, however, did have legitimate reasons for stressing their distinction from the Republic, whose political and social system was dominated by the Catholic Church which insisted on its own confessional privileges. The Republic's economy then made the North's seem relatively advanced. Unionism itself was a political position born of defensiveness, of 'what we have we hold' and for historical reasons its adherents valued successful resistance – to Home Rule in 1912–14 and the Irish rebellion in 1916–20 – more than the mundane, Reggie-ish, political virtues of flexibility and adaptation. The groundswell against O'Neill was expressed through normal politics, but also through the reactivation of the Ulster Volunteer Force (UVF) in some still rather mysterious circumstances in 1966.

In 1967, inspired by the success of the civil rights movement in the southern United States, students and Catholic activists set up the Northern Ireland Civil Rights Association (NICRA), demanding an end to discrimination in voting, housing, employment and the abolition of the sectarian reserve police force known as the B Specials. In 1968 the civil rights movement carried out protest rallies and marches, which had particular resonance in Northern Ireland where marches had been a traditional way of celebrating the ascendancy of Orange culture. On 5 October a civil rights march was brutally dispersed by B Specials in Londonderry, a city whose Unionist local authority depended on outrageous electoral manipulation to survive despite a majority of nationalist voters. The problems of the 'democratic slum' under Britain's rule were now becoming urgent and the British government set aside its long tradition of non-intervention in Northern Ireland affairs. O'Neill and his colleagues were summoned to Downing Street by Harold Wilson and pressured into agreeing to faster reforms. O'Neill appealed directly to his electorate, speaking of 'Ulster at the crossroads' and arguing that Ulster would be shamed if they failed to sort out their own problems and had to accede to Westminster legislating over their heads. Despite initial success, divisions emerged within the Unionists and O'Neill's hardline Minister for Home Affairs, William Craig, resigned. A provocative march over the New Year by the student radical 'People's Democracy' movement was broken up by Protestant thugs at Burntollet bridge and groups of policemen went on an undisciplined rampage in the Catholic Bogside area of Londonderry. The Deputy Prime Minister, Brian Faulkner, resigned in January 1969. O'Neill held a general election for Stormont in February 1969 in an attempt to gain a new mandate for reform, but the election was a confused business. Party branches divided into pro and anti O'Neill factions, just as Stormont MPs had, although sometimes the MP and the local branch were in different camps.

At this point terrorism made its first substantial contribution to events. Protestant extremists of the UVF set bombs at several electricity and water installations, succeeding in April 1969 in depriving most of Belfast of running water for a few days. It was part of a deliberate 'strategy of tension', to use the Italian term for a basically similar concept. The UVF – accurately –

assumed that the IRA would get the blame. They also hoped that chaos would discredit the moderates in government and lead to a surge in support for hardline policies. O'Neill resigned, but he was succeeded by James Chichester-Clark, who promised to continue the reform programme. In July and August the marching season was accompanied by mob violence and back in London the Home Office and the Ministry of Defence watched the disorder with growing alarm. On 13 August Home Office Minister Lord Stonham warned Maudling (in his capacity as Deputy Leader of the Opposition) that the arrival of British troops in Northern Ireland might not be long delayed, and Maudling signalled his assent.[4] The crunch came that evening as reports reached the Home Secretary, Jim Callaghan, of a collapse in law and order in towns across the province; the next morning he and Wilson, already decided on action, received a message from Chichester-Clark requesting troops. The situation in West Belfast had completely broken down, with Protestant mobs rampaging in Catholic areas burning down houses. The police (RUC) were ill equipped to control mass violence of this sort, and their auxiliary force, the B Specials, were an ill-disciplined and sectarian rabble.

At first, the army operation was a great success. Through superior force, and a certain amount of moral authority, the army were able to stop the violence and stop mob sectarian attacks. In the breathing space this provided, it was obvious that political progress had to be accelerated. Chichester-Clark and Harold Wilson agreed a 'Downing Street Declaration' in August 1969 which essentially provided the 'official' way forward for Northern Ireland. The B Specials were to be scaled back, an official review would take place into policing, an inquiry would take place into the disturbances, and action would be taken on the most glaring grievances such as local government and housing. The Declaration envisaged the withdrawal of the troops taking place fairly rapidly once satisfactory internal security arrangements were in operation. The two reports on disorder (Cameron) and policing (Hunt) found considerable reason to criticise the way in which the Northern Ireland government was operating and the British government attempted to enforce reforms. Callaghan was in his element in dealing with Northern Ireland. From August 1969 until June 1970 he was ever-present, somewhat to the irritation of the Stormont government and the British army. He and Roy Hattersley, the army minister, would micro-manage military and police decisions with the aim of keeping a balance that would allow a tenuous peace to be preserved.

Despite this, there were serious problems under the surface. The Ulster Unionist Party's hold on the politics of the province was weakening, but this was not the birth of political pluralism, despite the foundation of the avowedly cross-community Alliance Party in April 1970. The centre ground was disappearing as more extreme forces appeared on the Unionist right under pressure from the fearful and discontented Protestant electorate at large. In March 1970 five rebel Stormont MPs were expelled; in April Ian

Paisley and an ally of his won two Stormont seats in by-elections. From this point on, the option of a new Stormont election was pretty much closed, as both the mainstream Unionists and the British feared the election of a regime dominated by Paisley and his fellow-travellers. The Westminster general election confirmed that a wheel had come off the Unionist electoral machine, with the party reduced to only eight of the twelve seats – three Catholics of various shades won seats, as did Ian Paisley who triumphed in Antrim North. The election resulted in an extraordinarily diverse collection of Northern Ireland MPs, from Paisley representing new Unionism and Captain Orr of the old-style Orange Order, through moderates like Stratton Mills and the SDLP's Gerry Fitt to Frank McManus, a jovial veteran republican from the rural west who carried a revolver around, and the youthful republican Marxism of Bernadette Devlin. The Ulster debates of the 1970–4 parliament had an intense flavour all their own which fascinated new MPs such as Cecil Parkinson,[5] but appalled Reggie Maudling.

On the streets of Northern Ireland, the IRA had endured an ignominious few years. Its last 'military' campaign in 1956–62 had been a failure and at the end of the episode the organisation had abandoned armed tactics. In the succeeding years it split over political questions, between Marxism and a 'back to basics' Catholic-nationalist position. The IRA was in no position to make much of a contribution to the events of summer 1969 and its failure to deliver on its boast of being the defender of the Catholic community gave it the derisive nickname 'I Ran Away'. Its activists, particularly the traditionalist 'Provisional' faction which formed in December 1969, were determined to avenge this humiliation. Their opportunity came at the end of March 1970 when a provocative Orange march along Springfield Road in West Belfast aroused Catholic rioters and was helped through by the army.

Relations between the army and the Catholics of Belfast had been deteriorating since those first few days when they had ridden to the rescue in August 1969. Malachi O'Docherty, a moderate West Belfast resident, recalled the behaviour of soldiers even in the relatively peaceful days of autumn 1969 as being crude and undisciplined, shouting racist abuse in the street and swaggering around 'sometimes drunk and usually pig ignorant'.[6] However, despite this – and the use of CS gas and a public threat to shoot petrol-bombers in the Springfield Road and Ballymurphy riots – republicans who called for the total removal of 'Brits' from Northern Ireland were inhibited in attacking British forces. They lacked mass support for such action, and what sympathy they had was through a – misplaced – belief that the terrorists were effective defenders of the Catholic population against loyalist violence. The republicans had recovered somewhat from their ignominious failure in August 1969 and were gathering weapons, supposedly for defensive purposes, but they were hindered by a split between the 'Official' and 'Provisional' factions. The terrorists were not strong enough, and lacked sufficient support in the community, for a full-scale campaign in June 1970.

The British general election in June 1970 brought a new dimension to the problems. The Conservatives were, after all, officially titled the Conservative and Unionist Party and the depleted eight Ulster Unionists formed part of Heath's fairly slender parliamentary majority. The result was greeted with some simple-minded triumphalism by the Unionist right, and apprehension among the nationalists. This local reception was not the fault of the Conservatives, who had been scrupulous in supporting the Wilson government's policies while in opposition. But it did oblige them to demonstrate their neutral bona fides and give assurances that nothing had indeed changed in terms of policy. On the day after the 1970 election Quintin Hogg as Shadow Home Secretary telephoned Callaghan to ask for his views about the situation he was handing over. Hogg would probably have pursued a more activist policy than Maudling did, and Alec Douglas-Home had even speculated in May 1970 that 'a more far reaching approach' might be introduced to manage Northern Ireland and that in any case the Conservatives wanted to see 'the maximum progress made in the implementation of reforms . . . Any slackening in the pace of reform would be disastrous as it would be the surest means of bringing "reactionary elements" onto the streets again.'[7] Douglas-Home's attitude suggests that some Conservatives were already thinking about forcing the pace of Stormont's reforms from London.

Reggie Maudling's appointment at first gave considerable hope for progress in Northern Ireland. After all, he was calm, open-minded and liberal, a heavyweight political figure in the new government, and a man with a pleasant and persuasive personality it was very difficult to dislike. Ken Bloomfield, a senior Northern Ireland civil servant, had grown used to the 'tea and biscuits' hospitality of the Callaghan Home Office and recalled his first meeting under Maudling with some fondness: 'we were asked if it would be convenient to conduct our exchanges over lunch at Claridge's. Setting aside our natural austerity, we said we thought we could bear it.'[8]

Northern Ireland might have been the making of Maudling; it did not then have the reputation as a graveyard for political careers. It had rescued Callaghan who had previously been a discredited figure in the Labour government thanks to devaluation and plotting over *In Place of Strife* but emerged from Ulster with his reputation enhanced. Maudling attracted early support from liberal opinion in Britain such as Mark Arnold-Forster of the *Guardian* and Patrick Brogan of *The Times*.[9] He also received a fulsome welcome from Edmund Curran of the moderate *Belfast Telegraph*, who praised his intelligence and calmness and quoted him as saying that he relished the new job because 'The problems are human rather than intellectual and it is this human contact I like'.[10] While Maudling did enjoy human contact, he was unprepared for and alienated by the raw hatreds of Belfast he encountered within a fortnight.

Maudling's predecessor was first to worry about the appointment. Callaghan was surprised and concerned that Maudling did not approach him for a briefing along the lines he had given Hogg, but merely said in a short conversation at the State Opening of Parliament that he intended to continue the same policies but leave a lot of responsibility to the men on the spot.[11] This was a serious error, and it was Maudling's fault. A series of events followed which could have been designed to alienate the nationalists. Most of them were not actually initiated by Maudling, but a consequence of his philosophy of delegating as much as possible to the people on the ground, who were of course the security forces and the Northern Ireland government. The inclination of the army was to clamp down on trouble, and the Stormont government was tempted to slacken the pace of reform under pressure from the Unionist right. The combined outcome was a sudden shift in the nature of the Northern Ireland problem, and the end of Maudling's brief Ulster honeymoon.

The most senior figures of the new government considered Northern Ireland at a meeting on 22 June. Heath called Maudling, Douglas-Home and Carrington into Number 10 to consider what to do in the light of the imminent 'marching season', always a sensitive point in the Northern Ireland calendar. The army had advised that there was the prospect of serious disorder accompanying the Orange marches and the government had little option but to accede to their request for more troops. Over the longer term, Cabinet Secretary Burke Trend outlined the possibilities in an alarming secret briefing paper:

(a) It could improve of its own accord. But this would be so nearly a miracle that we can perhaps disregard it.

(b) It could remain much as it is – stabilised only by the presence of British troops and trembling on the edge of disaster but never quite tipping over. The resultant burden on ourselves, in terms both of men and money, would be so intolerable if it were maintained indefinitely that we ought not to contemplate it if it can be avoided.

(c) It could get worse and finally tip over the edge – the Northern Ireland Government proving incapable of holding the position, civil war breaking out within the Province and Dublin being compelled to intervene. This would present us with a political and constitutional crisis of the first order; and certain very secret contingency plans have already been prepared against this possibility.[12]

Trend had no illusions that the reform programme agreed with Stormont had much chance of calming matters. He advised Heath to 'ask the Home Secretary to devise some fresh political initiative to break out of the vicious circle in which we are at present trapped', while recognising that it was almost impossible to see what form such an initiative might take. Maudling also reviewed the contingency plans, one of which was the Bill that the Wilson government had prepared so that Stormont could be abolished and Westminster run the province through 'direct rule' overnight if necessary.

The security forces advised the ministers that little could be done about that year's marching season: 'They had concluded that to attempt at this stage to divert marches etc from their traditional routes, and *a fortiori* to ban them altogether, would create a situation which could be contained, if at all, only by the use of forces even larger than those at present contemplated.'[13] The officers took the view that legal marches would be easier to control than the apparently inevitable illegal marches that would go ahead if there was an attempt to ban them. However, other counsels advised doing something. James Chichester-Clark himself feared for public safety and although he could not openly call for a ban he would have been relieved if the decision had been taken out of his hands.[14] Callaghan had established a rather shadowy position of 'UK Representative' in Belfast, occupied in 1970 by Ronald Burroughs, whose role had essentially been as a channel of communication between non-Unionists and the government. Burroughs was extremely alarmed by the atmosphere around the 1970 parades, having been informed that if parades entered Catholic areas it was likely that the IRA would step in as 'defenders'.[15]

Heath left the decision on the marches to Maudling. Maudling, like General Freeland who thought marching was ridiculous behaviour for grown men to indulge in, had no love for Orange parades. Maudling once told Ian Paisley, 'I find you very hard to understand, Ian. So far as I can see, you and your supporters spend all your time getting drunk and marching all over the place.' Paisley claimed that he had never got drunk but he had sometimes marched, which struck Maudling as funny because 'I have sometimes got drunk but I have never marched'.[16] Try as he might, Maudling found it difficult to take marches as seriously as people in Northern Ireland did – either as essential expressions of their culture or as arrogant strutting designed to put the Catholics in their place. Maudling let the marches go ahead virtually unaltered, and also killed off a plan Callaghan had developed to augment the RUC by sending British police to some of the safer areas of Belfast to assist over the weekend of the marches.

The 22 June meeting also decided to send more troops over because the army were overstretched. Quite how overstretched became apparent the next weekend, as the start of the marching season sparked gun battles in two Catholic areas of Belfast on Saturday 27 June. In Short Strand, an isolated Catholic enclave in mainly Protestant East Belfast, there were fears that it was about to be overrun by loyalist thugs but the Protestants were repulsed by a Provisional IRA unit in what became famous as the battle of St Matthew's Church. The British army had not been able to protect the people of the area, and the IRA had expunged their failure of August 1969. To Protestants, the events of that weekend were seen in a different light; the shootings in Ardoyne in North Belfast and the battle of St Matthew's were seen as sectarian IRA killings and on 28 June Protestant workers expelled 500 Catholic workers from the Harland & Wolff shipyards. There was also violence in Derry after the clumsy arrest of the newly re-elected republican MP, Bernadette Devlin, and the deaths of three IRA men (and two young girls) after the premature detonation of a bomb. It was the grimmest few days Northern Ireland had endured since August 1969.

The smoke and CS gas had barely dispersed when Maudling flew into the province on his first official visit on 30 June, which had been hurriedly arranged as a fact-finding and people-meeting tour. The Home Secretary had a hectic round of meetings and engagements – the initial timetable allowed only one hour for meeting the Stormont Cabinet – and he was confused and had not properly absorbed his briefing materials. General Sir Ian Freeland, the army's General Officer Commanding (GOC), thought that on Maudling's first visit 'it did appear that he was completely ignorant . . . he didn't appear to have a great grip on the situation or to be desperately interested'.[17] Freeland charitably assumed that his apparent ignorance was a pose, to gather information and appear impartial, but even if this was the case this technique was ill-advised – all sides were afraid of the situation slipping out of control, and Maudling's approach increased this fear.

Maudling left a bad impression on most of those he met on his first visit. Paddy Devlin, a nationalist MP, met him and thought he was 'plainly out of his depth and bored rigid', although Devlin himself contributed to Maudling's dislike of Northern Ireland by throwing a rolled up copy of the *Daily Express* at him.[18] The British army were bemused by Maudling's approach. An officer based at army headquarters in Northern Ireland told ITN reporter Desmond Hamill:

> Reggie Maudling had no idea. He would never go out. We would get people to meet him and he would wander round and say things like 'Are you going to Ascot?' He was hopeless talking to community leaders on the streets. After his first visit here he sat in my office with his head in his hands and said, 'Oh, these bloody people! How are you going to deal with them?'[19]

The army, reasonably enough, did not consider 'dealing with them' was its job. It saw its role at that stage as being to hold the ring while the politicians came up with a longer-term solution; the military command never had any illusions that it was a problem that admitted a purely military solution.

Maudling's visit was a considerable contrast with Callaghan's visits to the province, which had involved walkabouts in the streets, media events and energetic bustling about. Callaghan had tried to inspire confidence. Maudling hoped to learn things quietly, but the situation was so far outside his experience that he let despair get the better of him. As his plane climbed away from Northern Ireland on 1 July Maudling sighed exasperatedly, 'For God's sake bring me a large Scotch. What a bloody awful country!'[20]

Maudling, to his credit, never attempted to deny the accuracy of the quotation when it was published, but rather unconvincingly claimed that it was because 'of all the places in the world, I found Belfast to be the most unhappy. The people were unhappy and that was why in a moment of pity more than anger or frustration that I said what a bloody awful place it was.'[21] Maudling, who was not an insensitive man, did feel pity at the situation he found, but it was pity akin to despair. The situation weighed on his conscience enough that he would say that the one thing he would love to have been able to do in politics was to find a solution for Ulster.[22] But this coexisted with feelings of anger that spilled over in unguarded moments to a contempt for the 'bloody Irish' and a resort to crude arguments of a sort the younger Maudling would have disowned.

A few days after Maudling gratefully accepted his Scotch as his plane climbed over the Irish Sea, Northern Ireland became bloodier and more awful with the infamous 'Lower Falls curfew' (or 'Rape of the Falls' in republican parlance). The army had been informed that the Official IRA had a cache of weapons hidden in the Lower Falls area and on 3 July soldiers swept into the area to face abuse and physical attacks from residents and nail bombs from the Provisional IRA. It was not a completely unprecedented event, but the army had decided that the next trouble would lead to a severe crackdown. The army swamped the Lower Falls. Helicopters patrolled the skies, soldiers barking orders from the air at residents to stay inside their houses, and 3,000 troops poured in to conduct house-to-house searches throughout the area. There was considerable damage to property and more permanent damage to community relations because of the bullying behaviour of many soldiers in the Falls, with particularly insensitive behaviour by some sectarian elements in a Scottish regiment. Both sections of the IRA attacked the army, and there were sporadic gun battles, but the five deaths during the curfew were all civilians. To make matters worse, two of the more insensitive Stormont ministers took a ride in army vehicles around the Falls, like colonial governors overseeing the suppression of rebellious natives. To the residents of the Falls, the army was from now on seen as a brutal and biased occupying force. 'Catholics are really afraid now' because of discriminatory searches and biased courts, reported Irish Military Intelligence.[23] The British army in turn felt that the raid was justified because a significant quantity of arms and ammunition was in fact recovered during the operation.[24]

The Falls Road curfew was a crucial episode in republican history. Twenty-five years later Sinn Fein memorialised it as an occasion on which the army 'were determined to teach the people of the Lower Falls a lesson . . . Families could only watch as their neighbours' doors were broken down, floorboards ripped up, furniture smashed and their meagre belongings destroyed by foul-mouthed British soldiers.' It was 'a watershed because it showed that never again would nationalists allow themselves to be bullied or intimidated. The fight-back had begun.'[25] The IRA's standing orders, the Green Book, observed that 'In September 1969 the existing conditions dictated that Brits were not to be shot, but after the Falls curfew all Brits were to the people acceptable targets'.[26] The British army could never walk the streets of nationalist areas of Belfast again without fear. A soldier's history of the conflict recorded that 'it can be argued that the failure to ban the 1970 Orange parades, and the massive arms searches and curfew in the Lower Falls area which followed, was the last chance to avoid the catastrophe that has since engulfed Ulster'.[27] In less emotive terms, historians of the province are agreed that, in the words of Martin Dillon, 'the Lower Falls curfew was a turning point militarily and politically. It contributed to the rise of the Provos, and should never be underestimated.'[28]

Maudling bears some responsibility for the Falls curfew. On 30 June the Stormont Cabinet had given him an ear-bashing about the situation, with Chichester-Clark asking whether the troops were inhibited by their orders and telling Maudling that it was 'essential that the army should deal toughly, and be seen to deal toughly, with thugs and gunmen'. The Home Affairs minister, Robert Porter, alleged that in the Ardoyne incident IRA men had reloaded their weapons with impunity in full view of troops. The Chief Whip weighed in and said that the credibility of the Northern Ireland government had been strained to breaking point in recent days. Maudling told the Stormont ministers that 'there was a very real problem and that it appeared that neither the police on their present instructions nor the army as present equipped were in a position to deal with it', and that he would take it up with the Chief Constable and Freeland. Freeland in turn told Maudling that the army alone were in a position to be tough. RUC morale was low and they had 'almost retired from the difficult business of controlling rioters' but the GOC thought the army was left with only two courses of action: to fire on rioters (which he thought was not a good idea because it would solve nothing and cause IRA retaliation) or put in a massive military presence to keep order. He told Maudling that 'searches of arms, interference with movement, and border security would be stepped up. More use would be made of helicopters to survey the ground and issue warnings.'[29]

Maudling expressed no misgivings about the army's idea, which was effectively a blueprint for the Falls curfew. He also passed on the comments of the Stormont ministers and told the army that it would get a quick decision on its request for new crowd control equipment, giving a green light for the crackdown. Callaghan knew enough about Northern Ireland not to be bounced like this; Maudling blundered into it out of inexperience rather than a desire to take a harder line.

The alienation of the Falls was not the only problem for the new government. After the violence of 27–28 June the British government had feared that real mayhem would kick off as a result of the 12 July parades. They took some comfort in the thought that if it did, it could be used as a reason to take drastic steps such as the abolition of Stormont. The Cabinet Office had prepared a plan to do this, which Burke Trend put before Heath and Maudling on 9 July:

> If, by Monday evening, public order is disintegrating in the cities, trouble is spreading to the countryside and the Chichester-Clark government is no longer either able or willing to cope with the situation, we must be prepared to take the action described in the Home Secretary's memorandum NI(70)2 – i.e. to suspend the Parliament at Stormont, to transfer its legislative authority to Westminster and to place the executive government of Ulster in the hands of a nominee of our own.[30]

However, the parades went off without significant problems. Chichester-Clark was the most relieved of all, writing to Heath about 'this happy outcome to a testing day'. The Stormont government felt in a stronger military and political position. But as it happened things might have been better if there had been trouble. If Stormont had fallen that week, the British would have had no option but to move at full speed towards political reconstruction and consider radical options, and presumably also to appoint a Cabinet minister who would be completely devoted to the province. Political initiatives would have then been starting from a position where terrorist organisations were still relatively small and unrepresentative. The radicalisation process would not have advanced so far; in December 1970 the SDLP was still keen on participating in Stormont and in new local institutions.[31] On the other hand, a successful operation by the British to confront Orange marchers and keep them out of Catholic areas would have helped repair a little of the damage from the Falls curfew. The temptation was there, and remained for the rest of 1970, to do very little while the Catholic ghettos festered and the Provisional IRA grew strong,[32] and Maudling found it difficult to resist the temptation.

In fairness, though, he cannot be blamed for giving Stormont's reforms another chance. He tried to persuade the Northern Ireland government to couple some more reform measures with the harder line on law and order, but received the unpromising answer from Chichester-Clark that the recent (and completely ineffective) Incitement to Hatred Bill 'had just about exhausted legislative remedies'.[33] Maudling resisted Stormont pressure to move to harsher law and order measures such as suspending trial by jury and extending the Special Powers Act (a law Maudling disliked in principle).[34] A deal was done with Chichester-Clark by which in exchange for policing resuming in 'no-go' areas the Northern Ireland government would ban marches for the rest of the year.[35]

In August 1970 Maudling had been obliged to issue a public statement threatening, in the most flimsily coded way, to introduce direct rule if the pace of reform slackened. To go back on reform 'would endanger the present constitutional arrangement under which Northern Ireland governs its own affairs'. This statement was made at the behest of James Chichester-Clark, who was threatened by a vote of no confidence from his constituency association; if he fell, his opponents hoped to replace him with a hardline Unionist government, probably under William Craig. Maudling's original draft was so bland and the threat so obscurely made that Chichester-Clark told the Home Office that it was insufficient to save the situation; the actual words used were written at the last minute by Home Office civil servants on the advice of Harold Black, the Northern Ireland Cabinet Secretary.[36] But it is doubtful whether there was any reality behind the threat at this stage, as internal documents indicate that direct rule was regarded as so unpalatable that while outright defiance was unacceptable, a certain amount of backsliding would be tolerated. The only definite prohibition was on the restoration of the B Specials.[37]

Later in 1970 Chichester-Clark did at least move forward with promised measures like one person one vote in local elections. There was a certain amount of cautious optimism on the part of the army and Home Office at the low level of violence in recent months, but the Chichester-Clark government was in a shaky position, threatened by right-wing unionists and buffeted by demands for ever-harder law and order policies.[38] The Chichester-Clark government's majority was so unstable that it had to dragoon its right-wing backbenchers by reminding them that London was insisting on the reforms and that there was, to coin a phrase, no alternative. Unfortunately, Chichester-Clark could not carry the day with a principled appeal for support of reforms he favoured and had devised, so he had to call London into aid all the time.[39] This in turn called into question the usefulness of Stormont itself; the institution, which was still the central feature of British thinking about the future of the province, was steadily being undermined without much thought being given to what might be put in its place.

Maudling visited the unhappy province for the first time since July 1970 at the beginning of March 1971. The origins of the trip were in an invitation issued in December 1970 to address the Ulster Unionist Party council, which his civil servants advised him to decline unless it was made part of a larger, formal visit.[40] The centrepiece of his trip was a formal address to both houses of Stormont, which took place amid much pomp and, more importantly, after a build-up of hype in which people were led to expect a significant initiative. Maudling delivered a pedestrian speech, full of bland reassurance and observations which, although possibly interesting and true, did not seem to be answering the sense of crisis that had developed. He opined that the reform programme implemented by Stormont had led to 'a considerable reduction in communal or sectarian strife . . . But we must all recognise on both sides of the water that what has recently emerged is a new and altogether more vicious threat . . . This new situation I believe has arisen just because of the progress that was being made.'[41]

The response was derisive. Simon Winchester of the *Guardian* called it 'pious, pointless pontificating' and reported that a Catholic Stormont member said it was 'a load of platitudinous nonsense' and that John Hume called it 'an insult to our intelligence'.[42] The Unionists were no more impressed, as Maudling had failed to provide more troops or sound sufficiently solid on the constitution. Brian Faulkner was unimpressed by 'a very ordinary speech' which damaged Maudling's standing.[43] Chichester-Clark, whose premiership was hanging by a thread, was depressed by Maudling's failure to offer anything of substance in a political – and literal – life and death situation.[44] Burroughs, the official UK representative in Belfast, commented that 'in sum, virtually no-one is happy either in the North or the South; but there is something to be said for displeasing both sides equally'.[45]

The rest of the visit was a rather routine series of meetings with Stormont ministers, opposition members and backbenchers, the police and army, plus an address to the Ulster Unionist Party council. The programme omitted any 'meet the people' events. The hospitality was of a high standard, particularly a formal dinner at Stormont (roast duckling with, suitably enough, orange salad) on Thursday at which he and Beryl were guests of honour. They stayed both nights as guests of Chichester-Clark at his country house of Moyola and enjoyed some country sports at the estate. It was a much more congenial visit for Maudling than his previous trip to Ulster.[46]

The Northern Ireland situation took a drastic turn for the worse within a week of Maudling's departure, with the murder on 10 March of three Scottish soldiers who had been out for a drink in Belfast only to be lured to a lonely hillside by some IRA men and shot in gangland style. One of the soldiers was only 17. This atrocity raised the political temperature in Northern Ireland and caused a collapse in confidence in the Stormont government.

One option at this point was to introduce internment without trial of IRA suspects. Right-wing unionists had favoured the policy for some time, but after the murder of the young Scots it was a demand that gained wider currency. Technically, the Northern Ireland government could introduce it without further legislation but in practice it required the consent of the British government. The British knew that internment was more or less the last shot in their locker. There had been preliminary discussions in December 1970 about the practicalities, at which the troopship HMS *Maidstone* was considered as a holding centre. Maudling and Carrington were not keen for public relations reasons, fearing pictures of a 'prison hulk' being broadcast around the world. In early 1971 there were further studies, which started off as a cosmetic exercise partly to give Chichester-Clark some 'welcome news' to take home from his next trip to London.[47] The army officer who looked at the issue in February 1971 found a page and a half of notes in a folder, suggesting the Isle of Man as a suitable place for the camp. This had the problem, he discovered, that the special powers law did not apply there and the internees would become free as soon as they landed. Instead, the army study identified a disused airfield at Long Kesh near Lisburn as being suitable.[48]

There was a case that a small-scale internment operation might have succeeded in March. Opinion in nationalist areas, some in the army believed, was sufficiently revolted by the murders of the soldiers that people would have acquiesced.[49] The SDLP MP for West Belfast, Gerry Fitt, had even before the murders urged Burroughs to introduce 'the immediate internment of all Provisional IRA men known to the police in order to rid Belfast of intimidation'.[50] But first the security forces had to work out whom to lock up if the order came – and, even more important, work out who should *not* be interned.

The list of potential internees was compiled mainly from RUC Special Branch files, whose intelligence effort was, as even Chichester-Clark admitted, 'not very good'.[51] Maudling tried to shore it up somewhat, by lending Metropolitan Police officers to them (although the Scotland Yard men found there was not much they could add to what the RUC were doing) and by sending over Sir Dick White of MI5 to report on intelligence arrangements in Northern Ireland in early March 1971, but this work was far from root-and-branch and in any case had only just begun at the time of the March crisis. White's mission led to some better coordination of RUC intelligence but intelligence improvement also resulted in the RUC being given 'training facilities in interrogation techniques' by the army, which turned out not to be a particularly good idea. This was done without ministerial approval, a signal that parts of the security forces were out of control.[52]

On 13 March Burroughs reported to London, the Head of the RUC Special Branch

has now advised the Prime Minister that he considers internment to be essential. Not because he believes it will be effective (Director of Intelligence believes we might pick up about 20 percent and then mostly small fry) but because he fears that the Protestants will take the law into their own hands if internment is not introduced before Easter.[53]

But he added that there was no point in introducing internment to save the Chichester-Clark government, which was on its way out anyway. Chichester-Clark flew over to London on 16 March to plead with the British government.

Somewhat to the surprise of the British, Chichester-Clark did not ask for internment. He disliked the policy and believed that it would be ineffective and counter-productive at quelling republican violence, and was content to accept the RUC and army view that it was not worth doing. The police had advised him that it would generate street protests and that 'they would have to take in about 300 to 400 people, but there would be a lot of younger people whom the police did not know and who would not be picked up'.[54] He did not remind Maudling about the 'studies' into the practical aspects of internment. Chichester-Clark's main hope had actually been to clarify the control of the security forces, ideally from his point of view to take it for the Northern Ireland government but he was prepared to see it transferred entirely to London. He also wanted something done about the no-go areas that were developing in Londonderry and Belfast. His principal request was for more troops. He described a 'panic reaction' to the three murders and the prospect of a 'general uprising' by those most opposed to the IRA. He wanted a massive increase in troop numbers to enable the army to take up positions within IRA areas and enforce curfews and cordons. The Chief of General Staff was horrified at the idea of his men becoming sitting targets and Carrington 'said that there appeared at present to be no military justification for sending additional troops. There might be a political reason now, but this could recur in a few weeks' time and there would then be renewed pressure for still further reinforcements.'[55] Sending troops in for political reasons was a bottomless pit. The British were only prepared to offer 1,300 extra troops, as opposed to Chichester-Clark's minimum demand of 3,000.

The Northern Ireland Prime Minister reported his failure to Stormont on 18 March and resolved to resign. The resignation took place in farcical circumstances. Chichester-Clark attempted to reach Maudling on Friday 19 March only to find that the Home Secretary was delivering a lecture at Merchant Taylors' school. Word was passed to Maudling's Special Branch minders who found him having lunch with the Headmaster – a lunch 'made up almost entirely of whiskey' according to one of those present.[56] Maudling made his excuses and left, but his car broke down in Watford and he was unable to talk to Chichester-Clark.[57] This, at least, is what Chichester-Clark was told; it seems possible that the 'car breakdown' was a diplomatic way of making sure that Maudling, drunk, could not make matters worse. The official chronology filed in the National Archives raises some discrepancies. Maudling was apparently capable of talking to Heath on a radio-telephone but unable to communicate with Chichester-Clark. Heath handled the matter instead and took Chichester-Clark's call at 5p.m. The Northern Ireland premier was intending to blame his resignation on lack of support from the British government, but Heath successfully argued him out of this course of action. By the end of the conversation Chichester-Clark was acknowledging 'all that you have done to try to help us', and was instead blaming the 'impossible' political situation in Northern Ireland.[58] When he made his decision public, he ascribed his resignation to the need to dramatise the severity of the situation. Rather than confront the British government, Chichester-Clark had allowed Stormont one more chance under the leadership of Brian Faulkner.

Faulkner was a professional politician, widely regarded in the small world of Northern Ireland politics as a cunning and devious operator. Chichester-Clark's reputation as a bumbling toff has been grossly overdone, but Faulkner's accession certainly marked an increase in the sophistication of

Northern Ireland government thinking. Despite his prior reputation as a hardliner, he quickly became the last chance of reformist Unionism. He started quite positively. In June 1971 he offered what was then perceived as quite a radical reform. He proposed to set up several scrutiny committees at Stormont – at a time when there was not a systematic set of select committees at Westminster – and give the opposition power by letting them chair the committees. The SDLP members at Stormont reacted positively and it seemed that an internal deal could be done – something that would have greatly relieved Maudling.

Faulkner's initiative produced another depressing false dawn in Northern Ireland politics. It was destroyed by the politics of the streets, in particular the hostility between urban Catholics and the British army. Two men were killed in rioting in Derry on 8 July, and feeling in the city ran high – John Hume, the city's Stormont MP, called a meeting at which the SDLP decided to withdraw from Stormont unless there was an inquiry into the deaths. Angry crowds were in the streets outside, which cast a pall of fear over the meeting. The party was split on the issue and Gerry Fitt flew to London for a private chat with Maudling to see if there could be a compromise. Maudling wanted to help but he had no statutory power to call an inquiry, although other possibilities that might have helped reach agreement were a special investigation undertaken by the Metropolitan Police or some sort of special status for the Londonderry inquest.[59] However, the following week the government announced that there would be no such gesture; the Faulkner government was completely intransigent to anything that smacked of surrender to SDLP blackmail. The SDLP withdrew from Stormont on 16 July.

Faulkner was angry at the SDLP's behaviour, and increasingly concerned at the wave of bombings in Northern Ireland in the first half of 1971. There had been 12 explosions in January, 37 in April and 91 in July.[60] The IRA was demonstrating its increasing capabilities, with a series of city centre bombings on 11 July and then on 17 July their first real 'spectacular' – the complete destruction of a *Daily Mirror* printing plant at Dunmurry on the outskirts of Belfast. Faulkner became convinced that something dramatic needed to be done and there was only one option left – internment. He notified Heath that he was going to insist on it.

On 23 July the army tried to disrupt IRA activities with a series of early-morning arrests. This had a dual purpose. The army hoped that they could surprise the suspects, interrogate them, search their houses and hopefully find evidence to charge them with possession of weapons or some other offence. The army leadership hoped that this operation would satisfy the Unionists but they only managed to arrest forty-eight out of the original 100 targets and found few weapons. The response among nationalists was hostile – Ivan Cooper of the SDLP called it 'virtual internment'.[61] A statement issued under Maudling's name struck a tough note, describing the need for 'utmost vigour' in security force action and the aim of policy as 'to maintain the constitutional position of Northern Ireland as enacted in the Government of Ireland Act 1949 by whatever means may be necessary'. This was uncharacteristic stuff from Maudling, and there were briefings to the effect that it did not really represent his views.[62] But thereafter Maudling repeatedly referred to a 'new phase' or 'new tactics' against the IRA and said that the raids were 'a very important development . . . The answer to those who may not think it sufficient is that it will be the first operation of this kind. There will be more . . . This is now an open war between the IRA and the security forces.'[63] Field Marshal Lord Carver criticised this high profile, saying later that 'unfortunately Reggie Maudling . . . blew this up, making an announcement that this was going to be something of a far greater scale and far more important than it obviously was going to be'.[64]

The other purpose of the raid was as the nationalists believed to gather evidence for a later internment sweep. This raid, and another raid on 28 July, ended up telegraphing the internment operation to the most dangerous suspects. Gerry Adams, rousted by British troops on 23 July, made sure that he was not at home when they came calling with internment orders.[65]

The Northern Ireland Cabinet formally approved internment on 3 August, and Brian Faulkner contacted Maudling on 4 August asking for a secret meeting in London to discuss 'a grave security matter' which was a pretty transparent agenda. The next day he met Heath, Maudling, Douglas-Home and Carrington and obtained their agreement for internment. They walked into the disaster with eyes open. The official note of the meeting acknowledged that:

> Internment was a major decision, which could not be said – as the GOC made clear – to be justified by any military necessity. It must therefore be regarded as a political act, which would be thought to be directed against one faction and must accordingly be matched by some political action, in the form of a ban on marches, which would represent its counterpart in relation to the other faction.[66]

Agreement was given conditionally, on the understanding that Faulkner would ban marches and parades, that it should be even-handed and that 'it would provide an opportunity for fresh initiatives to promote political reconciliation and the economic development of the province'. The British attempt to salvage something from internment was to come to nothing because Stormont was in charge of law and order and thus the arrests.

On the morning of 9 August the security forces moved in on republicans across Northern Ireland. A total of 342 people were rounded up, but a high proportion of the internees were not in fact active members of terrorist groups. The leadership of the Provisionals, helped by some advance warning about what was coming, escaped. In any case, preparations at Long Kesh were visible to passing motorists on the M1 motorway and there were extra advertisements in Belfast newspapers for prison officers, so it came as little surprise.[67] The impact of the first sweeps fell heavily on older IRA men whose names were known to the RUC and British intelligence but had stopped violent activity with the IRA ceasefire of 1962. Making up numbers in the internment round-up were a number of people with no terrorist involvement at all who had the misfortune of irritating the security forces or the Stormont government through civil rights or trade union activity. Internees included the People's Democracy activist Michael Farrell and most of the executives of NICRA and PD. There were even cases of relatives being picked up when the intended targets were not at home.

Maudling took little active part while the operation unfolded. He spent the day sitting by the swimming pool at Essendon, while two middle-ranking civil servants and a secretary handled the Whitehall end of the process. His contribution was limited to asking them on the phone every now and then to arrest some Protestants. He did not give the impression of taking this, or anything else, terribly seriously.[68]

After the round-up had taken place, he spoke to a series of media figures about internment in a broadly successful attempt to spin the episode in the best light possible. He stooped to telling one outright lie, informing the *Guardian*'s Alastair Hetherington that both Faulkner and Tuzo had convinced him that it must be introduced, but for the most part he blandly recited army propaganda, which he seems to have believed implicitly.[69] He told the press that the operation was a success, that there were well over a hundred IRA men from each faction under arrest and that nobody had been lifted for civil rights activity. He even claimed that 'the security on their plans after Thursday's visit had been astonishingly good'.[70] Journalists in Belfast had come to distrust army press pronouncements, particularly after a preposterous claim that only fifteen rounds had been fired in a long gun battle in July 1970, but Maudling accepted what he was told. It was only later that the British realised that they had made a colossal mistake in trusting Faulkner and the Northern Ireland intelligence effort.

Not a single loyalist was arrested on 9 August, despite Maudling's urgings on the day and before. Reggie had known that an entirely one-sided internment sweep would be politically unhelpful. He told Faulkner to 'lift some Protestants if you can' but Faulkner left the details of the round-up entirely to the RUC and Maudling adopted his usual hands-off policy to security issues.[71] The British government found themselves giving misleading assurances to the Irish republic on the day of internment that it would be non-discriminatory.[72] Maudling argued in public that there was no problem arising from Protestants – asked about Protestant detainees in a *Panorama* interview by Robin Day he said:

As far as I know I don't think any are, but I don't think any members of the IRA are Protestants . . . To say you should go and collect some

Protestants who are not doing the same thing, for the sake of achieving a balance, to my mind makes no sense. If any Protestant organisations were behaving like the IRA we should treat them in precisely the same way. This is what the British Army is there for, they're impartial between Protestant and Catholic.[73]

This was an utterly preposterous answer, even acknowledging that Reggie had to disown publicly his private view that some Protestants should be rounded up in the interests of balance. The claim that there were no Protestant terrorist groups was nonsense. In July 1970 British officials told the Americans that Protestant groups were responsible for bombings, including some attributed to the IRA.[74] On the very evening the *Panorama* interview was broadcast a man belonging to a new organisation, the Ulster Defence Association, was killed by his own bomb in North Belfast.[75] The Ulster Volunteer Force had been engaged in sabotage bombings before the IRA was active and was responsible for the bombings which toppled O'Neill in spring 1969. The UVF inflicted the first police casualty of the Troubles when RUC officer Victor Arbuckle was shot dead in October 1969. Just as the IRA incited unrest in Catholic areas, the UVF and assorted militias brought toughs, snipers and guns to riots in Protestant areas. The UVF also attempted assassinations of political opponents such as the nationalist politician Austin Currie in March 1970, although in the year 1970 there were no fatalities from loyalist activities. There were sporadic security force discoveries of loyalist arms dumps in the first half of 1971. In the month that Maudling made his bland assertion there was a serious escalation in tit-for-tat pub bombings around Belfast. In December 1971 this reached a horrific climax with the explosion at McGurk's bar in which a UVF bomb killed fifteen people; the army press operation attempted to blame a premature detonation of an IRA weapon.[76] Maudling's assessment that only the IRA were conducting serious terrorist operations was tautologous: the security forces were attributing all such operations to the republicans, so of course only the IRA seemed to be carrying them out. It is alleged that even in these early days armed Loyalism was fostered by elements of the RUC and seemingly respectable politicians, and the British army was certainly unhappy at the prospect of opening a second front, so there may be sinister reasons for the blind eye that was turned to loyalist extremism in 1971. Collusion has been another murky current in Northern Ireland almost since the beginning of the Troubles.

Maudling's argument was also flawed because many of the detainees had nothing to do with the IRA. No doubt the Northern Ireland government and the military saw civil rights activists as a tiresome presence on the scene whose activities stirred up unrest and led to violence even if they did not carry out violence themselves. Leaving aside the principles involved, there were certainly Protestants in a similar category, who stirred up loyalist mobs and indulged in fiery rhetoric while disclaiming responsibility for the consequences. Maudling's intellectual and moral laziness in accepting what he was told and not thinking these matters through had severe consequences.

Internment unleashed a spasm of violence in the province. Catholic areas erupted into riots and the army moved in again. Mass communal violence resembling the fear and hatred of August 1969 returned to the cities and around 7,000 people – mostly Catholic – were forced from their homes. Within a couple of days, seventeen people were dead, ten of them Catholic civilians killed by the British army; one of those was Hugh Mullan, a Catholic priest shot dead while giving an injured man the last rites. The British had expected a hostile reaction but they were taken aback by the strength of the response: 'the political and social consequences have been serious – more serious than many people in Northern Ireland expected. It is too soon to reach conclusions about the permanence of public reaction, but there has undoubtedly been a greater polarisation between the two communities.'[77] American State Department analysis was that it had changed the nature of terrorism in the province:

> Up until the August 9 arrests, and indeed for some time thereafter, terrorist activities, except for assaults on soldiers, were virtually entirely directed against installations and physical plant, both public and private. Attacks were usually made at night time or during the weekends, when the place attacked would be free of people.

But by the end of August, attacks had become indiscriminate and lethal.[78]

Maudling and Faulkner were reluctant to admit that internment had failed. In their memoirs they both continued to claim that the security situation had improved. It was clear that it had not. By the end of internment week the Provisionals had managed to organise a press conference in Belfast at which Joe Cahill and other leaders of the Belfast IRA appeared to show that they were still in business; even in his memoirs Faulkner did not acknowledge that these were indeed the principal commanders of his enemy. According to the IRA, only fifty-six of their men had been arrested.[79] On the streets of nationalist areas of Northern Ireland the IRA found that there was little vehement opposition to a policy of attacking British forces and the death toll took a rapid turn for the worse. Thirty people died in political violence in 1971 in the seven months before internment; 141 were killed in the remaining five months. The toll slackened a bit after the initial bloodshed (although September 1971 was still worse than any previous month except August), but the momentum picked up again in October when fatalities were averaging one a day. The IRA's ability to explode bombs across the province seemed unaffected. They had been swamped by volunteers in the days after internment, to the extent that the organisation in Derry had to impose a waiting list on new members.

Internment stands out as one of the great blunders of recent British political history. The rationale for it in August 1971 was exclusively political and rather muddled; nobody except Faulkner and the Unionist right (and even among them, some like Paisley spoke out against it) believed it would work. To give such a power to the creaking Stormont machine was to invite a fiasco; the regime used it to excess and with no sense of balance, as might have been predicted. When intelligence had improved and the central government had taken over law and order powers internment became a more effective weapon against terrorists, but that was in the future.

Internment also destroyed the prospects of a political settlement. Maudling had hoped to use it to launch some political initiatives, which was a ludicrous misapprehension and must have depended on suspending his disbelief about its effectiveness as a security measure. He told a ministerial meeting shortly after internment that 'The timing of such an initiative would need careful thought; no decision could begin in an atmosphere of violence, but it was necessary to hold out some hope that an end of violence would be accompanied by some political advance'.[80] Such an advance, he hoped, would be based on the continuance of Northern Ireland within the UK but with minority participation in government. But saying that there would be no progress until peace gave the IRA a veto on a constitutional agreement in Northern Ireland, and the loyalist paramilitaries a veto on reconstructing the government to include nationalists. This doctrine as such was abandoned, but its shadow as an excuse for inaction lasted for the rest of Maudling's time in charge. His attempt to modify this stance in December only landed him in more trouble.

It was all by now of little significance. Internment had completely alienated the constitutional nationalists, who followed up the withdrawal from Stormont after the Derry killings with a campaign of civil disobedience against the Northern Ireland administration. The SDLP withdrew from public bodies and local councils and organised a rent and rates strike. Before any further progress could be made on the political front, the SDLP had to be drawn back into the process, which in turn now seemed to require the end of internment, or at least moves in that direction. Maudling did want the SDLP to come back, and – ineffectively – asked Faulkner to talk to them.[81]

Heath started from a position of belligerent ignorance about Ireland. At a party in May 1969 he told the Irish Deputy Prime Minister 'in a somewhat hectoring tone of voice' that in his and the Tory party's opinion 'Northern Ireland is as much a part of the United Kingdom as Yorkshire'. 'Mr. Heath went on to say that any hope of good relations between "Eire" and the British Government – which would be a Tory Government very soon – had been put in jeopardy by the Irish government's decision to bring the [Northern] matter to the attention of the Secretary-General of the United Nations' and threatened to review the Free Trade Agreement.[82]

However, the ability to transcend one's prejudices is a rare and admirable one in political leadership, and Heath had increasingly come to the view that the solution to Northern Ireland's problems was to be found more in a dialogue between the three governments – British, Irish and Northern Irish – rather than in leaving Maudling to try to organise internal political talks. He hoped ultimately that European unity would lead in time to the end of the Irish problem. Heath believed that Wilson's 'Downing Street Declaration' was flawed in not recognising the all-Ireland context, and at root he was no intransigent pro-Unionist.[83] On the surface, relations between Heath and Irish Taoiseach Jack Lynch were poor. Lynch had repeatedly condemned British actions in the North, including internment, in strong language, and the Heath government responded by telling him, more or less in so many words, to mind his own business. However, these exchanges were mostly playing to the respective galleries and Lynch accepted Heath's invitation to talks at Chequers on 6–7 September. The talks had some stormy moments, particularly around Heath's insistence that the Irish government have nothing to do with internal talks within Northern Ireland that Maudling was to organise, but they were productive. Three weeks later Lynch returned to Chequers, this time for a tripartite meeting with Heath and Faulkner – it was the first time the three leaders had met since partition. Maudling was excluded from what turned out to be a rather congenial occasion. Faulkner 'felt sorry for Reggie Maudling, who was kept waiting at Chequers during the talks and had to ask various civil servants if they knew what was going on'.[84]

Maudling did at least try to put together a political initiative, on instructions from Heath after the meeting with Lynch in early September. There had been repeated pleas for urgency from Heath and Trend since June 1970, but it was now too late.[85] A few of the more obviously political detainees were released on 14 September. Maudling had a dilatory round of meetings in autumn 1971 with the constitutional parties and interest groups that were prepared to see him – the Ulster Unionists, the Alliance Party and the Ulster Liberals, whose membership could fit in the proverbial telephone box and still leave room for someone to make a call.[86] These discussions were supposed to lead to a joint meeting Maudling would chair, but did not reach that stage until months after Maudling had left the scene. The lack of urgency in the talks alarmed Lynch, who was disappointed to be told by Heath in December that the state of progress was uncertain and that there would not be any progress before Christmas on inter-party talks.[87]

Quite what the 'Maudling initiative' involved is vague, because he never developed a blueprint for political reform. There were considerable expectations in autumn 1971 that the British government would come up with something. Proportional representation for future elections to a Stormont body was certainly part of the plan at that stage. Maudling had developed a formula to describe desired future development of an 'active, permanent and guaranteed' (which became the acronym 'APG') role for the Catholic minority in the government of Northern Ireland.[88] This appeared to go a lot further than the concessions Faulkner was then offering about voluntary participation and a system of scrutiny committees at Stormont, and ran counter to the assumption among the Unionists that the British had agreed to maintain 'majority rule democracy' in Northern Ireland.[89] In later years Maudling claimed to have invented the phrase 'power-sharing', but authorship is also attributed to Ted Heath's think-tank, the Central Policy Review Staff (CPRS). There are differences between what is meant by APG and power-sharing; at least until the end of 1971 the British government understood APG to entail the appointment of a couple of Catholic ministers in a Stormont Cabinet on some sort of guaranteed basis.[90] APG was a stage in the development of British thinking towards power-sharing, which was a sensible enough policy, and did indeed become a lodestar of British policy towards the Northern Ireland constitution under one guise or another from then onwards. There is a thin thread of continuity leading from Maudling's initiative to the autumn 1972 Darlington talks and thence to the Sunningdale agreement. But the time to start talking about APG was months before, when it could have been presented as a dramatic initiative, not after the internment fiasco.

Maudling was occasionally overcome by bouts of fatalism, which led some participants in the talks and consultations of autumn 1971 to conclude that he had given up on Northern Ireland. Maurice Hayes of the Community Relations Commission, although he rather liked Maudling, was occasionally appalled by his levity and fatalism. Hayes had gathered an academic delegation who prepared a paper about the situation based on discussions with various interests, some of them such as the SDLP who were not cooperating with Maudling. After weeks of false starts, the delegation went to the Home Office in November 1971. Hayes found Maudling 'sprawled in a huge leather armchair at one side of a blazing open fire. The visit left my colleagues totally depressed at the apparent lack of information, poor understanding of the problem, and lack of strategic policy direction at the centre of the British government. Partly this was induced by the apparent torpor of Maudling, who having asked us over appeared not to be totally engaged by the issue.' Maudling asked to see Hayes again the next morning but 'the meeting did not last long. He opened with a question "What do we do? Arm the Protestants and get out?"'[91]

Allegations began to filter out shortly after internment was introduced that detainees had been maltreated. These were initially dismissed in public as IRA propaganda but it gradually became clear that something strange was going on. There had been a considerable amount of unfocused and undisciplined violence against detainees during and immediately after the round-up[92] which never received as much attention as it should have done, but in the days afterwards a more systematic set of abuses took place. Maudling and Carrington had given general permission on 10 August for a set of principles governing interrogation which the security forces had proposed to them:

That detainees should be subject to medical supervision, that there should be no brutal or degrading treatment, and that interrogation should be carried out humanely, but under strict discipline: techniques designed to isolate detainees subject to interrogation, to deprive them from obtaining any exact sense of time and location and to impose fatigue by exposure to insistent and disturbing noise ('white sound') were regarded as proper.[93]

In practice, the methods went even further and involved practices that did not have ministerial approval, such as hooding and 'spreadeagling', the use of bright lights and other indignities. The humane conditions in the ministerial guideline were sometimes ignored. Special treatment was meted out to eleven 'guinea pigs' whose selection was left to Faulkner. The responsibility for the abuses is still a murky business – it seems that there was a decision emanating from army interrogation specialists to experiment in going further than the guidelines suggested.[94] But those guidelines themselves allowed latitude and in the heat of interrogation their authors can hardly have been surprised that the balancing elements of the guidelines were not rigorously honoured.[95]

In any case, Maudling was not particularly bothered by the methods the army interrogators had been using in Northern Ireland. This was of a piece with his relativistic attitude to internment. If internment was a bad thing, but not as bad as murder, could the same not be said about torture? Although he shied away from expressing the logic in quite such brutal terms, Maudling basically accepted that it could.[96] He could well have been the author of the remark recorded in a Cabinet committee meeting that one should 'not be unduly squeamish' about interrogation methods,[97] as it faithfully reflected his attitude.

The outcry over interrogation methods had grown so strong by the end of August that the government appointed an official inquiry into the allegations, under Sir Edmund Compton. By the middle of October Compton had decided on the important point, that he would make a sophistical distinction between 'torture and brutality' (which required an element of sadism from the interrogators) and 'ill-treatment' (which did not), and 'a measure' of which had been carried out against the detainees. The Compton Report was published on 16 November and Maudling announced that the upshot of the report was that the internment operation 'was accomplished in a highly creditable manner'.[98] Publication of the Compton report was organised so that it came after Maudling's statement, giving MPs no chance to question him on the details, although a selective briefing had clearly been given to the Evening Standard, which called the timing 'an obvious attempt to muffle the parliamentary explosion'.[99]

Maudling's blithe, imperturbable style at the Despatch Box served him ill in the debates on interrogation. Maudling's infuriating calmness, the bland face of the professional politician seeming a world away from the degrading reality of brutalising men in windowless concrete cells, aroused almost elemental rage. Even Graham Greene wrote to *The Times* that 'If I, as a Catholic, were living in Ulster today I confess I would have one savage and irrational ambition – to see Mr Maudling pressed against a wall for hours on end, with a hood over his head, hearing nothing but the noise of a wind machine, deprived of sleep when the noise temporarily ceases by the bland voice of a politician telling him that his brain will suffer no irreparable damage'.[100]

Maudling's last visit to Northern Ireland as Home Secretary was, like his other forays, a public relations disaster. His trip in December 1971 was intended to be a signal that the government was still interested in political progress and on top of the security position, but this time the press had been briefed not to expect a dramatic initiative from a 'routine' visit.[101] Maudling managed to offend both sides. He failed to meet elected nationalist or Catholic representatives, although to be fair the SDLP had boycotted his visit on the grounds that it was pointless. He also engaged in a pointless spat with the Irish broadcasters RTE, when he refused to give them a television or radio interview on the grounds that 'if I thought it would do any good I would have given one'.[102] Everyone was offended by Maudling's remarks at a Belfast press conference on 15 December. The exact form of words he used varied as he repeated the remarks several times to different media, but the essentials were the same. The *Belfast Telegraph* reported that he said: 'You may not totally eliminate the IRA, but the Army has the power and certainly the intention of reducing the level of violence to something which is acceptable.'[103] The idea of an 'acceptable level of violence' was one that appalled Protestant opinion in particular, and it was immensely tactless of Maudling to present it to an on the record press conference. The Home Office had to 'put the record straight' in briefings and a note to an angry Brian Faulkner about what Maudling meant. Whitehall briefings stated that it had been intended to signal that new political initiatives might be brought forward when the security forces had reduced, rather than completely stopped, IRA violence; Maudling told Faulkner that he was referring to the precedent of the way the IRA was sidelined after the 1950s campaign and that he was saying that a lasting solution 'cannot be achieved by military action alone'.[104] Maudling's comment was not an offhand gaffe – the 'acceptable level' concept had been current in British military thinking after the failure of internment to shut down the paramilitaries, and he had picked it up in the briefings he had received in the province. To Maudling's logical mind, it made perfect sense. There is a background level of violence in any society and in Northern Ireland he understood enough history to know that violent republicanism would exist in some form for as long as the border did. A quiescent IRA as had existed for most of the period since 1921, and the odd bit of sectarian argy-bargy when the pubs closed, was what he understood as being acceptable. But most saw a more cynical meaning to the phrase – that the aim of policy was to stabilise the situation enough that

British public opinion could once again afford to ignore Northern Ireland while people there kept dying.

The combination of the botched implementation of internment and Maudling's apparent lack of concern led to an upsurge in activity by violent loyalist organisations. The Ulster Defence Association was formed in September 1971 as a federation of the vigilante groups which had appeared in Protestant areas and claimed to defend their people from IRA attacks. In the UDA's own history the organisation records:

> Protestant resentment towards the IRA and the nationalist community was reaching breaking point during 1971. I believe this proved to be a turning point for loyalists. They could no longer tolerate an inadequate security policy which seemed to favour 'an acceptable level of violence' which permitted the IRA to conduct its campaign of genocide and sectarianism against the protestant population.[105]

Unionist politicians such as Ian Paisley and Desmond Boal argued in favour of self-defence groups of the sort that evolved into the UDA. Maudling stated blandly at the same press conference as his 'acceptable level' remark that the principle of voluntary self-defence units was 'a good idea'.[106] To the nationalists it was not unreasonable to see British policy as the age-old good cop/bad cop routine, with the army playing a pretty tarnished good cop and the dirtiest activities subcontracted to the officially tolerated loyalist militias. Masked UDA men strutted around in their areas, did deals with the army, and remained legal – the organisation was only banned in 1992 despite carrying out sectarian murders almost from the very beginning of its existence in 1971.

The year 1972 began ominously. The IRA announced that it was 'The Year of Victory'[107] and made statements of intent with a bomb in central Belfast which injured over sixty people on 3 January, and a daring escape of seven IRA internees from HMS *Maidstone* on 17 January. The ever-shifting mood of the British government moved towards a crackdown. During his December 1971 visit, Maudling had met General Tuzo at army headquarters in Lisburn, where Tuzo told him that parts of Londonderry were out of control: 'a choice had to be made between accepting that Creggan and Bogside were areas where the army were not able to go, or to mount a major operation which would involve, at some stage, shooting at unarmed civilians.' Early in the New Year General Ford, Commander of Land Forces and a much more hardline officer than the subtle, politically aware Tuzo, wrote to Tuzo that the minimum necessary to restore order would be to 'shoot selected ringleaders' of a street gang called 'Derry Young Hooligans' who had been causing damage and disruption in the city. On 11 January Heath told the Northern Ireland Cabinet Committee, reflecting information from General Ford, that 'as to Londonderry, a military operation to re-impose law and order would be a major operation necessarily involving numerous civilian casualties'.[108] Under the prevailing view, propagated by Maudling, solving what was perceived as a law and order problem was a precondition for political progress. If the military, or part thereof, thought they could do it, the cost of achieving the defeat of the IRA and the restoration of law and order would be lower than the cost of letting the situation continue to deteriorate.

Faulkner announced a ban on marches and demonstrations on 18 January, but the anti-internment protests had gathered too much momentum to be stopped and despite the ban they continued. On 22 January a march near the internment camp at Magilligan strand on the coast of County Londonderry was broken up violently by British paratroopers, a regiment whose expertise was in combat rather than the sort of quasi-police role the army was carrying out in Northern Ireland. Another march was due to take place on 30 January in the city of Derry. The NICRA activists had talked to the local police, who favoured a soft approach to the illegal march and did not request army assistance,[109] but General Ford sent the Paras into Derry with instructions to 'scoop up' any rioters, particularly the Derry Young Hooligans. The Paras had been given a frightening briefing about the violence they might expect in Derry, and this rough regiment had scores to settle after suffering from snipers, and weeks of routine abuse, in Belfast.

The civil rights march degenerated into chaos. In a disputed sequence of events the soldiers opened fire and in several distinct incidents thirteen people were shot dead (another subsequently died from wounds) by troops. It became known as Bloody Sunday. In 1998 the events of late January 1972 became the subject of a public inquiry of exhausting thoroughness which aimed to clear up, in the interests of the peace process, one of the bitterest episodes of the conflict. The official account of the events, the quickly conducted Widgery inquiry, was regarded at the time by nationalists as a whitewash and cannot be regarded as a full version of events. Until the Saville inquiry reports – and maybe even after that – there will be unresolved questions about what happened and why. The army claimed that they had come under fire, but the most that could be demonstrated was a single ineffective shot, apparently fired by an Official IRA member, while army shootings took place in several separate incidents in the city. The coroner recorded that 'the army ran amok that day and shot people without thinking about what they were doing' and even the Widgery report found that the shooting 'bordered on the reckless'.

Saville will also report on the official chain of command, which was not part of Widgery's terms of reference. It is most unlikely that the inquiry will find anything resembling a Cabinet conspiracy to have rebellious Derry Catholics shot. Restoring a normal, stable democratic environment was the aim of government policy, and shooting people in the street is not generally considered conducive to this aim; Bloody Sunday was not what they wanted. There is no sign that sending in the Paras was anything other than an operational decision, no matter how mistaken it proved to be. But nor can one entirely excuse a political leadership which found discussions about inflicting civilian casualties acceptable in these circumstances. A more likely outcome is a finding that the government felt it was running out of options, and allowed itself to be convinced that General Ford had the answer in a more draconian enforcement of law and order. There was also a discreditable negligence in some official and political quarters about inflicting casualties in Northern Ireland. In 1971 the Lord Chancellor, Lord Hailsham, believed that the government was legally entitled to institute a shoot to kill policy, and after the shootings Reggie's agent, Arthur Fawcett, wrote to him saying, 'It is never pleasant when people are shot dead and wounded in circumstances such as these; but I must say I am glad that, at long last, the troops have started to get tough in riot situations, and I think that this attitude will have the support of everyone interested in the preservation of law and order.'[110] There was a widespread, vague tendency, in which Maudling was complicit, to favour clamping down in a manner that one might say bordered on the reckless. But it was reckless rather than calculated.

Bloody Sunday aroused rage against the British. Whatever was left of the government's moral authority after internment vanished and support for the IRA surged. It was a terrible blow for the country's reputation, particularly in the USA where Irish Americans became a source of funds for the IRA. There were riots in Northern Ireland, and most unusually in Dublin where the British Embassy was burnt down. The Irish government temporarily recalled their London ambassador. When Maudling stepped up to the Despatch Box the next day to make a statement, the situation was highly emotionally charged. Maudling was not at his best. He opened: 'The House will have heard with deep anxiety that a number of people were killed and injured in the course of disturbances in Londonderry yesterday.' He went on to condemn the march and matter-of-factly report the army's version of those events, before making the inflammatory and unjustified[111] assertion that 'The Army returned the fire directed at them with aimed shots and inflicted a number of casualties on those who were attacking them with firearms and with bombs'. Republican MP Bernadette Devlin, who had been present in Derry that day, tried to intervene to accuse Maudling of lying, but he continued:

> In view of the statements that have been made which publicly dispute this account, the Government have decided that it is right to set up an independent inquiry into the circumstances of the march and the incidents leading up to the casualties which resulted. We are urgently considering the most appropriate form and membership of such an inquiry and I will make a further statement to the House as soon as possible.[112]

He sat down, without a word of regret ('deep anxiety' was as far as he went), or sympathy for the relatives of those who had been killed, having smeared all those who died as having been armed with guns or bombs. It was a deplorable statement, inadequate to the occasion as well as inaccurate. 'Perhaps we failed him, we should have put something in' to express regret, thought Philip Allen,[113] but a politician like Maudling who was accustomed to making speeches from a few words scribbled on the back of an envelope cannot pass off responsibility to his civil servants. A few days later Reggie did tell Allen that he was 'slightly bothered' at the lopsided body count if the official version was to be believed, a sign that his critical faculties had been jarred into some sort of reflection.[114]

Bernadette Devlin, who failed to catch the Speaker's eye despite a reasonable expectation that she should be able to ask Maudling a question on his statement, rose in fury and launched herself across the floor of the House of Commons to pummel and punch Maudling and pull his hair, screaming that he was a 'murdering hypocrite'. Her gesture was not entirely spontaneous – it was noted that she was sitting on the end of the bench that day rather than her customary position in the middle – but it did authentically represent the feelings of her community. She landed three blows on him before she was restrained. Maudling was only slightly ruffled by the incident – Devlin's small fists made little impression on Maudling's imperturbable bulk and one observer commented that 'she almost woke him up'. He made light of the incident by saying that his grandchildren often pulled his hair and he was used to it, but Devlin commented afterwards that she wished she had got him by the throat.

Maudling's statement was not promising for the independence of the inquiry. He had given the government's version of events before announcing it, and he deflected Tory MP Hugh Fraser's question asking whether the terms of the inquiry could be broader and look into the chain of military command on that day. 'Certainly the inquiry will look into the circumstances in which the illegal march took place, and what happened thereafter,'[115] i.e. 'No', was his reply. When Heath appointed Widgery, the judge was told that 'it had to be remembered that we are in Northern Ireland fighting not only a military war but a propaganda war'.[116] An examination of the chain of military and political command had to wait until the Saville Inquiry.

Bloody Sunday was the end of Stormont. On 9 February the Cabinet committee on Northern Ireland noted:

> The alienation of the minority population is growing and world opinion is becoming increasingly critical. A purely military situation could not guarantee success and made a political initiative more urgent. The implementation of our plan might well involve an interregnum, during which Northern Ireland would be subject to direct rule.[117]

A mood of despair started to engulf the government in February 1972. David Butler encountered Willie Whitelaw on Constitution Hill one evening. Whitelaw spoke in bleak terms about the situation:

That can't do anything but get worse. It is those utterly impossible Unionists. They won't see reason and I fear it may come to direct rule. Quite level-headed people like Roy Hattersley are saying direct rule must come. But it has appalling side implications. Still what can you do? We have absolutely no control over the business of internment. We don't know who is interned and we cannot get explanations for why they are interned. We are put in a quite impossible position.[118]

Heath had become sick of responsibility without power and decided that he had to take control of the situation, which meant depriving Stormont of power over law and order and possibly abolishing it altogether. Some other radical options surfaced at this time, with Alec Douglas-Home arguing against direct rule on the grounds that 'The real British interest would be served best by pushing them towards a United Ireland rather than tying them closer to the United Kingdom'.[119] Maudling's own preference, since late 1971, had been for keeping Stormont but repartitioning the border to give the Protestants a more secure two to one majority in a smaller province. Repartition has had very little support in British or other circles since, because of its many drawbacks. However the border was drawn, short of organising 'population transfers' many Catholics would end up north of it – in West Belfast for instance – probably feeling even more threatened and isolated. While majority Catholic Derry could be transferred fairly readily, given the historical symbolism Unionists would be unlikely to accept its loss easily. And any new border through rural areas would throw up just as many anomalies as the old one, which the army was busily and unsuccessfully trying to shut by blowing up country lanes.[120] But most of all, repartition could never extinguish republicanism in Ireland.

Serious speculation about removing Maudling from the Irish scene, which had become an attractive idea for some Conservative MPs during 1971, began in earnest in early 1972. The message was coming through at the start of January to Cecil King, who was lunching with the great and the good as always and had his own idiosyncratic views (he favoured a united Ireland, but his favourite Ulster politician was Ian Paisley).[121] The discontent was becoming increasingly public. An Irish magazine commented:

The flies on the Cabinet Room wall say that Reggie is down to his last chance in Ulster, and Ted is in no mind to bail him out by giving him another job. If he continues to draw a blank or his policies are reversed, he's out and he knows it. Hence his total reliance on Brian, who still looks the best bet from Westminster.[122]

But Brian did not seem the best bet for much longer. Politics was still deadlocked and violence and bitterness were rampant in Northern Ireland. The conflict spilled over to England on 22 February[123], with an incompetent and brutal Official IRA attack on the Paras' Aldershot barracks which killed six civilians and a Catholic padre, Gerry Weston. But the focus of terror attacks remained Belfast, with appalling IRA bombings at the Abercorn restaurant on 4 March and in Donegall Street on 20 March.

On 22 March Brian Faulkner was summoned to Downing Street to hear Heath's demands. The British government proposed to assume control of security policy, relax internment and conduct a border plebiscite,[124] and wanted to reconstruct the Northern Ireland government as a coalition. Faulkner thought it unacceptable to surrender his powers on law and order and was not ready to accept nationalist members of his Cabinet. It was a tense meeting. Faulkner had, oddly, not expected to be faced with such demands and was unprepared. The British were surprised, as was Unionist MP Stratton Mills:

> all the intelligence I was picking up on the ground [at Westminster] and passing to people at Stormont was that the decision to abolish Stormont had been taken, it was just a matter of the detail between Bloody Sunday and March, and Faulkner refused to believe it. After it happened he said to his Cabinet, 'Sorry gentlemen, I got it wrong.' Quite a big error not to know . . . He was dealing with Maudling but towards the end Maudling was not so much involved.[125]

Maudling wondered aloud whether 'Brian was bluffing' in his refusal to contemplate the proposed changes.[126] Maudling was also extremely worried about a nightmare scenario in which Faulkner would walk out, return to Belfast and call a Stormont general election – leaving the British in the unenviable position of cancelling a free election or surrendering.[127] To Faulkner's right matters had got completely out of control, with William Craig leading a political movement called Vanguard and talking dangerously about 'liquidating the enemy' to a mass rally in Belfast where paramilitaries paraded around. The American representative in Belfast found it a distressing scene: 'Craig asked those who ascribed to the new movement's principles to raise their right hands three times and shout "I do". Back came the phrase three times in unison. It didn't sound too different from 'Sieg Heil.'[128] Ian Paisley had become, relatively, a voice of moderation and calm.[129]

Two days after the meeting with Faulkner, the public announcement was made – Stormont was suspended. Maudling's resistance to abolition had led to a deal that it would be suspended rather than closed down completely and that there would be a reformed version up and running within a couple of years;[130] perhaps after all he had been listening when Maurice Hayes and his group had talked about a 'caesura' the previous autumn. A new Cabinet post, the Secretary of State for Northern Ireland, was created and Willie Whitelaw took over. Maudling gratefully gave up his authority over the province.

The situation became even worse after Direct Rule despite Whitelaw's greater personal popularity. The IRA had become intoxicated by the massive political changes of the previous few years and believed that it might be possible to force the British out within months by stepping up the violence. When Whitelaw invited a group of Republicans, including the young Gerry Adams, to talks at the Cheyne Walk home of his junior minister Paul Channon, the delegation were completely intransigent. When talks broke down the IRA carried out some of the most horrific bombings of the Troubles, reducing parts of central Belfast to rubble and generating mass panic. The conviction that the end was near was also common on the Protestant side, a fear heightened by the suspension of 'their' parliament and the talks between the British and the IRA, and a siege mentality developed among the Protestants. The conflict went through its most vicious phase over the summer of 1972 as loyalist paramilitaries conducted a brutal campaign of sectarian abductions and murders of ordinary Catholics. These killings had a gruesome and sadistic quality taken to its greatest extreme by the Shankill butchers, essentially a gang of serial killers operating under Orange colours, but which reflected the fear, hatred and nihilism prevailing in the province. The year 1972 was easily the most lethal one of the conflict, with 479 killed.

Recovery was very gradual. Talks involving some political parties started at Darlington in October 1972, there were elections in June 1973 for a new Assembly and in January 1974 a power-sharing executive under Faulkner took office. It was brought down in May 1974 by loyalist paramilitaries who enforced a general strike. The death toll fell sharply in 1977; what the IRA called the 'Long War' and the British, behind closed doors, might call an acceptable level of violence, had begun.

The judgement about Maudling's role is whether the complete collapse of the situation into anarchy and murder was inevitable or whether his inactivity was partly responsible. Despite his failures, Maudling cannot be made to shoulder the responsibility alone. The botching of internment was mainly Faulkner's responsibility, and the Unionist insistence on Westminster-style majority rule in a situation far removed from Westminster conditions blocked progress. The constitutional nationalists of the SDLP were completely intransigent after July 1971; John Hume had decided to destroy the Stormont system rather than attempt to renovate it.[131] For the SDLP, 1972 was a radical period in which it was organising a campaign of civil disobedience; its leading Derry member, John Hume, was saying 'It's a united Ireland or nothing'. The IRA were callous and – at that time – politically unsophisticated, but the growth of such a movement is surely a symptom of deeper trouble. While nobody is a 'prisoner of history', a fundamental struggle had been awakened and the hopeful days of O'Neill and civil rights could not last.

The British government was poorly equipped to deal with the situation; Maudling's Northern Ireland responsibilities were a small part of his Home

Office job, which was busy with major reforms of immigration law and criminal justice, and he also had to take a view across the range of government business because of his senior status on Cabinet committees. Even a more energetic minister would have been overwhelmed. 10 Downing Street was also overloaded; Heath had to focus for much of 1970 and 1971 on the European entry negotiations and also faced world financial problems and industrial relations conflict in Britain. When Heath engaged with Northern Ireland, after September 1971, he made a real difference – but by then the situation had deteriorated badly.

Maudling at his best might have helped rather than harmed the situation. His attractive human qualities could have been put to good use in opening opportunities for dialogue. While he was capable of understanding, he did not try; he was shocked by the hatred on display during his first trip within a fortnight of his taking office and thought he could do nothing in the face of such forces. Maudling's logical, Hegelian mind could have grasped the peculiar synthesis (of unionist thesis and republican antithesis) represented by the 1998 Good Friday Agreement, but he was not thinking particularly creatively at the time and his 'initiatives' depended on a non-existent 'centre ground'.

The overall verdict on Maudling in Northern Ireland must be harsh. His initial mistakes – primarily those of omission – started the Heath government on a bad footing in Northern Ireland. His failure to act with more urgency in arranging talks between constitutional parties before the initiative passed to violent forces was a blunder; he made hardly any attempt until after internment, by which time it was too late. Even though he cannot be said to be complicit in the worst aspects of these events, he trod less than carefully on very dangerous ground. His bland acceptance of what the army and the Northern Ireland government told him was negligent, and his actions on internment, interrogation and the crackdown that led to Bloody Sunday reverberated for decades. Truly, the sleep of reason breeds monsters.

Chapter 21

ESSENDON MAN, 1970–1972

The appointment of Reginald Maudling to the Home Office was a sign that the Conservatives were not serious about the 'Selsdon Man' agenda, at least so far as it meant a law and order crackdown. The economics of Selsdon took a longer time to bury, but its purported Home Office policy was dead on arrival – if indeed it ever existed, as the minutes of the conference show that law and order was not central to the Shadow Cabinet discussion. This image of Selsdon arose from a successful spin-doctoring operation after the conference, to which Harold Wilson contributed with his brilliant but double-edged 'Selsdon Man' epithet. The home policy of the Heath government was completely different, reflecting Maudling's own civilised, tolerant weariness and cynicism. Britain may have expected Selsdon Man, but got Essendon Man instead.

In June 1970 Reginald Maudling was given an enormous, multifaceted job, covering criminal justice, prisons, police, drugs, licensing laws, immigration, the security services and broadcasting as well as Northern Ireland; the Home Office has always been rather a residual department for things that would not fit neatly into any other ministry.[1] Maudling himself called it a 'political dustbin' of odd jobs, but felt that what the tasks had in common was the central concern of society, the provision of a maximum level of freedom consistent with order and tolerance – that a Home Secretary should try to work for a society at peace with itself. In a diffuse sense the Home Secretary is responsible for much more, as representing the government's attitude to moral and social questions in the broadest sense. As an interviewer put it to Maudling in 1971, as Home Secretary he was the 'moral tone' of the Heath government. 'Oh dear,' lamented Reggie, 'what an awful thing to be.'[2]

A lot of Home Office work involves hard judgements on individual cases and command of detail – a storm can blow up apparently out of nothing from any of the corners of this vast bureaucratic empire. 'Whatever you do, you can't bloody well get it right,' Reggie grumbled to friends.[3] The Home Office was therefore rather an odd job to give a broad-brush man, whose interests lay primarily in economics and foreign affairs, but it was dictated by the need to give Maudling one of the top three jobs and Heath's verdict that he would be unsuitable as Chancellor because of the controversial legacy of his previous time at the Treasury. He had wanted a chance to show that he had been right in 1964 and felt that he could do the job well. Iain Macleod's sudden death in July 1970, only weeks after taking office, was Maudling's last chance, but Heath decided instead to appoint Anthony Barber to the Treasury and confirm Maudling in the Home Office post for which he had little interest or passion.

Furthermore, Maudling in 1970 was not the man he had been in 1960. He and his wife enjoyed good living. He had visibly aged at an alarming rate and lost all the freshness, eagerness and style he showed earlier in his career. Physically, he had gone to seed. The toll of late nights and long lunches was apparent in his expanding girth and an air of shabbiness and disorder in his appearance. His suits were more crumpled than ever, there was a slight dusting of dandruff on his shoulders, and his hair trailed back lankly towards his collar. This was only the superficial aspect of his loss of drive and interest, for Maudling was a weary soul who could not be revived by what the Home Office could offer. He had done things he ought not to have done in the previous years and feared the consequences. He seemed disengaged and bored, and far from cured of his depressed mood that had taken hold in late 1969. At the Home Office Maudling's reputation for idleness grew rapidly,[4] and there was this time more justification to the complaint than there had been in his previous ministerial jobs.

Despite Maudling's lack of energy, or perhaps because of it, the Home Office in 1970–2 was a happy ministry to work in. The Permanent Secretary was the legendary Sir Philip Allen, who had served in Whitehall since the days of Herbert Morrison and who knew deeply, and loved, the department. Allen was a drier, more serious man than Maudling but grew to regard Reggie with considerable affection and respect. While acknowledging that Maudling was not ideally suited to the Home Office, Allen regarded him as a great improvement on the previous Tory Home Secretary, the 'most unsuitable' Henry Brooke. As well as Reggie being politically astute, 'It was always quite a pleasure to come in for a chat. He was approachable, easy to talk to and indiscreet – but not as indiscreet as Rab. It was a very friendly relationship.'[5]

Reggie recruited Sir Clive Bossom as his Parliamentary Private Secretary. PPSs fall into two broad camps: either they are ambitious young MPs on the bottom rung of government, eager for a patron and an inside view of government, or they are a comforting presence, some light relief from the rigours of ministerial life. Bossom was decidedly the latter. He was the son of Sir Alfred Bossom, the MP about whom Winston Churchill had chortled, 'Bossom? Bossom? What a curious name. The man's neither one thing nor the other.' Bossom senior had entertained in grand style, throwing a ball at the start of each Parliament for all his colleagues. Bossom junior was a universally and deservedly popular bon viveur, without a malicious bone in his body and always ready with a stiff drink and a good story well told, but not exactly a political heavyweight. He was something of a sounding board for Reggie's more speculative thoughts, and could also be relied upon to administer a sharp dig in the ribs if Reggie dozed off, or looked like dozing off, in a debate.

The Home Office in those days had two Ministers of State (Lord Windlesham and Richard Sharples) and one Parliamentary Under-Secretary (Mark Carlisle) to serve under the Home Secretary. Windlesham, a languid, liberal and rather intellectual Tory, represented the department in the House of Lords. Windlesham later became Leader of the House of Lords and then Principal of Brasenose College, Oxford. Sharples, who took much of the flak over the government's Immigration Bill, was a competent but uninspiring minister, a staff officer rather than a general.[6] He left British politics in 1972, causing a celebrated Liberal by-election win in his Sutton and Cheam seat, to become Governor of Bermuda, but he was assassinated in March 1973. In 1977 his murderers became the last people to be executed under any British jurisdiction. Carlisle was a lawyer of some note and ended up with the main responsibility for the 1971–2 Criminal Justice Bill, and a certain amount more besides. Philip Allen recalls one important meeting when

> I had written a paper, and Reggie rolls back from lunch at quarter past three rather the worse for wear, read the papers, didn't take much interest and said 'I'll leave it to Mark' (Carlisle) and cleared off. Then he had the nerve to complain to me that it hadn't been a very satisfactory meeting! I did say that it was totally his fault, and he took it in good part.[7]

Another matter he 'left to Mark' was at a party conference, when he sent Carlisle in to answer a debate on hanging because he could not bear to do it himself. Maudling was usually more effective as a delegator of business than in these anecdotes. For a good junior minister, he was an admirable boss, following the same principle as at the Treasury, where he respected his juniors' expertise and stepped in only to head off trouble. 'Unless you make a complete ass of yourself, I'll back you,' he told Mark Carlisle. Reggie's mode of taking decisions resembled that of a barrister called in for advice. Even when he seemed disengaged, he could focus quickly on the heart of a matter once he had been briefed, and take strategic decisions quickly and efficiently. Having made the decisions that he considered needed to be made at Home Secretary level, he was happy to leave the detail and the implementation to his junior ministers. He was a courteous and patient boss to his junior ministers and his secretaries, including Viv Walker, whom he kept on to do what remained of his personal and political correspondence.

The loss of income that resulted from returning to public office was cushioned somewhat by a splendid official flat in Admiralty House, which was reached by a special lift whose doors opened into the main living room. Admiralty House became something of a social centre during Reggie's time as Home Secretary. Reggie and Beryl kept up the punishing routine of metropolitan social life throughout his term of office. Reggie did all he could to minimise official Home Office engagements outside London – even at the time, when ministerial visits were fewer than now, he did notably less in this direction than other Home Secretaries. There were few foreign trips as Home Secretary, much to their regret – with both the younger boys away at boarding school, in 1970 Beryl had been 'rather looking forward to the day I'd be free and we'd make some gorgeous journeys. Then the moment I'm free we get the election, so all the marvellous things we'd got lined up had to go.'[8]

Reggie was an energetic luncher, with journalists, business contacts and friends, and in the evenings he often booked one or two cocktail parties and a dinner party in the official diary. Very few of the events were political; he was bored and tired with the rubber chicken circuit and did not seek invitations to Conservative constituency events.[9] Reggie and Beryl often spent weekends in the country, shooting with his more affluent friends such as Sir Cyril Kleinwort and Sir Charles Forte. He enjoyed teasing Forte about the standards of his 'horrible motorway cafes'. Shooting had become something of a passion by the early 1970s, and in autumn 1971 after the party conference – which seems to have left him with surplus aggression to take out somehow or other – he was blasting birds from the sky for seven weekends out of nine.[10] When he was living at Chester Square, his secretary, Viv Walker, used to dread the Mondays after a shoot because she was allergic to feathers, and Reggie would hang pheasants up by the fridge door.[11]

When he was not shooting, he would also often have Sunday lunch in Barnet with his better friends among the constituency activists like Bob and Ann Brum. Another Barnet 'old friend and drinking companion' was Kingsley Amis, who lived at the time in a large house called 'Lemmons' in the constituency. Amis had been travelling from left to right rather more rapidly than Maudling had been edging from right to left, and they probably crossed over in the late 1960s; but much more than politics they shared interests in James Bond, middlebrow culture and alcoholic drink of all kinds. Reggie had a high opinion of Kingsley's version of a Bloody Mary, and appreciated the distinction he drew between physical and metaphysical hangovers.[12] Saturday 13 November 1971, when Reggie's engagements diary records 'Luncheon Mr and Mrs Kingsley Amis, dinner Mr and Mrs Kingsley Amis' must have been quite a day.[13] His holidays fell into the usual pattern he had established in the 1960s – staying at Formentor with Vane Ivanovic in the summer, and skiing in Norway with Sandy Glen at Easter.

The social climate had changed a great deal since Maudling was last in government. The year 1970 was a particularly difficult time for a Conservative Home Secretary to take over. Many Tories felt that the election result was a mandate to throw the permissive changes of the 1960s into reverse and clamp down on student demonstrators, hippies, layabouts and immigrants. Maudling had no intention of satisfying these demands. His instincts were clearly more liberal than Callaghan's and actually quite close to the right's permissive *bête noire* Roy Jenkins. Philip Allen, Permanent Secretary to all three men, thought that Reggie and Roy shared an approach to social matters while Jim was completely different.[14] Differences in style, as Maudling said in 1971, were not particularly about party allegiance. He believed that 'the object of a civilised society and government should be the maximum of freedom as long as the freedom of others is not infringed'.[15] It was absurd for the alternative magazine *Ink* to depict Maudling as 'the number one repressor in Britain',[16] much as some of the more atavistic Tories might have wanted him to be.

The limits of free expression were much discussed in the late 1960s and early 1970s, and there was a campaign led by Mary Whitehouse that had gathered strength during the 1960s, broadening its initial reaction against swearing in television programmes to cover a range of issues such as depictions of violence, nudity and sexual content in the mainstream media and the growth of pornography and alternative media. Several Conservative MPs fulminated about Britain 'sleepwalking into a cesspit'. Reggie was not greatly concerned about any of this, commenting that while he personally regretted that 'novelists and playwrights and film makers seem to have abandoned the emotion of love for the mechanics of sex' he would 'fight to the end for freedom to express, to entertain and to perform'.[17] He certainly wasn't going to restrict those freedoms just because a bossy woman like Mary Whitehouse told him to. He didn't bother to read Lord Longford's unofficial 1971 report into pornography. Maudling took a classic liberal, John Stuart Mill attitude to censorship, which he argued well but to no strong conclusion in his memoirs. 'If one adult wishes to write a book or produce a play and show it to other adults, and they wish to see it, what right has the State to object?'[18] He thought there were only three factors that might inhibit this: protection of children, the possibility that people might be influenced by scenes of violence and explicit advertising that is visible to people regardless of whether they wanted it. Maudling was quite sensibly agnostic about the effects of screen violence on behaviour, but explicit advertising he thought was clearly not acceptable (as indeed did the Williams Committee on obscenity in 1979). But he was much less concerned than Callaghan had been about 'sex and violence' on television and in films. Callaghan had called a meeting with the broadcasters in 1970 that ended up taking place early on in Reggie's time. Maudling did not take the meeting seriously. He started it by saying that he wasn't quite sure what all the fuss was about, he rather liked a bit of violence himself, 'but Philip here – and he gestured to his Permanent Secretary Philip Allen – will tell you what's worrying him'.[19] The broadcasters took heart that the new government was not going to back Whitehouse's campaign and merrily carried on pushing the envelope of how much sex and violence they could get away with.

The most notable sex-and-violence case of Maudling's term of office was over Stanley Kubrick's film *A Clockwork Orange* in January 1972. The imagery of oddly stylish hooligans dealing out random violence amid the concrete subways of some Heath-style city of the future generated an instant tabloid panic. Maudling added to the fuss by declaring that 'There is a new film out this week that I think I ought to go and see . . . If things are being shown which one could reasonably suppose are contributing to the degree of violence, I think I ought to know.'[20] Maudling went and secretly saw the film on 17 January at the Film Censors' headquarters in Soho Square, but then failed to pass any comment. He was criticised at the time for intervening at all, but he did nothing to suppress the film or feed the tabloid frenzy any further; the decision not to show it any more in Britain was made by Kubrick rather than the government. The only occasion on which he was heavy-handed towards the broadcasters was over a BBC television programme, *The Question of Ulster*. He summoned the chairman of the governors, Lord Hill, and the Director-General Charles Curran to see him and 'blew his top'; his intervention caused the broadcasters to amend the programme but he was unsuccessful in stopping it from being transmitted in January 1972. Maudling feared that it would contribute to despondency about the Northern Ireland situation among British public opinion, but as it turned out the programme was earnest and respectable to the point of dullness, as early 1970s current affairs output often was.[21]

Maudling's libertarianism was most apparent in his attitude to licensing, a subject in which he had a considerable personal interest. He would ideally have moved to a more or less complete free for all, allowing alcohol to be sold round the clock. He argued that the current licensing laws were bad in general, and also an absurd handicap for Britain's tourist industry.[22] Maudling wanted a quick and decisive study pointing in the direction he wanted, but according to his PPS, Clive Bossom, a complete bureaucratic meal was made of the question. Philip Allen insisted in July 1970 that he needed a full departmental committee of inquiry to achieve a radical reform because there was no consensus around a change: 'Notwithstanding your own lifetime's experience, there are fears held by a lot of people that if we follow the French example, for example, the number of people dying here of cirrhosis of the liver might mount up towards the French experience.'[23] Reggie acceded, and in December 1970 a committee was appointed. Reggie did his best to stack the committee, appointing his old ministerial colleague Freddy Erroll to chair it, but he simply could not manage to insert the measure into the government's legislative programme. There were big Home Office measures in each of the parliamentary sessions, the Immigration Bill in 1970–1 and the Criminal Justice Bill in 1971–2, and his colleagues were not inclined to make time for what many saw as a frivolous measure all too indicative of the later Maudling's priorities. Although the project for broad licensing reform came to nothing, Reggie did make a minor change to drinking in Britain – as Home Secretary part of his job was as overall proprietor of the pubs of Carlisle, which had been nationalised in 1916 on the grounds that private management was doing too good a job at selling alcohol to munitions workers. Maudling did not like his brief experience as a pub owner, and wanted to get rid of them. His Home Office did the preparatory work, and the pubs were denationalised in 1973.

Maudling never quite made up his mind about drugs other than alcohol. He was worried by the effects of hard drugs, but susceptible to libertarian arguments about soft drugs and in relaxed moments would say that he did not really think that cannabis should remain illegal.[24] He was intrigued by youth culture and not instinctively hostile to it as so many Tories were. His closeness to Caroline gave him an insight into the more glamorous end of the counter-culture and she reinforced some of his libertarian, permissive instincts. His younger sons were teenagers in 1970–2 and experimenting enthusiastically with cannabis. They would occasionally hold parties in Admiralty House where dope fumes hung heavy in the air. Thankfully in those days the press were less intrusive and young people, even the children of famous people, were allowed a bit more latitude. However, it was a considerable risk, which would have been less easy for Maudling to handle than it was for Jack Straw in slightly similar circumstances in the late 1990s because in the Maudling case social attitudes were harsher, an official residence was involved, and Maudling surely knew or guessed while Straw had been unaware.

Maudling also gave some serious thought to drugs in an official capacity, as the law was in a state of flux when he took over. The Labour government's legislation had fallen with the dissolution of Parliament and he had to decide whether to restore it, review the whole area, or write his own Bill. William Rees-Mogg said to him that it was absurd that here they were, writing *Times* leaders and making the law without any direct experience of cannabis. Maudling told him that he had asked the Home Office whether they could conduct an experiment, but was warned that they might face arrest. The proposed sampling did not take place.[25] However, he was not a convinced advocate of legalisation and was persuaded by the police that he should drop the idea. He persisted instead with the legislation he inherited from Callaghan – to which he added a couple of measures tipping the balance more towards treatment than punishment – which eventually became the Misuse of Drugs Act 1971.

Maudling's libertarianism was also apparent in some of the smaller issues of the Home Office, and his instinctive reaction to questions that were put to him. He dismissed the idea of a national identity card, and also praised the National Campaign for Civil Liberties – at the time widely regarded by Tories as being no more than leftist troublemakers – as 'hard working, conscientious people'.[26] He was also concerned about the conservative attitudes of magistrates, and believed that they had a tendency to become pompous and bossy after a few years on the bench; he encouraged friends whose judgement he respected to volunteer as magistrates, so that the bench was not full of authoritarians.[27] He was relaxed about the establishment of an office by the Palestine Liberation Organisation in London in 1972, which greatly angered Israel; if he had wanted to, he could have found a way to stop it, but he took the view that there was nothing he could do to stop a private organisation setting up shop as long as its personnel confined themselves to legal activities.

Oddly, given his own financial recklessness, more or less the only 'vice' he did anything to combat as Home Secretary was gambling, which in contrast to drinking in Carlisle he felt was somehow inappropriate in private hands. One of the minor Home Office issues that came up late in Reggie's term was the Tote. Financial problems caused by declining attendance at races and legal off-course betting made some legislation inevitable, either to let it collapse or to maintain it and enable it to continue in competition with the private bookmakers. The Home Office produced a Bill to allow the Tote to offer fixed odds betting and bets on events other than UK horse races. The intention was to open a few hundred offices off-course and put it in a competitive position with the large bookmakers. Philip Allen tried in vain to get Reggie to take an interest in the Tote, although Reggie did have a series of meetings about it. One memorable meeting was with George Wigg, a racing fanatic, although he was better known as Harold Wilson's former security sidekick, at which Wigg talked in riddles for an hour. Allen asked Reggie if he had understood what George was on about and he said, 'Not a word. But George seemed very happy, and I like to make people happy.'[28] Maudling did decide that he would oppose the interests of the private bookies.[29] When the legislation was introduced there was no official Labour opposition to this extension of the quasi-public sector, but in a strange role reversal there was a determined campaign by some Labour MPs such as Brian Walden to stop the Tote competing with the bookies.

Maudling did make an occasional move that offended liberal opinion and gave him some prestige on the right. One such was the decision to deport the German student revolutionary Rudi Dutschke who had been admitted to Britain for medical treatment after he was shot by a right-winger in 1968. His visa was renewed by Jim Callaghan to allow him to convalesce, and during the first half of 1970 he applied to Cambridge University to study. He was accepted by King's College on 3 June, and also offered a place at Balliol College, Oxford.[30] The matter of his immigration status was undecided at the time of the change of government in 1970. Dutschke had considerable support on the British left, and not just among the student revolutionaries; Michael Foot had rather adopted Dutschke and tried to persuade him of the merits of the parliamentary road to socialism, and had made most of the arrangements for his stay in Britain. Foot wrote in friendly terms to Reggie on 13 July and seemed optimistic about the case. At first Foot was puzzled by the lack of a reply from the Home Office for over a month, and then astonished when Maudling wrote on 25 August that he would not allow Dutschke to stay.

Maudling behaved most uncharacteristically over Dutschke. He became a bit obsessed with the case.[31] He became convinced, to an extent that was very unusual for him, of the righteousness of his decision.[32] While Foot was intrigued by Dutschke's views, Maudling could not understand how someone of Dutschke's intelligence could believe what he did, saw no reason why he should be allowed to stay and study and announced in September 1970 that he would have to go. The decision came at an opportune time, when he could make a rare conference-pleasing speech appealing to their prejudices about students and foreigners, but it appears that opportunism had nothing to do with his decision.

The reasons for his hard line are difficult to discern, but it was to some extent foreshadowed by his apparently genuine dismay at the prospect of another radical student, Dany Cohn-Bendit, being admitted to Britain in 1968. Initially Maudling attempted to defend the Dutschke decision on neutral administrative grounds but his line gradually hardened over the autumn. Until October 1970 no claims of any threat to national security from Dutschke were made, even in private meetings with Michael Foot.[33] This was only introduced later on, on ostensibly flimsy grounds concerning alleged meetings, most of which had taken place before June 1970 while Callaghan was Home Secretary. Foot refused to believe that Maudling had misled him, and it is still a mystery as to why Maudling's grounds for refusing Dutschke changed and why he had become so determined that he would proceed. He did so despite the lack of enthusiasm from his Cabinet colleagues and Home Office civil servants, and the evidence of Dutschke's doctor that his actions would be prejudicial to the young man's health.[34]

Dutschke, as was his right (although both Foot and Maudling were surprised that the right existed when this was pointed out by Philip Allen) took the case to a review tribunal,[35] and the hearing in December 1970 was a rather sinister affair at which guilt by association, wilful misreadings of his written work and the fruits of heavy security service surveillance were given as evidence, and government witnesses were not cross-examined.[36] The tribunal ruled for the government and Dutschke was accepted for studies in Denmark in 1971. However, Maudling would have deported Dutschke whatever the result because 'there are difficult problems involved here, of the security of the State, of the protection of British sources of intelligence'.[37] He would even have resigned rather than accept a Cabinet, or tribunal, decision that Dutschke might stay.[38] Maudling then announced that there would be no right of appeal in future on security cases, although in this case the security aspects seem to have been drummed up to justify a decision based on political prejudice. Either that, or Maudling uncritically accepted what he was told by MI5, whose peculiar mentality in the early 1970s is now well known. However, he was not the only 1970s Home Secretary to take controversial and arguably mistaken deportation decisions – Labour's Merlyn Rees, another basically liberal man, deported American journalists Agee and Hosenball in

1977 on security service advice. Maudling weighed in to support Rees in the parliamentary debate.[39] No evidence has since come to light, long after Dutschke died following years of ill-health from his wounds, to suggest that he was any sort of threat. His expulsion was an uncharacteristically shabby episode in Maudling's ministerial career; Reggie usually tried to make sure that individual cases were handled with justice and compassion. He extended this sympathy while Minister of Supply to aviation workers in the 1950s accused of being communist and therefore a security risk;[40] he thought hard about other justice cases he dealt with in the Colonial Office and the Home Office. But he had a strange blind spot over this crippled young German student who was moving gradually from revolutionary student to radical don.

The political situation in 1970 was also such that no Conservative Home Secretary could avoid introducing major legislation. Enoch Powell had whipped up anti-immigration feeling and inadvertently delivered votes to the Tories in the election campaign. Powell was a dangerous figure on the fringe and to fail to 'draw his horns' by introducing stricter legislation would have risked the government's political base. Many of the new Conservative voters in 1970 were working-class converts from Labour who had been persuaded that the Tories were sounder on immigration, and most of the Tory party faithful wanted controls. The Conservative manifesto had committed the party unambiguously to:

> Establish a new single system of control over all immigration from overseas. The Home Secretary of the day will have complete control, subject to the machinery of appeal, over the entry of individuals into Britain . . . These policies will mean that future immigration will be allowed only in strictly defined special cases. There will be no further large scale permanent immigration. We will give assistance to Commonwealth immigrants who wish to return to their countries of origin, but we will not tolerate any attempt to harass or compel them to go against their will.[41]

Reggie Maudling's own instincts on general policy concerning immigration were liberal. His PPS, Clive Bossom, was surprised one day when Maudling, in expansive mood, said that he did not really believe in immigration control and that ideally anyone who wanted to come should be able to do so.[42] As Colonial Secretary he had disliked the imposition of controls in 1962 and 'clung to the view, perhaps outmoded and sentimental, that subjects of the Queen should be allowed the right to come and live in the Mother Country'.[43] With great reluctance he had been persuaded intellectually, though hardly in his heart, that some controls had to be imposed. Reggie was uneasy about what he had to do, and a willing audience for Home Office civil servants who pointed out that in some respects the controls on Commonwealth immigrants were already more stringent than those on aliens, and the government had to choose whether to toughen up on aliens or relax these controls on

Commonwealth citizens. He promptly dictated a memo to this effect to Heath, who was exasperated that Reggie had been got at so quickly by his department.

The Bill that the Home Office produced was a complicated measure which did, basically, eliminate most of the distinctions between Commonwealth and 'alien' for immigration purposes and set up categories of permitted immigrants. More controversial were two other sections, one of which met the Powellite demand for assisted repatriation of Commonwealth immigrants, and the other which invented 'patriality'. This meant that people with a parent or grandparent born in the UK were entitled to enter the country, which neatly covered most of the white population of Australia, New Zealand and Canada. During the committee stage of the Bill this was amended to delete the grandparent clause, a defeat Maudling accepted but which was reversed before the end of the Heath government.[44]

Maudling did acknowledge privately that the Immigration Bill was discriminatory, something he strenuously denied in public. For a supposedly restrictive measure, the 1971 immigration changes actually allowed a large number of – white – immigrants to enter Britain uncontrolled, while making 'coloured immigration' more difficult. In setting out his case to the Cabinet in January 1971, Maudling wrote in terms that would now be considered unacceptable about how assimilation was 'all but impossible' for Asians, while the whites of the Old Commonwealth came from 'a cultural background fairly akin to our own'.[45] He added some reflections, not intended to be insulting, about how 'the smell of strange cooking probably had more effect in people's minds than almost anything else'.[46] It is safe to say that the British have, by and large, got over this problem, and learned to love their chicken tikka masalas. That Maudling could think and write in the terms he did is a reflection of his times – one need only watch comedy programmes of the time, or look at the blatantly racist cartoons in newspapers like the *Sunday Express*, to see how common and casual racism was in the early 1970s. Maudling's own attitudes were, however he expressed them, not motivated by racial prejudice or feelings of superiority, and neither were those of Heath, who had boldly denounced Powell's rivers of blood speech. Maudling was well travelled and his Colonial Office days had given him respect for people of other nationalities in the former Empire. He had many friends among the post-colonial leaders, and of course in the Arab world. In Maudling's case his attitude was also apparent from his personal life. In the late 1960s Caroline had a relationship with a black South African and Reggie was never anything less than welcoming, friendly and supportive.[47] George Hallett, a black Cape Town photographer, was left with deep memories of a dinner at Maudling's house; he felt that Reggie's liberal racial attitudes had taught him that Britain was a much more open and tolerant place than South Africa.[48]

Maudling's feelings that the Immigration Bill was distasteful but politically necessary meant that he did not play a very active part in steering it through

Parliament (although sitting about in the Bill's committee stages did occupy a great deal of his time during 1971). He did not focus on the Bill's details and left much of that to his junior minister, Richard Sharples. When he did appear to advocate the Bill, as in the Second Reading debate in March 1971, he produced some uncharacteristically poor Commons performances. He was ill at ease defending the detailed arrangements, giving the impression to one observer that he 'floundered like a stranded whale in his easygoing ignorance, whilst most of his backbenchers hurled greater or lesser harpoons at him'.[49] He became so muddled at one point that Jim Callaghan acidly commented that 'I am sure the Home Secretary understands his own Bill'.[50]

The Bill, despite its faults, was only weakly opposed and passed, rather arduously as it was a complex measure, through Parliament in 1971. The Tory right grumbled about the Bill's failure to make more effective provisions for dispersing future immigrants away from areas of previous settlement, and for maintaining UK voting rights for Commonwealth citizens, but Reggie refused to do anything to meet their objections.[51] The Bill gave a great deal of administrative discretion to future Home Secretaries and Employment Secretaries, which was by and large used humanely.

Maudling's Act continues to form the basis of immigration law, although the Thatcher government redefined British nationality in 1981. The repatriation provisions, which Powell cared most about, were sabotaged by the government when the details were drawn up and became a dead letter. 'I would be averse to a policy based on a theory saying we want to get rid of these chaps,' said Reggie characteristically in 1971.[52] The Immigration Act, together with entry to the EC, was part of the decisive turn towards Europe and away from the Commonwealth that took place – or, at least, was at last officially consummated – during the Heath government. The patriality rule has, despite its unsatisfactory underpinnings, stuck and as primary emigration from Britain to the Old Commonwealth has slowed it will be a back door for fewer and fewer people in future.

In tandem with the moderately restrictive Immigration Bill, Maudling relaxed the Labour government's restrictions on the immigration to Britain of Asians from the East African nations of Kenya and Uganda, raising the annual quota of admissions from 1,500 heads of households to 3,000, at the expense of other Commonwealth countries and aliens.[53] Maudling won some praise from the liberal Labour MP Alex Lyon about his treatment of East African Asians. Lyon spoke of 'the compassion he has shown in dealing with this difficult problem, which eluded the last [Labour] administration'.[54] When Idi Amin started his persecution of the Ugandan Asians, Reggie was clear about the moral issues involved in this matter; to him there was 'a duty of honour and decency to do this and people recognise it' and there was 'no alternative whatsoever'. He had an unusually positive opinion of the October 1972 Conservative conference at which his successor Robert Carr and 'youth, decency and moderation' triumphed.[55]

In the 1971 Queen's Speech the main Home Office legislation was a Criminal Justice Bill. These are passed every few years to change the criminal law and amalgamate a variety of loosely related matters in a single Bill. Some matters are pet schemes of Home Office civil servants, others are the result of political imperatives. Maudling's Bill emerged from round table discussions within the Home Office and owed a lot to its officials, but the selection of items and its placing in the government's legislative programme were Maudling's responsibilities. It was a rather uncontentious liberalising Bill.

Maudling explained the philosophy of the Bill as 'being designed to differentiate between violent crime for which there should be tougher penalties and other types of crime for which new, even experimental, penalties should be applied'. The most important change was the introduction of non-custodial sentencing through community service orders, a liberal measure that Roy Jenkins had not managed to introduce. Maudling later called community sentencing 'one of the great developments in this country in recent years'.[56] Reggie and his team rejected the simplistic idea that 'prison works'. The prison system was in a poor state in 1970. Rising crime and stiff sentencing had caused an unsustainable escalation in the prison population and there was an imminent danger that there would simply not be enough room to accommodate everyone. The prison population had risen over 40,000 – a record – and was increasing at a rate of 1,000 a month rather than the projected 1,000 a year.[57] Prison policy had started to change in the 1960s, when Roy Jenkins legislated for the introduction of suspended sentences and the abolition of corporal punishment in prisons in his 1967 Criminal Justice Act. However, suspended sentencing did not work as intended, because judges in sentencing seemed to be using it as an alternative to fines rather than to a full prison sentence. A programme of prison construction had started under Callaghan, and it continued and accelerated under Maudling, although Mark Carlisle and Philip Allen were largely responsible for the drive and detail. Maudling's actions in introducing community service orders and stepping up prison construction were appropriate and successful responses to the situation and the prison crisis was defused. While prison building may not seem a liberal policy, as Robert Carr pointed out there is nothing liberal about confining people in crumbling old jails.[58]

The 1971 Criminal Justice Bill also proposed to upgrade the Probation Service, whose work Reggie valued greatly, and a separate inquiry into pay and conditions was announced. People whose criminal behaviour was largely caused by alcoholism would be treated in drying-out clinics rather than being given prison or fines, and powers were taken to allow deferred sentences, to give people found guilty a chance to put things right and avoid prison. A few sentences for violent crimes were toughened, including the rather illogical change in the maximum penalty for carrying a firearm with intent to endanger life to a life sentence (the same as murder). Although it was a ragbag of measures, Maudling's Criminal Justice Bill was motivated by a consistent philosophy that distinguished between violent criminals, people whose character would be worsened by prison, for whom other forms of sentence should be found, and those whose offences were the product of inadequacy, who Maudling felt should be given more help for their own sake as well as society in general.[59]

As well as straightforward liberalism, Maudling's criminal justice policy had a more radical philosophical strand. In 1975 he wrote: 'For the simple fact is that concepts of morality are going to be influenced by the advance of science. It is not merely that conventions change from generation to generation. If it is possible by treatment to cure criminal tendencies, how can you distinguish between crime and illness?'[60] This was less an unintended lesson from his viewing of *A Clockwork Orange*, whose model of treatment to cure criminal tendencies might not be considered attractive, than a development from his meditations on technological change in recent years,[61] somewhat under the influence of Williams and Poulson. It is an indication of Reggie's intellectual curiosity, but also of his highly situational approach to morality. His interest in what might be called toughness on the causes of crime is apparent in some of the Home Office working groups on questions like the role of alcohol in crime, and engaging entries in the Home Office diary such as 'Lunacy and Criminality' booked in for 10a.m. on Friday morning.

The debates on the Criminal Justice Bill were good-natured. Maudling's introduction of the Bill on 22 November 1971 was welcomed on all sides. The Deputy Speaker was even lulled by the general consensus into a mistake, calling for next business before even the formality of a debate, until Jim Callaghan put him right. The Tory whip Bernard Weatherill noted that: 'There were so many nods of approval as Mr Maudling was outlining his plans that the Deputy Speaker should be forgiven for putting the question to the House as he sat down.'[62] Absent from the Bill was any move towards restoring the death penalty. Maudling remained in favour of capital punishment, although he did nothing to further the cause of restoration while he was Home Secretary. He commented that 'it was wrong to suppose that the burden on the Home Secretary of confirming a death sentence was an intolerable one' although it was certainly a heavy one, as he knew from having approved executions while he was Colonial Secretary.[63] Whenever Reggie was accused of being a knee-jerk liberal he was able to point to his support of the death penalty to refute the charge, but it was really only window-dressing. The death penalty had been debated fairly conclusively in 1965 and 1969 and it would have been unproductive to reopen it, particularly as any kind of official government initiative, even had Reggie felt more strongly about the issue than he did.

Maudling felt that it was even more difficult to decide on whether to accept advice on the release of convicted murderers and other dangerous prisoners. He took this particularly seriously in the light of the Graham Young case.

Young had been detained in Broadmoor secure hospital several years earlier after committing several serious poisonings, and according to the psychiatric advice that reached Maudling he was not a risk to the public any more. Maudling approved the release. Young, however, was not cured but a cunning psychopath, and when he came out he resumed his crimes and killed four people by poisoning before he was captured. Broadmoor frightened Maudling anyway – he received distressing letters and drawings from patients[64] – but the Young case was particularly horrible.[65] It was also politically dangerous. Maudling had some lead time while the murders were *sub judice* and set about preparing for the inevitable furore. He appointed two review committees into the procedures for releases from Broadmoor and the provision of semi-secure hospitals for people who could no longer be confined to Broadmoor, the latter chaired by Rab Butler. When Maudling came to make his statement in June 1972 he had headed off political trouble, and former Home Office ministers from the Labour government expressed sympathy for his predicament.

As Home Secretary Reggie rarely deviated from his emphasis on freedom – freedom combined with responsibility, to be sure, but he did not indulge in the sort of scapegoating of minorities and demonstrators that comes naturally to 'law and order' politicians. A rare exception, early in his term, was Reggie's description of a few scuffles in Notting Hill in summer 1970 as a 'black power conspiracy', and his strange interest in the case.[66] The harder line momentarily apparent in police practice after the election softened for lack of high-level support. But these were strange times, and a real if vague threat did exist, not from black power but in the form of the 'Angry Brigade', a loosely organised anarchist group responsible for several violent incidents in the early 1970s including a bomb attack on Robert Carr in Barnet. This pre-dated the IRA's bombings in England, and the anti-terrorist squad's origins were in fact in the Barnet police's investigation of these attacks – DI Habershon of Barnet was the squad's first chief. Additional security precautions were introduced for ministers, including of course Maudling himself because of the double threat from anarchists and the IRA. Reggie found the constant presence of his Special Branch detectives wearisome, and would occasionally give them the slip when he was socialising. As in 11 Downing Street in 1963, he was obdurate about not compromising his freedom to live family and social life, and the police were never satisfied with the security arrangements around Bedwell Lodge.[67] As in private, Maudling as minister did not overreact to the threat from terrorists, and did not play into their hands by introducing repressive legislation. His junior minister, now Lord Carlisle of Bucklow, has continued to uphold the Maudling Home Office liberal tradition in debates on counter-terrorist measures in the House of Lords in 2003.

Maudling was departmentally responsible for MI5, and had the task of choosing the new director-general in 1971. He accepted Home Office advice to bring in an outside candidate, in fact drawn from the Home Office, but he was overruled by Heath, who chose the internal MI5 candidate, Michael Hanley.[68] Reggie shrugged his shoulders and did not fight the decision, but the mid-1970s proved to be a particularly regrettable period in the history of MI5. Reggie was not particularly interested in spying and spooks, although he tended to defer to the agency in such matters, particularly in domestic affairs. He was a little more inclined to question its judgement in the larger Cold War issues, as he felt he understood something about Russia. The most serious security incident during Reggie's term of office was the mass expulsion of 105 Soviet diplomats whom the security agencies had identified as spies; the number of Soviet intelligence officers in London had, at least according to MI5, started to assume excessive proportions. The Trade Mission in Highgate, to whose growth Maudling had contributed as President of the Board of Trade, was a particular concern. Subtle approaches through Foreign Minister Gromyko had come to nothing, and a small committee of Heath, Douglas-Home, Maudling and Denis Greenhill, Permanent Secretary at the Foreign Office, considered the issue. Heath and Douglas-Home were for high-profile expulsions, but Maudling argued that 'after a mass expulsion, the Government would be the laughing-stock of the British public and we should all look very foolish'. Reggie was overruled on this occasion, but as Home Secretary agreed that he and Douglas-Home would jointly announce the decision, which was to opt for a mass expulsion. The British public, if anything, were impressed, and the chill in Anglo-Soviet relations was short-lived, as the Russians knew they had been pushing their luck. A little later, Reggie confessed his misjudgement to his colleagues.[69]

Maudling was one of three Home Secretaries – with Jenkins and Carr – who set Home Office policy on a course from which it did not seriously deviate until Michael Howard took over in 1993. Leo Abse regarded him as a good Home Secretary, with 'the authority to lead the Conservatives away from punitive and primitive thinking', rather than pandering to it.[70] Reggie's time was another 'liberal hour', all the more unexpected for coming on the back of a right-wing backlash. Maudling was altogether a more highly evolved creature than Selsdon Man. As well as actual liberal measures, Maudling fixed in place a top-level liberal consensus that despite rhetorical differences and occasional gestures survived for twenty years. Nearly all of Roy Jenkins's policies survived a change in government, and indeed probably fared better than they would have if Jim Callaghan had remained in place. In criminal justice, modernisation of prison conditions was accompanied by the search for non-custodial alternatives to prison. Maudling's failure even to try to move the clock back on censorship and personal liberty ensured that the frontiers of free expression moved steadily outward. It is hard to imagine any Tory Home Secretary taking office in 1970 being significantly more liberal than Maudling. Foreign comparisons, of right-wing administrations elected on a backlash vote in France and the United States in 1968, are instructive. In both countries law and order politics was pushed much further, to the paradoxical point of state illegality in clamping down on dissent, telephone tapping and the diminution of the civil rights of the individual; in the USA it was accompanied by ugly, divisive rhetoric against young people, minorities and people who exercised their right to protest. Under Maudling, and Carr, there was hardly any of this sort of thing in Britain.

As in his previous two government offices, Colonial Secretary and Chancellor, Maudling took over after a major change in direction. He cannot be claimed as a great innovator, but he was a first-class reconciler of traditionalists to new policies. While there was real division and bad feeling in the Tory party about the dissolution of empire in 1960–1, by the time he had finished – with the exception of Southern Rhodesia – the imperial issue had been put to rest. As Chancellor, Reggie managed to make the Tories accept planning and incomes policy, which Selwyn Lloyd had introduced but gave little impression of understanding. His liberal term as Home Secretary was a great work of reconciliation and settling down in turbulent times.

Maudling was Deputy Prime Minister as well as Home Secretary, although he was not given the official title, which comes and goes according to fashion and political expediency. Heath as Prime Minister was more than usually a chief executive, and while Maudling had second place in terms of protocol and certain coordinating functions, there was no division of the chief executive role and Heath disclaims having had any Deputy Prime Minister in his government.[71] But, more than any other minister except Heath, Maudling had a view over the entire waterfront of government affairs between June 1970 and July 1972.

When the Heath government was established Maudling was given the chairmanship of several Cabinet committees and membership of nearly all the important ones, including Defence and Overseas Policy, Economic Strategy, Home and Social Affairs, Emergencies, Rhodesia, Northern Ireland and Whitehall redevelopment. When Heath was not in attendance Maudling would chair most of them. As one of the most experienced ministers in the government, he was well qualified to comment on most of these matters. His twenty years of front bench service had been mostly about finance and economics, but he also had several years of colonial and international experience. The only major gaps in his direct knowledge were the public services, although even here he had exercised some sort of strategic direction as Chancellor and in opposition as head of the advisory committee on policy. Maudling was at his most effective in his role as committee chairman, conducting business with efficiency and good humour and adding considerably to the smooth running of the government. It was not unusual for committee work to finish before the allotted time because all the business had been done. His reports to Cabinet, on subjects such as the Third London Airport (which was then intended to be at Foulness mud bank on the Essex coast, later restyled 'Maplin Sands') and payment of benefits to strikers, were admirably concise and clear, and often only a couple of pages long plus annexes for those who cared to read them. They were usually impeccably logical and well argued.

Maudling would also take Prime Minister's Questions when Heath was absent. A particularly amusing occasion was in December 1971 when he turned up well lubricated after spending the entire morning at the annual wine taster of the year competition at the Savoy Hotel. He had announced his intention to go to this event to Philip Allen, who recalls him saying:

'You are going to be very cross with me, Philip.' I said 'Why, what have you done wrong now?' He said 'I am going off to a wine tasting party. You won't approve.' 'Well, no, it's not an occupation I endorse, but it's all right. Provided you don't win it and get some publicity.' He came back and said that he'd had very little difficulty in complying with my instructions.[72]

Bernard Weatherill, a Tory whip, observed Maudling's performance at Question Time that afternoon:

To a student of politics his style is a fascinating one. He appears to take very little trouble (it is rumoured that on the first occasion on which he stood in for the Prime Minister he refused to be briefed, saying that he preferred to play it by ear) but he seldom fails to score runs. This afternoon we raced through questions.[73]

Helped by the festive atmosphere, Reggie had an easy run, and his short and sometimes vague answers to questions generated no objections.[74]

Maudling was often seen at the time as being a 'left-wing' counterweight to Heath's right-wing leadership, or even as a minority left-wing faction leader within the Cabinet. This depended on a ludicrous misreading of Heath's political views which was strangely common at the time – that Heath was a hard-faced right-wing enthusiast for market forces and law and order. Neither was there anything in the perception of Maudling as faction leader, as he had never been in the business of forming personal or ideological cliques and was not about to start. However, there was a subtler sense in which Maudling was a counterweight to Heath.

The government's agenda was heavily influenced by Heath's impatient personality and his commitment to modernisation; it was indeed a 'quiet revolution'. Heath's government was a revolutionary undertaking, but it was a serious misunderstanding to see it as a right-wing revolution. It was actually about radical modernisation, about forcing Britain to accept the changes that had restructured the rest of Western Europe. Part of the project was joining the European Community. Part was about accelerating economic growth by any means available. Part was about technology and vast investment projects such as the Channel Tunnel and the enormous Maplin development in Essex, which started off as an airport and came to encompass a huge seaport and a New Town the size of Southampton. The Industrial Relations Act was not a crude piece of union-bashing but a flawed attempt to codify, modernise and reform a backward area of British life. In the same vein, the Conservative government demolished the traditional structure of local government. Maudling was no sort of revolutionary, quiet or otherwise, although he regarded Heath's project with benevolent, slightly sceptical goodwill. His more cautious Tory temperament was something of an anchor on the Heath government in its first two years.

Reggie played a small part in one of the two big political events of the Heath government – entry to Europe. He did not run the Cabinet committee concerned, and the negotiations were driven strongly from Number 10. But he was reconciled to the Heath policy of making the negotiations succeed. He was even more convinced than in 1965 that the economic strength of the European Community, changing trading patterns and the failure of the organisation to move rapidly towards a federal system made it a more palatable option than it had been in the early 1960s.[75] The Gaullist government in France had bullied its way to the 'Luxembourg compromise' on majority voting in 1966, which reassured Reggie that membership was compatible with his views on supra-nationalism, even though signing the Treaty committed Britain to 'ever closer union' and the prospect of a single currency by 1980. When he spoke in the great Europe debate of July 1971 he was teased by a former companion in Euro-scepticism, Labour's Michael Foot:

There has been a lot of talk about politicians coming off the fence in this issue. In the case of the Home Secretary maybe the fence just collapsed. At any rate, it is nice to see him. We shall welcome him later in the debate as another herald of the new dynamism with which we are going to be led into Europe. But there are those of us who will always retain an affection for the right hon. Gentleman in his earlier incarnation. As I see him, I always think of the limerick

> There was an old bear at the Zoo,
> Who could always find something to do.
> When it bored him, you know,
> To walk to and fro,
> He reversed it and walked fro and to.[76]

Reggie was rather amused by the image of the fence collapsing under him, and referred to it in his own speech. In fairness, he had never been, except as an emotional spasm in 1959–60, outright hostile to Europe, and tended when he was opposed to entry in 1960–5 to use pragmatic arguments rather than stating opposition in principle. A politician can have had few illusions, on accepting office from Edward Heath in 1970, that Europe was part of the package. Even if Reggie still had the occasional reservation about Europe, and lacked passion for the idea, his objections were not deeply rooted enough for him to refuse the high office he was hardly thirsting after.

The other big theme of the Heath government was industrial relations. The government came to office with a detailed plan worked out in opposition, which was intended to codify trade union and industrial relations law in a portmanteau Industrial Relations Act, an approach about which Maudling had justified misgivings in December 1970.[77] At the time, many in the unions saw the Industrial Relations Act as a piece of class warfare and union-bashing, but it was not. While it did impose some restrictions, such as the ability of the government to order strike ballots and cooling-off periods, it offered the carrot as well as the stick. Robert Carr, the Employment Secretary who saw it through Parliament in 1971, was a very pro-union Tory: 'all I wanted to be was an old-fashioned Minister of Labour, provided that there was a proper framework of laws around industrial relations.'[78] But the early 1970s were a period of industrial confrontation, not just in Britain but around the world. The end of wage restraint in 1969–70, in conditions of near full employment, rising living standards and rising expectations, produced a wave of militancy that swamped the Industrial Relations Act. Serious strikes had begun well before the Act was passed, with an early trial of strength in the docks in July 1970 leading to the declaration of a State of Emergency. Maudling chaired the Emergencies Committee of the Cabinet, and as Home Secretary had responsibility for emergency powers and 'civil contingencies'. He has the dubious honour of presiding over three declarations of a State of Emergency, more than any other minister: first in the docks and then in connection with a power workers' strike in December 1970 and the big coal strike of February 1972. A strike among local authority manual workers in October 1970 did not get to that stage, although Maudling ordered troops into east London to clear rubbish. In the December emergency he issued regulations banning floodlights and the use of electricity in advertising, and restricting Christmas decorations. It was, to some extent, psychodrama to play up the seriousness of the situation, but it was also the first intimation of the disruption of everyday life that could be produced by withdrawal of labour at innumerable key points in the economy, and a sign of things to come.

As 1971 began Maudling was seen as one of the more sure-footed ministers in the government. His reputation for wisdom and calmness and his long experience of government gave him a position, rare in that government, of some power independently of the Prime Minister. Only Sir Alec Douglas-Home, whose interest was largely confined to the Foreign Office, and who had no further interest in being Prime Minister, had comparable independent authority. In February 1971 Maudling was seen as the unchallenged candidate should Heath disappear from the scene, and the proverbial men in grey suits had apparently squared this with other potential contenders.[79] The article by Nora Beloff in which this story appeared was subsequently infamous, not so much for its content as because it substituted for a hard look at REFA by the *Observer* City desk. An internal *Observer* document ended up being leaked to *Private Eye*, whom Beloff had accused of a smear campaign in her article. Beloff ill-advisedly sued the *Eye*, and was made to look thoroughly ridiculous in what became known as the 'Ballsoff memorandum' case. Most political journalists still loved Reggie, despite his tendency to assume that they would pick up the tab for all his drinks when they met over lunch or in the Commons bar, and much preferred his company to that of Heath, or most other politicians. Despite the Ulster debacle, the Lobby wrote remarkably few disobliging things about him during 1971. There was a great difference in perception of Maudling between the Lobby, who knew him personally and either refused to believe any ill of him or didn't care what he had done, and the investigative journalists who were raking over REFA and Poulson during this period.

Maudling was also one of the most popular ministers in the government as far as public opinion was concerned, and became more popular as time went on. By January 1972 he was second only to Douglas-Home in his approval ratings, but within political circles his reputation had declined.[80] Maudling was now no longer the man most likely to succeed if Heath fell from the deck of *Morning Cloud*, although it was not particularly clear who had taken over from him. According to one commentator at the end of 1971 he 'now lumbers around Westminster like a great buffalo faced with extinction'.[81] Nora Beloff, who had sung his praises in February 1971, wrote in February 1972 that 'many of his parliamentary colleagues regard him as a disaster'.[82] His position was stronger within the inner circles of government, where his calmness and ability at chairing meetings were more appreciated, although negative stories that bore ministerial fingerprints had started to appear: 'the flies on the Cabinet Room wall say that Reggie is down to his last chance in Ulster, and Ted is in no mind to bail him out by giving him another job';[83] 'powerful perceptive observers believe that Mr Heath is now mulling over the question "How can I shift Reggie?"'[84]

February 1972 was a bad month for Maudling – first the realisation of the destruction that Bloody Sunday had visited on political prospects in Northern Ireland, and then a disaster on the home front with the decision of the coal miners to go out on strike in the second week of January over pay, where the National Union of Mineworkers (NUM) and the Coal Board had been miles apart since summer 1971. The miners, particularly the Yorkshire area under Arthur Scargill, had developed an effective technique of industrial action called 'flying pickets'. The strike being solid at the pits, striking miners would go to depots and persuade truck and train drivers not to shift coal around the country. At some places enormous mass pickets took place, at which the process of picketing became more like a tug of war than peaceful persuasion. Lines of police struggled to hold back sometimes unruly crowds, and passions were becoming dangerously heated. On 3 February a miner was killed in a picket line accident, and Reggie expressed sympathy with a sensitivity that had been so lacking in his Bloody Sunday statement only three days earlier.[85] But the success of the miners' picketing was putting great pressure on power resources, and on 9 February another State of Emergency was proclaimed and a rota of power cuts was announced. Conservative MPs murmured that Maudling seemed to lack authority and strolled up to the Despatch Box when he made the announcement.[86]

The principal trial of strength was at Saltley coke depot in Birmingham, where huge pickets had assembled in a largely symbolic bid to close the gates and stop coke deliveries. How such incidents were handled was technically up to the local Chief Constables, although the Home Office talked to them throughout the crisis. The Chief Constable of Birmingham told Maudling that the miners would get to the depot over his dead body. When the gates were closed, on 10 February, and the miners and Birmingham trade unionists had won, Reggie inquired solicitously after his health.[87] Maudling's personal instincts were to close the depot. He recalled in his memoirs: 'Some of my colleagues asked me afterwards, why I had not sent in troops to support the Police, and I remember asking them the simple question, "If they had been sent in, should they have gone in with their rifles loaded or unloaded?" Either course could have been disastrous.'[88] This was a very Maudlingesque way of looking at the proposition; while lacking a certain element of moral courage, and showing a very different attitude towards the maintenance of order in Birmingham from that he was prepared to allow a fortnight earlier in Londonderry, it did have the merit of logic. Within days, the government were backing down, with the Wilberforce inquiry appointed to review miners' pay reporting in only a week that the miners should have over 20 per cent. Even then, the miners held out for a few more concessions. As Heath's Political Secretary, Douglas Hurd, put it in his diary on 11 February: 'The Government now wandering all over the battlefield looking for someone to surrender to – and being massacred all the time.' It seemed the worst period of all for the government.[89] Maudling attracted a large share of the blame for the surrender: for his irresolute handling of the dispute and the State of Emergency, for his apparent failure to take it seriously, for the poor planning that meant that although there had been trouble brewing in the coal industry since the previous summer the coal stocks were still mostly held at the pitheads; but, most of all, because in defeat someone had to take the rap. The government undertook a review of emergencies legislation following the miners' strike, allegedly because Heath had lost confidence in Maudling's handling of the coal situation and wanted to get a better grip on future crises.[90]

While Maudling's own personal position was damaged by the miners' strike, the government's policies started to shift in the direction he had always supported – towards a search for consensus. Heath said in a prime ministerial broadcast on 27 February that 'we have to find a more sensible way to settle our differences'.[91] Emboldened by the new tone coming from Number 10, Reggie prepared a paper on economic policy and incomes after the miners' strike, but Heath asked him not to put it up to Cabinet and Reggie acceded. Heath's reason was presumably because of his own discussions that he opened with the TUC and CBI in March 1972, and therefore his desire for a free hand rather than the sort of concessions Maudling was advocating. Reggie published the memorandum instead in *The Times* on 12 September. The most striking phrase in it was: 'I conclude therefore that in modern political circumstances a capitalist economy must be prepared to accept a far greater degree of systematic control over the level of incomes and prices than we have ever contemplated before.' There needed to be an overall policy to restrain the overall growth of incomes and settle, on an acceptable basis, relativities between individual incomes. The 1972 Maudling memorandum was arguing for what is essentially corporatism. 'The old classical economics are no longer relevant to a wholly new political situation.' To Reggie, the politics of the 1970s was entirely new because of the power of organised labour. While his preference was for corporatism to grow out of voluntary arrangements, he was prepared to contemplate radical statutory intervention. It was an exceptionally radical intervention, which if what the Heath government performed in 1972 was a U-turn leaves one bereft of appropriate metaphors.

Maudling's prescriptions are now utterly unfashionable, but they had merit in their era and were not uniformly unsuccessful when tried at different times and in different places. The problem in Britain in 1972, as Richard Crossman pointed out, was that to implement the Maudling memorandum required a government with strong authority, which it did not have after the miners' strike, and goodwill, which it had lacked for a longer duration. It might have been possible to offer this and a change in industrial relations as a package deal on taking power in 1970, but it was now too late.[92] Maudling was proposing a brave leap of faith in the hope of a general agreement with the trade union leaders, and the hope that their writ could run as far as their members were concerned, both of which were questionable. The leaders of the large unions were hard men, but they were realistic and patriotic people who, if the circumstances were right, would do a deal; but, as was proved in 1978–9, there was a limit to how far they could take shop stewards and members with them. Heath proposed measures that went some way down the path advocated by Maudling at the end of September 1972, but the TUC did not agree to them and on 6 November 1972 Heath introduced a ninety-day freeze on wages and prices, followed by a statutory incomes policy.[93]

Reggie had frequently urged the government to conduct a reprise of his own economic experiment of 1962–4, and had even before the U-turn persuaded himself that Barber's 1971 Budget was 'aimed at putting new vitality and vigour into the British economy which since the war has been caught in a restrictive cycle of stop-go economics'.[94] Just as when his ambitions had outgrown the Colonial Office in 1962, he started firing off papers and comments about anything that took his fancy, which usually revolved around economic policy. His trespasses onto the field of economic and labour policy were tolerated by Anthony Barber and Robert Carr as they probably would not have been tolerated by Iain Macleod had he lived. The Maudling memorandum was a sign that Reggie was getting tired of being Home Secretary in spring 1972; there was the air of a forthcoming move onwards or outwards about Maudling after the advent of Direct Rule in Northern Ireland, but nothing had been resolved. That spring only Maudling himself, some business associates and a few of the most astute among journalists and civil servants, could have guessed that nemesis was already on its way, in the pudgy form of a pompous, bankrupt and highly disgruntled architect, who had unburdened himself to the Official Receiver as Reggie was busy thinking about Saltley Gate.

Chapter 22

'NOT FOR CRITICISM OR INVESTIGATION', 1970–1972

audling's business interests were a problem throughout his time as Home Secretary. His Permanent Secretary at the Home Office, Philip Allen, recalled that 'I was always very worried about his financial entanglements'.[1] The situation was much worse than it had been during his previous spell in government and he now seemed not greatly to care how it appeared to others. Maudling was recklessly indifferent to ministerial codes of conduct, but even so he was not without an ethical framework. His ministerial role, and Britain's position in the world, were important to him; being an MP was also a position he felt involved a certain dignity and he respected, even in the breach, the vague rules of parliamentary conduct. Business ethics were another matter. He had confidence in his own abilities to distinguish public and private interests, and operate a different morality in each sphere, but he was incapable of completely upholding the distinction. He also never understood the principle involved in accountability in public life, of being seen to do things properly.

The perennial question of Lloyd's membership was revived during the Heath government.[2] A revised version of the – then secret – governmental code of conduct called *Questions of Procedure for Ministers* (QPM) was circulated in spring 1971 and called upon ministers who were Names to submit applications to the Prime Minister and Cabinet Secretary if they wished to continue. A tightening up was envisaged, so that as well as the ministers specifically banned from membership, other ministers would not be allowed to be members of syndicates which could be seen as relevant to their jobs. To Allen's disquiet, Maudling blatantly ignored the new requirements and failed to send an application. When he was pursued about this, he fobbed off enquiries by saying that he was acting in line with an opinion Sir Lionel Heald had given him while Attorney General in the 1950s. No evidence of such an opinion was dug up when the Cabinet Office trawled the files in 1971 and Maudling vaguely said in October that it had been informal advice and that he 'now considers the matter closed'.[3]

The matter was not closed, and Heath returned to the issue with another minute at the start of December, to which Maudling at last gave an official reply saying that he saw no possibility of a conflict of interest with his job as Home Secretary and could see no reason why Lloyd's membership should be treated any differently from a shareholding in an insurance company. Number 10 replied in January 1972, disagreeing with Maudling's argument on the latter point but not wanting to argue the case any more if he was satisfied that he was immune from criticism on his position.[4] Behind closed doors, civil servants commented that 'not even *Private Eye* seems to have caught on, so far, to the fact that the Home Secretary is a "Name"'.

The Lloyd's saga was with Reggie from his arrival in Cabinet in 1957 to his departure in 1972. He did not do anything particularly wrong, but his attitude throughout displayed unattractive qualities when matters connected with his personal finances came to the fore. He exploited a loophole when he became a Name and evaded the rules established under *QPM* as long as he could after resuming office. He gave his colleagues vague self-justifying statements, or more often mulishly ignored the issue. The pattern was repeated with his more serious misdemeanours. With Lloyd's, Maudling got away with it. The *QPM* rules, as he realised in 1957, were essentially not enforced, and so they remained until the aftermath of their failure during the 1990s Jonathan Aitken scandal.

Lloyd's was far from the only concern about Reggie's finances in 1970–2. He still, as a ministerial colleague recalled, 'had a very strange relationship with Freddie Bennett. When Reggie became Home Secretary he insisted that any letter from Freddie should go straight to the Home Secretary. One always felt uncomfortable with and about Freddie.'[5] Maudling also had a thoroughly suspect relationship with Eric Miller throughout his time as Home Secretary. They used to meet frequently for lunch in the Executive Suite of Miller's headquarters at the Park West block of flats on Edgware Road, and occasionally for dinner. Reggie booked eight such appointments in 1971, and five during the first seven months of 1972, in his official Home Office diary.[6] In 1977 Maudling recalled that in total he had been to Miller's place seventy or eighty times, which seems plausible if perhaps an underestimate. Miller, ingratiatingly, pandered to Maudling's expensive tastes and Reggie enjoyed their meetings: 'I went to Sir Eric's home many times. And he to mine. It was the most convenient way to give advice. I ate his caviar. I love it. I cannot afford it myself. Who wouldn't eat caviar if it was offered? I remember having it with a baked potato.'[7] Strangely, in his 1977 interview Maudling specifically denied that Miller had taken him out for dinner at Annabel's, a highly fashionable nightspot of 1970s London, but his Home Office diary has just such a meeting written in for 8 July 1972. It is quite possible that Maudling had forgotten, but his incorrect denial also closed off questions about his links with Miller while in government. Given his description of the process of giving advice to Miller, there is no way of proving that his advisory relationship did not continue even after he became Home Secretary.

Maudling's links with Miller went further. Miller's company Peachey Property owned the freehold of Bedwell Lodge and had paid Poulson for the swimming pool. Given the terms of the agreement between the Maudlings and Peachey – it was not a commercial proposition but a form of remuneration – and that it continued in 1970–2, Maudling was still under some sort of obligation to Miller while Home Secretary despite the house being in Beryl's name. As well as baked potatoes with caviar, and the house arrangement, Miller was extremely generous at Christmas time. In December 1970 Miller gave Beryl a silver chess set from Asprey the jewellers; this cost the fantastic sum of £2,750 (well over £25,000 in modern terms), for which Miller's company picked up the bill. There is no reason to suppose that Maudling regarded it as anything other than a personal gift from a rich man, but it was still a startlingly generous one.[8] Another obligation was through his son Martin, who had joined Miller's staff in April 1970 and remained an employee until January 1973. Martin was also a company director of at least one of Miller's web of subsidiaries.[9] As his service for Poulson had demonstrated, Martin's talents as an office manager were limited, and his duties for Miller were sometimes of an unsavoury nature. One of Miller's lunch guests, whom Miller was trying to influence, recalled that 'At the end of the lunch he asked Martin to come over with the cigar box. Martin came with a large cigar box stuffed with £50 notes.'[10]

Reggie's transgressions often have an element of ambiguity to them, but his complicity in Martin's corruption, first through Poulson and then through Miller, was inexcusable. Martin was not the brightest of men, and most things to which he turned his own hand ended up in failure, but he was not wicked. That Reggie was prepared to see his son debased in this fashion, a bagman for a crooked property tycoon, may not have been a crime but it was among the worst things on his record. Quite whether the cigar box appeared during Reggie's lunches at Park West cannot be known, as he, Miller and Martin Maudling are all dead. One can only note that Reggie did enjoy cigars – real cigars – at the end of a meal, that Miller was crass enough to find some sort of reference to this difficult to resist, and also that Miller was repeatedly, extravagantly generous to Maudling.

Then there was Poulson. Maudling had hoped that the problems had been brought under control by the January 1970 Inter Planning and Design (IPD) takeover of Poulson's architectural practice. As far as its UK headquarters was concerned, ITCS continued to stagger on, its purpose ever more obscure; but the Abu Dhabi contracts were under way and producing income. Having been appointed Home Secretary he was obliged to dispose of his directorships, and he formally resigned from ITCS at the end of June. As with most aspects of the Poulson affair, it was not quite as simple as that. For a start, he was replaced on the board by Martin Maudling, and therefore had a line into the company's affairs. He was also, most improperly, still taking part in ITCS activities even as Home Secretary, in its tangled accounts and also in one appalling instance in obtaining money.

The bare fact is that Maudling, while Home Secretary, extracted £3,000 from Poulson's funds, which were then under the administration of IPD, the successor company to Poulson's architectural practice. The money was claimed as ITCS fees from a project in Nigeria. Maudling told IPD's Thomas Sweetman that ITCS was entitled to commissions on Poulson's projects, and also according to Sweetman: 'Mr Maudling had managed to obtain the payment for us from Nigeria, out of which that payment was made.' The Nigerian clients had been slow payers, but after a word from the Home Secretary they paid up. On 7 July 1970, on ITCS notepaper, Maudling wrote to Sweetman that '£3,000 will meet all my cash requirements for the foreseeable future', while noting that 'I have, of course, resigned from the Board'. Given that the revenue that arrived was £12,000, Maudling's cut amounted to 25 per cent – more than the supposed 20 per cent standard. It appears to have been worked out with reference to his vague estimate of his 'cash requirements' rather than the purported terms of the agreement between ITCS and Poulson. The payment was entered in the books on 29 July 1970 as 'ITCS Limited (R Maudling) £3,000'.[11]

The payment admits no innocent explanation. No reference to it appears in the IPD board meeting minutes of 29 July, while other payments (including £4,197 for Poulson's man in Nigeria, Mr Audifferen) were entered. On one reading of the evidence, the money was diverted into Maudling's own pocket, but Sweetman told the bankruptcy inquiry in a private hearing that he did not believe this to be the case. It is more likely that the Nigerian payment did go into ITCS but the company's accounts were so confused that they cannot completely resolve the question, and in any case they do not seem to have been prepared after the 1969 accounts were finally given a qualified audit in February 1972.

Maudling's reasons for doing what he did are a matter for speculation. Maudling told Sweetman in July 1970 that ITCS was in such financial trouble that it did not have enough money to pay its telephone bill, and keeping ITCS going was certainly a consideration in the minds of those who were running IPD. However, this explanation of ITCS's pathetic near or actual insolvency begs a couple of questions. After the economy measures Maudling had taken in 1969, including the closure of the company's plush offices in Grosvenor Place, ITCS business was conducted from his home at 27 Chester Square and therefore the company's running costs in London were hardly distinguishable from his domestic spending.[12] There was also the fact that at long last, thanks to the Abu Dhabi contracts and Reggie's rearrangement of the flow of funds, ITCS was receiving some income, and should have been able to stretch to a few phone calls.

Shortly after paying the ITCS money over to Maudling, Poulson's successors wrote to other creditors asking for a moratorium on payment; Maudling had jumped the queue for settlement against Poulson. He had done so by bamboozling a new director of the firm into paying the money while the overall financial position between ITCS and Poulson was hotly disputed. At the very least he was continuing as an active executive of ITCS despite his resignation on returning to office. It was grossly improper conduct, involving abuse of office, an unacceptable private interest, and quite probably fraud and theft against IPD and the Poulson creditors.

During all this, Reggie had responsibility for the maintenance of law and order in general, and policing in London in particular. At the time, London was unique in not having a local police authority. The police authority for the Metropolitan Police was the Home Secretary, who had overall responsibility for appointing the Commissioner and setting the general direction of policy. The Met was at a low ebb when Maudling took over in 1970, not through any deficiency in political leadership, as Jim Callaghan had been a competent and sympathetic Home Secretary, but through its own accumulated failings. There was a power vacuum at the top, as the incumbent Commissioner, Sir John Waldron, was a stopgap who had been utterly unable to get a grip on the problems afflicting the force. He had been put in while Robert Mark, a provincial officer whom Roy Jenkins had groomed for promotion, accumulated enough seniority to be placed in Britain's biggest policing job. This was ready by June 1970, but it actually took nearly two years before this necessary changing of the guard took place. According to Jim Callaghan: 'I have no idea why Waldron's departure was delayed for so long. Mark was ready and waiting and I left a note on Maudling's desk on the day of the changeover telling him so.'[13]

It was reasonable for Maudling to have wanted to get to know the personalities involved and make his own decision rather than his predecessor's, but it need not have taken so long. Reggie's attitude to the problems of the police was neglectful. The Met's CID detectives were a law unto themselves and there were significant numbers of corrupt officers. An extraordinary venture into investigative journalism by the normally staid *Times* revealed in November 1969 that some London detectives were extorting bribes in the form of protection money from career criminals and were sometimes even willing to help out in robberies. A detective was tape-recorded boasting about being a member of 'a little firm within a firm'.[14] As a result of the disclosures in *The Times* Callaghan called in an outsider, which was in itself a great affront to the Met, in the form of Frank Williamson of Her Majesty's Inspectorate, to investigate and recommend changes to the structure of the force. Williamson encountered obstruction and frustration at every turn at the hands of corrupt officers and their friends, and senior officers like Waldron who buried their heads in the sand. The inquiry became truly farcical in May 1970 when Chief Superintendent Bill Moody, the carnivorously corrupt head of the Obscene Publications Squad (aptly known as the Dirty Squad) who was subsequently jailed for his enthusiastic take-up of bribes, was appointed to assist Williamson with his investigation.[15]

Williamson appealed to Maudling in July 1971 for help and action, but received no support whatsoever.[16] According to Williamson in 1972:

> Callaghan was at least of some help. Maudling has been useless. At one point I wrote him a 30 page memo pointing out the grave difficulties I was having. He ignored it completely and has never spoken to me about it. Maudling appears quite ignorant of the facts of life so far as the police service is concerned and is concerned only with making as few waves as possible. But his refusal to take action on my memo, which was sent to him at least four months before I thought of quitting, is irresponsible in the extreme.[17]

Williamson eventually did resign, at the beginning of 1972, in protest at the obstruction from Scotland Yard and the indifference of the Home Secretary. But it was the dark before the dawn. The line could not hold much longer, with corrupt Drug Squad officers coming up for trial, the Dirty Squad racket on the verge of breaking open and the virtual vacancy in the Commissioner's office at last being filled by Robert Mark, who had endured four years in bureaucratic limbo. Reggie was receiving strong advice from his junior minister Mark Carlisle, who would have regarded it as a resigning matter if Robert Mark were not to be appointed.[18] Mark was summoned to the Home Secretary's office, where Reggie, flanked by Philip Allen, asked him bluntly, 'Will you do this fucking job for us?' 'His words did not remind me of the accession of the youthful Victoria,' the new Commissioner-designate reflected later.[19] Waldron was allowed to retire in his own sweet time, and chose to go five months later, in April 1972. Within weeks, a new anti-corruption squad, A10, was created at Scotland Yard, and a start was made at clearing out some of the worst elements of the Met.[20]

It has been suggested, most entertainingly by Peter Flannery's BBC television series *Our Friends in the North*, for which Williamson was an adviser, that there was some form of stand-off between Maudling and the Metropolitan CID about each other's activities. In exchange for the Home Secretary going slow on reforming the Met, and sabotaging the Williamson inquiry, they would not put any effort into following up the Poulson and REFA cases and keep his name out of the OSB–Wandsworth investigation. Such a bargain seems unlikely, although it must have been in the back of Maudling's mind that he was in a weak position to impose the necessary changes in the Met because of his own vulnerabilities. One does not need to look beyond Maudling's general political attitude of tolerating the idea that the ends justify the means and a world-weary sense that some things will never change, and the political context of the time. Williamson was asking Maudling to restructure the Met from top to bottom, which would have caused great ill will within the force at a time when there was considerable social and industrial unrest and the government would wish to enjoy reliable support from the police. The Thatcher government in 1979 made no mistake about matters when it gave the police enormous pay increases on coming to power, and the Heath government did not want to start its turbulent term of office by picking a fight with the police. There were enough other confrontations to be getting on with.

The stand-off theory also has the disadvantage of being unsupported by the evidence bundles from the Wandsworth case, in which Maudling's name hardly figures. Dan Smith was peripheral enough to the Wandsworth affair and Maudling's connection was only through him and the OSB firm. There was no evidence that he personally had done anything at all in connection with the case. The investigation into Wandsworth concentrated, as police inquiries do, on building a case against the principal wrongdoer in the area, who was Sidney Sporle, and they simply did not have time and resources to chase every lead. There is no sign from the police case notes that they looked into OSB in any depth, although the fact that Maudling's name came up in connection with the firm may well have piqued the interest of individual officers. At the trial, Sporle's efforts to bring Maudling's name into proceedings were quickly stopped by the judge. While Sporle was jailed for receiving a bribe from Dan Smith, Smith was acquitted of giving it at an extraordinary trial in July 1971, presided over by a judge who had stood as a Newcastle Labour candidate and for whom Dan had canvassed.[21] According to Smith, a senior police officer said to him after the acquittal that 'It won't be long before we meet again, this time with friend Poulson'.[22]

Even assuming that there was a stand-off between Maudling and the Met, it started to come undone during 1971 because of the infamous Oz trial. The publishers of a hippie magazine had been prosecuted with extreme rigour for its contents, but it did not escape the notice of the press or the Home Office that much stronger pornography was freely available in Soho. Reggie asked for an explanation of why this was – and it was something Philip Allen had been wondering about for some time – to receive a fob-off answer from Waldron in August 1971.[23] However, in February 1972 the Sunday Mirror published a story about the social links between Ken Drury of the OPS and pornography dealer James Humphreys, and the story unravelled from there. In 1977 several OPS officers including Bill Moody were sent to prison for corruption. A further Maudling–police conspiracy theory holds that, far from mutual blackmail going on, Metropolitan CID officers after the appointment of Mark and the destruction of the old-style OPS had a grudge against Maudling for ruining the good old days of London policing, and some of the officers who investigated Maudling in 1973–5 did have connections with OPS men. Maudling's ITCS colleague Ken Williams believes that the connections tie back to Malta – Maltese business interests were certainly prominent in post-war Soho – and that there was an element of revenge and even corruption in the pursuit of Maudling by the police.[24]

None of this, if there is any substance to it, was much apparent before 1972. The 1970 dossier from the Chief Inspector of Audit about Poulson,

Smith and local authority corruption, although it was apparently passed to the Director of Public Prosecutions and the police, disappeared from view before 1970 was out and no action was taken. The Bradford and Wandsworth cases trundled to their conclusions. Inquiries into the REFA affair by the police and the DTI proceeded at a dilatory pace, even dragging inconclusively into 1976. Even now, there is a puzzling veil cast over the REFA inquiries. Many papers are available in the National Archives dealing with the Poulson bankruptcy hearings and trial, and with the Wandsworth affair, but nothing to do with REFA even appears on the catalogue. However, parliamentary answers in 1972 disclosed that the IIG/ REFA group was under Fraud Squad investigation from October 1970 onwards – for a few weeks at the start, Reggie still nominally held his REFA management shares.[25] It has never been explained why it was proper for Maudling to continue as Home Secretary during 1970–2 when the Fraud Squad was examining the Real Estate Fund of America, and the audit dossier into Poulson was at least in the pending tray, while it became impossible as soon as there was a formal investigation of Poulson after the bankruptcy hearings in July 1972.

REFA was also a problem for Maudling because of a civil action started in New York in July 1971 by an aggrieved investor against REFA and its officials. At first he tried to dismiss it as nothing to do with him, on the grounds that the complainant's investment had taken place after he had resigned from the outfit and that he had never done any business in New York, but the American courts were unimpressed because of his continuing involvement in the management company part of Hoffman's rickety corporate structure. During September he evaded several attempts to serve legal documents on him – the server could not exactly rush up to him in a public place for fear of the quick reactions of Maudling's Special Branch minders – until they arrived by registered post at Essendon in October. Reggie tried to brush off the action as 'one of those strange American sue-everybody-in-sight type of litigations'.[26] Hoffman, meanwhile, had returned to New York with yet another financial project, been arrested in connection with an earlier mortgage swindle and pleaded guilty. Hoffman was shocked to receive a two-year prison sentence in the hellish Marion federal penitentiary in February 1972. As the cell door swung shut behind Hoffman, John Poulson too was throwing himself on the mercy of the judicial system.

During 1970 Poulson had continued to harbour desperate, delusional hopes of landing big contracts across the world: Argentina, Beirut . . . but he was on the way down. He was in shaky mental condition as his world crumbled. Maudling met him once during this period of decline and fall. By Reggie's own unguarded account in 1974:

The last time I saw Poulson was in the drawing room at No. 10. Ted had invited Conservative women leaders down to see him and Poulson's wife was chairman of the Yorkshire Conservative Women's Association. I was there and when Poulson walked in I nearly dived behind the sofa. By that time of course we all knew what was brewing. Not long after that I was stopped by a very prominent figure in the lobby of the House of Commons and he asked me: 'Now, then, when are we going to do something about that knighthood for old Poulson?' I said, 'Look here, old chap, if I were you I would forget all that very quickly. What! I should say so.'[27]

Reggie saw a little more of John King[28] while the corporate and financial mess that he had left was slowly being sorted out. Poulson alleged that 'King had always promised Maudling that he would see that the accounts of ITCS would not be an embarrassment to him, for which service Maudling would see that King received an honour'.[29] If there was such a deal – and Maudling and King both denied any such thing – it did not come off as intended, because there was no way of completely sanitising the ITCS accounts, and King received no honour from the Heath government. He did, for reasons unconnected with Maudling, get many appointments to boards and quangos, and a knighthood, during the 1974–9 Labour government, and a peerage and the chairmanship of British Airways under Thatcher. The process of squaring off the ITCS books was under way following Poulson's pressurised agreement to write off the alleged £70,000 debt in May 1970.[30] Poulson's personal position continued to deteriorate through 1971. In June he was obliged to move out of his pride and joy, his grand home 'Manasseh', and into what had previously been his secretary's house. He auctioned the contents of Manasseh to raise funds to pay his insistent creditors. In September a creditor petitioned for Poulson to be declared bankrupt, and after some legal confusion Poulson himself declared personal bankruptcy in January 1972 after the New Year holiday.[31] His case entered the files as Bankruptcy No.1 of 1972. It was soon to become the premier bankruptcy of the century.

The details of what happened when someone went bankrupt were an arcane area of law, at least until the Poulson hearings. The debtor's affairs are turned over lock, stock and barrel to the trustee in bankruptcy, who then has formidable powers of interrogation and information-gathering that date back to a law of 1571. As the law stood in 1972, there were public hearings in which the debtor and others could be questioned in public about their financial dealings, and also 'section 25' private hearings, which were supposed to be less confrontational and where more sensitive matters could be raked over. The purpose of bankruptcy hearings is to recover as much money as possible to pay the creditors, by finding any hidden financial assets of the debtor and collecting any money the debtor is owed; the trustee also has the power to recover gifts the bankrupt had given in the last ten years in order to sell and raise money. The point of a bankruptcy hearing is not to come to a judgement about criminal or moral responsibility, but to recover money.

The Poulson case was a particularly complicated one because of the strange interconnections between several companies – some at that point not actually owned by Poulson and still technically in business – and Poulson's own slack accounting methods. His long-suffering accountant, Vivian Baker, explained: 'I can only say that during the course of my employment I found Mr Poulson an impossible man to work for, particularly in relation to the financial side of the practice. There was only one bank account for the practice and out of this all the payments were made.'[32] Personal, practice and company payments were all jumbled together. However, Poulson's filing system, ably kept by his secretaries, passed into the hands of the trustee in early 1972 and could be excavated to track down where Poulson's money had gone.[33] It rapidly became apparent to the investigators that a can of worms had been opened. Very large amounts of money had obviously been channelled through Dan Smith, and there were other payments to dubious 'consultants' who not coincidentally had links with public bodies from which Poulson was seeking work. Then there were the enormous donations to the Adeline Genée Theatre in East Grinstead, and a mysterious paper trail leading to Beirut and the Persian Gulf. By June, the legal team – led by the leading practitioner of the bankruptcy Bar, Muir Hunter, QC – were ready to start conducting public examinations.

The first public hearing into Poulson's bankruptcy opened in the County Court in Wakefield on 13 June 1972. It passed off strangely quietly, despite the presence of many reporters in the public gallery and the evidence that Poulson money had gone to public figures such as T. Dan Smith and John Cordle, a Tory MP for Bournemouth. Mention was also made of the late 1969 dispute between Poulson and Maudling about £70,000 worth of fees, but all that resulted was a short piece in the *Leeds Evening Post* and a longer essay by Paul Foot in *Private Eye* of 30 June. Whitehall nerves, however, had started to twitch because of the evidence uncovered that George Pottinger, a senior Scottish Office civil servant, had received lavish gifts from Poulson, and it seemed entirely possible that there would have to be an inquiry into his case. Philip Allen, who had been reading *Private Eye*, pointed out the difficulties that might arise if Pottinger was the subject of an investigation but Maudling was treated differently.[34] Reggie's days in the Home Office were now numbered.

The next Poulson hearing took place in Wakefield on 3 July. It was a dramatic day in court. Poulson, who had crumpled under pressure during the first hearings, was now mercilessly confronted with the evidence of his sizeable payments to the Adeline Genée Theatre and his lavish spending on George Pottinger. When Muir Hunter moved on to ask him again about what Dan Smith had been doing for the £150,000 he had received, Poulson collapsed unconscious. The proud, abrasive businessman who had carved himself a place in local society and the political world was exposed as a fool, a crook or both. The hearing was adjourned, but this time the Poulson affair had become headline news.

Reggie, having been named in the hearing, felt obliged to issue a statement:

I was chairman of International Technical and Constructional Services, a company doing business wholly overseas. The fact that I was chairman was public knowledge. What was not public knowledge was that I received no payment for my work as chairman. Before I took on the chairmanship Mr Poulson made a substantial covenant in favour of a charity whose aims I strongly supported. I do not understand how helping a charity and running an export business can be regarded as a matter for criticism.[35]

This statement was true as far as it went, but it was carefully written. It did not volunteer the information, which would eventually surface, that Reggie had taken a salary for his activities for Construction Promotion and Open System Building, or that Martin had been such a beneficiary of his links with Poulson. Nor did Reggie add anything about his indirect remuneration such as the swimming pool or the extraordinarily open-handed attitude that ITCS (in fact, Poulson's own Ropergate) had been taking with his expenses. As for whether running an export business can be regarded as a matter for criticism, that all depends on whether it is well run and whether its business methods are acceptable. The statement was enough to stem any direct criticism of Maudling's conduct, but the Poulson hearings (added to the continuing rumblings of the REFA affair) had cast a lengthening shadow over his judgement in being associated with people such as Poulson and Hoffman.

On 5 July Jeremy Thorpe and his five Liberal colleagues in the Commons put down an Early Day Motion headed 'Allegations of Corruption in Public Life'. It called for an immediate inquiry into the Poulson allegations. Thorpe's intervention was a case of a man in a glass house lobbing a large stone. He had his own dubious business connections, although the subsequently infamous London & County Securities was not so unsavoury a firm as REFA. Thorpe also had reason to be grateful to Maudling for covering up a scandal on his behalf. Thorpe was mainly homosexual and in the early 1960s he had enjoyed an affair with a young man called Norman Josiffe. The hangover from this affair was not so enjoyable. Norman Josiffe (or Scott, as he called himself later on) was unstable and obsessed with Thorpe. To use a term of later coinage, Scott was a 'bunny boiler' (although ironically it was Scott's pet that was killed when the relationship went sour). Scott's allegations reached senior Liberals in 1971 and they conducted a secret inquiry. Maudling was approached for assistance in the investigation and, despite the existence of bulging police and MI5 files on Thorpe's relationship with Scott and his other sexual adventures, confined himself to a short statement that endorsed Thorpe's version of events and implicitly agreed with his assessment of Scott as a 'nutcase'.[36] Thorpe was off the hook. Not surprisingly, 'he of all people!' was the reaction of Tory Cabinet ministers to Thorpe's role in paving the way for Maudling's resignation.[37] Despite this, Maudling and Thorpe remained friends. Thorpe admitted to former Liberal MP Peter Bessell that he had acted impetuously and ungratefully, but then said that he had no choice but to sign a motion drafted by Emlyn Hooson, a Welsh QC who emerged as a strong critic of the MPs associated with Poulson. A month or so later Thorpe told Bessell: 'I was at a reception last night with Reggie. He couldn't have been more friendly. Christ – what a relief!'[38] It was a remarkable example of Reggie's inability to bear a grudge.

However, the hearing and the Liberal motion (which was discussed in Cabinet on 6 July) marked the start of the Poulson affair as a public scandal, and things were also moving behind the scenes. The Official Receiver, representing the Department of Trade and Industry (DTI), sat in on the hearings with a view to picking up any points of wider importance. Crates of documents arising from the bankruptcy investigation were delivered to the government on 10 July and on examination it became clear that there was a large corruption scandal in the offing. The pace of events started to accelerate. A meeting of ministers was called at short notice for the morning of 12 July to discuss the Poulson allegations, with representation from all the relevant departments except the Home Office.[39] Maudling's position was clearly becoming untenable.

In Cabinet on Thursday 13 July, Reggie withdrew for the discussion on Poulson, which started with a presentation by Peter Rawlinson, the Attorney General, which anticipated criminal charges being brought against several individuals (including, intriguingly, the prospect of corruption charges against two MPs associated with Poulson) and discussed Reggie's position. Rawlinson said that there was 'so far no evidence in the bankruptcy proceedings that the Home Secretary had been guilty of any impropriety in his dealings with Mr Poulson, although it might be necessary both to give further consideration to his position in the latter half of 1969 when he had remained a director of ITCS at a time when he might have been expected to have known that Mr Poulson was insolvent, and to inquire further into the taxation aspects of the payments which had been made on his behalf to the theatre trust'. It was hardly a clean bill of health for Reggie's position. In general, the Cabinet agreed with Rawlinson that they would not institute a Tribunal of Inquiry but let the legal process take its course, and see if the Official Receiver's initial report recommended a police investigation. In the meantime, they would wait.[40]

In answer to Questions in the House of Commons later that day, Heath stated that the evidence from the Poulson hearings was being considered and that the government was awaiting the preliminary report of the Official Receiver, to which Mr Bishop, the Receiver, was actually putting the finishing touches in Leeds as Heath spoke. The initial intention on 13 July had been to announce an inquiry and suspension in the Pottinger case only, but the government feared being overtaken by events and nothing happened for the time being. Douglas Haddow, according to Pottinger, told him that a

Commons statement would be delayed because 'the Cabinet cannot decide what to do about Maudling'.[41] William Armstrong, the head of the civil service and Heath's most influential general adviser, but who was not present at this meeting, privately favoured a full-scale Tribunal of Inquiry into Poulson.[42] His advice was not taken up, and the pattern of events moved inexorably towards the involvement of the Metropolitan Police. Developments were also crowding in from another direction. That Thursday afternoon Reggie was told by Peter Rawlinson, the Attorney General, that he might well be called upon to provide a witness statement for a police investigation into the Real Estate Fund of America.[43]

Friday 14 July was the grimmest day yet for Reggie. The *New Statesman* led boldly with the headline 'Maudling Must Go', and it was reported in the *Spectator* that a number of ministers had now concluded that Maudling should step aside at least until the air had been cleared. Worse than this was the outcome of a confidential meeting held at the Department of Trade and Industry to consider the Official Receiver's report. It was clear that there had been serious irregularities in the Poulson companies, and that it would not be surprising if ITCS turned out to have been involved in bribery overseas. The Receiver also passed on Hunter's comment that he had been informed that ITCS was 'dabbling in arms'. Even if this last allegation was unproved, there was enough to start secret section 109 DTI inquiries into ITCS and other Poulson-associated companies.[44] The Receiver also felt that the Adeline Genée payments were deserving of further investigation, alongside Dan Smith's activities and Poulson's relations with civil servants, but did not find either Maudling or Smith to have been culpable on the evidence then available.[45] The preliminary report and the note of the meeting's discussion of irregularities in ITCS were passed to Number 10.

After a weekend of further speculation that Maudling would resign, which went without a denial, William Armstrong came back on Monday determined to take official action. The Pottinger case was calling the integrity of the civil service into doubt and professional pride meant making an example of the suave, corrupt Scottish Office Permanent Under-Secretary. Sir Douglas Haddow, the Permanent Secretary at the Scottish Office, was determined to suspend Pottinger and see the matter dealt with. Armstrong's first drafts of the Prime Minister's statement on Poulson, written on Monday, announced a Metropolitan Police investigation into Poulson, and also unspecified action from the DTI. Members of the civil service and NHS bureaucracy involved in the police investigation would be suspended. There was no mention of Maudling in the draft statement, but by insisting on the Metropolitan Police being called in rather than a judicial inquiry Armstrong's advice was setting up a situation that made it impossible for Maudling to continue as Home Secretary.[46] It did not take long before the obvious conclusion was drawn and Heath summoned Maudling to a meeting at Number 10 on the Monday evening. Reggie had been out in the City with

Martin and with Eric Miller, who drove them to Downing Street. On the way to the meeting Reggie was in defiant mood and said that he was not intending to resign and that he had been pushed around long enough. He was not going to agree to another Cabinet post. Martin thought it would be best to leave the political scene entirely.[47]

Reggie's resolve to stand his ground or be sacked crumbled as his loyalty to Heath came into play; he eventually did agree to resign. Heath may well have seen the damaging material passed to Number 10 via the DTI, or at least have been told by William Armstrong that Maudling had to go, and the meeting was an uncomfortable one for both men. Heath did try to persuade Maudling to accept another Cabinet position, to take him away from the Home Office. Given the ostensible reason for his resignation Maudling could easily have switched to another job. The Department of the Environment was mentioned, but this would if anything have been even more inappropriate than the Home Office. It meant a lot of tedious detail and besides was the ministry dealing with local government and therefore Poulson and Smith's cronies. Better would have been a straight switch with Robert Carr, using Maudling's congenial relations with Labour and love of Westminster life to good effect as Leader of the House. He had served as acting Leader of the House for a couple of weeks earlier in the year after the transfer of Whitelaw to Northern Ireland. The arrangements after the resignation, when Carr temporarily took both jobs, kept this open as a possibility if Maudling were able to return quickly. There had also been speculation during the Heath government about Alec Douglas-Home's intentions; he was widely expected to stand down, perhaps after the elusive Rhodesian solution – a move for Maudling would have put him in the third 'great office of state' and given him a job he would have enjoyed and probably done well. However, his activities in the Persian Gulf would probably have ruled him out of this job as well.

Reggie dolefully left for Admiralty House and wrote out a resignation letter to Heath the next morning. After he had finished it he and Beryl retreated to Essendon. His letter read:

We discussed the assertions made by Mr Poulson during his bankruptcy hearing. Among them there was one referring to myself, to the effect that before I accepted his invitation to become Chairman of an export company, for which post I took no remuneration, he had made a covenant in favour of a charitable appeal which had my support. I do not regard this as matter either for criticism or investigation. However, there are matters not relating to me that do require investigation, and I entirely agree that this should be carried out in the normal way on behalf of the Director of Public Prosecutions. The difficulty arises that the task must fall on the Metropolitan Police, and in my particular office as Home Secretary I am Police Authority for the Metropolis. We agreed that it would not be appropriate for me to continue to hold this office while the investigations are being pursued, in view of the fact that my name has been mentioned at the Hearing. You were good enough to suggest that I might for the time being hold some other office in your Government, but this I do not wish to accept. For more than twenty years now I have held office continuously, as a Minister, or a member of the Shadow Cabinet. I think I can reasonably claim a respite from the burdens of responsibilities which, inevitably, surrounds a Minister and, inexcusably, engulfs the private lives even of his family.

Heath read it out to the House of Commons on the afternoon of 18 July. The letter was an extremely limited account of Reggie's relations with Poulson, but it sufficed as an 'official' reason for resignation. It did not, for instance, mention the question marks that the Attorney General had raised about the possibility of Reggie being in trouble over taxes and trading while insolvent. As it stood, it seemed that Maudling's action in resigning was a particularly pure example of a minister exercising individual responsibility and ensuring that the functioning of government was clearly seen to be above question or reproach. As later events unfolded, it came to seem much more complicated than that, but at the time it was taken at face value. The announcement of Reggie's resignation was greeted by gasps of shock and cries of 'shame!' on all sides. Ted Short, for Labour, praised Maudling for having 'acted in the best traditions of the public service in this country', and Jeremy Thorpe – whose motion had brought the issue to prominence – hoped that Reggie's resignation would only be temporary. Jim Callaghan, acting almost as if he was a trade union official representing Home Secretaries, expressed incredulity that Reggie should be forced out for such a reason. Callaghan pointed out that the Home Secretary did not determine what sort of police action takes place in an individual case, and that it was the Director of Public Prosecutions who took the decision on whether to prosecute.[48] In private Callaghan was even angrier. Mark Carlisle, the Home Office Minister of State, ran into him in the House, outside the Commons chamber; Callaghan grabbed Carlisle by the lapels and told him: 'You've let him down. He's a good man and he shouldn't have gone.'[49]

Maudling's resignation touched off a burst of sympathy and appreciation in the press, which contrasted with the previous gradual accumulation of complaint at his alleged indolence. Walter Terry in the *Daily Mail* wrote: 'It is frightening that someone so popular, and a politician of such substance who had contributed so much, can be tumbled so accidentally.'[50] Anthony Shrimsley of the *Sun* greeted it as 'one of the most sensational personal political tragedies of the century', and that paper's editorial hailed 'Maudling, man of honour'.[51] Praise for Maudling's honour ran through the press coverage, with the Labour-supporting *Daily Mirror* saying: 'in the circumstances he could not have acted more honourably.'[52] The *Daily Express* opined: 'There can be little wrong with public life when a man in Mr Maudling's position resigns as a matter of honour . . . Mr Maudling commanded respect as a Minister. Now he enhances the public by the manner of his going.'[53] The most excessive tribute came in a leader in the *Economist* entitled 'Reggie Agonistes'. It solemnly warned: 'it is time now for everyone in public life, politics and journalism to consider where the line should be drawn between responsible criticism and irresponsible, even if unwitting, support to the gravediggers of parliamentary democracy . . . It has been a bleak week in British politics. A few MPs, and rather more Pharisees in the press, have contrived to bring down a fine politician. In doing so they have shocked the country, and some of them may even have shocked themselves.'[54]

Some newspapers recorded in passing the fact that two men, whose names were not released but who were Thomas Sweetman and John King, were interviewed in conditions of tight security and confidentiality at the Wakefield bankruptcy court.[55] Among the subjects about which they were questioned was Maudling's £3,000 cut from the Nigeria payment in July 1970. His resignation would have looked very different if this transaction had been known at the time. The rest of Reggie's public and private life was spent in exploring his contradictory nature, his honourable public service combined with his capacity for such ugly and reprehensible behaviour, both of which were on display in very different surroundings on that dramatic July day in 1972.

Chapter 23

TEMPORARY EXILE,[1] 1972–1973

The loss of Reggie was another blow to the Heath government, which had been hobbled at the start by the death of Iain Macleod. It was not that Maudling was irreplaceable as Home Secretary. Robert Carr proved a capable replacement and showed if anything even greater liberalism. Carr continued his policies on prisons and took a courageous stand for decent values when he gave the Ugandan Asians sanctuary from persecution in August 1972 and faced down Enoch Powell at the party conference. But just as Maudling's best contribution to the government had been outside the department, his loss was felt in a diffuse, subtle way throughout the range of government activity. Douglas Hurd and David Butler had developed the phrase 'the big beasts of the jungle' to describe the dominant personalities of the political scene, and Maudling had been among them for thirteen years – fatter and greyer in 1972 than before, but a big beast none the less. Heath's Cabinet now lacked figures with authority and power independent of the Prime Minister. Both Barber and Carr were 'Heathmen', and it was well known that Alec Douglas-Home was in his last public office and somewhat remote from the main political game. Only Whitelaw, thrashing around in the Ulster elephant trap, showed signs of becoming a big beast, but for the rest of its term the government was, more than ever, the Heath government rather than a Tory government. Heath ended up taking a heavier personal workload, as no Deputy figure emerged to replace Maudling's coordinating work at the centre, and as Prime Minister depending more and more on the advice of senior civil servants Burke Trend and William Armstrong. It was more than Heath, and Armstrong in particular, could bear when the government's terminal crisis struck.

Maudling could also have been a steadying influence during the Heath government's U-turn phase. After all, the Heath government's policies in 1972–4 were very close to those Maudling had advocated for years[2] and he could, had he been able and willing, have been a convincing advocate of the new course from within government rather than cheering from the sidelines. Maudling at least could not be accused of abandoning his principles and panicking in the face of adversity, a charge that was levelled against Heath and his colleagues. Incomes policy, industrial conciliation, tripartite planning institutions and headlong economic expansion were all 'Maudlingite' policies, foreshadowed in the memorandum he wrote in the spring but published in

The Times in September 1972. More than ever, a Tory government needed Maudling to put over the human, acceptable face of its policies, but he was in ever-deepening trouble as a result of his own explorations of the unacceptable face of capitalism.

In contrast to Reggie's previous departure from office, this time the financial prospects were bleak. Loss of office meant another serious loss of earnings for Maudling. His salary dropped by about two-thirds and this time companies were not queuing up to employ him as a director or a consultant because of his reputation for poor judgement in his business affairs established by the Hoffman and Poulson connections. Cecil King, indiscreet recorder of lunchtime confidences, recorded Hartley Shawcross in February 1973 as telling him that 'there is nothing in the City for Reggie Maudling. He said Reggie was picking up pennies writing articles. Hartley sat with him for two to three years on some board, and in that period he never once opened his mouth. He seemed to think his duties as a director ended with the acceptance of his fee and the absorption of a champagne lunch after board meetings.'[3] Shawcross was extremely well connected in the City and industry, and views such as this did reflect a general opinion that Reggie had little to offer.

John Junor did indeed give Reggie regular opportunities to write for the *Sunday Express*, which for Reggie was money for old rope – in half an hour he could knock out something reasonable if platitudinous, sitting whisky in hand across the room from Viv Walker who typed as he spoke. It rarely needed more than one attempt to produce a viable article. There were occasional other pieces in *The Times* and *Spectator*, for instance, and broadcasting engagements like *Any Questions* and debates with Michael Foot and Roy Jenkins. Maudling was a good bet for a book review or two, which he wrote with his usual engaging intelligence whether the subject was Iain Macleod or the annual *Bedside Guardian* ('my trouble has always been waking up rather than going to sleep').[4] Reggie also accepted quirky offers such as writing for the *Radio Times* about his favourite television programmes.[5] The years 1972 and 1973 saw Reggie at his most active as a journalist, although he was almost completely inactive in the House of Commons. He was enjoying being the good-humoured and moderate elder statesman in temporary exile. The period just after his resignation was far from an unremittingly bleak time in his life.

Maudling did not have to eke out a living solely on his backbench pay and the proceeds of newspaper articles. Eric Miller was still interested in supporting Reggie, and put him on the Peachey Property payroll as a consultant for £7,000 a year, which pretty much compensated for his loss of office. There was also Mahdi Tajir, who 'kept him topped up', according to Viv Walker, Reggie's secretary at the time.[6] Maudling travelled frequently to the Middle East in 1972–3, in part to repair some of the damage the Poulson affair risked inflicting on him. When the new British ambassador arrived in Abu Dhabi in September 1973:

One of the first questions I asked my staff after arrival here was whether the Poulson affair was a local time bomb where Mr Maudling in particular was concerned. I was told that Mr Maudling had been out here mending fences and seemed to have succeeded in preserving his personal credit locally. I hope that that is right.[7]

Even so, Maudling had some serious outgoings after resignation that rapidly ate up the money he could earn. His legal expenses in connection with the Poulson bankruptcy investigation were considerable, and he had a long dispute with the Inland Revenue about the treatment of the proceeds of the sale of Chester Square. Part of the point of the Miller leaseback scheme had been for its supposed tax advantages relating to Chester Square – the transfer of ownership meant that it would be easier to claim that Chester Square, rather than Bedwell Lodge, had been the main residence and therefore not subject to Capital Gains Tax. As it turned out, the Revenue had their doubts about this, possibly also because part of Chester Square had been used as ITCS business premises, and CGT was eventually levied.[8] Like many of Reggie's more dubious financial wheezes, it ended up much more expensive than it was supposed to be, and possibly more expensive than playing it straight from the start. He might have heard the Maltese saying 'l-irħis għali'[9] on his travels (what's cheap in the end costs more), but the warning against false economy and financial short cuts never did sink in.

The year 1971 had been a particularly inopportune time to sell Chester Square, but Reggie had little choice. He could not afford to maintain it and Bedwell Lodge on a Cabinet salary. It was his bad luck that the London property boom took off shortly after he sold up for little more than he had paid for it in 1965. Given his reduced circumstances and the fact that by 1972 house prices in desirable areas of London had spiralled out of control, he decided on his eviction from Admiralty House to rent a flat in a block called Clunie House in Hans Place, behind Harrods in Knightsbridge. Apart from the location, it was a very ordinary flat and indeed rather small; his friend Michael Rice thought that when Reggie stood up in the front room he looked 'like a big fish in a small bowl'.[10]

Reggie's troubles in summer 1972 did not end with his walk into the wilderness in July. The weekend after his resignation there was more embarrassing publicity, this time promising the 'seedy truth' about REFA in the *Sunday Times*.[11] Maudling could put up with a certain amount of press criticism of his actions, although he did often threaten legal action, but he would become most indignant when, in his eyes, they dragged his family into it. This plea generated some sympathy, for the family did have its own private problems and just because one member of the family was a public figure the other members had not forfeited their right to privacy. Unfortunately for the Maudlings, Reggie had dragged them into the Poulson affair in the first place. It was mostly for the benefit of Beryl's theatre, and of Martin, that he signed up in the first place, and he distributed ITCS shares to other family members. In fact, Martin Maudling's conduct may not have received all the attention it deserved because of the fear of being seen to be engaged in a vendetta against the family. Reggie should have been angry with himself for his own behaviour, particularly in exposing Martin, a rather rudderless young man, to bad influences such as Poulson, Miller and business circles in Dubai.

When the Poulson bankruptcy hearings resumed on 1 August, Leonard Saffman, acting for Poulson, asked for the hearings to be adjourned arguing that the bankruptcy hearings might result in self-incrimination by Poulson. The morning session became a protracted legal argument as his cause was endorsed by two barristers who had popped up representing the offices of the Official Receiver and the Attorney General, arguing that the hearings might hinder the police investigation and prove prejudicial in eventual criminal cases. It was a multi-pronged attack on the continuing public embarrassment of the Poulson hearings. Hunter was astonished by this turn of events; in twenty-eight years of bankruptcy practice he had never seen an endorsement of an application to adjourn that resembled this one. The Registrar ruled that if necessary Poulson could be examined in private, but that the public hearings could continue.

There was further pressure after the conclusion of the 1 August hearing. Reggie issued a statement objecting to the procedure in court, which he said gave Poulson licence 'to make any allegation he liked about me without notice and in my absence, and without any opportunity to refute them'.[12] This is a common grievance by those named during inquisitorial proceedings, and although there is some substance to the objection, Reggie was overdoing it. There was no way of giving notice of any specifics of what was coming up, as it emerged from spontaneous exchanges between Hunter and Poulson, and this seeming expectation by Reggie that he was entitled to vet any criticism of him remained with him to the last. Poulson was answering questions put by Hunter – who was pulling his punches about the Maudling evidence in the files – and therefore only in a position to make allegations pertaining to the questions. Reggie in fact had the opportunity, which he took, of commenting publicly through the press on what Poulson said; in contrast to the adversarial criminal courts, there was no danger of contempt of court when Reggie accused the bankruptcy court witness, Poulson, of lying. The bankruptcy solicitors took the opportunity of inviting Maudling to write to the Official Receiver with his version, and to supply documents so that they could be used in the proceedings. Muir Hunter stated:

> I would have been very willing, if so instructed, to put to Mr Poulson any submissions of fact which Mr Maudling's advisers wished to supply to us, but it transpired that, no doubt owing to his many heavy commitments and public offices, Mr Maudling had either not retained, or was unable to find, his own file of correspondence[13]

After the 7 August public examination of Poulson, Maudling produced a further statement that went into more detail about ITCS, and gave his version challenging the alleged indebtedness of ITCS to Poulson. ITCS, he said, had won £1 million in overseas contracts, 'Not a bad job for this country considering that the contracts were won in competition with the Swedes, Japanese, French and everyone else'. This was a gloss, to put it mildly, as the contracts were hardly won in open competition in Malta, still less in the Gulf. Reggie further claimed that 'as far as I am aware OSB never did any business with Dan Smith at all', which flies in the face of OSB minutes that later emerged in evidence.[14] The press treated Maudling's statement respectfully, and the impression he gave that Poulson was either in a huge muddle or simply mudslinging and that ITCS was a normal overseas sales group, seemed convincing to most observers at the time. But the prospect of a long series of hearings meant that he was trying to explain away successive revelations as the Poulson files were explored in public. This statement, like the others, showed that Reggie's approach at each stage was never to volunteer disclosures, but manage and respond to revelations as they arose while complaining about a climate of smear and innuendo. It was, given the weight of evidence in the files, a poor strategy. He was continually retreating and relied increasingly upon professions of bad memory when the most damaging material emerged, which may in some cases have been true because of memory loss or confusion brought on by heavy drinking. From the autumn onwards, the impression was always there that there was more to it than had so far emerged. After his dignified resignation Reggie cut an increasingly unimpressive figure and the calls, so loud in July, for his rapid restoration were stilled.

During September 1972 there was a serious attempt to stitch together a package deal to settle the claims against Poulson and halt the hearings. John King and others, including ITCS, formed a consortium to negotiate a deal with the trustees, and things seemed to be going well until at the last minute Leeds City Council filed a large compensation claim for alleged negligence on Poulson's part in producing their international-sized swimming pool, and the Inland Revenue not surprisingly reassessed Poulson's tax returns. These larger holes in the Poulson accounts were too much for the consortium to settle, the hearings went on – and the investigating solicitors found more and more evidence, including 12,000 files seized only in January 1973, many of which concerned the Middle East.[15]

The resumed Poulson hearing on 25 September concerned mainly the network of 'consultants', including the Dan Smith operation, and Hunter was in particularly sarcastic mood, referring at one stage to 'poor old Pottinger' having to come up with a small share of the cost of his new house. John Cordle's name was kept out of this hearing, although he was regarded as a 'consultant' and Maudling appeared only fleetingly at the end of the day's session when Poulson was questioned about the November 1967 letter to

Maudling concerning the Lebanese politician who 'wants paying'.[16] Reggie issued a statement through his solicitors saying that no action was taken and no business was done with the man concerned.[17]

Coincidentally or not, that day Maudling at last 'found' some of the documents relating to Poulson and supplied them in a cumbersome file to the bankruptcy investigators, late at night and incorrectly addressed, hours before new hearings opened the next morning in Wakefield. It is quite possible for documents to go astray, particularly if one is untidy by nature and moving house (as Maudling had done twice since the 1970 election, at least regarding his London residence), and the explanation for this inconvenient form of disclosure may be innocent. On the other hand, it can be seen as a smart tactical move in relation to the inquiry. The bankruptcy investigators had warned Maudling after Poulson entered their care in early 1972 that he was required to preserve all documents relating to Poulson, so he had known for some time that the documents were wanted. By presenting his files to Hunter when he did, he ensured that in the short term Hunter would not be able to absorb their full contents, particularly as Poulson had also come up with a vanload of extra documents overnight.[18]

On 26 September Hunter had an incentive to try not to embarrass Maudling further, in order to recognise his assistance and to encourage further cooperation. However, there was no way to explore the bizarre accounts of ITCS, which was the subject of the day, without dealing with some material that reflected poorly on Maudling. Hunter did his best to put a favourable spin on matters. Some of the evidence produced that day, and put aggressively to Poulson by Hunter, did suggest that Maudling had not been aware of everything that was going on and two letters were cited to this effect – one in August 1968 expressing concern that contracts had been signed on behalf of ITCS without his knowledge, and in January 1969 when Poulson told Nasser that 'Mr Maudling would be horrified if he knew' about exchange control violations.[19] Despite this, the hearing threw up some sensitive matters – Nasser's practices in Beirut, for instance, and the name of Mahdi Tajir – and the government tried again to shut the hearings down.

At the beginning of October Prime Minister Edward Heath stepped in to try to stop the flow of revelations. His Private Secretary, Robin Butler, wrote to the Lord Chancellor's Office:

> The Prime Minister has been greatly disturbed, as no doubt have others of his colleagues, by the procedure in the Bankruptcy Court during the Poulson case . . . He would also like urgent consideration to be given to some effective means of dealing with the situation. He would be very grateful for suggestions on how this situation can be remedied.[20]

This looks a lot like an attempted cover-up. The 'urgent' intervention indicates that Heath's concern was to stop the embarrassing Poulson hearings rather than change things for the future. One option that was considered was that, in future, bankruptcy hearings should take place in private, but this would require legislation and be opposed by the DTI in the interests of commercial confidence, and also by the press. Legislation would also be needed to impose reporting restrictions on bankruptcies, of the sort that apply in divorce, juvenile and committal hearings. Another possibility might be to switch the hearings to London, as the Lord Chancellor, Lord Hailsham, blamed the 'inexperienced provincial registrar' for giving Muir Hunter too much latitude, or to put a circuit judge rather than a registrar in charge of particularly significant hearings. After inconclusive discussions, in which Hailsham argued against making far-reaching changes while Heath's wish was clearly to shut the Poulson hearings up if it was at all possible, nothing was done.[21]

Another public hearing took place on 29 January 1973, amid much sensational coverage. Labour's Tony Crosland was on the spot for having received a silver-plated coffee pot as a present when he opened a Poulson school in Bradford. He had written a grovelling letter of thanks, which was most embarrassing when it was read out at the hearing. The pot was actually sitting unused in the back of a cupboard in the Crosland kitchen, and was not worth nearly as much as Hunter supposed. There was another, more gratuitous, error when Hunter inquired about an admittedly peculiar holiday booked in 1964 for someone called George Brown, who 'to avoid publicity' would travel to Majorca under the name of T. Dan Smith. Hunter implied that this was the former Labour deputy leader, but it turned out that it could not have been as Brown had appeared in public in Durham and spoken in the House during the period in question, as a brief check should have revealed. Brown and Crosland's experiences illustrated the risks of the high-profile approach and aroused a backlash of sympathy for those whose names had come up in the hearings.

Then the Hunter became the hunted. Lord Chancellor Hailsham had already been angered by Muir Hunter's comments and questions at the hearings, and had now been converted to Heath's view that something should be done. He announced in the Lords that the law on bankruptcy hearings would be reviewed. The Bar Council decided to investigate Muir Hunter on charges of unprofessional conduct during the hearings. While he would occasionally drop tantalising hints to witnesses about what his investigations had uncovered, and would use rude and aggressive tactics if he felt that someone was being uncooperative, there was nothing unfocused or unprofessional about his approach. If being rude and aggressive were grounds for investigating a barrister, the Bar Council would spend its time doing little else. Hunter also had a telling turn of phrase in conducting the public examination – and some of the private hearings (he called Reggie's rearrangement of the flow of money from Abu Dhabi not so much a fiddle as 'a piece of carpentry') – and was fond of publicity, but this too is hardly unique or unprofessional among barristers. Nor is making mistakes unusual, however regrettable the George Brown and Tony Crosland incidents were; and these were errors in staff research rather than any decision of Hunter.

Inquiries into alleged unprofessional conduct are rare, and the Bar Council's decision to investigate Hunter while the case was going on was unprecedented. The charges were quickly dropped. It looked like the result of political pressure, designed to throw him off his stride, and with the adverse publicity from the errors he had made it dampened his relish for the task. The fascinated horror with which he had first explored the Poulson–ITCS books in summer 1972 was replaced by a more cautious manner in his later hearings, and he tiptoed carefully around Maudling, who was a more dangerous adversary than he had realised. David Graham, Hunter's colleague and not a natural radical, reflected later that 'I think we were battling against the establishment'.[22] They did not know then that the hostility went all the way up to the Prime Minister.

Hunter's fear of the opposition he had aroused was apparent in his attitude to a Granada *World In Action* documentary produced by Ray Fitzwalter which analysed the evidence so far that had come up in the hearings. He did his best to stop the programme and was particularly exercised at the broadcasters' plans to restage courtroom exchanges using actors. However, more direct pressure was brought to bear by the Independent Broadcasting Authority (IBA) who summarily banned the programme from transmission. IBA board members included Dame Evelyn Sharp, who had been a character witness at Dan Smith's Wandsworth trial, and Sir Fred Hayday, a union colleague of Andy Cunningham. Instead of the documentary, *The Flight of the Snow Goose* was broadcast on the night of 29 January. A revised version, without the staged reconstructions, and with the original title *The Friends and Influence of John Poulson* replaced with the less inflammatory *The Rise and Fall of John Poulson*, went out at the end of April 1973 after considerable pressure from the television unions and the press.

At the 29 January hearing Hunter had offered a preview of what was coming at the next session. Many people in the courtroom thought he had said that he would be opening 'the parliamentary file' and the press arrived at the hearing on 5 March agog with excitement. Hunter opened business by complaining about the acoustics in the courtroom and said that what he was going to do actually concerned 'the Beirut file. I will spell that. B-E-I-R-U-T'.[23] There was great puzzlement among the press corps, and the Poulson expert Ray Fitzwalter is sure that the parliamentary file did exist.[24] However, there were some problems with hearing in the court – in a private hearing the witness John King had heard 'technical book' when he was asked about a 'second report'. In another private hearing Poulson's solicitor, Leonard Saffman, assured Hunter that he did not hear him say the word 'parliamentary' at any stage.[25]

John Poulson's own comment on this was volunteered to the House of Commons Select Committee in January 1977. He believed that the 'parliamentary file' was nothing more than the records of his National Liberal and Westminster Forum meetings, which had been supplied to the Trustee, along with his Masonic records, after the September 1972 hearings.[26] The political – but not, one may note, the Masonic – material turned up in evidence bundles near the Beirut files when these were released in 2003. There were many names in this file, including Maudling, Heath, Thatcher, Douglas-Home, Barber and half the Shadow Cabinet, but all they had done was speak at political meetings and in some cases accept dinner at the Dorchester afterwards. While no doubt Poulson relished the opportunity of meeting such prominent figures, they had done absolutely nothing wrong in agreeing to attend. It is possible that rather than suppressing explosive revelations, Hunter's apparent retreat on the parliamentary file covered his own embarrassment at promising a big fuss about something minor, another mistake of that strangely flawed 29 January hearing.[27]

The 5 March hearing closed after only an hour and a half of examination of the Beirut file, whose contents were actually extremely murky but important. Poulson had sworn to the 25 September 1972 hearing that the file of correspondence with Maudling was the only file he had on ITCS,[28] and there was no more. However, the Beirut file, containing Costa Nasser's reports and correspondence with Poulson, was discovered in Poulson's former office in January 1973 and opened a whole new dimension to the Poulson investigation in which the investigators would have to tread very carefully. In spring 1973 they explored contacts in the Middle East; public discussion at that stage would have harmed the recovery operation and therefore not served the object of the investigation. They were also becoming aware of the international political dimensions of the case, and eventually fixed up an interview with the former Lebanese President Camille Chamoun, to ask him to use his influence with the Christian community there – which included Costa Nasser – to help. They saw Chamoun on 7 July.[29] Chamoun, according to Hunter, 'seemed genuinely interested in the trustee's problems and anxious to help, and called for and perused some of the documents. He concluded by offering to send for Mr Nasser, on his return to Beirut, and to ask him for explanations, and to seek to persuade him to agree to meet us for questioning somewhere outside the Lebanon.'[30]

The investigators recovered documents from contractors in the Middle East that provided proof of the commission payments, and there was a delicate process by which some of these documents were supplied to Maudling with the intention of bringing his influence with Nasser and others to bear. Quite what Maudling was up to during this period is far from clear. On the one hand, he had said to the investigators that he would help them, had occasional meetings with them, and claimed that he had travelled across the Middle East in this cause; on the other hand, the investigators never got anything out of Nasser despite his close friendship with Maudling. Maudling was seen with Nasser in Beirut in spring 1973 and whether he was urging him to come to Britain and help, or encouraging him to keep away from the hearings, cannot be known. Still, nothing Nasser said to him then deterred Maudling from claiming him as a friend and swearing to his honesty in the face of overwhelming evidence in July. And nothing Maudling said to Nasser prompted any more cooperation from the elusive Beirut businessman.

All of this was kept secret from the press. The failure of the 5 March bankruptcy hearing to provide any sensational stories brought the curtain down on the public fascination with the Poulson bankruptcy. In June 1973 the consortium paid up £130,000[31] in a voluntary agreed settlement that was, according to Hunter to Poulson in July 1973, 'in respect of the assets they took from you'.[32] Inter Planning and Design paid £90,000 of the sum; the origin of the remaining £40,000 is not known.[33] In among the lump sum was settlement of the £3,000 Nigeria payment which Maudling had extracted from Poulson's successors in July 1970. Hunter told Poulson, referring to the £3,000, 'You need not worry because we have got it all back again.'[34] Nor did Maudling have to worry, as Hunter's job was done once the money had been recovered; Reggie was not asked about it at his private examination and the matter was not aired publicly during the hearings. In July 1973 Poulson's criminal defence was refused access to the transcripts and documents relating to it.[35] The government's copy of the 'my immediate cash requirements' letter disappeared into a file that was mainly about George Pottinger's standing within the civil service.

The next public run of the scandal would be played out in the criminal courts. The Fraud Squad were given access to the Poulson bankruptcy papers, including the private hearings, on 19 April and it quickly became clear that there was an exceptionally strong case against Poulson for giving bribes in relation to contracts within Britain. Of the recipients of Poulson's generosity, the most exposed was George Pottinger, because the civil service was subject to a more stringent law, the Prevention of Corruption Act 1916, which required the accused to demonstrate that acceptance of gifts or money was innocent rather than the prosecution to prove that they were corrupt.

The police moved in on the evening of Friday 22 June 1973. In nearly simultaneous visits, Commander James Crane of the Fraud Squad arrested Pottinger and Inspector Kenneth Churchill-Coleman called on Poulson at his home in Pontefract to arrest the bankrupt architect. Poulson told the policeman, 'I think it's all wrong,' and started to weep.[36] The Poulson–Pottinger arrests came at a particularly important time. That very evening *The Times* was printing a leader column comparing the Poulson affair to the Watergate scandal which was then destroying Nixon's Presidency, and complaining that a cover-up was under way. It added weight to the demands for a full public inquiry into Poulson. The editorial did not appear in later editions because it was feared it would offend *sub judice* rules.[37] When the bankruptcy hearing resumed on 25 June, the public part was quickly stopped when Poulson's solicitor, Leonard Saffman, applied under a new rule that had come into force only in May.[38] Hunter did not object, as the public hearings had probably run their course and any further progress would come from other means.

Once the 25 June hearing had been converted to a private examination, Saffman commented: 'It is a matter for conjecture and opinion as to why this particular charge was brought so quickly. It may be, although I, of course, am not in a position to say, that it is as a result of the questions being raised in the House of Commons during the last week that it was felt that some positive step had to be taken.'[39] The Attorney General, Peter Rawlinson, who authorised the arrests, denies that there was anything unusual in the procedure. Rawlinson adds that Muir Hunter told him that the next hearing was intended to examine an (admittedly innocent) transaction that involved Anthony Barber – and was horrified to realise that nobody would believe that he had timed the arrests without intending to suppress discussion of the Chancellor's relations with Poulson.[40]

While the public hearings had been stopped by the arrests, the private section 25 hearings could continue. Maudling, accompanied by Martin and a legal adviser, travelled to the County Court in Barnsley on 19 July 1973, a year and a day after his resignation, to give his evidence in private to the Registrar and undergo questioning from Muir Hunter on behalf of the creditors. His hosts had hoped to evade the press by switching from the normal venue of Wakefield, but enterprising journalists had got wind of it and camped out in Barnsley. Reggie turned up, exuding charm and bonhomie and impressing Muir Hunter's junior, David Graham, with 'the friendliness, the warmth of the man'. Reggie, after fourteen years of answering parliamentary questions, and with his own quick intelligence and ability in logical argument, was more of a challenge for Hunter's forensic skills than the hapless Poulson or the confused Dan Smith could be, and according to Graham it was 'the only time when Muir Hunter met his match'.[41]

The Maudling private hearing was an ambiguous occasion, even in the making of the appointment. The investigators had more than enough by way of grounds to order a summons for Reggie's attendance, including the startling submission from the Trustee that:

10. The books of account of ITCS are in my respectful opinion in a deplorable state and it is quite impossible to disentangle its true financial position and worth. It appears that the income of ITCS may have been derived from two main sources: a. from fees paid by clients for whom buildings were designed the majority of whom were in the event either rulers of Middle Eastern States, or members of their families or State governments; b. from commissions payable to ITCS by firms whose products or services were through the instrumentality of ITCS used in connection with such building projects.

Still, despite a large number of counts in the summons, Maudling was allowed to suggest his own date to attend and was technically giving evidence voluntarily, through a face-saving agreement with the trustees.[42] He certainly claimed to be present in Barnsley as an 'amicus curiae', helping the investigators with their enquiries in the literal rather than customary sense of that phrase, but in the background there was an agenda of investigating him in connection with the disappearance of large sums of money from both ITCS and OSB, for which at least as an active director of both firms he bore a share of responsibility. Subsequently, some among the investigators regretted not pursuing him more aggressively for large sums of money while they hunted down other relatively minor amounts.[43]

During the examination, despite some rather confrontational periods, Maudling was also treated with some deference, particularly by the Registrar. Hunter started the hearing gently by thanking Maudling for coming voluntarily, and took him quickly into the tangled matter of the Adeline Genée covenants and the relationship between ITCS and Poulson. Reggie stated again and again that, despite there being no documentary evidence of the agreement on fee-sharing, common sense dictated that there must have been one: 'It is sheer common sense. Even a bunch of lunatics couldn't have set up a company which was going to borrow money to spend for someone else's benefit and get nothing in exchange.'[44] Reggie seems to have been exasperated about questioning on the relationship between Ropergate and ITCS, but he became really rattled when the questioning moved on to the convoluted treatment of the payment and loan-back of the fee for his ITCS chairmanship. The key exchanges were on the April 1968 £9,875 cheque which, in the opinion of the DTI, amounted to perjury,[45] although Maudling also gave an inconsistent and shifty account of the £2,000 Poulson had paid him and he in turn made over to the theatre production company in October 1967. After repeated questioning on these matters, Reggie lost patience and exploded:

> I don't see – I really don't see where this line of argument helps Mr Poulson's creditors to obtain any more money. I just don't see that. It is really extraordinary.

> Q. I must put it this way, Mr Maudling; it relates to your conduct of the company's affairs?
> A. With respect, am I here to talk about the conduct of the company's affairs or am I here within the terms of the Act, to give any information I have about the debtor, his dealings and his properties? I am not on trial here for my conduct of ITCS, I am here to try to help people.[46]

Hunter then returned to the question of the ITCS accounts, and the existence of two separate sets of accounts for 1968 which he called Mark 1 and Mark 2 – signed off by Maudling in June 1969 and July 1970 respectively, with their different treatment of directors' fees, the late 1969 accounts and the non-appearance of 1970 accounts because of the disappearance of necessary documents. At that point a halt was called for lunch. Reggie had brought his own picnic hamper up the M1 from London, and there was some good-natured banter between him and the legal team, who invited him to sample a local delicacy called a Barnsley chop.[47]

The afternoon session, when they resumed, was much less prickly than the morning's exchanges on the creative accountancy of the ITCS directors' fees and the ITCS–Ropergate relationship. The questioning moved to the Middle East, via the infamous meeting with Grimwood and Poulson in August 1969 at which the dispute over the £70,000 had come up. Hunter produced the 19 December 1967 'green light' letter from Nasser to Maudling and Reggie asked the Registrar to impose a 'stop order' on the transcript in order to protect Tajir in his capacity as UAE Ambassador in London. This was granted. According to Reggie:

> The position is that Mahdi Tajir was an old friend of mine and an Ambassador in London, and the right-hand man of the Rulers there. He started life as a clerk in the Customs of Bahrain and is now a very rich man. This happens in the Middle East. It is assumed, if you become rich, you do it by taking bribes, and I think what Costa is saying in his letter is that Mahdi required bribing. He was quite wrong, Mahdi was never bribed; I would not dream of offering him a bribe.

When asked about the passage 'You will notice in your letter from Costa that he mentions Mahdi requires a particular favour from us before giving the green light. Whatever you arrange, Reggie, will be alright with me,' Reggie replied: 'Yes, I can only comment on that, that it appears now that Mr Poulson was not unused to the idea of bribes being made. That is not on the record, is it? . . . There is no question whatever of being bribed. I did arrange for his son to go to a school somewhere. Whether that is a bribe, I don't know.' Asked further about Nasser's suggestion that Tajir should be bribed, Reggie commented that: 'I think what he was saying was "If you are doing business in the Middle East, this is the normal way business is conducted in the Middle East." This again probably ought to be off the record.'

Towards the end of the hearing, Maudling was asked about the position regarding Costa Nasser. Reggie defended his friend:

> I know him, I like him, I trust him . . . I checked up on him with ambassadors at various places and I have always got a good reply.

Q. Well, I understand that he is not permitted to enter Saudi Arabia?
A. What does that mean? I think you are thinking of Abu Dhabi, and that is not the case any more. I cleared that with the Ruler.[48]

Hunter asked Maudling whether Costa Nasser was a member of Al-Fatah; Reggie professed amazement. 'There is every sort of tittle-tattle and gossip in the Middle East – I have never known a place like it. I have been there many times. Ninety-nine percent of what you hear in the Middle East is bunkum.'[49] Reggie was then confronted with documentary evidence of Costa Nasser's activities in seeking commission from equipment suppliers and denied all knowledge, telling them to ask Nasser themselves. 'It is no good asking me, I don't know. I know the man, he is a friend of mine, I trust him. Would you please ask him and don't assume he is a rogue.'[50] Hunter asked Maudling to use his influence over Nasser to persuade him to meet the bankruptcy investigators in some neutral territory, but Reggie repeatedly told them that they should just write to him and see what he said. Maudling also, in correspondence, discouraged them from attempting to contact Sheikh Khalifa about overcharging on the Abu Dhabi contracts.[51]

Costa Nasser's elusiveness was a huge problem in gaining any information about the Beirut activities of ITCS. Maudling flatly refused to comment on the papers that Hunter produced demonstrating a pattern of commission payments, and had obtained telexes from Nasser on 4 July denying what seemed to be fairly plain documentary evidence.

As well as Maudling, the relevant section of the Foreign Office was doing its best to shield this area from further inquiries; they told Hunter that 'it would be highly undesirable for us to go and see Mr Nasser in Beirut'.[52] This was part of a pattern of official behaviour in response to the Poulson case. Hunter, the Trustee's solicitor from Moorhouse & Co., approached the Foreign Office on several occasions in 1973, not so much for help as to ask advice in relation to the Middle Eastern aspects of the Poulson affair. In July Hunter was asked to, and agreed to, supply any information in the files about links between the case and Al-Fatah to the security authorities. Hunter – following a letter in which Maudling urged the bankruptcy hearings to keep their names out of it – was also concerned about the possible political implications of naming Zayed, Rashid and Tajir. The official response was that 'mention of Sheikh Zayid and Sheikh Rashid could cause political embarrassment. Mahdi Tajir on the other hand was not a ruler and had been so notoriously involved in hankie-pankie of various kinds that a little more dirt was not likely to cause much fuss.'[53]

In general, the Foreign Office were extremely reluctant to do anything to help the bankruptcy investigation, although their legal adviser warned that 'the FCO must not be put in the position where it could ever be thought that we were trying to suppress evidence'. The view from Antony Parsons, Under-Secretary at the Near East department, was: 'my strong feeling is that we must disengage from this whole affair as much as possible, volunteer as little as possible, certainly nothing in writing. Mr M.H. is a dangerous man . . . Pl. keep me informed if we are asked for anything else.'[54]

The effect of the Foreign Office line was to shield the whole sordid mess of the Middle East end of the Poulson operation, and no doubt many more unpleasant pieces of business as well, from inquiry. There were political ramifications, given the links between Nasser and Palestinian politics, and also the protection of wider British business interests. It was another intervention from the government that had the effect of limiting and diverting the Poulson inquiry away from the Middle East and Maudling. Costa Nasser was supposed to come and give evidence in private at a bankruptcy hearing in September 1973, but he refused to attend, arguing that the warrant of service he had been issued in London shortly after the Chamoun interview was somehow defective. The Registrar observed: 'I think you are dealing with a difficult customer here.'[55] The hearings were adjourned *sine die* and Nasser's version was never heard.

The end of the Maudling hearing was amicable, with Hunter praising 'Mr Maudling's very helpful attitude' and not wishing to recall him. Future business would be via Reggie's solicitors. Reggie's own legal adviser, though, wanted a quick recess to see if there were 'any points that are necessary on which to re-examine him', and although the Registrar noted that it was 'rather irregular' it was allowed; however, Reggie was happy with things as they stood and there was no re-examination.[56] It was the toughest questioning he ever faced about his involvement with Poulson, and he gave a reasonably convincing account of himself. The hearing closed with Reggie disingenuously expressing his willingness to help in any way possible in future.

However, it was far from the end of Maudling's entanglement with the bankruptcy investigation. He had not been questioned about the design work Poulson staff had done on his swimming pool at Essendon, and when the investigators found these files they entered into a long correspondence about the matter. The trustees wished to recover money for the Poulson professional work on the swimming pool, but Maudling stalled and disputed whether there was any liability for the matter. In October 1973 it was agreed that Poulson had spent £1,136 on the pool design work, and settlement was referred to RIBA for arbitration. In October 1974, after the election, Maudling settled the claim with a payment of £250.[57] His attitude, of refusing to help until he was backed into a corner, conflicted with his protestations in public and to Hunter that he was motivated by a desire to help the Poulson creditors. As well as the swimming pool repayment, and the matters which had been included in the £130,000 consortium settlement, there was another £500 recovery from Reginald (or Martin) Maudling 'under statutory provisions' at some stage between 1972 and May 1977.[58]

Neither was Maudling unconcerned with the criminal and DTI investigations that had been concurrent with the bankruptcy hearings. In autumn 1973 the Fraud Squad started to regard prosecuting Maudling as a realistic proposition. The Fraud Squad had a heavy workload in preparing for the Poulson–Pottinger and the Poulson–Smith trials that were soon to take place, and were working their way through Poulson's public sector cohorts.

There were fifty-six headings under which the Fraud Squad were building Poulson-related cases,[59] and each officer in the London Fraud Squad was dealing with an average of seven cases overall during 1974, which could be expected to take two years each.[60] With the arrest of Dan Smith in early October they were now examining evidence that pointed to Maudling. Commander Crane obtained evidence from the bankruptcy hearings that related to Maudling, including the stopped sections of the Maudling examination in which he discussed his relationships with Tajir and Nasser. Later in October DTI Inspectors produced a secret report as a result of their section 109 inquiry into Ropergate, which alleged criminal offences on the part of Maudling and Poulson relating to transfers of money from Ropergate to the Adeline Genée Theatre, and the inspectors moved on to look at other Poulson companies including ITCS. 'The Attorney General has, as you probably know,' the Inspector General in Bankruptcy wrote in early November to the Permanent Secretary of the DTI, 'recently been concerned with the activities of one individual.'[61] The most dangerous phase of the Poulson affair had begun for Maudling.

Politically, the skies were darkening too. After Reggie gave up his role on the Conservative Party's Advisory Committee on Policy he had no formal role at all in the party leadership, although he was a keen supporter of the Heath government in all his many comments on politics and economics in the period after his resignation.

Reggie was particularly interested in economic policy, which since the great U-turn of 1972 had come to bear a close resemblance to his own dash for growth in 1962–4. Despite the great similarities, the Barber boom differed in several important ways from Maudling's. Britain was now free of the fixed exchange rate which Maudling had realised had obstructed the way in 1963–4 and would have been glad to abandon, had been accepted into the European Community and was likely to benefit from the lowering of trade barriers. It was clearer now that Britain could afford to run a deficit for a while. But in most ways the conditions were less favourable than in the early 1960s. While the TUC had joined the NEDC and publicly praised the 1963 Budget, relations with the trade unions in 1972 were poisoned by the bitterness over the Industrial Relations Act and several legal cases (notably the briefly imprisoned Pentonville Five dockers). Inflationary pressures were greater and the unions were not going to help out.

In a more diffuse sense industry's expectations were lower. While in 1963 business was ready to believe politicians when they talked about moving to a higher level of growth, and invest accordingly, the government carried little credibility in 1972 after the economic policy reversals of 1964–7. When Heath complained to industrialists that British businessmen seemed unwilling to invest north of a line from Bristol to the Wash, one told him bluntly that he wouldn't invest north of Oxford Street the way things were going.[62] There was an unattractive and cynical quality to some of the enterprises that were doing well in the early 1970s, such as the Slater Walker conglomerate, property speculators and dubious financial operations of all sorts, including offshore investment schemes and secondary banks; why make things when one could just make money?

Nevertheless, in 1973 the policy seemed to be working and economic growth reached a staggering 7 per cent, Britain's best performance on record. In May Maudling wrote of the uncanny similarities with the situation he had created in 1964, in which the problem the government now faced was to decelerate to a more sustainable pace of high growth without shattering confidence. His recommendation was to tighten up a little on consumer credit,[63] which since the 1971 'Competition and Credit Control' relaxation of credit had let rip. In September Maudling urged the government to ignore the 'gnomes of Zurich', carry on with expansion and incomes policy, and not lose its nerve.[64] Reggie eagerly looked forward to the Heath government seeing his unfinished experiment through to completion, but it was not to be. While Maudling's experiment was sunk by the balance of payments and political circumstances, the Barber boom ended even more disastrously when the world changed abruptly in October 1973 as war broke out in the Middle East and the oil price soared.

Although floating the pound in 1972 had loosened the overseas payments constraint on expansion, the balance of payments was still important and was deteriorating badly by the second half of 1973, just as it had in 1964. Once again, an inflationary boom was sucking in imports. Reggie had already written, in his Cabinet memorandum, about the increased power of organised labour and the need for a corporatist consensus; he now presciently identified the other fatal flaw in the strategy – the risk of a shock to the British economy coming from a possible oil crisis with its roots in the Middle East.

Maudling shared this insight with readers of the *Sunday Express* in June 1973. His contacts in the rich Arab oil states were exceptionally good, and the future of oil had been discussed at the May 1973 Bilderberg Group meeting in Saltsjöbaden, Sweden.[65] Denis Healey, the other senior British Bilderberg member, had tried to write about the looming oil crisis in the *Sunday Times* but his article was spiked on the grounds that the argument was 'so preposterous it was embarrassing'.[66] This was not a problem for the *Sunday Express*, and on 3 June Reggie's article[67] made it to the nation's breakfast tables, where it seems to have been ignored.

This was a pity, because Reggie was right even on fairly minor details. He outlined the facts of the situation, that the West was increasingly dependent on oil, that demand was projected to increase massively over the next ten years, and that the producers were becoming increasingly well organised through OPEC. Reggie pointed out that Western governments, through taxation, were getting more out of oil production than the Arab governments whose resources were being depleted, and warned that the producers were now in a position of great economic power to do something about it. He quoted 'one very shrewd Arab Minister' as having recently said to him, 'We do not want to become responsible for other people's comfort'. Reggie warned that the oil issue was related to a just settlement of the Arab-Israeli conflict, and that political instability in the Middle East could trigger problems. In the longer term there was the prospect of greater oil production in the USA in particular becoming economic on the basis of higher prices, coal becoming more important, and greater fuel economy in the West. Maudling also warned of the risks to stability in the world financial system from the need to accommodate large surpluses generated by the oil producers. Reggie's solution, as with many questions, was for men of goodwill to get together and come to a 'general agreement between producers and consumers', for which Reggie Maudling would no doubt be a suitable negotiator although he was too modest to advertise the fact.

Even if his article had been heeded, June 1973 was probably too late for any action to be taken. On 6 October Israel's Arab neighbours launched a military attack, but Israel managed to drive them back and on 16 October crossed the Suez Canal. A day later, Arab oil producers announced production cuts of 5 per cent per month until the United States changed its Middle East policies. A ceasefire was organised by the end of the month, but panic buying had already taken hold in the oil markets and OPEC, in two stages in October and at the end of December, took the opportunity to stabilise the oil price at four times what it had been at the start of 1973. The oil price rise was a disastrous blow for the Heath government, whose incomes policy was already coming under massive strain at the end of 1973. The oil shock came at the worst moment, when the miners were already preparing for a second round of strikes and the economy was overheating. A State of Emergency was declared on 13 November and petrol ration coupons were printed up. The year 1973 ended with the government, and Britain, in panicky mood, preparing for power blackouts and rationing and the Three Day Week. Cecil King, admittedly never the calmest commentator, described a conversation with Cabinet Minister Geoffrey Rippon in which Rippon compared the situation to the Weimar Republic, the fragile democratic regime that preceded the rise of Hitler.[68] The stage was set for 1974, the strangest and most dramatic year of modern British politics, in which Reggie's own troubles played a full part.

Chapter 24

REGINALD'S NOT THERE! 1974

The terminal crisis of the Heath government arose because of a second confrontation with the miners, now with their bargaining position much enhanced by the oil crisis. Unlike the first time round, Maudling was hawkish because a successful claim would destroy the government's elaborate incomes policy. Reggie desperately wanted the incomes policy to work and underpin a successful transition to a high-growth economy, and if the Barber boom had worked it would have been a retrospective vindication of the 1962–4 Maudling economic strategy. The year 1974 began with the Three Day Week to conserve fuel supplies, but at the end of January the miners voted for an all-out strike. Paralysis and panic started to grip central government, with the smoothly efficient William Armstrong breaking down completely. Throughout January there had been pressure among some Conservatives for a general election to gain a strengthened mandate for Heath's incomes policy. Maudling, on 20 January, wrote that unless a comprehensive agreement could be reached with the TUC the government should put the issues before the electorate.[1] Having attempted fruitlessly to find another solution, Heath announced on 7 February that there would be a general election.

One of Maudling's first acts as Home Secretary in 1970 had been to approve the Boundary Commission's review of parliamentary constituencies. This had become a Tory cause célèbre in 1969 when the Labour government, using the pretext of impending local government reform, had postponed the boundary changes. The real reason had been that the changes would favour the Tories because of the abolition of undersized Labour inner-city seats and the creation of new Tory seats in the suburbs. Barnet was one of the constituencies altered in the review because the Greater London boundary now ran through the area. Borehamwood and Elstree disappeared into a new South Hertfordshire constituency, which also swept up Potters Bar and other spare parts from Enfield West, Iain Macleod's constituency for twenty years but since his death represented by Cecil Parkinson. Maudling stayed with the bulk of his old seat which spread southwards and became known as 'Barnet, Chipping Barnet', which has a strange echo of James Bond about it. The new version of the seat was considerably safer for the Conservatives than the old Barnet had been.

Reggie played little part in the national campaign in February 1974. He had an unpleasant shock just before it opened, when he opened an IRA letter bomb at Bedwell Lodge and the blast damaged his thumb and a hall table.[2] He was in a peculiar public position, the subject of references in the Poulson–Pottinger trial and of course in private the target of exhaustive investigations, but not actually himself yet subject to any specific charges or allegations. It did seem that his complaint that he was being judged through innuendo and guilt by association had some merit. A minor irritation during the campaign occurred when a man called Bernard Jones distributed a leaflet to several households in Barnet making allegations about Maudling's links with Poulson and Hoffman. Maudling quickly obtained an injunction against Jones, halting the leafleting, and settled the case quietly after the election for a small sum.[3] Early on in the short campaign the Poulson–Pottinger trial came to an end, with guilty verdicts announced on both men on 11 February. They were both given prison sentences of five years, and the trial judge lashed out at Poulson as 'an incalculably evil man'.

For Reggie, the end of the first Poulson trial was an opportunity to challenge the allegations that had been made about him during the trial and on which it would previously have been contempt of court to make public comment. He released a statement that claimed to 'at last make public the true facts about my dealings with Mr Poulson' after eighteen months of silence. Like his earlier statements it was carefully written and concentrated on rebutting Poulson and Hunter's claims about the financial relationship between Poulson and ITCS. It also called, with the 'drunk in shirt sleeves' allegation no doubt uppermost in Reggie's mind, Poulson's statement to the Official Receiver full of 'highly offensive' allegations, and that 'I do not accept one single statement that he made'.[4] The prospect of further trials in the immediate future concerning Poulson's relationships with Coal Board, NHS and local government figures, and the plausible account Maudling gave, headed off further public discussion of the matter for a few months. However, things were moving behind the scenes.

Poulson had been publicly shredded once again during a long cross-examination in the witness box, and hobbled off to prison, broken and humiliated. He had just crossed a financial line and joined the select company of the 'minus millionaires'. A Fraud Squad memo noted that his liabilities now totalled £1,075,012.40, of which nearly two-thirds was to the Inland Revenue.[5] Poulson was facing a string of further charges, to which he had no real defence, including what John Cobb, QC, believed 'would have been one of the largest tax-frauds of all time'.[6] Poulson had nothing left to lose. On 21 February 1974 he offered the police a plea bargain – to plead guilty to the charges during the Dan Smith trial (and presumably face a minimal amount of time added on his sentence), and in return to 'spill the beans' to Superintendent Etheridge of the Fraud Squad about Maudling. News of the deal spread rapidly within the small circle of Poulson legal experts, as did the

view that 'Poulson's Counsel Mr Herod QC has heard this story and was said
to be horrified'.[7] But the Attorney General, Peter Rawlinson, decided on
22 February, one of his final days in office, to offer Poulson 'full immunity
from prosecution' in relation to Maudling and others for corruption and
fraudulent trading.[8] There was an almost tangible sense of excitement
and fear in early 1974 in high legal, political and civil service circles about
the Maudling situation.

Etheridge came to visit John Poulson in Armley jail in Leeds to ask
questions about Maudling, and spent some of election day talking to him. The
interviews were obviously conducted with a view to establishing a criminal
case against Maudling, as well as to assist the bankruptcy inquiry in tracing
Poulson money. Poulson was questioned about any allegations he had to
make about Maudling, including those in relation to Zayed, Tajir and the
financial relationship between Poulson and ITCS, and because Poulson's cause
was already lost Etheridge was fairly gentle with the prisoner. However, it was
a frustrating encounter because Poulson rambled, and his record of
dishonesty and hypocrisy meant that his uncorroborated word was of limited
evidential value. The police were handicapped by the need to find a charge
against Maudling that could be brought to court under the Attorney
General's guidelines and the interviews were of little use to the Fraud Squad,
fascinating though they were.

Poulson did not feature to a large extent during the rest of the election,
which was veering off Heath's chosen agenda of 'who governs Britain?' to
cover the record of the government since 1970, in particular on inflation and
general economic management. Harold Wilson, in his fourth election, was
fighting an astute, negative campaign, and while at the outset the general
expectation was for a considerable Tory victory, as the campaign wore on this
was replaced by uncertainty. The Liberals were gaining ground as voters
reacted against the confrontational circumstances of the election. Maudling,
in his election campaign, tried to bring attention back to what he thought of
as the fundamental question: 'Do the people in this country wish to see a
policy for incomes and prices based on Parliamentary authority, and the
maximum degree of mutual agreement, or are they willing to see everything
determined by the extreme use of industrial power?'[9] Reggie's opposition to
the miners' 1974 claim was because he saw it as opening the gates to a
collapse into a Hobbesian war of all against all, the replacement of reason by
brute force. He feared that the confrontation would wreck any attempt to
make consensus politics work in Britain, and was keen to see the 1974 Tory
manifesto – which was a thoroughly Maudlingite document in contrast to its
1970 predecessor – endorsed and put into practice. It was not to be, even
though Maudling himself won a convincing victory in the battle for his new
seat thanks to a near-even division in the opposition vote, as shown in the
results table. The turnout in Barnet was particularly high, although the
dramatic circumstances of the February campaign had brought large

numbers of people to the polls. His opposition in this election were an interesting pair. Glamorous journalist Nesta Wyn Ellis went on to write a sympathetic instant biography of John Major in 1991. John Mills, a Camden Labour councillor, was the husband of Barbara Mills, who went on to become head of the Serious Fraud Office and the Crown Prosecution Service in the 1990s.

Electorate		56,007	
Turnout			82.1
Reginald Maudling	Conservative	22,094	48.0
John Mills	Labour	12,183	26.5
Nesta Wyn Ellis	Liberal	11,714	25.5
Conservative majority		9,911	21.5

The national result of the election, however, was complex and confusing. For the first – and so far only – time since 1929 an election produced no outright majority in the House of Commons. Labour had won 301, the Conservatives (perversely, despite winning more votes and the boundary changes) only 297 while Liberals, Scottish Nationalists and Ulster Unionists made gains. Heath stayed in Downing Street a few more days, attempting to build a parliamentary coalition that would allow his government to stay in business. He offered the position of Home Secretary to Jeremy Thorpe, whose problems made him even less suitable for the post than Maudling. Reggie, from the sidelines that weekend, argued that the result was a victory for moderation and that whatever government emerged from the situation should pursue consensus policies like a prices and incomes policy, even extending this further, for instance, to cover bank profits, no further nationalisation, renegotiation of the terms of membership of the EEC, revision of industrial relations law, devolution to Scotland, Wales and Northern Ireland and a broad agreement between government and unions.[10] His response was a demonstration, in most unfavourable circumstances, of his political optimism. The Maudling proposals essentially combined some of the most attractive features of each of the party manifestos, and were not a million miles away from what Callaghan's Labour government ended up trying to do in 1976–9. There was certainly nothing in them that Roy Jenkins or Jeremy Thorpe, or even in their heart of hearts Tony Crosland and Harold Wilson, could not have swallowed in 1974. However, few then saw any great opportunity for a national consensus, particularly not the left of the Labour Party which had won the battle for a radical policy statement the previous autumn. The dictates of party politics meant that Heath's efforts to stay in power were in vain, and Wilson formed a minority Labour government on 4 March 1974.

Although not the outcome he would have chosen in the national interest, in some still mysterious way the advent of the Labour government was followed by one of the most decisive moves in the curtailment of the Poulson investigation. Since July 1972 the Department of Trade and Industry (DTI) Companies Investigation Branch had been investigating the affairs of the Poulson companies, and the range of these inquiries had been widened by the liquidation of the companies and the cooperation between the liquidators and the bankruptcy trustees in uncovering their activities. A senior officer, Alan Ford, had been assigned to conduct these inquiries, which took place under the secret section 109 procedure.

Ford, and his colleague Frederick Littlefield, produced several reports between October 1973 and March 1974. There were two reports into Ropergate, one into ITCS concentrating on Maudling's pay and share ownership, one into OSB, and one each into two more Poulson-associated companies, Ovalgate Investments and World Wide Interiors (which was finished by another inspector in October 1974). Inquiries were started but never completed into Construction Promotion and another company called Water and General Engineering Co.[11] Three of the reports (Ropergate 1, OSB, ITCS)[12] specified several criminal offences concerning which charges could be brought against Maudling, and were submitted to the Director of Public Prosecutions when they were completed. Some of the charges Ford proposed were, it is fair to say, minor – one on the OSB report would only attract a £20 fine if it were proved that Maudling had knowingly (and there lies the problem) authorised an increase in share capital without informing the Registrar of Companies.[13] Others had more substance, particularly in relation to expenses fraud and false accounting relating to overseas accounts operated by ITCS. Section 109 reports are highly secret as a rule. In the Poulson case there were exceptional measures to conceal them, to the extent of denying access to them to the trustees in bankruptcy and liquidators of the Poulson companies; even at the end of 1976 these parties were still complaining that they could not gain access to the reports.[14] The problem was undoubtedly Ford's recommendations of criminal charges against Maudling.

Shortly after the ITCS report was submitted on 15 March 1974 Ford was exiled from the Companies Investigation Branch, and sent to more routine work as Official Receiver for the bankrupt of Birmingham. He, and Littlefield, both died within five years. The removal of Ford is one of the most dubious aspects of the Maudling–Poulson investigation. The fatal sentence in his ITCS report may have been in the introduction, when he wrote that 'A further report will be submitted as soon as possible, covering the remainder of the company's trading activities'. He also pointed out that eight aspects of the 'interim' Maudling investigation deserved further inquiry.[15] Even if it stopped short of further criminal charges under UK jurisdiction, any such DTI investigation would surely have found Maudling unfit to be a director.[16] Ford and Littlefield did not approach Maudling for information; Maudling disingenuously claims in his memoirs that this was because he had not been sufficiently involved, but the real reason was because the investigation was aborted at an early stage and the DTI men were wary of cutting across the police investigations.[17] In September 1974 the remaining Poulson-related DTI investigations were abandoned when the police informed the DTI that no useful purpose would be achieved.[18] Given the guidelines for prosecutions the police had been given, there was little chance of getting a fraud or false accounting case into court. Ford complained that, in the police inquiry, 'Corruption was concentrated on to the exclusion of all else'. Ford's complaint was justified. According to a DPP memorandum in 1976: 'the police were given express instructions at a meeting with the Attorney General and the DPP on 17th May 1973 to concentrate on evidence of corruption and not to divert scarce investigatory resources into inquiring into other possible offences'.[19]

It had been known at a high level since July 1972 that Maudling's position in relation to trading while insolvent, and taxation, was shaky, and the effect of this decision was to make it extremely difficult to mount any fraud or company law prosecutions in relation to Poulson. The force of the police investigation was concentrated on councillors and nationalised industry officials against whom corruption offences under English law could be proved. The Fraud Squad had been disbarred from investigating other matters almost from the start, and the efforts of Ford and Littlefield in investigating seven Poulson companies plus Dan Smith's corporate web which spread out to eleven companies directly and twenty indirectly, all in a period of several months under time pressure[20] was all the investigation there was on company offences.

Even though the threat from the DTI dissipated in March, three of the worst weeks in the life of Reggie Maudling began when his mother-in-law, Florence Laverick, died at Essendon on 20 April 1974. She was no longer the proud social climber of ten years earlier, whose urgings had helped set Reggie on his disastrous course, but a bedridden shadow of her former self, who had lost the charm that could arouse feelings of considerable fondness in people she met.[21] Since the death of her husband in 1967 she had increasingly sought solace in the gin bottle and become another querulous, demanding burden on Reggie.[22] For all that, she was the nearest thing Reggie had left to his own family and her passing left him more on his own than ever, with an understandably upset wife to comfort while troubles were raining in on him from all directions.

The Poulson hearings had aroused the interest of the Inland Revenue. Illegal income has always been taxable and they were not unnaturally interested to see whether payments and benefits received from Poulson had been fully declared by everyone involved. Soon after the hearings began a small group at a high level in the Revenue established a 'watching brief' over the Poulson affair. The documents from this have been closed for seventy-five years, as are many Revenue papers, but there is other evidence showing that Maudling's complicated tax affairs were a major part of the Inland Revenue inquiry. The review of Maudling, which had not been limited to the Poulson connection, found, in the words of a tax inspector to Maudling, that 'the situation portrayed in the tax files differed in some respects from that now brought out by other evidence'. The Revenue had provisionally assessed Reggie's back tax liability at £25,000, including £12,000 relating to ITCS, and the senior officer, L.S. Stratford, questioned him politely but firmly at Clunie House on 25 April 1974 about the Adeline Genée payments and his business expenses, including his foreign travel. Reggie had his story reasonably straight about Genée, but was less convincing about expenses, particularly the trip to Australia for Martin's wedding, relating to which he claimed not to recall which companies would have been billed for this trip (if any) as he often did work for more than one company while abroad.[23] There was some unproductive verbal jousting about whether it was a business element to a personal trip, or a personal element to a business trip. In Poulson evidence there was an unconvincing attempt to argue that there was interest in Open System Building techniques in Australia, but the Poulson cash book entry for 18 January 1968 (£80 for 'R fare Australia i.e. RMM Wedding'), and the lack of any such mention in the OSB minutes, seems to suggest it was predominantly a private trip. The 25 April meeting ended with many questions about Reggie's taxes unresolved.[24]

The end of another Poulson trial produced, a couple of days after the private Inland Revenue interview, another burst of public interest in the affair. Dan Smith and Andy Cunningham were sentenced to prison for corruption at this trial, although before sentencing, Smith had given a revealing interview to the BBC's *The Money Programme*, disclosing among other things that he had given Labour's Deputy Leader, Ted Short (MP for Newcastle Central) payments during the mid-1960s that remained confidential at Short's request. It was intensely embarrassing for Short, who protested that these were simply reimbursed expenses, but it left the strong impression of, as far as public life was concerned, yet more fog on the Tyne. Several more events followed the Smith verdict. Labour MP Joe Ashton wrote a column for *Labour Weekly* that alleged that 'the number of Labour MPs who can be hired can be counted on the fingers of one hand. And the rest of us know who they are,' and that some MPs rarely declared their financial interests.[25] Ashton, for his pains, ended up under investigation. Harold Wilson tried to dispel some of the foul atmosphere of politics by setting up a Royal Commission into Standards of Conduct in Public Life under Lord Salmon. Wilson himself, and his Political Secretary, Marcia Williams, had been under sustained attack over allegations concerning land development in Wigan (the 'slag heaps' affair) since shortly after the election – although according to later witnesses this seems to have missed the main point of the bizarre, Gothic tale of the last Wilson government.[26] Hartley Shawcross piped up with allegations of corruption against unnamed public figures in the past, which seemed to hark back to the early 1950s but were never elaborated.

While the whole political climate was unhealthy, Maudling's position was particularly bad. DTI, police and Inland Revenue investigations, and the demands of the Trustee in Bankruptcy for payment on the Essendon swimming pool, were bad enough but a more immediate threat was from Ray Fitzwalter and the Granada *World In Action* television investigation into the construction of the Gozo hospital. The investigation was nearly over and it was time to ask questions of Maudling, whom the programme alleged had used his influence to secure the contract for Poulson as part of a dubious enterprise. The Granada journalists went to Clunie House, in the footsteps of the taxmen, on the last Wednesday before transmission. When they spoke to him they found him apparently unruffled, although he had a strange mannerism of sucking his teeth and puffing out his cheeks when the questioning touched on the Malta lobbying operation. They had obtained copies of his letters, and without actually saying that they had them they put it to Reggie that he had been 'hustling for Poulson', a suggestion at which he bridled. They then read him the content of the letters, which he denied.[27]

When *World In Action* asked Maudling whether he had been involved in Malta lobbying he told them that 'I was in no way concerned in getting the contract for the Poulson organisation. That had been arranged before I came on the scene.' This rapidly turned out to be demonstrably untrue, as the letters from Maudling to Maltese officials written in October 1966 surfaced quickly after he spoke. While it was true that Poulson had made the opening to Malta before he recruited Maudling, Reggie had in fact helped to unblock the way to getting the contract agreed. Why Reggie said what he did to the journalists is difficult to understand, as they already had the letters and Reggie was certainly able to recall the correct version to the bankruptcy investigators less than a year earlier in July 1973.[28] He was under such appalling strain in April and May 1974 that he did not seem to be acting rationally, although he was keeping up a good front in public. However, after all this something seemed to snap and he disappeared for a lost weekend in Paris.

When the Malta letters surfaced journalists raced to find Reggie. The *Daily Mail's* Harry Longmuir won, having heard that Maudling was in Paris. Knowing Maudling's tastes, Longmuir had a very short shortlist of hotels where he might be staying. Longmuir checked into the George V and found Reggie and Beryl in the 'Le President' suite. Reggie told him 'I'll come and see you.' Longmuir spoke at length to a confused, disorientated Reggie Maudling on Sunday morning. During the interview Maudling, in a dressing gown, worked his way through the entire contents of Longmuir's mini-bar and it is perhaps hardly surprising that Maudling was not clear about what he had said to the journalist or under what conditions; he said that it had been off the record, but the paper disagreed. Longmuir himself asked the paper to hold back the story until he had managed to obtain more support for it, but Reggie's unbuttoned and rambling interview, in which he gave away much

more than he could have intended, was published under the headline
'Maudling: The Letters I Forgot'.

The *World In Action* programme, under the slightly punning title 'Business
in Gozo', went out on the evening of 6 May 1974. Reggie had already been
put on the back foot during the Longmuir interview, when he had been
obliged to apologise to Granada for misleading them about the letters. It told
the story of the Malta contract from start to finish, which in May 1974 was
as a huge white elephant of a hospital stranded unoccupied on an
underpopulated island. The programme was the first sustained public
discussion of Poulson's overseas operations, and Maudling's role, and it was
not a pretty sight. Reggie was appalled by the programme. He spoke solemnly
in the House of Commons the next day, making a Personal Statement which,
as is the custom of the House, went uninterrupted and unquestioned. Beryl
watched, nodding in support, from the Gallery. He said of the programme: 'It
was clearly implied that I had used my position as a Member of Parliament
to further a private interest which I had not disclosed. I can think of no
graver or more evil allegation to make against a Member of this House.' He
went on:

> The facts are as follows. There was never any secret about my connection
> with Mr. Poulson so far as the Malta contract was concerned. The House
> should be aware, as the compilers of the programme clearly were not
> aware, that I took steps to ensure that my interest was known in full, not
> only to the Government of Malta but to the British Government as well.
> The Library of the House has provided me with a list of any references I
> made to Malta in the House of Commons at the relevant time. Not one of
> these contains any reference to hospital projects or had any relevance
> whatever to them.[29]

Reggie went on to announce that he was instructing solicitors to bring legal
proceedings 'against those who were in any way concerned with this
programme'. He then sat down, to cheers and murmurs of support from both
Conservative and Labour benches.

It is impossible to justify some of the assertions in Maudling's statement of
7 May 1974. It is particularly difficult to defend the claim that 'There was
never any secret about my connection with Mr. Poulson so far as the Malta
contract was concerned', which sits oddly with his statement as late as 2 May
1974 that 'I was in no way concerned in getting the contract for the Poulson
organisation. That had been arranged before I came on the scene.'[30] His
interest was hardly known 'in full', although he had taken care on several
occasions to describe Poulson as a 'business associate' in documents; this
could cover varying degrees of involvement. It was also a stretch to say that
none of his speeches on Malta had 'any relevance whatever' to hospital
projects, as the flow of British Overseas Development funds for Malta had a

direct effect on the size and scale of infrastructure projects in Malta and this was the subject of the debates in question.

Lying in a personal statement to the House is one of the most serious parliamentary offences, of an arguably greater magnitude than the original allegation of an undisclosed private interest. When Maudling made his statement he was under enormous pressure – the attentions of the Inland Revenue, the Fraud Squad, Granada's TV revelations and the publication of a book on the REFA affair all came at the same time. While John Profumo in 1963 had been hard pressed by his colleagues to deny the allegations against him, he had not been embattled on all fronts in the same way as Maudling was in 1974. But this is a plea of mitigation for Maudling rather than a defence; he was either lying, or sufficiently close to a breakdown to have lost his grip on what was true. The personal statement compounded his offence, even if he honestly believed or had managed to convince himself that it was the truth.

Later in May, Michael Gillard's book on the REFA affair was published under the title *A Little Pot of Money*, with a preface by Paul Foot. It had originally intended to cover Poulson as well, but this was legally impossible at the time and its scope was reduced to REFA only. Gillard's researches into Poulson were published in 1980 as *Nothing to Declare*, after Maudling's death. *A Little Pot of Money* was actually not at all bad for Reggie, as it found no evidence of anything worse than bad judgement and negligence, which is surely the minimum anyone who had promoted such a scam could be accused of. Reggie conceded the truth of much of what it said in an interview with the *Daily Telegraph*, and while he announced that his lawyers would be reading the book closely, no legal action against the book followed. However, the confluence of the Granada and Gillard investigations led to a Maudling counter-attack, in which he alleged that the book's publication 'this week after the Granada programme is obviously part of a concerted plot by Paul Foot and his usual gang of Granada-type people'. He accused Foot of conducting a personal vendetta against him, which Foot naturally denied.[31] Neither Foot nor Gillard had any connection with the 'Business in Gozo' programme, although Gillard had recently joined *World In Action* to research other projects, and the programme-makers found the coincidence and the plot allegation an embarrassing distraction.[32] Nothing more was heard of the 'plot', although the interrelation between the two actions caused some legal problems. His usual libel lawyers, Allen & Overy, also worked for the IBA and were concerned about the possibility of a perceived conflict of interest, but when he asked his next choice, the hawkish firm of Oswald Hickson Collier, they turned out to have advised the publishers on *A Little Pot of Money*.[33] He could either look further, or else choose one or other of the actions to pursue. By June Oswald Hickson Collier had opened preliminary discussions with Granada's solicitors, the formidably well-connected firm of Goodman Derrick.[34]

While the Granada case was gearing up, the REFA business wound down. Shortly after the publication of the Gillard book, in June 1974, an arrest warrant was issued for Hoffman, but the charge was not serious enough to count as extraditable from the United States. Without Hoffman, any legal action in Britain against the principals associated with REFA would have been Hamlet without the Prince, or at least King Lear without the Fool, and as long as he stayed out of British jurisdiction the REFA affair could be considered at an end. The file remained technically open until 1976, and in July 1977 it was announced that no prosecutions were pending.[35] The egregious Hoffman, when he came out of prison, could not resist returning to his old ways. He declared personal bankruptcy in Houston in 1976, but shortly afterwards was founding a company called Coastal & Offshore and generating a trail of unpaid bills. Hoffman attempted on at least two occasions to persuade development agencies in the USA to part with money to help with a scheme to build an aluminium smelter. In 1980 he surfaced in the guise of D. Jerald Hoffman, promising $1 billion of investment in North Carolina, incidentally claiming to have more than twenty years' experience managing construction projects in the Middle East, but he was exposed by the local media.[36] In 1985 he tried the same stunt at Lackawanna in the west of New York state, with the same result.[37]

The Poulson affair's main institutional legacy was the Register of Members' Interests, which was finally approved by resolution on 22 May. The demand for a public declaration of outside interests on the part of MPs had been current for some time. In the late 1960s, after revelations concerning the relationships between lobbying firms and MPs, the issue was examined by a Commons committee but its rather half-hearted recommendations lapsed with the 1970 election. The Poulson hearings started a new push for the introduction of a register of interests, with sixty Labour MPs led by Joe Ashton and Phillip Whitehead signing a petition in July 1972 in the wake of Maudling's resignation.[38] With the return of Labour to power in 1974, combined with the convictions in the Poulson cases, the momentum was irresistible and on 22 May the House voted to establish a Select Committee to work out the details of a compulsory register. Maudling was one of 168, nearly all Conservatives, who opposed the setting up of the register. However, even though the resolution was for a compulsory register, it became clear in 1975, when Enoch Powell refused to make a return for the register, that there were no sanctions against MPs who defied registration. When it was published in November 1975 Maudling's own declaration, like that of several other MPs, was extremely vague: 'Member of Lloyd's, occasional journalism and broadcasting. Financial and economic adviser.' It was not until the 1990s that an enforceable registration procedure came into force and the rules were tightened up to prevent uninformative and unclear declarations such as 'financial and economic adviser'.

The inconclusive result in February meant that the 1974 Parliament, action-packed though it was, was doomed to be short. It was no surprise when Harold Wilson announced on 18 September that there would be another election, on 10 October. An hour after Wilson called the election, Reggie issued his long-threatened writ against Granada's 6 May *World In Action* programme on the Malta deal. He could hardly leave it any longer, as he was being taunted in *Private Eye* for failing to come good on his threat to sue Granada and for his sabre rattling against *A Little Pot of Money*. But in taking on Granada and its chairman Sidney Bernstein he was confronting a powerful enemy who had never lost a case and who showed no interest in a 'commercial settlement', i.e. an unconvincing public statement and an out of court payment to the plaintiff to go away. Granada had every intention of defending it, and the company's journalistic and financial resources were formidable. Reggie, too, had his strengths and the libel case was to be a brutal fight to the finish. However, in the short term it stifled further allegations and enabled Reggie to fight the October 1974 election in a more or less normal fashion.

While the February election was dramatic, the October 1974 election was a placid business. There was not much doubt that Labour would win, although Heath's Tories battled gamely and – despite Reggie's own exile from the centre of things – had a manifesto along very Maudlingesque lines. They even suggested that they might not form a Tory-only government, but work for a government of national unity: 'After the election we will consult and confer with the leaders of other parties, and with the leaders of the great interests in the nation, in order to secure for the Government's policies the consent and support of all men and women of goodwill.'[39]

Reggie's own contribution to the national election was modest, consisting of a couple of newspaper letters and articles, and his campaign in Chipping Barnet was a routine victory against the same opponents as in February plus an unwelcome incursion from the extreme right National Front. Nationally, Heath's Tories held up surprisingly well and Labour's parliamentary majority was much less than expected – a paltry overall lead of three. However, as long as the Labour government did not get all the variegated opposition parties voting against it at the same time – there were Liberals, Scottish and Welsh Nationalists, and none of the twelve Northern Ireland MPs was affiliated to a British party any more – its position was more comfortable than the overall majority might indicate.

Electorate		56,473		
Turnout			73.6	
Reginald Maudling	Conservative	19,661	47.3	–0.7
John Mills	Labour	11,795	28.4	+1.9
Nesta Wyn Ellis	Liberal	8,884	21.4	–4.1
R.A. Cole	National Front	1,207	2.9	
Conservative majority		7,866	18.9	

The police inquiries into Poulson were reaching a climax in October 1974. The Poulson trials up to that point had been a string of successes and the evidence was building well against other civil servants, councillors and nationalised industry officials. The time now came for a decision on the MPs, including Maudling. The interviews with Poulson in February and March 1974 had included allegations relating to companies and perjury charges but also expenses fraud, bribery in Arabia and Maudling's relationship with Mahdi Tajir. A report by Superintendent Etheridge in May 1974 raised the possibility that there had been a secret arrangement between Maudling and Poulson in spring 1969 to pay the £9,500 ITCS fee off the books.[40] During the year the Fraud Squad investigation of Maudling had been narrowed down to the Gozo hospital contract and the prospect of establishing a corruption charge; shortly after Etheridge's first report relating to Maudling the prosecution guidelines were narrowed to focus on bribery and corrupt misuse of office cases which did not raise problems of jurisdiction or foreign nationality. Etheridge flew to Malta in July 1974 to investigate the activities of John Abela and his company, and spoke to a rather unhelpful Carmelo Caruana, and pursued inquiries in Britain into Malta and the Essendon swimming pool. The Maudling file, plus material relating to MPs Cordle and Roberts, was sent to the DPP in October 1974 and referred to two senior barristers, Sir John Cobb and Peter Taylor, for their opinion. Cobb and Taylor finished their report on 7 November 1974. Its contents were explosive.

The police investigation and the bulk of the Cobb–Taylor opinion were devoted to establishing whether any of the MPs could be charged with offences of corruption. There were two prongs to this – the payment of £5,000 to John Abela in Malta to grease the wheels there, and the MPs' own activities on behalf of Poulson in Britain. Before getting to the corruption angle, Cobb and Taylor noted that:

> Neither the Police reports nor our own advices have explored the possibility of any other type of offence: for example, in relation to taxation. However, it is right that we should point out that Department of Trade and Industry Inspectors' Reports [re Ropergate and ITCS] have been laid before us, and that possible offences by the Right Honourable Reginald Maudling have been specified as follows:

They go on to list several possible charges, including conspiracy with Poulson to obtain money from Ropergate, two perjury charges relating to his examination in the bankruptcy hearings, a larceny charge relating to the ITCS accounts and a charge under the Theft Act referring to a false and deceptive ITCS balance sheet. There were actually several more charges to which the DTI Reports relating to the Poulson companies alluded, including expenses fraud. The careful and specific exclusion of taxation from the report is a clear reference to the continuing inquiries into Maudling's tax returns.

The problem with the corruption charge was, according to Cobb and Taylor and a previous secret look at the law concerning bribery of MPs in March 1970, that there was a loophole that meant that the corruption laws did not apply to Members of Parliament. The statutory definition of corruption depended on an agent–principal relationship. Only someone who was acting as the agent of another could, in the strict sense, commit the crime of corruption – by betraying that interest in exchange for personal favours. Unlike civil servants, or serving ministers, it was held that MPs have no 'principal'.[41] They are not obliged to favour the interests of the government – the existence of parliamentary opposition would be impossible otherwise; they are not at all times expected to favour the interests of their constituents; the role of individual conscience is important in determining what an MP should do. Cobb and Taylor concluded that 'A Member of Parliament using his position to show favour to an individual for private reward commits no criminal offence. This situation might well be thought to be anomalous.' This doctrine on the immunity of MPs from prosecution for corruption has become part of the accepted understanding of what the law is, without ever being tested in court. It is not accepted in other Commonwealth jurisdictions whose law on these matters has the same root. Some government legal advice in October 1975 was to test the alleged immunity by bringing prosecutions of three MPs, but the Attorney General turned it down as a breach of privilege.'[42] The loophole doctrine was officially published in the July 1976 report of the Salmon Commission, which invited Parliament to consider whether it should bring bribery of MPs within the criminal law.[43] Governments since 1996 have supposedly been about to reform this anomaly, but as of 2004 nothing had happened.

Cobb and Taylor also considered the possibility that Maudling was in a different position as a Privy Councillor, but felt this was a dubious line of argument. The legal precedents in such a matter were extremely old, with the judgement in a case of 1769 seeming to offer an argument that the Privy Council was different, but Cobb and Taylor argued that references in this decision to a Privy Councillor 'are really, in our view, to be construed as references to a Minister'. Even so, there was what appeared to be a legal window through which a prosecution might be brought against Maudling; Cobb and Taylor stated that 'if the Privy Councillor is in a position e.g. as a minister to make an appointment, or to do, or to refrain from doing any act, and he receives a sum of money intended, and known by him to be intended, to influence him with regard to the advice which he gives, he commits the common law offence of corruption'. Maudling was in a position as a shadow minister (a position unknown at the time of the 1769 ruling) to give 'advice'. Etheridge argued in 1974 that because the Queen had the power to dismiss a Privy Councillor, the Crown was in the position of principal. Legal opinion consulted in the *Maudling v Daily Mirror* libel case later in the 1970s could not see any way round other than to argue that the loophole in respect of MPs did not exist, although the Granada side were more optimistic about the Privy Council argument.[44]

But here again a prosecution would have run into trouble because of the probable inadmissibility of parliamentary proceedings as evidence. Even without these, it was apparent from letters and the pattern of events that Maudling had for reward used his influence over Maltese ministers and in Britain in Poulson's interests, but whether this amounted to indictable corruption was another matter. To prosecute Maudling on this basis would have been to set a dangerous precedent; it would have thrown the whole accustomed system of former ministers seeking jobs in industry into doubt, and to do so in what still seemed like a borderline case would have been a great risk for the prosecuting authorities and the fragile Labour government. Another possible avenue would have been the common law offence of corruption. Although the case law on common law corruption was old, as it had been overlaid by statutes passed in 1889, 1906 and 1916, it seemed to the Attorney General's office in 1970 that the offence was broadly defined: 'It is a common law misdemeanour for an officer who has a duty to do something in which the public are interested to receive a bribe either to act in a manner contrary to his duty or to show favour in the discharge of his functions.' The 1970 opinion gave an example of conduct that its author believed might come under the common law:

> The exact scope of the offence at common law is uncertain, but, to take an illustration, if the company sponsoring the Brighton Marina Bill offered £1000 to any MP who voted for it, it is not inconceivable that an MP accepting the offer would be held guilty of an offence, or at least that he and the company would be guilty of conspiracy.[45]

From this argument, it might have been worth charging Cordle, against whom the case was particularly clear, with conspiracy and common law corruption and seeing what happened before taking any action against anyone else. However, the Salmon Commission disagreed with or ignored the 1970 opinion on MPs and common law corruption, stating that it did not apply because being an MP did not count as holding public office. In 1992, in *R v Greenway*, a judge decided that MPs are after all subject to the common law of bribery. However, in the specific matter of the accused MP Harry Greenway, it was decided that there was no case to answer on the facts of the matter, and Greenway was cleared before the issues of legal principle could be explored in any further detail.[46] The 1995 Nolan Report had little option but to state that it was likely that bribed MPs would be subject to the common law. It was only in the mid-1970s, when there was a realistic chance of charging MPs – particularly Cordle and possibly Maudling – that common law bribery mysteriously disappeared from the legal agenda.[47]

Even so, although the pattern of action on the Malta issue and reward from Poulson was clear, it is still extremely doubtful whether Maudling's conduct constituted bribery in the simple sense required by the common law of corruption. While Cordle and Roberts were hired agents, Maudling was a director and shareholder of Poulson companies and his relationship with Poulson was closer and more mutually dependent than that normally considered bribery. The case involved loopholes within loopholes.

The convoluted, but defensible, logic of the Cobb–Taylor opinion of 7 November was influenced by political considerations. It reads like an attempt to find reasons not to proceed against Maudling, while leaving some sort of secret official record that he had behaved in a 'reprehensible' fashion. In a review meeting in June 1976 Peter Taylor told the Attorney General that his opinion on Williams and Malta 'was given at short notice and could be subject to change should it be necessary to consider political or practical implications'.[48] John Cobb, according to Ken Etheridge and others, apparently decided that they could not proceed against Maudling without a 'one hundred per cent, copper-bottomed guarantee of winning'. This is not the usual standard for the DPP to decide on whether to prosecute someone – better than 50/50 is normally good enough. The prosecutors baulked rather than put a former Home Secretary in the dock and face the slightest chance of losing. Maudling was protected from the consequences of his actions by his high office.

Another possibility, in which the Fraud Squad seemed interested despite a blast of scepticism from the 7 November Cobb–Taylor opinion, was to tie Maudling to the bribery of Abela and Caruana in Malta and charge him with bribery or conspiracy. Etheridge, disappointed by the 7 November opinion, came back with a revised report on 19 November which covered the swimming pool and Malta and came up with a couple of fragments that indicated that Maudling may have been complicit in the bribery. There was a Maudling letter that referred to having 'read the files' on Malta which, if he had done so with any attention, would have made it absolutely plain to him that Poulson and Abela had struck a corrupt bargain. One particular item should have been food for thought; Poulson wrote to Abela on 3 August 1966 that 'I must say I admire the way in which you handle the politicians: you do it exactly the same as I do in this country . . .'. Poulson seemed to have realised halfway through dictating this sentence that it was somewhat incriminating, and concluded it unconvincingly and ungrammatically 'and you are obviously able to do this by loyalty thus commanding their respect'.[49]

The other fragment was the evidence of a Poulson architect, Barry Ibbetson, who had been perturbed by the methods used in gaining the contract. When he reported back to Poulson that Caruana was complaining about the failure of the money to arrive with the Nationalist Party, Poulson told him that Maudling and Williams were the people to sort it out, and in May or early June 1968 Ibbetson brought John Abela to the ITCS offices at

Grosvenor Place and then left. A few days later Ibbetson heard that at the meeting Abela had admitted to having spent the £5,000 himself and not passed it over. Although he did not see Maudling himself that day, Ibbetson had a strong impression from others in the offices that Maudling had been at the meeting.[50]

This was far too thin to prosecute Maudling, but in a supplementary opinion of 29 November 1974 Cobb and Taylor regarded it as worth further investigation. However, in the absence of further documents it came down to the evidence of the participants of the meeting, and Abela had already claimed not to remember it. This left Maudling himself, and Ken Williams. Since he left Vickers and ITCS, Williams had remained involved in the grandiose King Faisal Hospital in Riyadh and was living in Saudi Arabia as a counsellor to the King. Etheridge applied to the Saudi authorities for permission to question Williams but this was turned down. Maudling, perhaps coincidentally, was visiting Saudi Arabia in January 1975. Poulson had started to move down the Fraud Squad list of priorities, and Etheridge now also had to deal with the case of former Labour minister John Stonehouse, who faked his own death in November 1974 to escape from his fraudulent debts and had been arrested in Australia.

The taxation and company law charges were still on the table, as were matters concerning the pool and bribery in Malta, but the 7 November Cobb–Taylor opinion had removed what had seemed the best chance of prosecuting Maudling. There was considerable bitterness within the Fraud Squad about Maudling. One of the investigating officers, Dick Chitty, resigned his membership of the Conservative Party when Maudling was restored to the front bench in February 1975, complaining that 'the Shadow Cabinet is made up of fascists and crooks'. Chitty indicated that he believed that there had been 'a big cover-up over Maudling's role'.[51] Police frustration spilled out in the form of leaks, to *Private Eye* (which was well informed about the progress of the investigation)[52] and later to the *Granada* and *Mirror* defences against Maudling's libel actions in 1975–8.

The Fraud Squad kept the secret annexes to Maudling's bankruptcy examination until March 1976, pondering whether there was any way of bringing charges in relation to the Tajir or Nasser connections.[53] Their reasons for not proceeding on the Gulf case are easy to reconstruct. They would have needed better evidence than Poulson's word for it, and in the absence of Ken Williams and the unlikelihood of either Maudling or Tajir incriminating themselves, short of an extremely risky high-profile raid on Bedwell Lodge and Clunie House, there was unlikely to be any more than they had from the documents. Establishing, even if the allegations were true, that a crime under English law had been committed was still more complicated. Police work has a large element of triage about it – officers need to make a quick assessment on which lines of enquiry are probably going to result in arrest and conviction, and those which do not pass the test are abandoned.

Fraud Squad work is not popular among detectives because of its low ratio of collars felt to effort involved, and there are budget constraints that prevent intensive investigations of frauds with a substantial foreign component.[54] What is striking about the Maudling case is how hard Etheridge and his colleagues worked on a long-shot case.

Even had the police managed to assemble a case, 'reasons of state' might well have come into the picture, as few British businesses operating in the Middle East could have withstood such a degree of scrutiny. Added to this, Mahdi Tajir was the ambassador of a friendly – and, since the oil crisis – extremely powerful and important country. A criminal case involving him would have led to severe international repercussions, and possibly even to the collapse of sterling, as UAE balances held in London were a vital support on the international money markets. Even in the bankruptcy hearings, precautions were taken to keep discussion of Poulson, Maudling and Nasser's conspiracy to bribe Tajir over the Dubai airport contract out of the main transcript of Reggie's private hearing. The Foreign Office would not lift a finger even to assist in the recovery of the £4,000 debt Tajir owed the Bankruptcy Trustee, while they had been happy to intervene in another dispute between Tajir and a British firm in 1973.[55] John Cobb as early as October 1973 tried to halt any investigation of Maudling and the Middle East, making the odd claim in an official report that there was no evidence of any impropriety on Maudling's part in the files.[56] Tajir was, quite simply, above the law, and his status protected his friend Reggie Maudling.

The year 1974 was a hellish one for Maudling: the collapse of the Heath government, death in the family, financial crisis, public accusation and private travails at the hands of the police, DTI, Bankruptcy Trustee and the Inland Revenue. At the worst moment, in early May, he seemed close to the edge. But still he survived, while by the end of the year Poulson, Smith and Cunningham were all in prison, an arrest warrant was out for Hoffman and Williams and Nasser were well advised in keeping out of British jurisdiction. The Poulson affair was seen primarily in terms of greedy and essentially small-time Labour councillors, and the international ramifications seemed confined to Malta.

His journalistic opponents saw Maudling's hand in everything, and those officials who investigated him certainly had a way of being taken off the case when they were getting somewhere; the DTI's Alan Ford, Inland Revenue inspector Alan Wright and DCS Etheridge all ended up pursuing other inquiries by the end of 1974. Maudling still had many friends and sympathisers in government and the bureaucracy, who could not reconcile the allegations against him with his apparently benign and pleasant nature, and did not want to believe that he had done wrong. It is perhaps this feeling, rather than a knowing and malicious conspiracy to sabotage the case against him, that hampered efforts to investigate him. It is difficult not to believe that Maudling escaped official censure because the establishment was still organised and cohesive enough to make sure that one of its own (and what a perverse welcome to its ranks this was for Maudling) was protected. After Cobb–Taylor, and as long as that document remained secret, Reggie could think about a return to front-line politics. An incredulous journalist composed a poetical tribute in the style of T.S. Eliot in honour of his ability to survive:

> Reginald is a mystery cat: he's called the Hidden Paw –
> For he's the arch-illusionist who can defy the Law.
> He's the bafflement of Scotland Yard, the Flying Squad's despair:
> For when they reach the scene of crime, well –
> *Reginald's not there.*
> Ah, Reginald, that Reginald! There's nobody like Reggie:
> He's always On The Other Hand, his bets are ever hedgy;
> His powers of levitation would make a fakir stare,
> And when you reach the scene of crime, blast!
> *Reginald's not there!*
> You may seek him on the letterheads or on a boardroom chair –
> I tell you once, and once again, that *Reginald's not there!*
> Now, Reginald's a portly cat, he's rather tall and stout.
> You would know him if you saw him, for his tongue is hanging out.
> Some say that this is due to greed (or, even due to sin)
> But others claim it's laziness that leaves it on his chin.
> He sways his head from side to side, with movements like a snake,
> But when you think he's half-asleep, he's really half-awake.
> Ah, Reginald, old Reginald! There's no one quite like Reggie,
> A tower of equanimity, a cat that's never edgy.
> You may chuck him out of office, you may threaten him with clink,
> You may call him welsher, mountebank or charlatan or fink,
> He will merely beam and chortle (or, more likely, simply stare)
> But when a crime's discovered, why then *Reginald's not there!*[57]

Chapter 25

A Shadow of a Minister,
1975–1976

As Maudling's *annus horribilis* of 1974 drew to a close, he had grounds for some optimism about resurrecting his political career. John Junor had been banging the drum increasingly loudly in the *Sunday Express* that Reggie should be recalled to the front bench.[1] The *Sun* joined in, lamenting that the Tories were 'missing the Maudling magic'.[2] In November 1974 Edward Heath offered Maudling the chance of returning to the front bench as part of his attempt to shore up his leadership, but Reggie declined. Reggie was not sure he was out of the woods as far as the Poulson investigation went – as indeed he was not, as the Cobb–Taylor report had only recently been submitted, the police file was still open on Malta and the charges relating to company law were still on the docket – and he was confident that he could rely on Heath to renew the invitation at any time. But Reggie was back in play in the big leagues of politics.

Heath was increasingly embattled as leader of the opposition. His success in snatching a narrow defeat from the jaws of disaster in October 1974 was barely appreciated and Conservatives despaired of winning under the leadership of a three-time loser. Some wondered if the Tories could ever hold power again; others plotted to get rid of Heath but faced the problem that Willie Whitelaw, the most attractive alternative leader, was firmly loyal to Heath. But there was a chance for Heath's opponents to force the issue, because the rules had just changed and there would now be an annual opportunity for a leadership election.

In late 1974 Keith Joseph had been shaping up as a potential challenger, with a series of speeches announcing his conversion to monetarist economics and his anguished reflections on what he saw as the faults of the Heath government and his own role as a high-spending, bureaucratic Secretary of State for Health and Social Security. Maudling feigned amused indifference to Joseph's change of heart, commenting in his memoirs that 'Keith was fully entitled to measure himself for a hair shirt if he wanted to, but I was blowed if I could see why he should measure me and Ted at the same time'.[3] In private he was more scathing, calling Joseph 'nutty as a fruitcake'.[4] It was a judgement that became more widely shared after Joseph spoke at Edgbaston on 19 October and appeared to be saying that Britain was in danger because the lower orders were breeding too excessively. His efforts to explain the speech away only attracted more ridicule and he bowed out of the putative leadership election in November. At the end of that month the former Education Secretary, Margaret Thatcher, told Heath that if nobody else would come forward she would stand against him. Heath was dismissive, but as the February election date approached the momentum was with Thatcher. Her campaign was organised by Maudling's Merton contemporary Airey Neave, who proved masterful at manipulating his fellow MPs. Most of them wanted Thatcher to score respectably, either to give Heath a jolt or to open the contest to other contenders, but Neave cunningly persuaded some of them that Thatcher was facing a humiliating defeat and attracted their tactical and sympathy votes.

Maudling had no doubt about where he stood. He was a hardline Heath supporter for personal and political reasons. While never personally close, he always held Heath's abilities in high regard and, particularly after the 1972 'U-turn', supported his policies. Heath had also been supportive during Reggie's period of exile. In contrast, Maudling's feelings about Thatcher were extraordinarily, bitterly hostile. He was not a hater by nature, but he made an exception for Margaret Thatcher. She had, when she first arrived in Parliament in 1959, looked up to Maudling as a coming man and had good neighbourly relations with him as MP for Finchley. She had supported him in 1965 until the very end of the campaign when she switched her support to Heath, ironically giving Heath his two-vote overall lead in the first ballot. His private comments about her after 1965 grew more and more scathing. When outlining the factional balance within the Shadow Cabinet in 1969 for David Butler he commented that 'the right were welcome to Margaret Thatcher', almost as if his side of the argument would have been embarrassed by her support. Later in that interview he commented rudely that Thatcher was sceptical about entry to Europe because she was 'worried about the price of hats'.[5] This contempt became outright hatred by the mid-1970s and he would refer to her as 'that bitch' in his increasingly frequent unbuttoned moments.

The origin of his hatred was not her support for Heath in 1965. He had cordial relations with many Heath supporters including the bulk of his Home Office team in 1970–2. He may have resented her late switch and felt betrayed because he had been counting on her support, but this does not explain the virulence of his views. Maudling, it must be said, had sexist attitudes and Thatcher was precisely the sort of woman who set them off – bossy, strident and suburban. It is doubtful whether he would ever have supported a woman as party leader, but he regarded the prospect of submitting to Thatcher's leadership with particular horror.

Maudling was incredulous when the result of the first ballot of the 1975 Tory leadership election took place on 4 February. Thatcher was in the lead, with 130 votes, to Heath's 119 and 16 for the quixotic candidacy of

Sir Hugh Fraser. The balance was very close to those of his own surprising, narrow defeat in 1965. While he responded then to his personal disappointment with stunned, frozen disbelief and an attempt at putting a good face on it, he was openly furious with the Tories for having spurned Heath ten years later. He went to Heath's office to express his condolences and burst out that 'This is the worst day in the history of the Tory party. They've gone mad!'[6] Others heard him saying openly in the Smoking Room that 'the party's taken leave of its senses!'

Heath resigned immediately, leaving Robert Carr acting leader of the party until the next ballot took place a week later. His resignation opened the way for loyal ministers like Whitelaw and Geoffrey Howe to enter the contest, but the momentum was now with Thatcher and she won an easy victory in the second round, with 140 votes to 79 for Whitelaw and much less for the others. From Reggie's point of view, the lunatics had taken over the asylum.

Reggie was staggered a little later when Thatcher offered him the job of Shadow Foreign Secretary. He gratefully accepted, on the basis that while Ted would always ask again, he would probably only have one opportunity with a new leader. It was a surprising and incongruous appointment. Having promised a harder-edged approach, Thatcher had restored one of the most consensus-minded Conservatives in the House to a very senior position. Not only that, she was willing to overlook Maudling's loudly expressed views about the Tory party's mental health in choosing her. She was also taking a risk because Maudling was still under police investigation. All the Attorney General had been able to say was that he could not see a prosecution being brought on the evidence as yet available. When asked whether Maudling was in the clear, Thatcher could only mutter 'I think so'.[7]

Thatcher had no experience in foreign policy and badly needed an old hand as her Shadow Foreign Secretary, and there were hardly any alternatives to Maudling. It was only after she had appointed Reggie that Anthony Eden reminded her that Robert Carr had served for four years as his PPS in the Foreign Office, but she was not inclined to appoint Carr to any role in her Shadow Cabinet. Maudling, for all his problems from her point of view, was an intelligent and experienced man. Despite his scathing opinion of her, Thatcher touchingly held Reggie in high regard. An American diplomat who had lunch with Thatcher in May 1973 noted that 'Mrs Thatcher lamented that Maudling, whom she clearly ardently admires, was no longer in the Government. She commented that along with Keith Joseph and Hailsham, Maudling had one of the best minds in the Party.'[8] Before two years were up, she was utterly disillusioned with him, for reasons that reflect both on Reggie's decline and on the state of politics.

Reggie's routine as Shadow Foreign Secretary was leisurely. He would tend to work from home in the mornings, with a slow start leafing through all the newspapers and reading anything he could find about foreign affairs. He would sit in his study at Clunie House or Essendon listening to classical music and working through his papers, telephoning to catch up with the Conservative Research Department foreign affairs desk officers, one of whom was Robert Shepherd, later biographer of Iain Macleod and Enoch Powell. Reggie was still, as ever, a charming and considerate boss, impressing Shepherd with his open-mindedness and willingness to listen and think about what even junior colleagues had to offer. He would attend the Commons in the afternoon, often going to an evening dinner or reception and then sometimes returning to socialise in the bars of the Palace of Westminster.[9]

Reggie's Commons speeches were infrequent and perfunctory, although there were occasionally flashes of the old brilliance. He did his duty at Foreign Office Questions, but his interventions were often on the most obvious subjects. He tried to say things that would be acceptable to Tory opinion when he could, and particularly on the subject of Rhodesia he was ever more sympathetic to some sort of internal solution that broadened the base of the Smith regime and could lead to recognition and the lifting of sanctions. But even moderate Tory MPs were unimpressed, Peter Blaker calling Reggie's performance 'totally idle . . . he had not done his homework at all. He really was a disaster.'[10]

While his political profile was low, Maudling was involved in a considerable amount of work behind the scenes. He went on as many foreign trips as he could, often combining political and business travel, although, as he noted, it was difficult for a Shadow Foreign Secretary in particular to finance necessary travel in an entirely satisfactory way.[11] He regarded maintaining personal relationships with foreign diplomats and politicians as an essential part of the job, particularly given the fragility of the Labour government's hold on power and the possibility that he might have to assume office as a result of some sudden crisis. Reggie's shadow diplomacy was a very personal business. He burnished his contacts with people such as Henry Kissinger, and was particularly fond of the African leaders he had dealt with as Colonial Secretary such as Julius Nyerere of Tanzania. He always looked forward to Joshua Nkomo's visits to London – the Rhodesian rebel leader stayed at Claridges or the Savoy, and Reggie was amused by the dissonance and always glad of an excuse to go to either place for lunch.[12]

There was another side to Maudling's personal approach to the job of Shadow Foreign Secretary. It is possible, provided one takes or feigns an interest in enough countries, to attend an embassy reception nearly every evening and drink for free, and Reggie did take advantage of this side of his duties. He was struggling with his own fatalism and dissolution during his time as Shadow Foreign Secretary. Once all the excuses are made, his personal problems were interfering with his performance. In discussion with Roy Hattersley, the Minister of State dealing with issues such as Europe and the Cod War with Iceland, he shocked Hattersley – himself no slouch as a luncher – with his alcohol intake. Hattersley recalled a morning briefing meeting at which Maudling worked his way steadily through a jug of

Dubonnet and gin, a sticky-sweet and highly potent concoction that is powerful stuff as an aperitif, let alone a morning eye-opener.[13] In summer 1976, on an official visit to Paris, Ambassador Nicholas Henderson and his Private Secretary were amused to see that 'the picture of a public personality as depicted by *Private Eye* turned out to be, if anything, an understatement'. Leaving aside snoozes on the plane, the Shadow Foreign Secretary fell asleep three times and in an evening discussion, only a short way into a bottle of Pétrus 1953, dozed off and from then on 'contributed nothing to the party except loud snores'.[14]

Maudling was still capable of standing up for his own political beliefs. He did not regard Shadow Foreign Secretary as a particularly party political job. He was aware of his limitations as a platform speaker and in any case did not feel that it was appropriate to stir up party feeling about foreign policy. He was just as passionately committed to bipartisanship in this area as he was in 1950, but he was now in a position to make this, for a while, the official Conservative line. This was a fundamentally different position from that of his leader, which caused an increasingly public split in the Shadow Cabinet. Once again, Reggie was shadowing Jim Callaghan, one of his favourite Labour politicians and a man with whom he had a cordial relationship. The two had a unique record of having shadowed each other in the 'three great offices of state' – Chancellor, Home Secretary and Foreign Secretary – and had a high opinion of each other despite Callaghan's serious misgivings about Maudling's Northern Ireland policy. Callaghan found Maudling a useful ally in occasional crises, telling the Labour Cabinet in June 1975 that Maudling and the opposition 'were behaving very responsibly' over the deranged Idi Amin's threats to execute British citizens in Uganda.[15]

The cross-party spirit was most evident during the campaign for the June 1975 European referendum. The referendum was a device, first mooted by Tony Benn and taken up by Wilson and Callaghan, to get around the deep split within the Labour Party on Europe. After a cosmetic renegotiation of the terms agreed by Heath, the government decided that yes, it could recommend the new terms. Most establishment figures in politics and business favoured a Yes vote, while the No campaign suffered because its adherents were split between the socialist left and the nationalistic right. The Yes campaign in particular was an exercise in consensus politics of a kind congenial to Reggie, with speakers and organisers drawn from the three main political parties working alongside each other. While it was noted on his appointment that Reggie was not a Euro-enthusiast and that, with the replacement of Heath by Thatcher, the Tories would now be cooler on Europe, Reggie had drifted ever further into believing in the European idea. While he was not particularly effective in his short span as the Tory representative on the Britain In Europe campaign committee (he had 'in a very sleepy way, drifted through two meetings' according to David Steel), he spoke with unusual passion in private. He told David Butler in May 1975 that 'he didn't give a damn what the referendum said, he'd still vote for us staying in. His convictions are not going to be made a fool of by the voter. They could throw him out at the next election if they wanted to.'[16] He expressed the same thought, that the referendum was advisory not binding, in a more mannered form in a letter to his constituents published in *The Times*.[17] He took an active part in press conferences and speaking engagements for the Yes campaign, and was satisfied when Britain voted by two to one to stay in the European Community.

Reggie would, as he had before, range into other areas of policy in his regular *Sunday Express* pieces[18] and in speeches and policy papers. A particular cause was incomes policy, for which he had fought in opposition in 1964–70. He continued to make the case, although the tide in Conservative politics had turned decisively against incomes policy and in favour of the use of monetary policy to restrict demand. He put up a paper to the Shadow Cabinet in May 1976 that once again argued for it, but in terms that could easily be presented as advocating surrender to union power.[19] He also defended liberal Home Office policies, a sign that he had, contrary to superficial impressions, thought deeply about the issues while he was there and cared about them. An essay on this theme for the *Spectator* in July1975 was given the perhaps unfortunate title 'Reginald Maudling – Alternatives to Prison', which raised a smile at *Private Eye*.[20] Earlier that month the Fraud Squad had called on Maudling at his London flat in connection with the Poulson affair.

In contrast to the private bankruptcy hearing two years earlier there was very little bonhomie when Deputy Assistant Commissioner Crane and Detective Sergeant Adrian Keech interviewed Maudling on 4 July 1975. Crane started by cautioning Maudling: 'you are not obliged to say anything unless you wish to do so, but what you say may be put in writing and given in evidence.' The police had a long questionnaire to ask Maudling, which they worked through steadily. For the most part, Maudling, under the watchful eye of his solicitor Sir John Charles, gave monosyllabic answers – principally the monosyllable 'No'. He refused even to confirm that the Adeline Genée Theatre had been in financial difficulties, and purported not to recall anything about the circumstances in which he signed several letters, or meetings such as those that took place with Sir Andrew Cohen. One of his longer answers was when the police put it to him that Poulson had not submitted a bill for the swimming pool work; Maudling answered that 'a bill has been submitted and is a matter of dispute between myself and the trustees', which was technically true but deliberately evasive. Some of his 'No' answers stretch credulity. At the end Maudling refused to sign the interview notes or acknowledge the caution.[21] It was an almost entirely uninformative and frustrating interview. The police themselves thought they were no further forward as a result, and were hemmed in by even tighter prosecution guidelines introduced in April 1975 which ruled out borderline cases. The 'copper-bottomed' doctrine was officially expressed as being 'if there is disclosed in the papers a "runnable" defence which, however un-meritorious, might succeed' or if 'the trial is likely to be contested, lengthy and costly and a successful outcome could not be forecast'.[22] It could almost have been designed to keep Maudling out of the criminal courts. The hopes of the police Poulson squad – greatly reduced in number after redeployments in May 1975 – now rested on the slender reed of getting something incriminating out of Ken Williams.

As well as the criminal investigation, Maudling was also pursuing his increasingly complicated libel action against Granada over the May 1974 *World In Action* programme on Malta. In October 1975 there was what is known in the charming legal terminology as an order for 'further and better discovery' from Granada's solicitors, who were trying to broaden out the action to reflect the totality of the relationship between Maudling and Poulson. Maudling was anxious to avoid this, arguing that it was an oppressive move and fearing what might arise from the discovery process. However, his sense of humour remained intact and, at least according to *Private Eye*'s gossip column, Reggie had the chutzpah to appear at the Granada reception at the Tory party conference. 'I'm Reginald Maudling,' he introduced himself to a Granada executive, 'and I'm suing your company for £1 million. But if you get me a large brandy I'll be prepared to settle for a lower figure.'[23]

Things became more serious in January 1976 when the Granada legal team applied for a copy of the transcript of his July 1973 private examination in bankruptcy. Up to this point, there had been an agreement between the two sides that they would, to simplify matters, cooperate in obtaining documents from the bankruptcy papers from their guardians. Until 19 January everyone was under the impression that this included transcripts of the section 25 hearings, particularly Reggie's, but Reggie phoned his solicitors to say that he was not happy for his private examination to be disclosed, arguing that he had given evidence under the seal of confidentiality. Particularly weighing on his mind must have been the secret 'stopped' sections dealing with his relationships with Costa Nasser and Mahdi Tajir. Much to the surprise of Granada's team, the bankruptcy solicitors had become most unhelpful and reluctant to provide documents and in fact joined the action on Maudling's side when Granada tried to obtain a court order to gain access to the transcript.

The Granada case had drifted into some very dangerous waters. The solicitors, representing the interests of Poulson's creditors, had recently received the first promising news from the Middle East for a while, and wrote to the Registrar:

a few weeks ago we got a positive approach in writing from our original source of information to the effect that he was in a position to introduce us to an individual who had positive and exact information as to the whereabouts of no less than £450,000, the property of Poulson's estate or of his companies. In the past this source of information has never failed and we arranged an early meeting. Unfortunately the individual we were to meet, whose identity we know, was delayed in Damascus of all places and we are not to meet him for at least a fortnight. Meanwhile, we have been reminded that the position is of the utmost delicacy. Nothing must be done to alarm our informants and we were specifically reminded there were those who had quite sufficient influence to prevent the withdrawal of monies from Arab countries even if their whereabouts could be identified. It is in this context that we are finding considerable difficulty in satisfying at least the Solicitors acting for Granada Television that we are complying with the spirit and letter of your Order. We felt it right then to place this report before you.

A sealed copy of this letter, as well as the stopped sections of the Maudling transcript, was sent to the appeal judge hearing the Granada application. Granada lost the case. A mainstay of the judgement was the legitimacy of the Registrar's stop order, which it appears from the published judgement applied to the whole transcript while in fact there were only particular sections that had been stopped. Not only that, but the judges also ruled that the transcript would not have been useful in the libel case, which was a dubious line of argument.[24] While it had little to do with Malta, it was certainly relevant to Goodman Derrick's broader claim for Granada. Ray Fitzwalter, for Granada, thought the disclosure case was 'very nasty' and that there was something strange going on behind the scenes.[25] But the disclosure case was a skirmish on the edges rather than the main battle. The disclosure case had confounded expectations that *Maudling v Granada Television Ltd* would be heard in 1976, and this was postponed to some time in the future while both sides assessed the position after Walton's decision, and Granada conducted more research.

The offer of help from the Middle East turned out not to be particularly productive, and little if any more money came through from this source. It is not known what happened to the Middle Eastern ITCS money. The Lebanese banks were ransacked during the 1975–6 civil war, but the money may well not have been held there – it could have ended up in Abu Dhabi, Paris, Switzerland or more or less anywhere.

The Arab connection, which had provided the hidden agenda behind the disclosure appeal, continued with Maudling in his shadow job. When he was appointed Reggie did warn Thatcher that he might be seen as too pro-Arab, but she brushed this aside by saying that there was also a danger that she could appear to be too pro-Israeli.[26] On the big issue of the conflict between Israel and the Palestinians he was statesmanlike. However, he was again avidly supporting the traditional Arab monarchies, although he avoided speaking about them in the House, mixing political connections with commercial interests. He was still travelling frequently to Saudi Arabia and the Gulf, talking about contracts and giving economic and financial advice, although the exact nature of what was going on is not clear. Reggie devoted two whole pages in his memoirs, rather more than he had given to the 1965 Conservative leadership election, to extolling the merits of Saudi Arabia and various ministers in the Saudi government. Reggie commented that the Saudis 'deserve great admiration for the way they have developed their domestic policy' and 'Certainly the Saudi influence on international affairs has always been a beneficent one'.[27] Democrats and minorities within Saudi Arabia, and Israelis, would find these statements highly objectionable. 'He did suck up to the Arabs, unfortunately,' noted his secretary Viv Walker, 'they were all charming and had so much money.'[28]

Less discreditably, one of Reggie's causes in his shadow office was Rhodesia. The perennial, tangled problem had been getting steadily more brutal throughout the 1970s as guerrilla war and repression escalated. The collapse of the Portuguese colonies of Mozambique and Angola in 1975 had cut off supply lines to the Smith regime and at last they seemed more willing to negotiate. Reggie, while doing his best to preserve Conservative Party unity on the divisive Rhodesia issue, felt he could do something because of his strong relationships with the leaders of independent African countries from his time as Colonial Secretary. In 1976 he started a mission of his own to try to come to an agreement, and felt that his talks in Kenya and Tanzania were promising, but his African trip was aborted when he received a message from Thatcher calling him back to London to attend a futile House of Commons vote. He did as he was told, but he was incandescent with anger at, as he saw it, the destruction of his initiative on something important for such a trivial and party-political reason. It was the only time Robert Shepherd ever saw him in a bad mood, 'white with rage' about Thatcher and Westminster party games.[29] Whether Maudling's mission would have borne fruit is doubtful; it was followed by Henry Kissinger's unsuccessful attempt to do something similar, and it was not until the end of 1976 that Smith at last recognised the principle of majority rule, but he still tried to finesse and delay. The 'internal settlement' with moderate African nationalists of 1978, which created a coalition government, did not stick, although Reggie voted for the first time to lift British sanctions against Rhodesia on the strength of this concession by the regime. It was not enough to satisfy the Labour government, nor indeed its Conservative successor under Thatcher. In 1980 Zimbabwe emerged from the Lancaster House talks, although without the land settlement or constitutional consensus that Maudling had negotiated for Kenya. In perspective, Thatcher's Foreign Secretary, Lord Carrington, thought that 'on Africa Reggie was right, she was wrong. She had never been there and her instinct was to support Smith. After 1979 her brain took over from her gut and it was settled.'[30] Reggie and other members of the foreign affairs team dreaded the possibility that Thatcher's private utterances on the subject of Africa would leak out.[31] Rhodesia, in itself and in Maudling's perception that she would rather play politics than help him work for a settlement, was another issue that divided Thatcher and her Shadow Foreign Secretary.

Thatcher and Maudling were an extraordinarily poisonous and distrustful partnership, even for high-level Conservative politics, where such things are not unknown. The bad relationship was most evident in their attitude to the Cold War. An early sign came in July 1975 with the East–West Helsinki conference on arms reduction and human rights. Thatcher, like many on the right, was in an apocalyptic frame of mind in 1975, having witnessed the fall of Saigon, revolution in Portugal and the post-Watergate uncertainties of American power, and saw 'détente' as little more than appeasement.[32] In a hurriedly arranged speech in Chelsea, written with unofficial adviser Robert Conquest without consulting Reggie or any other member of the Shadow Cabinet, she set out an uncompromising Cold War viewpoint, calling for a military build-up and attacking communism in almost religious terms. Maudling was furious; he went angrily to see Thatcher at home to criticise her speech for its content and for not consulting him before making it.[33]

In Thatcher's sidelining of her official spokesman and reliance on a personal, irregular group of advisers in foreign policy in 1975–6 lay the origins of her style of government that led eventually to the alienation of Nigel Lawson and Geoffrey Howe in 1989–90; Maudling was the first of Thatcher's colleagues to undergo this unpleasant experience. He was also perturbed by Thatcher's refusal to take him with her on foreign visits and not inform him, either beforehand or afterwards, about meetings she was having with foreign leaders.[34] In 1975–6 the Conservatives effectively had two foreign policies, and it was hardly surprising that nobody found this satisfactory.

Further, Reggie was no cold warrior. He and Thatcher both wrote that the essential question was whether the Soviet leaders were engaged in a conspiracy for world domination or whether they were just hidebound and repressive but primarily interested in the welfare of Russia and its people. But they came to opposite conclusions. Thatcher shared the almost theological view current at the time, and given particular intellectual emphasis by Solzhenitsyn, of communism as an implacable and essentially evil system, while Maudling did not.[35] He pointed out in 1977 that 'Lenin did not introduce tyranny in Russia; he merely institutionalised it on the basis of a new dynasty'.[36] When asked in 1973 about the USSR, in a question that mentioned the 20 million casualties of Stalin's purges, Maudling said:

> One cannot underestimate the achievements of the USSR. One is entitled, rightly, to condemn what has happened but one should not underestimate what has been achieved. The people of Russia, the ordinary peasant people, the factory workers in Russia, from what little I have seen of that country, live a happier and better life now than their counterparts fifty years ago.[37]

Reggie believed in the competition of ideas in conditions of peaceful coexistence, and steady pressure on the Soviet bloc to implement the human rights provisions of Helsinki. He was not against military readiness, and even spoke favourably about the CIA, which had recently been in disgrace because of revelations about its role in corruption and assassination,[38] but he was always for a calm, non-dogmatic approach, having confidence that in the end democracy and freedom would prevail. It was Reggie's Hegelian philosophy again – that the Soviet antithesis to capitalism was not capable of prevailing in the world, but that the challenge it represented – of planning and equality – could be absorbed and transcended.[39]

In private Maudling gave the Russians the impression that he had more time for them than he did for Thatcher. In April 1976 Vladimir Semyonov, the minister-counsellor at the Soviet Embassy, had a cordial meeting with the Shadow Foreign Secretary in which Reggie apparently made a series of sympathetic remarks about the current Soviet attitude to Britain. According to the embassy report:

> Maudling said he fully understands and believes that the Soviet Union doesn't threaten British interests. More than that, it is ready to 'take Britain into account' and talk to her [Britain] 'on an equal footing'. He sees genuine evidence that the Soviet Union is not trying to exploit the decline in Britain's role and influence.[40]

He dismissed Thatcher and other cold warriors as people who did not understand contemporary realities and even told the Soviet diplomat, 'I beg you not to take some of our leader's statements seriously', before indicating that he did not expect Thatcher to be leader for very much longer. It was an extraordinarily disloyal performance. In the past Reggie had been very loyal to successive leaders, particularly Heath, but he felt differently about Thatcher.

His hope that she would not be leader much longer was not completely unrealistic in spring 1976, with Labour recovering some ground under a new Prime Minister, Reggie's old sparring partner Jim Callaghan, but over the summer and autumn Thatcher consolidated her position. She grew in confidence about her Cold War foreign policy and her monetarist free market economics, and the political position shifted the balance of power in her favour. As the economic situation deteriorated the Callaghan government's popularity slumped and the Conservatives took a lead of over 20 percentage points in the opinion polls. Reggie was far from indispensable, while Thatcher could mould her team and her policies with a bit more freedom.

The autumn of 1976 was a particularly turbulent time in politics, with sterling sinking fast and the Labour government becoming obliged to apply to the International Monetary Fund for assistance. Given that the government had no majority in the House of Commons, and the Labour Party was bitterly split, it seemed that the government itself might fall apart and the

Conservatives sweep to power in an election early in 1977. Harold Macmillan popped up in October urging the formation of a national coalition government, whose ranks would surely have included Maudling, but this was an impossible scheme in the confrontational politics of 1976. Maudling's performance had been increasingly coming under threat. He narrowly survived the Shadow Cabinet reshuffle in July despite the whips having come to the conclusion that he was dispensable ('good, shrewd, lazy *: Go, but difficult' they noted).[41] Still, over the hot summer of 1976 Reggie had cause to think that a return to power might only be months away. He seemed to be getting clear of the Poulson affair over the summer, as active police investigation tailed off.

In June 1976 the police learned, coincidentally, that Williams was in the south of France and established contact with his solicitor in Geneva. At first, Williams seemed willing to talk but wanted to know what it was about; when Etheridge elaborated and referred to an interview under caution about Gozo, Williams seemed a lot less keen. On 8 August his solicitor informed Etheridge that 'no useful purpose would be served' by meeting.[42] Even if they had managed to interview Williams, he would not have incriminated Maudling, and had his own interests to consider. His case remained on file until after his return to Britain. He was arrested in Bournemouth in June 1981, although the case at Winchester Crown Court in October 1982 collapsed when the alleged offence was ruled to be outside British jurisdiction; Williams denied that the charges were true in any case.[43]

While the possibility of a Gozo prosecution faded, so did the other potential charges against Maudling. The company finance charges were dealt with separately from the corruption charges. The possible charges had been the subject of a continuing argument involving the DTI and the Treasury Solicitor's Department after Cobb and Taylor had reported. Ford's reasoning came under attack from the DTI's in-house lawyers in the winter of 1974–5, who argued that there was either insufficient evidence to prove them, or that they were minor infringements that did not merit bringing a case to court.[44] The lack of a clearly understandable, major charge against Maudling was a problem – particularly as no effort was made to add to Alan Ford's work on violations of company law during the Poulson affair even though it was obvious that something fishy had happened. Sir Basil Hall of the Treasury Solicitor's department wrote in June 1976 that 'while it may become possible for a statement to be made to the effect that there is no evidence that Mr Maudling had been guilty of any corrupt practice, it would not be possible for it to be said that he had committed no impropriety, or even that he had committed no other offence, as director of companies in the Poulson group'.[45]

The matter rested until the corruption investigation had been concluded in July 1976, although no new investigative work was done even at this point. Legal counsel's opinion was finally consulted, although this was more to cover the Attorney General and DPP than to produce new findings, as they agreed with the DTI solicitor's view that charges should not be brought.[46] After a rapid study of the case their counsel, David Smout, QC, tended to agree.

The only point on which Smout thought a case might be brought was over the tax implications of the payment to Maudling in April 1968, and the relevant s.109 report was passed on to the Revenue in 1976, but the Board of Inland Revenue concluded that it did not add anything to what was known about Maudling through the inquiries of Wright and Stratford in 1974 and 'accordingly it is not proposed to bring criminal proceedings against either ITCS or Mr Maudling'.[47] The Inland Revenue is extremely reluctant to prosecute except in the most flagrant and high-value cases where the evader continues to make deceptive statements during the investigation. According to Michael Levi's academic study of fraud:

> The pressure to be cost-effective in the use of resources encourages settlement by the Revenue for less than is owed, so that they can move on to another case. Much of the negotiation in tax cases arises in the context of assessments of how much tax is payable (and how much the Revenue will settle for) rather than in the context of criminal investigation.[48]

Like bankruptcy trustees, the Revenue's purpose in taking action is to recover money rather than to come to a judgement about guilt or responsibility. It would have been easy to prosecute Maudling over the contents of his 1967 and 1968 tax returns but in a situation like this it was usual practice to put pressure on him and reassess his liability rather than drag him through the courts. By 1976 the questions relating to the 1968 directors' fees had been settled, although other matters may well still have been outstanding.[49]

Maudling's pleasant summer – apparent political renaissance and the end of any realistic prospect of a criminal prosecution – came abruptly to an end in October as he was assailed for his lethargy in his front bench job, and a long-buried scandalous letter – with which Reggie had no direct connection – surfaced with explosive consequences. Reggie had an even more unpleasant time at the party conference than normal. He was the target of an outspoken attack from a Harrogate representative, Philip Taylor, who lectured him from the rostrum: 'I openly urge him to play a more prominent and noticeable role in matters of foreign policy. If he does not wish to do this there is the alternative of resignation.' Reggie managed a half-smile at this comment. Reggie's closing speech in the foreign affairs debate was greeted with isolated calls of 'resign' and very perfunctory applause. A Young Conservative leaflet jibed that his term as Shadow Foreign Secretary was a remake of 'The Invisible Man' and criticised him for his 'failure to declare UDI' from the Labour government's foreign policy.[50] On 14 October, after the conference, the right-wing Selsdon Group publicly called for him to be fired.[51] Reggie should have been able to read the signs, but he was unaware, indifferent or preoccupied.

Maudling's new problem on the Poulson front was the report of the Salmon Commission. This was not because the July 1976 Salmon Report itself was gripping stuff, nor because it inquired much into Maudling's conduct. It had been a confusing and unsatisfactory Royal Commission in many ways, set up without a clear remit, and while it had access to various Poulson papers it was not a committee of inquiry into the Poulson affair. When asked what its mission was, Lord Allen (Reggie's former Permanent Secretary at the Home Office) said:

I wish I knew. We had the Redcliffe-Maud working party on corruption in local government, of which I was a member. Just as we were reaching our conclusions Harold Wilson had the idea of setting up a Royal Commission, but we had just done the work! It was the worst Royal Commission I ever sat on. It is a pure accident whether a judge makes a good chairman or a bad one, and Salmon I fear was not a good one. Spent all his time rowing with Douglas Houghton, who thought he ought to have been chairman. I made my maiden speech on the Report in the House of Lords, in a debate that was notable for Douglas Houghton getting up and criticising the chairman. It was really rather a waste of time.[52]

Salmon was dead in the water. It was not even debated in the Commons, because of its own inadequacies and because of the Labour government's discomfort with its subject matter. It was only debated in the Lords because Rab Butler arranged it in order to give the new Lord Allen an opportunity to make a maiden speech, and this debate was enlivened by an open argument between Salmon and Houghton, two of its authors. Its text, however, did contain a number of clues and hints to those who followed the intricacies of the Poulson affair. Dan Smith, adjusting to life in a prison cell in Leyhill after his defeat in a prisoners' council election to a sex offender who ran on the slogan 'Up with the bummer, down with the briber', read it over and noticed that its preamble on Poulson was contradictory. On the one hand, it noted that in 1970 the Chief Inspector of Audit had compiled his dossier of 'detailed and disturbing information, about Poulson, Smith et al.; on the other hand:

We doubt whether Mr Poulson would ever have been prosecuted but for his bankruptcy and his habit of meticulously preserving copies of everything he wrote or was written to him – however incriminating these pieces of paper might be. It is disturbing that, had it not been for the combination of these two factors, Mr Poulson and his accomplices might well still be carrying on their corrupt practices today.[53]

However, what had really exercised the Commission was the position of the MPs who had been involved with Poulson, and the information from the

DPP's office that nothing could be done through the courts about parliamentary corruption. Salmon and Houghton again disagreed about whether the apparent loophole in the corruption law should be closed or whether Parliament itself should deal with allegations against its members. The result was an inconclusive recommendation, seemingly detached from the rest of the report and evidence, to the effect that 'Parliament should consider bringing corruption, bribery and attempted bribery of a Member of Parliament acting in his Parliamentary capacity within the ambit of the criminal law'.[54] The impetus for this was the case of John Cordle, Tory MP for Bournemouth East.

Cordle was a blustering moraliser with an intriguing private life and business links that stretched from West Africa to the Church of England newspaper. His connections in West Africa attracted Poulson, who put him on the payroll for his help to Construction Promotion. In March 1965, after complaints from Poulson about his work rate, Cordle sent the architect a letter cataloguing his efforts, which included the brazen sentence, 'It was largely for the benefit of Construction Promotion that I took part in a debate in the House of Commons on The Gambia and pressed for HMG to award contracts to British firms'. As the Cobb–Taylor opinion of November 1974 commented, 'it would be hard to imagine a clearer admission of improper motive on the part of a Member of Parliament'. But Cordle could still not be prosecuted and there was no sign that anything else would be done officially. Behind closed doors, Lord Salmon had spoken to the Attorney General, Sam Silkin, about the case of John Cordle, and was surprised that it was not referred for parliamentary investigation once the Royal Commission had concluded its work.[55] The Cordle letter had angered and distressed Lord Salmon, who opined that it was such flagrant corruption that it made his hair stand on end.[56] If action had been taken on the Cordle case at this stage, Maudling may well have escaped further inquiry into his actions. A member of the Commission found the thought of Cordle getting away with his outrageous behaviour so unbearable that he sent a copy of the incriminating letter and other documentation in a brown paper parcel to *Observer* journalist Adam Raphael. The result was a splash story on 17 October 'Corruption – 3 MPs escape prosecution'. It was illustrated with a large picture of Reginald Maudling.

The *Observer* piece read very strangely because of the attentions of the newspaper's legal advisers. It pretended that Maudling was not one of the three MPs involved, on the grounds that the police had not concluded the investigation into his case, and the picture was captioned 'No decision yet'. Although they may not have known it, and although the Attorney General untruthfully denied it in the House on 19 October, the Maudling file was indeed still open and remained so until Maudling died. Its open status was reaffirmed at a police–DPP case conference as late as November 1978.[57] Reggie wrote Raphael a stiff, wounded letter and instructed his solicitors Allen & Overy to fire off a writ against the newspaper.[58] The *Daily Mirror*, on the

Wednesday after the *Observer* piece, wrote a much less confused version of the story: 'Three MPs – Shadow Foreign Secretary Reginald Maudling, Tory MP John Cordle and Labour MP Albert Roberts – have already been the subject of a report to the Director of Public Prosecutions. However, no criminal charges have been brought against any MP because of a loophole in the law.'[59] They too received a writ. This brought the total of Reggie's Poulson-related libel actions to three, with the long-running and complicated Granada case continuing in the background. A case against the BBC, brought because journalist Denis MacShane had tried to spice up a phone-in programme by describing Maudling as a 'fat crook', was settled quickly on Reggie's terms, but these others were not so unsupportable or quickly dealt with.

The *Observer* story lit yet another fuse and on Wednesday 20 October there was an almighty row in the House of Commons. Neither Callaghan nor Thatcher had any appetite for an inquiry, or for any debate on Salmon and what Callaghan called its 'obscure recommendation' in the bribery of MPs. In 1975 and 1976 officials had studied the case for a public inquiry into Poulson and corruption in general, but after long, tortuous reasoning decided that there was not a general crisis of confidence that would justify it.[60] The official complacency was challenged by the new Liberal leader, David Steel, and Labour backbencher Dennis Skinner, followed by other MPs and the press, made such a fuss that the government felt obliged to backtrack. In Cabinet the next day the matter was discussed and while a proposal for a full tribunal of inquiry to investigate the whole Poulson affair only attracted two supporters,[61] it was announced in the Commons that after all there would be a Select Committee to examine the conduct of the MPs associated with Poulson. It was established after another debate on 1 November.

Early in November, Reggie could not resist a joke at Thatcher's expense in a Shadow Cabinet meeting. When she expressed doubt about the abilities of the American President-elect Jimmy Carter, Reggie quoted Churchill at her, to the effect that if you feed a grub on royal jelly it becomes a queen bee. She did not find it funny, and Jim Prior felt that Reggie had sealed his fate.[62] Later that month, Thatcher decided to have another reshuffle of her front bench and Maudling was sacked completely rather than just moved to another shadow ministry. Thatcher recalled in her memoirs that:

> Reggie Maudling's performance as Shadow Foreign Secretary had long been a source of embarrassment. He did not agree with my approach to either the economy or foreign affairs; he was increasingly unwilling to disguise his differences with me; and he was laid back. But when I told him that he had to go, he summoned up enough energy to be quite rude. Still, out he went.[63]

Maudling's own account of the meeting is more mannered and evasive. He seemed most affronted about the fact that Thatcher had never expressed any criticism to him directly, before he was sacked, and he refused to write a resignation letter: 'as I had not the slightest desire to resign, I did not see why I should. We then parted with mutual, and I believe sincere, expressions of personal goodwill.'[64] This last sentence was something of a private Maudling joke, as a sincere expression of their mutual feelings would surely have turned the air blue. Maudling was not a bitter or angry man by nature, but his sacking was more than he could bear. As he had done in February 1975, he stomped around Westminster uttering scathing comments about Thatcher and the state of the Tory party. Dripping contempt, he summed up his career as 'hired by Winston Churchill, fired by Margaret Thatcher'. Unlike Thatcher, he could refer to 'Winston' on the basis of actual personal knowledge of the man, and when she took his name in vain Reggie's hackles rose.[65] He regarded her as the least among Churchill's successors and felt humiliated about being dismissed by such a negligible political figure.

The press obituaries on his career were cruel. Andrew Alexander wrote in the *Daily Mail* that 'few political meteors rose so fast: few have fizzled out so pathetically'. His sacking did not generate much of a splash: 'there is nothing so positive about his end. He has merely been "phased out" rather like an abandoned coal mine . . . Good old Reggie was not only indolent he was also, not to put too fine a point on it, greedy. He was greedy but not greedy enough for power.'[66]

However, in truth Maudling was fired not only for his personal failings but also for his belief in consensus politics. His dispute with Thatcher over foreign policy was a manifestation of the fundamental differences in attitude between the two of them, and the change that was taking place in British politics. His strong belief that foreign policy should be, as far as possible, above party politics was becoming unfashionable. The end of Maudling's front bench career represented a new ruthlessness and bitterness, the snapping of many of the threads making up the fabric of British politics. Maudling had always disliked the Labour Party for its excessive concern for the sectional interest represented by the trade unions, and disliked the thought of the Conservative Party abandoning its One Nation ideals to become a sectional party of the middle class or the rich. Within the Labour Party and the government, the IMF crisis had polarised opinion between the pragmatism of Callaghan and Healey, and the socialist fundamentalism of Benn. Crosland's social democracy seemed to have little to add to the debate. Maudling, too, was out of his time, his weary pragmatism swept aside by new Thatcherite certainties.[67] He left in anger at his humiliation, full of foreboding for the future of the Conservative Party and the nation as well as his own.

Chapter 26

OUT TO THE UNDISCOVERED
ENDS, 1976–1979

Maudling's final years in Parliament were a sad time, with the Indian summer of his return to the front bench followed by the onset of a cold winter. At 59, he was very young for an elder statesman, but he had an air of weariness and wisdom that seemed to fit the part. His return to the backbenches after the interlude in Thatcher's Shadow Cabinet was followed by several independent-minded speeches, the first of which was in an economics debate in November 1976. The IMF crisis had reached its terminal stage and the Labour government had agreed a package of cuts that at last stopped the slide in sterling that had been taking place all year. Part of the resolution was also the adoption of published targets for the money supply, a pragmatic concession under pressure towards monetarism that Maudling opposed more strongly than Labour's Chancellor, Denis Healey. There was something glorious in Maudling's completely unreconstructed Keynesian economics, which he developed in a series of speeches. They often attracted approving comment from Labour MPs, the left in particular finding common ground with Maudling in regretting monetarism and retrenchment. After his sacking he was constructing, in his own way, an intellectual case against Thatcherism. Maudling was preparing to be a leading dissenter in the event of her taking power and attempting to implement her economic policy. He looked forward to being proved right about economics, and perhaps even to restoration to power if a Thatcher government fell apart.[1] He was in the sad position of the prophet without honour, or of Cassandra whose warnings were destined never to be listened to.

Maudling's speech in the IMF debate on 30 November was a bold statement of intent. In his Commons speeches after his sacking, he spoke as a more than semi-detached Tory; his tone was more like that of a lone dissident, almost an Independent, even if he was still very much a Conservative in the way he voted. He opened with a deliberately provocative rebuttal of the fashionable ideas that had gained so much ground in the Conservative Party and opinion-forming circles since 1974:

I gather that I have become one of the neo-Keynesians who appear to be rather despised by some individuals. I do not mind being associated with

John Maynard Keynes. After all, he, together with Freud, was one of the great innovative intelligences in this century, just as Hegel was in the last century. If his theories do not wholly apply at present, it is simply because there are new political circumstances which he could not have foreseen. He would have adapted his principles to those circumstances – not deserted them, as they have been deserted by some of those who are so frightened by or so disapproving of modern society that they seek to take refuge in the last century.[2]

No Victorian values for Reggie. This was Reggie almost at his finest; a defiant statement of his consistency, intellectualism and modernity in the face of the takeover of the Tory party by a leader who totally disagreed with him. It is hard to overstate the radicalism of the break from Thatcher, Joseph *et al.*, that he made in this speech. In his comments on the IMF he was even rather to the left of the centre of gravity within the Labour government:

How can anyone, looking at the face of Britain today, argue that we are spending too much? We are no doubt spending unwisely – too much on some things, and too little on others. But, looking at the face of Britain and of our society, can anyone really argue that we are spending too much as a whole? Of course not.[3]

While accepting that there was a case for short-term public spending cuts in the circumstances at the time, he felt that 'the purpose should be to lay the foundations of expansion'. His speech also reflected his essential optimism, which was a contrast to the doom-mongering that was so common on the right of British politics at the time:

I believe that our economic prospects are better than they have been for many a long year if we have the wit to grasp them. We have a substantial amount of spare capacity available. We have a highly competitive currency. We have the signs of a development of international trade. We have the growing substance of North Sea oil. Taking all these things together, what a mark we could make on the world if we could unite to develop and use them. Despite this, all we seem to talk about in public is how much we should cut and how soon.

Economics was not the only subject in which Maudling challenged the front bench Tory line. In December 1976 the Labour government brought forward the Scotland and Wales Bill in an attempt to answer the rise of nationalism in Scotland in particular, which had shaken up British politics in the two elections of 1974. Constitutional change of some sort had been in the wind for some time – actually, since the Scottish Nationalists won the Hamilton by-election in 1967. The Conservatives had pronounced in favour of some sort of devolution in the Declaration of Perth in 1968, and the Royal Commission on the Constitution started under Labour but reported in 1973 under the Tories. Labour performed a U-turn between the elections of 1974 because of the risk that unless there was a gesture towards Scottish self-government the SNP would sweep the party aside. The 1976 Bill was the product of fear in contrast to the long years of planning that lay behind the creation of devolved government in Scotland and Wales in 1997–9. If Labour's motives were not exactly pure, the Conservative front bench were also playing some pretty hard politics – Thatcher changed party policy, shifting against devolution and sacking the most ardent devolutionists from the front bench, but hoping to use the issue to bring down the fragile Callaghan government.

Maudling was not particularly identified with either side of the devolution debate, although in March 1974 he had proposed it as part of the agenda for a consensus government. His December 1976 speech in the Commons admitted a certain amount of ignorance about the subject and a feeling that 'foreigners start slightly to the north of St. Albans'. But Maudling could be at his best when approaching a subject from first principles. He observed that 'devolution' was a matter of degree rather than kind – that there is always some level of devolved decision-making in any system and it is a question of 'how much to devolve, in what circumstances, and to whom'. He had no particular objection to the Scots running their affairs, on two conditions:

> First, they must not present us with the bill. If they want to run their own affairs, they must pay for it. That is fair enough. Second, if in Scotland they want to run their own housing, industry and social services, they cannot run ours as well. If it should be decided that the Scottish dimension in these matters should be independent or devolved, why should not the English dimension equally be devolved?[4]

Perhaps one should really talk about the 'Chipping Barnet Question' rather than the West Lothian Question, but Maudling at least was intellectually interested in finding an answer rather than using it as a pretext to derail the devolution proposals. He, correctly, doubted that the official Conservative line of favouring a Scottish committee within and subject to Westminster was going to be enough to meet Scottish aspirations. Maudling made two prescient and entirely justified comments about the Labour government's Bill. 'My main objection is the inclusion of Wales with Scotland, thereby making the Bill a dog's breakfast. Surely different considerations apply.' The Labour government realised the force of this objection during the next year as the Scotland and Wales Bill was bogged down in Parliament and finally defeated on a procedural vote about precisely this issue. Maudling also believed that it was 'extremely important to try to obtain a more definite appreciation of what the Scottish people really want when they know what they are being given as a choice. I am coming more and more to the view that some form of referendum is necessary.' In 1978 separate Acts for Scotland and Wales were passed, with provision for referendums. A lot of time and effort could have been saved if Maudling's reasonable observations had been taken on board.

There is no sign that Reggie's financial affairs took much of a turn for better or for worse after his 1976 sacking. He was still involved in business in the Arab world, travelling to Saudi Arabia in January 1977. 'I wish I could declare an interest,' he told the Commons when he returned, 'I have been trying my best to promote British exports there but without much success so far.'[5] It is not clear which projects he was promoting in Saudi Arabia, but he expressed interest in the same speech in 'jumbo projects', presumably like the King Faisal Hospital.

Not particularly remunerative, nor much of a substitute even for a shadow job but a mild diversion during some unpleasant times, was the process of writing his memoirs. In February 1977 Reggie went out to lunch with Lord Longford, in the latter's capacity as the chairman of the publishers Sidgwick & Jackson. Over some fine claret (Rausan-Ségla 1962, Reggie recalled), the publishers offered him a contract. Reggie was a bit reluctant, but was persuaded that the opportunity for self-expression was reason enough to write, and duly signed.[6] His secretary, Viv Walker, helped with research and typing up. For the most part the memoirs were written as they read, a story told by a pleasant old boy in a comfortable armchair with a stiff drink in his hand. Viv Walker sat with him, taking notes as he spoke, and Caroline did a little research where it was required. Viv Walker remembers:

> He did quite enjoy writing them. He did it without drafts – he would write some words on a piece of paper and then just pour it out. He was capable of working at a very high level right until the end. He wanted to call the book 'Laughter and the Love of Friends' but the publisher would not let him as it sounded too frivolous.[7]

While life went on, the Select Committee on the Poulson affair went about its work in conditions of some secrecy until the report was ready. It was an unsatisfactory process in many ways, with the MPs involved having to try to get a grip on an enormous mass of material on their occasional days in session without much by way of expert assistance. It was to be chaired by Michael Stewart, the former Labour Foreign Secretary (1965–6, 1968–70). Stewart was a very establishment choice for the role, a cautious, senior Privy Councillor and someone who, like Maudling, believed in consensus in foreign policy; also like Maudling, Stewart was past his best by 1976 and his effectiveness was reduced by alcohol. The rest of the committee was, even more than the House of Commons in general, top-heavy with barristers. The most active questioners were Labour's Max Madden, a journalist, and the Liberal QC Emlyn Hooson, who had inspired the 1972 Liberal motion on corruption and had been a critic of Jeremy Thorpe's dubious activities.

Immediately after the formation of the Select Committee the solicitors for the bankruptcy trustees came forward offering all sorts of help, including their network maps of the Poulson operation, indexes and guidance notes to the vast Poulson archive and names of helpful individuals. Alan Ford, the author of the DTI reports, Leslie Clarkson of the Official Receiver's Department ('we venture to suggest that no inquiry would be complete without reference to him'), and Alan Wright of the Inland Revenue special investigation, were suggested as being people with whom the committee should talk, and indeed a meeting was held with Ford and Clarkson and the secretary-designate of the committee at the end of November 1976. The bankruptcy trustees clearly hoped that the Select Committee would undertake a wide-ranging inquiry into Poulson that would prove a substitute for the tribunal of inquiry that had been repeatedly refused since 1969, and pointed out that no investigation to date could be regarded as complete. 'We should tell you that whilst many investigations into Mr Poulson's affairs have overlapped there has been no overall investigation, only a series of investigations by the various Departments concerned, each for their separate purpose and of necessity limited to some extent to separate areas.' The clearest possible hint was given that the overseas activities of ITCS and Maudling were deserving of particular attention from the committee: 'Indeed we think even now that the Trustee and his advisers are the only ones conversant with Mr Poulson's activities abroad in any detail. These have never been investigated by anyone other than the Trustee and they could well be relevant to your purpose.'

This, in November 1976, was an astonishing admission that the truth about the Poulson affair had not come out, and that nobody had even properly looked at one of its most serious aspects except with a view to recovering money for the Poulson creditors. It does not appear to have been seriously followed up by the Select Committee. Neither Ford nor Clarkson were called before the committee. After a scan through the transcripts of the private hearings, the Treasury Solicitor's envoy asked for copies of some of them, though strangely the Sweetman hearing was not among them, and nor was the Civil Service Department asked to provide its evidence, including the 'my immediate cash requirements' letter which had been on file for four and a half years.[8] These may well have been honest errors from an overworked government lawyer.[9] The stopped section of the Maudling transcript concerning Tajir was a delicate matter – the Attorney General had to 'explain the situation to the committee'. A signal was given, early on, that the Dubai connection was off-limits, and it attracted only the most fleeting references in Maudling's interview with the committee. Tajir's name was actually suppressed from the transcript when Reggie was questioned about his September 1967 expenses claim.[10]

The time allowed to the committee was short and discontinuous – meetings were usually fortnightly on Tuesdays. The MPs lacked time, had no investigative support and no counsel to the inquiry to assist in asking questions. The office of the Attorney General, Labour's Sam Silkin (who had refused to prosecute the three Poulson MPs in 1975), took an active part in steering the committee, and the Treasury Solicitor's Department handled liaison with the bankruptcy trustees. The MPs were given briefing notes by the Attorney General's office when they interviewed some of those involved, and these notes were basic indeed. Some of the questioning revealed startling ignorance about even the best-established facts of the Poulson affair.[11] The inquiry was quickly diverted along well-worn tramlines – the local government network in Britain and the Gozo hospital.

The main hearings of oral evidence began at the very end of December 1976. The parliamentary committee questioned very few witnesses. The first was Ken Etheridge, who with a colleague appeared to answer questions solely about a forged DPP memorandum from 1973 in which several – innocent – Labour MPs were named. Having cleared this up, Etheridge does not seem – unless the transcripts were censored – to have been asked about the Maudling corruption and false accounting investigations he had painstakingly conducted. When Poulson was summoned in January 1977, for some reason he failed to mention many of the allegations he had made against Maudling in his bankruptcy hearings and police interviews in 1972–4, and the MPs – if they had read the transcripts – did not press him. Dan Smith was also questioned, as were the three accused MPs and two former MPs (John Binns and Ted Short, now Lord Glenamara) who were not censured in the report.

Reggie himself appeared before the committee on 22 March 1977, only a day before a no-confidence motion was due to go before the House of Commons. Westminster was buzzing with rumours about what might happen. The Labour government had no overall majority and if the opposition parties united – and it looked as if they might – an election might be called immediately. With an election, the Select Committee's work would lapse. Labour ministers were in anxious talks to strike a deal with the Liberals, which in the end proved successful and prolonged the government's life by two years. With the best will in the world, the MPs could be forgiven for not having their minds completely on the Poulson affair that day. Reggie was questioned for two hours, with the MPs concentrating on the Adeline Genée covenant and the other payment he had received from Poulson, and they did manage to get a fairly clear picture of the relationship between the Maudling family finances and Poulson. They also probed on the Gozo hospital contract. After this, they had little time to get involved in the other aspects of the Poulson affair, still less the complexities of the ITCS accounts – that baffled experienced, full-time investigators who had years to look at them – or the sensitive Middle East business which the Attorney General had indicated was not something they should examine. Reggie easily stonewalled with flat denials the few questions he faced about whether there had been any bribery in overseas contracts, and the matter was not pursued. Yet in his July 1973 bankruptcy examination, to which the committee had supposedly been given access, he more or less admitted that Poulson was not unfamiliar with giving bribes, and if they had reconstructed the 'green light' correspondence on Dubai airport Reggie could have been asked some difficult questions. In the end, as he often did, he charmed his interrogators and he escaped, having apparently given a good account of himself, even though he had compounded his parliamentary offences by misleading the committee.

The Select Committee report was published on 14 July 1977. It was harshest about John Cordle. The evidence against him, in the form of the notorious letter to Poulson listing his dubious activities in the House, was open and shut. The committee had found that he had been guilty of conduct amounting to 'a contempt of the House',[12] a much more serious matter than the criticisms made of Roberts and Maudling. What the report failed to note about Cordle was that he had the extraordinary chutzpah to threaten to sue Poulson in 1967 to remain on a £1,000 a year retainer right up to 1970; Poulson's solicitor advised him that Cordle had been extremely cunning in framing his letters acknowledging receipt of Poulson's money in such a way as to set up such an obligation.[13] Small wonder that Poulson blurted out in the bankruptcy hearing that he considered himself to have been conned by the smooth Tory MP.

John Cordle initially tried to suggest that he had been vindicated by the report, and that he would remain in Parliament to defend himself and argue his case, but over the next couple of days it became clear that he had very little support even from his Tory colleagues. Cordle was a man with an unsavoury private life about whom none other than John Poulson said that he had 'low morals'. He had launched an attack on John Profumo after Profumo had admitted his offence and resigned. Cordle was sanctimonious, unpopular, hypocritical and obscure. The Conservative whips were increasingly conscious that if Cordle tried to hang on through the debate on the report, many of their MPs would probably stay away, having the stomach neither to vote to expel Cordle nor to uphold him as a fit person to serve in Parliament. A mass Tory stay-away would be bad news for Maudling. In a meeting of the 1922 Committee on 21 July there was concern that if Cordle were only reprimanded it would fuel public cynicism, while two Labour MPs suggested that it might be possible under the rules of Parliament to imprison Cordle in a cell at the foot of the clock tower of Big Ben.[14] The next day, Cordle gave in to the pressure and decided to resign his seat.[15] He made a resignation speech to a nearly empty House before walking from the Chamber for the last time, tearful and propped up by two fellow MPs. Cordle the perfect scapegoat walked into the wilderness bearing the sins of his colleagues. It was a wretched, embarrassing occasion, but Cordle had served as the lightning rod for MPs' fickle sense of parliamentary honour. The passion was spent.

The cases of the other two were more complicated. The committee was not particularly harsh about Albert Roberts, whose activities for Poulson were at least related to a constituency interest. Roberts, while an odd and not particularly popular Labour MP for his pro-Franco activities, had more friends than Cordle. He represented a significant demographic among Labour MPs – a rather reactionary mining representative muttering into his pint of Federation bitter – which the Labour whips needed to keep marching obediently through the division lobbies in order to sustain the government in office. Roberts also managed to give quite a convincing account of himself in response to the committee report, apologising for 'transgressing in the shallow waters' and complaining with some justice that MPs were never given much guidance on what the rules actually were. Roberts could stay, and was re-elected as MP for Normanton in 1979.

The crux of the report was its verdict on Maudling. While he was cleared of knowledge of the Abela bribe, and the committee accepted his assurances that he had looked into Poulson before joining him and did not know of irregularities in the companies, they did find matters of concern. One was the general question of the interests of shadow ministers, on which it noted that Maudling was not in a unique position; another was that in the case of the February 1967 Malta debate: 'Your committee are satisfied that if the House had, shortly after the speech had been made, become aware of the facts, they would have taken the view that a declaration ought to have been made; and to this extent Mr Maudling was at fault.' It drew attention to the 'close chronological interlocking of actions by Mr Poulson on behalf of the Theatre Trust and actions by Mr Maudling in the House and contacts with the Maltese Government and senior British officials which were to the benefit of Mr Poulson'. It also criticised his July 1972 resignation letter, which Edward Heath had read to the House, as 'lacking in frankness' and 'inconsistent with the standards which the House is entitled to expect from its Members'.[16] No particular penalty was recommended. The report's findings on Maudling were certainly critical, but they stopped well short of categorising him with Cordle. MPs since have survived worse, and Reggie could have lived with the mild rebuke for his February 1967 speech, but he read the criticism of his resignation letter with 'astonishment and disbelief . . . It was a bitter and wounding blow.'[17] Reggie therefore decided that the verdict of the Select Committee should be challenged, an extremely rare move in respect of an all-party, unanimous report. His cause received influential support from Conservative barristers Derek Walker-Smith and Peter Rawlinson at the 1922 Committee meeting on 21 July,[18] and after the disposal of Cordle there was clearly an undercurrent of sympathy for Maudling and a desire to make the issue go away. A temporary suspension, which had seemed a real option on Friday, had ceased to appear likely by Monday.[19] On the morning of Tuesday 26 July, the day of the debate, the *Daily Mail* reported that 'Last night Commons bars and restaurants were seething with arguments on whether one of the great hero figures of Westminster should be punished at all'.[20]

The House of Commons was at its worst in the much anticipated debate on the report of the Select Committee. Considering that this was supposed to be the High Court of Parliament, a substitute for the rigours of a criminal prosecution, which would have been the lot of ordinary citizens who had behaved in a similar way, it was a pathetic failure. Few MPs had read or understood the Select Committee report, or knew much about Poulson. The debate took place at an unpromising time, a summer evening near the end of term, when the charms of the bar and the terrace were even more winning than usual. It started with personal statements by the MPs concerned, namely Maudling and Roberts.

Reggie stated, once again, his version of events regarding Poulson, downplaying his involvement and stating that one police interview concerning the Malta bribe was all he had heard from either the police or the DTI during the Poulson investigations. 'This, I suggest, is a certain measure of the degree to which I was involved in the affairs of Mr Poulson,' he said, although it was more a measure of the care with which the DTI and the police proceed against such eminent people, and the curtailing of the DTI investigation in 1974. He welcomed the Select Committee's finding that rejected a charge of corruption, but gave his objections to the criticisms the Committee had made of him. He concluded: 'I am confident that the House will accept that what I have said is the truth, the whole truth and nothing but the truth, and that now for the first time the House has before it the facts upon which to reach a judgment.'[21] As was the custom, Reggie then withdrew from the Chamber, although at the end of his speech he expressed regret that others would then have the opportunity to criticise him without rebuttal. He went to the tea room and approached Leo Abse, the Labour MP and psychoanalyst:

> I felt sorry for his predicament. He was utterly amazed, bemused by the fact that he should be condemned. There was no anger expressed at what was done to him; no contriteness either. He was just bewildered at being criticised. He said the House of Commons is a strange place that they should do this to him. He did ask 'how can they behave like this to me?'[22]

Abse, who generally took the view that there was no point being an MP and not voting in Commons divisions, could not bring himself to condemn Reggie, and nor could many others. While Reggie was out of the Chamber, two Tory MPs had piped up and asked the Speaker to allow Maudling (and Roberts, who spoke after him) to return to the Chamber and hear the debate, and amid cries of 'Hear hear!' Speaker George Thomas overrode the customary practice and let them back in.

It fell to Michael Foot, as Leader of the House, to introduce the report. He did so with a heavy heart. Foot had a kind and gentle, even indulgent, nature. His instinct was always to understand rather than condemn. Very early in his parliamentary career he (like Reggie from his vantage point at the Research Department) had witnessed the 1948–9 Board of Trade scandal, in which a junior minister, John Belcher, had been harshly pilloried for minor misjudgements in a tribunal of inquiry. While Reggie had been censorious, Foot was one of the few MPs who spoke up for Belcher in the debates of 1949. The misery inflicted on poor Belcher, and the damage caused to the government by a whirlwind of rumour and innuendo, had made Foot most reluctant to see anything like this happening again. 'Sometimes the scare and mood becomes so, so poisoned that individuals suffer great injustices, and that's why some of us were not in favour of having all these questions, because we thought that a lot of innocent people got caught up with the guilty.'[23] Foot, in the one resonant phrase uttered that day, warned that 'the House of Commons has occasionally in the past operated a liberal form of lynch law. It can act as a mob, and of all mobs the most objectionable is a sanctimonious mob.' His message was that 'I believe the House of Commons can combine to act firmly but with forbearance and that the best way to do this is to accept the unanimous Report of the Select Committee, but to carry the matter no further than that'.

A peculiar aspect of the July 1977 debate was that Foot was cast in the role of prosecuting counsel. Some Labour MPs wished to suspend or expel Maudling, but these amendments stood no chance of passage and so the key vote of the evening was on the right-wing Conservative Ronald Bell's amendment to 'take note of' rather than 'agree with' the report's findings on Maudling. After Foot's highly equivocal argument for the report, Bell made an eloquent case that the Select Committee's condemnation of Maudling was sufficiently flawed to vote against it with clear conscience. Maudling and Bell had a good argument that the criticism of his letter of resignation lacked natural justice. Even if the criticism of the resignation letter was justified, it was certainly a procedural error to fail to question Maudling about it when he appeared before the committee. It falsified the statement in the report that 'no new evidence or accusation emerged that was not fully described and put to the Members concerned during their evidence'.[24] While the resignation letter was certainly not a complete picture of Maudling's links with Poulson, it did not entirely purport to be either, as it was a response to the 5 July Liberal motion and the decision to call in the Metropolitan Police. A simple statement of why Maudling felt unable to continue in government was all that was needed for the purpose, particularly as he had already given a longer (although also highly selective) public statement on 3 July. If writing a resignation letter that could legitimately be described as 'lacking in frankness' was a serious parliamentary offence, few resigning ministers could escape censure. Thanks to Norman Fowler's own – no doubt frank and complete – explanation in 1990 that he wanted to spend more time with his family, we now even have a stock phrase for such occasions.

The other criticism, for failing to declare his interest in Malta, was also flawed, but at least did not lack an element of natural justice. Maudling had tried to cover himself retrospectively with his letter from Lord Maybray-King, and from that and the Select Committee's opinion it seems clear that while Reggie had fallen below the standards expected, it was perhaps not a grave or even unusual event for the time. This is not to question the Cobb–Taylor opinion of his conduct as reprehensible, nor quibble with the Select Committee's description of the interlocking pattern of his actions, speeches and reward over Malta; it is to point out that it was selective enforcement which on this occasion went against Reggie. As Reggie himself had put it to the Committee when he gave evidence, 'I can give you many previous Prime Ministers who have been chairmen and directors of businesses for business with overseas Governments and who have not in any way felt inhibited in taking part in foreign policy debates or making comments on those policies.'[25] If the conduct of others had been scrutinised as intensely as Reggie's Malta activities in early 1967 had been, it may well have been found just as wanting. While 'but they're all at it' is a poor defence in law, it has its merits in a political tribunal such as the Select Committee and, even more so, the House of Commons. The vote on the report in any case took the two counts against Reggie together, so if either one fell the whole verdict was in question. It looked like, and was, a matter of the Committee reaching to find something to say against Reggie without being willing to engage in the really damaging stuff.

Reggie had decided that if the House agreed with the report, he would resign his seat and leave politics at once.[26] But the tide in his favour that had been flowing since the weekend after the report was still coming in during the debate. Francis Pym and Derek Walker-Smith argued against approving the report's criticisms of Maudling, while Emlyn Hooson in defending the report faced barracking from Tory MPs. Edward Heath made a particularly telling intervention, dismissing the criticism of the resignation letter: 'If I had believed for one moment that that letter of resignation sent to me as Prime Minister by the Home Secretary contained anything of any kind which was in the least untrue or inadequate for the purpose, I should not have accepted the letter.' Heath closed his speech, 'I believe that my right honourable Friend is an honourable man and that he should be supported.' Maudling was deeply grateful for Heath's speech, which may well have tipped the balance.[27]

After Michael Foot had wound up for the report, and Patrick Cormack had said a few words for the 'take note' amendment, the House divided in a tense vote. Maudling waited, inwardly anxious, for the declaration, and to his relief the 'take note' amendment was passed by 230 votes to 207. Some Labour MPs were angry. George Strauss, the Father of the House, believed that there had been an unofficial 'Save Reggie' whip applied on the Conservative side, and former Home Office minister Alex Lyon made a point of order about this after the vote. The vote was nearly along party lines, with only eleven Tories voting against Reggie[28] and twelve Labour and one Liberal voting for him.[29] Having decided this way on Maudling, many Labour MPs saw no reason to let the verdict on Roberts stand and the report as it affected him was 'taken note of' rather than 'agreed with' by 288 votes to 144. Journalists who had followed the case and were watching from the gallery reacted with disgust and believed that a high proportion of those voting were 'totally pissed', in the jaundiced view of the *Mirror*'s Richard Stott.[30] The last word in the House that day went to Labour MP Martin Flannery, who asked the Speaker, 'Would it be possible for the two Front Benches to get together and ask the former Member for Bournemouth East, Mr Cordle, to come back and tell him all is forgiven?'

Nothing good came of the Select Committee or the debate. It was a chance for the exercise of justice with mercy, but in the end neither was achieved. It could have been an opportunity to establish some ground rules for public life, so that nobody could again claim like Roberts to have been confused about some basic principles of how to behave in Parliament. Perhaps inevitably in a parliamentary vote, there were other considerations than justice to the accused at work. The most censorious were partisans of the Labour left – like the genuinely incorruptible Dennis Skinner – who felt that capitalist morality of any sort was oxymoronic. Their puritanical view was a repudiation of everything about Reggie, not just his Malta speech or his resignation letter. If Roberts, a man for whom they had little time, was the price of bringing down Reggie, so be it. But in general the mood in the middle ground was like that of Leo Abse who, without knowing the details, was aware that Reggie had transgressed but had no desire to humiliate him.

Maudling's amiability has a lot to answer for. The lack of appetite for condemnation of a much-loved man like Reggie, who was already suffering self-inflicted torments, was one of the reasons for this public failure to keep Parliament's own house in order. After the 1977 debate it was clear that not only was parliamentary corruption not punishable in the criminal courts but, unless someone happened to be already personally unpopular and on record admitting in explicit terms that he was motivated by improper considerations (as Cordle had done in the letter to Poulson), Parliament would do nothing either. It was a lesson that ambitious Tories on the make, in the permissive climate of the 1980s, took to heart. Maudling's offences against the rules of Parliament were not trivial ones, and deserved some element of censure, but they were certainly less serious than some that went unpunished before him (like Boothby's corruption) or the 'cash for questions' scandal that followed.

The Select Committee report had also done investigative journalism a great disservice. By its feeble and inconclusive response, Parliament had thrown up an obstacle to the courts taking anything that looked like a different decision in the *Granada* and *Mirror* libel cases that were still pending; the legal situation became even more complicated. A botched inquiry was worse than nothing at all. At this point, Reggie had the opportunity of pulling out and declaring victory – he could have abandoned the libel actions, probably claiming some costs in the process, and announced that the House of Commons had cleared his name.

However, despite the damage it might have done to the libel defendants (and Ray Fitzwalter and Richard Stott revile the committee with passion to this day), it did not actually offer much consolation to Reggie. It was another step towards personal destruction. He was, as Leo Abse observed, genuinely bewildered to find himself in the dock. The Select Committee from start to finish had been 'hateful' for him.[31] He had some hopes after the vote, which could be presented as an exoneration, of being restored to front bench office but he had no realistic chance of this. What hopes he may have held out disappeared when he read the weekend press, which had briefings obviously inspired by Thatcher and her allies that there was no way back. While – of course – any connection with the Poulson affair was disclaimed, the discontent that the party and its leader felt with his performance in the Shadow Cabinet was enough reason. A senior Tory told the *Sunday Telegraph* that 'there is no way in which I can see him again becoming a major figure in the party'.[32]

Despite his faults, public service was very important to Reggie's character and he was mortified to be told, so soon after his brutal sacking from the front bench, that there was indeed no future for him in politics. It was a death sentence; Ken Williams, his comrade from the Poulson time, felt that Maudling was effectively murdered in a campaign of character assassination,[33] a view that attracted some sympathy among loyal friends of Reggie. It was another turn of the ratchet of Reggie's constantly increasing tendency towards excessive drinking, which had taken a drastic turn since the investigations of 1974. His last years were sad and lonely. He was aimless, bored and depressed, drinking himself distractedly towards oblivion at receptions and in the bars of the House of Commons night after night.

Reggie was a disappointed, unhappy man who had known triumph for most of his life but had more recently endured mortifying defeat and humiliation. When his old deputy John Boyd-Carpenter ran into him at a party and asked routinely how he was, Reggie sighed, 'Not well, bored, frustrated'.[34] His career had collapsed, he was short of money, and Beryl could no longer protect him. She was sliding into alcoholism even faster than he was, appearing obviously drunk at constituency events and in the presence of journalists. As Reggie's life crumbled so did Beryl's dreams of social success and opulent living. Although she loved him as much as ever, her own anger and frustration boiled over into ferocious recriminations against him and even occasional physical violence. She would throw things at him and even hit him.[35] Reggie took it all, stolidly, sadly, calmly.

Reggie was also, mortifyingly, taken less seriously than he should have been as an elder statesman in the House of Commons. His later speeches are better known for an interjection by Dennis Skinner than for their content.

Reggie was returning to a point he often made about the need for higher productivity in British industry: 'it takes a German worker one day and a half to build a car, whereas it takes his British equivalent more than three days,' at which point Skinner chipped in 'An' 'ow long would it tek *you*, fats?'[36]

It was, in its brutal way, an appropriate question. In his public utterances Maudling often urged self-discipline, restraint, hard work and deferred gratification, qualities that he conspicuously lacked in his own life. But it would be a crude reading to see this as hypocrisy. The psychological mechanism of projection, in which undesirable characteristics of the self are attributed to others, was at work. Maudling's exhortations were unconsciously self-directed. Speaking in November 1977, Maudling talked in terms that suggest his attitudes to his own career and the British economy were closely entangled:

There is not enough will in this country to be efficient. There is not enough regard for competence and efficiency at all levels. There is not enough desire to make things work well. Such attitudes have been eroded over many years, for many social and political reasons. We cannot get back to the sort of prosperity we should enjoy unless we can restore the right sense of ethos and of purpose and a desire to get results. It could all be done so easily. In a matter of one or two years, this country could be infinitely more prosperous and happy than it is today. Cannot Parliament, management and unions together try to find the answer?[37]

The hope that a psychological change in British attitudes, plus tripartite talks, could improve the situation was not unreasonable but the idea that infinite prosperity and happiness were only a couple of years away was obviously excessive. But for Maudling himself, his own inefficiency and distraction from 'the right sense of ethos and purpose' had eroded his position from rising star to burnt-out case within twenty years.

However, even as a broken man, Maudling could still command reserves of intellectual power, human warmth and even dignity. He read as widely as ever, and developed a strong appreciation for poetry, particularly Robert Graves. He was a model grandfather to Caroline's daughter, Melissa, who came to look upon him as a father figure. He gave her 'a hundred per cent sense of security and safety . . . he seemed to be a solid oak tree' when he was with her, a stable presence for her; his masculine scent of Brylcreem and cigar smoke a source of comfort. He impressed her as a man who cared about justness, about what was right and wrong, and was kind and generous with gifts and his time. When he returned to Essendon at weekends he would take the little girl for walks in Brookmans Park, talking or just thinking and looking around as they walked.[38] Given all Maudling's own problems, his gentle and loving presence in the life of his granddaughter shows great strength and something essentially decent that could not be washed away by drink or despair.

Maudling was also, Dennis Skinner notwithstanding, still capable of making a fine Commons speech and standing up for what he believed in. He would appear at every budget debate with some elegantly crafted, unrepentantly Keynesian analysis of Denis Healey's latest measures. The economic circumstances of the late 1970s being what they were, sound budgets resembled London buses, in that one could wait years and then three would come along in short succession. From Reggie's standpoint, Healey's policies after the IMF crisis were about right: 'After 10 or 11 boss shots, it is about time he did. It almost restores one's faith in the law of averages, but not quite.'[39] Reggie had more sympathy for critics from the left such as Eric Heffer than those of the free market right. He sympathised with Healey's 'pink monetarism' of 1976–9: 'The Chancellor of the Exchequer makes obeisance towards the money supply myth. He makes the appropriate remarks, but this afternoon I did not think that he believed in it. He is far too wily.' In April 1978 he mocked the monetarist theories of his front bench, saying that 'To try to regulate the economy by changing the money supply is like trying to regulate the speed of a motorcar by twisting the needle on the speedometer'.[40] In the early 1980s 'wet' ministers would make genteel coded speeches, but no senior Tory, not even Edward Heath, was as early or as direct as Maudling.

Maudling's speeches were rather out of step with the general tone of the economic debates. He frequently looked wistfully back to his time as Chancellor, blaming the 1964 election result and the premature end of his experiment for most of Britain's economic woes. He was wryly envious of the Labour government's luck in enjoying the bonus of North Sea Oil: 'If in 1963 or 1964 we had had but one of the major oilfields now available to this country our whole subsequent economic and political history would have been different, and I believe much more satisfactory to the general public.' To Reggie, the conditions in the late 1970s were shaping up for another determined attempt to break through the barrier that had defeated his and Barber's efforts in the past.[41] Reggie rather approved of Healey's 1978 Budget, although he regretted that Healey's political style was not more like his own: 'Why does he always hide his natural intelligence in a desire to be combative and controversial? He can talk sense if he tried. Why does he not try to do so a little more often?'[42] Reggie suggested that he might have failed to support Conservative amendments, but, as he tended to in this part of his life, he did not have all the courage of his convictions. He was being, at least in the division lobbies, a good party man regardless of his contempt for those in charge of it, and he would make the occasional speech such as one on 8 June 1978 in which he referred to supporting 'our friends' in Africa, terms at which his liberal admirers would wince.

In Maudling's penultimate Commons speech, which had a strange visionary quality, he at last committed himself on the great issue of European unity. The Conservative opposition were criticising the Labour government's decision to stay out of the exchange rate mechanism of the European Monetary System, the newly devised attempt to control the parities of European currencies with each other. This was familiar territory to Reggie, and in contrast to the party line he thought Britain was best staying out. 'If the bus is doomed to run into a lamp-post, I would rather miss it,' he commented, evoking one of his favourite cartoons that depicted his 1958 European negotiations crashing into a De Gaulle-shaped lamp-post. The others could go ahead and we could go in at the right time, which would be later. In a sense, it was a classic example of the awkward partner mentality that dogged Britain's relations with Europe. But Reggie was actually making a different point. He always believed that economics was subordinate to politics, and felt that monetary integration, even a single currency, should flow from political integration rather than coming before it. Pressed by Enoch Powell and Nicholas Ridley during his speech on whether such integration was desirable, Reggie conceded that 'Yes, of course. I want to see European unity, but I want it to grow organically out of the reality of the economy rather than have it imposed by some system which will break down in the process.' In the meantime, there were practical problems arising from sterling's role as a reserve currency and the large amounts traded on world markets, which Reggie feared could destabilise the system. And so it proved when Britain finally joined the ERM in 1990, at the wrong time and the wrong rate. Reggie's combination of practical scepticism and, after a long time wavering, idealistic aims, were all too rare in the 1980s and 1990s.[43]

Maudling's *Memoirs* were published in June 1978. The book is an attractive record of his life in many ways: lacking in malice, open-minded and studded with appealing stories not always told to Reggie's advantage. It is the book of a raconteur rather than a historian; Reggie conceded that 'what I have to say will be impressionistic and selective. It may well at times be inaccurate, though I have done my best to avoid that where I can.'[44] At times, the memoirs are infuriatingly bland and elusive, particularly about Poulson, Hoffman and above all Tajir and Miller, who do not appear within its pages. Strangely, the Adeline Genée Theatre appears in the index but not in the published text.[45] On his business life, the book was not an honest settling of accounts, but it was more candid than many political memoirs about his experiences on the way up the greasy pole. He had the ability, like Rab Butler, of conveying a great deal through apparently casual asides, such as the revealing description of Margaret Thatcher as 'Selsdon Woman', and his very human recollections of Winston Churchill. His observations have often proved too good for historians not to quote, even if the book as a whole is rather light. It is also the book of a public man. Reggie did not write much about his parents, and kept Beryl and his own children out of it as far as he could, commenting that 'some things matter too deeply to parade them in print'.[46]

The reviews of *Memoirs* were generally mildly positive, if puzzled. Most commented on the book's rather bumbling narrative style, either with some affection like Janet Morgan or with vitriol as in a vindictive piece by Christopher Hitchens.[47] One particularly perceptive review was by John Mortimer in the *Sunday Times*, which noted that 'He is very pleased with a cartoon which shows him removing a blandly smiling mask to reveal an identical blandly smiling face. How many masks are there to go before we encounter the grimace of agony, or is he, and this is what gives the book its curiously eerie quality, the same all the way through like the skins of an onion?'[48] The eerie blankness of *Memoirs* arises from its failure to deal with his life behind the public masks – the Hegelian extreme moderate behind the mask of the clever pragmatist, in turn behind the mask of lazy goodwill, are all revealed. There is a glimpse, if one is aware enough to see it, of Reggie the drinking man, and even of Reggie the adopted Arab. But of Reggie the rejected son, the faithful husband, the cynic, the amoral man of business, there is no sign.

The *Memoirs* represented how Reggie wished to be remembered, but there were several hurdles left to overcome before he had finally buried the Poulson affair, and more questions over his business activities. Sir Eric Miller was found in his garden, dead of gunshot wounds, on 22 September 1977, the Day of Atonement. He and Maudling were not as close as they had been, although Maudling had been put on the Peachey payroll in 1972; with the return to power of Harold Wilson in 1974 Miller cultivated his Labour connections more avidly and received his reward in Wilson's 1976 resignation honours list, one of the most off-colour knighthoods of the infamous 'lavender list'. He did still see Maudling from time to time, at least once flying him off to Paris for lunch for no apparent reason,[49] but he lavished most attention on Wilson's Political Secretary, Marcia Falkender. In the last few years of his life Miller had developed some extremely unpleasant associations with people such as the intimidating 'financier' Judah Binstock and allegedly even the American mafia moneyman Meyer Lansky. Miller was spending money from the Peachey company account in a pathological spiral of fraud and excess until it eventually came crashing down. The Peachey board fired Miller and a Department of Trade investigation into his management was ordered in April 1977. He killed himself shortly before the DTI Inspectors were due to call. Reggie did not attend the funeral, saying that nobody had told him about it.[50] The inspectors interviewed Maudling, and recalled him as a cooperative witness who seemed to have nothing to hide,[51] and their report published in January 1979 cleared Reggie of any wrongdoing in relation to Peachey.[52] However, it neglected to deal with Martin's role and came to no conclusion as to whether the advice the company received for its payments to Maudling was worth the considerable salary.

Then there were the outstanding libel actions against Granada, the *Mirror* and the *Observer*, which had dragged into 1978. The Granada action had been put back and back, and there was merit from Reggie's point of view in closing down the other two actions on agreed terms before the colossal confrontation that would have taken place if he and Granada had got to court. While he did not attempt to strike a deal with Granada,[53] in January 1978 he opened back-channel discussions on the *Mirror* case with Hugh Cudlipp, who had been a good friend as a journalist and was now a senior executive at the *Mirror*. This approach had worked in 1969 when he won damages for Alan Watkins's article on REFA, but it did not bear fruit in 1978 when the stakes were much higher. Reggie's intervention served only to muddy the waters; it took place without reference to his solicitors and, ill-advisedly, he did not seem to have covered himself by stipulating that the letter to Cudlipp was 'without prejudice'. By writing, Reggie had endangered his claim to exemplary damages from the *Mirror*. In March, the two sides were still much too far apart to settle, with Maudling's advisers being willing to accept £50,000 or thereabouts including contribution to costs, while the *Mirror* would not offer more than £10,000.[54] The *Mirror* stayed in the battle, but both they and Granada were frightened that Maudling would win. Wherever Sidney Bernstein went, he found MPs of all parties saying how much they liked Maudling and could not believe he had done anything wrong,[55] and the libel defendants feared that a jury would respond in a similar way to his warmth and likeability.

The *Observer* case, because of the peculiar way in which the original story had been published, was perhaps the least defensible of the three because it was far from clear whether the paper should attempt to defend itself by pleading justification, or by saying that there was no defamation in the article. Counsel consulted by the *Observer* took a gloomy view of the paper's prospects and the case looked like being the first of the three to come to trial. In April 1978 a 'commercial settlement' was reached with Reggie, with an insincere statement in court and payment of £5,000 in costs and £12,500 in damages.[56] It was not a huge score for him given the continuing costs of the other two cases, which by March 1978 amounted to £10,000 on the *Mirror* case alone.

The *Observer* was unlucky to be taken off the field when it was, because the balance of power in the legal cases was to shift as 1978 wore on and the solicitors for Granada and the *Mirror* gained access to more and more damaging paperwork on Reggie's complex financial affairs. He was forced to disclose some of his tax records to the other side, but when they were delivered they were blatantly incomplete, with visible paperclips on the photocopies where blank pieces of paper had been placed to erase sections of the documentation. On one letter there was virtually nothing left visible. Reggie tried again with an informal approach to Ellis Birk at the start of October, offering a settlement in which he would drop the claim of malice and bad faith but he would still want some damages; the *Mirror*, while willing to give him some money towards costs, had no intention of conceding damages. Bad though the tax disclosure was, his biggest problem was the Cobb–Taylor report for the DPP in November 1974 on whether to prosecute Maudling and the other MPs for corruption. The other side in the libel cases obtained a copy of the report during 1978 and it was supplied to his side later in October through disclosure. Reggie was shaken to read its contents, having believed that if such a document had existed it would have turned up in the evidence bundles for the House of Commons Select Committee in 1976–7. He told Birk that 'This is the first time I have seen it, which seems a little strange as I am extensively referred to in it. My understanding was that it was a confidential document.' Reggie should not have been surprised, as it was not usual procedure to give secret prosecution opinions to their subjects.[57]

The Cobb report knocked a huge hole in Maudling's case in the libel actions, particularly in the *Mirror* case, which was narrowly based around the issue of whether Maudling escaped prosecution for corruption because of his status as an MP. His first response was to attempt to argue that it did not show this at all, but in the opinion of the *Mirror*'s barrister Alexander Irvine, it did, and the *Mirror*'s argument was certainly easier to sustain than Maudling's. While pointing out that Cobb–Taylor cleared him of being involved in the Abela bribe, Maudling was silent on the company finance charges. If the report did appear in evidence, he would surely have been sunk, but there was another legal manoeuvre that was open to his team. If he could manage a claim of comprehensive parliamentary immunity, in which anything which went on in Parliament could not be referred to in legal proceedings, the libel case would collapse. This was what a judge ruled in 1995 when Neil Hamilton sued the *Guardian* over cash for questions allegations, and it was only when Hamilton and his allies had amended the 1689 Bill of Rights that the case could resume in 1996. According to Richard Stott of the *Mirror*, their case was 'still years from trial in 1979', mainly because the subsidiary case on parliamentary privilege would have itself been appealed all the way up to the House of Lords before the main libel case could have been heard. The Granada case, because of its even greater complexity, would have taken even longer.[58]

But Reggie was never to see the inside of a courtroom in either case. 'I am sick and tired to death', he told the House at the end of November 1978, 'of hearing Britain described as a weak country. If it is a weak country, it is our fault and nobody else's. We have great industry, great skills, great commerce, and the best agriculture in the world. We also have North Sea Oil. If we are weak, it is our own fault. We should not ask for sympathy. We should accept the shame of it and set our own house in order.'[59] He was sick and tired to death literally as well as metaphorically, and in his words regretting wasted talents and accepting the shame of it there is another echo of his own predicament. His last speech in the House was on 13 December 1978, in a fateful debate on the use of sanctions to back up the government's incomes policy. The failure to have the election in October meant that the government went into the winter with no overall majority in Parliament and industrial relations in a restive condition after the severity of successive years of incomes policy. Callaghan was hoping to hold wage rises in the next year down to 5 per cent in order to continue the downward pressure on inflation, but this stage of the incomes policy, like its predecessor in 1974, started to come apart under pressure. The first breach came with the settlement of a major strike at the Ford motor company at 17 per cent. If the policy was to survive at all, the government would have to implement sanctions against Ford, including the withdrawal of subsidies and public sector contracts, and to do this a resolution needed to go through Parliament. Despite his general support for incomes policy, Reggie managed to convince himself that he should vote with the rest of the Conservatives against sanctions, on the grounds that sanctions themselves were an arbitrary and unfair way of enforcing wage restraint – just as much, he insisted, as was restricting the money supply. His preferred alternative, which he spelled out in his last words in Parliament, was:

In the private sector, I should like to see, in one form or another, independent arbitration made compulsory in major disputes. I agree that it would be difficult and complicated and would need the authority of the House, but I believe it would be possible for the House to authorise legislation so that, on major matters, independent arbitration was compulsory. The Government could be given the authority of the House to ensure that when an independent award is made, it is carried out. Those are my suggestions and my attempt to make a positive contribution. I must stress that a policy for productivity is our greatest national problem. No doubt all the difficulties will be paraded, but the present difficulties parade themselves. The Government are tinkering with the problem. The nation must be told clearly what lies before us if we go on as we are at present.[60]

Compulsory arbitration became an SDP-Liberal Alliance policy during the 1980s. By favouring it in 1978 Reggie distinguished himself from the simplistic monetarism of his Tory colleagues – that by restricting the money supply (which amounted to jacking up interest rates) inflation could be made to disappear. He still saw economic problems as essentially problems of social and political organisation, to which a solution had to be found through political techniques. Still, flawed as sanctions were, the alternative at that time was anarchy. Callaghan lost the sanctions resolution that night, the victim of the Tory determination to destroy the government and several left-wing Labour MPs' determination to destroy the incomes policy. The floodgates were opened, and a succession of strikes followed, at first by powerful groups like Shell tanker drivers who settled for 20 per cent, and then in January by millions of poorly paid public sector workers. The 'winter of discontent' was a heartbreaking failure not only for Callaghan's benign labourism but also for Maudling's hopes for a society of voluntary restraint in the use of power, common purpose, productivity and the planning of incomes. With the nastiness of those industrial disputes, and the nearly equal blindness and callousness of the Thatcherite response, the benevolence and optimism for which Maudling stood throughout his life seemed to have nothing left to offer.

As well as this terrible public destruction of what he had spent his political life trying to achieve, private tragedy – of his own making – closed in on Reggie at the same time. In reading Cobb–Taylor, he had been confronted by what he had done, not by accusatory journalists but by two eminent establishment figures who were anxiously looking for a reason not to put him in the dock. During late 1978 Reggie had been steadfastly ignoring friends and family who had been warning him that he looked ill and should see the doctor, but he was becoming visibly bloated through gastritis and getting ever more tired. If he had sought medical help earlier, his doctor thought he might have survived, but for whatever reason he ignored his physical deterioration.[61] He was always unobtrusive about his personal sufferings, feeling it was self-indulgent to make a fuss and impose them on others, but over Christmas 1978 he ignored the obvious. He had more or less given up on life. He was too intelligent not to realise the damage that alcohol was doing to him, but he simply could not stop drinking. Reggie effectively committed suicide; he took a gradual, initially pleasant path to that destination, but by the end the odds he was playing with his health were much riskier than Russian roulette.

Reginald Maudling's death, at the age of only 61, was deeply tragic and horrible. One morning in January 1979 his condition suddenly became worse. He woke to find the pillow soaked in blood; a vein in his neck had ruptured into his oesophagus. This is a not unusual complication of cirrhosis, caused by the blockage of the liver. He spent time in Welwyn Garden City Hospital and Westminster Hospital – for which Beryl had raised money – and was finally taken to the modern Royal Free Hospital in north London at the beginning of February. Nearly half of Britain's hospitals were only accepting emergency cases, although Reggie certainly counted as that. At the gates of the hospitals, as the ambulance drove through the snow, were pickets, braziers and placards as the 'winter of discontent' continued its destruction of his brand of politics.

For official consumption it was put out that Reggie was suffering from hepatitis, but in fact he was dying of cirrhosis.[62] The doctors tried to save him but the damage was too severe to be repaired and his condition worsened in hospital. His liver had effectively stopped working, and his kidneys also failed. He had several hours when he knew that the end was coming and nothing could be done, and summoned family and friends to see him for one last time. Sandy Glen, a fond and loyal friend to Reggie, arrived at the hospital at around midnight and was shown up to see Reggie and Beryl. Reggie looked very ill, his skin showing the obvious signs of liver failure. Reggie thanked him for coming and said 'I haven't got long to go'. Reggie's last words to his friend were something affectionate along the lines of 'you bloody Scotsman!'[63] Reggie faced the end of his life with touching bravery, dignity and good humour.

When the end came, early in the morning of 14 February 1979, it was a release from acute pain. His first two children received the news at the hospital; William was travelling, trying in vain to find himself in India. Martin, of the children the one who saw most even of the dark side of Reggie, said sadly to Caroline that he never felt that he really knew his father.[64] The real Reggie was elusive to the last, even to those he loved. Perhaps in his final moments he recalled his sadly appropriate motto from his student days, and went with one last self-deprecating smile into the darkness.

> Meum est propositum
> In taberna mori
> Ut sint vina proxima
> Morientis ori.
>
> Tunc cantabunt laetius
> Angelorum chori:
> 'Sit Deus propituis
> Huic potatori!'

I desire to end my days in a tavern drinking
May some Christian lift the glass when I am shrinking
That the Cherubim may cry, when they see me sinking:
God be merciful to a soul of this gentleman's way of thinking.

Chapter 27

THE TRAGEDY OF OUR TIMES

Reggie's death was not the last tragedy to afflict the Maudling family. The financial implications of the settlement with Peachey properties meant that there was a certain amount of confusion in the months after his death. Beryl moved out of Bedwell Lodge, although only across the road, and a few years later sold up again and lived in the Midlands near her son Edward. Her post-Reggie life was unhappy; she was heartbroken by the loss of her devoted husband. Touchingly, her cousin James Haw said that they decided to go down together on the sinking ship;[1] but Beryl was left floating with the wreckage until she died in August 1988. Her doctor did not mention alcohol on the death certificate. Beryl's dream of the Adeline Genée Theatre, for which Reggie had compromised himself so much and suffered so much embarrassment, closed in summer 1989. The theatre had been rescued from bankruptcy in 1979 by the Bush-Davies ballet school, but ten years later the school itself shut its doors because of financial difficulties.[2] The expensive building, little altered and with its ballet stage intact, is now owned by a security firm called Sabrewatch and used for training sessions.[3]

Martin only outlived his mother by a month. He was struck down by an aggressive form of multiple sclerosis that left him nearly unable to write by 1987 and killed him at the age of only 44. After his unsuccessful time at university, and his disastrous business life with his father and Poulson, he had turned his hand to other things, hoping at one time to make a living from his interest in fast cars. At long last, he found something he enjoyed and was good at in estate management, working at Knebworth in Hertfordshire and living in modest circumstances in Stevenage, but his happiness was sadly short-lived.

William Maudling died in mysterious circumstances in 1999 at the age of 42. He was the most restless of the Maudling children, a scintillatingly bright man who despite his gentleness had difficulty connecting with other people, forming relationships and coping with everyday things like jobs and flats. Alone of the Maudling children he was interested in politics, becoming involved with the Labour Party in north London and supporting the campaign to legalise cannabis. In January 1999 he expressed sympathy with Jack Straw's son who had been set up by the tabloids for using cannabis, finding it all to easy to imagine how he would have been treated if his parties at Admiralty House had been raided. William enjoyed cannabis but struggled with dependence on heroin. He was acutely sensitive and kind-hearted and sought a dimmer switch on his life in drugs, dingy flats with walls painted black and the company of nihilistic losers. In summer 1999 he seemed to be genuinely hopeful about quitting heroin and was trying a new approach. A couple of weeks later he was dead, having fallen from a tower block in Kentish Town in north London. It was not clear whether he had fallen accidentally, deliberately taken his own life, or been pushed over in an argument. Caroline decided to scatter his ashes in India, the place where he had felt most happy and at peace.

In some press coverage of William Maudling's death, it was suggested that the root of his problems was in his father's disgrace in the 1970s, but this was a gross oversimplification. He was troubled before then, and as a vulnerable, sensitive child of two alcoholics who encouraged him to drink from an early age was in obvious danger of drug or alcohol dependency. The fault, if one needs to allocate blame, is with his father's moral breakdown in 1966–8 rather than the public scandal that followed it.

Caroline and Edward are both still alive and well – and entitled to their privacy. Caroline's life has been full of incident and variety, while Edward lives with his family in rural tranquillity. They are both decent and admirable people.

Maudling was not the only politician of his time to leave a disastrous, disordered personal legacy. Older families, like the Churchills or the Macmillans, have had their tragedies too. But the ruins that Reggie left behind were all the more pathetic because of his near obsession with providing for the family after his death. He had hoped so fervently that he would be the one who managed to move the Maudling family from the upper middle class to among the greatest in the land, but his death left them with chaos and remarkably little money. In trying to provide for them, he had destroyed himself. Perhaps Beryl in particular can be said to have killed the goose that laid the golden eggs.

Most of Reggie's obituaries were kind. They concentrated on the nearly universal affection in which he was held, and how closely he had missed out on the party leadership. It was 'dear old Reggie', 'the nearly man', 'Tragedy of the brilliant Tory who never quite made it'.[4] Even the *Mirror*, Reggie's antagonist in one of the libel cases, was affectionate as well as critical, but the *Telegraph* struck a discordant note with its dismissal of Reggie as solid, sane and sensible but having embraced the 'disastrous post war consensus'.[5]

As Maudling lay dying, Britain was convulsed by a series of strikes which were dubbed the 'winter of discontent' by the media. On the day he died the government and the TUC had reached a 'Concordat' which, they hoped, would settle the situation. The Concordat was the last throw of the dice for the politics of consensus and social partnership that Maudling had championed all his life, but it had less than three months to run. Labour lost a vote of no confidence in the House of Commons on 28 March and a general election followed. Maudling's memorial service was on Tuesday 1 May 1979, only two days before Thatcher won the election. It was a memorial service for an era in politics as much as for a man.

Maudling's reputation slid lower and lower in the years after his death. Neither Granada nor the *Mirror* put the boot in, and the *Mirror* even gave Beryl some money when she wrote to them asking for help in settling Reggie's estate. However, the way was at last clear to publish books about the Poulson affair. Michael Gillard and Martin Tomkinson's *Nothing to Declare* came out in 1980 and David Taylor and Ray Fitzwalter's *Web of Corruption* followed in 1981. John Poulson's bankruptcy examination formally ended in September 1979, and in January 1980 he was conditionally discharged from bankruptcy.[6] Part of the agreement with the Trustee had been that the proceeds from his memoirs, which he had agreed to publish with Michael Joseph, would help to pay off the creditors. Poulson's book, *The Price*, was published in 1981 but quickly withdrawn. The problem with *The Price* was that it demonstrated in full measure Poulson's tendency towards vitriolic ranting against people he disliked, and his carelessness regarding accuracy, and was therefore an unacceptable libel risk. One of his most unpleasant tower blocks in Gateshead was blown up in 1987, amid much celebration by former residents, and more have followed over the years. John Poulson died in 1993.

The *Telegraph* view gradually replaced respect and affection as being the usual Tory view of Maudling. Thatcherism's political success in the 1980s enabled its exponents to dismiss the previous set of Tory politicians as trimmers and failures, Maudling most of all. He was a social permissive, a Keynesian who went beyond Keynes in his approach to the economy, a believer in decolonisation, racial equality and peaceful coexistence with the Soviet Union. He was also an exponent of a good-humoured, low-temperature form of politics that was anathema to the Thatcherite revolutionary guard. As a politician, he faded from view exceptionally quickly in the 1980s and his achievements were forgotten. The unconcluded libel case left a vague miasma of suspicion about his reputation, although this too faded into nothing. In 1996 Edmund Dell, a serious and thoughtful contemporary historian as well as a former Treasury minister, could write about Maudling's 'involvement, however innocent, in the Poulson affair'.[7] Many of the details of his far from innocent involvement remained a secret until the publication of this book, known only to a few appalled, and sometimes, like Alan Ford, embittered, investigators sworn to silence.

Maudling's political career neatly brackets the age of consensus politics. He arrived in the Treasury just after the defeat of 'Robot' in 1952. His final departure from the front bench was in November 1976 during the IMF crisis, which is widely held to have marked the end of the Keynesian welfare state consensus. He died during the winter of discontent in February 1979. To the Thatcherite his career summarises some of the worst aspects of the postwar settlement – consensus for the sake of it, meeting challenges with a cotton-wool blanket of reassuring words, a basic laziness and escape from reality. Even without being unduly polemical, his approach to the unreformed trade union movement did have a 'kiss the hand you cannot bite' mentality about it. He hoped, as did Callaghan – and, in fairness, some of the best trade union leaders like Woodcock, Feather and Jones – that the unions could become a full partner in a tripartite social contract, but the unions were too oppositionist to function in this fashion for more than two or three years at a time.

Maudling already disliked Thatcher for her personality, her instincts and her prejudices and he would have been horrified at the full programme of 'Thatcherism' that unfolded after May 1979. Maudling regarded monetarism itself as dangerous nonsense, and would have had nothing but contempt for the bastardised version put into practice by the Thatcher government in 1979–81. Maudling was not an unprincipled man; he was a genuine believer in 'one nation' and consensus. Had he survived – and had his reputation survived the Granada/*Mirror* libel cases – he would have felt obliged to speak out for the 'wet' cause. It is impossible to know whether he would have restricted himself, as did most other wets, to making genteel coded speeches and writing hostile articles in the newspapers, or whether he would have reached breaking point with Thatcher during the *annus horribilis* of 1981. However, he did leave a tantalising clue in one of his very last *Sunday Express* pieces in November 1978, which was given the heading 'Why Doesn't Mr Callaghan Quit the Labour Party?' Maudling, accurately, pointed to the huge gap between Callaghan's views and the left-wing policies to which the Labour Party was increasingly committed in the late 1970s. He acknowledged that there were divisions in the Conservative Party as well, but blandly assured his readers that this was normal in opposition and 'will in any case disappear when the Tories are returned to office'. He asked: 'Is it not time that Mr Callaghan tried to make some common cause with those in our nation, the great silent majority who are to be found in all parties who want to see reason and sense and moderation and justice?'[8] Maudling certainly saw himself in this camp, but could he have described Thatcher in this way? The challenge he was making to the Labour right, as he must have been aware, could also be made to the Conservative left and it is possible to see it as another piece of psychological projection on his part. He was arguing explicitly that it made political sense for the social democrats to break away from the increasingly socialist Labour Party and form a centre alliance. Although Callaghan stayed with Labour, the breakaway took place. Could Maudling have recognised the strength of his own logic and joined the SDP, whose leader Roy Jenkins held very similar political views and was also not averse to fine wine and interesting company?

Maudling hardly disagreed with Roy Jenkins. Their record in office demonstrated the extent of consensus, particularly in the continuity of their Home Office policies. Jenkins was if anything a more cautious, conservative Chancellor than Maudling. In a radio discussion with Jenkins in 1973 Maudling said that 'we're both aiming at the same thing: a continuation of the civilised traditions of this country in a world that can be more prosperous in the future if we are sensible about it' – civilised, prosperous and sensible all being terms beloved of the liberal centre ground. The only real disagreement was over redistribution and the related issue of equality, where Jenkins was willing to countenance a considerable move towards greater equality. Maudling was less keen, agreeing with Jenkins 'about the abolition of poverty, but I don't think this necessarily entails, as some of Mr Jenkins's colleagues seem to think, the abolition of wealth at the same time'.[9] In a private conversation over dinner shortly after the February 1974 election they acknowledged that there was very little separating them politically.[10] There was even less a few years later, when Jenkins no longer felt obliged to describe himself as a socialist.

The SDP would have appealed to Maudling's Hegelian side, as being the culmination of consensus politics – a synthesis of his own liberal Toryism with the politics of the social democrats he admired within the Labour Party. He was, at least in abstract, not unsympathetic to the idea. In 1973 Maudling said that 'I would like to see the emergence of a party of the extreme centre that held centre views with extreme conviction', but thought it would never happen, and that the risk of a third party was that it would just confuse things.[11] There was little in terms of SDP policy to which he could object, having argued consistently for incomes policy, planning, and in 1978 for compulsory arbitration in industry; he was also one of comparatively few Conservative MPs to vote for Proportional Representation for the European Parliament. At the beginning of his career he had argued against PR in an article for the *National and English Review* in September 1950 – but then, in the same issue, there was also an anti-reform argument from Roy Jenkins.[12] There was little in Jenkins's November 1979 Dimbleby Lecture foreshadowing a realignment of British politics with which Maudling could have disagreed:

The paradox is that we need more change accompanied by more stability of direction. It is a paradox but not a contradiction. Too often we have superficial and quickly reversed political change without much purpose or underlying effect. This is not the only paradox. We need the innovating stimulus of the free market economy without either the unacceptable brutality of its untrammelled distribution of rewards or its indifference to unemployment . . . The state must know its place, which must be an important but far from omnipotent one. You recognise that there are certain major economic objectives, well beyond merely regulatory ones like the control of the money supply, which can only be achieved by public action, often on an international scale . . .[13]

On the other hand, Maudling was a weary man, sceptical of grand new schemes and highly pragmatic. In his first departmental command he had, after all, killed off the V1000 and would have had reservations about taking a ride in what Roy Jenkins labelled in his 1980 remarks to the Press Gallery 'an experimental plane'. If Maudling spurned the Tories he would have feared their reprisals. The only Tory MP to defect, Christopher Brocklebank-Fowler, was harshly treated by his old party and Maudling could have expected brutal character assassination given his great vulnerabilities.

Maudling believed in consensus politics. There are few figures even in postwar British politics of whom this can be said so unequivocally. He is distinct from both components of Mr Butskell, his political parent according to Henry Fairlie in 1955. Butler had the traditional Tory approach of adaptation to circumstances, but also had some quite traditional Tory instincts about the free market and an ordered society. Gaitskell, for all his practical convergence with Butler on the assumptions underlying economic policy, was a passionate believer in equality and social change. Maudling had far fewer fixed ideological points; his politics was flexible to a much greater degree, and although he did have deep feelings about his party, he never lost his sense of perspective. There is something very appealing about a politician who recognises, even if the other side are in power, that not everything is triumph or disaster; a rationality and emotional balance that is not a common gift among politicians. Even those who have it generally feel obliged to conceal it from public view. Often the most moderate figures, like Macleod and Hogg on the Conservative side and Gaitskell for Labour, felt obliged to demonstrate that they really were members of the tribe by making slashing partisan attacks on the enemy.

Consensus was central to Maudling's self-definition as a political figure throughout his life, from his flirtation with National Labour in the late 1930s to his hostility to 'Selsdon Woman' in the late 1970s. The core of his philosophy was the Hegelian dialectic, which he regarded as 'the essential principle of human progress' and explicitly equated with the Middle Way (a 1930s slogan associated with left-wing Conservatives, particularly Harold Macmillan), Butskellism and consensus in politics.[14] To Maudling, progress came not from creating a lowest common denominator but in the synthesis of competing forces.

Was Maudling a Blairite before his time? The 'Third Way' also claims to be more than lowest common denominator centrist politics, and to be an expression of 'One Nation' politics. Some commentators, such as Robert Skidelsky, have perceived Blair as 'a Hegelian idealist'.[15] Maudling was certainly a Hegelian and believed in the same sort of synthesising politics of national unity, the absorption of ideas from right and left. The pragmatism of 'what matters is what works' would not have gone against the grain for Maudling. Neither would the global idealism of Blair; after all, Maudling defended Suez as doing the UN's job for it, much as Blair argued for the 2003 invasion of Iraq. Blair also spoke to the 2001 Labour conference about Britain's global moral mission of improving the living standards of the Third World. Would Blair dissent from Maudling's peroration about the purpose of a prosperous society, delivered to an unmoved Tory audience in 1963?

> There are great things to be done; meeting the passion for education, clearing up the pools of squalor that still disfigure some parts of our national life, bringing light and air and beauty to our cities, bringing aid and succour to the people of Asia and Africa who live at the edge of subsistence. These are the purposes which we disguise under the name of economic policy. They are noble purposes.[16]

There are some very obvious differences. Maudling was inclined to corporatism and a strong government involvement in the economy through incomes policy, but this reflects the times he lived in rather than his deeper beliefs. The values underlying the thesis and antithesis were almost immaterial to Maudling compared to the process of forming the synthesis. In the 1940s he saw the contemporary Conservative Party as a synthesis of the once-hostile forces of conservatism and liberalism. During his front-line political career he rapidly came to see the labour and socialist movement as an antithesis whose energies could be absorbed and used in the great progressive dialectic of politics. Maudling described himself in 1970 as being in the 'extreme centre' – meaning that he held moderate views but did so with extreme conviction, but his Hegelianism meant that he appreciated the role the extremes played in politics. 'Without the struggles of the extremes, the policies of moderation could not develop. So while it seems highly unlikely that either the extreme Left or the extreme Right will ever gain control of this country, their existence is essential to the dynamism of the centre, the position from which, broadly speaking, the country is governed.'[17]

Maudling's recognition of the validity and usefulness of the far left marks him out sharply from most of his Conservative colleagues. Tory discourse in the 1970s had heavy traces of paranoia. While on some weeks Maudling's contributions graced the pages of the *Sunday Express*, on others Angus Maude – who should have known better – and other writers worked themselves into a lather about 'Marxist wreckers'. To read the mid-market tabloids of the time is to enter a strange world where powerful conspirators stalked the land and the hand of Moscow lay behind every strike, every new teaching method and even every dirty bookshop. This thinking influenced Thatcher and some of her advisers. Maudling never lowered himself to such nonsense. To Maudling, Marxists were not demonic enemies, just people who had not read their Hegel properly.

Maudling lacked some of the elements of a true conservative temperament, despite his love of traditional Englishness. He was essentially an optimist about scientific and social progress and even, perhaps, the perfectibility of human beings. What sort of Tory has as his intellectual heroes Hegel, Freud and Keynes? Few liberals or social democrats would have been able to disagree very strongly with his creed, while it put him fundamentally at odds with socialists and real conservatives.

Maudling had no sense of being in politics to achieve anything in particular. He was an executive politician par excellence – uncomfortable, and frankly inadequate, in opposition, but at home taking decisions and running Cabinet committees. The life of a minister suited him, with the Private Office there to impose some discipline on aspects of life that could otherwise be problematic, such as his tendencies to avoid the more boring among his duties, mix with unsuitable company and drink too much. A strong Private Office and a department in which he was interested, as at the Treasury, could make Maudling a formidable minister.

Maudling's unique political talent of reconciliation was well used in several of his offices, particularly the Home Office, the Treasury and the Colonial Office. He could take over a situation after a virtual revolution had taken place, and within a year or two have people wondering what the fuss had ever been about. As Colonial Secretary his talent was used brilliantly to forge a consensus in Kenya, a deeply divided and potentially violent country before his intervention. As Prime Minister, he might have been able to say something sensible to a Britain obsessed with the idea of 'decline'. Maudling told an interviewer in September 1967 that it was nonsense for newspapers to talk in terms of national economic survival. 'We shall go on surviving, and we shall go on getting richer on average. The problem is that we just do not get richer fast enough, or regularly enough.'[18] Edward Boyle remembered that Maudling was the first minister to venture the view, in early 1956, that Britain must look on herself as 'at the top of the second league' rather than as a superpower.[19] If anyone was capable of creating a European-style social market government in Britain, and transcending the sterilities of 'decline' it was Maudling. But the later Maudling was inclined to a rather futile optimism interspersed with the wry pessimism expressed in remarks like 'we have lost our pride, but still have our conceit'.

But alongside Maudling's undoubted ability as a man of the executive, there is a question over his political courage. There are not many occasions in his career when he did the right thing even though it was difficult. He ducked away from reforming Resale Price Maintenance in the early 1960s, while Edward Heath took the strain of actually seeing it through. Although there is much to say in favour of his time as Chancellor, it was hardly a period in which he courted unpopularity in a good cause. It is notable that on the occasions when he exercised power his policies resembled his personal inclinations rather than his public rhetoric. While the Chancellor he most admired in the abstract was Stafford Cripps, his own policies in 1962–4 made a positive virtue out of expansion, consumption and deficit spending.

Strangely, he took the most difficult, unpopular decisions in his ministerial afterlife of 1970–2 – to admit the East African Asians, to exclude Dutschke, to let the 'civilised society' flourish. Although by any objective criteria – because of his general dissolution reflected in his declining powers and his corrupt behaviour in opposition – he was unfit for office, he managed as Home Secretary to achieve some measure of redemption.

The Maudling of 1968 is barely recognisable as the same man he was in 1963. Maudling's domestic life showed a tragic plunge, from the warmth of William's Downing Street birthday in March 1964 to the chronic dissolution and neglect of a few years later. There was a coarseness and crudity about him sometimes later on, in casual asides and in his political thought there was a loss of sensibility in someone who had once been capable of great insight and sensitivity. His decline was most apparent in the failure of his moral compass. Maudling could speak eloquently and apparently sincerely in the early 1960s about the purposes of affluence being to drain 'pools of squalor' at home and lift the majority of the world's people out of poverty. The uncomfortable choice in interpreting Maudling's actions is between dismissing his earlier words as just so much meaningless verbiage, and accepting them as genuine – which makes his decline all the more tragic because the potential for good was such a strong part of his nature. He spoke movingly, if unappreciated, at Blackpool in 1963 about 'bringing light and air and beauty to our cities'; in 1968 he was helping Poulson sell his shoddy, ugly tower blocks all over Britain. In 1963 he said that the main aim of economic policy was 'bringing aid and succour to the people of Asia and Africa who live at the edge of subsistence'. But in 1967–8 he was doing all he could to pressurise the Overseas Development Ministry into squandering money on the grotesquely oversized Gozo hospital, for the financial benefit of a corrupt associate. While Iain Macleod was a driving force behind Crisis at Christmas, which offered help to the homeless and desperate, Maudling's principal charitable venture was a failed theatre in Sussex.

Some aspects of his personality did manage to survive intact. He was always kind, self-effacing, rarely pompous, and he was to the end a lovely man to work for. He could be charming and generous to people without making a great fuss about it. His political thought, except as regards Northern Ireland, was always based around principles of one nation, civil liberties and a sense of decency; if his thinking became rigid in later life, it never became harsh or punitive. As Chancellor he had confidently overruled his officials, telling them that that was the point of having a minister in charge. As Home Secretary he deferred to the security forces and, often, his civil servants. He was capable of innovative and thoughtful approaches to new problems such as devolution, but he elevated his Keynesian economic thinking into a dogma and was negative and contemptuous of the Irish situation. In some ways, though, he became more tolerant as he went on, less bothered by the way other people lived their lives, less conscious of rank or status. The progressive loss of focus, both in its mostly negative effects but also his tolerance, has much to do with Maudling's relationship with alcohol.

Alcohol was a steadily deepening stream in Maudling's life. He first encountered beer at an early age and by the time he was at Oxford he was a regular imbiber of several different kinds of hard liquor. Maudling's consumption was initially an advantage. His enthusiasm for cognac was a bond with Churchill and his ability to hold his drink was important in Westminster society, which then and now is a hard-drinking environment. Maudling was a cheerful dispenser of six o'clock whisky and soda to the Lobby journalists and an entertaining companion during long evenings of voting.

From the mid-1960s onwards Maudling's increasing alcohol consumption damaged him. Even his iron constitution could not sustain this barrage without ill effect, and he started visibly to age and go to seed. He was occasionally spectacularly and obviously drunk at private occasions, while in previous years he could put away large amounts without showing it. His drinking started to interfere with his public functions when he was Home Secretary in the early 1970s. His disgrace after 1972 accelerated his decline and he turned increasingly to alcohol as a comfort in adversity. In the mid-1970s his consumption can only be described as escalating alcoholism, with incidents of solitary drinking, morning drinking, an inability to stop until supplies were exhausted and possibly memory blackouts such as the occasion of his George V interview in Paris. In the end, it killed him with his tacit consent.

The formation of Maudling's character predisposed him to alcoholism. His comfortable childhood as an only son, in which he was indulged by his parents, gave him a tendency to self-indulgence and an inability to deal with frustration and defeat, which lasted throughout his life. He doused the discomfort that came with failure – and perhaps also with excessively conspicuous success – with alcohol. Maudling had a self-defeating element to his personality. Enoch Powell, sensitively, observed that as a speaker 'He failed only on occasions to which it was necessary to rise'.[20] This was never more apparent than at the 1963 party conference when he blew his chances of victory in the leadership contest. Although there was no disastrous speech in 1965, his defeat was the product of complacency, disorganisation and an already spreading sense that he was disengaged and spending too much time at City lunches. Throughout his life, heavy drinking was a self-inflicted handicap. Like his son William, he seemed to need to sedate his extremely quick mind so that he could relate to the world on its own terms rather than being constantly waiting for others to catch up. He liked to turn in the occasional sparkling House of Commons performance or perform the parliamentary high-wire act of taking questions or winding up without notes, just to show that he could do it. But to perform consistently at that level would have taken some of the fun out of the game.

Maudling himself wrote as a 'final conclusion' of his memoirs and his life that 'there is no such thing for human beings as content. Man can never be content. He would very soon find himself bored in Paradise. Eternal happiness would soon pall.'[21] The failure to acknowledge contentment is often associated with excessive drinking. In his own life Maudling found himself bored in Paradise. He had everything during that most creative and industrious period of his life, 1959–64 – a happy family, an infectious sense of fun and jollity, friends, admiration, popularity, respect . . . But then it all started to go wrong.

A card-carrying Freudian would not hesitate to categorise Maudling as a classic oral personality, constantly sucking in food and drink, smoking big cigars, never entirely free of the influence of his mother. His mother's disowning of him at the age of 22 was cruel. A mother's love is supposedly unconditional, and Maudling learned then that even this could be taken away – and not, as is usual, by death but by a deliberate act of cruelty that lasted for seventeen years. It is much to Beryl Maudling's credit that he felt such love and comfort in his marriage, but there was still a damaged area of his emotional landscape that the always dependable, available, gratification of drink could temporarily cover over.

Westminster culture must take some of the blame for Maudling's drink problem. The incidence of alcohol-related death by profession is closely related to access to drink, with publicans leading the charts by a long way, bar staff, hoteliers and cooks also suffering disproportionately from cirrhosis. Politics is one of those industries where alcoholics can pass for normal. Alcohol is readily accessible at Westminster and the hours of work – from around 3p.m. to around 11p.m. – mean that drinking, socialising and work all take place at the same time. During the 1970s it was a particular problem because the parliamentary situation was so narrowly balanced and MPs were required to hang around all evening voting and killing time. Each Parliament contains a number of helpless alcoholics, who have generally been left to flounder by their colleagues who are unwilling to face up to the reality of alcoholism.

It must count against Maudling's colleagues and friends that he was allowed to destroy himself through drink, but he was a difficult man to advise. He could sometimes bridle and be huffy – rarely pompous – but was more usually blandly reassuring and evasive when challenged. The phenomenon of alcoholics like him, utterly dependent but with high tolerance and few blatant drunken episodes, warding off any therapeutic or other intervention with 'jaunty superficiality' has been noted.[22] 'Many people hold the view that alcohol is less essential than petrol,' Reggie observed in a budget debate on excise duty increases in April 1977, as if wondering whether to argue against this conventional wisdom. Maudling had poor judgement in friends and refused to believe ill of people he had decided to like and trust. This was true also of his relationship with alcohol. By the time he wrote his memoirs he must have been able to recognise the physical damage that alcohol had done to him, but the memoirs are full of affectionately rendered drinking anecdotes.

Reggie himself wrote, while under criminal investigation in 1975, although with no sign of recognising its applications to his own situation: 'For the simple fact is that concepts of morality are going to be influenced by the advance of science. It is not merely that conventions change from generation to generation. If it is possible by treatment to cure criminal tendencies, how can you distinguish between crime and illness?'[23]

The elusiveness and ambiguity of Reginald Maudling is never more apparent than in his criminal career. The sheer weight of evidence against him seems compelling – that he was up to no good with Poulson, that he received money he should not have done from the Middle East, that his tax returns were wilfully incomplete, that he was devious and dishonest in relation to money, all seem clear. But when specific allegations are considered, most of it dissolves into a vague miasma of minor breaches of the rules and loopholes successfully exploited. The portrait of Maudling as criminal is definitely painted from the Impressionist school. Looked at from a distance, it is perfectly clear what one is seeing – but peering at the detail, all one can make out are meaningless coloured dots and brushstrokes. The frustration of Alan Ford and Ken Etheridge, who investigated Maudling respectively for the DTI and the Fraud Squad, is palpable in the documentary record. They both knew he was guilty of something, but pinning down exactly what that was proved extremely difficult. In the absence of a single, major charge that could be conclusively proved, Ford ended up citing a host of infringements – the most piffling of which actually served to discredit the more serious – and Etheridge chased the mirage of a corruption prosecution. The House of Commons Select Committee, in reaching for a moderately serious charge against Maudling, tripped up badly in citing his 1972 resignation letter without first putting this to him.

Maudling, in his earlier career, did not so much lack integrity as have too sophisticated a sense of its meaning. He could speak, with conviction, of integrity in the sense of 'to thine own self be true'. He believed in his own honesty and integrity and with some rather circular reasoning he felt that his own confidence in his honesty should be enough to satisfy everyone else. He had an idealist – in the philosophical sense – approach to rules and regulations. Rules about, for instance, disclosure of interests, were there to ensure honest conduct of government. The point was not the rules themselves, but the underlying aim of honest government; ergo, given that he was satisfied that he was acting honestly the letter of the rule itself was insignificant. It may not be a convincing defence to the outside observer for matters such as Lloyd's, but Maudling himself seems to have been genuinely convinced by it.

It might be possible to see Maudling's violations of the law relating to companies in the same light as his evasion of the ministerial rules regarding Lloyd's. Company law is there to ensure honest and efficient management of companies, and protect shareholders and customers. Perhaps, as long as these interests are not prejudiced, the letter of the law might be said to be secondary, and with ITCS and the other Poulson companies it was all in-house to some degree. There was no significant separation of interest between the directors and shareholders of the Poulson firms. Counsel to the Director of Public Prosecutions in 1976 weighed these considerations in deciding whether to prosecute Maudling on the company law offences specified in the reports prepared by the Department of Trade and Industry Inspectors.

However, the 'deplorable state' of the company's books, payments contrary to law, and retrospective false accounting, can never be considered acceptable, and the laws do not exist just to protect certain interests but to uphold the integrity of the economic system as a whole. The conclusion must be that Maudling had morally lost his way by the late 1960s and was willing to commit and connive at acts of dishonesty and corruption. There is at least a case to answer for fraud, in terms of the appropriation of the income stream from Abu Dhabi.

Maudling's criminal activities belong to that white-collar territory where the offender finds it relatively easy to rationalise the offences as not being crimes at all. The attitude of the agencies that enforce some of these laws encourages the offender to do so, particularly with the Inland Revenue which hardly ever prosecutes except under gross and persistent provocation – even Mohammed Al-Fayed had a charmed life with the Revenue, let alone Maudling. Customs and Excise is in a similar position, in that it is – unless illegal goods of some sort are involved, which was never the case with Maudling – a revenue-raising body first and a law-enforcement agency second. Maudling, like many people, did not regard customs violations as really criminal, but rather in the same category as parking and speeding fines. Just as one can trace a fascination with prostitutes and insider dealing in the writings of Jeffrey Archer,[24] smuggling pops up here and there in the Maudling story, from youthful stories in the *Memoirs* to references in speeches in Parliament, and then the Middle Eastern gifts. By any reckoning tax and customs evasion are not suitable activities for a former Chancellor of the Exchequer or Home Secretary, and his behaviour does cast a deep shadow over his fitness for public office.

Corruption involves these issues, and others as well. It is hard, particularly from within, to see where corruption begins and normal social bonds of friendship and corporate goodwill end. A box of chocolates or bottle of whisky is usually considered an acceptable Christmas gift in the context of a business relationship, but at some point up the hierarchy of gifts from there to a case of whisky, a holiday, a new car, a house, a suitcase of untraceable banknotes . . . a line must be drawn, even in cases where there is no provable return on the investment. Was George Pottinger, who took Poulson for tens of thousands but whose contribution to Poulson's business is difficult to pin down as more than having a kept man at court, more legally and morally respectable than Andy Cunningham, who took less and actually put business Poulson's way?

Part of the complexity of the reckoning in the Maudling case is that he operated in several different environments with different sets of standards, and he tried to operate in each according to its own atmosphere rather than any overall set of moral principles of his own. In public life, he was generally honest even when genuine conflicts of interest did exist, although there were serious lapses, such as his Persian Gulf speeches in 1968 and his use of influence with Nigeria in 1970. In his British business affairs, he was less upright, although the standards prevailing in the construction industry in particular in the 1960s were low. 'You can't get business in the Middle East by putting up a brass plate,' as Reggie said himself in 1972. In the Middle East, where commissions and bribes are part of doing business, he participated but was not particularly predatory in doing so. He also, and this counts for something in the morality of commission agents in the Persian Gulf, used the money to provide for his family, and did some work for deals rather than sit back and rake in money.

Why did he do it? The simple answer, of greed, cannot be sustained. Reggie was no miser or hoarder of money. He did have expensive tastes, and as with many of us the best things in life are even better if someone else is paying for them. But the money flowed out as quickly as it flowed in. Reggie was impulsively generous and soft-hearted, and after he died his family found many instances, of which they had previously been completely unaware, of his kindness to strangers. He was particularly indulgent to his family. The running costs of being Beryl Maudling were very high, and Martin was also a drain on resources. The family were very demanding on Reggie, to the disquiet of some of his friends, who felt he was carrying an unfair burden. It was not in Reggie's psychological make-up to resist and Beryl in particular kept pushing and pushing at the open door.

During the weekend between the publication of the 1977 Select Committee report on Maudling's links with Poulson and the parliamentary debate, Peregrine Worsthorne wrote a characteristically quirky right-wing piece about the ethics of public service.[25] Worsthorne, always more thoughtful than his imitators, saw the Poulson quagmire as an example of the problems of running a semi-socialist society. The socialist ethic of public service as its own reward, and of the abnegation of the acquisitive spirit, had not been fully accepted; but then neither was the capitalist ethic that regarded making money as a healthy and praiseworthy activity. The result, said Worsthorne, was that 'most public men will both want to be rich for perfectly respectable reasons, and find it exceedingly difficult to achieve this honourable ambition without behaving in ways which their predecessors would have found unacceptable'. The same basic point had been made by a solicitor consulted in summer 1976 about the possibility of a public inquiry into Poulson: 'The political system into which we are moving will, in my view, make increased corruption inevitable, since to remove all reward from honest effort is to place a premium on dishonesty . . . contemporary Britain is a society where "fiddling" of one sort and another is almost universal.'[26]

It is not a negligible point. Once Maudling had started down the route of making money, he fairly quickly encountered penal rates of income tax on higher earnings without any of the standard ways round it that inherited wealth has always managed to discover. He quickly resorted to tax avoidance, for instance through his leaseback arrangement with Eric Miller in 1965. By definition, tax avoidance is legal; but it does involve some degree of distortion in the relationship between the avoider and the truth – from the minor tweaking of putting things in the name of one's spouse to the convoluted and artificial avoidance schemes devised in the late 1970s by specialist accountants such as Rossminster. A court in the early 1980s found that some schemes could fall in a middle ground between legal avoidance and illegal evasion.[27] A higher rate of 98 per cent, as existed on unearned income in the late 1970s, was an open invitation to find ways round it; human nature would not adjust to fit the law, any more than it would for Prohibition in 1920s America.

The problem with Worsthorne's argument is that a more wholehearted embrace of capitalist values, under Thatcher in the 1980s, did nothing to improve standards of conduct in business and public life – perhaps in the latter case, it even made matters worse. The celebration of acquisitiveness, combined with deprecation of the public service ethic and a huge programme of disposal of public assets, was a recipe for scandals. Even Maudling's murky behaviour in the United Arab Emirates must be weighed in comparison with the enormous arms-equipment-commission deals with Saudi Arabia known as Al-Yamamah and Al-Yamamah 2.

Maudling can be seen in a European context, in which his follies and even crimes seem less grotesque and exceptional. Take the case of Reginald Maudling's diamonds (presuming they existed – there is ample evidence of other gifts anyway), and Valéry Giscard d'Estaing's diamonds. The two men were contemporaries as finance ministers and Giscard went on to become President of France in 1974. He received several gifts of diamonds from Jean-Bedel Bokassa, the self-proclaimed Emperor of the Central African Empire. Bokassa was a much more revolting figure than anyone Maudling was associated with – a corrupt tyrant whose coronation cost a quarter of his impoverished country's GDP in 1977, whose excesses may not have stopped short of personal involvement in murders and cannibalism. Bokassa enjoyed the financial and diplomatic support of France during Giscard's time, until serious unrest broke out in his Empire in 1979. Giscard suffered some bad publicity in the French equivalent of *Private Eye*, but came under no serious scrutiny and nearly managed to win re-election in 1981. His active political career is still not over; as a respected elder statesman he has recently been involved in drafting a new European constitution. Maudling, in taking money and gifts out of office from a basically friendly, and in Middle Eastern terms liberal and constructive, country like Dubai, was nowhere near as morally tainted.

From the late 1950s onwards, part of Maudling's life was lived in a kind of international political fast lane, where the 'statesman' can expect to have a comfortable life without worrying too much about where the money comes from or being unduly concerned with 'local' rules and regulations. Prince Bernhard of the Netherlands, the guiding spirit of the Bilderberg Group and a friend of Maudling's, was himself a man with an extremely expensive lifestyle whom a Dutch official inquiry found had 'showed himself open to dishonourable requests and offers' in his relationship with the Lockheed aviation corporation.[28] There is a sense among the very grand that these things may be wrong, but that they don't matter very much, and this atmosphere influenced Maudling particularly when he was out of office after 1964.

Reggie Maudling's life, though productive in many ways, was a tragic waste. He was capable of so much more. Maudling had so many characteristics that could have made him a fine leader. These were not just the obvious ones of intelligence, compassion, moderation and amiability. Despite his problems, he was also emotionally balanced in a way that few politicians manage. He was not driven or obsessive about his political career, and did not have a grand fixed idea that he wanted to impose on the rest of the world. He could separate political differences – and even political defeats – from personal relationships and refused to bear grudges. He was able to shrug his shoulders, literally and metaphorically, and move on. He could work with institutions and ideas without reifying or sanctifying them. His calmness and lack of malice, even in trying circumstances, were solid and impressive qualities. There was more than a trace of Stanley Baldwin about Maudling's style of politics and leadership. When given a serious job, Maudling had the ability to knuckle down and master it quickly. It could well have been the same with the Premiership, although he did lack many of the street-fighting instincts that make for a successful opposition leader.

Maudling's memoirs end with a strange, personal epilogue in which he attempts to describe his philosophy of life. Having dismissed contentment as non-existent, happiness as insufficient, he concludes that he agrees with Hilaire Belloc that:

> There's nothing worth the wear of winning
> Save laughter and the love of friends.

Reginald Maudling was a most unusual politician. His gentle and decent political creed and his occasional deeply reprehensible behaviour had a common root in his desire to please and placate, to bring harmony where his cruel mother brought discord. He believed in peace between capital and labour, the old and the young, and he believed in his capacity as a capitalist and a member of the older generation to provide for the vulnerable in society and his own more immediate responsibilities, his family dependents. His sins were the sins of the warm-hearted, which should be weighed in a different balance from those of the wicked or the callous. He was a good man who did wrong, for very human reasons. He came into public life to do good and make things better, and for all the tragedy and waste and corruption, the world is better off for Reggie. He, more than most, did know 'laughter and the love of friends', and no life so blessed by these qualities can be accounted an unmitigated failure.

The grave of Reginald Maudling lies near the wall of the parish church of Little Berkhamsted, near Essendon in Hertfordshire. Beryl lies next to him. Theirs is a very modest final resting place. It is marked with a plain, unadorned stone with their names and dates, and a line from St Paul's letter to the Corinthians more usually quoted in wedding services:

> And now abideth faith, hope, love these three;
> But the greatest of these is love.

NOTES

PROLOGUE

1. Sir Sandy Glen, interview, 11 September 2002.
2. Interviews with Caroline Maudling.
3. Reginald Maudling, *Memoirs* (London: Sidgwick & Jackson, 1978), pp. 19–20. Hereafter *Memoirs*.
4. He was generally known as 'Reginald' but for the sake of clarity he is described here as R.G.
5. Basil Cottle, *The Penguin Dictionary of Surnames* (Harmondsworth: Penguin, 1967, 1978), p. 239.
6. *OMT News Sheet* (Winter 1963/4), p. 17.
7. *Taylorian* (December 1953), obituaries, 'R.G. Maudling'.
8. PRO BT 31/19050/105582, Board of Trade, Omnium files.
9. 'The Failures Among Insurance Offices', *The Times*, 28 June 1912, p. 19.
10. PRO BT 31/19050/105582, Board of Trade, Omnium files.
11. House of Commons Oral Answers, 2 April 1913, col. 392.
12. *Taylorian* (December 1953).
13. In 2002 Peter Clark, the current President of the Institute of Actuaries, was told by his doctor that he was the only actuary the GP had met who had a sense of humour. *Financial Times*, 1 June 2002.
14. R.G. Maudling, 'On the Classification and Duration of Compensation Claims in the Mining Industry', *Journal of the Institute of Actuaries* (November 1929).
15. *Economic Journal*, 33/131 (September 1923), p. 432.
16. *Journal of the Royal Statistical Society*, 91/1 (1928), p. 49.
17. Empire House, at the time of writing, stood empty and was due to be demolished at some time in the mid-2000s. The building was owned by the Kuwaiti Investment Office. R.G.'s granddaughter Caroline worked in an office only two doors away.
18. *Post Office Commercial Directory*, 1921.
19. *North London Guardian*, 7 October 1910.
20. Caroline Maudling, interview, 28 January 2002.
21. *Memoirs*, p. 19.
22. Lucille Iremonger, *The Fiery Chariot* (London: Secker & Warburg, 1970).

CHAPTER 1

1. He was sometimes erroneously assumed, like his father, to have had a middle initial G.
2. *Memoirs*, pp. 20–1.
3. PRO file WO 339/39469, personal file A.J. Farnfield, letter, Farnfield to War Office, 17 October 1918.
4. Obituary of Bernard Farnfield, *Chislehurst Times*, 4 March 1949, p. 5.
5. Although the rates were considerably lower for day boys. PRO file ED 109/2284, HMI Inspection of Bickley Hall school, October 1933.

6. Ashley Courtenay, *Bickley Hall* (Manchester: Cross-Courtenay, *c.* 1920). A copy of this booklet survives in the local studies section of Bromley Central Library.

7. *Ibid.*

8. PRO file ED 109/2284, HMI Inspection of Bickley Hall school, October 1933.

9. 'Bombshell for Bickley Hall', news cutting n.d. filed as L25.6, Bromley local studies collection.

10. *Memoirs*, p. 21.

11. In *Memoirs*, p. 21, Reggie remembers it as a day school, but it was not; in the 1920s the school promoted itself as a boarding establishment and in 1933 it was half boarders and half day boys. PRO file ED 109/2294.

12. Reggie's parents' residential arrangements were always obscure; this information comes from Post Office Directories.

13. *OMT News Sheet* (summer 1963), p. 15.

14. *Memoirs*, pp. 22–3.

15. *Memoirs*, p. 22.

16. *OMT News Sheet* (winter 1963/4), p. 17.

17. Letter, A.F.A. Powles to author, 17 December 2002.

18. *OMT News Sheet* (winter 1963/4), pp. 17–18.

19. Interview with Dennis Nicholson, 18 June 2002.

20. *OMT News Sheet* (summer 1963), p. 17.

21. Michael Rice, interview, 3 July 2003.

22. *OMT News Sheet* (summer 1963), p. 17.

23. *Memoirs*, p. 23; *OMT News Sheet* (summer 1963), p. 15. Cherrett had also heard about the beer bottles – Cherrett interview for *Panorama*, BBC 1, April 1963 (transcript in Edward Boyle Papers, MS 660/52345/2).

24. *Memoirs*, p. 23.

25. Letter, A.F.A. Powles to author, 17 December 2002.

26. *OMT News Sheet*; Douglas Clark, interview for *Panorama*, April 1963.

27. *Taylorian*, 56/2 (June 1934), pp. 124–6.

28. *Taylorian*, 56/4 (December 1934), 5 (March 1935).

29. *Taylorian*, 56/5 (March 1935), pp. 366–9, report of debate, 17 February 1935.

30. *OMT News Sheet* (summer 1963), p. 19.

31. *Taylorian*, 56/5 (March 1935), pp. 366–9, report of debate, 22 February 1935.

32. *Memoirs*, p. 29.

33. Steven Watson, interview for *Panorama*, April 1963.

34. G. Martin and J. Highfield, *A History of Merton College* (Oxford: OUP, 1997), pp. 335–6.

35. Charles Moritz (ed.), *Current Biography 1960* (New York: HW Wilson & Co., 1960), p. 268.

36. *Sunday Pictorial*, 4 March 1962, p. 17.

37. Henry Baskerville, interview, *Panorama*, April 1963.

38. *Isis*, 20 November 1935, 'College notes' p. 19.

39. Moritz, *Current Biography*, p. 268; *Sunday Times*, 29 September 1957.

40. Reginald Maudling, interview, *Panorama*, April 1963.

41. There are no records from the Floats for most of Maudling's time, but he did sign a programme in their album shortly after he left Oxford. The records of the societies are kept in Merton College Library.

42. 'College Comments', *Isis*, 10 March 1937, p. 14.

43. For Neave's life and career see Paul Routledge, *Public Servant, Secret Agent* (London: Fourth Estate, 2002).

44. Steven Watson, interview, *Panorama*, April 1963.

45. *Memoirs*, pp. 24–5.

46. Leigh Hunt translated the whole poem as follows:
    I desire to end my days in a tavern drinking
    May some Christian lift the glass when I am shrinking
    That the Cherubim may cry, when they see me sinking:
    God be merciful to a soul of this gentleman's way of thinking.
47. Steven Watson, interview, *Panorama*, April 1963.
48. Merton College Archives, meetings of Warden and Fellows, 11 and 14 March 1936.
49. This distinctive feature of his handwriting persisted. The author thinks graphology is nonsense, but was curious enough to consult some publications on what high dots and crosses displaced to the right, and other peculiarities of his writing, mean. 'Fast thinker, in a hurry, curiosity seeker, impatience, enthusiasm, daydreamer, high – maybe unrealistic – goals, optimistic, good communicator, taste, intelligence, charitable, expends energies without expecting remuneration', were some that emerged from Ruth Gardner, *Handwriting Secrets Explained* (St Paul, MN: Chancellor Press, 2000). Even on the last point this is actually not too bad as a description of the young Maudling. His 'I' supposedly indicates an absent father and some stress or resentment in his relationship with his mother.
50. Perhaps the JCR committee would consider naming the room after Maudling? A suggestions book from the 1930s thought that the origins of the games room would be 'lost in the mists of antiquity'.
51. Middle Temple records: Harmsworth scholarship applications 1937 and 1938.
52. 'Geoffrey Mure', appreciation by W.H. Walsh, *Postmaster* (1980).
53. 'Reggie Maudling', appreciation by Geoffrey Mure, *Postmaster* (1980).
54. For an insight into the content and style of Mure's teaching, see G.R.G. Mure, *An Introduction to Hegel* (Oxford: Oxford University Press, 1940). It is a difficult treatment of difficult concepts, and ends with no little irony on p. 175: 'If you once sever the good from the intelligible, sooner or later you will find that you have divorced it also from the real.'
55. 'Maudling: the Man in the Middle', interview with Lewis Chester, *Sunday Times*, 4 April 1971.
56. As cited by Peter Singer, *Hegel* (Oxford: Oxford University Press, 1983), p. 28. Singer's treatment of Hegel is more comprehensible than Mure's, but naturally has its own perspectives and does not pretend to be an exhaustive account.
57. *Memoirs*, pp. 29–30. Maudling claims that he despaired at a particularly intricate chapter, but having grappled with Hegel there was surely relatively little in Smith that could have caused him difficulty.
58. As, for instance, in his first letter to his constituents in 1962 as reproduced in *Memoirs*, pp. 260–3, and in his 1943 *Spectator* piece – see Chapter 3.

CHAPTER 2

1. Atticus, interview with Beryl Maudling, *Sunday Times*, 21 July 1963, p. 7.
2. *Stage*, 12 January 1936.
3. Atticus, 'A Heart to Heart with Reggie and Beryl', *Sunday Times*, 24 July 1977, p. 32.
4. Steven Watson, interview, *Panorama*, April 1963, as filed in Edward Boyle Papers MS 660/52345/2.
5. James Haw, interviews, 17 June 2003, 3 July 2003. However, families have legends, and Mr Haw is not completely sure about the distant origins of Beryl's family; it should also be noted that Laverick is a not uncommon family name in the north-east.
6. Joan White (ed.), *20th Century Dance in Britain* (London: Dance Books, 1983), p. 11.
7. *Dancing Times* (May 1924), p. 791. Beryl's medal in 1924, and other years except 1932, was silver, although silver was the highest available in each of several

categories – only one gold was awarded for the best performance in any category.

8. *Sunday Times*, 21 July 1963, p. 7.

9. *The Dancer* (July 1929), p. 505.

10. Ivor Guest, *Adeline Genée: A Lifetime in Ballet under Six Reigns* (London: A&C Black, 1958), p. viii.

11. Derek Parker, *The Royal Academy of Dance: The First Seventy-Five Years* (London: RAD, 1995).

12. Guest, *Adeline Genée*, p. 2.

13. *Dancing Times* (April 1930), p. 35.

14. Guest, *Adeline Genée*, pp. 179–80.

15. *Stage*, 30 December 1932.

16. 'Diary of the District', *Barnet Press*, 4 March 1950, p. 4.

17. *Stage*, 29 December 1933, p. 16.

18. Churchman's *In Town Tonight* cigarette card series 1938, No. 26.

19. Sir Sandy Glen, interview, 11 September 2002.

20. This is a slightly curious matter in itself. On his travels Reggie would sometimes call in on friends and business colleagues of his father, who were scattered through the English-speaking world, and presumably the ICI man was one of these; Maudling also mentions an Anglo-Irish couple called the Martins who lived in Buenos Aires. But Reggie's uncle, Leonard Hugh Maudling, was in the late 1930s listed as being on the staff of the Buenos Aires and Pacific Railway (*MTS Yearbook*). Perusal of English-language newspapers circulating in Buenos Aires at the time has failed to add any information to Maudling's own account.

21. *Memoirs*, pp. 31–2.

22. 'Reggie Maudling', appreciation by Geoffrey Mure, *Postmaster* (1980).

23. Email from Warden's office, All Souls College, to the author, 9 October 2002.

24. Middle Temple records: Harmsworth scholarship papers.

25. Middle Temple Library, attendance book.

26. Harold Nicolson, *Diaries and Letters 1930–39* (London: Collins, 1966), p. 406.

27. *Ibid.*, p. 406n.

28. Ramsay MacDonald Papers, PRO, file PRO 30/69/1329, National Labour.

29. There is no direct evidence of Maudling's own views about appeasement, but the indirect evidence from his juvenilia (of his lack of sympathy with German demands, distaste for Nazi diplomatic methods and anti-Semitic policies and implied criticism of inaction in the face of Japanese aggression in China) suggests that at the time he was instinctively more with Churchill than Chamberlain.

30. Caroline Maudling, interview, 2 July 1999.

31. Caroline Maudling, interview, 2 July 1999.

32. Probate records. R.G.'s 1940 will was a complicated document and it is completely improbable that she failed to make arrangements at the same time. She would have had to make an effort to destroy her will after his death.

33. Trudi Fawcett Kotrosa, interview, 20 May 2003.

34. Some records refer to Orchard Close, a suburban development in Edgware, as being his home in 1939 or 1940 but he did not seem to be there for very long and it cannot have been a permanent family house.

35. Caroline Maudling, interview, 28 January 2002.

36. Yearbooks of the Grotius Society 1939–59. He first appeared in the 1939 Yearbook compiled in 1940 although under the guise of 'Reginald Mandling'; this detail was corrected in 1943 and he remained a passive member at least until 1959.

37. Middle Temple Library, Harmsworth Scholarship committee records 1952.

38. National Sound Archive NP2705R Radio London talk, 9 April 1976.

Chapter 3

1. Sir Alexander Glen with Leighton Bowen, *Target Danube* (Lewes: Book Guild, 2002), describes his extraordinary mission, which led to Glen being called the real James Bond – a label he disclaimed.
2. Ronald G. Stansfield, 'Harold Larnder: Founder of Operational Research: An Appreciation', *Journal of the Operational Research Society*, 34/1 (1983), pp. 2–7, at 6.
3. Sebastian Cox, 'The Organisation and Sources of RAF Intelligence', Royal Air Force Historical Society, *Air Intelligence Symposium* (Bracknell Paper No. 7), 1997, pp. 6–7.
4. *Memoirs*, p. 33.
5. Edward Maudling, interview, 27 October 1999.
6. Derek Mitchell, interview, 28 January 2003.
7. Two such examples are preserved in Churchill College archives: CHAR 7/61B p. 209, 29 August 1942; CHAR 2/440, 2 July 1942.
8. Churchill College, CHAR 20/59/1–10; Maudling to Martin (Number 10), 10 August 1942.
9. Sinclair's personal papers for the war period have been lost or destroyed, but there seems to be no record of postwar correspondence between him and Maudling.
10. Gerard De Groot, *Liberal Crusader: The Life of Sir Archibald Sinclair* (London: Hurst, 1993), pp. 155–7.
11. *Memoirs*, p. 34.
12. Sir Ronald Melville died in 2002. I am most grateful to his son Michael Melville for his help in providing me with a copy of the order of service for Maudling's memorial service, and for telling me about Melville's role in Maudling's decision to go into politics. Michael Melville, letter to author, October 2002.
13. *The War and After* (London: Liberal Publication Department, 1941); text of speech given on 19 March 1941 by Sir Archibald Sinclair. Emphasis in original.
14. Conservative Party Archive, CCO 220/3/9/7, letter Maudling to Booth, 8 August 1946. Emphasis added. The following quotation is from the same source.
15. CPA CCO 220/3/9/7, Booth to Maudling, 13 August 1946; Maudling to Marjorie Maxse, 15 August 1946; *Barnet Press*, 8 March 1952.
16. Enquiries made in 2002 to the two constituency Conservative associations in the areas Maudling was known to be living in 1939–44, Hampstead and Greenwich, produced no information.
17. Obituary, *The Times*, 31 August 1964.
18. CPA CCO 220/3/9/7, Maudling personal file, note of interview, 17 December 1941.
19. CPA CCO 220/3/9/7, Maudling personal file, Greig to Dugdale, 22 January 1942.
20. This and other quotations preceding it in this passage are from Reginald Maudling, 'Conservatives and Control', *Spectator*, 12 November 1943, and reproduced as Appendix 1 in *Memoirs* (pp. 257–60). Emphasis in original.
21. Maudling interview, BBC *Panorama*, April 1963, transcript in Edward Boyle Papers MS 660/52345/8.
22. Reginald Maudling, 'Moderation in Politics', *Crossbow* (January–March 1970), pp. 9–10.
23. *Spectator*, 19 November 1943, Letters, p. 480.
24. CPA CCO 220/3/9/7, Maudling personal file, note of interview with 'HPM', 12 July 1944.
25. De Groot, *Liberal Crusader*, pp. 192–3.
26. 'New Constituency: The Conservative Candidate', *Middlesex Chronicle*, 14 April 1945, p. 2.
27. Letter from W.J. Berridge, *Middlesex Chronicle*, 26 May 1945, p. 5.

28. *Memoirs*, p. 37.
29. 'Conservatives' Meeting', *Middlesex Chronicle*, 26 May 1945, p. 2.
30. 'Great Welcome for Mr Churchill', *Middlesex Chronicle*, Hounslow edition, 7 July 1945, p. 5.
31. 'Loudspeakers and the General Election', *Barnet Press*, 4 February 1950, p. 5.
32. 'Round the Division', *Middlesex Chronicle*, Hounslow edition, 7 July 1945, p. 5.
33. 'The General Election', *Middlesex Chronicle*, Hounslow edition, 28 July 1945, p. 1.
34. Internet Movie Database search; *Middlesex Chronicle*, 2 June 1945, p. 5.

CHAPTER 4

1. 'A set of pink pansies!' Churchill once growled after a meeting with some of the new Conservative MPs in 1945, according to Harold Nicolson, *Diaries 1945–62* (London: Weidenfeld & Nicolson, 1968), p. 45. Although it didn't apply specifically to Maudling, he was part of the same change in attitude within the Conservative Party.
2. *Memoirs*, p. 38.
3. *Ibid.*
4. CPA CRD 2/53/1, R.A. Butler notes on 1945–51, 'Mechanism of the CRD'.
5. CPA CRD 2/53/5, 'Conservative Research Department', David Clarke, 3 August 1951.
6. Lord Butler, *The Art of the Possible* (London: Hamish Hamilton, 1971), p. 142.
7. CPA CCO 4/2/116.
8. CPA, Reginald Maudling, personal file: letter Maudling to Thomas, 24 November 1945.
9. Lord Taylor of Harlow, *A Natural History of Everyday Life* (London: Memoir Club, 1988).
10. Minutes of the two selection meetings are reproduced in *Reginald Maudling: An Informal, Affectionate and Unconcluded Record* (Barnet: Barnet Conservative Association, 1971), p. 2.
11. Lord Carr of Hadley, interview, 29 July 1999.
12. *Ibid.*
13. *Barnet Press*, 2 March 1946.
14. *Barnet Press*, 9 November 1946.
15. *Barnet Press*, 13 April 1946.
16. Avon Papers, AP 11/12/13A, Maudling to Eden, 16 August 1946.
17. Robert Shepherd, interview, 14 September 1999.
18. R.A. Butler Papers, H93, David Clarke to R.A.B., 4 January 1946.
19. Churchill Papers, CHUR 2/78: RM/CO, 27 February 1948, 'Parliamentary Questions on Nationalised Industries', Memorandum PCC 48(7).
20. CPA CRD 2/53/5, 'Conservative Research Department History', paper by Michael Fraser, August 1961; 'CRD record 1945–51'. Output of research papers was down to 120, with a larger staff, in 1959.
21. Enoch Powell, *Reflections of a Statesman* (London: Bellew, 1991), pp. 329–31, 'The Maudling I Knew'.
22. *Memoirs*, p. 28.
23. *Memoirs*, p. 43.
24. 'Reginald Maudling on the Complexity of Iain Macleod', *Spectator*, 12 May 1973, p. 589.
25. Robert Shepherd, *Iain Macleod* (London: Hutchinson, 1994).
26. 'Reginald Maudling on the Complexity of Iain Macleod', *Spectator*, 12 May 1973, p. 589.
27. Even though a sincere abolitionist, Macleod confirmed death sentences as Colonial Secretary in 1959–61. Shepherd, *Iain Macleod*, pp. 486–8.

28. Lord Butler interview (with Anthony Teasdale), 12 June 1980, David Butler Papers.

29. *The Robert Hall Diaries 1954–61*, ed. Alec Cairncross (London: Unwin Hyman, 1991), 28 September 1954, p. 11.

30. Robert Rhodes James, *Anthony Eden* (London: Weidenfeld & Nicolson, 1986), p. 329.

31. Avon Papers, AP 11/12/13, Letter from Maudling to Eden, 16 August 1946.

32. Rhodes James. *Anthony Eden*, pp. 327–8.

33. Eden was irritated that this was sometimes attributed to Butler, 'who had as much to do with that quotation as he did with the battle of Agincourt'. Eden credited Noel Skelton for having coined the phrase in the 1920s. Avon Papers, AP 23/16/71, Avon to Carr, 11 April 1972.

34. Lord Carr of Hadley, interview, 29 July 1999.

35. *Memoirs*, p. 44.

36. Churchill Papers, CHUR 4/49, pp. 61, 108. Maudling's former boss, Archibald Sinclair, with whom Churchill had a good relationship, was under 'other political friends'.

37. CHUR 2/375, Maudling to Churchill, 19 September 1947.

38. CHUR 2/381, Churchill to Maudling, telegram, September 1949.

39. *Barnet Press*, 26 March 1949, p. 4.

40. CHUR 2/59, Maudling to Churchill, 25 September 1947; Churchill memorandum, 25 September 1947.

41. CHUR 2/64, Maudling to Churchill, 30 April 1948.

42. *Sunday Pictorial*, 7 December 1947; CPA CCO 220/3/9/7.

43. CHUR 2/60 on the Manchester speech preparation and arrangements. Churchill asked Maudling to accompany him on the way up as well, but Maudling had to refuse because of a prior engagement. Maudling to Churchill, 1 December 1947.

44. Butler Papers RAB H 92 4–5, note on meeting in Birmingham, 19 December 1946.

45. CPA CRD 2/53/1, Butler notes on 1945–51.

46. *Barnet Press*, 3 May 1947.

47. Butler Papers, RAB H 92/152, Maudling to Butler, 22 September 1947.

48. *Ibid.*

49. *The Times*, 3 October 1947, p. 2.

50. CHUR 2/59, Chapman-Walker to Churchill, 2 October 1947.

51. As cited *Barnet Press*, 18 October 1947.

52. As quoted *The Times*, 6 October 1947, p. 6.

53. *Memoirs*, pp. 45–6.

54. Butler, *The Art of the Possible*, pp. 148–9.

55. CPA CCO 220/3/9/7, Brant to Dodd, 22 October 1947.

56. *The Times*, 30 December 1946, p. 5.

57. Maudling also used some of the same line of argument in a New Year message to his prospective Barnet constituents; *Barnet Press*, 17 January 1948, p. 4.

58. CHUR 5/16B, Maudling memorandum, 17 January 1948.

59. *Ibid.*

60. *Barnet Press*, 21 February 1948, p. 3.

61. CHUR 2/69, Maudling to Churchill, 22 June 1948.

62. *Barnet Press*, 15 January 1949.

63. CPA CRD 2/53/71, R.A. Butler notes on 1945–51, 'Mechanism of the CRD'.

64. CPA CRD 2/53/5, note by David Clarke, 8 August 1951, p. 8.

65. Robert Shepherd, interview, 14 September 1999.

66. CPA CRD 2/53/5, note by David Clarke, 8 August 1951, p. 8.

67. James Haw, interview, 17 June 2003.

68. R.A. Butler Papers, H33, Maudling to Butler, 23 November 1949.

69. *Memoirs*, p. 28.

70. For the main opposing views on consensus, see Harriet Jones and Michael Kandiah (eds), *The Myth of Consensus* (London: Macmillan, 1996); and Dennis Kavanagh and Peter Morris, *Consensus Politics from Attlee to Major* (Oxford: Basil Blackwell, 1994); and the debate in various issues since 1988 of *Contemporary Record* and *Contemporary British History*. Maudling is an under-recognised witness that there was something real, with more than a retrospective gloss, that was consensus; but I have also drawn attention in this chapter to some of his most non-consensual interventions.
71. CHUR 5/16B, memorandum by Maudling, 17 January 1948.
72. CHUR 2/84, Maudling to Gilliatt (Churchill's Private Secretary), 14 April 1949.
73. *Barnet Press*, 30 April 1949, p. 5.
74. CHUR 2/79, 'Brief on the Iron and Steel Bill', 10 November 1948.
75. *Barnet Press*, 29 November 1947.
76. CHUR 2/99, Maudling to Churchill, 1 February 1950.
77. *The Times*, 6 October 1947.
78. CHUR 2/16B, Maudling memorandum, 17 January 1948.
79. CHUR 5/16B, Maudling memorandum, 17 January 1948.
80. For instance, see *Barnet Press*, 24 April 1948, p. 5; 1 May 1948, p. 5; 15 January 1949, p. 5; 26 February 1949, p. 4.
81. CHUR 2/163, Maudling to Churchill, 23 May 1949.
82. CHUR 2/81, Maudling to Churchill, 14 September 1949.
83. Chris Bryant, *Stafford Cripps* (London: Hodder & Stoughton, 1997), pp. 424–34.
84. CHUR 2/84, Maudling to Eden, 6 October 1949.
85. *Barnet Press*, 29 October 1949, p. 5.
86. Brian Brivati and Lewis Baston, *The Future Labour Offered You* (forthcoming).
87. *The Times*, 30 December 1946, p. 5.

CHAPTER 5

1. Chipping Barnet Conservative archives, Barnet borough local studies file 21,109/1, Well House ward minutes.
2. *Barnet Press*, 15 January 1949, p. 4.
3. *Barnet Press*, 26 June 1948, p. 5.
4. The version of events in John Junor, *Listening for a Midnight Tram* (London: Chapmans, 1990), p. 197, is not supported by Lord Carr of Hadley, who completely understood Reggie's position and does not feel that Reggie acted inconsiderately. Letter, Lord Carr of Hadley to author, 18 July 2003.
5. *Barnet Press*, 3 December 1949, pp. 4–5.
6. Hertfordshire County Council records: Hertfordshire archives, HCC1/85–7, HCC2/208, 210, HCC50/1–2, HCC51/1–2.
7. 'Mrs Maudling to Retire from County Council', *Barnet Press*, 19 January 1952, p. 5.
8. Michael Rice, interview, 3 July 2003.
9. *Boreham Wood and Elstree Post*, 16 February 1950.
10. *Barnet Press*, 4 February 1950, p. 5.
11. Reginald Maudling, *Election Address February 1950* (Barnet: Barnet Conservative Association).
12. CPA CCO 1/8/322, Re: Barnet constituency reports: Annual report for 1950.
13. *Barnet Press*, 25 March 1950, p. 5; 29 April 1950, p. 6.
14. CHUR 2/99, Maudling to Churchill, 15 February 1950.
15. *The Times*, 21 February 1950.
16. H.G. Nicholas, *The British General Election of 1950* (London: Macmillan, 1951), pp. 286–7.
17. *Barnet Press*, 4 March 1950, p. 5.

18. *Barnet Press*, 25 March 1950, p. 10.
19. *Observer*, 5 March 1950, as cited *Barnet Press*, 11 March 1950, p. 4.
20. Michael Rice, interview, 3 July 2003.
21. *HC Debates* (series 5), vol. 472, cols 678–81, 10 March 1950.
22. *Barnet Press*, 25 March 1950, p. 10.
23. Michael Rice, interview, 3 July 2003.
24. *Memoirs*, p. 52.
25. Maudling quickly worked out that Bromley-Davenport was a man to be reckoned with, commenting in March 1950 that 'even I can't get past him' to get much time off from Westminster. *Barnet Press*, 25 March 1950, p. 10.
26. CHUR 2/99, Maudling to Eden, 9 January 1950.
27. *HC Debates*, vol. 476, cols 898–902, 19 June 1950.
28. Penny Junor, *Home Truths* (London: HarperCollins, 2002).
29. *Sunday Express*, 13 August 1950, p. 4.
30. RAB H 34/34, Butler to Macleod, 25 August 1950; Macleod to Butler, 28 August 1950.
31. David Butler, interview, 7 July 2003.
32. CPA CCO 1/8/322, Barnet constituency reports, Barnet annual report, 1950.
33. 'An MP and his Constituents', *Barnet Press*, 25 March 1950, p. 6.
34. Robert Shepherd, *Iain Macleod* (London: Hutchinson, 1994), p. 55.
35. CPA CCO 1/8/322, Barnet constituency reports.
36. *HC Debates*, vol. 473, cols 614–18, 30 March 1950.
37. *HC Debates*, vol. 485, cols 1009–13, 9 March 1951.
38. *The Times*, 12 September 1951.
39. Brian Brivati and Lewis Baston, *The Future Labour Offered You* (forthcoming).
40. Churchill Papers, CHUR 2, personal correspondence 1951.
41. 'Holiday Theft at Home of Barnet's MP', *Barnet Press*, 29 September 1951, p. 1.
42. *Barnet Press*, 12 May 1951, p. 3.
43. *Barnet Press*, 13 October 1951, p. 8.
44. *Barnet Press*, 13 October 1951, p. 8.
45. *Barnet Press*, 13 October 1951, pp. 1, 8.
46. Arthur Fawcett diary, 13 December 1951.
47. *Barnet Press*, 24 November 1951, p. 1.
48. Report of speech to Totteridge Conservatives, 6 January 1951, *Barnet Press*, 13 January 1951, p. 8.
49. *BBC Homes and Antiques Magazine*, August 2000, pp. 87–93.
50. *Sunday Express*, 20 April 1952.
51. Arthur Fawcett diary, 25 January 1951.
52. *Barnet Press*, 6 October 1951, p. 1.
53. *Barnet Press*, 24 November 1951, p. 1; 1 December 1951, letters.
54. *Barnet Press*, 26 January 1952.
55. Alport Papers, Box 37, One Nation Group minutes, 5 April 1951.
56. Alport Papers, Box 37, One Nation Group minutes, 7 April 1952.

Chapter 6

1. *Memoirs*, p. 52.
2. Sir William Teeling, *Corridors of Frustration* (London: Johnson, 1970), p. 178.
3. University of Glasgow, Maclay Papers, DC 371/2/4, Letter, Lord Muirshiel of Kilmacolm to Anthony Seldon, 10 February 1980.
4. PRO PREM 11/175, '1952 Government Machinery', Note from Norman Brook to PM, 2 May 1952.

5. *HC Debates*, vol. 509, col. 685 et seq., 11 December 1952.
6. Philip Murphy, *Alan Lennox-Boyd* (London: I.B. Tauris, 1999), pp. 91–6.
7. *Ibid.*, pp. 96–7.
8. 'Mr Maudling Talks to the Teachers', *Barnet Press*, 17 May 1952, p. 9.
9. *Barnet Press*, 31 May 1952.
10. Michael Rice, interview, 3 July 2003.
11. *The Times*, 25 November 1952, p. 8.
12. *HC Debates*, vol. 501, col. 143, 19 May 1952.
13. Lord Butler, *The Art of the Possible* (London: Hamish Hamilton, 1971), p. 156.
14. John Marshall, interview, 23 April 2003.
15. John Boyd-Carpenter, *Way of Life* (London: Sidgwick & Jackson, 1980), pp. 96–101.
16. 'Barnet MP Tipped for High Office', *Barnet Press*, 24 May 1952, p. 1; the speculation also appeared in the London evening press.
17. University of Essex, Alport Papers Box 37, One Nation Group minutes, 24 July 1952.
18. *The Times*, 25 November 1952, p. 9.
19. PRO T 199/631, draft job description, 29 November 1952.
20. PRO T 199/631, Roger Makins to Norman Brook, 'Operation Counter-Smike', 2 April 1958.
21. 'The Following Have Arrived', *Truth*, 15 April 1955, p. 445.
22. John Marshall, interview, 23 April 2003.
23. *Ibid.*
24. *Ibid.*
25. Robot aroused fierce arguments in the Treasury at the time, and continues to divide historians. There is a considerable literature – Edmund Dell, *The Chancellors* (London: HarperCollins, 1996), pp. 166–95 is a good place to pick it up. Reggie not being involved in Robot as such, I see no reason to go deeply into the issue in this book.
26. *Barnet Press*, 3 May 1952, p. 5.
27. *HC Debates*, vol. 497, col. 1980, 17 March 1952.
28. *Memoirs*, p. 56.
29. John Marshall, interview, 23 April 2003.
30. *HC Debates*, vol. 959, col. 495, 29 November 1978.
31. PRO T 236/3708, Maudling note on visit to Scandinavia, June 1954.
32. PRO T 172/2124, Butler to Salter, 31 July 1953.
33. *Economist*, 3 October 1953, p. 46.
34. *Memoirs*, p. 57.
35. *Memoirs*, pp. 148–9.
36. PRO DO 35/5589 contains a mass of information.
37. Barry Eichengreen, *Reconstructing Europe's Trade and Payments* (Manchester: Manchester University Press, 1993); Graham Rees, *Britain and the Postwar European Payments Systems* (Cardiff: University of Wales Press, 1963).
38. See PRO T 236/3708 for Maudling's positive reception on a trip to Scandinavia in June 1954.
39. *Fortune*, June 1954, p. 89.
40. *HC Debates*, vol. 514, col. 1273, 22 April 1953.
41. Henry Fairlie, 'Political Commentary', *Spectator*, 15 April 1955, p. 461.
42. *Economist*, 10 April 1954, p. 129.
43. As cited Samuel Brittan, *The Treasury Under the Tories 1951–64* (Harmondsworth: Penguin, 1964), p. 167.
44. Avon Papers, AP 11/10/166D, Buchan-Hepburn to Eden, 3 March 1954.
45. Avon Papers, AP 11/10/166A, Buchan-Hepburn to Eden, 12 March 1954.
46. *The Robert Hall Diaries 1954–61*, ed. Alec Cairncross (London: Unwin Hyman, 1991), 28 September 1954, p. 11.

47. Joseph Retinger, *Memoirs of an Eminence Grise*, ed. John Pomian (Brighton: Sussex University Press, 1972), pp. 250–60.

48. PRO PREM 11/1965, Maudling to Eden, 3 April 1956.

49. UCL, Gaitskell Papers, file C304.

50. PRO PREM 11/1965, note on February 1957 meeting by Lord Chancellor.

51. PRO PREM 11/1965, 'A note on the Bilderberg group', probably from 1957.

52. Arthur Fawcett, diary, 11 March 1955.

53. Richard Lamb, *The Failure of the Eden Government* (London: Sidgwick & Jackson, 1987), pp. 4–5, cites evidence that Eden and Butler had been discussing election timing before the formal succession had taken place. It is quite possible that Butler took Maudling into his confidence about the matter.

CHAPTER 7

1. Arthur Fawcett diary, 12 April 1955.

2. Birmingham University, Avon Papers, AP 11/11/8A.

3. *Memoirs*, p. 60.

4. *HC Debates*, vol. 549, col. 1230, 29 February 1956.

5. PRO SUPP 16/29, Maudling to Lloyd, 23 August 1956.

6. D.R. Thorpe, *Selwyn Lloyd* (London: Jonathan Cape, 1989), pp. 181–2.

7. Lord Hill of Luton, *Both Sides of the Hill* (London: Heinemann, 1964), p. 164.

8. *Economist*, 16 April 1955, p. 183.

9. *Time* (US), 18 April 1955, p. 29.

10. 'Review of the Week', *Time and Tide*, 16 April 1955, p. 484.

11. David Butler, *The British General Election of 1955* (London: Macmillan, 1955), p. 64.

12. *HC Debates*, vol. 540, cols 349–65, 21 April 1955.

13. 'Diary', *Time and Tide*, 30 April 1955, p. 553.

14. *Time* (US), 23 May 1955.

15. Arthur Fawcett diary, 9 November 1953.

16. *Barnet Press*, 4 June 1955, p. 9.

17. *Barnet Press*, 30 June 1978.

18. Arthur Fawcett diary, 26 October 1953, 28 October 1954.

19. CPA CCO 1/10/322, Barnet annual report for meeting, 9 April 1954.

20. CPA CCO 1/10/322, Barnet memorandum from General Director, 27 November 1953 and report, 30 November 1953.

21. Arthur Fawcett diary, 22 January 1953.

22. *Barnet Press*, 21 May 1955, p. 1.

23. Speech at Church House, Cockfosters as quoted *Barnet Press*, 21 May 1955, p. 9.

24. *Barnet Press*, 4 June 1955, p. 9.

25. Arthur Fawcett diary, 26 May 1955.

26. MRC Warwick; Crossman Papers, letter to Gilbert Baker, 2 June 1955.

27. *HC Debates*, vol. 543, cols 1559–63, 11 July 1955.

28. Keith Hayward, *Government and British Civil Aerospace* (Manchester: Manchester University Press 1983), pp. 13–19.

29. As cited *ibid.*, p. 19.

30. *Ibid.*, pp. 20–2.

31. PRO AIR 20/7734, Maudling to Butler, 14 October 1955.

32. Derek Wood, *Project Cancelled* (London: Tri-Service Press, 1990), p. 83.

33. *HC Debates* vol. 546, col. 669, 8 December 1955.

34. PRO SUPP 16/26, File note, 8 February 1956.

35. *Memoirs*, pp. 62–3.

36. *HC Debates*, vol. 547, cols 1931–5, 20 December 1955.

37. *Memoirs*, p. 62.
38. *Memoirs*, p. 61.
39. PRO SUPP 16/26, Minute 965/162, 3 August 1956.
40. PRO SUPP 16/26, Maudling to Watkinson, 6 February 1956.
41. PRO SUPP 16/26, Watkinson to Maudling, 29 June 1956.
42. 'Supersonic Bust', *Atlantic Monthly*, January 1977.
43. Sir Sandy Glen, interview, 11 September 2002.
44. *HC Debates*, vol. 550, cols 167–8, 12 March 1956.
45. Tom Caulcott, interview, 9 April 2003.
46. *Daily Telegraph*, 18 September 2002.
47. Andrew Roth, 'Sir Frederic Bennett', *Guardian*, 20 September 2002.
48. Letter Sir Frederic Bennett to author, 10 July 2002.
49. PRO T 231/1256.
50. Butler Papers, RAB G 28/57, Maudling to Butler, 26 October 1955, and reply.
51. For a full account of the Suez crisis, see Keith Kyle, *Suez* (London: IB Tauris, 2003).
52. *Memoirs*, p. 63.
53. *Memoirs*, p. 64.
54. *Barnet Press*, 5 January 1957, p. 5, reporting speech to Brunswick Park Conservatives.
55. *Barnet Press*, 9 February 1957, p. 2, reporting speech at East Barnet dinner-dance.
56. *Memoirs*, p. 64.
57. Anthony Nutting, *No End of a Lesson* (London: Constable, 1967), p. 171.
58. As cited Michael Foot and Mervyn Jones, *Guilty Men 1957* (London: Victor Gollancz, 1957), p. 221.
59. Arthur Fawcett diary, 2 December 1956.
60. Michael Rice, interview, 3 July 2003.
61. Arthur Fawcett diary, 9 January 1957.
62. Michael Rice, interview, 3 July 2003.
63. *Memoirs*, p. 64.
64. *Barnet Press*, 19 January 1957, p. 1, reporting dinner at Totteridge, 12 January 1957.
65. Arthur Fawcett diary, 9 January 1957.
66. Butler Papers, RAB G 46/5(21), 'Cabinet', January 1957

CHAPTER 8

1. Fawcett Papers, Arthur Fawcett diary, 12 January 1957.
2. Carmarthenshire Archives, Cilcennin Papers, Macmillan to Thomas, 1954.
3. *Memoirs*, p. 65.
4. Alistair Horne, *Macmillan 1894–1956* (London: Macmillan, 1988–9), pp. 453–7.
5. Anthony Howard, *RAB* (London: Jonathan Cape, 1987), p. 241.
6. *The Macmillan Diaries 1950–57*, ed. Peter Catterall (London: Macmillan, 2003), 3 February 1957, p. 614. Emphasis in original.
7. Sir Sandy Glen, interview, 11 September 2002.
8. Speech to Building Societies Association, as cited Michael Gillard and Martin Tomkinson, *Nothing to Declare* (London: John Calder, 1980), p. 168. Another such office, Lord Privy Seal, once attracted a similar disclaimer from its occupant: 'I am not a Lord. Nor am I a privy. Nor am I, thank God, a seal.'
9. Private interview.
10. *HC Debates*, vol. 563, cols 1198–9, 31 January 1957.
11. Roger Williams, *The Nuclear Power Decisions* (London: Croom Helm, 1980), p. 29.
12. *Ibid.*, pp. 60–1, 80–1.
13. *HC Debates*, vol. 562, col. 940, 17 December 1956; Williams, *Nuclear Power Decisions*, pp. 82–3.

14. ITN archive, 17 January 1957, Reginald Maudling interview with John Hartley.
15. *Memoirs*, pp. 66–7.
16. Lorna Arnold, *Windscale 1957*, 2nd edn (London: Macmillan, 1995), pp. 82–5.
17. *HC Debates*, vol. 566, cols 184–90, 5 March 1957.
18. 'Londoner's Diary', *Evening Standard*, 17 January 1957, p. 4.
19. R.G. Maudling's complicated will was executed following his death in 1953; it created trust funds with Reggie as beneficiary; with the 1945–9 subsidy of £2,000 Reggie had already been in receipt of substantial funds from his parents for some time, but Elsie's legacy was certainly a significant lump sum addition.
20. D.R. Thorpe, *Selwyn Lloyd* (London: Jonathan Cape, 1989), p. 149.
21. *HC Debates*, vol. 573, col. 222, 9 July 1957.
22. Geoffrey Wakeford, 'Maudling's Chance?', *Truth*, 29 November 1957, p. 1338.
23. PRO FO 371/128356, note of meeting, 15 August 1957; PRO T 337/16, Leslie to Liverman, 21 August 1957.
24. PRO T 337/16, prime ministerial minute, M357/57, 26 July 1957; Maudling to Macmillan, 5 August 1957, 13 August 1957.
25. As cited *Barnet Press*, 21 September 1957, p. 16.
26. See www.oecd.org/about/origins/oeec.htm.
27. PRO FO 371/128356, minute on UK and FTA negotiations, 16 August 1957.
28. PRO FO 371/134504, for papers connected with Maudling's missions.
29. William Clark Papers, f. 97, Maudling to Clark, 26 September 1957.
30. Sir Peter Carey, interview, 14 May 2003.
31. Adam Raphael, *Ultimate Risk* (London: Corgi, 1995), pp. 68–72.
32. PRO T 215/664, note to Prime Minister from Norman Brook, 31 December 1957.
33. PRO PREM 11/1484, Derek Mitchell (Treasury) to David Pitblado (Number 10), 15 July 1955.
34. PRO PREM 11/1484, Pitblado to Mitchell, 28 July 1955.
35. PRO T 215/664, note to Prime Minister from Norman Brook, 31 December 1957.
36. PRO T 199/486, note, 15 November 1957.
37. Richard Lamb, *The Macmillan Years* (London: John Murray, 1995), pp. 49–50.
38. PRO T 199/631, Division of ministerial responsibilities, note, 9 January 1958, from Roger Makins.
39. *HC Debates*, vol. 584, cols 227–8, 11 March 1958.
40. *The Robert Hall Diaries 1954–61*, ed. Alec Cairncross (London: Unwin Hyman, 1991), 31 March 1958, p. 153.
41. Horne, *Macmillan*, p. 67.
42. *HC Debates*, vol. 581, cols 1105–15, 4 February 1958.
43. Ben Pimlott, *Harold Wilson* (London: HarperCollins, 1992), pp. 216–17.
44. Paul Ferris, *The City* (London: Victor Gollancz, 1960).
45. Sir Sandy Glen, interview, 11 September 2002.
46. *Memoirs*, p. 75.
47. Nora Beloff, *The General Says 'No'* (Harmondsworth: Penguin Special, 1963), p. 80.
48. *Memoirs*, p. 72.
49. Lamb, *The Macmillan Years*, pp. 102–57, is an account of the negotiations from the British perspective with the PRO documents. Miriam Camps, *Britain and the European Community 1955–1963* (London: Oxford University Press, 1964), pp. 130–72, did an admirable job without the PRO files. I consider that Lamb, Camps and others have done enough for me to consider Reggie's challenge (*Memoirs*, p. 75), 'I will not go into the details of the negotiations; that is for the historians', to have been met already.
50. *HC Debates*, vol. 592, cols 1369–72, 30 July 1958.
51. Camps, *Britain and the European Community*, p. 155; Victoria Curzon, *The Essentials of Economic Integration* (London: Macmillan, 1974), p. 32.

52. *HC Debates*, vol. 595, cols 350–4, 11 November 1958.
53. Roy Denman, *Missed Chances* (London: Indigo, 1997), pp. 203–6.
54. FRUS 1958–60, vol. VII.1 (Washington DC: Government printing office, 1993) Memcon, 21 November 1958, with Ernst van der Beugel.
55. Camps (*Britain and the European Community*, pp. 168–9, 374) mentions some of these points.
56. Curzon, *The Essentials*, p. 34, develops this point; also Beloff, *The General*, pp. 84–5.
57. Command Papers 648 and 651 relating to Negotiations for a European Free Trade Area.
58. Douglas Jay, *Change and Fortune* (London: Hutchinson, 1980), pp. 281, 324.
59. *HC Debates*, vol. 599, cols 1380–3, 12 February 1959.
60. *HC Debates*, vol. 599, col. 1387, 12 February 1959.
61. Beloff, *The General*, p. 79.
62. Boyle Papers, MS 669/52274 et seq., Boyle to Barnes, 29 April 1981.
63. Haruko Fukuda, 'First Decade of EFTA's realization', in Hugh Corbet and David Robertson (eds), *Europe's Free Trade Experiment* (Oxford: Pergamon, 1970), pp. 43–77.
64. Fawcett Papers, Arthur Fawcett diary, 4 March 1957.
65. *HC Debates*, vol. 603, col. 232, 8 April 1959.
66. Beloff, *The General*, p. 87.
67. David Butler and Richard Rose, *The British General Election of 1959* (London: Macmillan, 1960), p. 63.
68. *Barnet Press*, 5 September 1959, letters; *Barnet Press*, 3 October 1959, p. 1.
69. Fawcett Papers, Maudling to Fawcett, 12 March 1959.
70. Fawcett Papers, Fawcett to Maudling, 2 August 1957; Maudling to Fawcett, 7 August 1957; Fawcett to Maudling, 6 September 1957.
71. 'Tory Landslide Surprised Mr Maudling', *Barnet Press*, 30 October 1959, p. 5.

CHAPTER 9

1. *HC Debates*, vol. 612, col. 276, 28 October 1959.
2. *Memoirs*, pp. 76–7.
3. Lord Erroll obituary by D.R. Thorpe, *Independent*, 26 September 2000.
4. Lord Erroll obituary, *The Times*, 18 September 2000.
5. Sir Peter Carey, interview, 28 April 2003.
6. PRO BT 11/5771, Macmillan to Maudling, 25 October 1959.
7. PRO BT 11/5771, Maudling to Macmillan, 27 October 1959.
8. Victoria Curzon, *The Essentials of Economic Integration* (London: Macmillan, 1974), p. 34.
9. Timothy Sherwen, 'British Business Attitudes towards EFTA', in Hugh Corbet and David Robertson (eds), *Europe's Free Trade Experiment* (Oxford: Pergamon, 1970), pp. 189–204.
10. *HC Debates*, vol. 615, col. 1168, 14 December 1959.
11. *HC Debates*, vol. 615, cols 1162–75, 14 December 1959.
12. Richard Lamb, *The Macmillan Years: The Emerging Truth* (London: John Murray, 1995), pp. 131–2; Nora Beloff, *The General Says 'No'* (Harmondsworth: Penguin Special, 1963), p. 86.
13. Lamb, *The Macmillan Years*, pp. 134–5.
14. *Ibid.*, pp. 138–9.
15. LSE, Hetherington Papers, interview with Reginald Maudling, 11 February 1960.
16. Roy Denman, *Missed Chances* (London: Indigo, 1997), pp. 208–13; Hugo Young, *This Blessed Plot* (London: Macmillan, 1999), pp. 122–5.

17. *HC Debates*, vol. 627, cols 1206–18, 25 July 1960.
18. 'Lord Erroll of Hale', obituary by D.R. Thorpe, *Independent*, 26 September 2000.
19. Edward Heath, *The Course of My Life* (London: Hodder & Stoughton, 1998), pp. 201–5.
20. Sir Peter Carey, interview, 28 April 2003.
21. *The Robert Hall Diaries 1954–61*, ed. Alec Cairncross (London: Unwin Hyman 1991), 1 January 1960, p. 224.
22. PRO BT 64/5223, Maudling to Macmillan, 29 June 1961.
23. PRO BT 64/5223, internal note Board of Trade, 30 June 1961.
24. Conservative Party archive contains a transcript of the 1954 broadcast.
25. *HC Debates*, vol. 613, col. 33, 9 November 1959.
26. Peter Scott, 'The Worst of Both Worlds: British Regional Policy 1951–64', *Business History*, 38 (October 1996), p. 41.
27. The problems were apparent in the election results, in which Scotland and Lancashire produced relatively poor results for the Conservatives.
28. Scott, 'The Worst of Both Worlds', citing K. Warren, *The British Iron and Steel Sheet Industry since 1840* (London: Bell, 1970).
29. Scott, 'The Worst of Both Worlds', citing PRO CAB 134/1624, Distribution of Industry Committee, 6 January 1960.
30. Alastair Hetherington Papers, LSE Library, interview with Reginald Maudling, 11 February 1960.
31. Scott, 'The Worst of Both Worlds'.
32. Sir Sandy Glen, interview, 10 March 2003.
33. Boyle Papers, MS 669/52274 et seq., Boyle to Lord Blake, 10 June 1981.
34. Sir Peter Carey, interviews, 28 April 2003, 14 May 2003. This was a general view within the department, not a personal view of Carey's.
35. Sir Peter Carey, interview, 28 April 2003.
36. Sir Peter Carey, interview, 14 May 2003.
37. For more on Marples, a man whose strange career has been insufficiently studied, see Richard Stott, *Dogs and Lampposts* (London: Metro, 2002), pp. 166–71.
38. PRO PREM 11/4945, *Hansard*, 28 January 1960, cols 372–3.
39. PRO reference BT 58/1482.
40. Sir Peter Carey, interview, 28 April 2003.
41. John Poulson, *The Price* (London: Michael Joseph, 1981), p. 99.
42. They were also guests at the same party in 1957 but neither Poulson nor Maudling remembered talking to each other on that occasion.
43. PRO BT 278/33, Export promotion group 1960–2, Export promotion campaign, Ninth Progress Report (January 1962).
44. Sir Sandy Glen, interview, 10 March 2003.
45. *Board of Trade Journal*, 180/3349, 26 May 1961.
46. Sir Peter Carey, interview, 28 April 2003.
47. *Memoirs*, p. 83.
48. Sir Peter Carey, interview, 28 April 2003.
49. *Memoirs*, p. 85.
50. PRO 11/5844, note on visit to Canada and USA, 24–30 September 1961.
51. Sir Peter Carey, interview, 28 April 2003.
52. Rhodes House Library, MSS Brit Emp s.484 p. 1, Reginald Maudling, interview, 24 April 1968.
53. 'How Big a Prize for Mr Maudling?', *The Director* (March 1961), pp. 455–7.
54. Sir Peter Carey, interview, 28 April 2003.
55. Churchill College, Hailes Papers, HAIS 4/13, Cary to Patrick Buchan-Hepburn, 11 April 1955.

56. Cecil King, *The Cecil King Diary 1965–70* (London: Jonathan Cape, 1972), 19 August 1965, p. 32.

57. *Statist*, Westminster Commentary, July 1963, filed RAB G 38/241.

Chapter 10

1. *Economist*, 14 July 1962, p. 159, citing a Kenyan newspaper.

2. A.N. Porter and A.J. Stockwell, *British Imperial Policy and Decolonization 1938–64*, vol. 2 *1951–64* (Cambridge Commonwealth Studies; London: Macmillan, 1989), p. 558, Document 80: Macleod to Conservative Party Conference, 11 October 1961.

3. Patrick Wall Papers, DPW48/161, Wall to Welensky, 10 October 1961.

4. Philip Murphy, *Party Politics and Decolonisation* (Oxford: Clarendon Press, 1995), p. 194.

5. Sir Roy Welensky, *Welensky's 4000 Days* (London: Collins, 1964), pp. 315–16.

6. Robert Shepherd, *Iain Macleod* (London: Pimlico, 1995), p. 255.

7. *HC Debates*, vol. 646, col. 354, 19 October 1961.

8. *HC Debates*, vol. 646, cols 345–54, 19 October 1961.

9. Macmillan diary, as cited in Horne, *Macmillan*, p. 408.

10. Lord Butler Papers, RAB G 38/2–28, 'The Africa Choice', 10 March 1962.

11. Jack Howard-Drake, interview, 12 May 2003.

12. Andrew Lycett, *Ian Fleming* (London: Phoenix, 1996), p. 393.

13. Logan Gourlay interview, 'Not Ruthless, but I Had Luck', *Daily Express*, 27 August 1962, p. 4.

14. David Cannadine, 'Ian Fleming and the Realities of Escapism', in *In Churchill's Shadow* (London: Allen Lane/ Penguin, 2002), pp. 279–311, provides an extended and interesting discussion of Bond in the context of contemporary British history.

15. 'Sex, Snobbery and Sadism', *New Statesman*, 5 August 1958, pp. 430–43, as cited by Cannadine, 'Ian Fleming', p. 302.

16. 'A Calypso Welcome for Reginald Maudling', filed in CCC Hailes Papers, HAIS 7/36.

17. Rhodes House Library, MSS Brit Emp s.484, Transcript of interview, 25 April 1968, W.P. Kirkman with Reginald Maudling, p. 16.

18. Jack Howard-Drake, interview, 12 May 2003; *Memoirs*, p. 92.

19. Jack Howard-Drake, interview, 12 May 2003.

20. Rhodes House, interview, p. 16.

21. Kim Johnson, 'How the Independence Deal was Hammered Out', *Trinidad Express Politics*, 30 August 1998.

22. David Holden, 'Bitter Days for British Guiana', *Guardian*, 16 May 1962.

23. Hector Parekh, 'Subversion in British Guiana', citing full declassified version of Schlesinger to Bruce, 1 March 1962, *Monthly Review* (October 1999).

24. FRUS documents on http://lasalle.edu/~daniels/guyexp/bg263.htm: Tyler to Rusk, 18 February 1962.

25. PRO PREM 11/3666, Fraser to Maudling, 20 March 1962. There are still a surprising number of documents withheld from this very revealing file. The American administration also admitted privately that it had failed to implement the policy of working with Jagan: FRUS, Tyler to Rusk, 18 February 1962.

26. PRO PREM 11/3666, Maudling to Macmillan, 10 January 1962.

27. Cheddi Jagan, Broadcast on Fight for Independence, January 1962; www.jagan.org/articles2.htm

28. PRO PREM 11/3666, Rusk to Home, 20 February 1962.

29. PRO PREM 11/3666, Macmillan to Home, 21 February 1962; Home to Rusk, 26 February 1962. Home's letter to Rusk was worded in extremely angry, pointed terms: he reminded the Americans that they had installed a regime in Guatemala that

was now making threats in 'language reminiscent of Hitler' against another British territory, British Honduras.

30. FRUS (Lasalle), Schlesinger to Bruce, 1 March 1962, and declassified version as cited by Parekh.
31. FRUS (Lasalle), Schlesinger to Kennedy, 8 March 1962.
32. FRUS (Lasalle), Schlesinger to Bruce, 1 March 1962.
33. PRO PREM 11/3666, Maudling to Jagan, 3 May 1962.
34. PRO PREM 11/3666, de Zulueta to Macmillan, 15 May 1962.
35. PRO PREM 11/3666, Macmillan to Brook, M112/62, 3 May 1962.
36. PRO PREM 11/3666, Fraser to British Ambassador, Washington, DC, 1 May 1962.
37. FRUS (Lasalle), McGeorge Bundy to Kennedy, 13 July 1962.
38. PRO CO 1013/3761 deals in more detail with the arguments about electoral systems in Guyana. Because the PPP failed to stand in six constituencies out of thirty-five, its vote share – actually 42.7 per cent – is understated. Depending on which form of PR was used, the PPP may have had a majority in 1961 and given demographic trends would be likely to win an election taking place in 1965 or later. 'British Guiana: Proportional Representation', 30 August 1962.
39. PRO PREM 11/3666, Fraser to Maudling, 20 March 1962.
40. PRO CAB 128/36 CC26(62), 5 April 1962. Maudling reported that there was no prospect of sufficient agreement at the constitutional conference to permit either internal self-government or independence in Zanzibar.
41. Rhodes House, interview, 1968, p. 24.
42. PRO CO 1015/2287, Watson to Martin, 5 December 1961, for instance, alludes to this; Maudling was afraid that Sandys would give Welensky commitments to which he, and the Colonial Office, could not be bound.
43. PRO PREM 11/3497, Maudling to Macmillan, 6 November 1961.
44. Rhodes House, interview, 1968, p. 2.
45. DPW 64/52, note of meeting with Reginald Maudling, 6 January 1962; also Welensky, *Welensky's 4000 Days*, p. 316.
46. PRO PREM 11/3497, Maudling to Macmillan, 6 November 1961. Double underlining in original.
47. *Memoirs*, p. 98.
48. Rhodes House, interview, 1968, p. 5.
49. RAB G 38/2–28, 'The Africa Choice', 10 March 1962.
50. Frank Heinlein, *British Government Policy and Decolonisation 1945–1963* (London: Frank Cass, 2002), pp. 258–9.
51. Harold Evans, *Downing Street Diary* (London: Hodder & Stoughton, 1981), 3 February 1962, p. 182.
52. DPW 64/52, note of meeting with Reginald Maudling, 6 January 1962.
53. Alistair Horne, *A Savage War of Peace* (London: Papermac, 1996).
54. Trevor Royle, *Winds of Change* (London: John Murray, 1996), pp. 197–8.
55. PRO CAB 128/35 CC61(61), 9 November 1961.
56. Rhodes House, interview, 1968, p. 8.
57. PRO CAB 134/1560, Maudling notes, 14 November 1961, 15 November 1961; cited in Keith Kyle, *The Politics of the Independence of Kenya* (London: Macmillan, 1999), pp. 141–2.
58. PRO CAB 128/35 CC63(61), 16 November 1961.
59. B.A. Ogot and W.R. Ochieng, *Decolonisation and Independence in Kenya 1940–93* (London: James Currey, 1995), pp. 48–79 deals with this period.
60. Rhodes House, interview, 1968, p. 11.
61. Rhodes House, interview, 1968.
62. Ogot and Ochieng, *Decolonisation*, pp. 72–3.

63. Rhodes House, interview, 1968, p. 12.
64. Interview, Jack Howard-Drake, 12 May 2003.
65. Rhodes House, interview, 1968, p. 12.
66. DPW 64/52, Patrick Wall note of meeting with Maudling, 9 January 1962. Bennett was regarded with suspicion for allegedly breaching confidences he was given at the Lancaster House talks: PRO CO 822/3275, MacDonald to Sandys, 22 November 1963.
67. Interview, Sir Philip Goodhart, 16 July 2002.
68. Rhodes House, interview, 1968, p. 11.
69. F.R.S. de Souza, 'Building on the Lancaster House Experience', 14 September 2001, presented to the Kenya constitutional review commission http://www.kenyaconstitution.org/docs/03d002/htm.
70. Ogot and Ochieng, *Decolonisation*, p. 74.
71. Rhodes House, interview, 1968 p. 12.
72. 'Uphill Work', *The Times*, 12 July 1962, p. 11.
73. National Sound Archive, Reginald Maudling, Radio London talk, 9 April 1976.
74. Rhodes House, interview, 1968, p. 20.
75. John Darwin, *Britain and Decolonisation* (Basingstoke: Macmillan Education, 1988), pp. 259–61.
76. *Africa News*/New Vision (Kampala), 31 December 2000, 'Our History: Did the British Leave too Soon?'
77. Interview, Jack Howard-Drake, 12 May 2003.

CHAPTER 11

1. Letter to the constituents of Barnet, 1962, as published in *Memoirs*, pp. 260–3.
2. Ken Young, 'Orpington and the "Liberal Revival"', in Chris Cook and John Ramsden (eds), *By-elections in British Politics* (London: UCL Press, 1997), pp. 157–79.
3. Arthur Fawcett Papers, Fawcett to Maudling, 1 June 1962.
4. *Primrose League Gazette*, June 1962, Reginald Maudling, 'Be Ready to Meet a Changing World', speech to Primrose League Grand Habitation, 11 May 1962.
5. Letter to the constituents of Barnet, 1962, as published in *Memoirs*, pp. 260–3.
6. *Ibid.*
7. Alistair Horne, *Macmillan 1957–1986* (London: Macmillan, 1989), pp. 339–47.
8. *Spectator*, 20 July 1962, pp. 71–2, 'Let's Go'.
9. NARA State Department Central Decimal File 741.00, Box 1656, Telegram from London No. 226, 17 July 1962.
10. *Statist*, Westminster Commentary, July 1963, filed Lord Butler Papers, RAB G 38/241.
11. *Barnet Press*, 5 July 1963, p. 1; Beryl Maudling speech to Osidge branch.
12. Caroline Maudling, interview, 28 January 2002.
13. *Sunday Express*, 8 March 1964, p. 15.
14. *Sunday Express*, 23 June 1963, p. 5.
15. Private interview.
16. Private interview.
17. *Daily Mail*, 16 March 1967, p. 5.
18. Sir Sandy Glen, interview, 10 March 2003.
19. Logan Gourlay, 'Not Ruthless but I Had Luck', *Daily Express*, 27 August 1962, p. 4.
20. Caroline Maudling, interview, 28 January 2002.
21. *Barnet Press*, 2 October 1964, p. 14.
22. *Radio Times*, 10–16 March 1973, p. 5; Basil Brush was another favourite in the 1970s.
23. Edward Boyle Papers, MSS 669/52274 et seq., transcript of BBC *Panorama* profile of Maudling, 1 April 1963; *Observer*, 21 June 1970.

24. Peregrine Worsthorne, *Tricks of Memory* (London: Weidenfeld & Nicolson, 1993), pp. 218–19.
25. *Star*, 11 November 1959, p. 6.
26. Tom Caulcott, interview, 9 April 2003.
27. *Daily Express*, 27 August 1962.
28. Lord Hill of Luton, *Both Sides of the Hill* (London: Heinemann, 1964), p. 241.
29. BBC *Panorama*, 1 April 1963. In his August 1962 *Express* interview Maudling said that although he did not believe in astrology the description of his star sign, Pisces, as 'two fish swimming in different directions, conflicting personalities, split slightly but not schizophrenic', 'may be right in my case'.
30. Sir Derek Mitchell, interview, 28 January 2003.
31. Tom Caulcott, interview, 9 April 2003.
32. Sir Richard Clarke, *Public Expenditure, Management and Control*, ed. Alex Cairncross (London: Macmillan, 1978), p. 55.
33. University of Glasgow Cairncross Papers, DC 106/10/3, Cairncross diary, 29 August 1962.
34. Tom Caulcott, interview, 9 April 2003.
35. *Ibid.*
36. *Ibid.*
37. Cairncross diary, 23 January 1963.
38. Sir Samuel Brittan, 'A Backward Glance: The Reappraisal of the 1960s', April 1997, available at http://www.samuelbrittan.co.uk/spee4_p.html
39. *Time and Tide*, 15–21 August 1963.
40. Cairncross diary, 1 January 1964.
41. Letter Lord Callaghan of Cardiff to author, 3 August 2002.
42. Cairncross diary, 14 December 1963.
43. National Sound Archive, C409/043 F1060B, Lord Cromer, 'City Lives', interview with David Phillips, 10 October 1990.
44. Tom Caulcott, interview, 9 April 2003.
45. *Economist*, 21 July 1962, pp. 212–14, 'Recipe for the Chancellor'.
46. Cairncross diary, 29 August 1962.
47. *HC Debates*, vol. 663, cols 1853–62, 26 July 1962.
48. Nicholas Davenport, 'No Rope for the Chancellor', *Spectator*, 27 July 1962, p. 140.
49. Alec Cairncross, *Managing the British Economy in the 1960s* (London: Macmillan, 1996), pp. 65–6, 67.
50. PRO T 236/2735, Mitchell to Rickett, 26 July 1962; also Lee to Peterson, 23 August 1962.
51. PRO T 236/2736, Lee to Caulcott, 31 August 1962.
52. PRO T 236/2736, Foreign Office Press Summary, 20 September 1962; Washington Embassy, 'Reactions to Chancellor's Speech'; Washington to FO, 21 September 1962.
53. Edmund Dell, *The Chancellors* (London: HarperCollins, 1996), pp. 288–90.
54. PRO T 236/2735, Lee to Peterson, 23 August 1962.
55. *Sunday Times*, 3 September 1967.
56. For example: Nicholas Davenport in *Spectator*, 26 October 1962; ITN report, 14 December 1962, 'Unemployment – the Crisis Facing Britain'.
57. ITN News Report, 30 January 1961, 'Car Workers' Protest March'.
58. US State Department Box 16 Central Numeric File 741.00 1960–63, Telegram to State Department, 11 October 1962, No. 1524, Report, 22 October 1962, A-835.
59. Humphrey Carpenter, *That Was Satire That Was* (London: Gollancz, 2000), pp. 132, 254. Maudling took it in good part, and attended a recording of *That Was the Week that Was* in April 1963.
60. Clarke, *Public Expenditure*, p. 66.

61. Cairncross, *Managing the British Economy*, p. 79.
62. *HC Debates*, vol. 666, cols 620–40, 5 November 1962.
63. *Economist*, 10 November 1962, pp. 543–5.
64. Nicholas Davenport, 'New Light at the Treasury', *Spectator*, 9 November 1962, p. 735.
65. Cairncross, *Managing the British Economy*, p. 272, criticises his choices over this as 'ministerial misjudgement'.
66. Clarke, *Public Expenditure*, p. 78.
67. LSE, Hetherington Papers, note of meeting with Maudling, 21 November 1962.
68. *HC Debates*, vol. 671, col. 1242, 12 February 1963.
69. Maudling's remarks as reported, ITN report, 1 February 1963.
70. Cairncross diary, 23 January 1963.
71. Cairncross Papers, DC 106/24/5, Cairncross to Armstrong, 1 February 1963.
72. PRO PREM 11/4202, note of meeting, 21 February 1963.
73. *Banker*, June 1968, p. 491.
74. Andrew Roth, interview, 2 February 2002.
75. Cairncross Papers, DC 106/24/5, Cairncross to Mitchell, 20 March 1963.
76. ITN report, 30 March 1963, 'UK Pre-Budget situation'.
77. PRO PREM 11/4202, annotation on Mitchell to Bligh, 6 March 1963.
78. PRO PREM 11/4202, Cromer to Maudling, 18 March 1963.
79. PRO PREM 11/4202, Macmillan aide memoire, 20 February 1963.
80. PRO PREM 11/4202, note on meeting between Chancellor and Prime Minister, 22 March 1963.
81. *Sunday Express*, 21 March 1963, p. 16.
82. Tom Caulcott, interview, 9 April 2003.
83. *Newcastle Journal*, 17 March 2000, p. 43. Also Richard Holt, *Second Among Equals* (London: Profile, 2001).
84. Geoffrey Wakeford, 'Maudling's Chance?', *Truth*, 29 November 1957, p. 1338.
85. LSE, Hetherington Papers, note of interview with Maudling, 21 November 1962.
86. PRO PREM 11/4202, Cromer to Maudling, 18 March 1963.
87. Tom Caulcott, interview, 9 April 2003.
88. The advice from the Research Department submitted as 'Taxation 1963' (filed as RAB G 38/40) concurred and advised that it would help middle-income groups.
89. ITN news report, 18 October 1967.
90. PRO PREM 11/4196, Maudling to Macmillan, 15 January 1963. Maudling had been one of the ministers most in favour of a profits tax in discussion in 1961. In 1963 Maudling did halve stamp duty on securities, which was a long-sought objective of many in the City and helped London as a financial centre.
91. *Memoirs*, p. 112.
92. Clarke, *Public Expenditure*, p. 78.
93. *Memoirs*, p. 113.
94. *Economist*, 6 April 1963, p. 15.
95. Dell, *The Chancellors*, p. 294.
96. PRO PREM 11/4363, note of meeting between Macmillan and Maudling, 29 November 1962.
97. Cairncross diary, 17 April 1963.
98. *Gallup Political Index*, report of poll, April 1963.
99. *Sunday Express*, 21 March 1963, p. 16.
100. Edward Boyle Papers, MS 660/54920, Boyle to Vaizey, 17 June 1963.
101. Derek Mitchell, interview, 28 January 1963.
102. Tom Caulcott, interview, 9 April 2003.
103. Richard Crossman, *The Backbench Diaries of Richard Crossman*, ed. Janet Morgan

(London: Jonathan Cape, 1981), June 1963, p. 1005.

104. *Gallup Political Index*, July 1963.
105. Philip Goodhart, *1922* (London: Macmillan, 1973).
106. *Westminster Confidential*, 11 July 1963.
107. *Daily Telegraph*, 12 July 1963, p. 15. The survey covered 66 MPs. Of 25 Maudling supporters in June, 22 were still supporting him while three had switched to Butler. Of 25 who did not support him in June, 14 did in July; of 16 MPs not asked before, 12 supported Maudling to two each for Macmillan and Butler.
108. *Time and Tide*, 27 June–3 July 1963, p. 6.

CHAPTER 12

1. Tom Caulcott, interview, 9 April 2003.
2. *Sunday Times*, 7 July 1963, p. 1 'Tories must appeal to youth, says Maudling'.
3. *Sunday Times*, 14 July 1963, p. 10.
4. *Daily Telegraph*, 8 July 1963, p. 10.
5. *Westminster Confidential*, 11 July 1963.
6. Alan Watkins, interview, 26 November 2002.
7. *Memoirs*, p. 125.
8. *Sunday Times*, 14 July 1963, p. 3.
9. Enoch Powell Papers, POLL 1/6/28, 'Narrative of the events of 8–19 October 1963 so far as known to me directly', dictated 20–23 October 1963.
10. R.A. Butler Papers, RAB G 40/83, Ashton to Butler, 19 September 1963.
11. PRO PREM 11/5008, Brooke to Macmillan, 8 October 1963.
12. POLL 1/1/14f53, Maddan to John Morrison, 11 October 1963, bcc to Powell. Maddan had supported Maudling in a previous letter of 17 July; POLL 3/1/24.
13. Cairncross Papers, DC 106/10/3, diary, 16 October 1963.
14. *Sunday Times*, 28 July 1963.
15. Arthur Fawcett Papers, Fawcett to Maudling, 21 September 1963, cited below.
16. Richard Crossman, *The Backbench Diaries of Richard Crossman*, ed. Janet Morgan (London: Jonathan Cape, 1981), June 1963, p. 1015.
17. *Sunday Times*, 28 July 1963.
18. *Memoirs*, p. 125.
19. R.A. Butler Papers, RAB G 40/83, note of conversation, 31 July 1963.
20. Harold Macmillan diary, 5 September 1963, as cited in Alistair Horne, *Macmillan 1957–1986* (London: Macmillan, 1989), p. 531.
21. Alec Cairncross Papers, DC 106/10/3, diary, 16 October 1963; *Yorkshire Post*, 10 October 1963.
22. Robin Chichester-Clark, interview, 6 August 2002.
23. Cairncross Papers, DC 106/10/3, diary, 16 October 1963.
24. Andrew Alexander, 'Treachery and Lies – Business as Usual', *Daily Mail*, 20 June 1997.
25. For instance, Arthur Fawcett greatly distrusted him, and Patrick Wall's agent reported that of people who contacted the Haltemprice association during the 1963 leadership crisis 'under no circumstances do they wish to have Rab Butler'. Patrick Wall Papers, DPW 1/88, note to Wall, 14 October 1963.
26. Arthur Fawcett Papers, Fawcett to Maudling, 21 September 1963.
27. Edward Du Cann, *Two Lives* (Upton-upon-Severn: Images Publishing, 1995), pp. 85, 86.
28. *Daily Express*, 4 October 1973.
29. *The Times*, 12 October 1963.
30. *Ibid.*; *Daily Express*, 4 October 1973.
31. POLL 1/6/28, 'Narrative of the events of 8–19 October 1963 so far as known to me

directly', dictated on 20–23 October 1963.

32. Trudi Fawcett Kotrosa, interview, 22 April 2003.

33. *The Times*, 12 October 1963.

34. Sir Philip Goodhart, letter to *The Times*, 17 March 2001.

35. ITN report interview with Cyril Stein, 15 October 1963. He had been at 6–1 before the Conference speech.

36. PRO PREM 11/5008, Butler to Macmillan, 15 October 1963.

37. *The Times*, 1 July 1963, p. 7; *The Times*, 2 July 1963, p. 6.

38. PRO PREM 11/5008, Macmillan memorandum, 15 October 1963.

39. PRO PREM 11/5008, Dilhorne to Macmillan, 8 October 1963.

40. *The Times*, 20 January 1964, 'Keeping the Home Fires Burning'. This article was based on a conversation with Maudling in the aftermath of Iain Macleod's revelations in the *Spectator*. Maudling had also read Macleod's article before publication and agreed with it. RAB G 43/1, Macleod to Butler, 15 January 1964.

41. Enoch Powell's account in POLL 1/6/28 is additional evidence that Dilhorne's rendering of sometimes quite subtle reasoning into first, second and third preferences was inaccurate.

42. Robert Shepherd, *Iain Macleod* (London: Hutchinson, 1994), pp. 325–7. Andrew Alexander in the *Daily Mail*, 20 June 1997, wrote that Macleod had briefed journalists at Blackpool about Home's qualities, but it seems unlikely that he would have continued to support Home for tactical reasons during the Cabinet survey. Boyle considered resigning but stayed on at Education in order to see that the Robbins Report was implemented.

43. Derek Mitchell, interview, 28 January 2003.

44. According to Dilhorne, Hare's second preference after Home was for Hailsham; in this reckoning I have assumed that Dilhorne was correct in saying that Hare had positive views about Hailsham. In a Butler v Home run-off, one can be utterly confident that Maudling and Erroll, plus Hailsham and Hare, plus the original five, supported Butler, making nine; Boyd-Carpenter almost certainly made ten, as he participated in pro-Butler meetings on the Friday.

45. PRO PREM 11/5008, Redmayne to Bligh, 18 October 1963.

46. PRO PREM 11/5008, Redmayne to Macmillan, 16 October 1963.

47. PRO PREM 11/5008, Lord St Aldwyn to Macmillan, 17 October 1963.

48. *The Times*, 17 October 1963.

49. Derek Mitchell, interview, 28 January 2003.

50. *Ibid.*

51. *Ibid.*

52. *Ibid.*

53. Iain Macleod, 'The Tory Leadership', *Spectator*, 17 January 1964, confirmed by POLL 1/6/28, 'Narrative of the events of 8–19 October 1963 so far as known to me directly', dictated 20–23 October 1963.

54. Derek Mitchell, interview, 28 January 2003.

55. D.R. Thorpe, *Alec Douglas-Home* (London: Sinclair-Stevenson, 1996), p. 314; Thorpe obtained this account from Maudling in a letter in September 1975.

56. Derek Mitchell, interview, 28 January 2003.

57. *Memoirs*, p. 130. This was surely a little joke of Reggie's; not only did he know that pencil doesn't fade, but he knew everyone knew.

58. *The Times*, 20 January 1964.

59. Derek Mitchell, interview, 28 January 2003.

60. POLL 1/6/28, 'Narrative of the events of 8–19 October 1963 so far as known to me directly', dictated 20–23 October 1963.

61. Lord Butler interview with Anthony Teasdale, 12 June 1980; David Butler Papers.

CHAPTER 13

1. PRO T 199/1033, Caulcott to Derbyshire, 31 July 1963.
2. Derek Mitchell, interview, 28 January 2003.
3. James Haw, interview, 17 June 2003.
4. www.sixtiescity.com/Popmovies/Popfilm64.htm
5. See www.alphadeltaplus.20m.com/fsguestbook.html; email Tony Poulter to author June 2002. For Reggie's opinion about pigeons see *Daily Express*, 27 August 1962.
6. Edward Maudling, interview, 27 October 1999.
7. PRO T 199/1033, memo, 23 April 1963; Caulcott to Derbyshire, 31 July 1963.
8. *Memoirs*, p. 120.
9. D.R. Thorpe, *Alec Douglas-Home* (London: Sinclair-Stephenson, 1996), p. 257.
10. Peter Hennessy, *Muddling Through* (London: Gollancz, 1996), p. 240.
11. In the first draft of the title, it was 'Trade, Industry and Regional Development' until it was pointed out that this abbreviated to TIRED or TIRD.
12. Cairncross Papers, DC 106/10/3, diary entry, 28 October 1963.
13. Tom Caulcott, interview, 9 April 2003.
14. Private interview; letter, Sir Edward Heath to author, 21 August 2002. I should emphasise that the 'never rated' quotation is not from Sir Edward Heath.
15. PRO T 311/260, note by Selwyn Lloyd, 4 June 1962.
16. PRO T 311/260, Mitchell to Allen, 11 January 1963; Maudling annotation to Mitchell, 25 February 1963.
17. PRO T 311/260, Maudling to Douglas-Home, 24 December 1963.
18. Lord Butler Papers, RAB H 96/77, Channon to Butler, 24 January 1964.
19. PRO T 311/262, *passim*; John Boyd-Carpenter did dissent somewhat but was not supported by Maudling.
20. *Economist*, 18 January 1964, pp. 179–80.
21. Cairncross diary, 11 December 1964.
22. PRO CAB 129/116 CP(64)18, 'Decimalisation', 21 January 1964; CAB 128/38 CM9(64).
23. Eric Roll, *Crowded Hours* (London: Faber & Faber, 1995), pp. 143–4.
24. John Dickie, *The Uncommon Commoner* (London: Pall Mall Press, 1964), pp. 196–7.
25. Robert Taylor, *The TUC* (Basingstoke: Palgrave, 2000), pp. 160–1.
26. Geoffrey Goodman, *The Awkward Warrior* (Nottingham: Spokesman, 1984), pp. 366–7. Cousins, of course, was a member of that government and resigned in July 1966 over incomes policy.
27. Cairncross Papers, DC 106/24/5, Cairncross to Mitchell, 4 December 1963.
28. Cairncross diary, 11 December 1963.
29. PRO PREM 11/5014, note of meeting between Douglas-Home and Maudling, 4 December 1963.
30. *Sunday Times*, 8 December 1963.
31. Robert Shepherd, *Enoch Powell* (London: Hutchinson, 1996), pp. 269–71.
32. Enoch Powell Papers, POLL 3/1/29, Maudling to Powell, 3 February 1964. Maudling often signed himself 'Reggy' to old friends like Arthur Fawcett and Enoch Powell.
33. David Butler Papers, David Butler and Anthony King, interview with Reginald Maudling, 24 June 1965.
34. PRO T 117/611, Maudling to Douglas-Home, 25 August 1964.
35. PRO CAB 123/38, Cabinet minutes, 12 November 1963.
36. Sir Richard Clarke, *Public Expenditure, Management and Control* (London: Macmillan, 1978), p. 83.
37. *Ibid.*, p. 81.
38. *Ibid.*, p. 83.

39. PRO CAB 128/38 CM21(64), 9 April 1964.

40. Alec Cairncross and Frances Cairncross, *The Legacy of the Golden Age* (London: Routledge, 1992), p. 103.

41. John Boyd-Carpenter, *Way of Life* (London: Sidgwick & Jackson, 1980), pp. 158–9.

42. Alec Cairncross, *Managing the British Economy in the 1960s* (London: Macmillan, 1996), p. 82.

43. Cairncross diary, 3 March 1964.

44. Cairncross diary, 'Monday', mid-February 1964.

45. PRO PREM 11/4774, Maudling to Douglas-Home, 3 February 1964.

46. PRO PREM 11/4774, Bligh to Douglas-Home, 2 April 1964.

47. *Sunday Express*, 26 January 1964.

48. PRO PREM 11/4774, Bligh to Douglas-Home, 2 April 1964.

49. *Sunday Express*, 26 January 1964.

50. David Butler Papers, David Butler and Anthony King, interview with Reginald Maudling, 29 June 1964.

51. Cairncross diary, 'Monday', mid-February 1964.

52. David Watt, 'Cold Comfort Farm', *Spectator*, 17 April 1964, p. 505.

53. 'End of the Line?', *Economist*, 18 April 1964, pp. 239–40.

54. Nicholas Davenport, 'What Reggie Did', *Spectator*, 17 April 1964, p. 526.

55. 'End of the Line?', *Economist*, 18 April 1964, pp. 239–40.

56. 'Shortening the Odds', *Economist*, 18 April 1964, p. 288; *Memoirs*.

57. *Memoirs*, p. 122.

58. 'Budget 1964', ITN report, 14 April 1964.

59. Nicholas Davenport, 'Is Mr Maudling "With-It"?', *Spectator*, 5 June 1964, p. 771.

60. Cairncross Papers, DC 106/24/7, Cairncross to Rickett, 18 February 1964.

61. Cairncross Papers, DC 106/24/7, Cairncross note, 23 June 1964.

62. Cairncross Papers, DC 106/24/7, Cairncross to Bancroft, 24 March 1964.

63. Cairncross diary, 3 July 1964.

64. Cairncross diary, 16 July 1964.

65. *Guardian*, 1 January 1995, citing Cromer to Maudling, July 1964.

66. Cairncross diary, 3 July 1964.

67. Cairncross Papers, DC 106/24/7, Cairncross to Caulcott, 21 January 1964.

68. Cairncross, *Managing the British Economy*, p. 86; Cairncross diary, 3 July 1964.

69. PRO T 171/611, Maudling to Edwards *et al.*, 13 May 1964.

70. Tom Caulcott, interview, 9 April 2003.

71. Alec Cairncross, *The Wilson Years: A Treasury Diary 1964–69* (London: The Historians' Press, 1997), 18 October 1964, p. 6.

72. Cairncross, *Managing the British Economy*, pp. 86–7.

73. Cairncross Papers, DC 106/24/7, Cairncross to Pitblado, 16 March 1964. Even in August 1962 the Treasury avoided criticising the Canadian import surcharge (PRO T 235/6736 Canada briefing 17 August 1962), presumably on the grounds that this was an option that Britain should keep open.

74. Eric Roll, *Crowded Hours* (London: Faber & Faber, 1995), p. 146.

75. *Barnet Press*, 2 October 1964, p. 14; 'Our Girl in Tokio', *Daily Mail*, 15 September 1964.

76. *Barnet Press*, 14 August 1964 and 21 August 1964.

77. *Barnet Press*, 2 October 1964, p. 14.

78. *Barnet Press*, 2 October 1964, p. 15.

79. *Barnet Press*, 25 September 1964, p. 15.

80. Cairncross diary, 18 October 1964.

81. 'Election Diary', *New Statesman*, 2 October 1964.

82. David Butler and Anthony King, *The British General Election of 1964* (London:

Macmillan, 1965), p. 115.

83. Anthony Howard and Richard West, *The Making of the Prime Minister* (London: Jonathan Cape, 1965), p. 179.

84. Butler and King, *The British General Election of 1964*, p. 117.

85. Howard and West, *The Making of the Prime Minister*, pp. 175–6.

86. For instance Brian Reading, *The Great Mess Myth*, Old Queen Street Paper 15, Conservative Research Department, May 1970.

87. Conservative Central Office, *Weekend Talking Point no. 32*, 20 September 1952.

88. PRO PREM 11/4777, Cromer to Maudling, 1 October 1964, Number 10 Note for the Record, 2 October 1964, Maudling to Douglas-Home, 6 October 1964; T 171/611, Maudling to Cromer, 7 October 1964.

89. 'True Gold Loss Cloaked', *The Times*, 3 October 1964.

90. David Butler Papers, David Butler interview with Peter Goldman, 28 October 1964.

91. David Butler Papers, David Butler interview with Nigel Lawson, n.d. September 1964.

92. *Economist*, October 1964.

93. PRO CAB 21/5316, note by Rogers, Palmer and Armstrong, 22 October 1964.

94. The swing was 4.7 per cent in Barnet, and 3.2 per cent nationally.

95. *Barnet Press*, 23 October 1964, p. 19.

96. Cairncross diary, 16 October 1964.

97. *Memoirs*, p. 131.

98. *Memoirs*, p. 132.

99. Cairncross diary, 16 October 1964.

100. James Callaghan, *Time and Chance* (London: Collins, 1987), p. 162; letter Lord Callaghan of Cardiff to author, 3 August 2002.

CHAPTER 14

1. Roy Jenkins, *A Life at the Centre* (London: Macmillan, 1991), p. 291.

2. www.bankofengland.co.uk/press30.htm, Mervyn King lecture, 17 October 1996.

3. Edmund Dell, *The Chancellors* (London: HarperCollins, 1996), p. 303.

4. Ben Pimlott, *Harold Wilson* (London: HarperCollins, 1993), pp. 349–50.

5. University of Glasgow, Cairncross Papers, DC 106/10/3, diary entry, 21 November 1963.

6. David Butler, interview with Reginald Maudling, 29 June 1964.

7. Alec Cairncross, *Managing the British Economy in the 1960s* (London: Macmillan, 1996), p. 76.

8. *Ibid.*, pp. 264–9.

9. *Memoirs*, p. 112.

10. Robert Taylor, *The TUC* (Basingstoke: Palgrave, 2000), p. 158.

11. Statistics derived from those cited David McKie and Chris Cook, *Election '70* (London: Panther, 1970), p. 134. As a share of GDP, Maudling's departing share of 0.53 per cent was higher than that given by the succeeding Labour government.

12. *Barnet Press*, 30 October 1964, p. 26.

13. *HC Debates*, vol. 701, col. 240, 4 November 1964.

14. *HC Debates*, vol. 720, col. 1264, 17 November 1965.

15. Samuel Brittan, *Steering the Economy* (London: Secker & Warburg, 1969), pp. 190–6.

16. ITN report, 23 November 1964.

17. Harold Wilson, *The Labour Government 1964–70* (London: Weidenfeld & Nicolson, 1971), pp. 60–6.

18. *HC Debates*, vol. 705, col. 1010, 2 February 1965.

19. Historian John Barnes has written an entertaining 'extract from the memoirs of Lord Maudling of Barnet' on what might have happened had the Conservatives won in

1964 and continued the Maudling experiment. Iain Dale and Duncan Brack (eds), *Prime Minister Portillo and Other Things that Never Happened* (London: Politico's, 2003).

20. *HC Debates*, vol. 828, col. 1306, 21 December 1971.

21. BBC News report, 16 February 1965.

22. Boyle Papers, MS 660/23047, Maudling paper to Leader's Consultative Committee, 30 March 1965, Maudling draft, 25 March 1965.

23. Indeed, in his memoirs Maudling forgot that it was Home rather than Heath who appointed him to the job. *Memoirs*, p. 137.

24. *HC Debates*, vol. 709, cols 1960–72, 1 April 1965; vol. 716, cols 1145 et seq., 19 July 1965.

25. ITN report, 25 June 1965.

26. LSE, Hetherington Papers, interview with Reginald Maudling, 21 November 1962.

27. *Barnet Press*, 23 October 1964, p. 19.

28. James Haw, interview, 17 June 2003.

29. 'What Now for Those who Used to Rule?', *Daily Mail*, 19 October 1964.

30. 'Mr Maudling's First Day at his New City Job', *Daily Mail*, 17 November 1964.

31. Jehanne Wake, *Kleinwort Benson: The History of Two Families in Banking* (Oxford: Oxford University Press, 1997). Wake notes that significant quantities of Kleinwort Benson documentation were destroyed in 1989 (p. 443).

32. *Ibid.*, pp. 383–7.

33. Clive Bossom, notes made in 1979.

34. *Barnet Press*, 27 November 1964, 4 December 1964.

35. Sir Sandy Glen, interview, 11 September 2002.

36. James Haw, interview, 17 June 2003.

37. 'The Reginald Maudlings at Home', *Ideal Home*, November 1968, pp. 27–31.

38. David Butler Papers, interview with Reginald Maudling, 11 November 1969.

39. Westminster City Council, local archives file Chester Square, cutting dated 31 March 1964.

40. Department of Trade, *Peachey Property Corporation Limited*, January 1979.

41. Edward Maudling, interview, 27 October 1999.

42. *Peachey Property* report, paras 429–32.

43. *Ibid.*, paras 431–7.

44. *Daily Mail*, 28 September 1977, p. 1.

45. Certainly, as well as the inadequate documentation, there is the same convoluted, and possibly conveniently back-calculated, look to the leaseback as there is to the Adeline Genée covenant and the ITCS books.

46. David Butler Papers, Reginald Maudling interviews with David Butler and Anthony King, 19 May 1966, 24 June 1965.

CHAPTER 15

1. Cecil King, *The Cecil King Diary 1965–70* (London: Jonathan Cape, 1972), 25 July 1965, p. 24–5.

2. Ted Short, *Whip to Wilson* (London: Macdonald, 1989), p. 152.

3. Stratton Mills, interview, 11 July 2002.

4. Short, *Whip to Wilson*, pp. 152–9.

5. *Daily Express*, 22 July 1965, p. 1.

6. Harold Macmillan diary, MSS Macmillan dep d53, 27 July 1965.

7. James Margach, 'The Bloodless Victory that Put Heath on Top', *Sunday Times*, 1 August 1965, p. 4.

8. See for instance *Observer*, 25 July 1965, p. 1.

9. King, *Diary*, 25 July 1967, p. 134.

10. Michael Rice, 'Can I Go Round Again?', unpublished MS, p. 120.
11. Sir Philip Goodhart, interview, 16 July 2002.
12. Patrick Wall Papers, DPW 1/108, handwritten list of those invited to the initial meeting.
13. Lord Carr of Hadley, interview, 29 July 1999.
14. *Sunday Times*, 25 July 1965, p. 9.
15. Patrick Wall Papers, DPW 1/108, list of MPs with handwritten voting intention added. Heath was given 86 votes, the rest undecided. This appears to have been an early canvass sheet, as Alan Watkins was told on election day that the Maudling campaign reckoned they had over 160 votes (*Spectator*, 30 July 1965).
16. Peter Walker, *Staying Power* (London: Bloomsbury, 1991), pp. 42–3.
17. Jim Prior, *A Balance of Power* (London: Hamish Hamilton, 1986), pp. 37–8.
18. Howe had originally intended to support Powell, but switched to Heath. Geoffrey Howe, *Conflict of Loyalty* (London: Macmillan, 1994), p. 39.
19. Margaret Thatcher, *The Path to Power* (London: HarperCollins, 1995), pp. 135–6.
20. Charles Longbottom, interview, 25 June 2002.
21. Prior, *A Balance of Power*, p. 38.
22. Other sources give a lower figure for double promises; four or five, thought another Heath man. Sir Robin Chichester-Clark, interview, 6 June 2002.
23. William Teeling, *Corridors of Frustration* (London: Johnson, 1970), p. 202. Maudling may well have been having a joke at Teeling's expense; Caroline Maudling doubts he went to church at all that weekend.
24. Caroline Maudling, interview, 28 January 2002.
25. Sir Sandy Glen, interview, 11 September 2002.
26. Charles Longbottom, interview, 25 June 2002; Stratton Mills, interview, 11 July 2002.
27. *New Statesman*, 30 July 1965.
28. *Observer*, 25 July 1965, pp. 1, 3.
29. *Daily Mail*, 27 July 1965, p. 1.
30. Walker, *Staying Power*, p. 44.
31. King, *Diary*, 25 July 1965, 19 August 1965, pp. 25, 32.
32. *Daily Express*, 27 July 1965, pp. 1–2.
33. Sir Robin Chichester-Clark, interview, 6 August 2002; David Butler, interview with Willie Whitelaw, 1966.
34. Stratton Mills, interview, 11 July 2002.
35. Teeling, *Corridors of Frustration*, p. 202; Gerald Kaufman, 'The End of the Phoney War', *New Statesman*, 30 July 1965.
36. *Daily Mail*, 29 July 1965, p. 8.
37. *Memoirs*, p. 136.
38. *Daily Mirror*, 3 August 1965, p. 3.
39. *Memoirs*, p. 137.
40. Butler Papers, RAB G 44/123, 'The Leadership Change', 2 August 1965.
41. Lord Carrington, interview, 15 October 2002.
42. Edward Boyle Papers, MS 660/52298, letter to Sir Robert Armstrong, 25 March 1981.
43. Caroline Maudling, interview, 2 July 1999.

CHAPTER 16

1. Alex Saville, interview, 29 July 2003; Viv Walker, interview, 11 July 2003.
2. N. Kessel and H. Walton, *Alcoholism*, 2nd edn (Harmondsworth: Penguin, 1989), pp. 49–51.
3. *Ibid.*
4. For some of the best see Peter Paterson, *Tired and Emotional* (London: Chatto & Windus, 1993).

5. 'The Reginald Maudlings at Home', *Ideal Home*, November 1968, p. 28.
6. Private interview.
7. Private interview.
8. Alex Saville, interview, 29 July 2003.
9. Private interview.
10. Alex Saville, interview, 29 July 2003.
11. Sir Sandy Glen, interview, 10 March 2003.
12. Edward Maudling, interviews, 29 October 1999, 27 July 2004.
13. Alex Saville, interview, 29 July 2003.
14. Edward Maudling, interview, 29 October 1999.
15. Sir Sandy Glen, interview, 11 September 2002.
16. Michael Rice, interview, 3 July 2003.
17. *Ibid.*
18. Timothy Green, 'Gold Smuggling in the Seventies', *Euromoney* (August 1971), gold supplement.
19. PRO file FCO 8/1510, Annual Review of 1970: Dubai, p. 6.
20. Michael Rice, interview, 3 July 2003.
21. *Time*, 10 September 1990.
22. James Paul, 'The New Bourgeoisie of the Gulf', *Middle East Report*, September–October 1986, pp. 18–22.
23. Michael Rice, interview, 3 July 2003.
24. David Butler Papers, interview with Reginald Maudling, 4 June 1965; David Butler and Anthony King, *The British General Election of 1966* (London: Macmillan, 1966), pp. 63–4.
25. Alex Saville, interview, 29 July 2003.
26. Butler and King, *The British General Election of 1966*, p. 130.
27. David Butler Papers, interview with Edward Heath, 17 May 1966.
28. David Butler Papers, interview with Reginald Maudling, 19 May 1966.
29. Cecil King, *The Cecil King Diary 1965–70* (London: Jonathan Cape, 1972), 5 January 1967, p. 107.
30. MEPO (pending), Poulson to Maudling, 10 June 1966; Maudling to Poulson, 15 June 1966; Poulson to Maudling, 5 July 1966.
31. Ken Williams, interview, 9 November 2002.
32. Murray Martin, interview, 10 May 2001.
33. *House of Commons Select Committee on the Conduct of Members*, July 1977 (hereafter HCSC), Minutes of hearing, 22 March 1977, para. 1540.
34. Tom Caulcott, interview, 9 April 2003.
35. PRO MT 118/308.
36. Sir Sandy Glen, interview, 10 March 2003.
37. In fairness to RIBA, serious investigations had begun in 1971 and been deferred to allow Poulson time to prepare a defence (*Architect's Journal*, 4 October 1972). However, there were enough complaints on file to justify action at an earlier date.
38. *Architect's Journal*, 16 August 1972, leader, p. 348.
39. MEPO (pending), Poulson to Marr, 22 December 1966, annexed as Document 58 to s.109 report on ITCS.
40. Ray Fitzwalter and David Taylor, *Web of Corruption* (St Albans: Granada, 1981) is much the most approachable account of John Poulson's career and his operations in British local government and Malta.
41. HCSC, Evidence, 22 February 1977, para. 1513.
42. PRO J 291/93 J.G.L. Poulson, 'Payments in the nature of commission to persons other than employees: Year ended 5 April 1967'.
43. MEPO (pending), Adeline Genée Trust minutes, 10 October 1966.

44. PRO J 291/63, Poulson evidence, 3 January 1974, p. 45.
45. PRO J 291/85, Poulson to McCowan, 10 October 1966.
46. Ken Williams, interview, 9 November 2002.
47. Or, at least, this was Muir Hunter's reading of the books. PRO J 291/101, Poulson private examination, 18 July 1973, paras 477–524.
48. Ken Williams, interview, 9 November 2002.
49. PRO J 291/101, Exchange between Hunter and Poulson at Poulson private examination, 16 July 1973, paras 204–5. This was confirmed by Maudling at his own hearing.
50. Edgar Mizzi, *Malta in the Making* (Malta: Edgar Mizzi, 1995), p. 73.
51. *HCSC*, Evidence, July 1977, Appendices 43–9.
52. Fitzwalter and Taylor, *Web of Corruption*, pp. 140–1.
53. Ken Williams, interview for *Sleaze*, Channel 4, 1999.
54. *Times of Malta*, 9 January 1967, 11 January 1967.
55. *HCSC*, Evidence, Appendix 50, Poulson to Maudling, 11 January 1967.
56. *HC Debates*, vol. 740, cols 818–25, 2 February 1967.

CHAPTER 17

1. The title of the memoirs of John Stonehouse (London: W.H. Allen, 1975), the former Labour minister who faked his own death in 1974 to escape from fraudulent debts, in which he describes his deteriorating mental state.
2. *HC Debates*, vol. 740, cols 818–25, 2 February 1967.
3. *HC Debates*, vol. 740, cols 36–8, 30 January 1967. A similar question was raised a week earlier, *HC Debates*, vol. 739, cols 1276–7, 24 January 1967.
4. Ray Fitzwalter, interview, 28 October 1999.
5. *HC Debates*, vol. 740, col. 813, 2 February 1967.
6. *Dance and Dancers* (March 1967), p. 41; *Brighton Evening Argus*, 26 January 1967.
7. *Brighton Evening Argus*, 27 October 1967; Michael Rice, interview, 3 July 2003.
8. Edward Boyle Papers, MS 660/34273, Beryl Maudling to Lord Goodman, 9 March 1967.
9. Edward Boyle Papers, MS 660/34273, Lord Goodman to Beryl Maudling, 10 March 1967.
10. Edward Boyle Papers, MS 660/34273, Beryl Maudling to Lord Goodman, 9 March 1967.
11. PRO J 291/95, Maudling private examination, 19 July 1973, paras 6–14, 211–12.
12. PRO J 291/95, Maudling private examination, 19 July 1973, paras 211–12. Emphasis in original document, held by Metropolitan Police.
13. The agreement was the basis for one potential criminal charge against Maudling and Poulson for 'conspiracy to obtain money ultra vires' from Ropergate: November 1974, Cobb-Taylor report to the Director of Public Prosecutions, November 1974. In July 1976 another counsel's report thought that this was a 'wholly artificial' offence and that there would be difficulty in demonstrating that Maudling's claim that he had assumed that Ropergate was entitled to make such payments was knowingly incorrect. PRO BT 296/833, David Smout advice, 22 July 1976.
14. DTI Inspectors wondered whether this in itself was a corrupt practice, but legal counsel disagreed. PRO BT 296/833, Opinion of David Smout, QC, 22 July 1976.
15. *House of Commons Select Committee on the Conduct of Members*, July 1977 (hereafter *HCSC*), Evidence, Appendices 60–1. Baker to Maudling, 5 April 1968; Maudling to Poulson, 6 April 1968. *HCSC* wrongly records 'account' as 'amount' – original in police files.
16. PRO J 291/68, Poulson to Smith, 13 July 1967.
17. Mcleod to Maudling, 22 February 1967. Poulson evidence, as cited in Michael Gillard and Martin Tomkinson, *Nothing to Declare* (London: John Calder, 1980), p. 292. Jack

Merritt, at his examination in bankruptcy, stated that he had not met Maudling and there is no reason not to believe this to be the case. It was a favour done by Maudling to Poulson, rather than particularly to Merritt. PRO J 291/95, Merritt private examination, 24 July 1972, para. 223.

18. According to Williams, the whole Mexican project was a chimera; there was never the remotest chance of getting anything built and it was all about promoting the political career of Echeverria senior. Ken Williams, interview, 5 December 2003. Poulson was clearly taken for a ride in Mexico to an even greater extent than he was elsewhere.

19. PRO J 291/101, Poulson evidence, 18 July 1973, para. 572.

20. PRO FCO 7/643.

21. PRO J 291/63, Valerie Richmond evidence, 11 December 1973, p. 55. She was not referring to the Mexican trip, but this serves as a general example of the Poulson attitude to foreign travel.

22. Ken Williams, interview, 7 November 2002.

23. MEPO (pending), DTI s.109 report, ITCS Board Minute, 3 April 1967.

24. MEPO (pending), DTI s.109 report, Document 58. The figures are US dollars. The total claim came to £622.

25. PRO J 291/68, Poulson to Smith, 13 July 1967; for the arrangement on houses see PRO J 291/65, agreement between Poulson and Smith, 4 August 1966.

26. PRO J 291/68, Poulson to Smith, 13 July 1967; WYAS WCC 3/1/2 OSB board minutes, 11 July 1967.

27. PRO J 291/84, Hilton to Poulson, 20 September 1967.

28. PRO J 291/68, Poulson to Smith, 2 February 1968.

29. HCSC, Evidence, Appendix 68, Statement by John Brennan, 28 November 1974.

30. PRO J 291/99, William Sales evidence at bankruptcy hearing, 15 May 1973, paras 2566-74.

31. Sunday Times, 17 June 1973.

32. PRO J 291/92, Poulson to Kenyon, 2 June 1967.

33. US State Department files PO 12 UK Box 2565, Note of briefing from Maudling and Michael Fraser, 21 January 1967.

34. BBC News report, 3 October 1966.

35. Guardian, 13 October 1966.

36. PRO FCO 8/137, Foreign Office to Jeddah, Kuwait, Bahrain, Abu Dhabi, Amman, Dubai, 14 July 1967.

37. PRO FCO 17/227, Maudling note of meeting with King Hussein, 3 August 1967.

38. PRO FCO 17/227, Letter from Cable (Beirut) to Morris (Foreign Office), 7 August 1967.

39. Memoirs, p. 148.

40. David Gilmour, Lebanon: The Fractured Country (Oxford: Martin Robertson, 1983), pp. 3-10, describes the situation. Tax evasion was almost a national pastime, even though rates were low – it was estimated that companies evaded 75 per cent and the liberal professions 90 per cent of what they owed.

41. WYAS WCC 3/1/3, Poulson evidence, 13 June 1972, para. 168.

42. PRO J 291/91, Nasser to Poulson, 4 August 1967.

43. WYAS WCC 3/1/2, Moorhouse to Registrar, 19 March 1976.

44. PRO J 291/87, Jowett to Poulson, 25 September 1967. Poulson's secretary noted that there was no copy of the earlier letter in the filing system.

45. PRO J 291/91, Nasser to Poulson, 6 October [incorrectly dated September] 1967.

46. PRO J 291/91, Nasser to Poulson, 20 September 1967.

47. PRO J 291/91, Poulson to Nasser, 29 September 1967.

48. WYAS WCC 3/1/1, Application for summons of Nasser to section 25 hearing, July 1973.

49. PRO J 291/90, Nasser to Poulson, 1 December 1967. Poulson's response to the

proposition is not clear from the files.

50. PRO J 291/101, Poulson evidence, 16 July 1973, paras 340–2; WYAS WCC 3/1/2, Application for summons of Costa Nasser, July 1973.

51. It should be noted that British officials were anxious to keep on reasonably friendly terms with Al-Fatah, who in the late 1960s distanced themselves from the outright international terrorism of the Popular Front for the Liberation of Palestine; PRO FCO 17/691. But, even so, they were a guerrilla movement which planned to reoccupy Palestine from the Israelis by armed force and were responsible for terrorist attacks within Israel.

52. The bankruptcy investigators were told that Nasser was a member of Al-Fatah, and Poulson also said this; Maudling himself denied the suggestion as 'bunkum'. Nasser's feelings, though, are not in doubt – he had family connections with Palestinian leaders, the Cattans, and wrote on several occasions to Maudling and Poulson about Palestine.

53. PRO J 291/101, Poulson evidence, 18 July 1973, paras 855–8.

54. PRO J 291/89, Poulson to Nasser, 31 January 1969; Poulson to Gomershall, telex, 16 April 1968.

55. PRO FCO 8/864, Foreign Office to Bahrain Agency, 4 August 1967.

56. PRO FCO 8/864, Archie Lamb to Foreign Office, 29 July 1967.

57. PRO J 291/87, Jowett to Poulson, 1 November 1967.

58. PRO J 291/90, Poulson to Nasser, 16 January 1968. Poulson didn't agree – 'Did you ever hear such humbug and misrepresentation in your life! He gave it to us because Booth's design was excellent.'

59. HCSC, Report para. 30 makes the point in relation to Malta that it was a general issue, although it did not doubt that the Maltese when dealing with Maudling would consider the benefit of gratifying someone who now, and even more in the future, would be able to help. The same is true in the Gulf.

60. PRO J 291/101, Poulson evidence, 18 July 1973, paras 684–92.

61. PRO BT 296/833, Opinion of David Smout, QC, 22 July 1976, citing ITCS s.109 Report, paras 51, 62, 65, 66. Smout concluded that even though the Revenue form may have been absent, 'As it is not doubted that the expenses were bona fide and properly recorded, my own view is that this aspect does not merit further investigation'. In the light of the considerable doubt over, for instance, the validity of these September 1967 expenses and the Acapulco trip, this view is open to serious challenge.

62. PRO J 291/76, John Poulson to Alice Poulson, 19 September 1967.

63. PRO J 291/95, Maudling evidence, 19 July 1973, paras 180–91.

64. PRO J 291/95, Maudling evidence, 19 July 1973, para. 211; HCSC, Evidence, 22 March 1977, paras 1685–91.

65. Poulson never understood the distinction between the two separate Adeline Genée organisations; in his police interview in 1974 and his 1981 memoir, The Price, he claimed that he had continued to pay the covenant after the theatre had gone bust and that the difference was pocketed by Maudling. This accusation was false, because the covenant was with the Trust – still in existence – not the production company which had indeed gone out of business.

66. In disclosure for the Mirror libel case, parts of a 29 April 1974 letter relating to this £2,000 were blacked out. In police files (MEPO pending) there is a 6 October 1967 letter from Maudling to the theatre trust asking them to 'treat this as a loan, to be repaid when you receive a similar amount in the relatively near future from a company in which I have an interest'.

67. Brighton Evening Argus, 24 November 1967.

68. Michael Rice, interview, 3 July 2003.

69. WYAS WCC 3/1/2, OSB minutes, 11 October 1967.
70. Private interview.
71. PRO J 291/100, Telex, 16 November 1967, cited Poulson evidence, 18 July 1973, para. 742; J291/87, Jowett to Macleod, 17 November 1967 and 18 December 1967.
72. Private interview.
73. MEPO (pending), Poulson to Abela, 17 May 1967.
74. PRO J 291/84, Ibbetson to Poulson, 19 June 1967.
75. *HCSC*, Evidence, Appendices 56–7, Maudling to Borg Olivier, 13 October 1967, 25 October 1967.
76. *HCSC*, Evidence, Appendix 57, Maudling to Borg Olivier, 25 October 1967.
77. PRO FCO 27/321, Commonwealth Office note on corruption in Malta, January 1968; Brown (High Commissioner in Valletta) to Redpath (CO), 30 January 1968. The British diplomats in Malta found these allegations all too credible.
78. Gillard and Tomkinson, *Nothing to Declare*, pp. 263–7.
79. PRO FCO 24/29, Johnston to Moreton, 21 November 1967.
80. PRO PREM 13/1668; *The Times*, 7 December 1967, p. 8.
81. PRO FCO 8/137, Brehony to Ibbott, 13 August 1967.
82. WYAS WCC 3/1/3, Poulson to Maudling, 27 November 1967, cited by Hunter during Poulson hearing, 25 September 1972.

Chapter 18

1. Ray Fitzwalter, interview, 28 October 1999.
2. PRO J 291/89, Nasser to Poulson, 26 April 1968.
3. Sir Albert Costain, *Reflections* (Cirencester: New Wellington Press, 1987), an uncompleted memoir, gives the basic biographical details and comments (p. 88) that the firm's prior success in Iran had given it experience in winning contracts in the Persian Gulf. There is no mention of Maudling in Costain's memoirs.
4. PRO FO 1016/838, Dubai to FO, telegram, 1 June 1966. If Nasser is correctly quoting Maudling, and that Maudling himself was right, the introduction probably took place in late 1966, as Foreign Office files show Costain as a contender in early 1967. FO 1016/839.
5. PRO FCO 8/893, Roberts to Mason, 28 September 1967.
6. Tom Bower, *Fayed* (London: Macmillan, 1998), pp. 31–41, particularly p. 40.
7. PRO FCO 8/840, Roberts to Crawford, 25 January 1968.
8. PRO file FCO 8/1510, Note from Bullard to Weir, 18 May 1970, 'Mehdi Tajir and the Dubai government'.
9. PRO J 291/74, Telex, Poulson to Nasser, n.d. ? December 1967.
10. PRO J 291/90, Nasser to Poulson, 16 October 1967.
11. PRO J 291/90, Nasser to Maudling, 19 December 1967.
12. PRO J 291/101, cited in Maudling private examination, 19 July 1973, para. 423.
13. PRO J 291/90, Poulson to Nasser, 1 January 1968.
14. PRO J 291/93, Maudling private examination, 19 July 1973, para. 424.
15. PRO FCO 93/299, Wright to Evans, 9 October 1973; Simpson to Wright, 1 October 1973.
16. PRO CAB 131/28, 9 February 1963, as cited in Frank Heinlein, *British Government Policy and Decolonisation 1945–1963* (London: Frank Cass, 2002), p. 224.
17. *HC Debates*, vol. 756, col. 2072, 18 January 1968.
18. For instance, in conversation with King Faisal of Saudi Arabia in July 1967 Maudling 'pointed out to him the clear commitment made by HMG in the Defence debate that they had no intention of withdrawing from the Gulf'. PRO FCO 8/137, Maudling note of visit to Faisal, 31 July 1967.

19. He intervened on the issue on 24 January, 25 January (debate), 30 January, 31 January, 14 February, three times on 26 February, 7 March, and twice on 1 May.
20. *HC Debates*, vol. 757, col. 639, 25 January 1968.
21. PRO FCO 8/137, background note for meeting with Maudling, 5 January 1968. The personal details refer to his Kleinwort Benson job and state that the Ruler of Dubai had asked him to be his Financial Director. But there is no reference in this note for his meeting with the minister that he was engaged in trying to win business for ITCS.
22. PRO FO 1016/760, file note by Crawford, 24 January 1968.
23. *HC Debates*, vol. 757, col. 639, 25 January 1968.
24. PRO FO 1016/760, Weir to Crawford, 15 February 1968.
25. PRO J 291/90, Poulson to Nasser, 16 January 1968.
26. Michael Rice, interview, 3 July 2003.
27. PRO file FCO 8/1186, Saudi economic links – letter from Hilary Sinclair to FCO, 10 July 1969.
28. Andrew Roth, interview, 2 February 2002.
29. PRO file FCO 8/1186, Saudi economic links – documents relating to Margaret Mackay 1967.
30. *Parliamentary Profiles/Westminster Confidential*, 1 January 1970.
31. NARA State Department Registry Box 2652 (1967–9) POL 7, 25 April 1968, note.
32. PRO FCO 8/137, Palmer to Asprey, 2 March 1968. Page was suspicious because Poulson had appeared to produce designs so quickly; although he was probably not aware that Poulson had in fact been alerted to the contract in autumn 1967.
33. PRO FCO 8/862, Roberts to Asprey, 8 February 1968.
34. PRO FCO 8/137, Foreign Office cables to Kuwait, 29 January 1968, Bahrain, 31 January 1968.
35. Police interview with John Poulson, 27 February 1974, Tape 2, p. 6.
36. BBC News report, 16 September 1967. The burglary appears to have been a professional operation, and the criminals apparently managed to open a safe in which the jewels were stored.
37. 'The Reginald Maudlings at Home', *Ideal Home* (November 1968). The pearl was the subject of rumour among investigative journalists in the 1970s, who cannot be blamed for failing to consult this unlikely source for confirmation.
38. Poulson police interview, 27 February 1974.
39. PRO FCO 8/137 is the main source on official reactions to the Dubai airport wrangle, but FCO 8/862 is also relevant and the files show some signs of having been pruned.
40. PRO FCO 8/137, Lamb to Crawford, 8 February 1968.
41. Poulson police interview, 27 February 1974.
42. PRO FCO 8/137, Strachan to Asprey, 12 February 1968.
43. PRO FCO 8/137, Strachan to Asprey, 12 February 1968. The letter relating to Poulson does not appear to be on file.
44. PRO FCO 8/137, Kay to Stirling, 22 February 1968.
45. PRO FCO 8/137, Asprey to Roberts, 28 February 1968.
46. PRO FCO 8/137, Asprey to Kay, 10 June 1968.
47. PRO J 291/90, Nasser to Maudling, 1 March 1968.
48. PRO J 291/89, Poulson to Nasser, 21 March 1968. The ECGD approval was necessary for major sources of finance to consider lending. At some point in the winter of 1967/8 Maudling himself went to see ECGD officials in connection with the Dubai airport project but when the files were trawled in 1976 it was noted that 'so far all efforts to track down the papers recording this interview have failed'. PRO BT 296/833 Walton (ECGD) to Hetherington (Deputy Treasury Solicitor), 13 December 1976.
49. PRO J 291/89, Tajir to Maudling, 15 April 1968.

50. PRO J 291/89, Nasser to Maudling, 17 April 1968.
51. PRO J 291/93, Maudling private examination, 19 July 1973, stopped section.
52. Said Aburish, *Pay-Off* (London: André Deutsch, 1984).
53. PRO J 291/89, Poulson to Nasser, 10 October 1968.
54. PRO J 291/84, Camm to Macleod, 23 November 1967, states that Poulson hoped that the airport terminal building and runway would have been worth £1 million while the Bandar Abbas complex could have been £7 million. This latter is unlikely to be a realistic estimate.
55. This dispute should probably have been referred to RIBA for arbitration, as the work done and not paid for on Maudling's swimming pool was in 1973–4; see Chapters 19 and 23.
56. PRO J 291/92, Poulson to Kenyon, 23 November 1970.
57. PRO FCO 8/833, Despatch No. 3 from Political Agency Abu Dhabi (Simon Nuttall) to Stewart Crawford (British Residency, Bahrain), 12 August 1967.
58. PRO J 291/92, Poulson to Kenyon, 17 June 1968.
59. PRO J 291/101, Poulson evidence, 16 July 1973, paras 330–6.
60. PRO FCO 65/1 relates to the corruption round-robin and replies; Curle to FCO, 29 January 1969.
61. MEPO (pending), minute of CP (Africa) board meeting, 12 February 1967.
62. PRO J 291/73, Poulson to Grimwood, draft, 17 June 1970.
63. *HC Debates*, vol. 769, col. 1435, 27 August 1968.
64. PRO FCO 38/261, notes of meetings between Thomson and Maudling, 25 August 1967, 13 October 1967, 31 January 1968, 8 March 1968.
65. PRO J 291/88, Poulson to Gomershall, 30 August 1968.
66. Ray Fitzwalter and David Taylor, *Web of Corruption* (St Albans: Granada, 1981), pp. 147–9; also PRO J 291/101, Poulson examination, 18 July 1973. WYAS C 391/1/16, Poulson account books.
67. PRO J 291/92, Marr to Poulson, 1 June 1968.
68. Fitzwalter and Taylor, *Web of Corruption*, p. 149, citing Poulson to Maudling, 30 July 1968.
69. WYAS WCC 3/1/3, Poulson examination, 25 September 1972, para. 3571 et seq.
70. University of Warwick Modern Records Centre, MSS 154/8/169, Crossman diary, May 1970, pp. 220–1.
71. David Butler Papers, David Butler interview with James Douglas, 8 February 1968.
72. NARA State Department central files, Box 2564 PO 12, UK Telegram, 18 March 1968.
73. *The Banker* (June 1968), p. 488.
74. Ken Williams, interview, 5 November 2002.
75. Jack Howard-Drake, interview, 12 May 2003.
76. *HC Debates*, vol. 763, cols 147–57, 23 April 1968.
77. PRO FCO 8/89, McCarthy to Burroughs, 19 August 1968, 'The Persian Gulf: Conservative Party Statements'.
78. PRO FCO 8/979, McCarthy note, 21 April 1969.
79. PRO FCO 8/9, note of conversation between Crawford and the Ruler of Bahrain.
80. PRO T 312/1983, note, 23 July 1968, P.C. Petrie.
81. PRO T 312/1983, Armstrong to Houghton, 9 August 1968; note of meeting, 15 August 1968.
82. John Poulson, *The Price* (London: Michael Joseph, 1981), p. 144.
83. Police interview with John Poulson, 28 February 1974, Tape 3, p. 2.
84. PRO J 291/101, Poulson evidence, 18 July 1973, para. 735.
85. PRO FCO 8/139, McCarthy to Burroughs, 20 June 1968.
86. PRO J 291/89, Poulson to Nasser, 31 January 1969.

87. PRO J 291/92, Poulson to Marr, 30 April 1968; Maudling to Poulson, 22 April 1968.
88. T. Dan Smith, unpublished memoirs, pp. 94–5.

CHAPTER 19

1. Viv Walker, interview, 11 July 2003; Sir Sandy Glen, interview, 11 September 2002.
2. Sir Sandy Glen, interview, 10 March 2003.
3. Viv Walker, interview, 11 July 2003.
4. WYAS C 391/1/16, Financial records, May 1968.
5. Other documents relating to the swimming pool were obtained during a libel action by the *Daily Mirror* legal team in the late 1970s.
6. WYAS WCC 3/1/3, Poulson evidence, 13 June 1972, paras 205–9.
7. PRO J 219/63, Valerie Richmond evidence, 13 December 1973, p. 63.
8. As cited Michael Gillard and Martin Tomkinson, *Nothing to Declare* (London: John Calder, 1980), p. 285.
9. MEPO pending; Maudling to Baker, 27 February 1969; Poulson to Maudling, 25 April 1969.
10. Note of meeting between L.S. Stratford and Maudling, 25 April 1974.
11. PRO J 291/95, Maudling private examination, 19 July 1973, para. 282.
12. PRO BA 119/116, Official Receiver's Preliminary Report Re John Garlick Llewellyn Poulson, July 1972.
13. WYAS WCC 3/1/3, Poulson examination, 13 June 1972, para. 394.
14. John Dodd, 'The Clamping Stay King', *Independent on Sunday*, 15 July 1990.
15. Martyn Gregory, *Dirty Tricks* (London: Little, Brown, 1994), pp. 16–25.
16. *Who's Who*, 1997.
17. WYAS WCC 3/1/3, Poulson evidence, 13 June 1972, para. 314.
18. The REFA story is told in Michael Gillard, *A Little Pot of Money* (London: André Deutsch/Private Eye, 1974). This book, although critical, was never the subject of legal action from Maudling's solicitors despite public statements that his lawyers were reading it closely. Given Maudling's sensitivity, as shown by the Alan Watkins libel settlement (see below) and the action against the Granada programme on Malta in May 1974, this would suggest that Gillard's book is a reliable account of events as they relate to Maudling. Limitations of time and resources and the apparent destruction of most REFA paperwork mean that there is little to add in these pages to what is covered in Gillard's book, and the reader with a deeper interest in REFA is referred to that work.
19. *Ibid.*, p. 23.
20. Charles Raw, Bruce Page and Godfrey Hodgson, *Do You Sincerely Want to be Rich?* (London: André Deutsch, 1971), pp. 81–2.
21. Gillard, *Little Pot*, pp. 39–45.
22. *HC Debates*, vol. 517, col. 1303, 8 July 1953.
23. Gillard, *Little Pot*, pp. 52–68.
24. Miriam Camps, *Britain and the European Community 1955–1963* (London: Oxford University Press, 1964), pp. 125–6.
25. Gillard, *Little Pot*, pp. 84–91.
26. This story, originally told by Poulson in his police interviews and repeated in *The Price*, was confirmed by Ken Williams (1999 interview for Channel 4, *Sleaze*).
27. Gillard and Tomkinson, *Nothing to Declare*, p. 334 fn. 265.
28. Gillard, *Little Pot*, pp. 69–72.
29. This may have contravened section 13(1) or section 13(2) of the Prevention of Fraud (Investments) Act 1958 by which 'Any person who, by any statement, promise or forecast which he knows to be misleading, false or deceptive, or by any dishonest

concealment of material facts, or by the reckless making (dishonestly or otherwise) of a statement, promise or forecast which is misleading, false or deceptive, induces or attempts to induce another person' to make investments, or conspires to do the same, is guilty of an offence. The fact that REFA products were not permitted for sale in the UK, under part of the same legislation, may not have been a sufficient loophole to avoid such a charge.

30. PRO FCO 17/848, Beirut to FCO, 14 July 1969; FCO to Beirut, 21 July 1969.

31. Gillard, *Little Pot*, pp. 99–101.

32. As cited *ibid.*, p. 161.

33. Department of Trade, *London and County Securities*, 1976.

34. Raw, Page and Hodgson, *Do you Sincerely Want*, pp. 319–26.

35. *Ibid.*, p. 306.

36. Robert Hutchison, *Vesco* (New York: Avon, 1976); Arthur Herzog, *Robert Vesco* (New York: Doubleday, 1987). Vesco was closely involved in the Bahamas in the 1970s, as was Sir Frederic Bennett. 'Offshore' by its nature remains obscure, as do any links between Vesco and British politics.

37. Alan Watkins, *A Short Walk Down Fleet Street* (London: Duckworth, 2000), pp. 136–9; Alan Watkins, interview, 26 November 2002; Richard Stott, interview, 7 January 2003.

38. PRO FCO 8/995/1, Abu Dhabi to FCO, 1 May 1969.

39. PRO J 291/89, Poulson to Nasser, 8 November 1968.

40. PRO FCO 93/299, Wright to Evans, 13 September 1973.

41. PRO J 291/89, Williams to Nasser, 14 January 1969.

42. Letter cited in Poulson private examination, 18 July 1973, para. 538. The shadowy existence of ITCS (Middle East) is a loose end of the affair. When asked about this letter, Reggie said 'I don't think it ever was incorporated actually', but references to the existence of shares in the company appear elsewhere in the Poulson documents.

43. PRO J 291/95, Maudling private examination, 19 July 1973, para. 351.

44. PRO J 291/101, Poulson private examination, 18 July 1973, paras 528–70.

45. PRO J 291/95, Maudling private examination, 19 July 1973, para. 354. This rather contradicts the statement in para. 351 above, in which paying ITCS creditors was the point of the exercise.

46. MEPO (pending), ITCS minute, 12 August 1969.

47. PRO J 291/101, Poulson private examination, 18 July 1973, paras 578–85, Hunter citing Maudling to Nasser, 10 September 1969.

48. MEPO (pending), DTI s.109 report on ITCS, para. 108. Alan Ford was investigating this matter when he was removed from the inquiry in 1974. Martin Maudling was paid £2,500 as 'compensation for loss of office' in September 1971.

49. PRO J 291/101, Poulson private examination, 18 July 1973, para. 471; Maudling private examination, 19 July 1973.

50. PRO J 291/95, Maudling private examination, 19 July 1973, para. 278.

51. To muddy the waters even further, a Poulson letter suggests that 'Maudling' (not 'ITCS' although that is probably what he meant) was entitled to 2 per cent commission on overseas projects, but he seems to have imagined that this was in addition to the 10 per cent that was going to his practice. However, some deals had been negotiated in the Middle East that entailed fees of only 5 per cent; these seem to have been loss-leaders to get Poulson established in the region; Poulson at one point seemed to think that Maudling would end up out of pocket as a result of these deals, but when questioned was entirely unclear about what he had meant in this letter. PRO J 291/101, Poulson private examination, 18 July 1973, paras 425–58.

52. PRO J 291/101, exchange between Hunter and Poulson at Poulson private examination, 18 July 1973, paras 458 et seq. This contention seems to be supported by an affidavit produced by Sweetman on 16 June 1972 that stated that 'It appears to

me that prior to May, 1970, there was no clear understanding or accord between ITCS and Ropergate, particularly between the Right Honourable Reginald Maudling and Mr Poulson, as to the terms and effect of an oral agreement which I am informed by the former directors of ITCS was made between the directors of those two companies . . .' (as cited at Maudling private examination 19 July 1973, para. 274). When asked why the oral agreement was not reduced to writing, Maudling plaintively said that 'There was no need to do so because we had to trust one another at that time' (para. 277). If true, this displayed utter naivety and folly on the part of both parties.

53. PRO J 291/95, Maudling private examination, 19 July 1973, para. 370.
54. PRO J 291/95, Maudling private examination, 19 July 1973, para. 342.
55. ITCS accounts as supplied to Companies House, file 00893892 (ITCS).
56. *Architect's Journal*, 4 October 1972, p. 749.
57. Gillard and Tomkinson, *Nothing to Declare*, p. 287, from Poulson testimony to the Official Receiver entered as evidence at Poulson trial, 13 December 1973.
58. PRO J 291/61, Wilson *et al.* to Poulson, 9 November 1969.
59. WYAS WCC 3/1/2, Sales note, 14 October 1969.
60. PRO BT 296/833, Opinion of David Smout, QC, 22 July 1976, citing OSB Report 1973. Smout did not accept that there was proof of loss to other traders from OSB continuing in business and therefore not a prima facie offence; this was one of the less convincing aspects of his opinion, because while this assertion could be made on the evidence before him at the time, the bankruptcy hearings had explored the effects of the collapse of OSB in more detail. Maudling's resignation suggests that he was aware of the dangers of continued association with OSB.
61. PRO BA 119/116, Official Receiver's Preliminary Report, July 1972.
62. WYAS WCC 3/1/3, Poulson evidence, 3 July 1972, paras 1217–22; the last payment of the covenant was in March 1969. However (MEPO pending) the Trust still seemed to be expecting the payment in May 1970 (de Rougemont to Clifford Turner, 21 May 1970).
63. PRO J 291/94, Sweetman evidence, 18 July 1972, paras 581–624.
64. WYAS WCC 3/1/3, Poulson evidence, 13 June 1972, paras 725–52; Muir Hunter's examination of Poulson explored this question; see also para. 836.
65. PRO J 291/95, John King private examination, 18 July 1972, paras 164–7.
66. PRO J 291/95, John King private examination, 18 July 1972, paras 1–4; 76–87.
67. PRO J 291/95, John King private examination, 18 July 1972, para. 187.
68. WYAS WCC 3/1/3, Poulson evidence, 1 August 1972, p. 36.
69. PRO J 291/92, Poulson to Kenyon, 23 November 1970.
70. Sir Roy Strong, *The Roy Strong Diaries 1967–87* (London: Weidenfeld & Nicolson, 1997), 6 January 1970, p. 55. Gulf Arabs often find the frivolous wearing of their traditional clothes by Westerners offensive; the Maudlings were sensitive enough to know this and must have been confident that the gesture would not be taken badly.
71. DPW 59/102, 'Persian Gulf Reassessment', 16 October 1969.
72. PRO FCO 8/1292, Hayman to Arthur, 12 February 1970.
73. DPW 59/103, 'Report on visit to the Gulf', September 1970.
74. PRO DPP 2/4679, Report by Inspector Mees, 2 December 1969.
75. PRO DPP 2/4680, Richardson report made 28 November 1969.
76. PRO DPP 2/4679, Elwyn Jones to Skelhorn, 9 December 1969; further opinion from Richardson, 16 December 1969.
77. Hetherington Papers, interview with Harold Wilson, 19 July 1972.
78. *Royal Commission on Standards of Conduct in Public Life 1974–76* (Salmon Report) (London: HMSO, 1976), Cmnd 6524, para. 23.
79. Private information.
80. PRO DPP 2/4680, Note on file, 12 August 1969.

81. PRO DPP 2/4680, 'Observations'.

82. 'My Baby and Me: Caroline Maudling Tells All', *News of the World*, 28 September 1969, p. 3.

83. Unfortunately, the press was not always so kind to Caroline and others in difficult family circumstances.

84. Although the main interview was to the *Rand Daily Mail* in South Africa and not intended for British publication. Reginald Maudling to *News of the World*, 5 October 1969. Hull archives, NCCL 582/16.

85. *Evening News*, 24 September 1969.

86. *Daily Sketch*, 24 September 1969.

87. 'What Caroline Means to Us', *Daily Express*, 24 September 1969.

88. Leo Abse, interview, 10 February 2003.

89. *Westminster Confidential*, 25 September 1969.

90. *Guardian*, 8 October 1969.

91. Cecil King, *The Cecil King Diary 1965–70* (London: Jonathan Cape, 1972), 27 October 1969, p. 286.

92. Boyle Papers, MS 660/54927 et seq., Boyle to Vaizey, 11 September 1975.

93. Arthur Fawcett Papers, Maudling to Fawcett, n.d. (October 1969).

94. Reginald Maudling, interview with David Butler and Austin Mitchell, 2 June 1968.

95. Reginald Maudling, interview with David Butler and Michael Pinto-Duschinsky, 11 November 1969.

96. Reginald Maudling, interview with David Butler and Michael Pinto-Duschinsky, 11 November 1969; Boyle Papers, MS 660/23454 et seq. Minutes of Advisory Committee on Policy.

97. Boyle Papers, MS 660/52274 et seq., Boyle to Fraser, 6 May 1981.

98. CPA CCO 500/56/1, Selsdon Park notes; Thatcher archive URL.

99. 'An Incomes Policy or Bust', *Spectator*, 25 April 1970, p. 556.

100. King, *Diary*, 7 March 1970, p. 315.

101. David Butler Papers, MPD note of 1969 Conservative Party conference.

102. David Butler Papers, Reginald Maudling interview with David Butler and Austin Mitchell, 2 June 1968.

103. David Butler and Michael Pinto-Duschinsky, *The British General Election of 1970* (London: Macmillan, 1971), pp. 221–3.

104. Douglas Hurd, *Memoirs* (London: Little, Brown, 2003), p. 185.

105. *Barnet Press*, 5 June 1970, p. 1.

106. *Barnet Press*, 26 June 1970, p. 13.

107. *Observer*, 21 June 1970.

108. Alec Cairncross, *The Wilson Years: A Treasury Diary 1964–69* (London: The Historians' Press, 1997), 24 September 1968, p. 326.

109. State Dept SNF 1970–73, Box 2651, Telegram London to State, 24 June 1970.

110. Edward Heath, *The Course of My Life* (London: Hodder & Stoughton, 1998), p. 310.

111. State Dept SNF 1970–73, Box 2651, Telegram London to State, 24 June 1970.

CHAPTER 20

1. Brian Faulkner, *Memoirs of a Statesman* (London: Weidenfeld & Nicolson, 1978), after title page.

2. Alexis de Tocqueville, *L'Ancien Régime* (Paris, 1856).

3. Jim Callaghan, *A House Divided* (London: Collins, 1973), p. 5.

4. *Ibid.*, p. 38.

5. Cecil Parkinson, interview, 22 October 2002.

6. Malachi O'Docherty, *The Trouble with Guns* (Belfast: Blackstaff, 1998), pp. 64–5.

7. NAI 2002/19/384, Confidential reports from the London Embassy; note from Ambassador Donal O'Sullivan to Ministry of Foreign Affairs, 1 May 1970.
8. Ken Bloomfield, *Stormont in Crisis* (Belfast: Blackstaff, 1994), p. 127.
9. NAI 2002/19/384, Notes on conversations by Con Howard (Irish Embassy), 23 June 1970.
10. 'Clever and Casual, Manly and Matey, Maudling Steps into Ulster', *Belfast Telegraph*, 24 June 1970.
11. Callaghan, *A House Divided*, pp. 143–4.
12. PRO PREM 15/100, Trend to Heath, 21 June 1970.
13. PRO PREM 15/100, minutes of Cabinet committee meeting, 22 June 1970.
14. Clive Scoular, *James Chichester-Clark* (Killyleagh: Clive Scoular, 2000), p. 108.
15. Sunday Times Insight Team, *Ulster* (Harmondsworth: Penguin Special 1972), p. 207.
16. *Memoirs*, p. 179.
17. Interview with Thames TV, as reported in *Irish Press*, 13 August 1974.
18. Paddy Devlin, *Straight Left* (Belfast: Blackstaff, 1993), p. 127.
19. Desmond Hamill, *Pig in the Middle* (London: Methuen, 1986), p. 36.
20. Sunday Times Insight Team, *Ulster* p. 213 is the canonical version of the quotation (different versions have sometimes been cited). The comment was first cited in the *Sunday Times* in November 1971.
21. *Irish Press*, 15 February 1979; this explanation had been given to reporter John McEntee in conversation in June 1978.
22. National Sound Archive, BBC, *Analysis* interview with Ian McIntyre, 1971.
23. NAI Jack Lynch Papers 2001/8/8, Report on situation, 15 July 1970.
24. Quite how significant the arms haul was is disputed. According to reports to the Stormont government at the time, the age and variety of arms suggested that there had been no recent large-scale acquisition of arms by the IRA. PRONI file CAB 4/1532, Cabinet conclusions, 7 July 1970.
25. Anon., *Three Days in July: The Story of the Falls Road Curfew* (Belfast: Sinn Fein, 1995).
26. As cited Tim Pat Coogan, *The IRA* (London: HarperCollins, 1995), p. 552.
27. Lt-Col Michael Dewar, *The British Army in Northern Ireland* (London: Arms and Armour, 1985), p. 39.
28. Martin Dillon, *The Enemy Within* (London: Doubleday, 1994), p. 97; Peter Taylor, *Brits* (London: Bloomsbury, 2002), pp. 50–1.
29. PRO CJ 4/21, notes of meetings, 30 June 1970, at Belfast and Lisburn.
30. PRO PREM 15/100, Ireland I: Note Trend to Heath, 9 July 1970.
31. NAI Jack Lynch Papers 2001/8/15, report of conversation between Patrick Hillery and Gerry Fitt, 13 December 1970.
32. According to Lt-Col Dewar, Provisional IRA membership increased from fewer than 100 in May–June to roughly 800 in December 1970. The label 'Provisional' was dropped by the organisation during 1970 but persisted in British army and political usage.
33. PRONI CAB 4/1535, report on meeting with Home Secretary, 17 July 1970.
34. PRONI CAB 4/1535, report on meeting with Home Secretary, 17 July 1970 and PRONI CAB 4/1558, Cabinet conclusions, 3 November 1970.
35. PRO PREM 15/101, note of meeting, 17 July 1970. This deal was less than it seemed – in Derry the no-go areas rapidly reappeared and the Northern Ireland government softened its line on 'celebrations'.
36. PRO CJ 4/4, statement on 10 August 1970, drafts.
37. PRO CJ 3/48, memorandum by A.J. Langdon, 11 September 1970.
38. 'Maudling's Unenviable Mission', *Financial Times*, 5 March 1971.
39. Sir Robin Chichester-Clark, interview, 6 August 2002.
40. PRO CJ 4/65, Private Office note to Maudling, 7 December 1970; 15 February 1971.

41. 'Warning on the Alternative to Peaceful Co-existence', *News Letter*, 5 March 1971.
42. Simon Winchester, *In Holy Terror* (London: Faber & Faber, 1974), p. 129.
43. Faulkner, *Memoirs of a Statesman*, pp. 90-1.
44. Scoular, *Chichester-Clark*, pp. 126-7.
45. PRO CJ 4/62, Burroughs to Wakefield, 10 March 1971.
46. PRO NI CAB 9A/7/232, file on arrangements for Maudling visit to Northern Ireland, March 1971.
47. PRO PREM 15/475 NI (3), 'Note on internment', 12 February 1971.
48. Taylor, *Brits*, pp. 62-3.
49. *Ibid.*, pp. 59-60.
50. PRO PREM 15/476, cable from UKREP NI, 2 March 1971.
51. PRO PREM 15/475, note of meeting at Chequers, 13 February 1971; also CJ 4/50 on the RUC Special Branch in 1971 in more detail.
52. PRO CAB 130/522, note of meeting of GEN 47 (NI Cabinet Committee), 18 October 1971.
53. PREM 15/476, cable from UKREP NI, 13 March 1971.
54. PRO PREM 15/475, note of meeting, 13 February 1971.
55. PRO PREM 15/476, note of meeting, 16 March 1971.
56. Private information.
57. PRO PREM 15/476.
58. PRO PREM 15/476, note of conversation between Heath and Chichester-Clark, 19 March 1971.
59. PRO CJ 4/85 on meetings following the Derry shootings.
60. Henry Kelly, *How Stormont Fell* (Dublin: Gill & Macmillan, 1972), p. 56.
61. *Ibid.*, p. 56.
62. 'Concern at UK's Hard Line Move: British Statement Seen as Bid to Avoid Direct Rule', *Irish News*, 24 July 1971.
63. *Belfast Telegraph*, 27 July 1971.
64. BBC interview with Field Marshal Lord Carver conducted in 2001 for *UK Confidential*, January 2002.
65. Gerry Adams, *Before the Dawn* (London: Mandarin, 1996), pp. 151-6.
66. PRO PREM 15/478, note of meeting, 5 August 1971.
67. The operation was launched a day earlier than planned because of fears of leaks.
68. Jack Howard-Drake, interview, 12 May 2003.
69. In 1978 he recalled that 'I was always frightened that the IRA might reply by kidnapping a lot of innocent children and holding them hostage', which has the ring of something Colin Wallace, the gifted army PR man based in Lisburn, might have made up to frighten people. *Irish Press*, 30 June 1978.
70. LSE, Hetherington Papers, note of meeting with Maudling, 9 August 1971.
71. Faulkner, *Memoirs*, p. 119.
72. NAI 2002/19/385, note of meeting between Donal O'Sullivan and Stewart Crawford (FCO), 9 August 1972.
73. BBC *Panorama*, interview with Robin Day, 21 September 1971. The first Protestants interned were in fact John McGuffin, a civil rights activist and Ronnie Bunting, a member of the Official IRA; Stormont politicians hoped that pointing out that the existence of Protestant detainees of this kind might deflect allegations about the one-sided nature of internment! The first detentions of loyalist paramilitaries were not until February 1973.
74. NARA Box 2653 POL 23-8 UK, Belfast to State, 21 August 1970.
75. David McKittrick, Seamus Kelters, Brian Feeney and Chris Thornton, *Lost Lives* (Edinburgh: Mainstream, 1999), 'James Glenn Finlay', pp. 101-2.
76. Jim Cusack and Henry McDonald, *UVF* (Dublin: Poolbeg, 1997), pp. 73-97 for UVF

activities in the period. It was not until 1978 that a UVF man was tried for involvement in the bombing and the real sequence of events was apparent.

77. PRO CAB 164/879, briefing note for Heath before meeting with Faulkner, 19 August 1971.

78. NARA Box 2654 L 23–8 UK, 7 September 1971, 'The Changing Pattern of Terror', memorandum to State Department.

79. Seán MacStiofáin, *Memoirs of a Revolutionary* (London: Gordon Cremonesi, 1975), p. 192.

80. PRO CAB 130/522, minutes of meeting of GEN 47, 12 August 1971.

81. PRO NI CAB 4/1610, Cabinet conclusions, 20 August 1971, report on meeting, 19 August 1971.

82. NAI DFA 2003/17/296, note by ambassador on conversation between Edward Heath and the Tanaiste, 5 May 1969.

83. Edward Heath, *The Course of My Life* (London: Hodder & Stoughton, 1998), pp. 423–4. NAI DFA 2003/13/6 Chequers I: Heath is quoted in the Irish official record as saying infelicitously that Europe could offer 'a final solution to the Irish problem'.

84. Faulkner, *Memoirs*, p. 129; Bloomfield, *Stormont in Crisis*, p. 157.

85. NAI 2002/8/487, transcript of press conference after Chequers talks, 7 September 1971; PRO CAB 130/522, minutes of GEN 47, 11 August 1971.

86. Records of the talks are filed at PRO CJ 4/47.

87. NAI 2002/8/489, note of Jack Lynch meeting with Edward Heath, 6 December 1971.

88. 'APG' was actually the phrase of Brian Faulkner rather than Maudling, whose original draft referred to 'an active and permanent role, guaranteed by the UK government'. PRO CJ 4/47, note of conversation between Maudling and Faulkner, 3 September 1971.

89. PRO NI CAB 4/1610, Cabinet conclusions, 20 August 1971, report on meeting, 19 August 1971.

90. I am grateful to Peter Neumann for elaborating this point to me. Email Peter Neumann to author, 17 December 2002.

91. Maurice Hayes, *Minority Verdict* (Belfast: Blackstaff, 1995), p. 144.

92. John McGuffin, *Internment* (Tralee: Anvil Books, 1973), chapter 11: 'Torture and Brutality'; now available on www.cain.ulst.ac.uk/events/intern.

93. PRO CAB 130/522, minutes of Cabinet Committee GEN 47(71), 18 October 1971.

94. Taylor, *Brits*, pp. 68–74. There was another spate of torture incidents in police custody in May 1972 which self-evidently had no political approval, so it is quite probable that the August–September 1971 experiments did not either. Whitelaw reacted with 'shock and horror' when shown evidence of the May 1972 cases. NARA POL 29, UK Dublin Embassy cables 0512, 0520 May 1972.

95. The ministers ordered that such practices be stopped without specific authorisation (which was apparently never given) at their meeting on 18 October. In January 1972 the government agreed with Lord Gardiner's minority report from the Parker Committee that the original techniques approved on 10 August were themselves not acceptable and henceforth never to be used.

96. Private information.

97. PRO CAB 130/522, minutes of Cabinet Committee, GEN 47(71), 18 October 1971.

98. *HC Debates*, vol. 826, cols 215–17, 16 November 1971.

99. *HC Debates*, vol. 826, cols 224–6, 16 November 1971.

100. *The Times*, 12 December 1971.

101. *Belfast Telegraph*, 9 December 1971.

102. *Irish Times*, 16 December 1971.

103. *Belfast Telegraph*, 15 December 1971. According to the *Irish Times* (16 December 1971) he said that 'would not be defeated, not completely eliminated, but have their violence reduced to an acceptable level'.

104. *Irish News*, 17 December 1971.

105. Anon., *A Brief History of the UDA/UFF in Contemporary Conflict* (Belfast: Prisoners' Aid and Post-Conflict Resettlement Group, 1995) (NIPC P11254).

106. *Guardian*, 16 December 1971.

107. *Republican News*, 2 January 1972.

108. Documents released to the Saville inquiry, as cited by Eamonn McCann, 'In Derry it's Still Personal', *Scotsman*, 17 January 2002.

109. The local police commander favoured taking photographs of those involved in violence and arresting them later, not trying to do so amid a chaotic march. Taylor, *Brits*, pp. 89–90.

110. Arthur Fawcett Papers, Fawcett to Maudling, 1 February 1972.

111. The QC for most of the soldiers at the Saville inquiry, in his opening statement, announced that it was not part of their argument that any of the known dead had been armed, but that they had been shot at from elsewhere. Cited in Eamonn McCann, 'In Derry it's Still Personal', *Scotsman*, 17 January 2002.

112. *HC Debates*, vol. 830, cols 31–3, 31 January 1972.

113. Lord Allen of Abbeydale, interview, 22 July 2003.

114. Rory Rapple, 'Maudling bothered by killings', 5 January 2003, cutting, source unknown. The article cites a letter from Allen to the Ministry of Defence, 8 February 1972.

115. *HC Debates*, vol. 830, col. 34, 31 January 1972.

116. As cited by Taylor, *Brits*, p. 103.

117. PRO CAB 130/560, ministerial committee on Northern Ireland, 9 February 1972.

118. David Butler Papers, Willie Whitelaw interview, 19 February 1972.

119. PRO PREM 15/1004, Douglas-Home to Heath, 13 March 1972.

120. *Guardian*, 13 April 2002, p. 9.

121. Cecil King, *The Cecil King Diary 1970–74* (London: Jonathan Cape, 1975), 5 January 1972, p. 165.

122. Calvin Macnee, 'Reggie's Last Stand', *Fortnight*, 23 February 1972.

123. The first mainland attack related to the Troubles is sometimes said to have been the bombing of the Post Office Tower in October 1971 but according to the usually well-informed US London Embassy this was the work of the British anarchist Angry Brigade as a protest against joining the EEC. NARA Box 2653 POL 23–8, UK Belfast consulate to State, 17 February 1972.

124. NARA Box 2655 POL 23–9, UK London 2694, 24 March 1972.

125. Stratton Mills, interview, 11 July 2002.

126. Bloomfield, *Stormont in Crisis*, p. 163. According to Bloomfield, Maudling was 'distinctly abstracted' over lunch.

127. Letter to author from Lord Molyneaux, 14 July 2002.

128. NARA Box 2653 POL 23–8, UK Belfast consulate to State, 17 February 1972.

129. It is a curious fact about Northern Ireland that the political positions of individuals are oddly flexible. Faulkner, after all, started off as a hardliner and ended up power-sharing after Sunningdale; Craig moved in the mid–1970s to advocating voluntary coalition with the SDLP, and several of his Vanguard followers – such as David Trimble and Reg Empey – became thoughtful men of peace who operated the Good Friday Agreement after 1998.

130. Heath, *The Course of My Life*, p. 436.

131. Paul Routledge, *John Hume* (London: HarperCollins, 1998), pp. 102–3.

CHAPTER 21

1. Lord Windlesham, *Politics in Practice* (London: Jonathan Cape, 1975), pp. 15–20, paints a vivid portrait of the ramshackle administrative structure of the department at the time.

2. National Sound Archive, BBC *Analysis*, March 1971, Reginald Maudling interview with Ian Macintyre; also interview, Lord Carlisle of Bucklow, 28 October 2002.

3. Private interview.

4. Cecil King, *The Cecil King Diary 1970–74* (London: Jonathan Cape, 1975) *passim* illustrates the point.

5. Interview, Lord Allen of Abbeydale, 22 July 2002.

6. Clive Bossom notes, 1979.

7. Interview, Lord Allen of Abbeydale, 22 July 2002.

8. *Daily Telegraph*, 20 October 1971.

9. Clive Bossom notes, 1979.

10. PRO HO 317/22, Appointments diary 1971.

11. Viv Walker, interview, 11 July 2003.

12. National Sound Archive, 'Now Read On' radio programme, Reginald Maudling on two books on drink, 1976, NSA M4670R BD1, http://cadensa.bl.uk/uhtbin/cgisirsi/NFVRgO1suW/196230046/9.

13. PRO HO 317/22, Appointments diary 1971.

14. Interview, Lord Allen of Abbeydale, 22 July 2002.

15. National Sound Archive, BBC *Analysis*, March 1971, Reginald Maudling interview with Ian Macintyre.

16. Alan Watkins, 'The Man in the Middle', *New Statesman*, 20 August 1971.

17. Nora Beloff, 'Optimist in the Wings', *Observer*, 28 February 1971.

18. *Memoirs*, pp. 170–2.

19. Lord Allen of Abbeydale, interview, 22 July 2002.

20. *The Sun*, 10 January 1972, as quoted by Christian Bugge, 'The *Clockwork Orange* Controversy', available on www.virtual-memory.co.uk/amk/doc/0012.html.

21. Roger Bolton, *Death on the Rock and Other Stories* (London: W.H. Allen, 1990), pp. 20–3.

22. Clive Bossom notes, 1979.

23. PRO HO 295/68, Allen to Maudling, 28 July 1970.

24. Clive Bossom notes, 1979; Sir Clive Bossom, interview, June 2002.

25. William Rees-Mogg, 'We've got to face it, Britain's gone to pot', *The Times*, 2 July 2001.

26. National Sound Archive, BBC *Analysis*, March 1971, Reginald Maudling interview with Ian Macintyre.

27. Private interview.

28. Lord Allen of Abbeydale, interview, 22 July 2002.

29. Lord Carlisle of Bucklow, interview, 28 October 2002.

30. Michael Foot Papers, MF/4, contains considerable documentation on Dutschke.

31. Lord Allen of Abbeydale, interview, 22 July 2002.

32. Patrick Cosgrave, 'Reginald Maudling: Temporary Exile', *Spectator*, 22 July 1972.

33. *Tribune*, 15 January 1971.

34. Dr C. Pallis to Maudling, 15 September 1970; Michael Foot Papers, MF/4. Reggie did at least say that he would be prepared to consider extending his stay on grounds of convalescence: Maudling to Foot, 23 September 1970.

35. *Private Eye*, 1 January 1971, suggests that it was the realisation that the decision would have to be defended before a tribunal that led to the calling in aid of 'national security' and the use of special powers in relation to evidence.

36. Alan Watkins, 'Rudi and Reggie', *New Statesman*, 25 September 1970; 'An Abuse of

Power', *New Statesman*, 6 November 1970; 'Star Chamber in the Strand', *New Statesman*, 25 December 1970.

37. *Memoirs*, p. 166; Maudling devoted twice as much space in his memoirs to the Dutschke affair as to the 1965 leadership contest.

38. In *Memoirs*, p. 166, Maudling's implication that he would have resigned is pretty clear. Patrick Cosgrave in *The Lives of Enoch Powell* (London: Bodley Head, 1989, p. 301) states it explicitly, adding that 'few of the Cabinet could see much reason to deny residence'. The prospect of resignation was also referred to in the press at the time, see for instance letter to *The Times* from Geoffrey Marshall, 12 January 1971.

39. *HC Debates*, vol. 931, cols 373–6, 3 May 1977.

40. M.R.C. Crossman, MSS 154/8/8 f743/1, diary, 28 October 1955. The incident was a constituency case of Crossman's.

41. *A Better Tomorrow*, Conservative Party manifesto, 1970 general election.

42. Sir Clive Bossom, interview, June 2002.

43. *Memoirs*, pp. 157–8.

44. PRO CAB 129/157/8, 'Immigration Policy', 10 May 1971, memorandum by Home Secretary.

45. PRO CAB 128/48, Cabinet minute, CM(71)1/3.

46. *Memoirs*, p. 158 repeats the sense of the Cabinet papers reference.

47. Caroline Maudling, interview, 6 October 1999.

48. *Birmingham Post*, 22 October 2002, p. 12.

49. 'Genial Mr Maudling', *Socialist Commentary* (April 1971), pp. 7–8.

50. *Ibid.*

51. DPW 37/8, Wall to Pym, 16 March 1971; Maudling to Pym, 2 April 1971.

52. National Sound Archive, BBC *Analysis*, March 1971, Reginald Maudling interview with Ian Macintyre.

53. PRO CAB 128/47, Cabinet minute CM(70)41, 26 November 1970.

54. *HC Debates*, vol. 835, col. 1764, 27 April 1972.

55. National Sound Archive, BBC *Analysis*, October 1972, Reginald Maudling and Roy Jenkins.

56. *HC Debates*, vol. 945, col. 68, 27 February 1978.

57. *Daily Telegraph*, 22 June 1970, p. 2.

58. Lord Carr of Hadley, interview, 29 July 1999.

59. *HC Debates*, vol. 826, cols 965–76, 22 November 1971.

60. Reginald Maudling, 'Alternatives to Prison', *Spectator*, 26 July 1975.

61. Reginald Maudling, *The Ever-Changing Challenge* (London: Conservative Political Centre, 1969).

62. UKC Weatherill Papers, WEA/PP R13, Whips' Office note, 22 November 1971.

63. *Memoirs*, pp. 161–2.

64. Edward Maudling, interview, 27 October 1999.

65. Anthony Holden, *The St Albans Poisoner* (London: Corgi, 1995).

66. On this peculiar business, there are references in an article by Darcus Howe, *New Statesman*, 12 December 1997; Mike Phillips and Trevor Phillips, *Windrush* (London: HarperCollins, 1998), p. 280; the official file on Maudling's interest in the case, PRO HO 325/144, has been retained by the Department and is unavailable for consultation.

67. Private interview; also *Memoirs*, pp. 164–5.

68. Private interview.

69. Denis Greenhill, *More By Accident* (York: Wilton 65, 1992), pp. 158–9.

70. Leo Abse, interview, 10 February 2003.

71. Letter Sir Edward Heath to author, 21 August 2002. Nevertheless, Maudling was sometimes referred to as Deputy Prime Minister in civil service correspondence.

72. Lord Allen of Abbeydale, interview, 22 July 2002.

73. UKC Weatherill Papers, WEA/PP R30, Bernard Weatherill diary, 21 December 1971.
74. *HC Debates*, vol. 828, cols 1297–306, 21 December 1971.
75. *HC Debates*, vol. 822, cols 155–66, 26 July 1971.
76. *HC Debates*, vol. 822, col. 56, 26 July 1971.
77. King, *Diary*, 3 November 1970, p. 52.
78. Interview, Lord Carr of Hadley, 29 July 1999.
79. Nora Beloff, 'Optimist in the Wings', *Observer*, 28 February 1971.
80. *Sunday Express*, 16 January 1972.
81. Hugh MacPherson, 'Political Commentary', *Spectator*, 27 November 1971, p. 758.
82. Nora Beloff, 'Why Maudling is taking the rap', *Observer*, 13 February 1972, p. 8.
83. Calvin Macnee, 'Reggie's Last Stand', *Fortnight*, 23 February 1972.
84. Derek Marks, 'The Big Fish among the Minnows', *Sunday Express*, 16 January 1972.
85. *HC Debates*, vol. 830, col. 800, 3 February 1972.
86. Nora Beloff, 'Why Maudling is Taking the Rap', *Observer*, 13 February 1972, p. 8.
87. Lord Allen of Abbeydale, interview, 22 July 2002.
88. *Memoirs*, pp. 160–1.
89. Douglas Hurd, *An End to Promises* (London: Collins, 1979), pp. 102–3.
90. *Sunday Times*, 22 February 1976.
91. Edward Heath, *The Course of My Life* (London: Hodder & Stoughton, 1998), p. 353.
92. *The Times*, 13 September 1972.
93. Robert Taylor, 'The Heath Government and Industrial Relations: Myth and Reality', in Stuart Ball and Anthony Seldon, *The Heath Government 1970–74* (Harlow: Longman, 1996), pp. 161–90.
94. NAI 2002/19/384, Irish Embassy reports: Con Howard's report on Maudling's lunch with the Foreign Press Association, 31 March 1971.

CHAPTER 22

1. Lord Allen of Abbeydale, interview, 22 July 2002.
2. This discussion of Maudling and Lloyd's in 1971 is based on the documents in the PRO file CAB 164/1663.
3. PRO CAB 164/1663, Armstrong to Trend, 8 October 1971. My own research found something that Maudling might have meant. Heald contributed to the 1951–2 review of policy on ministerial directorships, saying in December 1951 that he was not sure being a Name should count, as it was a 'nominal and technical' interest. The government did not accept this view and the rules were framed in July 1952 on a different basis (PRO PREM 11/4945, Heald memorandum, 28 December 1951). This if anything makes Maudling's behaviour in 1971 more reprehensible – either he was deliberately using an outdated precedent, or he was misrepresenting as a legal opinion something Heald had said as an expression of personal opinion.
4. PRO CAB 164/1663, Heath to Maudling, 17 January 1972. A fine distinction, but Maudling had not actually claimed that he was immune from criticism on the Lloyd's matter – just that he felt there was no conflict of interest and that he would be happy to defend the position in Parliament. He had given no assurances that a perceived conflict would not arise and cause difficulties with the press. If Number 10 had wanted to pursue the matter, instead of accepting an assurance that had been at best ambiguously given, they would have had grounds. Peter Walker, who was in a somewhat similar position, made exhaustive enquiries and decided that it would be best to resign from Lloyd's altogether.
5. Private interview.
6. 1971: 29 January, 22 February, 18 March, 13 May, 24 June, 12 October, 19 November; 1972: 28 January, 8 February, 9 March, 28 April, 8 July. The 1970

diary seems to have been lost.

7. 'Maudling Agrees to Buy Back his £2 a Week Home', *Daily Mail*, 28 September 1977, p. 1.

8. Department of Trade, *Peachey Property Corporation Limited*, section 165 inquiry, January 1979, paras 438–9.

9. *Sunday Times*, 9 July 1978, p. 62.

10. Private interview.

11. PRO J 291/94, Evidence produced in private examination of Thomas Sweetman, 18 July 1972, paras 790–874; Sweetman to Maudling, 6 July 1970, Maudling to Sweetman, 7 July 1970. Copies of these letters were sent to Whitehall and arrived shortly after Maudling's resignation.

12. PRO J 291/95, Maudling private examination, 19 July 1973, paras 353–4. 'I provided out of my own pocket office space and everything . . . and I provided a secretary to do the work. I said "send any money they don't need for local expenditure back here and we will pass it on to Poulson." We may have kept a small reserve to meet our own creditors, but I don't know.'

13. Letter, Lord Callaghan of Cardiff to author, 3 August 2002.

14. *The Times*, 29 November 1969; John Grigg, *The History of the* Times *1966–1981* (London: Times Books, 1993), pp. 116–21. In fairness to the much-maligned tabloid press, one should note that a similar exposé had been published about different officers by the *People* in 1968; it was allegedly investigated by the Met but no action followed.

15. Barry Cox, John Shirley, Martin Short, *The Fall of Scotland Yard* (Harmondsworth: Penguin, 1977) is the most detailed account of the Williamson, Dirty Squad and other police scandals of the time.

16. Obituary, Frank Williamson, *The Times*, 30 December 1998.

17. LSE, Hetherington Papers, Reporter's note of conversation with Frank Williamson, 20 March 1972.

18. Lord Carlisle, interview, 28 October 2002.

19. Sir Robert Mark, *In the Office of Constable* (London: Collins, 1978), p. 118. Mark gives a slightly bowdlerised version of the encounter.

20. David Ascoli, *The Queen's Peace* (London: Hamish Hamilton, 1979), pp. 302–17.

21. One of the very few cuts from Fitzwalter and Taylor's *Web of Corruption* made on legal advice was the suggestion that senior Labour legal figures had pulled strings to give Dan Smith the best possible judge. Ray Fitzwalter, interview, 28 October 1999.

22. T. Dan Smith, unpublished memoirs, p. 119.

23. Alan Travis, *Bound and Gagged* (London: Profile, 2001), pp. 231–54, particularly pp. 248–53.

24. Ken Williams, interview, *Sleaze*, Channel 4, 1999.

25. Parliamentary answers, Peter Rawlinson, 21 February 1972 (when he announced that the police and DTI were still investigating the REFA 'group') as cited Michael Gillard, *A Little Pot of Money* (London: Private Eye/André Deutsch, 1974), pp. 137–8; Carlisle, *HC Debates*, vol. 852, cols 174–5, 3 August 1972; Rawlinson, *HC Debates*, vol. 842, col. 8, 31 July 1972.

26. Gillard, *Little Pot*, pp. 130–2; *Daily Mail*, 2 November 1971.

27. *Daily Mail*, 6 May 1974, p. 2.

28. Lunch engagements were booked in the 1971 and 1972 Home Office diaries on 21 January and 28 July 1971, and 28 June 1972 – there were no subsequent engagements that day until 6p.m.

29. Poulson statement to Official Receiver, read at trial, 13 December 1973.

30. PRO J 291/63, Poulson trial evidence, 4 January 1974 (Day 26), p. 30.

31. Ray Fitzwalter and David Taylor, *Web of Corruption* (St Albans: Granada, 1981), pp. 195–203.

32. PRO J 291/60, Vivian Baker witness statement, 10 October 1973.
33. Poulson's secretaries were extremely efficient. Often four or five copies of the same document would appear in the archive in different files relating to all the subjects it touched upon. This was an important reason for the staggering size of the Poulson archive – 27,000 documents or so – but it also impeded any efforts to destroy evidence because even if Poulson or others managed to get rid of one file, most of its contents were to be found elsewhere anyway. David Graham interview for *Sleaze*, Channel 4, 1999.
34. *Private Eye*, 30 June 1972; PRO BA 19/116, Sermon to Chilcot, 30 June 1972.
35. Reginald Maudling, press statement 3 July 1972, as cited Fitzwalter and Taylor, *Web of Corruption*, p. 208.
36. David Steel, *Against Goliath* (London: Weidenfeld & Nicolson, 1989), p. 93. See also Simon Freeman and Barrie Penrose, *Rinkagate* (London: Bloomsbury, 1996), pp. 156–7. Barrie Penrose and Roger Courtiour, *The Pencourt File* (London: Secker & Warburg, 1978), p. 153.
37. UKC Weatherill Papers, WEA/PP R102, Whips' Office note, 18 July 1972.
38. Peter Bessell, *Cover-Up* (Oceanside, CA: Simons Books, 1980), p. 225.
39. PRO CAB 164/1062, note from Simcock (Number 10) to Owen (Lord Chancellor's Office), 11 July 1972.
40. PRO CAB 128/50, minutes of Cabinet meeting, 13 July 1972.
41. Fitzwalter and Taylor, *Web of Corruption*, p. 209.
42. Lord Baker, interview, 19 September 2000. There is also evidence from the PRO file BA 19/117 indicating that until shortly before Maudling's resignation a judicial inquiry was considered likely – the Inspector General in Bankruptcy was asked to advise on whether the bankruptcy proceedings could continue alongside the inquiry, and stated that it could.
43. Statement by Reginald Maudling, 20 July 1972. The date for this meeting with the Attorney General is given as 14 July in some accounts, but appears in his Home Office diary for 13 July.
44. PRO BA 19/116, note of meeting, Antony Part, 14 July 1972.
45. PRO BA 19/116, Interim Report, 14 July 1972.
46. PRO BA 19/116, draft statement, 17 July 1972.
47. LSE, Hetherington Papers, note of meeting with Harold Wilson, 19 July 1972; interview, Joe Haines, 30 May 2002.
48. *HC Debates*, vol. 841, cols 402–8, 18 July 1972.
49. Lord Carlisle, interview, 28 October 2002.
50. *Daily Mail*, 19 July 1972.
51. *The Sun*, 19 July 1972.
52. *Daily Mirror*, 19 July 1972.
53. *Daily Express*, 19 July 1972, leader and Derek Marks article.
54. *Economist*, 22 July 1972, pp. 13–15.
55. *Financial Times*, 19 July 1972, p. 24; *The Times*, 19 July 1972, p. 2; *Guardian*, 19 July 1972, p. 5. Reggie's Home Office diary shows meetings booked in with King on 28 June and Sweetman on 4 July.

CHAPTER 23

1. The title of a perceptive profile of Maudling by Patrick Cosgrave, *Spectator*, 22 July 1972.
2. This point was noted by Alan Watkins as early as 10 November 1972 in 'The Rehabilitation of Reggie', *New Statesman*, p. 662.
3. Cecil King, *The Cecil King Diary 1970–74* (London: Jonathan Cape, 1975),

17 February 1973, p. 264.

4. *Guardian*, 6 November 1972.

5. *Radio Times*, 10–16 March 1973, p. 5.

6. Viv Walker, interview, 22 July 2003.

7. PRO FCO 93/299, McCarthy to Wright, 25 September 1973.

8. *Daily Mail*, 26 September 1977.

9. Edgar Mizzi, *Malta in the Making* (Malta: Edgar Mizzi, 1995), p. 6.

10. Michael Rice, interview, 3 July 2003.

11. *Sunday Times*, 23 July 1972, p. 13.

12. WYAS WCC 3/1/3. Maudling's statement was read into the record of the 7 August hearing, p. 7.

13. WYAS WCC 3/1/3, Statement by Muir Hunter in court, 7 August 1972, p. 11.

14. *Daily Telegraph*, 9 August 1972.

15. MEPO (pending), Attorney General's evidence to the Salmon Commission, para. 39.

16. WYAS WCC 3/1/3, Poulson evidence, 25 September 1972, paras 3617–25.

17. Statement dated 26 September 1972. Despite being Costa Nasser's base, ITCS accomplished remarkably little in Lebanon.

18. WYAS WCC 3/1/3, Poulson evidence, 26 September 1972, p. 1.

19. WYAS WCC 3/1/3, Poulson evidence, 26 September 1972, para. 4160 et seq.; Maudling to Poulson, 29 August 1968; Poulson to Nasser, 14 January 1969.

20. PRO PREM 15/1059, Butler to Owen, 2 October 1972.

21. PRO PREM 15/1059, Owen to Butler, 16 October 1972, Butler to Heath, 27 October 1972, Owen to Butler, 19 December 1972.

22. David Graham interview for *Sleaze*, Channel 4, 1999.

23. Ray Fitzwalter and David Taylor, *Web of Corruption* (St Albans: Granada, 1981), p. 221.

24. Ray Fitzwalter, interview, 28 October 1999. Given Poulson's secretaries' practice of making multiple file copies of documents it is likely that even if a compromising parliamentary file does exist, it might not contain much that was not made public later through the *Observer* in October 1976 and the Select Committee report in July 1977. If a 'parliamentary file' was suppressed in 1973 the principal beneficiary was probably John Cordle, whose scandalous letter was not revealed until October 1976. See Chapters 25 and 26.

25. PRO J 291/95, examination of John King, 18 July 1972, paras 44–5; PRO J 291/100, Poulson private examination, 25 June 1973, p. 8.

26. WYAS WCC 3/1/3, Poulson evidence, 25 September 1972, pp. 78–9. In the September 1972 hearing Saffman referred to files on 'political matters' and Hunter said, 'I do not know what is meant by "political file" exactly'.

27. PRO J 291/80 contains National Liberal files; Poulson's comment is para. 607 of the Select Committee's evidence. Saffman's comment given above (and Poulson was unpleasant about Saffman in his Commons evidence) may therefore have been a professional courtesy. Poulson further alleged in his House of Commons evidence that the 'parliamentary file' allegation was made in an informal announcement by Hunter to the press, of which there was no transcript. Arguably, it would have been legitimate for Hunter to ask questions about the National Liberal hospitality to check whether they were gifts and therefore recoverable for Poulson's creditors. Being named in such a context in bankruptcy proceedings does not imply any criminal or moral censure.

28. WYAS WCC 3/1/3, Poulson evidence, 25 September 1972, paras 2736–40.

29. WYAS WCC 3/1/2, Moorhouse to Registrar, 19 March 1976; application for section 25 hearing with Costa Nasser, 1973. Chamoun was hostile to the PLO presence in Lebanon, while Nasser was pro-Palestinian. Lebanese politics in the period was so spectacularly corrupt and devious that it is hard to know who was playing on which side and why. According to the *Washington Post*'s man in Beirut, a Gulf oil state kept

former Lebanese Prime Ministers on monthly retainers of thousands of dollars in case they came in useful again. Jonathan Randal, *The Tragedy of Lebanon* (London: Hogarth Press, 1990), p. 57. British official documents note that Sheikh Zayed of Abu Dhabi had influence in Lebanon and subsidised several newspapers, including one 'quasi fascist' organ. Note from British Embassy, Beirut, 31 July 1969, PRO FCO 8/1275.

30. PRO FCO 93/299, Hunter to Craig, 11 July 1973.
31. WYAS WCC 3/1/1, Statement of account, 1 February 1978.
32. PRO J 291/101, Poulson evidence, 16 July 1973, para. 252.
33. IPD accounts, 28 February 1974, as filed with Companies House. IPD's payment was made without admission of liability, and the company was still regarded as a creditor, although the agreement with the Trustee established that it was last in the queue and therefore most improbable that it would see any of the money again. The £90,000 was written off in the 1974 accounts.
34. PRO J 291/100, Poulson evidence, 16 July 1973, para. 247–50.
35. WYAS WCC 3/1/2, Saffman to Registrar, 10 July 1973.
36. PRO J 291/61, report from Churchill-Coleman, 19 July 1973.
37. *The Times*, 23 June 1973. Hunter objected strongly to *The Times* statement that there had been large anonymous payments; the only anonymous payment had been £100 from an individual who had received gifts from Poulson. But this was something of a technicality, as the consortium settlement could be regarded as a disguised form of settlement.
38. WYAS WCC 3/1/3, Poulson evidence, 25 June 1973, p. 1: public section.
39. PRO J 291/100, Poulson examination, 25 June 1973: private section.
40. Peter Rawlinson, *A Price Too High* (London: Weidenfeld & Nicolson, 1989), pp. 195–7.
41. David Graham interview for *Sleaze*, Channel 4, 1999.
42. WYAS WCC 3/1/1, Summons for attendance of Reginald Maudling, July 1973.
43. Private interview.
44. PRO J 291/95, Maudling examination, 19 July 1973, para. 113.
45. Cobb-Taylor opinion; PRO BT 296/833, Opinion of David Smout, QC, comments that 'Neither of the subjects on which Mr Maudling was inaccurate appear to have been material in those proceedings though they were of course relevant to his credibility. There is accordingly in my view an insufficient case to justify any prosecution for perjury, and I could not recommend it.'
46. PRO J 291/95, Maudling examination, 19 July 1973, paras 264–5.
47. David Graham interview for *Sleaze*, Channel 4, 1999.
48. PRO J 291/95, Maudling examination, 19 July 1973, paras 441–2.
49. *Ibid.*, para. 447.
50. *Ibid.*, para. 510.
51. PRO FCO 93/299, Wright to Evans, 13 September 1973.
52. PRO J 291/93, Maudling examination, 19 July 1973, stopped section para. 513.
53. PRO FCO 93/299, James Craig note of meeting between Hunter and Foreign Office officials, 6 July 1973. Spelling and emphasis in original. Also Maudling to Sutton, 26 February 1973.
54. PRO FCO 93/299, Sinclair to Craig, 11 July 1973, annotation initialled by recipient (A. Parsons – see annotation on Evans to Wright, 12 September 1973, for attribution), 16 July 1973.
55. PRO J 291/101, Nasser examination, 6 September 1973.
56. PRO J 291/95, Maudling examination, 19 July 1973, exchanges after para. 546. What passed between Maudling and his legal adviser cannot be known, but it is notable that the 1974 DPP counsel's assessment of Maudling's evidence was that there were two counts of perjury on which he might be prosecuted.
57. *House of Commons Select Committee on the Conduct of Members*, July 1977, Report

Appendix 69; WYAS WCC 3/1/1, Trustee in Bankruptcy Statement of Account 1974, entry for 23 October 1974.

58. WYAS WCC 3/1/1, Trustee in Bankruptcy Analysis of Recoveries, 11 May 1977. The extra £500 may well refer to a payment from Martin, rather than Reggie Maudling – because Martin's initials were R.M.M. they were sometimes confused, and in a schedule of payments dated 19 November 1973, filed in PRO BT 296/833, there is an entry that suggests that this is the case.

59. PRO BT 296/833 contains a list of these as of July 1975. The Malta corruption case, which is the only police file still open on Maudling at that time, is number 20 and 'awaits counsel's decision'. Incidentally, this suggests there might be in existence somewhere a supplementary counsel's opinion in 1975 or 1976 covering Malta only, following the broader corruption inquiry of the 1974 Cobb–Taylor opinion and before the 1976 Smout opinion on company law.

60. Michael Levi, *The Regulation of Fraud* (London: Tavistock, 1987), p. 171.

61. PRO BT 296/833, Taylor to Part, 2 November 1973.

62. Phillip Whitehead, *The Writing on the Wall* (London: Michael Joseph, 1985).

63. *The Times*, 15 May 1973, p. 16.

64. *Sunday Express*, 9 September 1973.

65. Robin Ramsay, 'Was the 1974 Oil Price Hike Engineered by the Bilderberg Group?', *Lobster* 41 (Summer 2001), pp. 32–3. The question was posed as a result of Sheikh Yamani, the Saudi oil minister for most of the 1970s and 1980s, commenting in an interview (*Observer*, 14 January 2001) that the Americans had orchestrated the crisis and it had been agreed at a meeting in Sweden. Although there are many unsatisfactory aspects to the conventional version of the oil crisis (see also Jack Anderson with James Boyd, *Fiasco* (New York: Times Books, 1983)), the claim that it was planned by the Bilderberg Group simply does not stand up.

66. Denis Healey, *The Time of My Life* (London: Michael Joseph, 1989), p. 348.

67. 'The Oil Warning Light Glows Red for the West', *Sunday Express*, 7 June 1973, p. 3.

68. King, *Diary*, 18 December 1973, p. 331.

Chapter 24

1. *Sunday Express*, 20 January 1974.

2. *Barnet Press*, 8 February 1974.

3. *Private Eye*, 4 October 1974.

4. Reginald Maudling statement, 11 February 1974, as cited *The Times*, 12 February 1974.

5. PRO J 291/70, Fraud Squad memo, 8 March 1974.

6. MEPO (pending), Cobb to Gasson, 24 August 1975.

7. PRO BT 296/833, Taylor to Part, 22 February 1974. Replying, Part to Taylor, 26 February 1974, the Permanent Secretary asked 'please keep me closely informed'.

8. MEPO (pending), Rawlinson to Skelhorn, 22 February 1974.

9. *Sunday Express*, 17 February 1974.

10. *Sunday Express*, 3 March 1974.

11. PRO BT 296/833, 'The first schedule' attached to report on DTI and Poulson, March 1977. Dates are: Ropergate 1: 18 October 1973; Ropergate 2: 13 November 1973; OSB: 10 December 1973; Ovalgate: 18 January 1974; WWI: 31 October 1974.

12. Cobb and Taylor cite Ropergate 2 but not OSB; Smout cites OSB but not Ropergate 2.

13. PRO BT 296/833, Opinion of David Smout, QC, 22 July 1976.

14. WYAS WCC 3/1/1, Simpson to Boulton, 3 November 1976.

15. MEPO (pending), DTI section 109, Report on ITCS, filed as Appendix F to the Maudling police investigation.

16. In addition, non-compliance, false evidence and destruction of documentation relating

to a section 109 or other inquiry are Companies Act offences punishable by fines and imprisonment. Given the state of the ITCS books it is not impossible that such offences took place.

17. *Memoirs*, p. 199; MEPO (pending).
18. PRO BT 296/833, memorandum by P.A.R. Brown, 15 March 1977.
19. PRO BT 296/833, Hetherington to Hall, 21 June 1976. The DTI seem to have been unaware of this ruling, and in February 1977 the Companies Investigation Branch were under the impression that the police were covering company matters and that there was therefore no need to appoint an inquiry under section 165, which would have been more probing than the s.109 reports. Gill to Trapnell, 22 February 1977.
20. PRO BT 296/833, Taylor to Part, 2 November 1973 lists six Dan Smith company investigations completed, four still pending and two 'frustrated' because Smith's accountant and fellow director, Bill Kirkup, was resident in Spain; about another twenty companies were expected to come under investigation in looser connection with Dan Smith in the Midlands. This also notes that the ITCS investigation was expected to be completed in mid-December 1973 'in line with the AG's timetable' – that it was late is not surprising given the complexity of the issues.
21. Alex Saville, interview, 29 July 2003. She came to the Saville wedding and Mrs Saville still recalls her with affection.
22. Private interview.
23. PRO J 291/92, Poulson files. Some of this cost was clearly therefore from Poulson. In later correspondence with the Revenue Maudling reviewed his bank records for expenses cheques from Poulson but could not recall what each payment was for. Maudling to Stratford, 8 May 1974, 3 August 1974.
24. Note of interview between L.S. Stratford and Reginald Maudling, 25 April 1974.
25. *Labour Weekly*, 26 April 1974.
26. Joe Haines, *Glimmers of Twilight* (London: Politicos, 2003); Bernard Donoughue, *The Heat of the Kitchen* (London: Politicos, 2003).
27. Ray Fitzwalter, interview, 6 October 2003.
28. 'Gozo, certainly we had – I myself took part in the negotiations, I went out to Malta with him.' PRO J 291/95, Maudling private hearing, 19 July 1973, para. 390.
29. *HC Debates*, vol. 873, cols 219–20, 7 May 1974.
30. *Mirror* case cuttings, file 2, 2 May 1974, p. 11.
31. *The Times*, 11 May 1974; *Daily Telegraph*, 10 May 1974.
32. Ray Fitzwalter, interview, 6 October 2003.
33. *Guardian*, 14 May 1974.
34. Brian Brivati, *Lord Goodman* (London: Richard Cohen Books, 1999), describes the web of connections around Goodman Derrick's senior partner, which at the time extended to the leaders of the three main political parties.
35. *HC Debates*, vol. 936, col. 235, 27 July 1977.
36. *New York Times*, 7 December 1980, S3 p. 8.
37. *Business First – Buffalo*, 20 May 1985, p. 2.
38. *Labour Weekly*, 21 July 1972.
39. *Putting Britain First*, as cited David Butler and Dennis Kavanagh, *The British General Election of October 1974* (London: Macmillan, 1975), p. 68.
40. MEPO (pending), preliminary report, 10 May 1974, para. 54 in particular; Poulson police interviews, February and March 1974.
41. PRO CAB 164/433, 'Bribery of MPs and the law', note by H.J. Davies of the Attorney General's office, March 1970.
42. Private information.
43. *Royal Commission on Standards of Conduct in Public Life (Salmon)* (London: HMSO, 1976), Cmnd. 6524, paras 307, 311.

44. Richard Stott, interview, 8 January 2003; Ray Fitzwalter, interview, 6 October 2003.

45. PRO CAB 164/433, Davies opinion.

46. See Report of the Joint Parliamentary Committee on the Draft Corruption Bill, 27 July 2003, relating to Clause 12 on parliamentary privilege, available via www.parliament.uk.

47. *Salmon*, para. 307. The Nolan Report (*First Report of the Commission on Standards in Public Life* Cm 2850.I, para. 103) said that 'it is quite likely that Members of Parliament who accepted bribes in connection with their Parliamentary duties would be committing Common Law offences which could be tried by the courts. Doubt exists as to whether the courts or Parliament have jurisdiction in such cases.'

48. MEPO (pending), note of 'Poulson' meeting, 23 June 1976; date on note incorrectly given as 28 June.

49. MEPO (pending), report on Maudling, 19 November 1974; Poulson to Abela, 3 August 1966.

50. MEPO (pending), witness statement of Malcolm Barry Ibbetson, 9 October 1974.

51. Tony Benn, *Against the Tide Diaries: 1973–76* (London: Hutchinson, 1989), p. 322. Caroline Benn was a colleague of Chitty's son Clyde in the comprehensive schools movement.

52. For instance *Private Eye*, 16 May 1975, p. 5; 30 May 1975, p. 3; 11 July 1975, p. 3.

53. WYAS WCC3/1/1, Correspondence between Trustee and Fraud Squad, 15 March 1976, 22 March 1976.

54. Michael Levi, *Regulating Fraud* (London: Tavistock, 1987), pp. 173–5.

55. PRO FCO 93/299, Wright to Evans, 9 October 1973.

56. MEPO (pending), Taylor memorandum on the scope of a possible public inquiry into corruption, January 1976 refers (p. 62) to Cobb to DPP, 5 October 1973.

57. Richard Stott, *Dogs and Lampposts* (London: Metro, 2002), pp. 143–4. My thanks to Richard Stott for his permission to quote. Richard Stott, interview, 7 January 2003.

CHAPTER 25

1. *Sunday Express*, 14 April 1974, 20 October 1974.

2. *Sun*, 23 October 1974.

3. *Memoirs*, p. 209.

4. Mark Garnett, *Keith Joseph* (Chesham: Acumen, 2001), p. 259.

5. Reginald Maudling, interview with David Butler and Michael Pinto-Duschinsky, 11 November 1969.

6. Lord (Kenneth) Baker of Dorking, interview, 19 September 2000.

7. Lord (Robert) Carr of Hadley, interview, 29 July 1999.

8. US State Department, file POL15–1 UK, London embassy to State Department, 25 June 1973.

9. Robert Shepherd, interview, 14 September 1999; also Viv Walker, interview, 11 July 2003, on how pleasant he was to work for.

10. David Butler, interview with Peter Blaker, 20 May 1975.

11. *Memoirs*, p. 211.

12. Robert Shepherd, interview, 14 September 1999.

13. Roy Hattersley, interview for *Sleaze*, Channel 4, 1999.

14. Nicholas Henderson, *Mandarin: The Diaries of Nicholas Henderson* (London: Weidenfeld & Nicolson, 1994), pp. 124–6.

15. Barbara Castle, *The Castle Diaries 1974–76* (London: Weidenfeld & Nicolson, 1980), 12 June 1975, p. 417.

16. David Butler diary, 8 May 1975 (Steel and Maudling).

17. *The Times*, 26 May 1975.

18. A particularly notable one was on 11 May 1975, with the headline – written by the Features Editor rather than Reggie – 'For God's Sake, Harold, Wake Up!' Wilson was apparently annoyed and commented that Reggie hadn't woken up in thirty years. *Sunday Express*, 25 May 1975.

19. The memorandum is reprinted in *Memoirs*, pp. 265–7.

20. *Private Eye*, 8 August 1975, p. 3.

21. MEPO (pending), Reginald Maudling, interview, 4 July 1975; memorandum by DS Keech, 24 July 1975.

22. MEPO (pending), Joint opinion, 22 April 1975.

23. *Private Eye*, 31 October 1975, pp. 5–6.

24. Reported in *All England Law Reports* [1976]2 All ER 1020–1032 Re: Poulson (J.G.L.), a bankrupt, ex parte *Granada Television Ltd* v *Maudling and another*.

25. Ray Fitzwalter, interview, 6 October 2003.

26. *Memoirs*, p. 213.

27. *Memoirs*, pp. 151–4.

28. Viv Walker, interview, 11 July 2003.

29. Robert Shepherd, interview, 14 September 1999.

30. Lord Carrington, interview, 15 October 2002.

31. Private interview.

32. Margaret Thatcher, *The Path to Power* (London: HarperCollins, 1995), pp. 348–9.

33. *Ibid.*, pp. 351–3; John Campbell, *Margaret Thatcher, Volume 1: The Grocer's Daughter* (London: Jonathan Cape, 2000), pp. 339–42.

34. *Memoirs*, pp. 225–6.

35. Compare Thatcher, *Path to Power*, pp. 350–1; *Memoirs*, pp. 137–8.

36. *HC Debates*, vol. 932, col. 488, 18 May 1977.

37. National Sound Archive, Bow Dialogue with Revd McCullough, 6 February 1973.

38. *HC Debates*, vol. 927, col. 299, 1 March 1977.

39. In the 1970s the 'convergence hypothesis' suggested that the East and West would become more like each other – that the East would gradually liberalise and the West would become more centrally planned.

40. 'Thatcher: the Kremlin Files', *The Times*, 26 April 1992, p. 19.

41. Weatherill Papers, WEA M1, note of whips' discussion, 28 July 1976.

42. MEPO (pending), See to Etheridge, 16 June 1976; Etheridge to See, 5 July 1976; See to Etheridge, 8 August 1976. This at least is the paper trail in the Metropolitan Police archives. According to Williams, he offered to submit to a police interview outside UK jurisdiction, with both sides making tapes, but heard nothing more from the police. Williams was extremely suspicious of the motives of the Fraud Squad. Ken Williams, interview, 9 November 2002; Ken Williams, interview with R. Barry O'Brien, 1979.

43. The ruling came as a surprise to the prosecutors, as no previous legal advice had questioned whether it was justiciable in Britain: MEPO (pending). According to Williams, the ruling was something of a fix to sort out what had been an oppressive prosecution which he and his solicitor had successfully resisted. Ken Williams, interview, 5 December 2003. The prosecutors took a different view.

44. PRO BT 296/833, Trapnell to DPP, 2 December 1974, 27 January 1975.

45. PRO BT 296/833, Hall to Allen *et al.*, 25 June 1976.

46. PRO BT 296/833, memorandum by P.A.R. Brown, 15 March 1977.

47. PRO BT 296/833, Weston to Trapnell, 23 August 1976.

48. Michael Levi, *Regulating Fraud* (London: Tavistock, 1987), p. 185.

49. The *Mirror* team believed that Inland Revenue investigation files on Maudling were open well after summer 1976.

50. *Daily Mail*, 8 October 1976, p. 9.

51. *Daily Telegraph*, 15 October 1976.

52. Lord Allen of Abbeydale, interview, 22 July 2002.
53. Salmon, *Report of the Royal Commission on Standards of Conduct in Public Life* (London: HMSO, 1976), paras 23–4.
54. *Ibid.*, para. 311.
55. *Daily Mirror*, 25 October 1976, p. 5.
56. Adam Raphael, *My Learned Friends* (London: W.H. Allen, 1989), p. 112.
57. MEPO (pending), note of Poulson case conference, 10 November 1978, referenced Lawrence to Coussey, 7 March 1979.
58. Raphael, *My Learned Friends*, pp. 116–26.
59. *Daily Mirror*, 20 October 1976, p. 1.
60. PRO BT 296/833, report by Hetherington, 22 June 1976; Hall to Allen *et al.*, 25 June 1976.
61. Private information.
62. Jim Prior, *A Balance of Power* (London: Hamish Hamilton, 1986), p. 108.
63. Thatcher, *Path to Power*, p. 319.
64. *Memoirs*, p. 226.
65. Robert Shepherd, interview, 12 July 1999.
66. Andrew Alexander, 'The Decline and Fall of Reggie Maudling', *Daily Mail*, 20 November 1976.
67. *The Times*, 19 June 1999.

CHAPTER 26

1. I am grateful to Robert Shepherd, 14 September 1999, for putting this point to me.
2. *HC Debates*, vol. 921, col. 742, 30 November 1976.
3. *HC Debates*, vol. 921, col. 741, 30 November 1976.
4. *HC Debates*, vol. 922, cols 1281–2, 14 December 1976.
5. *HC Debates*, vol. 925, col. 72, 31 January 1977.
6. *Memoirs*, pp. 13–14.
7. Viv Walker, interview, 11 July 2003.
8. The transcripts that were available to the government, if not necessarily the full Select Committee, included those of John King, Dan Smith, Cynthia Poulson (plus an exhibit associated with her testimony), William Sales and Reginald Maudling. The contents of the Cynthia Poulson hearings and the exhibit are still not known. Treasury Solicitor to Wakefield court, 17 December 1976.
9. At the same time, several government departments were asked to conduct a trawl through their files for records connected with meetings between Maudling, Cordle, Short and Roberts and Ministers and Permanent Secretaries at relevant times. The results were limited, although the Foreign Office seems to have neglected to look at its Arabian and Near Eastern Department files touching on Maudling's commercial activities – perhaps on the grounds that it was not directly relevant to his parliamentary conduct. PRO BT 296/833.
10. Select Committee evidence, para. 1710, question by Max Madden. See also Chapter 17 above. In the Select Committee version it is given as 'Legerrotto, etc' whereas the true version is 'Legerrotto, Mahdi Tajir etc'.
11. *House of Commons Select Committee on the Conduct of Members*, July 1977 (hereafter HCSC), Evidence, para. 1583 for instance.
12. HCSC, Report, para. 23.
13. PRO J 291/93, Marr to Poulson, 26 October 1967.
14. *Daily Mail*, 22 July 1977, p. 1.
15. If Cordle had been sacrificed a year earlier at the time of the Salmon Report, it is quite possible that there would have been no parliamentary inquiry at all; the flagrancy of

his case was the principal reason that the Select Committee was set up in the first place.

16. *HCSC*, Report, paras 25–33.
17. *Memoirs*, p. 201.
18. *Daily Mail*, 22 July 1977, p. 1.
19. *Daily Mail*, 25 July 1977, p. 9.
20. *Daily Mail*, 26 July 1977, p. 3.
21. *HC Debates*, vol. 936, cols 333–9, 26 July 1977.
22. Leo Abse, interview, 10 February 2003.
23. Michael Foot interview for *Sleaze*, Channel 4, 1999.
24. *HCSC*, Report, para. 4. Maudling's speech in the debate on the report correctly points this out.
25. *HCSC*, Evidence, para. 1604. This may refer to Harold Wilson, who worked out of office for Montague Meyer, a timber company, and other companies.
26. *Memoirs*, p. 205.
27. *HC Debates*, vol. 936, cols 332–462, 26 July 1977, is the record of the debate.
28. John Biffen, Peter Bottomley, Alan Clark, Nigel Forman, M. Harvie Anderson, John Hunt, Michael Latham, Tim Smith (who twenty years later would stand down in disgrace in the cash for questions affair), Peter Temple-Morris, Peter Thomas and David Walder. Anderson and Thomas had served on the committee.
29. Gordon Bagier (who had been in trouble in 1969 for links with a lobbying firm), three North East members (Bernard Conlan, George Grant, Mark Hughes), three MPs from South Yorkshire (Patrick Duffy, Edwin Wainwright and Alec Woodall), Hugh Brown, Michael English, Ben Ford (of Bradford), James Lamond, Robert Sheldon for Labour, and Jeremy Thorpe for the Liberals. If these MPs had voted the other way, the 'take note' motion would have been defeated by one vote, 219–218.
30. Richard Stott, interview, 7 January 2003.
31. Private interview.
32. '"No Post" in Thatcher Team for Maudling', *Sunday Telegraph*, 30 July 1977, p. 4.
33. Ken Williams, interview, 7 November 2002.
34. John Boyd-Carpenter, *Way of Life* (London: Sidgwick & Jackson, 1980), p. 160.
35. Edward Maudling, interview, 27 October 1999.
36. As cited in Matthew Parris, *Great Parliamentary Scandals* (London: Robson, 1995), p. 170.
37. *HC Debates*, vol. 938, col. 927, 10 November 1977.
38. Melissa Maudling, interview, 17 October 2001.
39. *HC Debates*, vol. 938, cols 920 et seq., 10 November 1977.
40. *HC Debates*, vol. 948, col. 1703, 27 April 1978.
41. *HC Debates*, vol. 938, cols 920 et seq., 10 November 1977.
42. *HC Debates*, vol. 949, col. 818, 8 May 1978.
43. *HC Debates*, vol. 959, cols 493–9, 29 November 1978.
44. *Memoirs*, p. 14.
45. I am grateful to Michael Rice for pointing this out.
46. *Memoirs*, p. 15.
47. *Times Literary Supplement*, 28 July 1978, p. 841; *New Statesman*, 30 June 1978, pp. 887–8.
48. *Sunday Times*, 2 July 1978.
49. Alistair McAlpine, *Once a Jolly Bagman* (London: Weidenfeld & Nicolson, 1997), pp. 75–7.
50. *Daily Mail*, 28 September 1977. The funeral was organised very quickly, as is customary for Jewish funerals, and it is not unreasonable to take Maudling's answer at face value although there was some scepticism at the time.
51. Private information.

52. Department of Trade, *Peachey Property Corporation Limited*, Investigation under section 165(b), January 1979, paras 428–41. The inquiry also cleared Wilson and Falkender.
53. Ray Fitzwalter, interview, 6 October 2003.
54. From note of meeting between Ellis Birk and Sir John Charles, 7 March 1978.
55. Ray Fitzwalter, interview, 6 October 2003; Richard Stott, interview, 7 January 2003.
56. Adam Raphael, *My Learned Friends* (London: W.H. Allen, 1989), pp. 126–9.
57. Richard Stott, interview, 7 January 2003; Richard Stott, *Dogs and Lampposts* (London: Metro, 2002), pp. 156–7.
58. Richard Stott, interview, 7 January 2003; Ray Fitzwalter, interview, 28 October 1999.
59. *HC Debates*, vol. 959, col. 499, 29 November 1978.
60. *HC Debates*, vol. 960, cols 716–21, 13 December 1978.
61. Viv Walker, interview, 11 July 2003.
62. According to his family Reggie had picked up an infection in the Middle East that worsened his condition; this may be so but was not reflected on his death certificate which straightforwardly blames cirrhosis and its complications.
63. Sir Sandy Glen, interview, 10 March 2003.
64. Interview with Caroline Maudling, 28 January 2002.

CHAPTER 27

1. James Haw, interview, 17 June 2003.
2. *Daily Telegraph*, 29 October 1988.
3. Telephone call to Sabrewatch, 3 December 2003.
4. *Evening Standard*, 14 February 1979; *Daily Mail*, 15 February 1979; *Evening News*, 14 February 1979.
5. *Daily Telegraph*, 15 February 1979. Friends of Reggie also believed that the *Telegraph* obituary of Beryl was unnecessarily spiteful and that the paper had latterly run a vendetta against him; their reporter R. Barry O'Brien had been particularly thorough in covering the Poulson case, which was not a matter of discredit to him or the paper. But if an explanation is required it may be in some personal matter connected with the Maudlings' relationship with the Berry family.
6. WYAS WCC 3/1/1, documents on Poulson discharge. The winding up of the bankruptcy proceedings against Poulson and the claims against his companies were consolidated in 1977, although the companies retained a vestigial existence until 1995.
7. Edmund Dell, *The Chancellors* (London: HarperCollins, 1996), p. 302.
8. *Sunday Express*, 19 November 1978.
9. 'A Civilised Conversation between Roy Jenkins and Reginald Maudling', *Listener*, 13 July 1973.
10. Sir Sandy Glen, interview, 11 September 2002.
11. National Sound Archive, Radio 4 *Any Questions*, recorded at Hemel Hempstead, 1973.
12. 'PR: A Symposium', *National and English Review* (September 1950).
13. Roy Jenkins, *A Life at the Centre* (London: Macmillan, 1991), pp. 518–19.
14. *Memoirs*, p. 28.
15. 'Leap of Faith', *Financial Times* magazine, 26 April 2003, p. 16.
16. *The Times*, 12 October 1963; *Daily Express*, 4 October 1973.
17. Reginald Maudling, 'Moderation in Politics', *Crossbow* (January–March 1970), pp. 9–11.
18. *Sunday Times*, 3 September 1967.
19. Boyle Papers, MS 660/11046, Boyle to Childs, 28 February 1979.

20. Enoch Powell, 'The Maudling I Knew', *Reflections of a Statesman* (London: Bellew, 1991), pp. 329–31; originally in *Sunday Telegraph*, 18 February 1979.

21. *Memoirs*, p. 255.

22. N. Kessel and H. Walton, *Alcoholism*, 2nd edn (Harmondsworth: Penguin, 1989), pp. 70–2.

23. Reginald Maudling, 'Alternatives to Prison', *Spectator*, 26 July 1975.

24. Michael Crick, *Stranger than Fiction* (London: Hamish Hamilton, 1995), *passim*; particularly pp. 269–70, 400.

25. 'Can MPs Afford to be Honest?', *Sunday Telegraph*, 24 July 1977, p. 16.

26. PRO BT 296/833, Kerry to Thornton, 30 June 1976.

27. Michael Gillard, *In the Name of Charity* (London: Chatto & Windus, 1987) is about Rossminster.

28. Commissie van Drie report, 1976, as cited David Boulton, *The Lockheed Papers* (London: Jonathan Cape, 1978), p. 269.

BIBLIOGRAPHY

This bibliography is organised into the following sections.

PRIMARY SOURCES

Private Manuscript Collections
Other Manuscript Collections
Public Records
Official Papers

SECONDARY SOURCES

Works by Maudling
Other Published Works
Internet Resources

Private Manuscript Collections

Lord Alport Papers (Albert Sloman Library, University of Essex, Colchester)
Avon Papers (Main Library, University of Birmingham, Edgbaston)
Edward Boyle Papers (Leeds University Library, Leeds)
R.A. Butler Papers (Conservative Party Archive, Bodleian Library, Oxford)
Sir Alec Cairncross Papers (University of Glasgow, Glasgow)
Churchill Papers (Churchill Archives Centre, Cambridge University, Cambridge)
Cilcennin Papers (Carmarthenshire Archives Service, Carmarthen)
William Clark MSS (Bodleian Library, Oxford)
Crossman Papers (Modern Records Centre, Warwick University, Warwick)
Arthur Fawcett Papers (privately held)
Michael Foot Papers (Labour History Archive and Study Centre, Manchester)
Gaitskell Papers (University College, London)
Hailes Papers (Churchill College Archives, Cambridge University, Cambridge)
Hetherington Papers (London School of Economics Library, London)
Jack Lynch Papers (National Archives of Ireland, Dublin)
James Ramsay MacDonald Papers (National Archives, Kew)
Maclay Papers (Glasgow University Archive Services, Glasgow)
Macmillan Papers (Bodleian Library, Oxford)
John Enoch Powell Papers (Churchill Archives Centre, Cambridge University)
Patrick Wall Papers (Brynmor Jones Library, Hull University)
Weatherill Papers (Kent University Library, Canterbury)

Other Manuscript Collections

Bodleian Library of Commonwealth and African Studies at Rhodes House (Oxford)
Bromley Local Studies (Bromley Central Library, Bromley)
David Butler General Election Papers (Nuffield College, Oxford)
Chipping Barnet Conservative Association Papers (Barnet Archives and Local Studies Department, Mill Hill)
Churchill College Archive (Cambridge University, Cambridge)
Conservative Party Records (CPA) (Bodleian Library, Oxford)
Hertfordshire Archives and Local Studies (Hertford)
Merton College Archive (Oxford)
Records of the Metropolitan Police (London)
Middle Temple Records (Middle Temple Library, London)
Modern Records Centre (University of Warwick Library, Coventry)
National Council for Civil Liberties Archives (British Library of Political and Economic Science, Brynmor Jones Library, University of Hull)
Northern Ireland Political Collection (Linen Hall Library, Belfast)
Sleaze transcripts (Blakeway Productions, London)
West Yorkshire Archive Service (Wakefield)
City of Westminster Archives Centre (London)

Public Records

The National Archives, Kew

Air Ministry: AIR 20
Treasury, and Civil Service Department: Management [Personnel] Division: BA 19
Board of Trade: BT 31; BT 58; BT 64; BT 296
Cabinet Office: CAB 21; CAB 123; CAB 128; CAB 164
Home Office and Northern Ireland Office: CJ 3; CJ 4
Colonial Office: East Africa: CO 822
Colonial Office: Central Africa and Aden: CO 1015
Dominions Office and Commonwealth Relations Office: DO 35
Director of Public Prosecutions: DPP 2
Board of Education and successors: ED 109
Chancellor of the Exchequer's Office: T 171
Foreign Office and Foreign and Commonwealth Office: FCO 7; FCO 8; FCO 10; FCO 17; FCO 24; FCO 27; FCO 38; FCO 65; FCO 93
Foreign Office: FO 371; FO 1016
Home Office: HO 295; HO 317
Metropolitan Police Files: MEPO
Ministry of Supply: SUPP 16
Ministry of Transport: MT 118
Prime Minister's Office: PREM 11, 13, 15
Supreme Court of Judicature: The Crown Court at Leeds: Case Files 1959–86: J 291
Treasury: T 199; T 215; T 231; T 236; T 311; T 312; T 337
War Office: WO 339

The National Archives of Ireland, Dublin

Department of Foreign Affairs: DFA 2001–3

National Archives and Records Administration, Washington, DC

State Department Papers
Central Numeric Files
UK Embassy Files: POL 23–9
Registry Boxes: POL 12; POL 15–1 (UK)

Probate Department, Principal Registry of the Family Division, London

Registers of births, marriages and deaths

Public Record Office of Northern Ireland, Belfast

Cabinet Secretariat: CAB 4; CAB 9A

Official Papers

House of Commons Debates, 4th–5th series
Government documents published as Command Papers
All England Law Reports
House of Commons Select Committee on the Conduct of Members [1977]
ITCS Company Report, Companies House File 00893892
Department of Trade and Industry Reports into Peachey Property, Ropergate, ITCS, London and County

SECONDARY SOURCES

Note: Place of publication is London unless stated otherwise.

Works by Maudling

'Conservatives and Control', *Spectator*, 12 November 1943; repr. *Memoirs*, app. 1, pp. 257–60
Election Address February 1950, Barnet, Barnet Conservative Association, 1950
'Be Ready to Meet a Changing World', *Primrose League Gazette* (June 1962) [speech, 11 May 1962]
The Ever-Changing Challenge, Conservative Political Centre, 1969
'Moderation in Politics', *Crossbow* (January–March 1970), 9–10
BBC *Analysis*, March 1971, interview with Ian Macintyre, National Sound Archive
BBC *Analysis*, October 1972, Reginald Maudling and Roy Jenkins, National Sound Archive
Radio 4 *Any Questions*, recorded at Hemel Hempstead, 1973, National Sound Archive
Bow Dialogue with Revd McCullough, 6 February 1973, National Sound Archive
'Reginald Maudling on the Complexity of Iain Macleod', *Spectator*, 12 May 1973, p. 589
'Alternatives to Prison', *Spectator*, 26 July 1975
Radio London talk, 9 April 1976, National Sound Archive NP 2705R
Radio programme 'Now Read On', review of two books on drink, 1976, National Sound Archive M4670R BD1, http//cadensa.bl.uk/uhtbin/cgisirsi/NFVRgO1suW/196230046/9
Memoirs, Sidgwick & Jackson, 1978

Other Published Works

Aburish, Said K. *Pay-off: Wheeling and Dealing in the Arab World*, Deutsch, 1985
Adams, Gerry. *Before the Dawn*, pbk edn, Mandarin, 1996

Anderson, Jack with Boyd, James. *Fiasco*, New York, Times Books, 1983

Anon. *A Brief History of the UDA/UFF in Contemporary Conflict*, Belfast, Prisoners' Aid and Post-Conflict Resettlement Group, 1995

Anon. *Three Days in July: The Story of the Falls Road Curfew*, Belfast, Sinn Fein, 1995

Arnold, Lorna. *Windscale 1957: Anatomy of a Nuclear Accident*, 2nd edn, Macmillan, 1995

Ascoli, David. *The Queen's Peace: The Origins and Development of the Metropolitan Police 1829–1979*, Hamish Hamilton, 1979

Beloff, Nora. *The General Says 'No': Britain's Exclusion from Europe*, Penguin Special, no. 201, Harmondsworth, Penguin Books, [1963]

———. 'Optimist in the Wings', *Observer*, 28 February 1971

Benn, Tony. *Against the Tide: Diaries, 1973–76*, Hutchinson, 1989

Bessell, Peter. *Cover-Up, the Jeremy Thorpe Affair*, Oceanside, CA, Simons Books, 1980

A Better Tomorrow: The Conservative Programme for the Next 5 Years, Conservative Central Office, 1970

Bloomfield, Ken. *Stormont in Crisis: A Memoir*, Belfast, Blackstaff Press, 1994

Bolton, Roger. *Death on the Rock and Other Stories*, W.H. Allen, 1990

Bossom, Clive. Unpublished notes made in 1979

Bower, Tom. *Fayed: The Unauthorized Biography*, Macmillan, 1998

Boyd-Carpenter, John. *Way of Life: The Memoirs of John Boyd-Carpenter*, Sidgwick & Jackson, 1980

Brittan, Samuel. *The Treasury Under the Tories, 1951–64*, Harmondsworth, Penguin, 1964

———. *Steering the Economy: The Role of the Treasury*, rev. edn, Secker & Warburg, 1969 [new edn of *The Treasury Under the Tories*]

Brivati, Brian. *Lord Goodman*, Richard Cohen Books, 1999

———. and Baston, Lewis. *The Future Labour Offered You*, forthcoming

Bryant, Chris. *Stafford Cripps: The First Modern Chancellor*, Hodder & Stoughton, 1997

Butler, David. *The British General Election of 1955*, Macmillan, 1955

——— and Kavanagh, Dennis. *The British General Election of October 1974*, Macmillan, 1975

——— and King, Anthony. *The British General Election of 1964*, Macmillan, 1965

———. *The British General Election of 1966*, Macmillan, 1966

——— and Pinto-Duschinsky, Michael. *The British General Election of 1970*, Macmillan, 1971

——— and Rose, Richard. *The British General Election of 1959*, Macmillan, 1960

Butler, R.A. *The Art of the Possible: The Memoirs of Lord Butler*, Hamish Hamilton, 1971

Cairncross, Alec. *The Wilson Years: A Treasury Diary 1964–69*, The Historians Press, 1997

———. *Managing the British Economy in the 1960s: A Treasury Perspective*, Macmillan, 1996

——— and Cairncross, Frances. *The Legacy of the Golden Age: The 1960s and their Economic Consequences*, Routledge, 1992

Callaghan, James. *A House Divided: The Dilemma of Northern Ireland*, Collins, 1973

———. *Time and Chance*, Collins, 1987

Campbell, D. *The Prevention of Fraud*, 2nd edn, Chichester, Rose, 1979

Campbell, John. *Margaret Thatcher*, i. *The Grocer's Daughter*, Jonathan Cape, 2000

Camps, Miriam. *Britain and the European Community 1955–63*, Oxford University Press, 1964

Cannadine, David. 'Ian Fleming and the Realities of Escapism', in *In Churchill's Shadow: Confronting the Past in Modern Britain*, Allen Lane, 2002, pp. 279–311

Carpenter, Humphrey. *That Was the Satire That Was: Beyond the Fringe, The Establishment Club, Private Eye and That Was the Week That Was*, Gollancz, 2000

Castle, Barbara. *The Castle Diaries 1974–76*, Weidenfeld & Nicolson, 1980

Churchman's. *In Town Tonight*, cigarette card, no. 26, ser. 1938

Clarke, Richard. *Public Expenditure, Management and Control: The Development of the Public Expenditure Survey Committee (PESC)*, ed. Alec Cairncross, Macmillan, 1978

Coogan, Tim Pat. *The IRA*, new edn, HarperCollins, 1995

Cosgrave, Patrick. *The Lives of Enoch Powell*, Bodley Head, 1989

Costain, Albert. *Reflections*, Cirencester, New Wellington Press, 1987

Cottle, Basil. *The Penguin Dictionary of Surnames*, Harmondsworth, Penguin, 1967

Courtenay, Ashley R. *Bickley Hall, Bickley, Kent*, Manchester, Cross-Courtenay, *c.* 1920 [school prospectus]

Cox, Barry, Shirley, John, and Short, Martin. *The Fall of Scotland Yard*, Harmondsworth, Penguin, 1977

Cox, Sebastian. 'The Organisation and Sources of RAF Intelligence', in *Air Intelligence: A Symposium, 22 March 1996*, Bracknell Paper No. 7, Royal Air Force Historical Society, 1997

Crick, Michael. *Stranger than Fiction*, Hamish Hamilton, 1995

Crossman, Richard. *The Backbench Diaries of Richard Crossman*, ed. Janet Morgan, Jonathan Cape, 1981

Curzon, Victoria. *The Essentials of Economic Integration: Lessons of EFTA Experience*, Macmillan, 1974

Cusack, Jim, and McDonald, Henry. *UVF*, Dublin, Poolbeg, 1997

Dale, Iain, and Brack, Duncan (eds). *Prime Minister Portillo and Other Things That Never Happened*, Politicos, 2003

Darwin, John. *Britain and Decolonisation: The Retreat from Empire in the Post-War World*, The Making of the 20th Century, Basingstoke, Macmillan Education, 1988

De Groot, Gerard. *Liberal Crusader: The Life of Sir Archibald Sinclair*, Hurst, 1993

De Tocqueville, Alexis. *L'Ancien Régime et La Revolution*, 2nd edn, Paris, Michel Lévy Frères, 1856

Dell, Edmund. *The Chancellors: A History of the Chancellors of the Exchequer, 1945–90*, HarperCollins, 1996

Denham, Roy. *Missed Chances: Britain and Europe in the Twentieth Century*, pbk edn, Orion, 1997

Devlin, Paddy. *Straight Left: An Autobiography*, Belfast, Blackstaff Press, 1993

Dewar, Michael. *The British Army in Northern Ireland*, Arms and Armour, 1985

Dickie, John. *The Uncommon Commoner: A Study of Sir Alec Douglas-Home*, Pall Mall Press, 1964

Dillon, Martin. *The Enemy Within*, Doubleday, 1994

Donoughue, Bernard. *The Heat of the Kitchen: An Autobiography*, Politicos, 2003

Du Cann, Edward. *Two Lives: The Political and Business Careers of Edward Du Cann*, Upton-upon-Severn, Images Publishing, 1995

Eichengreen, Barry. *Reconstructing Europe's Trade and Payments: The European Payments Union*, Insights from Economic History, Manchester, Manchester University Press, 1993

Evans, Harold. *Downing Street Diary: The Macmillan Years 1957–1963*, Hodder & Stoughton, 1981

Faulkner, Brian. *Memoirs of a Statesman*, ed. John Houston, Weidenfeld & Nicolson, 1978

Ferris, Paul. *The City*, Victor Gollancz, 1960

Fitzwalter, Ray, and Taylor, David. *Web of Corruption: The Story of J.G.L. Poulson and T. Dan Smith*, Granada, 1981

Foot, Michael, and Jones, Mervyn. *Guilty Men, 1957*, Victor Gollancz, 1957

Freeman, Simon, with Penrose, Barrie. *Rinkagate: The Rise and Fall of Jeremy Thorpe*, Bloomsbury, 1996

Fukuda, Haruko. 'First Decade of EFTA's Realization', in Hugh Corbet and David Robertson (eds), *Europe's Free Trade Experiment*, Oxford, Pergamon, 1970, pp. 43–77

Gardner, Ruth. *Handwriting Secrets Explained*, St Paul, MN, Chancellor Press, 2000

Garnett, Mark. *Keith Joseph*, Chesham, Acumen, 2001

Gillard, Michael. *In the Name of Charity: The Rossminster Affair*, new edn, Chatto & Windus, 1987

——. *A Little Pot of Money: The Story of Reginald Maudling and the Real Estate Fund of America*, André Deutsch/Private Eye, 1974

—— and Tompkinson, Martin. *Nothing to Declare: The Political Corruptions of John Poulson*, John Calder, 1988

Gillman, Peter. 'Supersonic Bust: The Story of the Concorde', *Atlantic Monthly*, 239/1 (1977), 72–81

Gilmour, David. *Lebanon: The Fractured Country*, Oxford, Martin Robertson, 1983

Glen, Alexander, with Bowen, Leighton. *Target Danube: A River Not Quite Too Far*, Lewes, Book Guild, 2002

Goodhart, Philip, with Branson, Ursula. *1922: The Story of the Conservative Backbenchers' Parliamentary Committee*, Macmillan, 1973

Goodman, Geoffrey. *The Awkward Warrior: Frank Cousins, His Life and Times*, 2nd edn, Nottingham, Spokesman, 1984

Greenhill, Denis. *More By Accident*, York, Wilton 65, 1992

Gregory, Martyn. *Dirty Tricks: The Inside Story of British Airways' Secret War against Richard Branson's Virgin Atlantic*, Little, Brown, 1994

Grigg, John. *The History of The Times, 6: The Thomson Years 1966–1981*, Times Books, 1993

Guest, Ivor. *Adeline Genée: A Lifetime in Ballet under Six Reigns*, A & C Black, 1958

Haines, Joe. *Glimmers of Twilight: Harold Wilson in Decline*, Politicos, 2003

Hall, Robert. *The Robert Hall Diaries 1954–61*, ed. Alec Cairncross, Unwin Hyman, 1991

Hamill, Desmond. *Pig in the Middle: The Army in Northern Ireland*, rev. edn, Methuen, 1986

Hayes, Maurice. *Minority Verdict: Experiences of a Catholic Public Servant*, Belfast, Blackstaff Press, 1995

Hayward, Keith. *Government and British Civil Aerospace: A Case Study on Post War Technology Policy*, Manchester, Manchester University Press, 1983

Healey, Denis. *The Time of My Life*, Michael Joseph, 1989

Heath, Edward. *The Course of My Life: My Autobiography*, Hodder & Stoughton, 1998

Heinlein, Frank. *British Government Policy and Decolonisation 1945–1963*, Frank Cass, 2002

Henderson, Nicholas. *Mandarin: The Diaries of an Ambassador*, Weidenfeld & Nicolson, 1994

Hennessey, Peter. *Muddling Through: Power, Politics and the Quality of Government in Postwar Britain*, Gollancz, 1996

Herzog, Arthur. *Vesco, from Wall Street to Castro's Cuba: The Rise, Fall, and Exile of the King of White Collar Crime*, New York, Doubleday, 1987

Hill, Charles (Lord Hill of Luton). *Both Sides of the Hill*, Heinemann, 1964

Holden, Anthony. *The St Albans Poisoner: The Life and Crimes of Graham Young*, new edn, Corgi, 1995

Holt, Richard. *Second Amongst Equals: Chancellors of the Exchequer and the British Economy*, Profile, 2001

Horne, Alistair. *Macmillan 1894–1956*, 2 vols, Macmillan, 1988–9

——. *A Savage War of Peace: Algeria 1954–1962*, rev. edn, Papermac, 1996

Howard, Anthony. *RAB: The Life of R.A. Butler*, Cape, 1987

—— and West, Richard. *The Making of the Prime Minister*, Jonathan Cape, 1965

Howe, Geoffrey. *Conflict of Loyalty*, Macmillan, 1994

Hurd, Douglas. *An End to Promises: Sketch of a Government 1970–1974*, Collins, 1979

——. *Memoirs*, Little, Brown, 2003

Hutchinson, Robert A. *Vesco*, pbk edn, New York, Avon, 1976

Iremonger, Louise. *The Fiery Chariot: A Study of British Prime Ministers and the Search for Love*, Secker & Warburg, 1970

James, Robert Rhodes. *Anthony Eden*, Weidenfeld & Nicolson, 1986

Jay, Douglas. *Change and Fortune: A Political Record*, Hutchinson, 1980

Jenkins, Roy. *A Life at the Centre*, Macmillan, 1991

Jones, Harriet, and Kandiah, Michael (eds). *The Myth of Consensus: New Views on British History, 1945–64*, Basingstoke, Macmillan, 1996

Johnson, Kim. 'How the Independence Deal was Hammered Out', *Trinidad Express Politics* (30 August 1998)

Junor, John. *Listening for a Midnight Tram: Memoirs*, Chapmans, 1990

Junor, Penny. *Home Truths: Life around My Father*, HarperCollins, 2002

Kavanagh, Dennis, and Morris, Peter (eds). *Consensus Politics from Attlee to Major*, Making Contemporary Britain, Oxford, Basil Blackwell, 1994

Kelly, Henry. *How Stormont Fell*, Dublin, Gill & Macmillan, 1972

Kessel, Neil, and Walton, Henry. *Alcoholism*, 2nd edn, Penguin, 1989

Kidwell, Raymond Incledon, and Samwell, Stanley David. *Peachey Property Corporation Limited: Investigation under Section 165(b) of the Companies Act 1948*, Department of Trade, HMSO, 1979

King, Cecil. *The Cecil King Diary*, 1: *1965–70*; 2: *1970–74* (Jonathan Cape, 1972, 1974)

Kyle, Keith. *The Politics of the Independence of Kenya*, Macmillan, 1999

——. *Suez: Britain's End of Empire in the Middle East*, pbk edn, I. B. Taurus, 2003

Lamb, Richard. *The Failure of the Eden Government*, Sidgwick & Jackson, 1987

——. *The Macmillan Years 1957–1963: The Emerging Truth*, John Murray, 1995

Landa, Ronald D. *et al.* (eds). *Foreign Relations of the United States 1958–1960*, Washington, USGPO, 1993

Leggatt, Andrew Pete, and Hobson, David C. *London and County Securities Group Limited: Investigation under Section 165(b) of the Companies Act 1948*, Department of Trade, HMSO, 1976

Levi, Michael. *Regulating Fraud: White-Collar Crime and the Criminal Process*, Tavistock, 1987

Lycett, Andrew. *Ian Fleming*, pbk edn, Phoenix, 1996

McAlpine, Alistair. *Once a Jolly Bagman: Memoirs*, Weidenfeld & Nicolson, 1997

McGuffin, John. Internment, Tralee, Anvil Books, 1973

McKie, David, and Cook, Chris. *Election '70: The Guardian/Panther Guide to the General Election*, Panther Books, 1970

McKittrick, David, Kelters, Seamus, Feeney, Brian, and Thornton, Chris. *Lost Lives: The Stories of the Men, Women, and Children who Died as a Result of the Northern Ireland Troubles*, Edinburgh, Mainstream, 1999

Macmillan, Harold. *The Macmillan Diaries: The Cabinet Years 1950–1957*, ed. Peter Catterall, Macmillan, 2003

MacStiofáin, Seán. *Memoirs of a Revolutionary*, Gordon Cremonesi, 1975

Mark, Robert. *In the Office of Constable*, Collins, 1978

Martin, G.H., and Highfield, J.P.L. *A History of Merton College*, Oxford, Oxford University Press, 1997

Maudling, R.G. 'On the Classification and Duration of Compensation Claims in the Mining Industry', *Journal of the Institute of Actuaries* (November 1929)

Mizzi, Edgar. *Malta in the Making 1962–1987: An Eyewitness Account*, Malta, Edgar Mizzi, 1995

Mure, G.R.G. *An Introduction to Hegel*, Oxford, Clarendon Press, 1940

Murphy, Philip. *Party Politics and Decolonisation: The Conservative Party and British Colonial Policy in Tropical Africa*, Oxford, Clarendon Press, 1995

——. *Alan Lennox-Boyd: A Biography*, I.B. Tauris, 1999

Nicholas, H.G. *The British General Election of 1950*, Macmillan, 1951

Nicolson, Harold. *Diaries and Letters*, ed. Nigel Nicolson, 3 vols, Collins, 1966–8

Noring, Nina J. *et al.* (eds). *Foreign Relations of the United States 1961–1963*, Washington, USGPO, 1994

Nutting, Anthony. *No End of a Lesson: The Story of Suez*, Constable, 1967

O'Doherty, Malachi. *The Trouble with Guns: Republican Strategy and the Provisional IRA*, Belfast, Blackstaff Press, 1998

Ogot, Bethwell A., and Ochieng, William R. *Decolonisation and Independence in Kenya 1943–93*, James Currey, 1995

Parekh, Hector J. 'Subversion in British Guiana: How and Why the Kennedy Administration Got Rid of a Democratic Government', *Monthly Review*, 1 October 1999, 50–8

Parker, Derek. *The First Seventy-Five Years*, Royal Academy of Dancing, 1995

Parris, Matthew. *Great Parliamentary Scandals: Four Centuries of Calumny, Smear and Innuendo*, Robson, 1995

Paterson, Peter. *Tired and Emotional: The Life of Lord George-Brown*, Chatto & Windus, 1993

Paul, James. 'The New Bourgeoisie of the Gulf', in *Wealth and Power in the Middle East: With Profiles of the Region's Richest People*, Middle East Report No. 142, Washington, Middle East Research and Information Project, 1986, pp. 18–22

Penrose, Barrie, and Courtiour, Roger. *The Pencourt File*, Secker & Warburg, 1978

Phillips, Mike, and Phillips, Trevor. *Windrush: The Irresistible Rise of Multi-Racial Britain*, HarperCollins, 1998

Pimlott, Ben. *Harold Wilson*, HarperCollins, 1993

Porter, A.N., and Stockwell, A.J. *British Imperial Policy and Decolonization 1938–42*, ii. *1951–64*, Cambridge Commonwealth Studies; Macmillan, 1989

Poulson, John. *The Price: The Autobiography of John Poulson, Architect*, Michael Joseph, 1981

Powell, J. Enoch. 'The Maudling I Knew', in *Reflections of a Statesman: The Writings and Speeches of Enoch Powell*, ed. Rex Collings, Bellew, 1991, pp. 329–31

Prior, Jim. *A Balance of Power*, Hamish Hamilton, 1986

Ramsay, Robin. 'Was the 1974 Oil Price Engineered by the Bilderberg Group?', *Lobster: The Journal of Parapolitics*, 41 (2001), 32–3

Randal, Jonathan. *The Tragedy of Lebanon: Christian Warlords, Israeli Adventurers and American Bunglers*, rev. edn, Hogarth Press, 1990

Raphael, Adam. *My Learned Friends*, W.H. Allen, 1989

——. *Ultimate Risk*, updated edn, Corgi, 1995

Raw, Charles, Page, Bruce, and Hodgson, Godfrey. *Do You Sincerely Want to Be Rich? Bernard Cornfeld and I.O.S.: An International Swindle*, André Deutsch, 1971

Rawlinson, Peter. *A Price Too High: An Autobiography*, Weidenfeld & Nicolson, 1989

Reading, Brian. *The Great Mess Myth*, Old Queen Street Paper 15, Conservative Research Department, May 1970

Rees, Graham L. *Britain and the Postwar European Payments Systems*, Cardiff, University of Wales Press, 1963

Retinger, Joseph. *Joseph Retinger – Memoirs of an Eminence Grise*, ed. John Pomian, Brighton, Sussex University Press, 1972

Rice, Michael. 'Can I Go Round Again?', manuscript, 2003

Roll, Eric. *Crowded Hours*, Faber & Faber, 1995

Roth, Andrew, *Parliamentary Profiles*, 1964–76

Routledge, Paul. *John Hume: A Biography*, pbk edn, HarperCollins, 1998

——. *Public Servant, Secret Agent: The Elusive Life and Violent Death of Airey Neave*, Fourth Estate, 2002

Royle, Trevor. *Winds of Change: The End of Empire in Africa*, John Murray, 1996

Salmon, Cyril. *Report of the Royal Commission on Standards of Conduct in Public Life*, HMSO, 1976

Scott, Richard. 'The Worst of Both Worlds: British Regional Policy 1951–64', *Business History*, 38 (1996), 41–64

Scoular, Clive. *James Chichester-Clark: Prime Minister of Northern Ireland*, Killyleagh, Clive Scoular, 2000

Shepherd, Robert. *Enoch Powell*, Hutchinson, 1996

——. *Iain Macleod*, Hutchinson, 1994; pbk edn, Pimlico, 1995

Sherwen, Timothy. 'British Business Attitudes Towards EFTA', in Hugh Corbet and David Robertson (eds), *Europe's Free Trade Experiment*, Oxford, Pergamon, 1970, pp. 189–204

Short, Ted. *Whip to Wilson*, Macdonald, 1989

Sinclair, Archibald. *The War and After: A Speech Given at the National Liberal Club . . . March 19th, 1941*, Sutton, Surrey, Liberal Publication Department, 1941

Singer, Peter. *Hegel*, Oxford, Oxford University Press, 1983

Smith, T. Dan. Unpublished memoirs

Stansfield, Ronald G. 'Harold Lardner: Founder of Operational Research: An Appreciation', *Journal of the Operational Research Society*, 34/1 (1983), 2–7

Steel, David. *Against Goliath: David Steel's Story*, Weidenfeld & Nicolson, 1989

Stonehouse, John. *Death of an Idealist*, W.H. Allen, 1975

Stott, Richard. *Dogs and Lampposts: Secrets Behind the Headlines from Fleet Street's Number One Editor*, Metro, 2002

Strong, Roy. *The Roy Strong Diaries 1967–1987*, Weidenfeld & Nicolson, 1997

Sunday Times Insight Team. *Ulster*, Harmondsworth, Penguin Special, 1972

Taylor, Peter. *Brits: The War Against the IRA*, pbk edn, Bloomsbury, 2002

Taylor, Robert. 'The Heath Government and Industrial Relations: Myth and Reality', in Stuart Ball and Anthony Seldon (eds), *The Heath Government 1970–74: A Reappraisal*, Harlow, Addison Wesley Longman, 1996, pp. 161–90

——. *The TUC: From the General Strike to New Unionism*, Basingstoke, Palgrave, 2000

Taylor, Stephen James. *A Natural History of Everyday Life*, Memoir Club, 1988

Teeling, William. *Corridors of Frustration*, Johnson, 1970

Thatcher, Margaret. *The Path to Power*, HarperCollins, 1995

Thorpe, D.R. *Alec Douglas-Home*, Sinclair-Stevenson, 1996

——. *Selwyn Lloyd*, Jonathan Cape, 1989

Travis, Alan. *Bound and Gagged: A Secret History of Obscenity in Britain*, pbk edn, Profile, 2001

Wake, Jehanne. *Kleinwort Benson: The History of Two Families in Banking*, Oxford, Oxford University Press, 1997

Walker, Peter. *Staying Power: An Autobiography*, Bloomsbury, 1991

Watkins, Alan. *A Short Walk down Fleet Street: From Beaverbrook to Boycott*, Duckworth, 2000

Welensky, Roy. *Welensky's 4000 Days: The Life and Death of the Federation of Rhodesia and Nyasaland*, Collins, 1964

White, Joan, W. (ed.). *Twentieth-Century Dance in Britain*, Dance Books, 1985

Whitehead, Phillip. *The Writing on the Wall: Britain in the Seventies*, Joseph, 1985

Williams, Roger. *The Nuclear Power Decisions: British Policies 1953–78*, Croom Helm, 1980

Wilson, Harold. *The Labour Government 1964–70: A Personal Record*, Weidenfeld & Nicolson, 1971

Winchester, Simon. *In Holy Terror: Reporting the Ulster Troubles*, Faber & Faber, 1974

Windlesham, D.J.G. *Politics in Practice*, Jonathan Cape, 1975

Wood, Derek. *Project Cancelled: The Disaster of Britain's Abandoned Aircraft Projects*, rev. edn, Tri-Service Press, 1990

Worsthorne, Peregrine. *Tricks of Memory: An Autobiography*, Weidenfeld & Nicolson, 1993

Young, Hugo. *This Blessed Plot: Britain and Europe from Churchill to Blair*, rev. edn, Papermac, 1999

Young, Ken. 'Orpington and the "Liberal Revival"', in Chris Cook and John Ramsden (eds), *By-elections in British Politics*, rev. edn, University College of London Press, 1997, pp. 157–79

Internet Resources

Alpha Delta Plus Guestbook: www.alphadeltaplus.20m.com/fsguestbook.html

BBC Online Archive: www.bbc.co.uk

Brittan, Samuel. 'A Backward Glance: The Reappraisal of the 1960s' (April 1997): www.samuelbrittan.co.uk/spee4_p.html

Bugge, Christian. 'The *Clockwork Orange* Controversy': www.virtual-memory.co.uk/amk/doc/0012.html

De Souza, F.R.S. 'Building in the Lancaster House Experience', presented to the Constitution of Kenya Review Commission Workshop of the Interpretation of its Mandate (14 September 2001): www.kenyaconstitution.org/docs/03d002.htm

ITN Online Archive: www.itnarchive.com

Jagan, Cheddi. 'Broadcast by Premier on Fight for Independence' (January 1962): www.jagan.org/articles2j.htm

Joint Committee on the Draft Corruption Bill: www.parliament.the-stationery-office.co.uk/pa/jt200203/jtselect/jtcorr/157/3061102.htm

King, Mervyn, 'Monetary Stability; Rhyme or Reason?', *Economic and Social Research Council Annual Lecture*, 17 October 1996: www.bankofengland.co.uk/press30.htm

Organisation for Economic Cooperation and Development: www.oecd.org/about/origins/oeec.htm

Pop and Youth Culture Movies: www.sixtiescity.com/Popmovies/Popfilm64.htm

INDEX